Foundations of Cryptography

Cryptography is concerned with the conceptualization, definition, and construction of computing systems that address security concerns. The design of cryptographic systems must be based on firm foundations. This book presents a rigorous and systematic treatment of the foundational issues: defining cryptographic tasks and solving new cryptographic problems using existing tools. It focuses on the basic mathematical tools: computational difficulty (one-way functions), pseudorandomness, and zero-knowledge proofs. The emphasis is on the clarification of fundamental concepts and on demonstrating the feasibility of solving cryptographic problems rather than on describing ad hoc approaches.

The book is suitable for use in a graduate course on cryptography and as a reference book for experts. The author assumes basic familiarity with the design and analysis of algorithms; some knowledge of complexity theory and probability is also useful.

Oded Goldreich is Professor of Computer Science at the Weizmann Institute of Science and incumbent of the Meyer W. Weisgal Professorial Chair. An active researcher, he has written numerous papers on cryptography and is widely considered to be one of the world experts in the area. He is an editor of *Journal of Cryptology* and *SIAM Journal on Computing* and the author of *Modern Cryptography, Probabilistic Proofs and Pseudorandomness*, published in 1999 by Springer-Verlag.

Foundations of Cryptography

Basic Tools

Oded Goldreich

Weizmann Institute of Science

CAMBRIDGE
UNIVERSITY PRESS

CAMBRIDGE UNIVERSITY PRESS
Cambridge, New York, Melbourne, Madrid, Cape Town, Singapore, São Paulo

Cambridge University Press
The Edinburgh Building, Cambridge CB2 2RU, UK

Published in the United States of America by Cambridge University Press, New York

www.cambridge.org
Information on this title: www.cambridge.org/9780521791724

First published 2001
Reprinted with corrections 2003
This digitally printed first paperback version 2006

A catalogue record for this publication is available from the British Library

Library of Congress Cataloguing in Publication data
Goldreich, Oded.
Foundations of cryptography : basic tools / Oded Goldreich.
p.   cm.
Includes bibliographical references and index.
ISBN 0-521-79172-3
1. Coding theory.   2. Cryptography – Mathematics.   I. Title.
QA268.G5745   2001
652′.8 – dc21   00-049362

ISBN-13 978-0-521-79172-4 hardback
ISBN-10 0-521-79172-3 hardback

ISBN-13 978-0-521-03536-1 paperback
ISBN-10 0-521-03536-8 paperback

To Dana

Contents

Note: Asterisks throughout Contents indicate advanced material.

List of Figures

Preface

It is possible to build a cabin with no foundations,
but not a lasting building.
Eng. Isidor Goldreich (1906–1995)

Cryptography is concerned with the construction of schemes that should be able to withstand any abuse. Such schemes are constructed so as to maintain a desired functionality, even under malicious attempts aimed at making them deviate from their prescribed functionality.

The design of cryptographic schemes is a very difficult task. One cannot rely on intuitions regarding the typical state of the environment in which a system will operate. For sure, an *adversary* attacking the system will try to manipulate the environment into untypical states. Nor can one be content with countermeasures designed to withstand specific attacks, because the adversary (who will act after the design of the system has been completed) will try to attack the schemes in ways that typically will be different from the ones the designer envisioned. Although the validity of the foregoing assertions seems self-evident, still some people hope that, in practice, ignoring these tautologies will not result in actual damage. Experience shows that such hopes are rarely met; cryptographic schemes based on make-believe are broken, typically sooner rather than later.

In view of the foregoing, we believe that it makes little sense to make assumptions regarding the specific *strategy* that an adversary may use. The only assumptions that can be justified refer to the computational *abilities* of the adversary. Furthermore, it is our opinion that the design of cryptographic systems has to be based on *firm foundations*, whereas ad hoc approaches and heuristics are a very dangerous way to go. A heuristic may make sense when the designer has a very good idea about the environment in which a scheme is to operate, but a cryptographic scheme will have to operate in a maliciously selected environment that typically will transcend the designer's view.

This book is aimed at presenting firm foundations for cryptography. The foundations of cryptography are the paradigms, approaches, and techniques used to conceptualize, define, and provide solutions to natural "security concerns." We shall present some of these paradigms, approaches, and techniques, as well as some of the fundamental results obtained by using them. Our emphasis is on the clarification of fundamental concepts and on demonstrating the feasibility of solving several central cryptographic problems.

Solving a cryptographic problem (or addressing a security concern) is a two-stage process consisting of a *definitional stage* and a *constructive stage*. First, in the definitional stage, the functionality underlying the natural concern must be identified and an adequate cryptographic problem must be defined. Trying to list all undesired situations is infeasible and prone to error. Instead, one should define the functionality in terms of operation in an imaginary ideal model and then require a candidate solution to emulate this operation in the real, clearly defined model (which will specify the adversary's abilities). Once the definitional stage is completed, one proceeds to construct a system that will satisfy the definition. Such a construction may use some simpler tools, and its security is to be proved relying on the features of these tools. (In practice, of course, such a scheme also may need to satisfy some specific efficiency requirements.)

This book focuses on several archetypical cryptographic problems (e.g., encryption and signature schemes) and on several central tools (e.g., computational difficulty, pseudorandomness, and zero-knowledge proofs). For each of these problems (resp., tools), we start by presenting the natural concern underlying it (resp., its intuitive objective), then define the problem (resp., tool), and finally demonstrate that the problem can be solved (resp., the tool can be constructed). In the last step, our focus is on demonstrating the feasibility of solving the problem, not on providing a practical solution. As a secondary concern, we typically discuss the level of practicality (or impracticality) of the given (or known) solution.

Computational Difficulty

The specific constructs mentioned earlier (as well as most constructs in this area) can exist only if some sort of computational hardness (i.e., difficulty) exists. Specifically, all these problems and tools require (either explicitly or implicitly) the ability to generate instances of hard problems. Such ability is captured in the definition of one-way functions (see further discussion in Section 2.1). Thus, one-way functions are the very minimum needed for doing most sorts of cryptography. As we shall see, they actually suffice for doing much of cryptography (and the rest can be done by augmentations and extensions of the assumption that one-way functions exist).

Our current state of understanding of efficient computation does not allow us to prove that one-way functions exist. In particular, the existence of one-way functions implies that $\mathcal{NP}$ is not contained in $\mathcal{BPP} \supseteq \mathcal{P}$ (not even "on the average"), which would resolve the most famous open problem of computer science. Thus, we have no choice (at this stage of history) but to assume that one-way functions exist. As justification for this assumption we can only offer the combined beliefs of hundreds (or thousands) of researchers. Furthermore, these beliefs concern a simply stated assumption, and their validity is supported by several widely believed conjectures that are central to some fields (e.g., the conjecture that factoring integers is difficult is central to computational number theory).

As we need assumptions anyhow, why not just assume what we want, that is, the existence of a solution to some natural cryptographic problem? Well, first we need to know what we want: As stated earlier, we must first clarify what exactly we do want; that is, we must go through the typically complex definitional stage. But once this stage is completed, can we just assume that the definition derived can be met? Not really: The mere fact that a definition has been derived does *not* mean that it can be met, and one can easily define objects that cannot exist (without this fact being obvious in the definition). The way to demonstrate that a definition is viable (and so the intuitive security concern can be satisfied at all) is to construct a solution based on a *better-understood* assumption (i.e., one that is more common and widely believed). For example, looking at the definition of zero-knowledge proofs, it is not a priori clear that such proofs exist at all (in a non-trivial sense). The non-triviality of the notion was first demonstrated by presenting a zero-knowledge proof system for statements regarding Quadratic Residuosity that are believed to be difficult to verify (without extra information). Furthermore, contrary to prior belief, it was later shown that the existence of one-way functions implies that any $\mathcal{NP}$-statement can be proved in zero-knowledge. Thus, facts that were not at all known to hold (and were even believed to be false) were shown to hold by reduction to widely believed assumptions (without which most of modern cryptography would collapse anyhow). To summarize, not all assumptions are equal, and so reducing a complex, new, and doubtful assumption to a widely believed simple (or even merely simpler) assumption is of great value. Furthermore, reducing the solution of a new task to the assumed security of a well-known primitive task typically means providing a construction that, using the known primitive, will solve the new task. This means that we not only know (or assume) that the new task is solvable but also have a solution based on a primitive that, being well known, typically has several candidate implementations.

Structure and Prerequisites

Our aim is to present the basic concepts, techniques, and results in cryptography. As stated earlier, our emphasis is on the clarification of fundamental concepts and the relationships among them. This is done in a way independent of the particularities of some popular number-theoretic examples. These particular examples played a central role in the development of the field and still offer the most practical implementations of all cryptographic primitives, but this does not mean that the presentation has to be linked to them. On the contrary, we believe that concepts are best clarified when presented at an abstract level, decoupled from specific implementations. Thus, the most relevant background for this book is provided by basic knowledge of algorithms (including randomized ones), computability, and elementary probability theory. Background on (computational) number theory, which is required for specific implementations of certain constructs, is not really required here (yet a short appendix presenting the most relevant facts is included in this volume so as to support the few examples of implementations presented here).

Organization of the work. This work is organized into three parts (see Figure 0.1), to be presented in three volumes: *Basic Tools*, *Basic Applications*, and *Beyond the Basics*. This first volume contains an introductory chapter as well as the first part

> Volume 1: Introduction and Basic Tools
>   Chapter 1: Introduction
>   Chapter 2: Computational Difficulty (One-Way Functions)
>   Chapter 3: Pseudorandom Generators
>   Chapter 4: Zero-Knowledge Proof Systems
> Volume 2: Basic Applications
>   Chapter 5: Encryption Schemes
>   Chapter 6: Signature Schemes
>   Chapter 7: General Cryptographic Protocols
> Volume 3: Beyond the Basics
>   . . .

Figure 0.1: Organization of the work.

(basic tools). It provides chapters on computational difficulty (one-way functions), pseudorandomness, and zero-knowledge proofs. These basic tools will be used for the basic applications in the second volume, which will consist of encryption, signatures, and general cryptographic protocols.

The partition of the work into three volumes is a logical one. Furthermore, it offers the advantage of publishing the first part without waiting for the completion of the other parts. Similarly, we hope to complete the second volume within a couple of years and publish it without waiting for the third volume.

Organization of this first volume. This first volume consists of an introductory chapter (Chapter 1), followed by chapters on computational difficulty (one-way functions), pseudorandomness, and zero-knowledge proofs (Chapters 2–4, respectively). Also included are two appendixes, one of them providing a brief summary of Volume 2. Figure 0.2 depicts the high-level structure of this first volume.

Historical notes, suggestions for further reading, some open problems, and some exercises are provided at the end of each chapter. The exercises are *mostly* designed to assist and test one's basic understanding of the main text, not to test or inspire creativity. The open problems are fairly well known; still, we recommend that one check their current status (e.g., at our updated-notices web site).

Web site for notices regarding this book. We intend to maintain a web site listing corrections of various types. The location of the site is

> http://www.wisdom.weizmann.ac.il/~oded/foc-book.html

Using This Book

The book is intended to serve as both a textbook and a reference text. That is, it is aimed at serving both the beginner and the expert. In order to achieve that goal, the presentation of the basic material is very detailed, so as to allow a typical undergraduate in computer science to follow it. An advanced student (and certainly an expert) will find the pace in these parts far too slow. However, an attempt has been made to allow the latter reader to easily skip details that are obvious to him or her. In particular, proofs typically are presented in a modular way. We start with a high-level sketch of the main ideas and

Chapter 1: *Introduction*
    Main topics covered by the book (Sec. 1.1)
    Background on probability and computation (Sec. 1.2 and 1.3)
    Motivation to the rigorous treatment (Sec. 1.4)
Chapter 2: *Computational Difficulty (One-Way Functions)*
    Motivation and definitions (Sec. 2.1 and 2.2)
    One-way functions: weak implies strong (Sec. 2.3)
    Variants (Sec. 2.4) and advanced material (Sec. 2.6)
    Hard-core predicates (Sec. 2.5)
Chapter 3: *Pseudorandom Generators*
    Motivation and definitions (Sec. 3.1–3.3)
    Constructions based on one-way permutations (Sec. 3.4)
    Pseudorandom functions (Sec. 3.6)
    Advanced material (Sec. 3.5 and 3.7)
Chapter 4: *Zero-Knowledge Proofs*
    Motivation and definitions (Sec. 4.1–4.3)
    Zero-knowledge proofs for $\mathcal{NP}$ (Sec. 4.4)
    Advanced material (Sec. 4.5–4.11)
Appendix A: Background in Computational Number Theory
Appendix B: Brief Outline of Volume 2
Bibliography and Index

Figure 0.2: Rough organization of this volume.

only later pass to the technical details. The transition from high-level description to lower-level details is typically indicated by phrases such as "details follow."

> In a few places, we provide straightforward but tedious details in indented paragraphs such as this one. In some other (even fewer) places, such paragraphs provide technical proofs of claims that are of marginal relevance to the topic of the book.

More advanced material typically is presented at a faster pace and with fewer details. Thus, we hope that the attempt to satisfy a wide range of readers will not harm any of them.

Teaching. The material presented in this book is, on one hand, way beyond what one may want to cover in a semester course, and on the other hand it falls very short of what one may want to know about cryptography in general. To assist these conflicting needs, we make a distinction between *basic* and *advanced* material and provide suggestions for further reading (in the last section of each chapter). In particular, those sections marked by an asterisk are intended for advanced reading.

Volumes 1 and 2 of this work are intended to provide all the material needed for a course on the foundations of cryptography. For a one-semester course, the instructor definitely will need to skip all advanced material (marked by asterisks) and perhaps even some basic material; see the suggestions in Figure 0.3. This should allow, depending on the class, coverage of the basic material at a reasonable level (i.e., all material marked as "main" and some of the "optional"). Volumes 1 and 2 can also serve as a textbook for a two-semester course. Either way, this first volume covers only the first half of the material for such a course. The second half will be covered in Volume 2. Meanwhile,

Each lecture consists of one hour. Lectures 1–15 are covered by this first volume. Lectures 16–28 will be covered by the second volume.

Lecture 1: Introduction, background, etc.
  (depending on class)
Lectures 2–5: *Computational Difficulty (One-Way Functions)*
    Main: Definition (Sec. 2.2), Hard-core predicates (Sec. 2.5)
    Optional: Weak implies strong (Sec. 2.3), and Sec. 2.4.2–2.4.4
Lectures 6–10: *Pseudorandom Generators*
    Main: Definitional issues and a construction (Sec. 3.2–3.4)
    Optional: Pseudorandom functions (Sec. 3.6)
Lectures 11–15: *Zero-Knowledge Proofs*
    Main: Some definitions and a construction (Sec. 4.2.1, 4.3.1, 4.4.1–4.4.3)
    Optional: Sec. 4.2.2, 4.3.2, 4.3.3, 4.3.4, 4.4.4
Lectures 16–20: *Encryption Schemes*
    Definitions and a construction (consult Appendix B.1.1–B.1.2)
    (See also fragments of a draft for the encryption chapter [99].)
Lectures 21–24: *Signature Schemes*
    Definition and a construction (consult Appendix B.2)
    (See also fragments of a draft for the signatures chapter [100].)
Lectures 25–28: *General Cryptographic Protocols*
    The definitional approach and a general construction (sketches).
    (Consult Appendix B.3; see also [98].)

Figure 0.3: Plan for one-semester course on the foundations of cryptography.

we suggest the use of other sources for the second half. A brief summary of Volume 2 and recommendations for alternative sources are given in Appendix B. (In addition, fragments and/or preliminary drafts for the three chapters of Volume 2 are available from earlier texts, [99], [100], and [98], respectively.)

A course based solely on the material in this first volume is indeed possible, but such a course cannot be considered a stand-alone course in cryptography because this volume does not consider at all the basic tasks of encryption and signatures.

Practice. The aim of this work is to provide sound theoretical foundations for cryptography. As argued earlier, such foundations are necessary for any *sound* practice of cryptography. Indeed, sound practice requires more than theoretical foundations, whereas this work makes no attempt to provide anything beyond the latter. However, given sound foundations, one can learn and evaluate various practical suggestions that appear elsewhere (e.g., [158]). On the other hand, the absence of sound foundations will result in inability to critically evaluate practical suggestions, which in turn will lead to unsound decisions. Nothing could be more harmful to the design of schemes that need to withstand adversarial attacks than misconceptions about such attacks.

Relationship to another book by the author. A frequently asked question concerns the relationship of this work to my text *Modern Cryptography, Probabilistic Proofs and Pseudorandomness* [97]. That text consists of three brief introductions to the related topics in the title. Specifically, in Chapter 1 it provides a brief (i.e., 30-page) summary of this work. The other two chapters of *Modern Cryptography, Probabilistic Proofs and Pseudorandomness* [97] provide a wider perspective on two topics mentioned in this volume (i.e., probabilistic proofs and pseudorandomness). Further comments on the latter aspect are provided in the relevant chapters of this volume.

Remark 4.10.6 as well as Theorems 4.10.10, 4.10.14 and 4.10.16, seem to require trapdoor permutations in which the permutation's domain coincides with the set of all strings of certain length. This special case of Definition 2.4.5 can be implemented by modifying the RSA or the Factoring Trapdoors (cf. Canetti et al (in STOC'96) and [5]). For further detail on Remark 4.10.6, the reader is referred to [23].

A recent result by Boaz Barak (in FOCS'01), calls for re-evaluation of the significance of all negative results regarding black-box zero-knowledge (cf. Definition 4.5.10). In particular, relying on standard intractability assumptions, Barak presents round-efficient public-coin zero-knowledge arguments for NP (using non-black-box simulators), whereas only BPP can have such black-box zero-knowledge arguments (cf. comment following Theorem 4.5.11). Interestingly, Barak's simulator works in strict (rather than expected) probabilistic polynomial-time, addressing an open problem mentioned in Section 4.12.3.

In continuation to Sections 4.7 and 4.9.2, we mention that the round-efficient argument system of [77] is actually an "argument of knowledge" (with negligible error).

Acknowledgments

First of all, I would like to thank three remarkable people who had a tremendous influence on my professional development: Shimon Even introduced me to theoretical computer science and closely guided my first steps. Silvio Micali and Shafi Goldwasser led my way in the evolving foundations of cryptography and shared with me their ongoing efforts toward further development of those foundations.

I have collaborated with many researchers, but I feel that my work with Benny Chor and Avi Wigderson has had the most important impact on my professional development and career. I would like to thank them both for their indispensable contributions to our joint research and for the excitement and pleasure of working with them.

Leonid Levin deserves special thanks as well. I have had many interesting discussions with Leonid over the years, and sometimes it has taken me too long to realize how helpful those discussions have been.

Next, I would like to thank a few colleagues and friends with whom I have had significant interactions regarding cryptography and related topics. These include Noga Alon, Boaz Barak, Mihir Bellare, Ran Canetti, Ivan Damgard, Uri Feige, Shai Halevi, Johan Hastad, Amir Herzberg, Russell Impagliazzo, Joe Kilian, Hugo Krawcyzk, Eyal Kushilevitz, Yehuda Lindell, Mike Luby, Daniele Micciancio, Moni Naor, Noam Nisan, Andrew Odlyzko, Yair Oren, Rafail Ostrovsky, Erez Petrank, Birgit Pfitzmann, Omer Reingold, Ron Rivest, Amit Sahai, Claus Schnorr, Adi Shamir, Victor Shoup, Madhu Sudan, Luca Trevisan, Salil Vadhan, Ronen Vainish, Yacob Yacobi, and Da2id Zuckerman.

Even assuming I have not overlooked people with whom I have had significant interactions on topics related to this book, the complete list of people to whom I am indebted is far more extensive. It certainly includes the authors of many papers mentioned in the Bibliography. It also includes the authors of many cryptography-related papers that I have not cited and the authors of many papers regarding the theory of computation at large (a theory taken for granted in this book).

Finally, I would like to thank Alon Rosen for carefully reading this manuscript and suggesting numerous corrections.

CHAPTER 1

Introduction

In this chapter we briefly discuss the goals of cryptography (Section 1.1). In particular, we discuss the basic problems of secure encryption, digital signatures, and fault-tolerant protocols. These problems lead to the notions of pseudorandom generators and zero-knowledge proofs, which are discussed as well.

Our approach to cryptography is based on computational complexity. Hence, this introductory chapter also contains a section presenting the computational models used throughout the book (Section 1.3). Likewise, this chapter contains a section presenting some elementary background from probability theory that is used extensively in the book (Section 1.2).

Finally, we motivate the rigorous approach employed throughout this book and discuss some of its aspects (Section 1.4).

Teaching Tip. Parts of Section 1.4 may be more suitable for the last lecture (i.e., as part of the concluding remarks) than for the first one (i.e., as part of the introductory remarks). This refers specifically to Sections 1.4.2 and 1.4.3.

1.1. Cryptography: Main Topics

Historically, the term "cryptography" has been associated with the problem of designing and analyzing *encryption schemes* (i.e., schemes that provide secret communication over insecure communication media). However, since the 1970s, problems such as constructing unforgeable *digital signatures* and designing *fault-tolerant protocols* have also been considered as falling within the domain of cryptography. In fact, cryptography can be viewed as concerned with the design of any system that needs to withstand malicious attempts to abuse it. Furthermore, cryptography as redefined here makes essential use of some tools that need to be treated in a book on the subject. Notable examples include one-way functions, pseudorandom generators, and zero-knowledge proofs. In this section we briefly discuss these terms.

We start by mentioning that much of the content of this book relies on the assumption that one-way functions exist. The definition of one-way functions captures the sort of computational difficulty that is inherent to our entire approach to cryptography, an approach that attempts to capitalize on the computational limitations of any real-life adversary. Thus, if nothing is difficult, then this approach fails. However, if, as is widely believed, not only do hard problems exist but also instances of them can be efficiently generated, then these hard problems can be "put to work." Thus, "algorithmically bad news" (by which hard computational problems exist) implies good news for cryptography. Chapter 2 is devoted to the definition and manipulation of computational difficulty in the form of one-way functions.

1.1.1. Encryption Schemes

The problem of providing *secret communication over insecure media* is the most traditional and basic problem of cryptography. The setting consists of two parties communicating over a channel that possibly may be tapped by an adversary, called the *wire-tapper*. The parties wish to exchange information with each other, but keep the wire-tapper as ignorant as possible regarding the content of this information. Loosely speaking, an encryption scheme is a protocol allowing these parties to communicate *secretly* with each other. Typically, the encryption scheme consists of a pair of algorithms. One algorithm, called *encryption*, is applied by the sender (i.e., the party sending a message), while the other algorithm, called *decryption*, is applied by the receiver. Hence, in order to send a message, the sender first applies the encryption algorithm to the message and sends the result, called the *ciphertext*, over the channel. Upon receiving a ciphertext, the other party (i.e., the receiver) applies the decryption algorithm to it and retrieves the original message (called the *plaintext*).

In order for this scheme to provide secret communication, the communicating parties (at least the receiver) must know something that is not known to the wire-tapper. (Otherwise, the wire-tapper could decrypt the ciphertext exactly as done by the receiver.) This extra knowledge may take the form of the decryption algorithm itself or some parameters and/or auxiliary inputs used by the decryption algorithm. We call this extra knowledge the *decryption key*. Note that, without loss of generality, we can assume that the decryption algorithm is known to the wire-tapper and that the decryption algorithm needs two inputs: a ciphertext and a decryption key. We stress that the existence of a secret key, not known to the wire-tapper, is merely a necessary condition for secret communication.

Evaluating the "security" of an encryption scheme is a very tricky business. A preliminary task is to understand what "security" is (i.e., to properly define what is meant by this intuitive term). Two approaches to defining security are known. The first ("classic") approach is *information-theoretic*. It is concerned with the "information" about the plaintext that is "present" in the ciphertext. Loosely speaking, if the ciphertext contains information about the plaintext, then the encryption scheme is considered insecure. It has been shown that such a high (i.e., "perfect") level of security can be achieved only if the key in use is at least as long as the *total* length of the messages sent via the encryption scheme. The fact that the key has to be longer than the information exchanged using it is indeed a drastic limitation on the applicability of such encryption schemes. This is especially true when *huge* amounts of information need to be secretly communicated.

The second ("modern") approach, as followed in this book, is based on *computational complexity*. This approach is based on the fact that *it does not matter whether or not the ciphertext contains information about the plaintext,* but rather *whether or not this information can be efficiently extracted.* In other words, instead of asking whether or not it is *possible* for the wire-tapper to extract specific information, we ask whether or not it is *feasible* for the wire-tapper to extract this information. It turns out that the new (i.e., "computational-complexity") approach offers security even if the key is much shorter than the total length of the messages sent via the encryption scheme. For example, one can use "pseudorandom generators" (discussed later) that expand short keys into much longer "pseudo-keys," so that the latter are as secure as "real keys" of comparable length.

In addition, the computational-complexity approach allows the introduction of concepts and primitives that cannot exist under the information-theoretic approach. A typical example is the concept of *public-key encryption schemes*. Note that in the preceding discussion we concentrated on the decryption algorithm and its key. It can be shown that the encryption algorithm must get, in addition to the message, an auxiliary input that depends on the decryption key. This auxiliary input is called the *encryption key*. Traditional encryption schemes, and in particular all the encryption schemes used over the millennia preceding the 1980s, operate with an encryption key equal to the decryption key. Hence, the wire-tapper in these schemes must be ignorant of the encryption key, and consequently the *key-distribution problem* arises (i.e., how two parties wishing to communicate over an insecure channel can agree on a secret encryption/decryption key).[1] The computational-complexity approach allows the introduction of encryption schemes in which the encryption key can be known to the wire-tapper without compromising the security of the scheme. Clearly, the decryption key in such schemes is different from the encryption key, and furthermore it is infeasible to compute the decryption key from the encryption key. Such encryption schemes, called *public-key schemes*, have the advantage of trivially resolving the key-distribution problem, because the encryption key can be publicized.

In Chapter 5, which will appear in the second volume of this work and will be devoted to encryption schemes, we shall discuss private-key and public-key encryption schemes. Much attention is devoted to defining the security of encryption schemes. Finally, constructions of secure encryption schemes based on various intractability assumptions are presented. Some of the constructions presented are based on pseudorandom generators, which are discussed in Chapter 3. Other constructions use specific one-way functions such as the RSA function and/or the operation of squaring modulo a composite number.

1.1.2. Pseudorandom Generators

It turns out that pseudorandom generators play a central role in the construction of encryption schemes (and related schemes). In particular, pseudorandom generators

---

[1]The traditional solution is to exchange the key through an alternative channel that is secure, alas "more expensive to use," for example, by a convoy.

yield simple constructions of private-key encryption schemes, and this observation is often used in practice (usually implicitly).

Although the term "pseudorandom generators" is commonly used *in practice*, both in the context of cryptography and in the much wider context of probabilistic procedures, it is seldom associated with a precise meaning. We believe that using a term without clearly stating what it means is dangerous in general and particularly so in a tricky business such as cryptography. Hence, a precise treatment of pseudorandom generators is central to cryptography.

Loosely speaking, a pseudorandom generator is a deterministic algorithm that expands short random seeds into much longer bit sequences that *appear* to be "random" (although they are not). In other words, although the output of a pseudorandom generator is not really random, it is *infeasible* to tell the difference. It turns out that pseudorandomness and computational difficulty are linked in an even more fundamental manner, as pseudorandom generators can be constructed based on various intractability assumptions. Furthermore, the main result in this area asserts that pseudorandom generators exist if and only if one-way functions exist.

Chapter 3, devoted to pseudorandom generators, starts with a treatment of the concept of computational indistinguishability. Pseudorandom generators are defined next and are constructed using special types of one-way functions (defined in Chapter 2). Pseudorandom *functions* are defined and constructed as well. The latter offer a host of additional applications.

1.1.3. Digital Signatures

A notion that did not exist in the pre-computerized world is that of a "digital signature." The need to discuss digital signatures arose with the introduction of computer communication in the business environment in which parties need to commit themselves to proposals and/or declarations they make. Discussions of "unforgeable signatures" also took place in previous centuries, but the objects of discussion were handwritten signatures, not digital ones, and the discussion was not perceived as related to cryptography.

Relations between encryption and signature methods became possible with the "digitalization" of both and the introduction of the computational-complexity approach to security. Loosely speaking, a *scheme for unforgeable signatures* requires

- that each user be able *to efficiently generate his or her own signature* on documents of his or her choice,

- that each user be able *to efficiently verify* whether or not a given string is a signature of another (specific) user on a specific document, and

- that *no one be able to efficiently produce the signatures of other users* to documents that those users did not sign.

We stress that the formulation of unforgeable digital signatures also provides a clear statement of the essential ingredients of handwritten signatures. Indeed, the ingredients are each person's ability to sign for himself or herself, a universally agreed verification procedure, and the belief (or assertion) that it is infeasible (or at least difficult) to forge signatures in a manner that could pass the verification procedure. It is difficult to state to what extent handwritten signatures meet these requirements. In contrast, our discussion of digital signatures will supply precise statements concerning the extent to which digital signatures meet the foregoing requirements. Furthermore, schemes for unforgeable digital signatures can be constructed using the same computational assumptions as used in the construction of (private-key) encryption schemes.

In Chapter 6, which will appear in the second volume of this work and will be devoted to signature schemes, much attention will be focused on defining the security (i.e., unforgeability) of these schemes. Next, constructions of unforgeable signature schemes based on various intractability assumptions will be presented. In addition, we shall treat the related problem of message authentication.

Message Authentication

Message authentication is a task related to the setting considered for encryption schemes (i.e., communication over an insecure channel). This time, we consider the case of an active adversary who is monitoring the channel and may alter the messages sent on it. The parties communicating through this insecure channel wish to authenticate the messages they send so that the intended recipient can tell an original message (sent by the sender) from a modified one (i.e., modified by the adversary). Loosely speaking, a *scheme for message authentication* requires

- that each of the communicating parties be able *to efficiently generate an authentication tag* for any message of his or her choice,
- that each of the communicating parties be able *to efficiently verify* whether or not a given string is an authentication tag for a given message, and
- that *no external adversary* (i.e., a party other than the communicating parties) *be able to efficiently produce authentication tags* to messages not sent by the communicating parties.

In some sense, "message authentication" is similar to a digital signature. The difference between the two is that in the setting of message authentication it is not required that third parties (who may be dishonest) be able to verify the validity of authentication tags produced by the designated users, whereas in the setting of signature schemes it is required that such third parties be able to verify the validity of signatures produced by other users. Hence, digital signatures provide a solution to the message-authentication problem. On the other hand, a message-authentication scheme does not necessarily constitute a digital-signature scheme.

Signatures Widen the Scope of Cryptography

Considering the problem of digital signatures as belonging to cryptography widens the scope of this area from the specific secret-communication problem to a variety of problems concerned with limiting the "gain" that can be achieved by "dishonest" behavior of parties (who are either internal or external to the system). Specifically:

- In the secret-communication problem (solved by use of encryption schemes), one wishes to reduce, as much as possible, the information that a potential wire-tapper can extract from the communication between two designated users. In this case, the designated system consists of the two communicating parties, and the wire-tapper is considered as an external ("dishonest") party.

- In the message-authentication problem, one aims at prohibiting any (external) wire-tapper from modifying the communication between two (designated) users.

- In the signature problem, one aims at providing all users of a system a way of making self-binding statements and of ensuring that one user cannot make statements that would bind another user. In this case, the designated system consists of the set of all users, and a potential forger is considered as an internal yet dishonest user.

Hence, in the wide sense, *cryptography is concerned with any problem in which one wishes to limit the effects of dishonest users*. A general treatment of such problems is captured by the treatment of "fault-tolerant" (or cryptographic) protocols.

1.1.4. Fault-Tolerant Protocols and Zero-Knowledge Proofs

A discussion of signature schemes naturally leads to a discussion of cryptographic protocols, because it is a natural concern to ask under what circumstances one party should provide its signature to another party. In particular, problems like mutual simultaneous commitment (e.g., contract signing) arise naturally. Another type of problem, motivated by the use of computer communication in the business environment, consists of "secure implementation" of protocols (e.g., implementing secret and incorruptible voting).

Simultaneity Problems

A typical example of a simultaneity problem is that of simultaneous exchange of secrets, of which contract signing is a special case. The setting for a simultaneous exchange of secrets consists of two parties, each holding a "secret." The goal is to execute a protocol such that if both parties follow it correctly, then at termination each will hold its counterpart's secret, and in any case (even if one party cheats) the first party will hold the second party's secret if and only if the second party holds the first party's secret. Perfectly simultaneous exchange of secrets can be achieved only if we assume the existence of third parties that are trusted to some extent. In fact, simultaneous exchange of secrets can easily be achieved using the active participation of a trusted third party: Each party sends its secret to the trusted third party (using a secure channel). The third party, on receiving both secrets, sends the first party's secret to the second party and the second party's secret to the first party. There are two problems with this solution:

1. The solution requires the *active* participation of an "external" party in all cases (i.e., also in case both parties are honest). We note that other solutions requiring milder forms of participation of external parties do exist.

2. The solution requires the existence of a *totally trusted* third entity. In some applications, such an entity does not exist. Nevertheless, in the sequel we shall discuss the problem

of implementing a trusted third party by a set of users with an honest majority (even if the identity of the honest users is not known).

Secure Implementation of Functionalities and Trusted Parties

A different type of protocol problem is concerned with the secure implementation of functionalities. To be more specific, we discuss the problem of evaluating a function of local inputs each of which is held by a different user. An illustrative and motivating example is *voting*, in which the function is majority, and the local input held by user A is a single bit representing the vote of user A (e.g., "pro" or "con"). Loosely speaking, a protocol for securely evaluating a specific function must satisfy the following:

- *Privacy*: No party can "gain information" on the input of other parties, beyond what is deduced from the value of the function.

- *Robustness*: No party can "influence" the value of the function, beyond the influence exerted by selecting its own input.

It is sometimes required that these conditions hold with respect to "small" (e.g., minority) coalitions of parties (instead of single parties).

Clearly, if one of the users is known to be totally trustworthy, then there exists a simple solution to the problem of secure evaluation of any function. Each user simply sends its input to the trusted party (using a secure channel), who, upon receiving all inputs, computes the function, sends the outcome to all users, and erases all intermediate computations (including the inputs received) from its memory. Certainly, it is unrealistic to assume that a party can be trusted to such an extent (e.g., that it will voluntarily erase what it has "learned"). Nevertheless, the problem of implementing secure function evaluation reduces to the problem of implementing a trusted party. It turns out that a trusted party can be implemented by a set of users with an honest majority (even if the identity of the honest users is not known). This is indeed a major result in this field, and much of Chapter 7, which will appear in the second volume of this work, will be devoted to formulating and proving it (as well as variants of it).

Zero-Knowledge as a Paradigm

A major tool in the construction of cryptographic protocols is the concept of *zero-knowledge* proof systems and the fact that zero-knowledge proof systems exist for all languages in $\mathcal{NP}$ (provided that one-way functions exist). Loosely speaking, a zero-knowledge proof yields nothing but the validity of the assertion. Zero-knowledge proofs provide a tool for "forcing" parties to follow a given protocol properly.

To illustrate the role of zero-knowledge proofs, consider a setting in which a party, called Alice, upon receiving an encrypted message from Bob, is to send Carol the least significant bit of the message. Clearly, if Alice sends only the (least significant) bit (of the message), then there is no way for Carol to know Alice did not cheat. Alice could prove that she did not cheat by revealing to Carol the entire message as well as its decryption key, but that would yield information far beyond what had been required. A much better idea is to let Alice augment the bit she sends Carol with a zero-knowledge proof that this bit is indeed the least significant bit of the message. We stress that the foregoing statement is of the "$\mathcal{NP}$ type" (since the proof specified earlier can be efficiently verified), and therefore the existence of zero-knowledge proofs for $\mathcal{NP}$-statements implies that the foregoing statement can be proved without revealing anything beyond its validity.

The focus of Chapter 4, devoted to zero-knowledge proofs, is on the foregoing result (i.e., the construction of zero-knowledge proofs for any $\mathcal{NP}$-statement). In addition, we shall consider numerous variants and aspects of the notion of zero-knowledge proofs and their effects on the applicability of this notion.

1.2. Some Background from Probability Theory

Probability plays a central role in cryptography. In particular, probability is essential in order to allow a discussion of information or lack of information (i.e., secrecy). We assume that the reader is familiar with the basic notions of probability theory. In this section, we merely present the probabilistic notations that are used throughout this book and three useful probabilistic inequalities.

1.2.1. Notational Conventions

Throughout this entire book we shall refer to only *discrete* probability distributions. Typically, the probability space consists of the set of all strings of a certain length ℓ, taken with uniform probability distribution. That is, the sample space is the set of all ℓ-bit-long strings, and each such string is assigned probability measure $2^{-\ell}$. Traditionally, functions from the sample space to the reals are called *random variables*. Abusing standard terminology, we allow ourselves to use the term *random variable* also when referring to functions mapping the sample space into the set of binary strings. We often do not specify the probability space, but rather talk directly about random variables. For example, we may say that X is a random variable assigned values in the set of all strings, so that $\Pr[X = 00] = \frac{1}{4}$ and $\Pr[X = 111] = \frac{3}{4}$. (Such a random variable can be defined over the sample space $\{0, 1\}^2$, so that $X(11) = 00$ and $X(00) = X(01) = X(10) = 111$.) In most cases the probability space consists of all strings of a particular length. Typically, these strings represent random choices made by some randomized process (see next section), and the random variable is the output of the process.

How to Read Probabilistic Statements. All our probabilistic statements refer to functions of random variables that are defined beforehand. Typically, we shall write $\Pr[f(X) = 1]$, where X is a random variable defined beforehand (and f is a function). An important convention is that *all occurrences of a given symbol in a probabilistic statement refer to the same (unique) random variable*. Hence, if $B(\cdot, \cdot)$ is a Boolean expression depending on two variables and X is a random variable, then $\Pr[B(X, X)]$ denotes the probability that $B(x, x)$ holds when x is chosen with probability $\Pr[X = x]$.

Namely,

$$\Pr[B(X, X)] = \sum_x \Pr[X = x] \cdot \chi(B(x, x))$$

where χ is an indicator function, so that $\chi(B) = 1$ if event B holds, and equals zero otherwise. For example, for every random variable X, we have $\Pr[X = X] = 1$. We stress that if one wishes to discuss the probability that $B(x, y)$ holds when x and y are chosen independently with the same probability distribution, then one needs to define *two* independent random variables, both with the same probability distribution. Hence, if X and Y are two independent random variables, then $\Pr[B(X, Y)]$ denotes the probability that $B(x, y)$ holds when the pair (x, y) is chosen with probability $\Pr[X = x] \cdot \Pr[Y = y]$. Namely,

$$\Pr[B(X, Y)] = \sum_{x, y} \Pr[X = x] \cdot \Pr[Y = y] \cdot \chi(B(x, y))$$

For example, for every two independent random variables, X and Y, we have $\Pr[X = Y] = 1$ only if both X and Y are trivial (i.e., assign the entire probability mass to a single string).

Typical Random Variables. Throughout this entire book, U_n denotes a random variable uniformly distributed over the set of strings of length n. Namely, $\Pr[U_n = \alpha]$ equals 2^{-n} if $\alpha \in \{0, 1\}^n$, and equals zero otherwise. In addition, we shall occasionally use random variables (arbitrarily) distributed over $\{0, 1\}^n$ or $\{0, 1\}^{l(n)}$ for some function $l:$ $\mathbb{N} \to \mathbb{N}$. Such random variables are typically denoted by X_n, Y_n, Z_n, etc. We stress that in some cases X_n is distributed over $\{0, 1\}^n$, whereas in others it is distributed over $\{0, 1\}^{l(n)}$, for some function $l(\cdot)$, which is typically a polynomial. Another type of random variable, the output of a randomized algorithm on a fixed input, is discussed in Section 1.3.

1.2.2. Three Inequalities

The following probabilistic inequalities will be very useful in the course of this book. All inequalities refer to random variables that are assigned real values. The most basic inequality is the *Markov inequality*, which asserts that for random variables with bounded maximum or minimum values, some relation must exist between the deviation of a value from the expectation of the random variable and the probability that the random variable is assigned this value. Specifically, letting $E(X) \stackrel{\text{def}}{=} \sum_v \Pr[X = v] \cdot v$ denote the expectation of the random variable X, we have the following:

Markov Inequality: *Let X be a non-negative random variable and v a real number. Then*

$$\Pr[X \geq v] \leq \frac{E(X)}{v}$$

Equivalently, $\Pr[X \geq r \cdot E(X)] \leq \frac{1}{r}$.

Proof:

$$E(X) = \sum_x \Pr[X = x] \cdot x$$

$$\geq \sum_{x < v} \Pr[X = x] \cdot 0 + \sum_{x \geq v} \Pr[X = x] \cdot v$$

$$= \Pr[X \geq v] \cdot v$$

The claim follows. ∎

The Markov inequality is typically used in cases in which one knows very little about the distribution of the random variable; it suffices to know its expectation and at least one bound on the range of its values. See Exercise 1.

Using Markov's inequality, one gets a "possibly stronger" bound for the deviation of a random variable from its expectation. This bound, called Chebyshev's inequality, is useful provided one has additional knowledge concerning the random variable (specifically, a good upper bound on its variance). For a random variable X of finite expectation, we denote by $\mathsf{Var}(X) \stackrel{\text{def}}{=} E[(X - E(X))^2]$ the variance of X and observe that $\mathsf{Var}(X) = E(X^2) - E(X)^2$.

Chebyshev's Inequality: *Let X be a random variable, and $\delta > 0$. Then*

$$\Pr[|X - E(X)| \geq \delta] \leq \frac{\mathsf{Var}(X)}{\delta^2}$$

Proof: We define a random variable $Y \stackrel{\text{def}}{=} (X - E(X))^2$ and apply the Markov inequality. We get

$$\Pr[|X - E(X)| \geq \delta] = \Pr[(X - E(X))^2 \geq \delta^2]$$

$$\leq \frac{E[(X - E(X))^2]}{\delta^2}$$

and the claim follows. ∎

Chebyshev's inequality is particularly useful for analysis of the error probability of approximation via repeated sampling. It suffices to assume that the samples are picked in a pairwise-independent manner.

Corollary (Pairwise-Independent Sampling): *Let $X_1, X_2, \ldots, X_n$ be pairwise-independent random variables with the same expectation, denoted μ, and the same variance, denoted σ^2. Then, for every $\varepsilon > 0$,*

$$\Pr\left[\left|\frac{\sum_{i=1}^n X_i}{n} - \mu\right| \geq \varepsilon\right] \leq \frac{\sigma^2}{\varepsilon^2 n}$$

The X_i's are called *pairwise-independent* if for every $i \neq j$ and all a and b, it holds that $\Pr[X_i = a \wedge X_j = b]$ equals $\Pr[X_i = a] \cdot \Pr[X_j = b]$.

Proof: Define the random variables $\overline{X}_i \overset{\text{def}}{=} X_i - E(X_i)$. Note that the $\overline{X}_i$'s are pairwise-independent and each has zero expectation. Applying Chebyshev's inequality to the random variable defined by the sum $\sum_{i=1}^{n} \frac{X_i}{n}$, and using the linearity of the expectation operator, we get

$$\Pr\left[\left|\sum_{i=1}^{n} \frac{X_i}{n} - \mu\right| \geq \varepsilon\right] \leq \frac{\text{Var}\left[\sum_{i=1}^{n} \frac{X_i}{n}\right]}{\varepsilon^2}$$

$$= \frac{E\left[\left(\sum_{i=1}^{n} \overline{X}_i\right)^2\right]}{\varepsilon^2 \cdot n^2}$$

Now (again using the linearity of E)

$$E\left[\left(\sum_{i=1}^{n} \overline{X}_i\right)^2\right] = \sum_{i=1}^{n} E[\overline{X}_i^2] + \sum_{1 \leq i \neq j \leq n} E[\overline{X}_i \overline{X}_j]$$

By the pairwise independence of the $\overline{X}_i$'s, we get $E[\overline{X}_i \overline{X}_j] = E[\overline{X}_i] \cdot E[\overline{X}_j]$, and using $E[\overline{X}_i] = 0$, we get

$$E\left[\left(\sum_{i=1}^{n} \overline{X}_i\right)^2\right] = n \cdot \sigma^2$$

The corollary follows. ∎

Using pairwise-independent sampling, the error probability in the approximation is decreasing linearly with the number of sample points. Using totally independent sampling points, the error probability in the approximation can be shown to decrease exponentially with the number of sample points. (The random variables $X_1, X_2, \ldots, X_n$ are said to be *totally independent* if for every sequence $a_1, a_2, \ldots, a_n$ it holds that $\Pr[\wedge_{i=1}^{n} X_i = a_i]$ equals $\prod_{i=1}^{n} \Pr[X_i = a_i]$.) Probability bounds supporting the foregoing statement are given next. The first bound, commonly referred to as the *Chernoff bound,* concerns 0-1 random variables (i.e., random variables that are assigned values of either 0 or 1).

Chernoff Bound: *Let $p \leq \frac{1}{2}$, and let $X_1, X_2, \ldots, X_n$ be independent 0-1 random variables, so that $\Pr[X_i = 1] = p$ for each i. Then for all ε, $0 < \varepsilon \leq p(1 - p)$, we have*

$$\Pr\left[\left|\frac{\sum_{i=1}^{n} X_i}{n} - p\right| > \varepsilon\right] < 2 \cdot e^{-\frac{\varepsilon^2}{2p(1-p)} \cdot n}$$

We shall usually apply the bound with a constant $p \approx \frac{1}{2}$. In this case, n independent samples give an approximation that deviates by ε from the expectation with probability δ that is exponentially decreasing with $\varepsilon^2 n$. Such an approximation is called an (ε, δ)-*approximation* and can be achieved using $n = O(\varepsilon^{-2} \cdot \log(1/\delta))$ sample points. It is important to remember that the sufficient number of sample points is polynomially related to ε^{-1} and logarithmically related to δ^{-1}. So using poly(n) many samples, the error probability (i.e., δ) can be made negligible (as a function in n), but the accuracy of the estimation (i.e., ε) can be bounded above only by any fixed polynomial fraction (but cannot be made negligible).[2] We stress that the dependence of the number of samples on ε is not better than in the case of pairwise-independent sampling; the advantage of totally independent samples lies only in the dependence of the number of samples on δ.

A more general bound, useful for approximation of the expectation of a general random variable (not necessarily 0-1), is given as follows:

Hoefding Inequality:[3] *Let* $X_1, X_2, \ldots, X_n$ *be n independent random variables with the same probability distribution, each ranging over the (real) interval* $[a, b]$, *and let* μ *denote the expected value of each of these variables. Then, for every* $\varepsilon > 0$,

$$\Pr\left[\left|\frac{\sum_{i=1}^{n} X_i}{n} - \mu\right| > \varepsilon\right] < 2 \cdot e^{-\frac{2\varepsilon^2}{(b-a)^2} \cdot n}$$

The Hoefding inequality is useful for estimating the average value of a function defined over a large set of values, especially when the desired error probability needs to be negligible. It can be applied provided we can efficiently sample the set and have a bound on the possible values (of the function). See Exercise 2.

1.3. The Computational Model

Our approach to cryptography is heavily based on computational complexity. Thus, some background on computational complexity is required for our discussion of cryptography. In this section, we briefly recall the definitions of the complexity classes $\mathcal{P}$, $\mathcal{NP}$, $\mathcal{BPP}$, and "non-uniform $\mathcal{P}$" (i.e., $\mathcal{P}/\text{poly}$) and the concept of oracle machines. In addition, we discuss the types of intractability assumptions used throughout the rest of this book.

1.3.1. $\mathcal{P}$, $\mathcal{NP}$, and $\mathcal{NP}$-Completeness

A conservative approach to computing devices associates efficient computations with the complexity class $\mathcal{P}$. Jumping ahead, we note that the approach taken in this book is a more liberal one in that it allows the computing devices to be randomized.

Definition 1.3.1 (Complexity Class $\mathcal{P}$): *A language L is* **recognizable in** (deterministic) **polynomial time** *if there exists a deterministic Turing machine M and a polynomial* $p(\cdot)$ *such that*

- *on input a string x, machine M halts after at most* $p(|x|)$ *steps, and*
- $M(x) = 1$ *if and only if* $x \in L$.

[2]Here and in the rest of this book, we denote by poly() some fixed but unspecified polynomial.

[3]A more general form requires the X_i's to be independent, but not necessarily identical, and uses $\mu \stackrel{\text{def}}{=} \frac{1}{n}\sum_{i=1}^{n} \mathsf{E}(X_i)$. See [6, app. A].

$\mathcal{P}$ *is the class of languages that can be recognized in (deterministic) polynomial time.*

Likewise, the complexity class $\mathcal{NP}$ is associated with computational problems having solutions that, once given, can be efficiently tested for validity. It is customary to define $\mathcal{NP}$ as the class of languages that can be recognized by a non-deterministic polynomial-time Turing machine. A more fundamental formulation of $\mathcal{NP}$ is given by the following equivalent definition.

Definition 1.3.2 (Complexity Class $\mathcal{NP}$): *A language L is in $\mathcal{NP}$ if there exists a Boolean relation $R_L \subseteq \{0, 1\}^* \times \{0, 1\}^*$ and a polynomial $p(\cdot)$ such that R_L can be recognized in (deterministic) polynomial time, and $x \in L$ if and only if there exists a y such that $|y| \le p(|x|)$ and $(x, y) \in R_L$. Such a y is called a* **witness for membership** *of $x \in L$.*

Thus, $\mathcal{NP}$ consists of the set of languages for which there exist short proofs of membership that can be efficiently verified. It is widely believed that $\mathcal{P} \ne \mathcal{NP}$, and resolution of this issue is certainly the most intriguing open problem in computer science. If indeed $\mathcal{P} \ne \mathcal{NP}$, then there exists a language $L \in \mathcal{NP}$ such that every algorithm recognizing L will have a super-polynomial running time *in the worst case*. Certainly, all $\mathcal{NP}$-complete languages (defined next) will have super-polynomial-time complexity *in the worst case*.

Definition 1.3.3 ($\mathcal{NP}$-Completeness): *A language is $\mathcal{NP}$-**complete** if it is in $\mathcal{NP}$ and every language in $\mathcal{NP}$ is polynomially reducible to it. A language L is* **polynomially reducible** *to a language L' if there exists a polynomial-time-computable function f such that $x \in L$ if and only if $f(x) \in L'$.*

Among the languages known to be $\mathcal{NP}$-complete are *Satisfiability* (of propositional formulae), *Graph Colorability*, and *Graph Hamiltonicity*.

1.3.2. Probabilistic Polynomial Time

Randomized algorithms play a central role in cryptography. They are needed in order to allow the legitimate parties to generate secrets and are therefore allowed also to the adversaries. The reader is assumed to be familiar and comfortable with such algorithms.

1.3.2.1. Randomized Algorithms: An Example

To demonstrate the notion of a randomized algorithm, we present a simple randomized algorithm for deciding whether or not a given (undirected) graph is connected (i.e., there is a path between each pair of vertices in the graph). We comment that the following algorithm is interesting because it uses significantly less space than the standard (BFS or DFS-based) deterministic algorithms.

Testing whether or not a graph is connected is easily reduced to testing connectivity between any given pair of vertices.[4] Thus, we focus on the task of determining whether or not two given vertices are connected in a given graph.

Algorithm. On input a graph $G = (V, E)$ and two vertices, s and t, we take a *random walk* of length $O(|V| \cdot |E|)$, starting at vertex s, and test at each step whether or not vertex t is encountered. If vertex t is ever encountered, then the algorithm will accept; otherwise, it will reject. By a random walk we mean that at each step we uniformly select one of the edges incident at the current vertex and traverse this edge to the other endpoint.

Analysis. Clearly, if s is not connected to t in the graph G, then the probability that the foregoing algorithm will accept will be zero. The harder part of the analysis is to prove that if s is connected to t in the graph G, then the algorithm will accept with probability at least $\frac{2}{3}$. (The proof is deferred to Exercise 3.) Thus, either way, the algorithm will err with probability at most $\frac{1}{3}$. The error probability can be further reduced by invoking the algorithm several times (using fresh random choices in each try).

1.3.2.2. Randomized Algorithms: Two Points of View

Randomized algorithms (machines) can be viewed in two equivalent ways. One way of viewing randomized algorithms is to allow the algorithm to make random moves (i.e., "toss coins"). Formally, this can be modeled by a Turing machine in which the transition function maps pairs of the form ($\langle$state$\rangle$, $\langle$symbol$\rangle$) to two possible triples of the form ($\langle$state$\rangle$, $\langle$symbol$\rangle$, $\langle$direction$\rangle$). The next step for such a machine is determined by a random choice of one of these triples. Namely, to make a step, the machine chooses at random (with probability $\frac{1}{2}$ for each possibility) either the first triple or the second one and then acts accordingly. These random choices are called the *internal coin tosses* of the machine. The output of a probabilistic machine M on input x is not a string but rather a random variable that assumes strings as possible values. This random variable, denoted $M(x)$, is induced by the internal coin tosses of M. By $\Pr[M(x) = y]$ we mean the probability that machine M on input x will output y. The probability space is that of all possible outcomes for the internal coin tosses taken with uniform probability distribution.[5] Because we consider only polynomial-time machines, we can assume, without loss of generality, that the number of coin tosses made by M on input x is independent of their outcome and is denoted by $t_M(x)$. We denote by $M_r(x)$ the output of M on input x when r is the outcome of its internal coin tosses. Then $\Pr[M(x) = y]$

---

[4]The space complexity of such a reduction is low; we merely need to store the names of two vertices (currently being tested). Alas, the time complexity is indeed relatively high; we need to invoke the two-vertex tester $\binom{n}{2}$ times, where n is the number of vertices in the graph.

[5]This sentence is slightly more problematic than it seems. The simple case is when, on input x, machine M always makes the same number of internal coin tosses (independent of their outcome). In general, the number of coin tosses may depend on the outcome of prior coin tosses. Still, for every r, the probability that the outcome of the sequence of internal coin tosses will be r equals $2^{-|r|}$ if the machine does not terminate when the sequence of outcomes is a strict prefix of r, and equals zero otherwise. Fortunately, because we consider polynomial-time machines, we can modify all machines so that they will satisfy the structure of the simple case (and thus avoid the foregoing complication).

is merely the fraction of $r \in \{0, 1\}^{t_M(x)}$ for which $M_r(x) = y$. Namely,

$$\Pr[M(x) = y] = \frac{\left|\{r \in \{0, 1\}^{t_M(x)} : M_r(x) = y\}\right|}{2^{t_M(x)}}$$

The second way of looking at randomized algorithms is to view the outcome of the internal coin tosses of the machine as an auxiliary input. Namely, we consider deterministic machines with two inputs. The first input plays the role of the "real input" (i.e., x) of the first approach, while the second input plays the role of a possible outcome for a sequence of internal coin tosses. Thus, the notation $M(x, r)$ corresponds to the notation $M_r(x)$ used earlier. In the second approach, we consider the probability distribution of $M(x, r)$ for any *fixed* x and a uniformly chosen $r \in \{0, 1\}^{t_M(x)}$. Pictorially, here the coin tosses are not "internal" but rather are supplied to the machine by an "external" coin-tossing device.

Before continuing, let it be noted that we should not confuse the fictitious model of "non-deterministic" machines with the model of probabilistic machines. The former is an unrealistic model that is useful for talking about search problems whose solutions can be efficiently verified (e.g., the definition of $\mathcal{NP}$), whereas the latter is a realistic model of computation.

Throughout this entire book, unless otherwise stated, a *probabilistic polynomial-time Turing machine* means a probabilistic machine that always (i.e., independently of the outcome of its internal coin tosses) halts after a polynomial (in the length of the input) number of steps. It follows that the number of coin tosses for a probabilistic polynomial-time machine M is bounded by a polynomial, denoted T_M, in its input length. Finally, without loss of generality, we assume that on input x the machine always makes $T_M(|x|)$ coin tosses.

1.3.2.3. Associating "Efficient" Computations with $\mathcal{BPP}$

The basic thesis underlying our discussion is the association of "efficient" computations with probabilistic polynomial-time computations. That is, we shall consider as efficient only randomized algorithms (i.e., probabilistic Turing machines) for which the running time is bounded by a polynomial in the length of the input.

Thesis: *Efficient computations correspond to computations that can be carried out by probabilistic polynomial-time Turing machines.*

A complexity class capturing these computations is the class, denoted $\mathcal{BPP}$, of languages recognizable (with high probability) by probabilistic polynomial-time Turing machines. The probability refers to the event in which *the machine makes the correct verdict on string x*.

Definition 1.3.4 (Bounded-Probability Polynomial Time, $\mathcal{BPP}$): *We say that L is recognized by the probabilistic polynomial-time Turing machine M if*

- *for every $x \in L$ it holds that $\Pr[M(x) = 1] \geq \frac{2}{3}$, and*
- *for every $x \notin L$ it holds that $\Pr[M(x) = 0] \geq \frac{2}{3}$.*

———— **15** ————

$\mathcal{BPP}$ is the class of languages that can be recognized by a probabilistic polynomial-time Turing machine (i.e., randomized algorithm).

The phrase "bounded-probability" indicates that the success probability is bounded away from $\frac{1}{2}$. In fact, in Definition 1.3.4, replacing the constant $\frac{2}{3}$ by any other constant greater than $\frac{1}{2}$ will not change the class defined; see Exercise 4. Likewise, the constant $\frac{2}{3}$ can be replaced by $1 - 2^{-|x|}$ and the class will remain invariant; see Exercise 5. We conclude that languages in $\mathcal{BPP}$ can be recognized by probabilistic polynomial-time algorithms with a negligible error probability. We use *negligible* to describe any function that decreases faster than the reciprocal of any polynomial:

Negligible Functions

> **Definition 1.3.5 (Negligible):** *We call a function $\mu : \mathbb{N} \to \mathbb{R}$* **negligible** *if for every positive polynomial $p(\cdot)$ there exists an N such that for all $n > N$,*
>
> $$\mu(n) < \frac{1}{p(n)}$$

For example, the functions $2^{-\sqrt{n}}$ and $n^{-\log_2 n}$ are negligible (as functions in n). Negligible functions stay that way when multiplied by any fixed polynomial. Namely, for every negligible function μ and any polynomial p, the function $\mu'(n) \stackrel{\text{def}}{=} p(n) \cdot \mu(n)$ is negligible. It follows that an event that occurs with negligible probability would be highly unlikely to occur even if we repeated the experiment polynomially many times.

Convention. In Definition 1.3.5 we used the phrase "there exists an N such that for all $n > N$." In the future we shall use the shorter and less tedious phrase "for all sufficiently large n." This makes one quantifier (i.e., the $\exists N$) implicit, and that is particularly beneficial in statements that contain several (more essential) quantifiers.

1.3.3. Non-Uniform Polynomial Time

A stronger (and actually unrealistic) model of efficient computation is that of non-uniform polynomial time. This model will be used only in the negative way, namely, for saying that even such machines cannot do something (specifically, even if the adversary employs such a machine, it cannot cause harm).

A *non-uniform polynomial-time "machine"* is a pair $(M, \bar{a})$, where M is a two-input polynomial-time Turing machine and $\bar{a} = a_1, a_2, \ldots$ is an infinite sequence of strings such that $|a_n| = \text{poly}(n)$.[6] For every x, we consider the computation of machine M on the input pair $(x, a_{|x|})$. Intuitively, a_n can be thought of as extra "advice" supplied from the "outside" (together with the input $x \in \{0, 1\}^n$). We stress that machine M

---

[6]Recall that poly() stands for some (unspecified) fixed polynomial; that is, we say that there exists some polynomial p such that $|a_n| = p(n)$ for all $n \in \mathbb{N}$.

gets the same advice (i.e., a_n) on all inputs of the same length (i.e., n). Intuitively, the advice a_n may be useful in some cases (i.e., for some computations on inputs of length n), but it is unlikely to encode enough information to be useful for all 2^n possible inputs.

Another way of looking at non-uniform polynomial-time "machines" is to consider an infinite sequence of Turing machines, $M_1, M_2, \ldots$, such that both the length of the description of M_n and its running time on inputs of length n are bounded by polynomials in n (fixed for the entire sequence). Machine M_n is used only on inputs of length n. Note the correspondence between the two ways of looking at non-uniform polynomial time. The pair $(M, (a_1, a_2, \ldots))$ (of the first definition) gives rise to an infinite sequence of machines $M_{a_1}, M_{a_2}, \ldots$, where $M_{a_{|x|}}(x) \stackrel{\text{def}}{=} M(x, a_{|x|})$. On the other hand, a sequence $M_1, M_2, \ldots$ (as in the second definition) gives rise to a pair $(U, (\langle M_1 \rangle, \langle M_2 \rangle, \ldots))$, where U is the universal Turing machine and $\langle M_n \rangle$ is the description of machine M_n (i.e., $U(x, \langle M_{|x|} \rangle) = M_{|x|}(x)$).

In the first sentence of this Section 1.3.3, non-uniform polynomial time was referred to as a stronger model than probabilistic polynomial time. That statement is valid in many contexts (e.g., language recognition, as seen later in Theorem 1.3.7). In particular, it will be valid in all contexts we discuss in this book. So we have the following informal "meta-theorem":

Meta-theorem: *Whatever can be achieved by probabilistic polynomial-time machines can be achieved by non-uniform polynomial-time "machines."*

The meta-theorem clearly is wrong if we think of the task of tossing coins. So the meta-theorem should not be understood literally. It is merely an indication of real theorems that can be proved in reasonable cases. Let us consider, for example, the context of language recognition.

Definition 1.3.6: *The complexity class* non-uniform polynomial time *(denoted $\mathcal{P}$/poly) is the class of languages L that can be recognized by a non-uniform sequence of polynomial time "machines." Namely, $L \in \mathcal{P}$/poly if there exists an infinite sequence of machines $M_1, M_2, \ldots$ satisfying the following:*

1. *There exists a polynomial $p(\cdot)$ such that for every n, the description of machine M_n has length bounded above by $p(n)$.*

2. *There exists a polynomial $q(\cdot)$ such that for every n, the running time of machine M_n on each input of length n is bounded above by $q(n)$.*

3. *For every n and every $x \in \{0, 1\}^n$, machine M_n will accept x if and only if $x \in L$.*

Note that the non-uniformity is implicit in the absence of a requirement concerning the construction of the machines in the sequence. It is required only that these machines exist. In contrast, if we augment Definition 1.3.6 by requiring the existence of a polynomial-time algorithm that on input 1^n (n presented in unary) outputs the description of M_n, then we get a cumbersome way of defining $\mathcal{P}$. On the other hand, it is obvious that $\mathcal{P} \subseteq \mathcal{P}/\text{poly}$ (in fact, strict containment can be proved by considering non-recursive unary languages). Furthermore:

Theorem 1.3.7: $\mathcal{BPP} \subseteq \mathcal{P}/\text{poly}$.

Proof: Let M be a probabilistic polynomial-time Turing machine recognizing $L \in \mathcal{BPP}$. Let $\chi_L(x) \stackrel{\text{def}}{=} 1$ if $x \in L$, and $\chi_L(x) \stackrel{\text{def}}{=} 0$ otherwise. Then, for every $x \in \{0, 1\}^*$,

$$\Pr[M(x) = \chi_L(x)] \geq \frac{2}{3}$$

Assume, without loss of generality, that on each input of length n, machine M uses the same number, denoted $m = \text{poly}(n)$, of coin tosses. Let $x \in \{0, 1\}^n$. Clearly, we can find for each $x \in \{0, 1\}^n$ a sequence of coin tosses $r \in \{0, 1\}^m$ such that $M_r(x) = \chi_L(x)$ (in fact, most sequences r have this property). But can one sequence $r \in \{0, 1\}^m$ fit all $x \in \{0, 1\}^n$? Probably not. (Provide an example!) Nevertheless, we can find a sequence $r \in \{0, 1\}^n$ that fits $\frac{2}{3}$ of all the x's of length n. This is done by an averaging argument (which asserts that if $\frac{2}{3}$ of the r's are good for each x, then there is an r that is good for at least $\frac{2}{3}$ of the x's). However, this does not give us an r that is good for all $x \in \{0, 1\}^n$. To get such an r, we have to apply the preceding argument on a machine M' with exponentially vanishing error probability. Such a machine is guaranteed by Exercise 5. Namely, for every $x \in \{0, 1\}^*$,

$$\Pr[M'(x) = \chi_L(x)] > 1 - 2^{-|x|}$$

Applying the averaging argument, now we conclude that there exists an $r \in \{0, 1\}^m$, denoted r_n, that is good for *more than* a $1 - 2^{-n}$ fraction of the x's in $\{0, 1\}^n$. It follows that r_n is good for all the 2^n inputs of length n. Machine M' (viewed as a deterministic two-input machine), together with the infinite sequence $r_1, r_2, \ldots$ constructed as before, demonstrates that L is in $\mathcal{P}/\text{poly}$. ■

Non-Uniform Circuit Families. A more convenient way of viewing non-uniform polynomial time, which is actually the way used in this book, is via (non-uniform) families of polynomial-size Boolean circuits. A *Boolean circuit* is a directed acyclic graph with internal nodes marked by elements of $\{\wedge, \vee, \neg\}$. Nodes with no in-going edges are called *input nodes*, and nodes with no out-going edges are called *output nodes*. A node marked $\neg$ can have only one child. Computation in the circuit begins with placing input bits on the input nodes (one bit per node) and proceeds as follows. If the children of a node (of in-degree d) marked $\wedge$ have values $v_1, v_2, \ldots, v_d$, then the node gets the value $\wedge_{i=1}^{d} v_i$. Similarly for nodes marked $\vee$ and $\neg$. The output of the circuit is read from its output nodes. The *size* of a circuit is the number of its edges. A *polynomial-size circuit family* is an infinite sequence of Boolean circuits $C_1, C_2, \ldots$ such that for every n, the circuit C_n has n input nodes and size $p(n)$, where $p(\cdot)$ is a polynomial (fixed for the entire family).

The computation of a Turing machine M on inputs of length n can be simulated by a single circuit (with n input nodes) having size $O((|\langle M \rangle| + n + t(n))^2)$, where $t(n)$ is a bound on the running time of M on inputs of length n. Thus, a non-uniform sequence of polynomial-time machines can be simulated by a non-uniform family of polynomial-size circuits. The converse is also true, because machines with polynomial description lengths can incorporate polynomial-size circuits and simulate their computations in polynomial time. The thing that is nice about the circuit formulation is that there is no need to repeat the polynomiality requirement twice (once for size and once for time) as in the first formulation.

Convention. For the sake of simplicity, we often take the liberty of considering circuit families $\{C_n\}_{n \in \mathbb{N}}$, where each C_n has poly(n) input bits rather than n.

1.3.4. Intractability Assumptions

We shall consider as *intractable* those tasks that cannot be performed by probabilistic polynomial-time machines. However, the adversarial tasks in which we shall be interested ("breaking an encryption scheme," "forging signatures," etc.) can be performed by non-deterministic polynomial-time machines (because the solutions, once found, can be easily tested for validity). Thus, the computational approach to cryptography (and, in particular, most of the material in this book) is *interesting* only if $\mathcal{NP}$ is not contained in $\mathcal{BPP}$ (which certainly implies $\mathcal{P} \neq \mathcal{NP}$).[7] We use the phrase "not interesting" (rather than "not valid") because all our statements will be of the form "if $\langle$intractability assumption$\rangle$ then $\langle$useful consequence$\rangle$." Such a statement remains valid even if $\mathcal{P} = \mathcal{NP}$ (or if just $\langle$intractability assumption$\rangle$, which is never weaker than $\mathcal{P} \neq \mathcal{NP}$, is wrong); but in such a case the implication is of little interest (because everything is implied by a fallacy).

In most places where we state that "if $\langle$intractability assumption$\rangle$ then $\langle$useful consequence$\rangle$," it will be the case that $\langle$useful consequence$\rangle$ either implies $\langle$intractability assumption$\rangle$ or implies some weaker form of it, which in turn implies $\mathcal{NP} \setminus \mathcal{BPP} \neq \emptyset$. Thus, in light of the current state of knowledge in complexity theory, we cannot hope to assert $\langle$useful consequence$\rangle$ without any intractability assumption.

In a few cases, an assumption concerning the limitations of probabilistic polynomial-time machines shall not suffice, and we shall use instead an assumption concerning the limitations of non-uniform polynomial-time machines. Such an assumption is of course stronger. But also the consequences in such a case will be stronger, since they will also be phrased in terms of non-uniform complexity. However, because all our proofs are obtained by reductions, an implication stated in terms of probabilistic polynomial time is stronger (than one stated in terms of non-uniform polynomial time) and will be preferred unless it is either not known or too complicated. This is the case because a probabilistic

---

[7]We remark that $\mathcal{NP}$ is not known to contain $\mathcal{BPP}$. This is the reason we state the foregoing conjecture as $\mathcal{NP}$ *is not contained in* $\mathcal{BPP}$, rather than $\mathcal{BPP} \neq \mathcal{NP}$. Likewise, although "sufficiently strong" one-way functions imply $\mathcal{BPP} = \mathcal{P}$, this equality is not known to hold unconditionally.

polynomial-time reduction (proving implication in its probabilistic formalization) always implies a non-uniform polynomial-time reduction (proving the statement in its non-uniform formalization), but the converse is not always true.[8]

Finally, we mention that intractability assumptions concerning worst-case complexity (e.g., $\mathcal{P} \neq \mathcal{NP}$) will not suffice, because we shall *not be satisfied* with their corresponding consequences. Cryptographic schemes that are guaranteed to be *hard to break only in the worst case* are useless. A cryptographic scheme must be unbreakable in "most cases" (i.e., "typical cases"), which implies that it will be *hard to break on the average*. It follows that because we are not able to prove that "worst-case intractability" implies analogous "intractability for the average case" (such a result would be considered a breakthrough in complexity theory), our intractability assumption must concern average-case complexity.

1.3.5. Oracle Machines

The original utility of oracle machines in complexity theory was to capture notions of reducibility. In this book (mainly in Chapters 5 and 6) we use oracle machines mainly for a different purpose altogether – to model an adversary that may use a cryptosystem in the course of its attempt to break the system. Other uses of oracle machines are discussed in Sections 3.6 and 4.7.

Loosely speaking, an oracle machine is a machine that is augmented so that it can ask questions to the outside. We consider the case in which these questions (called queries) are answered consistently by some function $f : \{0, 1\}^* \rightarrow \{0, 1\}^*$, called the oracle. That is, if the machine makes a query q, then the answer it obtains is $f(q)$. In such a case, we say that the oracle machine is given access to the oracle f.

Definition 1.3.8 (Oracle Machines): *A (deterministic/probabilistic)* **oracle machine** *is a (deterministic/probabilistic) Turing machine with an additional tape, called the* **oracle tape**, *and two special states, called* **oracle invocation** *and* **oracle appeared**. **The computation of the deterministic oracle machine M on input x and with access to the oracle** $f : \{0, 1\}^* \rightarrow \{0, 1\}^*$ **is defined by the successive-configuration relation**. *For configurations with states different from* oracle invocation, *the next configuration is defined as usual. Let γ be a configuration in which the state is* oracle invocation *and the content of the oracle tape is q. Then the configuration following γ is identical to γ, except that the state is* oracle appeared, *and the content of the oracle tape is $f(q)$. The string q is called M's* **query**, *and $f(q)$ is called the* **oracle reply**. *The computation of a probabilistic oracle machine is defined analogously. The output distribution of the oracle machine M, on input x and with access to the oracle f, is denoted $M^f(x)$.*

We stress that the running time of an oracle machine is the number of steps made during its computation and that the oracle's reply to each query is obtained in a single step.

---

[8]The current paragraph may be better understood in the future, after seeing some concrete examples.

1.4. Motivation to the Rigorous Treatment

In this section we address three related issues:

1. the mere need for a rigorous treatment of the field,

2. the practical meaning and/or consequences of the rigorous treatment, and

3. the "conservative" tendencies of the treatment.

Parts of this section (corresponding to Items 2 and 3) are likely to become more clear after reading any of the following chapters.

1.4.1. The Need for a Rigorous Treatment

> *If the truth of a proposition does not follow*
> *from the fact that it is self-evident to us,*
> *then its self-evidence in no way justifies our belief in its truth.*
> Ludwig Wittgenstein, *Tractatus logico-philosophicus* (1921)

Cryptography is concerned with the construction of schemes that will be robust against malicious attempts to make these schemes deviate from their prescribed functionality. Given a desired functionality, a cryptographer should design a scheme that not only will satisfy the desired functionality under "normal operation" but also will maintain that functionality in face of adversarial attempts that will be devised after the cryptographer has completed the design. The fact that an adversary will devise its attack after the scheme has been specified makes the design of such schemes very hard. In particular, the adversary will try to take actions other than the ones the designer has envisioned. Thus, *the evaluation of cryptographic schemes* must take account of a practically infinite set of adversarial strategies. It is useless to make assumptions regarding the specific *strategy* that an adversary may use. The only assumptions that can be justified will concern the computational *abilities* of the adversary. To summarize, an evaluation of a cryptographic scheme is a study of an infinite set of potential strategies (which are not explicitly given). Such a highly complex study cannot be carried out properly without great care (i.e., rigor).

The design of cryptographic systems must be based on *firm foundations*, whereas ad hoc approaches and heuristics are a very dangerous way to go. Although always inferior to a rigorously analyzed solution, a heuristic may make sense when the designer has a very good idea about the environment in which a scheme is to operate. Yet a cryptographic scheme has to operate in a maliciously selected environment that typically will transcend the designer's view. Under such circumstances, heuristics make little sense (if at all).

In addition to these straightforward considerations, we wish to stress two additional aspects.

On Trusting Unsound Intuitions. We believe that *one* of the roles of science is to formulate, examine, and refine our intuition about reality. A rigorous formulation is required in order to allow a careful examination that may lead either to verification and justification of our intuition or to its rejection as false (or as something that is true only in certain cases or only under certain refinements). There are many cases in which our initial intuition turns out to be correct, as well as many cases in which our initial intuition turns out to be wrong. The more we understand the discipline, the better our intuition becomes.

At this stage in history, it would be very presumptuous to claim that we have good intuition about the *nature of efficient computation*. In particular, we do not even know the answers to such basic questions as whether or not $\mathcal{P}$ is strictly contained in $\mathcal{NP}$, let alone have an understanding of what makes one computational problem hard while a seemingly related problem is easy. Consequently, we should be extremely careful when making assertions about what can or cannot be efficiently computed. Unfortunately, *making assertions about what can or cannot be efficiently computed is exactly what cryptography is all about*. Worse yet, many of the problems of cryptography have much more complex and cumbersome descriptions than are usually encountered in complexity theory. To summarize, cryptography deals with very complex computational notions and currently must do so without having a good understanding of much simpler computational notions. Hence, our current intuitions about cryptography must be considered highly unsound until they can be formalized and examined carefully. In other words, the general need to formalize and examine intuition becomes even more acute in a highly sensitive field such as cryptography that is intimately concerned with questions we hardly understand.

The Track Record. Cryptography, as a discipline, is well motivated. Consequently, cryptographic issues are being discussed by many researchers, engineers, and laypersons. Unfortunately, most such discussions are carried out without precise definitions of the subject matter. Instead, it is implicitly assumed that the basic concepts of cryptography (e.g., secure encryption) are self-evident (because they are so natural) and that there is no need to present adequate definitions. The fallacy of that assumption is demonstrated by the abandon of papers (not to mention private discussions) that derive and/or jump to wrong conclusions concerning security. In most cases these wrong conclusions can be traced back to implicit misconceptions regarding security that could not have escaped the eyes of the authors if they had been made explicit. We avoid listing all such cases here for several obvious reasons. Nevertheless, we shall mention one well-known example.

Around 1979, Ron Rivest claimed that no signature scheme that was "proven secure assuming the intractability of factoring" could resist a "chosen message attack." His argument was based on an implicit (and unjustified) assumption concerning the nature of a "proof of security (which assumes the intractability of factoring)." Consequently, for several years it was believed that one had to choose between having a signature scheme "proven to be unforgeable under the intractability of factoring" and having a signature scheme that could resist a "chosen message attack." However, in 1984, Goldwasser, Micali, and Rivest pointed out the fallacy on which Rivest's 1979 argument had been based and furthermore presented signature schemes that could resist a "chosen message attack," under general assumptions. In particular, the intractability of factoring suffices to prove that there exists a signature scheme that can resist "forgery," even under a "chosen message attack."

To summarize, the basic concepts of cryptography are indeed very natural, but they are *not* self-evident nor well understood. Hence, we do not yet understand these concepts well enough to be able to discuss them *correctly* without using precise definitions and rigorously justifying every statement made.

1.4.2. Practical Consequences of the Rigorous Treatment

As customary in complexity theory, our treatment is presented in terms of asymptotic analysis of algorithms. (Actually, it would be more precise to use the term "functional analysis of running time.") This makes the treatment less cumbersome, but it is *not* essential to the underlying ideas. In particular, the definitional approach taken in this book (e.g., the definitions of one-way functions, pseudorandom generators, zero-knowledge proofs, secure encryption schemes, unforgeable signature schemes, and secure protocols) is based on general paradigms that remain valid in any reasonable computational model. In particular, the definitions, although stated in an "abstract manner," lend themselves to concrete interpolations. The same holds with respect to the results that typically relate several such definitions. To clarify the foregoing, we shall consider, as an example, the statement of a generic result as presented in this book.

A typical result presented in this book relates two computational problems. The first problem is a simple computational problem that is assumed to be intractable (e.g., intractability of factoring), whereas the second problem consists of "breaking" a specific implementation of a useful cryptographic primitive (e.g., a specific encryption scheme). The abstract statement may assert that if integer factoring cannot be performed in polynomial time, then the encryption scheme is secure in the sense that it cannot be "broken" in polynomial time. Typically, the statement is proved by a fixed polynomial-time reduction of integer factorization to the problem of breaking the encryption scheme. Hence, what is actually being proved is that if one can break the scheme in time $T(n)$, where n is the security parameter (e.g., key length), then one can factor integers of length m in time $T'(m) = f(m, T(g(m)))$, where f and g are fixed polynomials that are at least implicit in the proof. In order to determine the practicality of the result, one should first determine these polynomials (f and g). For most of the basic results presented in this book, these polynomials are reasonably small, in the sense that instantiating a scheme with a reasonable security parameter and making reasonable intractability assumptions (e.g., regarding factoring) will yield a scheme that it is infeasible to break in practice. (In the exceptional cases, we say so explicitly and view these results as merely claims of the plausibility of relating the two notions.) We actually distinguish three types of results:

1. *Plausibility results:* Here we refer to results that are aimed either at establishing a connection between two notions or at providing a generic way of solving a class of problems.

   A result of the first type says that, in principle, X (e.g., a specific tool) can be used in order to construct Y (e.g., a useful utility), but the specific construction provided in the proof may be impractical. Still, such a result may be useful in practice because it suggests that one may be able to use *specific* implementations of X in order to provide a practical construction of Y. At the very least, such a result can be viewed as a challenge to the researchers to either provide a practical construction of Y using X or explain why a practical construction cannot be provided.

A result of the second type says that any task that belongs to some class $\mathcal{C}$ is solvable, but the generic construction provided in the proof may be impractical. Still, this is a very valuable piece of information: If we have a specific problem that falls into the foregoing class, then we know that the problem is solvable in principle. However, if we need to construct a real system, then we probably should construct a solution from scratch (rather than employing the preceding generic result).

To summarize, in both cases a plausibility result provides very useful information (even if it does not yield a practical solution). Furthermore, it is often the case that *some* tools developed toward proving a plausibility result may be useful in solving the specific problem at hand. This is typically the case for the next type of results.

2. *Introduction of paradigms and techniques that may be applicable in practice:* Here we refer to results that are aimed at introducing a new notion, model, tool, or technique. Such results (e.g., techniques) typically are applicable in practice, either as presented in the original work or, after further refinements, or at least as an inspiration.

3. *Presentation of schemes that are suitable for practical applications.*

Typically, it is quite easy to determine to which of the foregoing categories a specific result belongs. Unfortunately, the classification is not always stated in the original paper; however, typically it is evident from the construction. We stress that all results of which we are aware (in particular, all results mentioned in this book) come with an explicit construction. Furthermore, the security of the resulting construction is explicitly related to the complexity of certain intractable tasks. Contrary to some uninformed beliefs, for each of these results there is an explicit translation of concrete intractability assumptions (on which the scheme is based) into lower bounds on the amount of work required to violate the security of the resulting scheme.[9] We stress that this translation can be invoked for any value of the security parameter. Doing so will determine whether a specific construction is adequate for a specific application under specific reasonable intractability assumptions. In many cases the answer is in the affirmative, but in general this does depend on the specific construction, as well as on the specific value of the security parameter and on what it is reasonable to assume for this value (of the security parameter).

1.4.3. The Tendency to Be Conservative

When reaching the chapters in which cryptographic primitives are defined, the reader may notice that we are unrealistically "conservative" in our definitions of security. In other words, we are unrealistically liberal in our definition of insecurity. Technically speaking, this tendency raises no problems, because our primitives that are secure in a very strong sense certainly are also secure in the (more restricted) reasonable sense. Furthermore, we are able to implement such (strongly secure) primitives using

---

[9]The only exception to the latter statement is Levin's observation regarding the existence of a *universal one-way function* (see Section 2.4.1).

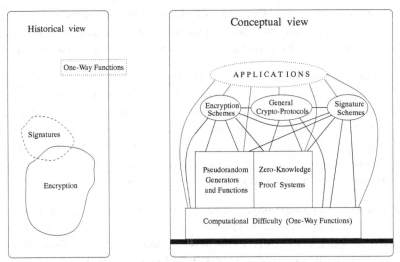

Figure 1.1: Cryptography: two points of view.

reasonable intractability assumptions, and in most cases we can show that such assumptions are necessary even for much weaker (and, in fact, less than minimal) notions of security. Yet the reader may wonder why we choose to present definitions that seem stronger than what is required in practice.

The reason for our tendency to be conservative when defining security is that it is extremely difficult to capture what is *exactly* required in a specific practical application. Furthermore, each practical application has different requirements, and it is undesirable to redesign the system for each new application. Thus, we actually need to address the security concerns of all future applications (which are unknown to us), not merely the security concerns of some known applications. It seems impossible to cover whatever can be required in all applications (or even in some wide set of applications) without taking our conservative approach.[10] In the sequel, we shall see how our conservative approach leads to definitions of security that can cover all possible practical applications.

1.5. Miscellaneous

In Figure 1.1 we confront the "historical view" of cryptography (i.e., the view of the field in the mid-1970s) with the approach advocated in this text.

1.5.1. Historical Notes

Work done during the 1980s plays a dominant role in our exposition. That work, in turn, had been tremendously influenced by previous work, but those early influences are not stated explicitly in the historical notes to subsequent chapters. In this section we shall

---

[10]One may even argue that it seems impossible to cover whatever is required in one reasonable application without taking our conservative approach.

trace some of those influences. Generally speaking, those influences took the form of setting intuitive goals, providing basic techniques, and suggesting potential solutions that later served as a basis for constructive criticism (leading to robust approaches).

Classic Cryptography. Answering the fundamental question of classic cryptography in a gloomy way (i.e., it is *impossible* to design a code that cannot be broken), Shannon [200] also suggested a modification to the question: Rather than asking whether or not it is *possible* to break a code, one should ask whether or not it is *feasible* to break it. A code should be considered good if it cannot be broken by an investment of work that is in reasonable proportion to the work required of the legal parties using the code. Indeed, this is the approach followed by modern cryptography.

New Directions in Cryptography. The prospect for commercial applications was the trigger for the beginning of civil investigations of encryption schemes. The DES block-cipher [168], designed in the early 1970s, has adopted the new paradigm: It is clearly *possible*, but supposedly *infeasible*, to break it. Following the challenge of constructing and analyzing new (private-key) encryption schemes came new questions, such as how to exchange keys over an insecure channel [159]. New concepts were invented: *digital signatures* (cf., Diffie and Hellman [63] and Rabin [186]), *public-key cryptosystems* [63], and *one-way functions* [63]. First implementations of these concepts were suggested by Merkle and Hellman [163], Rivest, Shamir, and Adleman [191], and Rabin [187].

Cryptography was explicitly related to complexity theory in the late 1970s [39, 73, 147]: It was understood that problems related to breaking a 1-1 cryptographic mapping could not be $\mathcal{NP}$-complete and, more important, that $\mathcal{NP}$-hardness of the breaking task was poor evidence for cryptographic security. Techniques such as "n-out-of-$2n$ verification" [186] and secret sharing [196] were introduced (and indeed were used extensively in subsequent research).

At the Dawn of a New Era. Early investigations of cryptographic protocols revealed the inadequacy of imprecise notions of security, as well as the subtleties involved in designing cryptographic protocols. In particular, problems such as *coin tossing over the telephone* [31], *exchange of secrets* [30], and *oblivious transfer* [188] (cf. [70]) were formulated. Doubts (raised by Lipton) concerning the security of the mental-poker protocol of [199] led to the current notion of secure encryption, due to Goldwasser and Micali [123], and to concepts such as computational indistinguishability [123, 210]. Doubts (raised by Fischer) concerning the oblivious-transfer protocol of [188] led to the concept of zero-knowledge (suggested by Goldwasser, Micali, and Rackoff [124], with early versions dating to March 1982).

A formal approach to the security of cryptographic protocols was suggested in [65]. That approach actually identified a *subclass* of insecure protocols (i.e., those that could be broken via a syntactically restricted type of attack). Furthermore, it turned out that it was much too difficult to test whether or not a given protocol was secure [69]. Recall that, in contrast, our current approach is to construct secure protocols (along with their proofs of security) and that this approach is *complete* (in the sense that it allows us to solve any solvable problem).

1.5.2. Suggestions for Further Reading

The background material concerning probability theory and computational complexity provided in Sections 1.2 and 1.3, respectively, should suffice for the purposes of this book. Still, a reader feeling uncomfortable with any of these areas may want to consult some standard textbooks on probability theory (e.g., [79]) and computational complexity (e.g., [86; 202]). The reader may also benefit from familiarity with randomized computation [167; 97, app. B].

Computational problems in number theory have provided popular candidates for one-way functions (and related intractability assumptions). However, because this book focuses on concepts, rather than on specific implementation of such concepts, those popular candidates will not play a major role in the exposition. Consequently, background in computational number theory is not really necessary for this book. Still, a brief description of relevant facts appears in Appendix A herein, and the interested reader is referred to other text (e.g., [10]).

This book focuses on the basic concepts, definitions, and results in cryptography. As argued earlier, these are of key importance for sound practice. However, practice needs much more than a sound theoretical framework, whereas this book makes no attempt to provide anything beyond the latter. For helpful suggestions concerning practice (i.e., applied cryptography), the reader may *critically* consult other texts (e.g., [158]).

Our treatment is presented in terms of asymptotic analysis of algorithms. Furthermore, for simplicity, we state results in terms of robustness against polynomial-time adversaries, rather than discussing general time-bounded adversaries. However, as explained in Section 1.4, none of these conventions is essential, and the results could be stated in general terms, as done in Section 2.6 and elsewhere (e.g., [155]). Our choice to present results in terms of robustness against polynomial-time adversaries makes the statement of the results somewhat less cumbersome, because it avoids stating the exact complexity of the reduction by which security is proved. This suffices for stating plausibility results, which is indeed our main objective in this book, but when using schemes in practice one needs to know the exact complexity of the reduction (for that will determine the actual security of the concrete scheme). We stress that typically it is easy to determine the complexity of the reductions presented in this book, and in some cases we also include comments referring to this aspect. We mention that the alternative choice, of presenting results in terms of robustness against general time-bounded adversaries, is taken in Luby's book [155].

1.5.3. Open Problems

As mentioned earlier (and further formalized in the next chapter), most of the content of this book relies on the existence of one-way functions. Currently, we assume the existence of such functions; it is to be hoped that the new century will witness a proof of this widely believed assumption/conjecture. We mention that the existence of one-way functions implies that $\mathcal{NP}$ is not contained in $\mathcal{BPP}$, and thus would establish that $\mathcal{NP} \neq \mathcal{P}$ (which is the most famous open problem in computer science).

We mention that $\mathcal{NP} \neq \mathcal{P}$ is not known to imply any practical consequences. For the latter, it would be required that hard instances not only exist but also occur quite frequently (with respect to some easy-to-sample distribution). For further discussion, see Chapter 2.

1.5.4. Exercises

Exercise 1: *Applications of Markov's inequality:*
1. Let X be a random variable such that $E(X) = \mu$ and $X \leq 2\mu$. Give an upper bound on $\Pr[X \leq \frac{\mu}{2}]$.
2. Let $0 < \varepsilon$ and $\delta < 1$, and let Y be a random variable ranging in the interval $[0,1]$ such that $E(Y) = \delta + \varepsilon$. Give a lower bound on $\Pr[Y \geq \delta + \frac{\varepsilon}{2}]$.
   Guideline: In both cases, one can define auxiliary random variables and apply Markov's inequality. However, it is easier simply to apply directly the reasoning underlying the proof of Markov's inequality.

Exercise 2: *Applications of Chernoff/Hoefding bounds:* Let $f : \{0,1\}^* \to [0,1]$ be a polynomial-time-computable function, and let $F(n)$ denote the average value of f over $\{0,1\}^n$. Namely,

$$F(n) \overset{\text{def}}{=} \frac{\sum_{x \in \{0,1\}^n} f(x)}{2^n}$$

Let $p(\cdot)$ be a polynomial. Present a probabilistic polynomial-time algorithm that on input 1^n will output an estimate to $F(n)$, denoted $A(n)$, such that

$$\Pr\left[|F(n) - A(n)| > \frac{1}{p(n)} \right] < 2^{-n}$$

Guideline: The algorithm selects at random polynomially many (how many?) sample points $s_i \in \{0,1\}^n$. These points are selected independently and with uniform probability distribution. (Why?) The algorithm outputs the average value taken over this sample. Analyze the performance of the algorithm using the Hoefding inequality. (Hint: Define random variables X_i such that $X_i = f(s_i)$.)

Exercise 3: *Analysis of the graph-connectivity algorithm:* Regarding the algorithm presented in Section 1.3.2.1, show that if s is connected to t in the graph G, then, with probability at least $\frac{2}{3}$, vertex t will be encountered in a random walk starting at s.

Guideline: Consider the connected component of vertex s, denoted $G' = (V', E')$. For any edge (u, v) in E', let $T_{u,v}$ be a random variable representing the number of steps taken in a random walk starting at u until v is first encountered. First, prove that $E[T_{u,v}] \leq 2|E'|$. (Hint: Consider the "frequency" with which this edge is traversed in a certain direction during an infinite random walk, and note that this frequency is independent of the identity of the edge and the direction.) Next, letting cover (G') be the expected number of steps in a random walk starting at s and ending when the last of the vertices of V' is encountered, prove that cover $(G') \leq 4 \cdot |V'| \cdot |E'|$. (Hint: consider a cyclic tour C going through all vertices of G', and show that cover $(G') \leq \sum_{(u,v) \in C} E[T_{u,v}]$.) Conclude by applying Markov's inequality.

Exercise 4: *Equivalent definition of BPP. Part 1:* Prove that Definition 1.3.4 is robust when $\frac{2}{3}$ is replaced by $\frac{1}{2} + \frac{1}{p(|x|)}$ for every positive polynomial $p(\cdot)$. Namely, show that $L \in \mathcal{BPP}$ if there exists a polynomial $p(\cdot)$ and a probabilistic polynomial-time machine M such that

- for every $x \in L$ it holds that $\Pr[M(x)=1] \geq \frac{1}{2} + \frac{1}{p(|x|)}$, and
- for every $x \notin L$ it holds that $\Pr[M(x)=0] \geq \frac{1}{2} + \frac{1}{p(|x|)}$.

   Guideline: Given a probabilistic polynomial-time machine M satisfying the foregoing condition, construct a probabilistic polynomial-time machine M' as follows. On input x, machine M' runs $O(p(|x|)^2)$ many copies of M, on the same input x, and rules by majority. Use Chebyshev's inequality (see Section 1.2) to show that M' is correct with probability at least $\frac{2}{3}$.

Exercise 5: *Equivalent definition of BPP. Part 2:* Prove that Definition 1.3.4 is robust when $\frac{2}{3}$ is replaced by $1 - 2^{-p(|x|)}$ for every positive polynomial $p(\cdot)$. Namely, show that for every $L \in \mathcal{BPP}$ and every polynomial $p(\cdot)$, there exists a probabilistic polynomial-time machine M such that

- for every $x \in L$ it holds that $\Pr[M(x)=1] \geq 1 - 2^{-p(|x|)}$, and
- for every $x \notin L$ it holds that $\Pr[M(x)=0] \geq 1 - 2^{-p(|x|)}$.

   Guideline: Similar to Exercise 4, except that you have to use a stronger probabilistic inequality (namely, Chernoff bound; see Section 1.2).

CHAPTER 2

Computational Difficulty

In this chapter we define and study one-way functions. One-way functions capture our notion of "useful" computational difficulty and serve as a basis for most of the results presented in this book. Loosely speaking, a one-way function is a function that is easy to evaluate but hard to invert (in an average-case sense). (See the illustration in Figure 2.1.) In particular, we define strong and weak one-way functions and prove that the existence of weak one-way functions implies the existence of strong ones. The proof provides a good example of a *reducibility argument*, which is a strong type of "reduction" used to establish most of the results in the area. Furthermore, the proof provides a simple example of a case where a computational statement is much harder to prove than its "information-theoretic analogue."

In addition, we define hard-core predicates and prove that every one-way function has a hard-core predicate. Hard-core predicates will play an important role in almost all subsequent chapters (the chapter on signature scheme being the exception).

Organization. In Section 2.1 we motivate the definition of one-way functions by arguing informally that it is implicit in various natural cryptographic primitives. The basic definitions are given in Section 2.2, and in Section 2.3 we show that weak one-way functions can be used to construct strong ones. A more efficient construction (for certain restricted cases) is postponed to Section 2.6. In Section 2.4 we view one-way functions as uniform collections of finite functions and consider various additional properties that such collections may have. In Section 2.5 we define hard-core predicates and show how to construct them from one-way functions.

Teaching Tip. As stated earlier, the proof that the existence of weak one-way functions implies the existence of strong ones (see Section 2.3) is instructive for the rest of the material. Thus, if you choose to skip this proof, do incorporate a discussion of the *reducibility argument* in the first place you use it (e.g., when showing how to construct hard-core predicates from one-way functions).

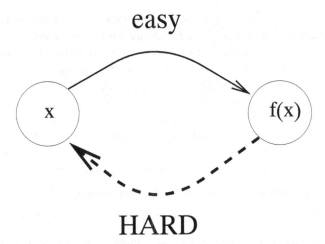

Figure 2.1: One-way functions: an illustration.

2.1. One-Way Functions: Motivation

As stated in the introductory chapter, modern cryptography is based on a gap between efficient algorithms provided for the legitimate users and the computational infeasibility of abusing or breaking these algorithms (via illegitimate adversarial actions). To illustrate this gap, we concentrate on the cryptographic task of secure data communication, namely, encryption schemes.

In secure encryption schemes, the legitimate users should be able to easily decipher the messages using some private information available to them, yet an adversary (not having this private information) should not be able to decrypt the ciphertext efficiently (i.e., in probabilistic polynomial time).[1] On the other hand, a non-deterministic machine can quickly decrypt the ciphertext (e.g., by guessing the private information). Hence, the existence of secure encryption schemes implies that there are tasks (e.g., "breaking" encryption schemes) that can be performed by non-deterministic polynomial-time machines, yet cannot be performed by deterministic (or even randomized) polynomial-time machines. In other words, a necessary condition for the existence of secure encryption schemes is that $\mathcal{NP}$ not be contained in $\mathcal{BPP}$ (and thus $\mathcal{P} \neq \mathcal{NP}$).

Although $\mathcal{P} \neq \mathcal{NP}$ is a necessary condition for modern cryptography, it is not a sufficient one. Suppose that the breaking of some encryption scheme is $\mathcal{NP}$-complete. Then, $\mathcal{P} \neq \mathcal{NP}$ implies that this encryption scheme is hard to break in the worst case, but it does not rule out the possibility that the encryption scheme is easy to break almost always. In fact, one can construct "encryption schemes" for which the breaking problem is $\mathcal{NP}$-complete and yet there exists an efficient breaking algorithm that succeeds 99% of the time. Hence, worst-case hardness is a poor measure of security. Security requires hardness in most cases, or at least "average-case hardness." A necessary condition for the existence of secure encryption schemes is thus the existence of languages in $\mathcal{NP}$

---

[1]This "private information" is called a key; see Chapter 5.

that are hard on the average. We mention that it is not known whether or not $P \neq NP$ implies the existence of languages in NP that are hard on the average.

Furthermore, the mere existence of problems (in NP) that are hard on the average does not suffice either. In order to be able to use such hard-on-the-average problems, we must be able to generate hard instances together with auxiliary information that will enable us to solve these instances fast. Otherwise, these hard instances will be hard also for the legitimate users, and consequently the legitimate users will gain no computational advantage over the adversary. Hence, the existence of secure encryption schemes implies the existence of an efficient way (i.e., probabilistic polynomial-time algorithm) to generate instances with corresponding auxiliary input such that

1. it is easy to solve these instances given the auxiliary input, but

2. it is hard, on the average, to solve these instances when not given the auxiliary input.

The foregoing requirement is reflected in the definition of one-way functions (as presented in the next section). Loosely speaking, a one-way function is a function that is easy to compute but hard (on the average) to invert. Thus, one-way functions capture the hardness of reversing the process of generating instances (and obtaining the auxiliary input from the instance alone), which is responsible for the discrepancy between the preceding two items. (For further discussion of this relationship, see Exercise 1.)

In assuming that one-way functions exist, we are postulating the existence of efficient processes (i.e., the computation of the function in the forward direction) that are hard to reverse. Note that such processes of daily life are known to us in abundance (e.g., the lighting of a match). The assumption that one-way functions exist is thus a complexity-theoretic analogue of daily experience.

2.2. One-Way Functions: Definitions

In this section, we present several definitions of one-way functions. The first version, hereafter referred to as a strong one-way function (or just one-way function), is the most popular one. We also present weak one-way functions, non-uniformly one-way functions, and plausible candidates for such functions.

2.2.1. Strong One-Way Functions

Loosely speaking, a one-way function is a function that is easy to compute but hard to invert. The first condition is quite clear: Saying that a function f is easy to compute means that there exists a polynomial-time algorithm that on input x outputs $f(x)$. The second condition requires more elaboration. What we mean by saying that *a function f is hard to invert* is that every probabilistic polynomial-time algorithm trying, on input y, to find an inverse of y under f may succeed only with negligible (in $|y|$) probability, where the probability is taken over the choices of y (as discussed later). A sequence $\{s_n\}_{n \in \mathbb{N}}$ (resp., a function $\mu : \mathbb{N} \to \mathbb{R}$) is called *negligible* in n if for every positive polynomial $p(\cdot)$ and all sufficiently large n's, it holds that $s_n < \frac{1}{p(n)}$ (resp., $\mu(n) < \frac{1}{p(n)}$). Further discussion follows the definition.

Definition 2.2.1 (Strong One-Way Functions): *A function $f : \{0, 1\}^* \rightarrow \{0, 1\}^*$ is called* **(strongly) one-way** *if the following two conditions hold:*

1. Easy to compute: *There exists a (deterministic) polynomial-time algorithm A such that on input x algorithm A outputs $f(x)$ (i.e., $A(x) = f(x)$).*

2. Hard to invert: *For every probabilistic polynomial-time algorithm A', every positive polynomial $p(\cdot)$, and all sufficiently large n's,*

$$\Pr[A'(f(U_n), 1^n) \in f^{-1}(f(U_n))] < \frac{1}{p(n)}$$

Recall that U_n denotes a random variable uniformly distributed over $\{0, 1\}^n$. Hence, the probability in the second condition is taken over all the possible values assigned to U_n and all possible internal coin tosses of A', with uniform probability distribution. Note that A' is not required to output a specific pre-image of $f(x)$; any pre-image (i.e., element in the set $f^{-1}(f(x))$) will do. (Indeed, in case f is 1-1, the string x is the only pre-image of $f(x)$ under f; but in general there may be other pre-images.)

The Auxiliary Input 1^n. In addition to an input in the range of f, the inverting algorithm A' is also given the length of the desired output (in unary notation). The main reason for this convention is to rule out the possibility that a function will be considered one-way merely because it drastically shrinks its input, and so the inverting algorithm just does not have enough time to print the desired output (i.e., the corresponding pre-image). Consider, for example, the function f_{len} defined by $f_{len}(x) = y$ such that y is the binary representation of the length of x (i.e., $f_{len}(x) = |x|$). Since $|f_{len}(x)| = \log_2 |x|$, no algorithm can invert f_{len} on y in time polynomial in $|y|$; yet there exists an obvious algorithm that inverts f_{len} on $y = f_{len}(x)$ in time polynomial in $|x|$ (e.g., by $|x| \mapsto 0^{|x|}$). In general, the auxiliary input $1^{|x|}$, provided in conjunction with the input $f(x)$, allows the inverting algorithm to run in time polynomial in the total length of the main input and the desired output. Note that in the special case of length-preserving functions f (i.e. $|f(x)| = |(x)|$ for all x's), this auxiliary input is redundant. More generally, the auxiliary input is redundant if, given only $f(x)$, one can generate $1^{|x|}$ in time polynomial in $|x|$. (See Exercise 4 and Section 2.2.3.2.)

Further Discussion

Hardness to invert is interpreted (by the foregoing definition) as an upper bound on the success probability of efficient inverting algorithms. The probability is measured with respect to both the random choices of the inverting algorithm and the distribution of the (main) input to this algorithm (i.e., $f(x)$). The input distribution to the inverting algorithm is obtained by applying f to a uniformly selected $x \in \{0, 1\}^n$. If f induces a permutation on $\{0, 1\}^n$, then the input to the inverting algorithm is uniformly distributed over $\{0, 1\}^n$. However, in the general case where f is not necessarily a one-to-one function, the input distribution to the inverting algorithm may differ substantially from the uniform one. In any case, it is required that the success probability, defined over the aforementioned probability space, be negligible (as a function of the length of x). To further clarify the condition placed on the success probability, we consider two trivial algorithms.

Random-Guess Algorithm A_1. On input $(y, 1^n)$, algorithm A_1 uniformly selects and outputs a string of length n. We note that the success probability of A_1 equals the collision probability of the random variable $f(U_n)$ (i.e., $\sum_y \Pr[f(U_n) = y]^2$). That is, letting U'_n denote a random variable uniformly distributed over $\{0, 1\}^n$ independently of U_n, we have

$$\Pr[A_1(f(U_n), 1^n) \in f^{-1}(f(U_n))] = \Pr[f(U'_n) = f(U_n)]$$
$$= \sum_y \Pr[f(U_n) = y]^2 \geq 2^{-n}$$

where the inequality is due to the fact that, for non-negative x_i's summing to 1, the sum $\sum_i x_i^2$ is minimized when all x_i's are equal. Thus, the last inequality becomes an equality if and only if f is a 1-1 function. Consequently:

1. For any function f, the success probability of the trivial algorithm A_1 is strictly positive. Thus, one cannot require that any efficient algorithm will *always* fail to invert f.

2. For any 1-1 function f, the success probability of A_1 in inverting f is negligible. Of course, this does not indicate that f is one-way (but rather that A_1 is trivial).

3. If f is one-way, then the collision probability of the random variable $f(U_n)$ is negligible. This follows from the fact that A_1 falls within the scope of the definition, and its success probability equals the collision probability.

Fixed-Output Algorithm A_2. Another trivial algorithm, denoted A_2, is one that computes a function that is constant on all inputs of the same length (e.g., $A_2(y, 1^n) = 0^n$). For every function f, we have

$$\Pr[A_2(f(U_n), 1^n) \in f^{-1}(f(U_n))] = \Pr[f(0^n) = f(U_n)]$$
$$= \frac{|f^{-1}(f(0^n))|}{2^n} \geq 2^{-n}$$

with equality holding in case $f(0^n)$ has a single pre-image (i.e., 0^n itself) under f. Again we observe analogous facts:

1. For any function f, the success probability of the trivial algorithm A_2 is strictly positive.

2. For any 1-1 function f, the success probability of A_2 in inverting f is negligible.

3. If f is one-way, then the fraction of x's in $\{0, 1\}^n$ that are mapped by f to $f(0^n)$ is negligible.

Obviously, Definition 2.2.1 considers all probabilistic polynomial-time algorithms, not merely the trivial ones discussed earlier. In some sense this definition asserts that for one-way functions, no probabilistic polynomial-time algorithm can "significantly" outperform these trivial algorithms.

Negligible Probability

A few words concerning the notion of negligible probability are in order. The foregoing definition and discussion consider the success probability of an algorithm to be *negligible* if, as a function of the input length, the success probability is bounded above by every polynomial fraction. It follows that repeating the algorithm polynomially (in the input length) many times yields a new algorithm that also has negligible success probability. In other words, events that occur with negligible (in n) probability remain negligible even if the experiment is repeated for polynomially (in n) many times. Hence, defining a negligible success rate as "occurring with probability smaller than any polynomial fraction" is naturally coupled with defining feasible computation as "computed within polynomial time."

A "strong negation" of the notion of a negligible fraction/probability is the notion of a noticeable fraction/probability. We say that a function $v : \mathbb{N} \to \mathbb{R}$ is *noticeable* if there exists a polynomial $p(\cdot)$ such that for all sufficiently large n's, it holds that $\mu(n) > \frac{1}{p(n)}$. We stress that functions may be neither negligible nor noticeable.

2.2.2. Weak One-Way Functions

One-way functions, as defined earlier, are one-way in a very strong sense. Namely, any efficient inverting algorithm has negligible success in inverting them. A much weaker definition, presented next, requires only that all efficient inverting algorithms fail with some noticeable probability.

Definition 2.2.2 (Weak One-Way Functions): *A function* $f : \{0, 1\}^* \to \{0, 1\}^*$ *is called* **weakly one-way** *if the following two conditions hold:*

1. Easy to compute: *As in the definition of a strong one-way function.*

2. Slightly hard to invert: *There exists a polynomial $p(\cdot)$ such that for every probabilistic polynomial-time algorithm A' and all sufficiently large n's,*

$$\Pr[A'(f(U_n), 1^n) \notin f^{-1}(f(U_n))] > \frac{1}{p(n)}$$

We call the reader's attention to the order of quantifiers: There exists a *single* polynomial $p(\cdot)$ such that $1/p(n)$ lower-bounds the failure probability of *all* probabilistic polynomial-time algorithms trying to invert f on $f(U_n)$.

Weak one-way functions fail to provide the kind of hardness alluded to in the earlier motivational discussions. Still, as we shall see later, they can be converted into strong one-way functions, which in turn do provide such hardness.

2.2.3. Two Useful Length Conventions

In the sequel it will be convenient to use the following two conventions regarding the *lengths* of the pre-images and images of one-way functions. In the current section we justify the use of these conventions.

2.2.3.1. Functions Defined Only for Some Lengths

In many cases it is more convenient to consider one-way functions with domains partial to the set of all strings. In particular, this facilitates the introduction of some structure in the domain of the function. A particularly important case, used throughout the rest of this section, is that of functions with domain $\cup_{n\in\mathbb{N}}\{0, 1\}^{l(n)}$, where $l(\cdot)$ is some polynomial. We provide a more general treatment of this case.

Let $I \subseteq \mathbb{N}$, and denote by $s_I(n)$ the successor of n with respect to I; namely, $s_I(n)$ is the smallest integer that is both greater than n and in the set I (i.e., $s_I(n) \stackrel{\text{def}}{=} \min\{i \in I : i > n\}$). A set $I \subseteq \mathbb{N}$ is called *polynomial-time-enumerable* if there exists an algorithm that on input n halts within poly(n) steps and outputs $1^{s_I(n)}$. (The unary output forces s_I to be polynomially bounded; i.e., $s_I(n) \leq$ poly(n).) Let I be a polynomial-time-enumerable set and f be a function with domain $\cup_{n\in I}\{0, 1\}^n$. We call f strongly (resp., weakly) *one-way on lengths in I* if f is polynomial-time-computable and is hard to invert over n's in I. For example, the hardness condition for functions that are strongly one-way on lengths in I is stated as follows:

> For every probabilistic polynomial-time algorithm A', every positive polynomial $p(\cdot)$, and all sufficiently large n's in I,

$$\Pr[A'(f(U_n), 1^n) \in f^{-1}(f(U_n))] < \frac{1}{p(n)}$$

Ordinary one-way functions, as defined in previous subsections, can be viewed as being one-way on lengths in $\mathbb{N}$.

One-way functions on lengths in any polynomial-time-enumerable set can be easily transformed into ordinary one-way functions (i.e., defined over all of $\{0, 1\}^*$). In particular, for any function f with domain $\cup_{n\in I}\{0, 1\}^n$, we can construct a function $g : \{0, 1\}^* \to \{0, 1\}^*$ by letting

$$g(x) \stackrel{\text{def}}{=} f(x') \tag{2.1}$$

where x' is the longest prefix of x with length in I. In case the function f is length-preserving (i.e., $|f(x)| = |x|$ for all x), we can preserve this property by modifying the construction to obtain a length-preserving function $g' : \{0, 1\}^* \to \{0, 1\}^*$ such that

$$g'(x) \stackrel{\text{def}}{=} f(x')x'' \tag{2.2}$$

where $x = x'x''$, and x' is the longest prefix of x with length in I.

> **Proposition 2.2.3:** *Let I be a polynomial-time-enumerable set, and let f be strongly (resp., weakly) one-way on lengths in I. Then g and g' (as defined in Eq. (2.1) and Eq. (2.2), respectively) are strongly (resp., weakly) one-way (in the ordinary sense).*

Although the validity of the foregoing proposition is very appealing, we urge the reader not to skip the following proof. The proof, which is indeed quite simple, uses (for the first time in this book) an argument that is used extensively in the sequel. The argument used to prove the hardness-to-invert property of the function g (resp., g') proceeds by assuming, toward the contradiction, that g (resp., g') can be efficiently inverted with unallowable success probability. Contradiction is derived by deducing that f can be efficiently inverted with unallowable success probability. In other words, inverting f is "reduced" to inverting g (resp., g'). The term "reduction" is used here in a stronger-than-standard sense. Here a reduction needs to preserve the success probability of the algorithms. This kind of argument is called a *reducibility argument*.

Proof: We first prove that g and g' can be computed in polynomial time. To this end we use the fact that I is a polynomial-time-enumerable set, which implies that we can decide membership in I in polynomial time (e.g., by observing that $m \in I$ if and only if $s_I(m-1) = m$). It follows that on input x one can find in polynomial time the largest $m \le |x|$ that satisfies $m \in I$. Computing $g(x)$ amounts to finding this m and applying the function f to the m-bit prefix of x. Similarly for g'.

We next prove that g maintains the hardness-to-invert property of f. A similar proof establishes the hardness-to-invert property of g'. For the sake of brevity, we present here only the proof for the case that f is strongly one-way. The proof for the case that f is weakly one-way is analogous.

The proof proceeds by contradiction. We assume, contrary to the claim (of the proposition), that there exists an efficient algorithm that inverts g with success probability that is not negligible. We use this inverting algorithm (for g) to construct an efficient algorithm that inverts f with success probability that is not negligible, hence deriving a contradiction (to the hypothesis of the proposition). In other words, we show that inverting f (with unallowable success probability) is efficiently reducible to inverting g (with unallowable success probability) and hence conclude that the latter is not feasible. The reduction is based on the observation that inverting g on images of arbitrary lengths yields inverting g also on images of lengths in I, and that on such lengths g collides with f.

Intuitively, any algorithm inverting g can be used to invert f as follows. On input $(y, 1^n)$, where y is supposedly in the image of $f(U_n) = g(U_m)$ for any $m \in \{n, \ldots, s_I(n) - 1\}$, we can invoke the g-inverter on input $(y, 1^m)$ and output the longest prefix with length in I of the string that the g-inverter returns (e.g., if the g-inverter returns an m-bit-long string, then we output its n-bit-long prefix). Thus, our success probability in inverting f on $f(U_n)$ equals the success probability of the g-inverter on $g(U_m)$. The question is which $m \in \{n, \ldots, s_I(n) - 1\}$ we should use, and the answer is to try them all (capitalizing on the fact that $s_I(n) = \text{poly}(n)$). Note that the integers are partitioned to intervals of the form $[n, \ldots, s_I(n) - 1]$, each associated with a single $n \in I$. Thus, the success probability of any g-inverter on infinitely many lengths $m \in \mathbb{N}$ translates to the success probability of our f-inverter on infinitely many lengths $n \in I$. Details follow.

Given an algorithm B' for inverting g, we construct an algorithm A' for inverting f such that A' has complexity and success probability related to those for B'. (For simplicity, we shall assume that $B'(y, 1^m) \in \{0, 1\}^m$ holds for all $y \in \{0, 1\}^*$ and $m \in \mathbb{N}$; this assumption is immaterial, and later we comment about this aspect in two footnotes.) Algorithm A' uses algorithm B' as a subroutine and proceeds as follows. On input y and 1^n (supposedly y is in the range of $f(U_n)$, and $n \in I$), algorithm A' proceeds as follows:

1. It computes $s_I(n)$ and sets $k \stackrel{\text{def}}{=} s_I(n) - n - 1 \geq 0$. (Thus, for every $i = 1, \ldots, k$, we have $n + i \notin I$.)

2. For $i = 0, 1, \ldots, k$, algorithm A' invokes algorithm B' on input $(y, 1^{n+i})$, obtaining $z_i \leftarrow B'(y, 1^{n+i})$; if $g(z_i) = y$, then A' outputs the n-bit-long prefix[2] of z_i.

Note that for all $x' \in \{0, 1\}^n$ and $|x''| \leq k$, we have $g(x'x'') = f(x')$, and so if $g(x'x'') = y$, then $f(x') = y$, which establishes the correctness of the output of A'. Using $s_I(n) = \text{poly}(n)$ and the fact that $s_I(n)$ is computable in polynomial time, it follows that if B' is a probabilistic polynomial-time algorithm, then so is A'. We next analyze the success probability of A' (showing that if B' inverts g with unallowable success probability, then A' inverts f with unallowable success probability).

Suppose that B' inverts g on $(g(U_m), 1^m)$ with probability $\varepsilon(m)$. Then there exists an n such that $m \in \{n, \ldots, \text{poly}(n)\}$ and such that $A'(f(U_n), 1^n)$ invokes B' on input $(f(U_n), 1^m) = (g(U_m), 1^m)$. It follows that $A'(f(U_n), 1^n)$ inverts f with probability at least $\varepsilon(m) = \varepsilon(\text{poly}(n))$. Thus, $A'(f(U_n), 1^n)$ inherits the success of $B'(g(U_m), 1^m)$. A tedious analysis (which can be skipped) follows.[3]

> Suppose, contrary to our claim, that g is not strongly one-way, and let B' be an algorithm demonstrating this contradiction hypothesis. Namely, there exists a polynomial $p(\cdot)$ such that for infinitely many m's the probability that B' inverts g on $g(U_m)$ is at least $\frac{1}{p(m)}$. Let us denote the set of these m's by M. Define a function $\ell_I : \mathbb{N} \to I$ such that $\ell_I(m)$ is the largest lower bound of m in I is both (i.e., $\ell_I(m) \stackrel{\text{def}}{=} \max\{i \in I : i \leq m\}$). Clearly, $m \geq \ell_I(m)$ and $m \leq s_I(\ell_I(m)) - 1$ for every m. The following two claims relate the success probability of algorithm A' with that of algorithm B'.
>
> **Claim 2.2.3.1:** Let m be an integer and $n = \ell_I(m)$. Then
>
> $$\Pr[A'(f(U_n), 1^n) \in f^{-1}(f(U_n))] \geq \Pr[B'(g(U_m), 1^m) \in g^{-1}(g(U_m))]$$
>
> (Namely, the success probability of algorithm A' on $f(U_{\ell_I(m)})$ is bounded below by the success probability of algorithm B' on $g(U_m)$.)
>
> **Proof:** By construction of A', on input $(f(x'), 1^n)$, where $x' \in \{0, 1\}^n$, algorithm A' obtains the value $B'(f(x'), 1^t)$ for every $t \in \{n, \ldots, s_I(n) - 1\}$. In particular, since $m \geq n$ and $m \leq s_I(\ell_I(m)) - 1 = s_I(n) - 1$, it follows that algorithm A' obtains the value $B'(f(x'), 1^m)$. By definition of g, for all $x'' \in \{0, 1\}^{m-n}$, it holds that $f(x') = g(x'x'')$. The claim follows. $\square$
>
> **Claim 2.2.3.2:** There exists a polynomial $q(\cdot)$ such that $m < q(\ell_I(m))$ for all m's.

---

[2] Here we use the assumption $z_i \in \{0, 1\}^{n+i}$, which implies that n is the largest integer that both is in I and is at most $n + i$. In general, A' outputs the longest prefix x' of z_i satisfying $|x'| \in I$. Note that it holds that $f(x') = g(z_i) = y$.

[3] The reader can verify that the following analysis does not refer to the length of the output of B' and so does not depend on the simplifying assumption made earlier.

Proof: Let q be a polynomial (as guaranteed by the polynomial-time enumerability of I) such that $s_I(n) < q(n)$. Then, for every m, we have $m < s_I(\ell_I(m)) < q(\ell_I(m))$. $\square$

By Claim 2.2.3.2, the set $S \overset{\text{def}}{=} \{\ell_I(m) : m \in M\}$ is infinite (as, otherwise, for u upper-bounding the elements in S we get $m < q(\ell_I(m)) \le q(u)$ for every $m \in M$, which contradicts the hypothesis that M is infinite). Using Claim 2.2.3.1, it follows that for every $n = \ell_I(m) \in S$, the probability that A' inverts f on $f(U_n)$ is at least

$$\frac{1}{p(m)} > \frac{1}{p(q(\ell_I(m)))} = \frac{1}{p(q(n))} = \frac{1}{\text{poly}(n)}$$

where the inequality is due to Claim 2.2.3.2. It follows that f is not strongly one-way, in contradiction to the proposition's hypothesis. ■

2.2.3.2. Length-Regular and Length-Preserving Functions

A second useful convention regarding one-way functions is to assume that the function f is *length-regular* in the sense that for every $x, y \in \{0, 1\}^*$, if $|x| = |y|$, then $|f(x)| = |f(y)|$. We point out that the transformation presented earlier (i.e., both Eq. (2.1) and Eq. (2.2)) preserves length regularity. A special case of length regularity, preserved by Eq. (2.2), is that of *length-preserving* functions.

Definition 2.2.4 (Length-Preserving Functions): *A function f is **length-preserving** if for every $x \in \{0, 1\}^*$ it holds that $|f(x)| = |x|$.*

Given a strongly (resp., weakly) one-way function f, we can construct a strongly (resp., weakly) one-way function f'' that is length-preserving, as follows. Let p be a polynomial bounding the length expansion of f (i.e., $|f(x)| \le p(|x|)$). Such a polynomial must exist because f is polynomial-time-computable. We first construct a length-regular function f' by defining

$$f'(x) \overset{\text{def}}{=} f(x)10^{p(|x|)-|f(x)|} \tag{2.3}$$

(We use a padding of the form 10^* in order to facilitate the parsing of $f'(x)$ into $f(x)$ and the "leftover" padding.) Next, we define f'' only on strings of length $p(n) + 1$, for $n \in \mathbb{N}$, by letting

$$f''(x'x'') \overset{\text{def}}{=} f'(x') , \text{ where } |x'x''| = p(|x'|) + 1 \tag{2.4}$$

Clearly, f'' is length-preserving.

Proposition 2.2.5: *If f is a strongly (resp., weakly) one-way function, then so are f' and f'' (as defined in Eq. (2.3) and Eq. (2.4), respectively).*

Proof Sketch: It is quite easy to see that both f' and f'' are polynomial-time-computable. Using "reducibility arguments" analogous to the one used in the preceding proof, we can establish the hardness-to-invert of both f' and f''. For example, given an algorithm B' for inverting f', we construct an algorithm A' for inverting f as follows. On input y and 1^n (supposedly y is in the range of $f(U_n)$), algorithm A' halts with output $B'(y10^{p(n)-|y|}, 1^n)$. ∎

On Dropping the Auxiliary Input $1^{|x|}$. The reader can easily verify that if f is length-preserving, then it is redundant to provide the inverting algorithm with the auxiliary input $1^{|x|}$ (in addition to $f(x)$). The same holds if f is length-regular and does not shrink its input by more than a polynomial amount (i.e., there exists a polynomial $p(\cdot)$ such that $p(|f(x)|) \geq |x|$ for all x). In the sequel, *we shall deal only with one-way functions that are length-regular and do not shrink their input by more than a polynomial amount.* Furthermore, we shall mostly deal with length-preserving functions. In all these cases, *we can assume, without loss of generality, that the inverting algorithm is given only $f(x)$ as input.*

On 1-1 One-Way Functions. If f is 1-1, then so is f' (as defined in Eq. (2.3)), but not f'' (as defined in Eq. (2.4)). Thus, when given a 1-1 one-way function, we can assume without loss of generality that it is length-regular, but we cannot assume that it is length-preserving. Furthermore, the assumption that 1-1 one-way functions exist seems stronger than the assumption that arbitrary (and hence length-preserving) one-way functions exist. For further discussion, see Section 2.4.

2.2.4. Candidates for One-Way Functions

Following are several candidates for one-way functions. Clearly, it is not known whether or not these functions are indeed one-way. These are only conjectures supported by extensive research that thus far has failed to produce an efficient inverting algorithm (one having noticeable success probability).

2.2.4.1. Integer Factorization

In spite of the extensive research directed toward the construction of feasible integer-factoring algorithms, the best algorithms known for factoring integers have sub-exponential running times. Hence it is reasonable to believe that the function f_{mult} that partitions its input string into two parts and returns the (binary representation of the) integer resulting by multiplying (the integers represented by) these parts is one-way. Namely, let

$$f_{\text{mult}}(x, y) = x \cdot y$$

where $|x| = |y|$, and $x \cdot y$ denotes (the string representing) the integer resulting by multiplying the integers (represented by the strings) x and y. Clearly, f_{mult} can be computed in polynomial time. Assuming the intractability of factoring (e.g., that given the product of two uniformly chosen n-bit-long primes, it is infeasible to find the prime factors), and using the density-of-primes theorem (which guarantees that at least $\frac{N}{\log_2 N}$ of the integers smaller than N are primes), it follows that f_{mult} is at least weakly one-way. (For further discussion, see Exercise 8.) Other popular functions related to integer factorization (e.g., the RSA function) are discussed in Section 2.4.3.

2.2.4.2. Decoding of Random Linear Codes

One of the most outstanding open problems in the area of error-correcting codes is that of presenting efficient decoding algorithms for random linear codes. Of particular interest are random linear codes with constant information rates that can correct a constant fraction of errors. An (n, k, d) *linear code* is a k-by-n binary matrix in which the vector sum (mod 2) of any non-empty subset of rows results in a vector with at least d entries of 1 (one-entries). (A k-bit-long message is encoded by multiplying it by the k-by-n matrix, and the resulting n-bit-long vector has a unique pre-image even when flipping up to $\frac{d}{2}$ of its entries.) The Gilbert-Varshamov bound for linear codes guarantees the existence of such a code provided that $\frac{k}{n} < 1 - H_2(\frac{d}{n})$, where $H_2(p) \overset{\text{def}}{=} -p \log_2 p - (1 - p) \log_2(1 - p)$ if $p < \frac{1}{2}$ and $H_2(p) \overset{\text{def}}{=} 1$ otherwise (i.e., $H_2(\cdot)$ is a modification of the binary entropy function). Similarly, if for some $\varepsilon > 0$ it holds that $\frac{k}{n} < 1 - H_2(\frac{(1+\varepsilon)d}{n})$, then almost all k-by-n binary matrices will constitute (n, k, d) linear codes. Consider three constants $\kappa, \delta, \varepsilon > 0$ satisfying $\kappa < 1 - H_2((1 + \varepsilon)\delta)$. The function f_{code} seems a plausible candidate for a one-way function:

$$f_{\text{code}}(C, x, i) \overset{\text{def}}{=} (C, xC + e(i))$$

where C is a κn-by-n binary matrix, x is a κn-dimensional binary vector, i is the index of an n-dimensional binary vector having at most $\frac{\delta n}{2}$ one-entries within a corresponding enumeration of such vectors (the vector itself is denoted $e(i)$), and the arithmetic is in the n-dimensional binary vector space. Clearly, f_{code} is polynomial-time-computable, provided we use an efficient enumeration of vectors. An efficient algorithm for inverting f_{code} would yield an efficient algorithm for decoding a non-negligible fraction of the constant-rate linear codes (which would constitute an earth-shaking result in coding theory).

2.2.4.3. The Subset-Sum Problem

Consider the function f_{ssum} defined as follows:

$$f_{\text{ssum}}(x_1, \ldots, x_n, I) = \left(x_1, \ldots, x_n, \sum_{i \in I} x_i \right)$$

where $|x_1| = \cdots = |x_n| = n$, and $I \subseteq \{1, 2, \ldots, n\}$. Clearly, f_{ssum} is polynomial-time-computable. The fact that the subset-sum problem is $\mathcal{NP}$-complete cannot serve as evidence to the one-wayness of f_{ssum}. On the other hand, the fact that the subset-sum problem is easy for special cases (such as having "hidden structure" and/or "low density") does not rule out this proposal. The conjecture that f_{ssum} is one-way is based on the failure of known algorithms to handle random "high-density" instances (i.e., instances in which the length of the elements approximately equals their number, as in the definition of f_{ssum}).

2.2.5. Non-Uniformly One-Way Functions

In the foregoing two definitions of one-way functions the inverting algorithm is a probabilistic polynomial-time algorithm. Stronger versions of both definitions require that the functions cannot be inverted even by non-uniform families of polynomial-size circuits. We stress that the easy-to-compute condition is still stated in terms of uniform algorithms. For example, the following is a non-uniform version of the definition of strong (length-preserving) one-way functions.

Definition 2.2.6 (Non-Uniformly Strong One-Way Functions): *A function f : $\{0, 1\}^* \rightarrow \{0, 1\}^*$ is called **non-uniformly one-way** if the following two conditions hold:*

1. Easy to compute: *There exists a polynomial-time algorithm A such that on input x algorithm A outputs $f(x)$.*

2. Hard to invert: *For every (even non-uniform) family of polynomial-size circuits $\{C_n\}_{n \in \mathbb{N}}$, every positive polynomial $p(\cdot)$, and all sufficiently large n's,*

$$\Pr[C_n(f(U_n)) \in f^{-1}(f(U_n))] < \frac{1}{p(n)}$$

The probability in the second condition is taken only over all the possible values of U_n. We note that any non-uniformly one-way function is one-way (i.e., in the uniform sense).

Proposition 2.2.7: *If f is non-uniformly one-way, then it is one-way. That is, if f satisfies Definition 2.2.6, then it also satisfies Definition 2.2.1.*

Proof: We convert any (uniform) probabilistic polynomial-time inverting algorithm into a non-uniform family of polynomial-size circuits, without decreasing the success probability. This is in accordance with our meta-theorem (see Section 1.3.3). Details follow.

Let A' be a probabilistic polynomial-time (inverting) algorithm. Let r_n denote a sequence of coin tosses for A' maximizing the success probability of A' (averaged over input $f(U_n)$). Namely, r_n satisfies

$$\Pr[A'_{r_n}(f(U_n)) \in f^{-1}(f(U_n))] \geq \Pr[A'(f(U_n)) \in f^{-1}(f(U_n))]$$

where the first probability is taken only over all possible values of U_n, and the second probability is also over all possible coin tosses for A'. (Recall that $A'_r(y)$ denotes the output of algorithm A' on input y and internal coin tosses r.) The desired circuit C_n incorporates the code of algorithm A' and the sequence r_n (which is of length polynomial in n). ∎

We note that, typically, averaging arguments (of the form applied earlier) allow us to convert probabilistic polynomial-time algorithms into non-uniform polynomial-size circuits. Thus, in general, non-uniform notions of security (i.e., robustness against non-uniform polynomial-size circuits) imply uniform notions of security (i.e., robustness against probabilistic polynomial-time algorithms). The converse is not necessarily true. In particular, it is possible that one-way functions exist (in the uniform sense) and yet there are no non-uniformly one-way functions. However, this situation (i.e., that one-way functions exist *only* in the uniform sense) seems unlikely, and it is widely believed that non-uniformly one-way functions exist. In fact, all candidates mentioned in the preceding subsection are believed to be non-uniformly one-way functions.

2.3. Weak One-Way Functions Imply Strong Ones

We first remark that not every weak one-way function is necessarily a strong one. Consider, for example, a one-way function f (which, without loss of generality, is length-preserving). Modify f into a function g so that $g(p, x) = (p, f(x))$ if p starts with $\log_2 |x|$ zeros, and $g(p, x) = (p, x)$ otherwise, where (in both cases) $|p| = |x|$.[4] We claim that g is a weak one-way function but not a strong one. Clearly, g cannot be a strong one-way function (because for all but a $\frac{1}{n}$ fraction of the strings of length $2n$ the function g coincides with the identity function). To prove that g is weakly one-way, we use a "reducibility argument."

Proposition 2.3.1: *Let f be a one-way function (even in the weak sense). Then g, constructed earlier, is a weakly one-way function.*

Proof: Intuitively, inverting g on inputs on which it does *not* coincide with the identity transformation is related to inverting f. Thus, if g is inverted, on inputs of length $2n$, with probability that is noticeably greater than $1 - \frac{1}{n}$, then g must be inverted with noticeable probability on inputs to which g applies f. Therefore, if g is not weakly one-way, then neither is f. The full, straightforward but tedious proof follows.

Given a probabilistic polynomial-time algorithm B' for inverting g, we construct a probabilistic polynomial-time algorithm A' that inverts f with "related" success probability. Following is the description of algorithm A'. On input y, algorithm A' sets $n \overset{\text{def}}{=} |y|$ and $l \overset{\text{def}}{=} \log_2 n$, selects p' uniformly in $\{0, 1\}^{n-l}$, computes $z \overset{\text{def}}{=} B'(0^l p', y)$, and halts with output of the n-bit suffix of z. Let S_{2n} denote the sets of all $2n$-bit-long strings that start with $\log_2 n$ zeros (i.e., $S_{2n} \overset{\text{def}}{=} \{0^{\log_2 n}\alpha : \alpha \in \{0, 1\}^{2n-\log_2 n}\}$). Then, by construction of A' and g, we have

$$\Pr[A'(f(U_n)) \in f^{-1}(f(U_n))]$$

$$\geq \Pr[B'(0^l U_{n-l}, f(U_n)) \in (0^l U_{n-l}, f^{-1}(f(U_n)))]$$

$$= \Pr[B'(g(U_{2n})) \in g^{-1}(g(U_{2n})) \mid U_{2n} \in S_{2n}]$$

$$\geq \frac{\Pr[B'(g(U_{2n})) \in g^{-1}(g(U_{2n}))] - \Pr[U_{2n} \notin S_{2n}]}{\Pr[U_{2n} \in S_{2n}]}$$

$$= n \cdot \left(\Pr[B'(g(U_{2n})) \in g^{-1}(g(U_{2n}))] - \left(1 - \frac{1}{n}\right) \right)$$

$$= 1 - n \cdot (1 - \Pr[B'(g(U_{2n})) \in g^{-1}(g(U_{2n}))])$$

---

[4] Throughout the text, we treat $\log_2 |x|$ as if it were an integer. A precise argument can be derived by replacing $\log_2 |x|$ with $\lfloor \log_2 |x| \rfloor$ and some minor adjustments.

———— 43 ————

(For the second inequality, we used $\Pr[A|B] = \frac{\Pr[A \cap B]}{\Pr[B]}$ and $\Pr[A \cap B] \geq \Pr[A] - \Pr[\neg B]$.) It should not come as a surprise that the above expression is meaningful only in case $\Pr[B'(g(U_{2n})) \in g^{-1}(g(U_{2n}))] > 1 - \frac{1}{n}$.

It follows that for every polynomial $p(\cdot)$ and every integer n, if B' inverts g on $g(U_{2n})$ with probability greater than $1 - \frac{1}{p(2n)}$, then A' inverts f on $f(U_n)$ with probability greater than $1 - \frac{n}{p(2n)}$. Hence, if g is not weakly one-way (i.e., for every polynomial $p(\cdot)$ there exist infinitely many m's such that g can be inverted on $g(U_m)$ with probability $\geq 1 - 1/p(m)$), then also f is not weakly one-way (i.e., for every polynomial $q(\cdot)$ there exist infinitely many n's such that f can be inverted on $f(U_n)$ with probability $\geq 1 - 1/q(n)$, where $q(n) = p(2n)/n$). This contradicts our hypothesis (that f is weakly one-way).

To summarize, given a probabilistic polynomial-time algorithm that inverts g on $g(U_{2n})$ with success probability $1 - \frac{1}{n} + \alpha(n)$, we obtain a probabilistic polynomial-time algorithm that inverts f on $f(U_n)$ with success probability $n \cdot \alpha(n)$. Thus, since f is (weakly) one-way, $n \cdot \alpha(n) < 1 - (1/q(n))$ must hold for some polynomial q, and so g must be weakly one-way (since each probabilistic polynomial-time algorithm trying to invert g on $g(U_{2n})$ must fail with probability at least $\frac{1}{n} - \alpha(n) > \frac{1}{n \cdot q(n)}$). ■

We have just shown that unless no one-way functions exist, there exist weak one-way functions that are not strong ones. This rules out the possibility that all one-way functions are strong ones. Fortunately, we can also rule out the possibility that all one-way functions are (only) weak ones. In particular, the existence of weak one-way functions implies the existence of strong ones.

Theorem 2.3.2: *Weak one-way functions exist if and only if strong one-way functions exist.*

We strongly recommend that the reader not skip the proof (given in Section 2.3.1), since we believe that the proof is very instructive to the rest of this book. Furthermore, the proof demonstrates that amplification of computational difficulty is much more involved than amplification of an analogous probabilistic event. Both aspects are further discussed in Section 2.3.3. An illustration of the proof in the context of a "toy" example is provided in Section 2.3.2. (It is possible to read Section 2.3.2 before Section 2.3.1; in fact, most readers may prefer to do so.)

2.3.1. Proof of Theorem 2.3.2

Let f be a weak one-way function, and let p be the polynomial guaranteed by the definition of a weak one-way function. Namely, every probabilistic polynomial-time algorithm fails to invert f on $f(U_n)$ with probability at least $\frac{1}{p(n)}$. We assume, for simplicity, that f is length-preserving (i.e. $|f(x)| = |x|$ for all x's). This assumption, which is not really essential, is justified by Proposition 2.2.5. We define a function g

as follows:

$$g(x_1, \ldots, x_{t(n)}) \overset{\text{def}}{=} f(x_1), \ldots, f(x_{t(n)}) \tag{2.5}$$

where $|x_1| = \cdots = |x_{t(n)}| = n$ and $t(n) \overset{\text{def}}{=} n \cdot p(n)$. Namely, the $n^2 p(n)$-bit-long input of g is partitioned into $t(n)$ blocks, each of length n, and f is applied to each block.

Clearly, g can be computed in polynomial time (by an algorithm that breaks the input into blocks and applies f to each block). Furthermore, it is easy to see that inverting g on $g(x_1, \ldots, x_{t(n)})$ requires finding a pre-image to each $f(x_i)$. One may be tempted to deduce that it is also clear that g is a strongly one-way function. A naive argument might proceed by assuming implicitly (with no justification) that the inverting algorithm worked separately on each $f(x_i)$. If that were indeed the case, then the probability that an inverting algorithm could successfully invert all $f(x_i)$ would be at most $(1 - \frac{1}{p(n)})^{n \cdot p(n)} < 2^{-n}$ (which is negligible also as a function of $n^2 p(n)$). However, the assumption that an algorithm trying to invert g works independently on each $f(x_i)$ cannot be justified. Hence, a more complex argument is required.

Following is an outline of our proof. The proof that g is strongly one-way proceeds by a contradiction argument. We assume, on the contrary, that g is not strongly one-way; namely, we assume that there exists a polynomial-time algorithm that inverts g with probability that is not negligible. We derive a contradiction by presenting a polynomial-time algorithm that, for infinitely many n's, inverts f on $f(U_n)$ with probability greater than $1 - \frac{1}{p(n)}$ (in contradiction to our hypothesis). The inverting algorithm for f uses the inverting algorithm for g as a subroutine (without assuming anything about the manner in which the latter algorithm operates). (We stress that we do not assume that the g-inverter works in a particular way, but rather use any g-inverter to construct, in a generic way, an f-inverter.) Details follow.

Suppose that g is not strongly one-way. By definition, it follows that there exists a probabilistic polynomial-time algorithm B' and a polynomial $q(\cdot)$ such that for infinitely many m's,

$$\Pr[B'(g(U_m)) \in g^{-1}(g(U_m))] > \frac{1}{q(m)} \tag{2.6}$$

Let us denote by M' the infinite set of integers for which this holds. Let N' denote the infinite set of n's for which $n^2 \cdot p(n) \in M'$ (note that all m's considered are of the form $n^2 \cdot p(n)$, for some integer n).

Using B', we now present a probabilistic polynomial-time algorithm A' for inverting f. On input y (supposedly in the range of f), algorithm A' proceeds by applying the following probabilistic procedure, denoted I, on input y for $a(|y|)$ times, where $a(\cdot)$ is a polynomial that depends on the polynomials p and q (specifically, we set $a(n) \overset{\text{def}}{=} 2n^2 \cdot p(n) \cdot q(n^2 p(n)))$.

Procedure I

Input: y (denote $n \overset{\text{def}}{=} |y|$).

$$\text{------} \quad \mathbf{45} \quad \text{------}$$

For $i = 1$ to $t(n)$ do begin

1. Select uniformly and independently a sequence of strings $x_1, \ldots, x_{t(n)} \in \{0, 1\}^n$.

2. Compute $(z_1, \ldots, z_{t(n)}) \leftarrow B'(f(x_1), \ldots, f(x_{i-1}), y, f(x_{i+1}), \ldots, f(x_{t(n)}))$.
(Note that y is placed in the ith position instead of $f(x_i)$.)

3. If $f(z_i) = y$, then halt and output z_i.
(This is considered a *success*).

end

Using Eq. (2.6), we now present a lower bound on the success probability of algorithm A'. To this end we define a set, denoted S_n, that contains all n-bit strings on which the procedure I succeeds with non-negligible probability (specifically, greater than $\frac{n}{a(n)}$). (The probability is taken only over the coin tosses of procedure I.) Namely,

$$S_n \stackrel{\text{def}}{=} \left\{ x : \Pr[I(f(x)) \in f^{-1}(f(x))] > \frac{n}{a(n)} \right\}$$

In the next two claims we shall show that S_n contains all but at most a $\frac{1}{2p(n)}$ fraction of the strings of length $n \in N'$ and that for each string $x \in S_n$ the algorithm A' inverts f on $f(x)$ with probability exponentially close to 1. It will follow that A' inverts f on $f(U_n)$, for $n \in N'$, with probability greater than $1 - \frac{1}{p(n)}$, in contradiction to our hypothesis.

Claim 2.3.2.1: For every $x \in S_n$,

$$\Pr[A'(f(x)) \in f^{-1}(f(x))] > 1 - \frac{1}{2^n}$$

Proof: By definition of the set S_n, the procedure I inverts $f(x)$ with probability at least $\frac{n}{a(n)}$. Algorithm A' merely repeats I for $a(n)$ times, and hence

$$\Pr[A'(f(x)) \notin f^{-1}(f(x))] < \left(1 - \frac{n}{a(n)}\right)^{a(n)} < \frac{1}{2^n}$$

The claim follows. $\square$

Claim 2.3.2.2: For every $n \in N'$,

$$|S_n| > \left(1 - \frac{1}{2p(n)}\right) \cdot 2^n$$

Proof: We assume, to the contrary, that $|S_n| \leq (1 - \frac{1}{2p(n)}) \cdot 2^n$. We shall reach a contradiction to Eq. (2.6) (i.e., our hypothesis concerning the success probability of B'). Recall that by this hypothesis (for $n \in N0$),

$$s(n) \stackrel{\text{def}}{=} \Pr\left[B'(g(U_{n^2 p(n)})) \in g^{-1}(g(U_{n^2 p(n)}))\right] > \frac{1}{q(n^2 p(n))} \tag{2.7}$$

Let $U_n^{(1)}, \ldots, U_n^{(n \cdot p(n))}$ denote the n-bit-long blocks in the random variable $U_{n^2 p(n)}$ (i.e., these $U_n^{(i)}$'s are independent random variables each uniformly distributed in $\{0, 1\}^n$). We partition the event considered in Eq. (2.7) into two disjoint events corresponding to whether or not one of the $U_n^{(i)}$'s resides out of S_n. Intuitively, B' cannot perform well in such a case, since this case corresponds to the success probability of I on pre-images out of S_n. On the other hand, the probability that all $U_n^{(i)}$'s reside in S_n is small. Specifically, we define

$$s_1(n) \stackrel{\text{def}}{=} \Pr\left[B'\left(g(U_{n^2 p(n)})\right) \in g^{-1}\left(g\left(U_{n^2 p(n)}\right)\right) \wedge \left(\exists i \text{ s.t. } U_n^{(i)} \notin S_n\right)\right]$$

and

$$s_2(n) \stackrel{\text{def}}{=} \Pr\left[B'\left(g\left(U_{n^2 p(n)}\right)\right) \in g^{-1}\left(g\left(U_{n^2 p(n)}\right)\right) \wedge \left(\forall i : U_n^{(i)} \in S_n\right)\right]$$

Clearly, $s(n) = s_1(n) + s_2(n)$ (as the events considered in the s_i's are disjoint). We derive a contradiction to the lower bound on $s(n)$ (given in Eq. (2.7)) by presenting upper bounds for both $s_1(n)$ and $s_2(n)$ (which sum up to less).

First, we present an upper bound on $s_1(n)$. The key observation is that algorithm I inverts f on input $f(x)$ with probability that is related to the success of B' to invert g on a sequence of random f-images containing $f(x)$. Specifically, for every $x \in \{0, 1\}^n$ and every $1 \le i \le n \cdot p(n)$, the probability that I inverts f on $f(x)$ is greater than or equal to the probability that B' inverts g on $g(U_{n^2 p(n)})$ conditioned on $U_n^{(i)} = x$ (since any success of B' to invert g means that f was inverted on the ith block, and thus contributes to the success probability of I). It follows that, for every $x \in \{0, 1\}^n$ and every $1 \le i \le n \cdot p(n)$,

$$\Pr[I(f(x)) \in f^{-1}(f(x))]$$
$$\ge \Pr\left[B'\left(g(U_{n^2 p(n)})\right) \in g^{-1}\left(g(U_{n^2 p(n)})\right) \mid U_n^{(i)} = x\right] \qquad (2.8)$$

Since for $x \notin S_n$ the left-hand side (l.h.s.) cannot be large, we shall show that (the r.h.s. and so) $s_1(n)$ cannot be large. Specifically, using Eq. (2.8), it follows that

$$s_1(n) = \Pr\left[\exists i \text{ s.t. } B'\left(g(U_{n^2 p(n)})\right) \in g^{-1}\left(g(U_{n^2 p(n)})\right) \wedge U_n^{(i)} \notin S_n\right]$$

$$\le \sum_{i=1}^{n \cdot p(n)} \Pr\left[B'\left(g(U_{n^2 p(n)})\right) \in g^{-1}\left(g(U_{n^2 p(n)})\right) \wedge U_n^{(i)} \notin S_n\right]$$

$$\le \sum_{i=1}^{n \cdot p(n)} \sum_{x \notin S_n} \Pr\left[B'\left(g(U_{n^2 p(n)})\right) \in g^{-1}\left(g(U_{n^2 p(n)})\right) \wedge U_n^{(i)} = x\right]$$

$$= \sum_{i=1}^{n \cdot p(n)} \sum_{x \notin S_n} \Pr\left[U_n^{(i)} = x\right] \cdot \Pr\left[B'\left(g(U_{n^2 p(n)})\right) \in g^{-1}\left(g(U_{n^2 p(n)})\right) \mid U_n^{(i)} = x\right]$$

$$\le \sum_{i=1}^{n \cdot p(n)} \max_{x \notin S_n} \left\{\Pr\left[B'\left(g(U_{n^2 p(n)})\right) \in g^{-1}\left(g(U_{n^2 p(n)})\right) \mid U_n^{(i)} = x\right]\right\}$$

$$\le \sum_{i=1}^{n \cdot p(n)} \max_{x \notin S_n}\{\Pr[I(f(x)) \in f^{-1}(f(x))]\}$$

$$\le n \cdot p(n) \cdot \frac{n}{a(n)} = \frac{n^2 \cdot p(n)}{a(n)}$$

(The last inequality uses the definition of S_n, and the one before it uses Eq. (2.8).)

We now present an upper bound on $s_2(n)$. Recall that by the contradiction hypothesis, $|S_n| \leq (1 - \frac{1}{2p(n)}) \cdot 2^n$. It follows that

$$s_2(n) \leq \Pr\left[\forall i : U_n^{(i)} \in S_n\right]$$

$$\leq \left(1 - \frac{1}{2p(n)}\right)^{n \cdot p(n)}$$

$$< \frac{1}{2^{n/2}} < \frac{n^2 \cdot p(n)}{a(n)}$$

(The last inequality holds for sufficiently large n.)

Combining the upper bounds on the s_i's, we have $s_1(n) + s_2(n) < \frac{2n^2 \cdot p(n)}{a(n)} = \frac{1}{q(n^2 p(n))}$, where equality is by the definition of $a(n)$. Yet, on the other hand, $s_1(n) + s_2(n) = s(n) > \frac{1}{q(n^2 p(n))}$, where the inequality is due to Eq. (2.7). Contradiction is reached, and the claim follows. □

Combining Claims 2.3.2.1 and 2.3.2.2, we obtain

$$\Pr[A'(f(U_n)) \in f^{-1}(f(U_n))]$$

$$\geq \Pr[A'(f(U_n)) \in f^{-1}(f(U_n)) \wedge U_n \in S_n]$$

$$= \Pr[U_n \in S_n] \cdot \Pr[A'(f(U_n)) \in f^{-1}(f(U_n)) \mid U_n \in S_n]$$

$$\geq \left(1 - \frac{1}{2p(n)}\right) \cdot (1 - 2^{-n}) > 1 - \frac{1}{p(n)}$$

It follows that there exists a probabilistic polynomial-time algorithm (i.e., A') that inverts f on $f(U_n)$, for $n \in N'$, with probability greater than $1 - \frac{1}{p(n)}$. This conclusion, which follows from the hypothesis that g is not strongly one-way (i.e., Eq. (2.6)), stands in contradiction to the hypothesis that every probabilistic polynomial-time algorithm fails to invert f with probability at least $\frac{1}{p(n)}$, and the theorem follows. ■

2.3.2. Illustration by a Toy Example

Let us try to further clarify the algorithmic ideas underlying the proof of Theorem 2.3.2. To do so, consider the following quantitative notion of weak one-way functions. We say that (a polynomial-time-computable) f is ρ-one-way if for all probabilistic polynomial-time algorithms A', for all but finitely many n's, the probability that on input $f(U_n)$ algorithm A' fails to find a pre-image under f is at least $\rho(n)$. (Each weak one-way function is $1/p()$-one-way for some polynomial p, whereas strong one-way functions are $(1 - \mu())$-one-way, where μ is a negligible function.)

Proposition 2.3.3 (Toy Example): *Suppose that f is $\frac{1}{3}$-one-way, and let $g(x_1, x_2) \stackrel{\text{def}}{=} (f(x_1), f(x_2))$. Then g is 0.55-one-way (where $0.55 < 1 - (\frac{2}{3})^2$).*

Proof Outline: Suppose, toward the contradiction, that there exists a polynomial-time algorithm A' that inverts $g(U_{2n})$ with success probability greater than

—— **48** ——

The Naive View   The Actual Proof

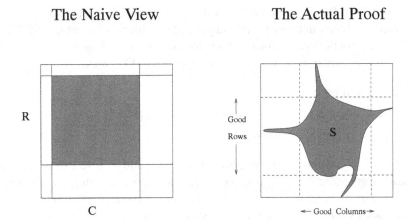

Figure 2.2: The naive view versus the actual proof of Proposition 2.3.3.

$1 - 0.55 = 0.45$, for infinitely many n's. Consider any such n, and let $N \stackrel{\text{def}}{=} 2^n$. Assume for simplicity that A' is deterministic. Consider an N-by-N matrix with entries corresponding to pairs $(x_1, x_2) \in \{0, 1\}^n \times \{0, 1\}^n$ such that entry (x_1, x_2) is marked 1 if A' successfully inverts g on input $g(x_1, x_2) = (f(x_1), f(x_2))$ and is marked zero otherwise. Our contradiction hypothesis is that the fraction of 1-entries in the matrix is greater than 45%.

The naive (unjustified) assumption is that A' operates separately on each element of the pair $(f(x_1), f(x_2))$. If that were the case, then the success region of A' would have been a generalized rectangle $R \times C \subseteq \{0, 1\}^n \times \{0, 1\}^n$ (i.e., corresponding to all pairs (x_1, x_2) such that $x_1 \in R$ and $x_2 \in C$ for some sets $R \subseteq \{0, 1\}^n$ and $C \subseteq \{0, 1\}^n$). Using the hypothesis that f is $\frac{1}{3}$-one-way, we have $|R|, |C| \leq \frac{2}{3} \cdot N$, and so $\frac{|R \times C|}{N^2} \leq \frac{4}{9} < 0.45$, in contradiction to our hypothesis regarding A'.

However, as stated earlier, the naive assumption cannot be justified, and so a more complex argument is required. In general, the success region of A', denoted S, may be an arbitrary subset of $\{0, 1\}^n \times \{0, 1\}^n$ satisfying $|S| > 0.45 \cdot N^2$ (by the contradiction hypothesis). Let us call a row x_1 (resp., column x_2) *good* if it contains at least 0.1% of 1-entries; otherwise it is called *bad*. (See Figure 2.2.) The main algorithmic part of the proof is establishing the following claim.

Claim 2.3.3.1: *The fraction of good rows (resp., columns) is at most 66.8%.*

Once this claim is proved, all that is left is straightforward combinatorics (i.e., counting). That is, we upper-bound the size of S by counting separately the number of 1-entries in the intersection of good rows and good columns and the 1-entries in bad rows and bad columns: By Claim 2.3.3.1, there are at most $(0.668N)^2$ entries in the intersection of good rows and good columns, and by definition the number of 1-entries in each bad row (resp., bad column) is at most $0.001N$. Thus, $|S| \leq (0.668N)^2 + 2 \cdot N \cdot 0.001N < 0.449 \cdot N^2$, in contradiction to our hypothesis (i.e., $|S| > 0.45 \cdot N^2$).

— 49 —

Proof of Claim 2.3.3.1: Suppose, toward the contradiction, that the fraction of good rows is greater than 66.8% (the argument for columns is analogous). Then, to reach a contradiction, we construct an algorithm for inverting f as follows. On input y, the algorithm repeats the following steps 10,000 times:

1. Select x_2 uniformly in $\{0, 1\}^n$.

2. Invoke A' on input $(y, f(x_2))$, and obtain its output (x', x'').

3. If $f(x') = y$, then halt with output x'.

Clearly, this algorithm works in polynomial time, and it is left to analyze its success in inverting f. For every good x_1, the probability that the algorithm fails to invert f on input $y = f(x_1)$ is at most $(1 - 0.001)^{10,000} < 0.001$. Thus, the probability that the algorithm succeeds in inverting f on input $f(U_n)$ is at least $0.668 \cdot 0.999 > \frac{2}{3}$, in contradiction to the hypothesis that f is $\frac{1}{3}$-one-way. $\square$

2.3.3. Discussion

2.3.3.1. Reducibility Arguments: A Digest

Let us recall the structure of the proof of Theorem 2.3.2. Given a weak one-way function f, we first constructed a polynomial-time-computable function g. This was done with the intention of later proving that g is strongly one-way. To prove that g is strongly one-way, we used a *reducibility argument*. The argument transforms efficient algorithms that supposedly contradict the strong one-wayness of g into efficient algorithms that contradict the hypothesis that f is weakly one-way. Hence g must be strongly one-way. We stress that our algorithmic transformation, which is in fact a randomized Cook reduction,[5] makes no implicit or explicit assumptions about the structure of the prospective algorithms for inverting g. Assumptions such as the "natural" assumption that the inverter of g works independently on each block cannot be justified (at least not at our current state of understanding of the nature of efficient computations).

We use the term *reducibility argument*, rather than just saying a reduction, so as to emphasize that we do *not* refer here to standard (worst-case-complexity) reductions. Let us clarify the distinction: In both cases we refer to *reducing* the task of solving one problem to the task of solving another problem; that is, we use a procedure solving the second task in order to construct a procedure that solves the first task. However, in standard reductions one assumes that the second task has a perfect procedure solving it on all instances (i.e., on the worst case) and constructs such a procedure for the first task. Thus, the reduction may invoke the given procedure (for the second task) on very "non-typical" instances. This cannot be done in our reducibility arguments. Here, we are given a procedure that solves the second task *with certain probability with respect to a certain distribution*. Thus, in employing a reducibility argument, we cannot invoke this procedure on any instance. Instead, we must consider the probability distribution,

---

[5]A (randomized) Cook reduction of one computational problem Π_1 to another problem, denoted Π_2, is a (probabilistic) polynomial-time oracle machine that solves Π_1, while making queries to oracle Π_2.

on instances of the second task, induced by our reduction. In many cases the latter distribution equals the distribution to which the hypothesis (regarding solvability of the second task) refers, but other cases can be handled too (e.g., these distributions may be "sufficiently close" for the specific purpose). In any case, a careful analysis of the distribution induced by the reducibility argument is due.

2.3.3.2. The Information-Theoretic Analogue

Theorem 2.3.2 has a natural information-theoretic (or "probabilistic") analogue that asserts that repeating an experiment that has a noticeable failure probability sufficiently many times will yield some failure with very high probability. The reader is probably convinced at this stage that the proof of Theorem 2.3.2 is much more complex than the proof of the information-theoretic analogue. In the information-theoretic context, the repeated events are independent by definition, whereas in our computational context no such independence (which corresponds to the naive argument given at the beginning of the proof of Theorem 2.3.2) can be guaranteed. Another indication of the difference between the two settings follows. In the information-theoretic setting, the probability that none of the failure events will occur decreases exponentially with the number of repetitions. In contrast, in the computational setting we can reach only an unspecified negligible bound on the inverting probabilities of polynomial-time algorithms. Furthermore, it may be the case that g constructed in the proof of Theorem 2.3.2 can be efficiently inverted on $g(U_{n^2 p(n)})$ with success probability that is sub-exponentially decreasing (e.g., with probability $2^{-(\log_2 n)^3}$), whereas the analogous information-theoretic bound is exponentially decreasing (i.e., e^{-n}).

2.3.3.3. Weak One-Way Functions Versus Strong Ones: A Summary

By Theorem 2.3.2, whenever we assume the existence of one-way functions, there is no need to specify whether we refer to weak or strong ones. That is, as far as the mere existence of one-way function goes, the notions of weak and strong one-way functions are equivalent. However, as far as efficiency considerations are concerned, the two notions are not really equivalent, since the above transformation of weak one-way functions into strong ones is not practical. An alternative transformation, which is much more efficient, does exist for the case of one-way permutations and other specific classes of one-way functions. The interested reader is referred to Section 2.6.

2.4. One-Way Functions: Variations

In this section we discuss several issues concerning one-way functions. In the first subsection we present a function that is (strongly) one-way, provided that one-way functions exist. The construction of this function is of strict abstract interest. In contrast, the issues discussed in the other subsections are of practical importance. First, we present an alternative formulation of one-way functions. This formulation is better suited for describing many natural candidates for one-way functions, and indeed we use it in order to describe some popular candidates for one-way functions. Next, we use this formulation to present one-way functions with additional properties; specifically, we consider (one-way) trapdoor permutations and claw-free function pairs. We remark that these additional properties are used in several constructions presented in other chapters of this book (e.g., trapdoor permutations are used in the construction of public-key encryption schemes, whereas claw-free permutations are used in the construction of collision-free hashing). We conclude this section with remarks concerning the "art" of proposing candidates for one-way functions.

2.4.1.*Universal One-Way Function

Using the notion of a universal machine and the result of the preceding section, it is possible to prove the existence of a *universal* one-way function; that is, we present a (fixed) function that is one-way, provided that one-way functions exist.

Proposition 2.4.1: *There exists a polynomial-time-computable function that is (strongly) one-way if and only if one-way functions exist.*

Proof Sketch: A key observation is that there exist one-way functions if and only if there exist one-way functions that can be evaluated by a quadratic-time algorithm. (The choice of the specific time bound is immaterial; what is important is that such a specific time bound exists.) This statement is proved using a padding argument. Details follow.

Let f be an arbitrary one-way function, and let $p(\cdot)$ be a polynomial bounding the time complexity of an algorithm for computing f. Define $g(x'x'') \stackrel{\text{def}}{=} f(x')x''$, where $|x'x''| = p(|x'|)$. An algorithm computing g first parses the input into x' and x'' so that $|x'x''| = p(|x'|)$ and then applies f to x'. The parsing and the other overhead operations can be implemented in quadratic time (in $|x'x''|$), whereas computing $f(x')$ is done within time $p(|x'|) = |x'x''|$ (which is linear in the input length). Hence, g can be computed (by a Turing machine) in quadratic time. The reader can verify that g is one-way using a "reducibility argument" (analogous to the one used in the proof of Proposition 2.2.5).

We now present a (universal one-way) function, denoted f_{uni}:

$$f_{\text{uni}}(\text{desc}(M), x) \stackrel{\text{def}}{=} (\text{desc}(M), M(x)) \tag{2.9}$$

where $\text{desc}(M)$ is a description of Turing machine M, and $M(x)$ is defined as the output of M on input x if M runs at most quadratic time on x, and $M(x)$ is defined as x otherwise. (Without loss of generality, we can view any string as the description of some Turing machine.) Clearly, f_{uni} can be computed in polynomial time by a universal machine that uses a step counter. To show that f_{uni} is weakly one-way (provided that one-way functions exist at all), we use a "reducibility argument."

Assuming that one-way functions exist, and using the foregoing observation, it follows that there exists a one-way function g that is computed in quadratic time. Let M_g be the quadratic-time machine computing g. Clearly, an (efficient) algorithm inverting f_{uni} on inputs of the form $f_{uni}(desc(M_g), U_n)$ with probability $p(n)$ can be easily modified into an (efficient) algorithm inverting g on inputs of the form $g(U_n)$ with probability $p(n)$. As in the proof of Proposition 2.3.1, it follows that an algorithm inverting f_{uni} with probability at least $1 - \varepsilon(n)$ on strings of length $|desc(M_g)| + n$ yields an algorithm inverting g with probability at least $1 - 2^{|desc(M_g)|} \cdot \varepsilon(n)$ on strings of length n. (We stress that $|desc(M_g)|$ is a constant, depending only on g.) Hence, if f_{uni} is not weakly one-way (i.e., the function ε is not noticeable), then also g cannot be (weakly) one-way (i.e., also $2^{|desc(M_g)|} \cdot \varepsilon$ is not noticeable).

Using Theorem 2.3.2 (to transform the weak one-way function f_{uni} into a strong one), the proposition follows. ∎

Discussion. The observation by which it suffices to consider one-way functions that can be evaluated within a specific time bound is crucial to the construction of f_{uni}, the reason being that it is not possible to construct a polynomial-time machine that is universal for the class of all polynomial-time machines (i.e., a polynomial-time machine that can "simulate" all polynomial-time machines). It is, however, possible to construct, for every polynomial $p(\cdot)$, a polynomial-time machine that is universal for the class of machines with running time bounded by $p(\cdot)$.

The impracticality of the construction of f_{uni} stems from the fact that f_{uni} is likely to be hard to invert only on huge input lengths (i.e., lengths allowing the encoding of non-trivial algorithms as required for the evaluation of one-way functions). Furthermore, to obtain a strongly one-way function from f_{uni}, we need to apply the latter on a sequence of more than 2^L inputs, each of length $L + n$, where L is a lower bound on the length of the encoding of potential one-way functions, and n is our actual security parameter.

Still, Proposition 2.4.1 says that, in principle, the question of whether or not one-way functions exist "reduces" to the question of whether or not a specific function is one-way.

2.4.2. One-Way Functions as Collections

The formulation of one-way functions used thus far is suitable for an abstract discussion. However, for describing many natural candidates for one-way functions, the following formulation (although being more cumbersome) is more serviceable. Instead of viewing one-way functions as functions operating on an infinite domain (i.e., $\{0, 1\}^*$), we consider infinite collections of functions each operating on a finite domain. The functions in the collection share a single evaluating algorithm that when given as input a succinct representation of a function and an element in its domain returns the value of the specified function at the given point. The formulation of a collection of functions is also useful for the presentation of trapdoor permutations and claw-free functions (see Sections 2.4.4 and 2.4.5, respectively). We start with the following definition.

Definition 2.4.2 (Collection of Functions): *A **collection of functions** consists of an infinite set of **indices**, denoted $\bar{I}$, and a corresponding set of finite functions,* *denoted $\{f_i\}_{i \in \bar{I}}$. That is, for each $i \in \bar{I}$, the domain of the function f_i, denoted D_i, is a finite set.*

Typically, the set of indices $\bar{I}$ will be a "dense" subset of the set of all strings; that is, the fraction of n-bit-long strings in $\bar{I}$ will be noticeable (i.e., $|\bar{I} \cap \{0, 1\}^n| \geq 2^n/\text{poly}(n)$).

We shall be interested only in collections of functions that can be used in cryptographic applications. As hinted earlier, a necessary condition for using a collection of functions is the existence of an efficient function-evaluating algorithm (denoted F) that on input $i \in \bar{I}$ and $x \in D_i$ returns $f_i(x)$. Yet this condition by itself does not suffice. We need to be able to (randomly) select an index specifying a function over a sufficiently large domain, as well as to be able to (randomly) select an element of the domain (when given the domain's index). The sampling property of the index set is captured by an efficient algorithm (denoted I) that on input an integer n (presented in unary) randomly selects a poly(n)-bit-long index specifying a function and its associated domain. (As usual, unary presentation is used so as to conform with the standard association of efficient algorithms with those running in times polynomial in the lengths of their inputs.) The sampling property of the domains is captured by an efficient algorithm (denoted D) that on input an index i randomly selects an element in D_i. The one-way property of the collection is captured by requiring that every efficient algorithm, when given an index of a function and an element in its range, fails to invert the function, except with negligible probability. The probability is taken over the distribution induced by the sampling algorithms I and D. All the preceding is captured by the following definition.

Definition 2.4.3 (Collection of One-Way Functions): *A collection of functions $\{f_i : D_i \to \{0, 1\}^*\}_{i \in \bar{I}}$ is called strongly (resp., weakly) **one-way** if there exist three probabilistic polynomial-time algorithms I, D, and F such that the following two conditions hold:*

1. Easy to sample and compute: *The output distribution of algorithm I on input 1^n is a random variable assigned values in the set $\bar{I} \cap \{0, 1\}^n$. The output distribution of algorithm D on input $i \in \bar{I}$ is a random variable assigned values in D_i. On input $i \in \bar{I}$ and $x \in D_i$, algorithm F always outputs $f_i(x)$.*

   (Thus, $D_i \subseteq \cup_{m \leq \text{poly}(|i|)} \{0, 1\}^m$. Without loss of generality, we can assume that $D_i \subseteq \{0, 1\}^{\text{poly}(|i|)}$. Also without loss of generality, we can assume that algorithm F is deterministic.)

2. Hard to invert (version for strongly one-way): *For every probabilistic polynomial-time algorithm A', every positive polynomial $p(\cdot)$, and all sufficiently large n's,*

$$\Pr[A'(I_n, f_{I_n}(X_n)) \in f_{I_n}^{-1}(f_{I_n}(X_n))] < \frac{1}{p(n)}$$

   where I_n is a random variable describing the output distribution of algorithm I on input 1^n, and X_n is a random variable describing the output of algorithm D on input (random variable) I_n.

   (The version for weakly one-way collections is analogous.)

We stress that the output of algorithm I on input 1^n *is not* necessarily distributed *uniformly* over $\bar{I} \cap \{0, 1\}^n$. Furthermore, it is not even required that $I(1^n)$ not be entirely concentrated on one single string. Likewise, the output of algorithm D on input i *is not* necessarily distributed *uniformly* over D_i. Yet the hardness-to-invert condition implies that $D(i)$ cannot be mainly concentrated on polynomially many (in $|i|$) strings. We stress that the collection is hard to invert with respect to the distribution induced by the algorithms I and D (in addition to depending, as usual, on the mapping induced by the function itself).

We can describe a collection of one-way functions by indicating the corresponding triplet of algorithms. Hence, we can say that a *triplet of probabilistic polynomial-time algorithms* (I, D, F) *constitutes a collection of one-way functions* if there exists a collection of functions for which these algorithms satisfy the foregoing two conditions.

Clearly, any collection of one-way functions can be represented as a one-way function, and vice versa (see Exercise 18), yet each formulation has its own advantages. In the sequel, we shall use the formulation of a collection of one-way functions in order to present popular candidates for one-way functions.

Relaxations. To allow a less cumbersome presentation of natural candidates for one-way collections (of functions), we relax Definition 2.4.3 in two ways. First, we allow the index-sampling algorithm to output, on input 1^n, indices of length $p(n)$ rather than n, where $p(\cdot)$ is some polynomial. Second, we allow all algorithms to fail with negligible probability. Most important, we allow the index sampler I to output strings not in $\bar{I}$ so long as the probability that $I(1^n) \notin \bar{I} \cap \{0, 1\}^{p(n)}$ is a negligible function in n. (The same relaxations can be used when discussing trapdoor permutations and claw-free functions.)

Additional Properties: Efficiently Recognizable Indices and Domains. Several additional properties that hold for some candidate collections for one-way functions will be explicitly discussed in subsequent subsections. Here we mention two (useful) additional properties that hold in some candidate collections for one-way functions. The properties are (1) having an efficiently recognizable set of indices and (2) having efficiently recognizable collection of domains; that is, we refer to the existence of an efficient algorithm for deciding membership in $\bar{I}$ and the existence of an efficient algorithm that given $i \in \bar{I}$ and x can determine whether or not $x \in D_i$. Note that for the non-relaxed Definition 2.4.3, the coins used to generate $i \in \bar{I}$ (resp., $x \in D_i$) constitute a certificate (i.e., an $\mathcal{NP}$-witness) for the corresponding claim; yet this certificate that $i \in \bar{I}$ (resp., $x \in D_i$) may assist in inverting the function f_i (resp., always yielding the pre-image x).

2.4.3. Examples of One-Way Collections

In this section we present several popular collections of one-way functions (e.g., RSA and discrete exponentiation) based on computational number theory.[6] In the exposition

---

[6] Obviously these are merely candidate collections for one-way functions; their hardness-to-invert feature either is a (widely believed) conjecture or follows from a (widely believed) conjecture.

that follows, we assume some knowledge of elementary number theory and some familiarity with simple number-theoretic algorithms. Further discussion of the relevant number theoretic material is presented in Appendix A.

2.4.3.1. The RSA Function

The RSA collection of functions has an index set consisting of pairs (N, e), where N is a product of two $(\frac{1}{2} \cdot \log_2 N)$-bit primes, denoted P and Q, and e is an integer smaller than N and relatively prime to $(P - 1) \cdot (Q - 1)$. The function of index (N, e) has domain $\{1, \ldots, N\}$ and maps the domain element x to $x^e \bmod N$. Using the fact that e is relatively prime to $(P - 1) \cdot (Q - 1)$, it can be shown that the function is in fact a permutation over its domain. Hence, the RSA collection is a collection of *permutations*.

We first substantiate the fact that the RSA collection satisfies the first condition for the definition of a one-way collection (i.e., that it is easy to sample and compute). To this end, we present the triplet of algorithms $(I_{\text{RSA}}, D_{\text{RSA}}, F_{\text{RSA}})$.

On input 1^n, algorithm I_{RSA} selects uniformly two primes, P and Q, such that $2^{n-1} \leq P < Q < 2^n$, and an integer e such that e is relatively prime to $(P - 1) \cdot (Q - 1)$. (Specifically, e is uniformly selected among the admissible possibilities.[7]) Algorithm I_{RSA} terminates with output (N, e), where $N = P \cdot Q$. For an efficient implementation of I_{RSA}, we need a probabilistic polynomial-time algorithm for generating uniformly (or almost uniformly) distributed primes. For more details concerning the uniform generation of primes, see Appendix A.

As for algorithm D_{RSA}, on input (N, e) it selects (almost) uniformly an element in the set $D_{N,e} \stackrel{\text{def}}{=} \{1, \ldots, N\}$. (The exponentially vanishing deviation is due to the fact that we implement an N-way selection via a sequence of unbiased coin tosses.) The output of F_{RSA}, on input $((N, e), x)$, is

$$\text{RSA}_{N,e}(x) \stackrel{\text{def}}{=} x^e \bmod N \qquad (2.10)$$

It is not known whether or not factoring N can be reduced to inverting $\text{RSA}_{N,e}$, and in fact this is a well-known open problem. We remark that the best algorithms known for inverting $\text{RSA}_{N,e}$ proceed by (explicitly or implicitly) factoring N. In any case, it is widely believed that the RSA collection is hard to invert.

In the foregoing description, $D_{N,e}$ corresponds to the additive group mod N (and hence will contain N elements). Alternatively, the domain $D_{N,e}$ can be restricted to the elements of the multiplicative group modulo N (and hence will contain $(P - 1) \cdot (Q - 1) \approx N - 2\sqrt{N} \approx N$ elements). A modified domain sampler may work by selecting an element in $\{1, \ldots, N\}$ and discarding the unlikely cases in which the selected element is not relatively prime to N. The function $\text{RSA}_{N,e}$ defined earlier induces a permutation on the multiplicative group modulo N. The resulting collection is as hard to invert as the original one. (A proof of this statement is left as an exercise to the reader.) The question of which formulation to prefer seems to be a matter of personal taste.

---

[7]In some sources, e is set to equal 3. In such a case, the primes (P and Q) are selected so that they are congruent to 2 mod 3. It is not known whether or not the assumption that one variant is one-way implies that the other also is.

2.4.3.2. The Rabin Function

The Rabin collection of functions is defined analogously to the RSA collection, except that the function is squaring modulo N (instead of raising to the eth power mod N). Namely,

$$\mathrm{Rabin}_N(x) \overset{\mathrm{def}}{=} x^2 \bmod N \tag{2.11}$$

This function, however, does not induce a permutation on the multiplicative group modulo N, but is rather a 4-to-1 mapping on this group.

It can be shown that extracting square roots modulo N is computationally equivalent to factoring N (i.e., the two tasks are reducible to one another via probabilistic polynomial-time reductions). For details, see Exercise 21. Hence, squaring modulo a composite is a collection of one-way functions if and only if factoring is intractable. We remind the reader that it is generally believed that integer factorization is intractable, and this holds also for the special case in which the integer is a product of two primes of the same length.[8]

2.4.3.3. The Factoring Permutations

For a special subclass of the integers, known by the name of *Blum integers*, the function $\mathrm{Rabin}_N(\cdot)$ defined earlier induces a permutation on the quadratic residues modulo N. We say that r is a *quadratic residue mod N* if there exists an integer x such that $r \equiv x^2$ (mod N). We denote by Q_N the set of quadratic residues in the multiplicative group mod N. For purposes of this paragraph, we say that N is a Blum integer if it is the product of two primes, each congruent to 3 mod 4. It can be shown that when N is a Blum integer, each element in Q_N has a unique square root that is also in Q_N, and it follows that in this case the function $\mathrm{Rabin}_N(\cdot)$ induces a permutation over Q_N. This leads to the introduction of the collection $\mathrm{SQR} \overset{\mathrm{def}}{=} (I_{\mathrm{BI}}, D_{\mathrm{QR}}, F_{\mathrm{SQR}})$ of permutations. On input 1^n, algorithm I_{BI} selects uniformly two primes, P and Q, such that $2^{n-1} \leq P < Q < 2^n$ and $P \equiv Q \equiv 3$ (mod 4), and outputs $N = P \cdot Q$. On input N, algorithm D_{QR} uniformly selects an element of Q_N by uniformly selecting an element of the multiplicative group modulo N and squaring it mod N. Algorithm F_{SQR} is defined exactly as in the Rabin collection. The resulting collection is one-way, provided that factoring is intractable.

2.4.3.4. Discrete Logarithms

Another computational number-theoretic problem that is widely believed to be intractable is that of extracting discrete logarithms in a finite field (and, in particular, of prime cardinality). The DLP collection of functions, which borrows its name (and its conjectured one-wayness) from the *discrete-logarithm problem*, is defined by the triplet of algorithms $(I_{\mathrm{DLP}}, D_{\mathrm{DLP}}, F_{\mathrm{DLP}})$.

On input 1^n, algorithm I_{DLP} selects uniformly a prime P, such that $2^{n-1} \leq P < 2^n$, and a primitive element G in the multiplicative group modulo P (i.e., a generator

---

[8]In fact, the latter case is believed to be the hardest.

of this cyclic group), and outputs (P, G). There exists a probabilistic polynomial-time algorithm for uniformly generating primes, together with the prime factorization of $P - 1$, where P is the prime generated (see Appendix A). Alternatively, one can uniformly generate a prime P of the form $2Q + 1$, where Q is also a prime. (In the latter case, however, one has to assume the intractability of DLP with respect to such primes. We remark that such primes are commonly believed to be the hardest for DLP.) Using the factorization of $P - 1$, we can find a primitive element by selecting an element of the group at random and checking whether or not it has order $P - 1$ (by raising the candidate to powers that non-trivially divide $P - 1$, and comparing the result to 1).

Regarding algorithm D_{DLP}, on input (P, G) it selects uniformly a residue modulo $P - 1$. Algorithm F_{DLP}, on input $((P, G), x)$, outputs

$$\mathrm{DLP}_{P,G}(x) \overset{\mathrm{def}}{=} G^x \bmod P \qquad (2.12)$$

Hence, inverting $\mathrm{DLP}_{P,G}$ amounts to extracting the discrete logarithm (to base G) modulo P. For every (P, G) of the foregoing form, the function $\mathrm{DLP}_{P,G}$ induces a 1-1 and onto mapping from the additive group mod $P - 1$ to the multiplicative group mod P. Hence, $\mathrm{DLP}_{P,G}$ induces a permutation on the set $\{1, \ldots, P - 1\}$.

Exponentiation in other groups is also a reasonable candidate for a one-way function, provided that the discrete-logarithm problem for the group is believed to be hard. For example, it is believed that the logarithm problem is hard in the group of points on an elliptic curve.

2.4.4. Trapdoor One-Way Permutations

We shall define trapdoor (one-way) permutations and review a popular candidate (i.e., the RSA).

2.4.4.1. Definitions

The formulation of collections of one-way functions is convenient as a starting point to the definition of trapdoor permutations. Loosely speaking, these are collections of one-way permutations, $\{f_i\}$, with the extra property that f_i is efficiently inverted once it is given as auxiliary input a "trapdoor" for the index i. The trapdoor for index i, denoted by $t(i)$, *cannot* be efficiently computed from i, yet one can efficiently generate corresponding pairs $(i, t(i))$.

Definition 2.4.4 (Collection of Trapdoor Permutations): *Let $I : 1^* \to \{0, 1\}^* \times \{0, 1\}^*$ be a probabilistic algorithm, and let $I_1(1^n)$ denote the first element of the pair output by $I(1^n)$. A triple of algorithms, (I, D, F), is called a* **collection of strong (resp., weak) trapdoor permutations** *if the following two conditions hold:*

1. The algorithms induce a collection of one-way permutations: *The triple (I_1, D, F) constitutes a collection of strong (resp., weak) one-way permutations.* *(Recall that, in particular, $F(i, x) = f_i(x)$.)*

2. Easy to invert with trapdoor: *There exists a (deterministic) polynomial-time algorithm, denoted F^{-1}, such that for every (i, t) in the range of I and for every $x \in D_i$, it holds that $F^{-1}(t, f_i(x)) = x$.*

A useful relaxation of these conditions is to require that they be satisfied with overwhelmingly high probability. Namely, the index-generating algorithm I is allowed to output, with negligible probability, pairs (i, t) for which either f_i is not a permutation or $F^{-1}(t, f_i(x)) = x$ does not hold for all $x \in D_i$. On the other hand, one typically requires that the domain-sampling algorithm (i.e., D) produce an almost uniform distribution on the corresponding domain. Putting all these modifications together, we obtain the following version, which is incomparable to Definition 2.4.4. We take the opportunity to present a slightly different formulation, as well as to introduce a non-uniformly one-way version.

Definition 2.4.5 (Collection of Trapdoor Permutations, Revisited): *Let $\bar{I} \subseteq \{0, 1\}^*$ and $\bar{I}_n \overset{\text{def}}{=} \bar{I} \cap \{0, 1\}^n$. A **collection of permutations** with **indices** in $\bar{I}$ is a set $\{f_i : D_i \to D_i\}_{i \in \bar{I}}$ such that each f_i is 1-1 on the corresponding D_i. Such a collection is called a **trapdoor permutation** if there exist four probabilistic polynomial-time algorithms I, D, F, and F^{-1} such that the following five conditions hold:*

1. Index and trapdoor selection: *For every n,*

$$\Pr[I(1^n) \in \bar{I}_n \times \{0, 1\}^*] > 1 - 2^{-n}$$

2. Selection in domain: *For every $n \in \mathbb{N}$ and $i \in \bar{I}_n$,*
   (a) $\Pr[D(i) \in D_i] > 1 - 2^{-n}$.

   (b) *Conditioned on $D(i) \in D_i$, the output is uniformly distributed in D_i. That is, for every $x \in D_i$,*

$$\Pr[D(i) = x \mid D(i) \in D_i] = \frac{1}{|D_i|}$$

   Thus, $D_i \subseteq \cup_{m \leq \text{poly}(|i|)}\{0, 1\}^m$. Without loss of generality, $D_i \subseteq \{0, 1\}^{\text{poly}(|i|)}$.

3. Efficient evaluation: *For every $n \in \mathbb{N}$, $i \in \bar{I}_n$, and $x \in D_i$,*

$$\Pr[F(i, x) = f_i(x)] > 1 - 2^{-n}$$

4. Hard to invert: *Let I_n be a random variable describing the distribution of the first element in the output of $I(1^n)$, and $X_n \overset{\text{def}}{=} D(I_n)$. We consider two versions:*
   Standard/uniform-complexity version: *For every probabilistic polynomial-time algorithm A', every positive polynomial $p(\cdot)$, and all sufficiently large n's,*

$$\Pr[A'(I_n, f_{I_n}(X_n)) = X_n] < \frac{1}{p(n)}$$

   Non-uniform-complexity version: *For every family of polynomial-size circuits $\{C_n\}_{n \in \mathbb{N}}$, every positive polynomial $p(\cdot)$, and all sufficiently large n's,*

$$\Pr[C_n(I_n, f_{I_n}(X_n)) = X_n] < \frac{1}{p(n)}$$

5. Inverting with trapdoor: *For every $n \in \mathbb{N}$, any pair (i, t) in the range of $I(1^n)$ such that $i \in \bar{I}_n$, and every $x \in D_i$,*

$$\Pr[F^{-1}(t, f_i(x)) = x] > 1 - 2^{-n}$$

We comment that an exponentially vanishing measure of indices for which any of Items 2, 3, and 5 does not hold can be omitted from $\bar{I}$ (and accounted for by the error allowed in Item 1). Items 3 and 5 can be relaxed by taking the probabilities also over all possible $x \in D_i$ with uniform distribution.

2.4.4.2. The RSA (and Factoring) Trapdoor

The RSA collection presented earlier can be easily modified to have the trapdoor property. To this end, algorithm I_{RSA} should be modified so that it outputs both the index (N, e) and the trapdoor (N, d), where d is the multiplicative inverse of e modulo $(P - 1) \cdot (Q - 1)$ (note that e has such inverse because it has been chosen to be relatively prime to $(P - 1) \cdot (Q - 1)$). The inverting algorithm F_{RSA}^{-1} is identical to the algorithm F_{RSA} (i.e., $F_{\text{RSA}}^{-1}((N, d), y) = y^d \bmod N$). The reader can easily verify that

$$F_{\text{RSA}}^{-1}((N, d), F_{\text{RSA}}((N, e), x)) = x^{ed} \bmod N$$

indeed equals x, for every x in the multiplicative group modulo N. In fact, one can show that $x^{ed} \equiv x \pmod{N}$ for every x (even in case x is not relatively prime to N).

The Rabin collection presented earlier can be easily modified in a similar manner, enabling one to efficiently compute all four square roots of a given quadratic residue $(\bmod N)$. The trapdoor in this case is the prime factorization of N. The square roots mod N can be computed by extracting a square root modulo each of the prime factors of N and combining the results using the Chinese Remainder Theorem. Efficient algorithms for extracting square roots modulo a given prime are known (see Appendix A). Furthermore, in case the prime P is congruent to 3 mod 4, the square roots of x mod P can be computed by raising x to the power $\frac{P+1}{4}$ (while reducing the intermediate results mod P). Furthermore, in case N is a Blum integer, the collection SQR, presented earlier, forms a collection of trapdoor permutations (provided, of course, that factoring is hard).

2.4.5.*Claw-Free Functions

The formulation of collections of one-way functions is also a convenient starting point for the definition of a collection of claw-free pairs of functions.

2.4.5.1. The Definition

Loosely speaking, a claw-free collection consists of a set of pairs of functions that are easy to evaluate, that have the same range for both members of each pair, and yet for which it is infeasible to find a range element together with a pre-image of it under each of these functions.

Definition 2.4.6 (Claw-Free Collection): A collection of pairs of functions *consists of an infinite set of indices, denoted $\bar{I}$, two finite sets D_i^0 and D_i^1 for each $i \in \bar{I}$, and two functions f_i^0 and f_i^1 defined over D_i^0 and D_i^1, respectively. Such a collection is called* **claw-free** *if there exist three probabilistic polynomial-time algorithms I, D, and F such that the following conditions hold:*

1. Easy to sample and compute: *The random variable $I(1^n)$ is assigned values in the set $\bar{I} \cap \{0, 1\}^n$. For each $i \in \bar{I}$ and $\sigma \in \{0, 1\}$, the random variable $D(\sigma, i)$ is distributed over D_i^σ, and $F(\sigma, i, x) = f_i^\sigma(x)$ for each $x \in D_i^\sigma$.*

2. Identical range distribution: *For every i in the index set $\bar{I}$, the random variables $f_i^0(D(0, i))$ and $f_i^1(D(1, i))$ are identically distributed.*

3. Hard to form claws: *A pair (x, y) satisfying $f_i^0(x) = f_i^1(y)$ is called a* claw *for index i. Let C_i denote the set of claws for index i. It is required that for every probabilistic polynomial-time algorithm A', every positive polynomial $p(\cdot)$, and all sufficiently large n's,*

$$\Pr[A'(I_n) \in C_{I_n}] < \frac{1}{p(n)}$$

where I_n is a random variable describing the output distribution of algorithm I on input 1^n.

The first requirement in Definition 2.4.6 is analogous to what appears in Definition 2.4.3. The other two requirements in Definition 2.4.6 are conflicting in nature. On one hand, it is required that claws do exist (to say the least), whereas on the other hand it is required that claws cannot be efficiently found. Clearly, a claw-free collection of functions yields a collection of strong one-way functions (see Exercise 22). A case of special interest arises when the two domains are identical (i.e., $D_i \stackrel{\text{def}}{=} D_i^0 = D_i^1$), the random variable $D(\sigma, i)$ is uniformly distributed over D_i, and the functions f_i^0 and f_i^1 are permutations over D_i. Such a collection is called a *collection of claw-free pairs of permutations*.

Again, a useful relaxation of the conditions of Definition 2.4.6 is obtained by allowing the algorithms (i.e., I, D, and F) to fail with negligible probability. An additional property that a (claw-free) collection may (or may not) have is an efficiently recognizable index set (i.e., a probabilistic polynomial-time algorithm for determining whether or not a given string is in $\bar{I}$).

2.4.5.2. The DLP Claw-Free Collection

We now seek to show that claw-free collections do exist under specific reasonable intractability assumptions. We start by presenting such a collection under the assumption that the discrete-logarithm problem (DLP) for fields of prime cardinality is intractable.

Following is the description of a collection of claw-free pairs of *permutations* (based on the foregoing assumption). The index set consists of triples, (P, G, Z), where P is a prime, G is a primitive element mod P, and Z is an element in the field (of residues mod P). The index-sampling algorithm selects P and G as in the DLP collection presented in Section 2.4.3, and Z is selected uniformly among the residues mod P. The domain is the same for both functions with index (P, G, Z) and equals the set $\{1, \ldots, P - 1\}$, and the domain-sampling algorithm selects uniformly from this set. As for the functions themselves, we set

$$f_{P,G,Z}^{\sigma}(x) \overset{\text{def}}{=} Z^{\sigma} \cdot G^{x} \bmod P \qquad (2.13)$$

The reader can easily verify that both functions are permutations over $\{1, \ldots, P-1\}$. In fact, the function $f_{P,G,Z}^{0}$ coincides with the function $\text{DLP}_{P,G}$ presented in Section 2.4.3. Furthermore, the ability to form a claw for the index (P, G, Z) yields the ability to find the discrete logarithm of $Z \bmod P$ to base G (since $G^{x} \equiv Z \cdot G^{y} \pmod{P}$ yields $G^{x-y} \equiv Z \pmod{P}$). Thus, the ability to form claws for a non-negligible fraction of the index set translates to the ability to invert the DLP collection presented in Section 2.4.3. Put in other words, if the DLP collection is one-way, then the collection of pairs of permutations defined in Eq. (2.13) is claw-free.

The foregoing collection *does not* have the additional property of having an efficiently recognizable index set, because it is not known how to efficiently recognize primitive elements modulo a prime. This can be remedied by making a slightly stronger assumption concerning the intractability of DLP. Specifically, we assume that DLP is intractable even if one is given the factorization of the size of the multiplicative group (i.e., the factorization of $P-1$) as additional input. Such an assumption allows one to add the factorization of $P-1$ into the description of the index. This makes the index set efficiently recognizable (since one can test whether or not G is a primitive element by raising it to powers of the form $(P-1)/Q$, where Q is a prime factor of $P-1$). If DLP is hard also for primes of the form $2Q+1$, where Q is also a prime, life is even easier: To test whether or not G is a primitive element mod P, one simply computes $G^{2} \bmod P$ and $G^{(P-1)/2} \bmod P$ and checks whether or not both of them are different from 1.

2.4.5.3. Claw-Free Collections Based on Factoring

We now show that a claw-free collection (of functions) does exist under the assumption that integer factorization is infeasible. In the following description, we use the structural properties of Blum integers (i.e., products of two primes both congruent to 3 mod 4), which are further discussed in Appendix A. In particular, for a Blum integer N, it holds that

- the Jacobi symbol of $-1 \bmod N$ equals 1, and

- half of the square roots of each quadratic residue have Jacobi symbol 1.

Let J_{N}^{+1} (resp., J_{N}^{-1}) denote the set of residues in the multiplicative group modulo N with Jacobi symbol $+1$ (resp., -1).

The index set of the collection consists of all Blum integers that are composed of two primes of the same length. The index-selecting algorithm, on input 1^{n}, uniformly selects such an integer by uniformly selecting two (n-bit) primes, each congruent to 3 mod 4, and outputting their product, denoted N. Both functions of index N, denoted f_{N}^{0} and f_{N}^{1}, consist of squaring modulo N, but their corresponding domains are disjoint. The domain of function f_{N}^{σ} equals the set $J_{N}^{(-1)^{\sigma}}$. The domain-sampling algorithm, denoted D, uniformly selects an element of the corresponding domain in the natural manner. Specifically, on input (σ, N), algorithm D uniformly selects polynomially many residues mod N and outputs the first residue with Jacobi symbol $(-1)^\sigma$.

The reader can easily verify that both $f_N^0(D(0, N))$ and $f_N^1(D(1, N))$ are uniformly distributed over the set of quadratic residues mod N. The difficulty of forming claws follows from the fact that a claw yields two residues, $x \in J_N^{+1}$ and $y \in J_N^{-1}$, such that their squares modulo N are equal (i.e., $x^2 \equiv y^2 \pmod{N}$). Since $-1 \in J_N^{+1}$ (and the latter is a multiplicative subgroup), it follows that $y \not\equiv \pm x \pmod{N}$, and so the greatest common divisor (g.c.d.) of $y \pm x$ and N yields a factorization of N.

The foregoing collection consists of pairs of functions that are 2-to-1 (and are defined over disjoint domains). To obtain a collection of claw-free *permutations*, we slightly modify the collection as follows. The index set consists of Blum integers that are the products of two primes P and Q of the same length, so that $P \equiv 3 \pmod{8}$ and $Q \equiv 7 \pmod{8}$. For such composites, neither 2 nor -2 is a quadratic residue modulo $N = P \cdot Q$ (and in fact $\pm 2 \in J_N^{-1}$). Consider the functions f_N^0 and f_N^1 defined over the set, denoted Q_N, of quadratic residues modulo N:

$$f_N^\sigma(x) \stackrel{\text{def}}{=} 4^\sigma \cdot x^2 \bmod N \tag{2.14}$$

Clearly, both f_N^0 and f_N^1 are *permutations* over Q_N. The difficulty of forming claws follows from the fact that a claw yields two quadratic residues, x and y, so that $x^2 \equiv 4y^2 \pmod{N}$. Thus, $(x/y)^2 \equiv 4 \pmod{N}$, and so $(2 - (x/y)) \cdot (2 + (x/y)) \equiv 0 \pmod{N}$. Since $\pm 2 \notin Q_N$ (and the latter is a multiplicative subgroup), it follows that $(x/y) \not\equiv \pm 2 \pmod{N}$, and so the g.c.d. of $(2 \pm x \cdot y^{-1} \bmod N)$ and N yields the factorization of N.

The foregoing collections are *not* known to possess the additional property of having an efficiently recognizable index set. In particular, it is not even known how to efficiently distinguish products of two primes from products of more than two primes.

2.4.6.*On Proposing Candidates

Although we do believe that one-way functions exist, their *mere* existence does not suffice for practical applications. Typically, an application that is based on one-way functions requires the specification of a concrete (candidate one-way) function.[9] Hence, the problem of proposing reasonable candidates for one-way functions is of great practical importance. Everyone understands that such a reasonable candidate (for a one-way function) should have a very efficient algorithm for evaluating the function. In case the "function" is presented as a collection of one-way functions, the domain sampler and function-evaluation algorithm should be very efficient (whereas for index sampling, "moderate efficiency" may suffice). However, people seem less careful about *seriously considering* the difficulty of inverting the candidates that they propose. We stress that the candidate has to be difficult to invert on "the average" and not only in the worst case, and "the average" is taken with respect to the instance-distribution determined by the candidate function. Furthermore, "hardness on the average" (unlike

---

[9]As explained in Section 2.4.1, the observation concerning the existence of a universal one-way function is of little practical significance.

worst-case analysis) is extremely sensitive to the instance-distribution. Hence, one has to be extremely careful in deducing average-case complexity with respect to one distribution from the average-case complexity with respect to another distribution. The short history of the field contains several cases in which this point has been ignored, and consequently bad suggestions have been made.

Consider, for example, the following (bad) suggestion to base one-way functions on the conjectured difficulty of the Graph Isomorphism problem. Let $F_{GI}(G, \pi) = (G, \pi G)$, where G is an undirected graph, π is a permutation on its vertex set, and πG denotes the graph resulting by renaming the vertices of G using π (i.e., $(\pi(u), \pi(v))$ is an edge in πG if and only if (u, v) is an edge in G). Although it is indeed believed that Graph Isomorphism cannot be solved in polynomial time, it is easy to see that F_{GI} is easy to invert in most instances (e.g., use vertex-degree statistics to determine the isomorphism). That is, the conjectured worst-case hardness does not imply an average-case hardness for the uniform distribution. Furthermore, even if the problem is hard on the average with respect to *some* distribution, one has to specify this distribution and propose an efficient algorithm for sampling according to it.

2.5. Hard-Core Predicates

Loosely speaking, saying that a function f is one-way implies that given y, it is infeasible to find a pre-image of y under f. This does not mean that it is infeasible to find some partial information about the pre-image of y under f. Specifically, it may be easy to retrieve half of the bits of the pre-image (e.g., given a one-way function f, consider the function g defined by $g(x, r) \stackrel{\text{def}}{=} (f(x), r)$ for every $|x| = |r|$). The fact that one-way functions do not necessarily hide partial information about their pre-images limits their "direct applicability" to tasks such as secure encryption. Fortunately, assuming the existence of one-way functions, it is possible to construct one-way functions that hide specific partial information about their pre-images (which is easy to compute from the pre-image itself). This partial information can be considered as a "hard-core" of the difficulty of inverting f.

2.5.1. Definition

Loosely speaking, a *polynomial-time* predicate b is called a hard-core of a function f if every efficient algorithm, given $f(x)$, can guess $b(x)$ with success probability that is only negligibly better than one-half.

Definition 2.5.1 (Hard-Core Predicate): *A polynomial-time-computable predicate* $b : \{0, 1\}^* \to \{0, 1\}$ *is called a* **hard-core** *of a function f if for every probabilistic polynomial-time algorithm A', every positive polynomial $p(\cdot)$, and all sufficiently large n's,*

$$\Pr[A'(f(U_n)) = b(U_n)] < \frac{1}{2} + \frac{1}{p(n)}$$

——— **64** ———

Note that for every $b : \{0, 1\}^* \to \{0, 1\}$ and $f : \{0, 1\}^* \to \{0, 1\}^*$ there exist obvious algorithms that guess $b(U_n)$ from $f(U_n)$ with success probability at least one-half (e.g., the algorithm that, obliviously of its input, outputs a uniformly chosen bit). Also, if b is a hard-core predicate (for any function), then $b(U_n)$ must be almost unbiased (i.e., $|\Pr[b(U_n) = 0] - \Pr[b(U_n) = 1]|$ must be a negligible function in n).

Since b itself is polynomial-time-computable, the failure of efficient algorithms to approximate $b(x)$ from $f(x)$ (with success probability non-negligibly higher than one-half) must be due either to an information loss of f (i.e., f not being one-to-one) or to the difficulty of inverting f. For example, the predicate $b(\sigma\alpha) = \sigma$ is a hard-core of the function $f(\sigma\alpha) \overset{\text{def}}{=} 0\alpha$, where $\sigma \in \{0, 1\}$ and $\alpha \in \{0, 1\}^*$. Hence, in this case the fact that b is a hard-core of the function f is due to the fact that f loses information (specifically, the first bit σ). On the other hand, in case f loses no information (i.e., f is one-to-one), hard-cores for f exist only if f is one-way (see Exercise 25). We shall be interested in the case where the hardness of approximating $b(x)$ from $f(x)$ is due to computational reasons and not to information-theoretic ones (i.e., information loss).

Hard-core predicates for collections of one-way functions are defined in an analogous way. Typically, the predicate may depend on the index of the function, and both algorithms (i.e., the one for evaluating it, as well as the one for predicting it based on the function value) are also given this index. That is, a polynomial-time algorithm $B : \{0, 1\}^* \times \{0, 1\}^* \to \{0, 1\}$ is called a *hard-core of the one-way collection* (I, D, F) if for every probabilistic polynomial-time algorithm A', every positive polynomial $p(\cdot)$, and all sufficiently large n's,

$$\Pr[A'(I_n, f_{I_n}(X_n)) = B(I_n, X_n)] < \frac{1}{2} + \frac{1}{p(n)}$$

where $I_n \overset{\text{def}}{=} I(1^n)$ and $X_n \overset{\text{def}}{=} D(I_n)$.

Some Natural Candidates. Simple hard-core predicates are known for the RSA, Rabin, and DLP collections (presented in Section 2.4.3), provided that the corresponding collections are one-way. Specifically, the least significant bit is a hard-core for the RSA collection, provided that the RSA collection is one-way. Namely, assuming that the RSA collection is one-way, it is infeasible to guess (with success probability significantly greater than $\frac{1}{2}$) the least significant bit of x from $\text{RSA}_{N,e}(x) = x^e \bmod N$. Similarly, assuming the intractability of integer factorization, it is infeasible to guess the least significant bit of $x \in Q_N$ from $\text{Rabin}_N(x) = x^2 \bmod N$, where N is a Blum integer (and Q_N denotes the set of quadratic residues modulo N). Finally, assuming that the DLP collection is one-way, it is infeasible to guess whether or not $x < \frac{P}{2}$ when given $\text{DLP}_{P,G}(x) = G^x \bmod P$. In the next subsection we present a general result of this type.

2.5.2. Hard-Core Predicates for Any One-Way Function

Actually, the title is inaccurate: We are going to present hard-core predicates only for (strong) one-way functions of a special form. However, every (strong) one-way function can be easily transformed into a function of the required form, with no substantial loss in either "security" or "efficiency."

Theorem 2.5.2: *Let f be an arbitrary strong one-way function, and let g be defined by $g(x, r) \overset{\text{def}}{=} (f(x), r)$, where $|x| = |r|$. Let $b(x, r)$ denote the inner product mod 2 of the binary vectors x and r. Then the predicate b is a hard-core of the function g.*

In other words, the theorem states that if f is strongly one-way, then it is infeasible to guess the exclusive-OR (XOR) of a random subset of the bits of x when given $f(x)$ and the subset itself. We stress that the theorem requires that f be strongly one-way and that the conclusion is false if f is only weakly one-way (see Exercise 25). Clearly, g is also strongly one-way. We point out that g maintains other properties of f, such as being length-preserving and being one-to-one. Furthermore, an analogous statement holds for collections of one-way functions with/without trapdoor, etc.

The rest of this section is devoted to proving Theorem 2.5.2. Again we use a reducibility argument: Here, inverting the function f is reduced to guessing $b(x, r)$ from $(f(x), r)$. Hence, we assume (for contradiction) the existence of an efficient algorithm guessing the inner product with an advantage that is non-negligible, and we derive an algorithm that inverts f with related (i.e., non-negligible) success probability. This contradicts the hypothesis that f is a one-way function.

We start with some preliminary observations and a motivating discussion and then turn to the main part of the actual proof. We conclude with more efficient implementations of the reducibility argument that assert "higher levels of security."

2.5.2.1. Preliminaries

Let G be a (probabilistic polynomial-time) algorithm that on input $f(x)$ and r tries to guess the inner product (mod 2) of x and r. Denote by $\varepsilon_G(n)$ the (overall) advantage of algorithm G in guessing $b(x, r)$ from $f(x)$ and r, where x and r are uniformly chosen in $\{0, 1\}^n$. Namely,

$$\varepsilon_G(n) \overset{\text{def}}{=} \Pr[G(f(X_n), R_n) = b(X_n, R_n)] - \frac{1}{2} \qquad (2.15)$$

where here and in the sequel X_n and R_n denote two independent random variables, each uniformly distributed over $\{0, 1\}^n$. Assuming, to the contrary, that b is not a hard-core of g means that there exists an efficient algorithm G, a polynomial $p(\cdot)$, and an infinite set N such that for every $n \in N$, it holds that $\varepsilon_G(n) > \frac{1}{p(n)}$. We restrict our attention to this algorithm G and to n's in this set N. In the sequel, we shorthand ε_G by ε.

Our first observation is that on at least an $\frac{\varepsilon(n)}{2}$ fraction of the x's of length n, algorithm G has at least an $\frac{\varepsilon(n)}{2}$ advantage in guessing $b(x, R_n)$ from $f(x)$ and R_n. Namely:

Claim 2.5.2.1: There exists a set $S_n \subseteq \{0, 1\}^n$ of cardinality at least $\frac{\varepsilon(n)}{2} \cdot 2^n$ such that for every $x \in S_n$, it holds that

$$s(x) \overset{\text{def}}{=} \Pr[G(f(x), R_n) = b(x, R_n)] \geq \frac{1}{2} + \frac{\varepsilon(n)}{2}$$

Here the probability is taken over all possible values of R_n and all internal coin tosses of algorithm G, whereas x is fixed.

Proof: The claim follows by an averaging argument. Namely, write $E(s(X_n)) = \frac{1}{2} + \varepsilon(n)$, and apply Markov's inequality. $\square$

In the sequel, we restrict our attention to x's in S_n. We shall show an efficient algorithm that on every input y, with $y = f(x)$ and $x \in S_n$, finds x with very high probability. Contradiction to the (strong) one-wayness of f will follow by recalling that $\Pr[U_n \in S_n] \geq \frac{\varepsilon(n)}{2}$.

We start with a motivating discussion. The inverting algorithm that uses algorithm G as subroutine will be formally described and analyzed later.

2.5.2.2. A Motivating Discussion

Consider a fixed $x \in S_n$. By definition, $s(x) \geq \frac{1}{2} + \frac{\varepsilon(n)}{2} > \frac{1}{2} + \frac{1}{2p(n)}$. Suppose, for a moment, that $s(x) > \frac{3}{4} + \frac{1}{2p(n)}$. Of course there is no reason to believe that such is the case; we are just doing a mental experiment. Still, in this case (i.e., of $s(x) > \frac{3}{4} + \frac{1}{\text{poly}(|x|)}$), retrieving x from $f(x)$ is quite easy. To retrieve the ith bit of x, denoted x_i, we randomly select $r \in \{0, 1\}^n$ and compute $G(f(x), r)$ and $G(f(x), r \oplus e^i)$, where e^i is an n-dimensional binary vector with 1 in the ith component, and 0 in all the others, and $v \oplus u$ denotes the addition mod 2 of the binary vectors v and u. (The process is actually repeated polynomially many times, using independent random choices of such r's, and x_i is determined by a majority vote.)

If both $G(f(x), r) = b(x, r)$ and $G(f(x), r \oplus e^i) = b(x, r \oplus e^i)$, then

$$G(f(x), r) \oplus G(f(x), r \oplus e^i) = b(x, r) \oplus b(x, r \oplus e^i)$$
$$= b(x, e^i)$$
$$= x_i$$

where the second equality uses

$$b(x, r) \oplus b(x, s) \equiv \sum_{i=1}^{n} x_i r_i + \sum_{i=1}^{n} x_i s_i \equiv \sum_{i=1}^{n} x_i(r_i + s_i) \equiv b(x, r \oplus s) \pmod{2}$$

The probability that both $G(f(x), r) = b(x, r)$ and $G(f(x), r \oplus e^i) = b(x, r \oplus e^i)$ hold, for a random r, is at least $1 - 2 \cdot (\frac{1}{4} - \frac{1}{\text{poly}(|x|)}) > \frac{1}{2} + \frac{1}{\text{poly}(|x|)}$. Hence, repeating the foregoing procedure sufficiently many times and ruling by majority, we retrieve x_i with very high probability. Similarly, we can retrieve all the bits of x and hence invert f on $f(x)$. However, the entire analysis was conducted under (the unjustifiable) assumption that $s(x) > \frac{3}{4} + \frac{1}{2p(|x|)}$, whereas we know only that $s(x) > \frac{1}{2} + \frac{1}{2p(|x|)}$.

The problem with the foregoing procedure is that it doubles the original error probability of algorithm G on inputs of the form $(f(x), \cdot)$. Under the unrealistic assumption that G's average error on such inputs is non-negligibly smaller than $\frac{1}{4}$, the error-doubling phenomenon raises no problems. However, in general (and even in the special case where G's error is exactly $\frac{1}{4}$), the foregoing procedure is unlikely to invert f. Note that the *average* error probability of G (which is averaged over all possible inputs of the form $(f(x), \cdot)$) cannot be decreased by repeating G several times (e.g., G may always answer correctly on $\frac{3}{4}$ of the inputs and always err on the remaining $\frac{1}{4}$). What is required is an *alternative way of using* the algorithm G, a way that does not double the original error probability of G. The key idea is to generate the r's in a way that requires applying algorithm G only once per each r (and i), instead of twice. Specifically, we shall use algorithm G to obtain a "guess" for $b(x, r \oplus e^i)$ and obtain $b(x, r)$ in a different way. The good news is that the error probability is no longer doubled, since we use G only to get a "guess" of $b(x, r \oplus e^i)$. The bad news is that we still need to know $b(x, r)$, and it is not clear how we can know $b(x, r)$ without applying G. The answer is that we can guess $b(x, r)$ by ourselves. This is fine if we need to guess $b(x, r)$ for only one r (or logarithmically in $|x|$ many r's), but the problem is that we need to know (and hence guess) the values of $b(x, r)$ for polynomially many r's. An obvious way of guessing these $b(x, r)$'s yields an exponentially vanishing success probability. Instead, we generate these polynomially many r's such that, on one hand, they are "sufficiently random," whereas, on the other hand, we can guess all the $b(x, r)$'s with noticeable success probability. Specifically, generating the r's in a particular *pairwise-independent* manner will satisfy both (seemingly contradictory) requirements. We stress that in case we are successful (in our guesses for all the $b(x, r)$'s), we can retrieve x with high probability. Hence, we retrieve x with noticeable probability.

A word about the way in which the pairwise-independent r's are generated (and the corresponding $b(x, r)$'s are guessed) is indeed in order. To generate $m = \text{poly}(n)$ many r's, we uniformly (and independently) select $l \stackrel{\text{def}}{=} \log_2(m + 1)$ strings in $\{0, 1\}^n$. Let us denote these strings by $s^1, \ldots, s^l$. We then guess $b(x, s^1)$ through $b(x, s^l)$. Let us denote these guesses, which are uniformly (and independently) chosen in $\{0, 1\}$, by σ^1 through σ^l. Hence, the probability that all our guesses for the $b(x, s^i)$'s are correct is $2^{-l} = \frac{1}{\text{poly}(n)}$. The different r's correspond to the different *non-empty* subsets of $\{1, 2, \ldots, l\}$. Specifically, we let $r^J \stackrel{\text{def}}{=} \oplus_{j \in J} s^j$. The reader can easily verify that the r^J's are pairwise independent, and each is uniformly distributed in $\{0, 1\}^n$. The key observation is that

$$b(x, r^J) = b(x, \oplus_{j \in J} s^j) = \oplus_{j \in J} b(x, s^j)$$

Hence, our guess for the $b(x, r^J)$'s is $\oplus_{j \in J} \sigma^j$, and with noticeable probability all our guesses are correct.

2.5.2.3. Back to the Actual Proof

Following is a formal description of the inverting algorithm, denoted A. We assume, for simplicity, that f is length-preserving (yet this assumption is not essential). On input y (supposedly in the range of f), algorithm A sets $n \stackrel{\text{def}}{=} |y|$ and $l \stackrel{\text{def}}{=} \lceil \log_2(2n \cdot p(n)^2 + 1) \rceil$, where $p(\cdot)$ is the polynomial guaranteed earlier (i.e., $\varepsilon(n) > \frac{1}{p(n)}$ for the infinitely many n's in N). Algorithm A proceeds as follows:

1. It uniformly and independently selects $s^1, \ldots, s^l \in \{0, 1\}^n$ and $\sigma^1, \ldots, \sigma^l \in \{0, 1\}$.

2. For every non-empty set $J \subseteq \{1, 2, \ldots, l\}$, it computes a string $r^J \leftarrow \oplus_{j \in J} s^j$ and a bit $\rho^J \leftarrow \oplus_{j \in J} \sigma^j$.

3. For every $i \in \{1, \ldots, n\}$ and every non-empty $J \subseteq \{1, \ldots, l\}$, it computes

$$z_i^J \leftarrow \rho^J \oplus G(y, r^J \oplus e^i).$$

4. For every $i \in \{1, \ldots, n\}$, it sets z_i to be the majority of the z_i^J values.

5. It outputs $z = z_1 \cdots z_n$.

Remark: An Alternative Implementation. In an alternative implementation of these ideas, the inverting algorithm tries all possible values for $\sigma^1, \ldots, \sigma^l$, computes a string z for each of these 2^l possibilities, and outputs only one of the resulting z's, with an obvious preference for a string z satisfying $f(z) = y$. For later reference, this alternative algorithm is denoted A'. (See further discussion in the next subsection.)

Following is a detailed analysis of the success probability of algorithm A on inputs of the form $f(x)$, for $x \in S_n$, where $n \in N$. One key observation, which is extensively used, is that for $x, \alpha, \beta \in \{0, 1\}^n$, it holds that

$$b(x, \alpha \oplus \beta) = b(x, \alpha) \oplus b(x, \beta)$$

It follows that $b(x, r^J) = b(x, \oplus_{j \in J} s^j) = \oplus_{j \in J} b(x, s^j)$. The main part of the analysis is showing that in case the σ^j's are correct (i.e., $\sigma^j = b(x, s^j)$ for all $j \in \{1, \ldots, l\}$), with constant probability, $z_i = x_i$ for all $i \in \{1, \ldots, n\}$. This is proved by bounding from below the probability that the majority of the z_i^J's equal x_i, where $z_i^J = b(x, r^J) \oplus G(f(x), r^J \oplus e^i)$ (due to the hypothesis that $\sigma^j = b(x, s^j)$ for all $j \in \{1, \ldots, l\}$).

Claim 2.5.2.2: For every $x \in S_n$ and every $1 \leq i \leq n$,

$$\Pr\left[|\{J : b(x, r^J) \oplus G(f(x), r^J \oplus e^i) = x_i\}| > \frac{1}{2} \cdot (2^l - 1) \right] > 1 - \frac{1}{2n}$$

where $r^J \overset{\text{def}}{=} \oplus_{j \in J} s^j$ and the s^j's are independently and uniformly chosen in $\{0, 1\}^n$.

Proof: For every J, define a 0-1 random variable ζ^J such that ζ^J equals 1 if and only if $b(x, r^J) \oplus G(f(x), r^J \oplus e^i) = x_i$. Since $b(x, r^J) \oplus b(x, r^J \oplus e^i) = x_i$, it follows that $\zeta^J = 1$ if and only if $G(f(x), r^J \oplus e^i) = b(x, r^J \oplus e^i)$.

The reader can easily verify that each r^J is uniformly distributed in $\{0, 1\}^n$, and the same holds for each $r^J \oplus e^i$. It follows that each ζ^J equals 1 with probability $s(x)$, which by $x \in S_n$ is at least $\frac{1}{2} + \frac{1}{2p(n)}$. We show that the ζ^J's are pairwise independent by showing that the r^J's are pairwise independent. For every $J \neq K$, without loss of generality, there exist $j \in J$ and $k \in K - J$. Hence, for every $\alpha, \beta \in \{0, 1\}^n$, we have

$$\Pr[r^K = \beta \mid r^J = \alpha] = \Pr[s^k = \beta \mid s^j = \alpha]$$
$$= \Pr[s^k = \beta]$$
$$= \Pr[r^K = \beta]$$

and pairwise independence of the r^J's follows. Let $m \overset{\text{def}}{=} 2^l - 1$, and let ζ represent a generic ζ^J (which are all identically distributed). Using Chebyshev's inequality (and $m \geq 2n \cdot p(n)^2$), we get

$$\Pr\left[\sum_J \zeta^J \leq \frac{1}{2} \cdot m\right] \leq \Pr\left[\left|\sum_J \zeta^J - \left(\frac{1}{2} + \frac{1}{2p(n)}\right) \cdot m\right| \geq \frac{1}{2p(n)} \cdot m\right]$$

$$\leq \frac{m \cdot \mathsf{Var}[\zeta]}{\left(\frac{1}{2p(n)} \cdot m\right)^2}$$

$$= \frac{\mathsf{Var}[\zeta]}{\left(\frac{1}{2p(n)}\right)^2 \cdot (2n \cdot p(n)^2)}$$

$$< \frac{\frac{1}{4}}{\left(\frac{1}{2p(n)}\right)^2 \cdot (2n \cdot p(n)^2)}$$

$$= \frac{1}{2n}$$

The claim follows. $\square$

Recall that if $\sigma^j = b(x, s^j)$ for all j's, then $\rho^J = \oplus_{j \in J} \sigma^j = \oplus_{j \in J} b(x, s^j) = b(x, r^J)$ for all non-empty J's. In this case, with probability at least $\frac{1}{2}$, the string z output by algorithm A equals x. However, the first event (i.e., $\sigma^j = b(x, s^j)$ for all j's) happens with probability $2^{-l} = \frac{1}{2n \cdot p(n)^2 + 1}$ independently of the events analyzed in Claim 2.5.2.2. Hence, in case $x \in S_n$, algorithm A inverts f on $f(x)$ with probability at least $\frac{1}{2} \cdot 2^{-l} = \frac{1}{4n \cdot p(|x|)^2 + 2}$ (whereas the alternative algorithm A' succeeds with probability at least $\frac{1}{2}$). Recalling that (by Claim 2.5.2.1) $|S_n| > \frac{1}{2p(n)} \cdot 2^n$, we conclude that for every $n \in N$, algorithm A inverts f on $f(U_n)$ with probability at least $\frac{1}{8n \cdot p(n)^3 + 4p(n)}$. Noting that A is polynomial-time (i.e., it merely invokes G for $2n \cdot p(n)^2 = \text{poly}(n)$ times, in addition to making a polynomial amount of other computations), a contradiction to our hypothesis that f is strongly one-way follows. $\blacksquare$

2.5.2.4.* More Efficient Reductions

The preceding proof actually establishes the following:

Proposition 2.5.3: *Let G be a probabilistic algorithm with running time $t_G : \mathbb{N} \to \mathbb{N}$ and advantage $\varepsilon_G : \mathbb{N} \to [0, 1]$ in guessing b (see Eq. (2.15)). Then there exists an algorithm A that runs in time $O(n^2/\varepsilon_G(n)^2) \cdot t_G(n)$ such that*

$$\Pr[A(f(U_n)) = U_n] \geq \frac{\varepsilon_G(n)}{2} \cdot \frac{\varepsilon_G(n)^2}{4n}$$

The alternative implementation, A', mentioned earlier (i.e., trying all possible values of the σ^j's rather than guessing one of them), runs in time $O(n^3/\varepsilon_G(n)^4) \cdot t_G(n)$ and satisfies

$$\Pr[A'(f(U_n)) = U_n] \geq \frac{\varepsilon_G(n)}{2} \cdot \frac{1}{2}$$

Below, we provide a more efficient implementation of A'. Combining it with a more refined averaging argument than the one used in Claim 2.5.2.1, we obtain the following:

Proposition 2.5.4: *Let G, $t_G : \mathbb{N} \to \mathbb{N}$, and $\varepsilon_G : \mathbb{N} \to [0, 1]$ be as before, and define $\ell(n) \overset{\text{def}}{=} \log_2(1/\varepsilon_G(n))$. Then there exists an algorithm A'' that runs in expected time $O(n^2 \cdot \ell(n)^3) \cdot t_G(n)$ and satisfies*

$$\Pr[A''(f(U_n)) = U_n] = \Omega(\varepsilon_G(n)^2)$$

Thus, the *time-versus-success ratio* of A'' is $\mathrm{poly}(n)/\varepsilon_G(n)^2$, which (in some sense) is optimal up to a $\mathrm{poly}(n)$ factor; see Exercise 30.

Proof Sketch: Let $\varepsilon(n) \overset{\text{def}}{=} \varepsilon_G(n)$, and $\ell \overset{\text{def}}{=} \log_2(1/\varepsilon(n))$. Recall that $E[s(X_n)] = 0.5 + \varepsilon(n)$, where $s(x) \overset{\text{def}}{=} \Pr[G(f(x), R_n) = b(x, R_n)]$ (as in Claim 2.5.2.1). We first replace Claim 2.5.2.1 by a more refined analysis.

Claim 2.5.4.1: There exists an $i \in \{1, \ldots, \ell\}$ and a set $S_n \subseteq \{0, 1\}^n$ of cardinality at least $(2^{i-1} \cdot \varepsilon(n)) \cdot 2^n$ such that for every $x \in S_n$, it holds that

$$s(x) = \Pr[G(f(x), R_n) = b(x, R_n)] \geq \frac{1}{2} + \frac{1}{2^{i+1} \cdot \ell}$$

Proof: Let $A_i \overset{\text{def}}{=} \{x : s(x) \geq \frac{1}{2} + \frac{1}{2^{i+1}\ell}\}$. For any non-empty set $S \subseteq \{0, 1\}^n$, we let $a(S) \overset{\text{def}}{=} \max_{x \in S}\{s(x) - 0.5\}$, and $a(\emptyset) \overset{\text{def}}{=} 0$. Assuming, to the contrary, that the claim does not hold (i.e., $|A_i| < (2^{i-1} \cdot \varepsilon(n)) \cdot 2^n$ for $i = 1, \ldots, \ell$), we get

$$E[s(X_n) - 0.5] \leq \Pr[X_n \in A_1] \cdot a(A_1)$$

$$+ \sum_{i=2}^{\ell} \Pr[X_n \in (A_i \setminus A_{i-1})] \cdot a(A_i \setminus A_{i-1})$$

$$+ \Pr[X_n \in (\{0, 1\}^n \setminus A_\ell)] \cdot a(\{0, 1\}^n \setminus A_\ell)$$

$$< \varepsilon(n) \cdot \frac{1}{2} + \sum_{i=2}^{\ell}(2^{i-1} \cdot \varepsilon(n)) \cdot \frac{1}{2^i \ell} + 1 \cdot \frac{1}{2^{\ell+1}\ell}$$

$$= \frac{\varepsilon(n)}{2} + (\ell - 1) \cdot \frac{\varepsilon(n)}{2\ell} + \frac{2^{-\ell}}{2\ell} = \varepsilon(n)$$

which contradicts $E[s(X_n) - 0.5] = \varepsilon(n)$. $\square$

Fixing any i that satisfies Claim 2.5.4.1, we let $\varepsilon \overset{\text{def}}{=} 2^{-i-1}/\ell$ and consider the corresponding set $S_n \overset{\text{def}}{=} \{x : s(x) \geq 0.5 + \varepsilon\}$. By suitable setting of parameters, we obtain that for every $x \in S_n$, algorithm A' runs in time $O(n^3/\varepsilon^4) \cdot t_G(n)$ and retrieves x from $f(x)$ with probability at least $\frac{1}{2}$. Our next goal is to provide a more efficient implementation of A', specifically, one running in time $O(n^2/\varepsilon^2) \cdot (t_G(n) + \log(n/\varepsilon))$.

The modified algorithm A' is given input $y = f(x)$ and a parameter ε and sets $l = \log((n/\varepsilon^2) + 1)$. In the actual description (presented later), it will be more convenient to use arithmetic of reals instead of Boolean. Hence, we denote $b'(x, r) = (-1)^{b(x,r)}$ and $G'(y, r) = (-1)^{G(y,r)}$. The verification of the following facts is left as an exercise:

Fact 1: For every x, it holds that $E[b'(x, U_n) \cdot G'(f(x), U_n + e^i)] = s'(x) \cdot (-1)^{x_i}$, where $s'(x) \stackrel{\text{def}}{=} 2 \cdot (s(x) - \frac{1}{2})$. (Note that for $x \in S_n$, we have $s'(x) \geq 2\varepsilon$.)

Fact 2: Let R be a uniformly chosen l-by-n Boolean matrix. Then for every $v \neq u \in \{0, 1\}^l \setminus \{0\}^l$, it holds that vR and uR are pairwise independent and uniformly distributed in $\{0, 1\}^n$.

Fact 3: For every $x \in \{0, 1\}^n$ and $v \in \{0, 1\}^l$, it holds that $b'(x, vR) = b'(xR^T, v)$.

Using these facts, we obtain the following:

Claim 2.5.4.2: For any $x \in S_n$ and a uniformly chosen l-by-n Boolean matrix R, there exists $\sigma \in \{0, 1\}^l$ such that, with probability at least $\frac{1}{2}$, for every $1 \leq i \leq n$, the sign of $\sum_{v \in \{0,1\}^l} b'(\sigma, v) \cdot G'(f(x), vR + e^i)$ equals the sign of $(-1)^{x_i}$.

Proof: Let $\sigma = xR^T$. Combining the foregoing facts, for every $v \in \{0, 1\}^l \setminus \{0\}^l$, we have $E[b'(xR^T, v) \cdot G'(f(x), vR + e^i)] = s'(x) \cdot (-1)^{x_i}$. Thus, for every such v, it holds that $\Pr[b'(xR^T, v) \cdot G'(f(x), vR + e^i) = (-1)^{x_i}] = \frac{1+s'(x)}{2} = s(x)$. Using Fact 2, $l = \log((2n/\varepsilon^2) + 1)$, and Chebyshev's inequality, the claim follows. $\square$

A last piece of notation: Let B be a 2^l-by-2^l matrix, with the (σ, v) entry being $b'(\sigma, v)$, and let $\bar{g}^i$ be a 2^l-dimensional vector, with the vth entry equal to $G'(f(x), vR + e^i)$. Thus, the σth entry in the vector $B\bar{g}^i$ equals $\sum_{v \in \{0,1\}^l} b'(\sigma, v) \cdot G'(f(x), vR + e^i)$.

Efficient implementation of algorithm A': On input $y = f(x)$ and a parameter ε, the inverting algorithm A' sets $l = \log((n/\varepsilon^2) + 1)$ and proceeds as follows:

1. For $i = 1, \ldots, n$, it computes the 2^l-dimensional vector $\bar{g}^i$ (as defined earlier).

2. For $i = 1, \ldots, n$, it computes $\bar{z}_i \leftarrow B\bar{g}^i$.

   Let Z be a 2^l-by-n real matrix in which the ith column equals $\bar{z}_i$.

   Let Z' be a 2^l-by-n Boolean matrix representing the signs of the elements in Z: Specifically, the (i, j)th entry of Z' equals 1 if and only if the (i, j)th entry of Z is negative.

3. Scanning all rows of Z', it outputs the first row z so that $f(z) = y$.

By Claim 2.5.4.2, for $x \in S_n$, with probability at least $\frac{1}{2}$, the foregoing algorithm retrieves x from $y = f(x)$. The running time of the algorithm is dominated by

Steps 1 and 2, which can be implemented in time $n \cdot 2^l \cdot O(t_G(n)) = O((n/\varepsilon)^2 \cdot t_G(n))$ and $n \cdot O(l \cdot 2^l) = O((n/\varepsilon)^2 \cdot \log(n/\varepsilon))$, respectively.[10]

Finally, we define algorithm A''. On input $y = f(x)$, the algorithm selects $j \in \{1, \ldots, \ell\}$ with probability 2^{-2j+1} (and halts with no output otherwise). It invokes the preceding implementation of algorithm A' on input y with parameter $\varepsilon \overset{\text{def}}{=} 2^{-j-1}/\ell$ and returns whatever A' does. The *expected* running time of A'' is

$$\sum_{j=1}^{\ell} 2^{-2j+1} \cdot O\left(\frac{n^2}{(2^{-j-1}/\ell)^2}\right) \cdot (t_G(n) + \log(n \cdot 2^{j+1}\ell)) = O(n^2 \cdot \ell^3) \cdot t_G(n)$$

(assuming $t_G(n) = \Omega(\ell \log n)$). Letting $i \leq \ell$ be an index satisfying Claim 2.5.4.1 (and letting S_n be the corresponding set), we consider the case in which j (selected by A'') is greater than or equal to i. By Claim 2.5.4.2, in such a case, and for $x \in S_n$, algorithm A' inverts f on $f(x)$ with probability at least $\frac{1}{2}$. Using $i \leq \ell$ $(= \log_2(1/\varepsilon(n)))$, we get

$$\Pr[A''(f(U_n)) = U_n] \geq \Pr[U_n \in S_n] \cdot \Pr[j \geq i] \cdot \frac{1}{2}$$

$$\geq 2^{i-1}\varepsilon(n) \cdot 2^{-2i+1} \cdot \frac{1}{2}$$

$$\geq \varepsilon(n) \cdot 2^{-\ell} \cdot \frac{1}{2} = \frac{\varepsilon(n)^2}{2}$$

The proposition follows. ∎

Comment. Using an additional trick,[11] one can save a factor of $\Theta(n)$ in the running time, resulting in an *expected* running time of $O(n \cdot \log^3(1/\varepsilon_G(n))) \cdot t_G(n)$.

---

[10]Using the special structure of matrix B, one can show that given a vector $\bar{w}$, the product $B\bar{w}$ can be computed in time $O(l \cdot 2^l)$. Hint: B (known as the Sylvester matrix) can be written recursively as

$$S_k = \begin{pmatrix} S_{k-1} & S_{k-1} \\ S_{k-1} & \bar{S}_{k-1} \end{pmatrix}$$

where $S_0 = +1$ and $\bar{M}$ means flipping the $+1$ entries of M to -1 and vice versa. So

$$\begin{pmatrix} S_{k-1} & S_{k-1} \\ S_{k-1} & \bar{S}_{k-1} \end{pmatrix} \begin{bmatrix} w' \\ w'' \end{bmatrix} = \begin{bmatrix} S_{k-1}w' + S_{k-1}w'' \\ S_{k-1}w' - S_{k-1}w'' \end{bmatrix}$$

Thus, letting $T(k)$ denote the time used in multiplying S_k by a 2^k-dimensional vector, we have $T(k) = 2 \cdot T(k-1) + O(2^k)$, which solves to $T(k) = O(k2^k)$.

[11]We further modify algorithm A' by setting $2^l = O(1/\varepsilon^2)$ (rather than $2^l = O(n/\varepsilon^2)$). Under the new setting, with constant probability, we recover correctly a constant fraction of the bits of x (rather than all of them). If x were a codeword under an asymptotically good error-correcting code (cf. [138]), this would suffice. To avoid this assumption, we modify algorithm A' so that it tries to recover certain XORs of bits of x (rather than individual bits of x). Specifically, we use an asymptotically good linear code (i.e., having constant rate, correcting a constant fraction of errors, and having efficient decoding algorithm). Thus, the modified A' recovers correctly a constant fraction of the bits in the encoding of x under such a code, and using the decoding algorithm it recovers x.

2.5.3.*Hard-Core Functions

We have just seen that every one-way function can be easily modified to have a hard-core predicate. In other words, the result establishes one bit of information about the pre-image that is hard to approximate from the value of the function. A stronger result may say that several bits of information about the pre-image are hard to approximate. For example, we may want to say that a specific pair of bits is hard to approximate, in the sense that it is infeasible to guess this pair with probability non-negligibly larger than $\frac{1}{4}$. Actually, in general, we take a slightly different approach and require that the true value of these bits be hard to distinguish from a random value. That is, a *polynomial-time* function h is called a hard-core of a function f if no efficient algorithm can distinguish $(f(x), h(x))$ from $(f(x), r)$, where r is a random string of length $|h(x)|$. For further discussion of the notion of efficient distinguishability, the reader is referred to Section 3.2. We assume for simplicity that h is length-regular (see next).

Definition 2.5.5 (Hard-Core Function): *Let $h : \{0, 1\}^* \to \{0, 1\}^*$ be a polynomial-time-computable function satisfying $|h(x)| = |h(y)|$ for all $|x| = |y|$, and let $l(n) \stackrel{\text{def}}{=} |h(1^n)|$. The function h is called a **hard-core** of a function f if for every probabilistic polynomial-time algorithm D', every positive polynomial $p(\cdot)$, and all sufficiently large n's,*

$$\left| \Pr[D'(f(X_n), h(X_n)) = 1] - \Pr[D'(f(X_n), R_{l(n)}) = 1] \right| < \frac{1}{p(n)}$$

where X_n and $R_{l(n)}$ are two independent random variables, the first uniformly distributed over $\{0, 1\}^n$ and the second uniformly distributed over $\{0, 1\}^{l(n)}$.

For $l \equiv 1$, Definition 2.5.5 is equivalent to Definition 2.5.1; see the discussion following Lemma 2.5.8. See also Exercise 31.

Simple hard-core functions with logarithmic lengths (i.e., $l(n) = O(\log n)$) are known for the RSA, Rabin, and DLP collections, provided that the corresponding collections are one-way. For example, the function that outputs logarithmically many least significant bits is a hard-core function for the RSA collection, provided that the RSA collection is one-way. Namely, assuming that the RSA collection is one-way, it is infeasible to distinguish, given $\text{RSA}_{N,e}(x) = x^e \bmod N$, the $O(\log |N|)$ least significant bit of x from a uniformly distributed $O(\log |N|)$-bit-long string. (Similar statements hold for the Rabin and DLP collections.) A general result of this type follows.

Theorem 2.5.6: *Let f be an arbitrary strong one-way function, and let g_2 be defined by $g_2(x, s) \stackrel{\text{def}}{=} (f(x), s)$, where $|s| = 2|x|$.[12] Let $b_i(x, s)$ denote the inner product mod 2 of the binary vectors x and $(s_{i+1}, \ldots, s_{i+n})$, where $s = (s_1, \ldots, s_{2n})$. Then, for any constant $c > 0$, the function $h(x, s) \stackrel{\text{def}}{=} b_1(x, s) \cdots b_{l(|x|)}(x, s)$ is a hard-core of the function g_2, where $l(n) \stackrel{\text{def}}{=} \min\{n, \lceil c \log_2 n \rceil\}$.*

---

[12]In fact, we can use $|s| = |x| + l(|x|) - 1$, where $l(n) = O(\log n)$. In the current description, s_1 and $s_{n+l(n)+1}, \ldots, s_{2n}$ are not used. However, the current formulation makes it unnecessary to specify l when defining g_2.

The proof of the theorem follows by combining a *proposition that capitalizes on the structure of the specific function h* and a *general lemma* concerning hard-core functions. Loosely speaking, the proposition "reduces" the problem of approximating $b(x, r)$ given $g(x, r)$ to the problem of approximating the XOR of any non-empty set of the bits of $h(x, s)$ given $g_2(x, s)$, where b and g are the hard-core and the one-way function presented in the preceding subsection. Since we know that the predicate $b(x, r)$ cannot be approximated from $g(x, r)$, we conclude that no XOR of the bits of $h(x, s)$ can be approximated from $g_2(x, s)$. The general lemma implies that for every "logarithmically shrinking" function h' (i.e., h' satisfying $|h'(x)| = O(\log |x|)$), the function h' is a hard-core of a function f' if and only if the XOR of any non-empty subset of the bits of h' cannot be approximated from the value of f'. Following are the formal statements and proofs of both claims.

Proposition 2.5.7: *Let f, g_2, l, and the b_i's be as in Theorem 2.5.6. Let $\{I_n \subseteq \{1, 2, \ldots, l(n)\}\}_{n \in \mathbb{N}}$ be an arbitrary sequence of non-empty sets, and let $b_{I_{|x|}}(x, s) \stackrel{\text{def}}{=} \oplus_{i \in I_{|x|}} b_i(x, s)$. Then for every probabilistic polynomial-time algorithm A', every positive polynomial $p(\cdot)$, and all sufficiently large n's,*

$$\Pr[A'(I_n, g_2(U_{3n})) = b_{I_n}(U_{3n})] < \frac{1}{2} + \frac{1}{p(n)}$$

where U_{3n} is a random variable uniformly distributed over $\{0, 1\}^{3n}$.

Proof: The proof is by a reducibility argument. Let X_n, R_n, and S_{2n} be independent random variables uniformly distributed over $\{0, 1\}^n$, $\{0, 1\}^n$, and $\{0, 1\}^{2n}$, respectively. We show that the problem of approximating $b(X_n, R_n)$ given $(f(X_n), R_n)$ is reducible to the problem of approximating $b_{I_n}(X_n, S_{2n})$ given $(f(X_n), S_{2n})$. The underlying observation is that for every $|s| = 2 \cdot |x|$ and every $I \subseteq \{1, \ldots, l(n)\}$,

$$b_I(x, s) = \oplus_{i \in I} b_i(x, s) = b(x, \oplus_{i \in I} \mathrm{sub}_i(s))$$

where $\mathrm{sub}_i(s_1, \ldots, s_{2n}) \stackrel{\text{def}}{=} (s_{i+1}, \ldots, s_{i+n})$. Furthermore, the reader can verify that for every non-empty $I \subseteq \{1, \ldots, l(n)\}$, the random variable $\oplus_{i \in I} \mathrm{sub}_i(S_{2n})$ is uniformly distributed over $\{0, 1\}^n$, and that given a string $r \in \{0, 1\}^n$ and such a set I, one can efficiently select a string uniformly in the set $\{s : \oplus_{i \in I} \mathrm{sub}_i(s) = r\}$. Verification of both claims is left as an exercise.[13]

Now assume, to the contrary, that there exists an efficient algorithm A', a polynomial $p(\cdot)$, and an infinite sequence of sets (i.e., I_n's) and n's such that

$$\Pr[A'(I_n, g_2(U_{3n})) = b_{I_n}(U_{3n})] \geq \frac{1}{2} + \frac{1}{p(n)}$$

[13]Given any non-empty I and any $r = r_1 \cdots r_n \in \{0, 1\}^n$, consider the following procedure, where k is the largest element in I. First, uniformly select $s_1, \ldots, s_k, s_{k+n+1}, \ldots, s_{2n} \in \{0, 1\}$. Next, going from $i = 1$ to $i = n$, determine s_{k+i} so that $\oplus_{j \in I} s_{i+j} = r_i$ (i.e., $s_{k+i} \leftarrow r_i \oplus (\oplus_{j \in I \setminus \{k\}} s_{j+i})$), where the relevant s_{i+j}'s are already determined, since $j < k$). This process determines a string $s_1 \cdots s_{2n}$ uniformly among 2^n strings s that satisfy $\oplus_{i \in I} \mathrm{sub}_i(s) = r$. Since there are 2^n possible r's, both claims follow.

We first observe that for n's satisfying the foregoing inequality we can easily find a set I satisfying

$$p_I \stackrel{\text{def}}{=} \Pr[A'(I, g_2(U_{3n})) = b_I(U_{3n})] \geq \frac{1}{2} + \frac{1}{2p(n)}$$

Specifically, we can try all possible I's and estimate p_I for each of them (via random experiments), picking an I for which the estimate is highest. (Note that using poly(n) many experiments, we can approximate each of the possible $2^{l(n)} - 1 = \text{poly}(n)$ different p_I's up to an additive deviation of $1/4p(n)$ and error probability of 2^{-n}.)

We now present an algorithm for approximating $b(x, r)$ from $y \stackrel{\text{def}}{=} f(x)$ and r. On input y and r, the algorithm first finds a set I as described earlier (this stage depends only on $n \stackrel{\text{def}}{=} |x|$, which equals $|r|$). Once I is found, the algorithm uniformly selects a string s such that $\oplus_{i \in I} \text{sub}_i(s) = r$ and returns $A'(I, (y, s))$.

Note that for uniformly distributed $r \in \{0, 1\}^n$, the string s selected by our algorithm is uniformly distributed in $\{0, 1\}^{2n}$ and $b(x, r) = b_I(x, s)$. Evaluation of the success probability of this algorithm is left as an exercise. ∎

The following lemma provides a generic transformation of algorithms distinguishing between $(f(X_n), h(X_n))$ and $(f(X_n), R_{l(n)})$ to algorithms that, given $f(X_n)$ and a random non-empty subset I of $\{1, \ldots, l(n)\}$, predict the XOR of the bits of X_n at locations I.

Lemma 2.5.8 (Computational XOR Lemma): *Let f and h be arbitrary length-regular functions, and let $l(n) \stackrel{\text{def}}{=} |h(1^n)|$. Let D be any algorithm, and denote*

$$p \stackrel{\text{def}}{=} \Pr[D(f(X_n), h(X_n)) = 1] \quad \text{and} \quad q \stackrel{\text{def}}{=} \Pr[D(f(X_n), R_{l(n)}) = 1]$$

where X_n and $R_{l(n)}$ are independent random variables uniformly distributed over $\{0, 1\}^n$ and $\{0, 1\}^{l(n)}$, respectively. We consider a specific algorithm, denoted $G \stackrel{\text{def}}{=} G_D$, that uses D as a subroutine. Specifically, on input and y, and $S \subseteq \{1, \ldots, l(n)\}$ (and $l(n)$), algorithm G selects $r = r_1 \cdots r_{l(n)}$ uniformly in $\{0, 1\}^{l(n)}$ and outputs $D(y, r) \oplus 1 \oplus (\oplus_{i \in S} r_i)$. Then,

$$\Pr[G(f(X_n), I_l, l(n)) = \oplus_{i \in I_l}(h_i(X_n))] = \frac{1}{2} + \frac{p - q}{2^{l(n)} - 1}$$

where I_l is a randomly chosen non-empty subset of $\{1, \ldots, l(n)\}$, and $h_i(x)$ denotes the i th bit of $h(x)$.

It follows that for logarithmically shrinking h's, the existence of an efficient algorithm that distinguishes (with a gap that is not negligible in n) the random variables $(f(X_n), h(X_n))$ and $(f(X_n), R_{l(n)})$ implies the existence of an efficient algorithm that approximates the XOR of a random non-empty subset of the bits of $h(X_n)$ from the value of $f(X_n)$ with an advantage that is not negligible. On the other hand, it is clear that any efficient algorithm that approximates an XOR of a random non-empty subset of the bits of h from the value of f can be easily modified to distinguish $(f(X_n), h(X_n))$ from $(f(X_n), R_{l(n)})$. Hence, for logarithmically shrinking h's, the function h is a hard-core of a function f if and only if the XOR of any non-empty subset of the bits of h cannot be approximated from the value of f.

Proof: All that is required is to evaluate the success probability of algorithm G (as a function of $p - q$). We start by fixing an $x \in \{0, 1\}^n$ and evaluating $\Pr[G(f(x), I_l, l) = \oplus_{i \in I_l}(h_i(x))]$, where I_l is a uniformly chosen non-empty subset of $\{1, \ldots, l\}$ and $l \stackrel{\text{def}}{=} l(n)$. The rest is an easy averaging (over the x's).

Let C denote the set (or class) of all non-empty subsets of $\{1, \ldots, l\}$. Define, for every $S \in C$, a relation $\equiv_S$ such that $y \equiv_S z$ if and only if $\oplus_{i \in S} y_i = \oplus_{i \in S} z_i$, where $y = y_1 \cdots y_l$ and $z = z_1 \cdots z_l$. Note that for every $S \in C$ and $z \in \{0, 1\}^l$, the relation $y \equiv_S z$ holds for exactly 2^{l-1} of the y's. Recall that by definition of G, on input $(f(x), S, l)$ and random choice $r = r_1 \cdots r_l \in \{0, 1\}^l$, algorithm G outputs $D(f(x), r) \oplus 1 \oplus (\oplus_{i \in S} r_i)$. The latter equals $\oplus_{i \in S}(h_i(x))$ if and only if one of the following two disjoint events occurs:

event 1: $D(f(x), r) = 1$ and $r \equiv_S h(x)$.

event 2: $D(f(x), r) = 0$ and $r \not\equiv_S h(x)$.

By the preceding discussion and elementary manipulations, we get

$$s(x) \stackrel{\text{def}}{=} \Pr[G(f(x), I_l, l) = \oplus_{i \in I_l}(h_i(x))]$$

$$= \frac{1}{|C|} \cdot \sum_{S \in C} \Pr[G(f(x), S, l) = \oplus_{i \in S}(h_i(x)]$$

$$= \frac{1}{|C|} \cdot \sum_{S \in C}(\Pr[\text{event } 1] + \Pr[\text{event } 2])$$

$$= \frac{1}{2 \cdot |C|} \cdot \sum_{S \in C}(\Pr[\Delta(R_l) = 1 \mid R_l \equiv_S h(x)] + \Pr[\Delta(R_l) = 0 \mid R_l \not\equiv_S h(x)])$$

where R_l is uniformly distributed over $\{0, 1\}^l$ (representing the random choice of algorithm G), and $\Delta(r)$ is shorthand for the random variable $D(f(x), r)$. The rest of the analysis is straightforward but tedious and can be skipped with little loss.

$$s(x) = \frac{1}{2} + \frac{1}{2|C|} \cdot \sum_{S \in C}(\Pr[\Delta(R_l) = 1 \mid R_l \equiv_S h(x)] - \Pr[\Delta(R_l)$$

$$= 1 \mid R_l \not\equiv_S h(x)])$$

$$= \frac{1}{2} + \frac{1}{2|C|} \cdot \frac{1}{2^{l-1}} \cdot \left(\sum_{S \in C} \sum_{r \equiv_S h(x)} \Pr[\Delta(r) = 1] - \sum_{S \in C} \sum_{r \not\equiv_S h(x)} \Pr[\Delta(r) = 1] \right)$$

$$= \frac{1}{2} + \frac{1}{2^l \cdot |C|} \cdot \left(\sum_r \sum_{S \in EQ(r, h(x))} \Pr[\Delta(r) = 1] \right.$$

$$\left. - \sum_r \sum_{S \in NE(r, h(x))} \Pr[\Delta(r) = 1] \right)$$

where $EQ(r, z) \stackrel{\text{def}}{=} \{S \in C : r \equiv_S z\}$ and $NE(r, z) \stackrel{\text{def}}{=} \{S \in C : r \not\equiv_S z\}$. Observe that for every $r \neq z$, it holds that $|NE(r, z)| = 2^{l-1}$ (and $|EQ(r, z)| = 2^{l-1} - 1$). On the other hand, $EQ(z, z) = C$ (and $NE(z, z) = \emptyset$) holds for every z. Hence, we get

$$s(x) = \frac{1}{2} + \frac{1}{2^l |C|} \sum_{r \neq h(x)} ((2^{l-1} - 1) \cdot \Pr[\Delta(r) = 1] - 2^{l-1} \cdot \Pr[\Delta(r) = 1])$$

$$+ \frac{1}{2^l |C|} \cdot |C| \cdot \Pr[\Delta(h(x)) = 1]$$

$$= \frac{1}{2} - \frac{1}{2^l |C|} \sum_{r \neq h(x)} \Pr[\Delta(r) = 1] + \left(\frac{1}{|C|} - \frac{1}{2^l |C|} \right) \cdot \Pr[\Delta(h(x)) = 1]$$

where the last equality uses $|C| = 2^l - 1$ (i.e., $\frac{1}{2^l} = \frac{1}{|C|} - \frac{1}{2^l |C|}$). Rearranging the terms and substituting for Δ, we get

$$s(x) = \frac{1}{2} + \frac{1}{|C|} \cdot \Pr[\Delta(h(x)) = 1] - \frac{1}{2^l |C|} \sum_r \Pr[\Delta(r) = 1]$$

$$= \frac{1}{2} + \frac{1}{|C|} \cdot (\Pr[D(f(x), h(x)) = 1] - \Pr[D(f(x), R_l) = 1])$$

Finally, taking the expectation over the x's, we get

$$E[s(X_n)] = \frac{1}{2} + \frac{1}{|C|} \cdot (\Pr[D(f(X_n), h(X_n)) = 1] - \Pr[D(f(X_n), R_l) = 1])$$

$$= \frac{1}{2} + \frac{1}{2^l - 1} \cdot (p - q)$$

and the lemma follows. ∎

2.6.* Efficient Amplification of One-Way Functions

The *amplification* of weak one-way functions into strong ones, presented in Theorem 2.3.2, has no practical value. Recall that this amplification transforms a function f that is hard to invert on a noticeable fraction (i.e., $\frac{1}{p(n)}$) of the strings of length n into a function g that is hard to invert on all but a negligible fraction of the strings of length $n^2 p(n)$. Specifically, it is shown that an algorithm running in time $T(n)$ that inverts g on a $\varepsilon(n)$ fraction of the strings of length $n^2 p(n)$ yields an algorithm running in time $\text{poly}(p(n), n, \frac{1}{\varepsilon(n)}) \cdot T(n)$ that inverts f on a $1 - \frac{1}{p(n)}$ fraction of the strings of length n. Hence, if f *is hard to invert in practice on 1% of the strings of length 1000*, then all we can say is that g *is hard to invert in practice on almost all strings of length 100,000,000*. In contrast, an efficient amplification of one-way functions, as given later, should relate the difficulty of inverting the (weak one-way) function f on strings of length n to the difficulty of inverting the (strong one-way) function g on the strings of length $O(n)$, rather than relating it to the difficulty of inverting the function g on the strings of length $\text{poly}(n)$. Consequently, we may get assertions such as this: If f *is*

——— 78 ———

hard to invert in practice on 1% of the strings of length 1000, then g is hard to invert in practice on almost all strings of length 5000. The following definition is natural for a general discussion of amplification of one-way functions.

Definition 2.6.1 (Quantitative One-Wayness): *Let $T : \mathbb{N} \to \mathbb{N}$ and $\varepsilon : \mathbb{N} \to \mathbb{R}$ be polynomial-time-computable functions. A polynomial-time-computable function $f : \{0, 1\}^* \to \{0, 1\}^*$ is called $\varepsilon(\cdot)$-***one-way with respect to time*** $T(\cdot)$ if for every algorithm A', with running time bounded by $T(\cdot)$ and all sufficiently large n's,*

$$\Pr[A'(f(U_n)) \notin f^{-1}(f(U_n))] > \varepsilon(n)$$

Using this terminology, we review what we already know about amplification of one-way functions. A function f is weakly one-way if there exists a polynomial $p(\cdot)$ such that f is $\frac{1}{p(\cdot)}$-one-way with respect to polynomial time.[14] A function f is strongly one-way if for every polynomial $q(\cdot)$, the function f is $(1 - \frac{1}{q(\cdot)})$-one-way with respect to polynomial time. (The identity function is only 0-one-way with respect to linear time, whereas no function is $(1 - \exp(\cdot))$-one-way with respect to linear time.[15]) The amplification result of Theorem 2.3.2 can be generalized and restated as follows: *If there exist a polynomial p and a (polynomial-time-computable) function f that is $\frac{1}{p(\cdot)}$-one-way with respect to time $T(\cdot)$, then there exists a (polynomial-time-computable) function g that is strongly one-way with respect to respect to time $T'(\cdot)$, where $T'(n^2 \cdot p(n)) = T(n)$, or, in other words, $T'(n) = T(n^\varepsilon)$ for some $\varepsilon > 0$ satisfying $(n^2 \cdot p(n))^\varepsilon \le n$.* In contrast, an efficient amplification of one-way functions, as given later, should state that the foregoing holds with respect to $T'(O(n)) = T(n)$ (in other words, $T'(n) = T(\varepsilon \cdot n)$ for some $\varepsilon > 0$). Such a result can be obtained for *regular* one-way functions. A function f is called *regular* if there exists a polynomial-time-computable function $m : \mathbb{N} \to \mathbb{N}$ and a polynomial $p(\cdot)$ such that for every y in the range of f, the number of pre-images (of length n) of y under f is between $\frac{m(n)}{p(n)}$ and $m(n) \cdot p(n)$. In this book we review the result only for one-way permutations (i.e., length-preserving 1-1 functions).

Theorem 2.6.2 (Efficient Amplification of One-Way Permutations): *Let $p(\cdot)$ be a polynomial, and $T : \mathbb{N} \to \mathbb{N}$. function. Suppose that f is a polynomial-time-computable permutation that is $\frac{1}{p(\cdot)}$-one-way with respect to time $T(\cdot)$. Then there exists a constant $\gamma > 1$, a polynomial q, and a polynomial-time-computable permutation F such that for every polynomial-time-computable function $\epsilon : \mathbb{N} \to [0, 1]$, the function F is $(1 - \epsilon(\cdot))$-one-way with respect to time $T'_\epsilon(\cdot)$, where $T'_\epsilon(\gamma \cdot n) \overset{\text{def}}{=} \frac{\epsilon(n)^2}{q(n)} \cdot T(n)$.*

The constant γ depends only on the polynomial $p(\cdot)$.

---

[14] Here and later, *with respect to polynomial time* means with respect to time T, for every polynomial T.

[15] The identity function can be "inverted" with failure probability zero in linear time. On the other hand, for every function f, the algorithm that, given y, outputs $0^{|y|}$ inverts f on $f(U_n)$ with failure probability of at most $1 - 2^{-n} < 1 - \exp(-n)$.

2.6.1. The Construction

The key to the amplification of a one-way permutation f is to apply f on many different arguments. In the proof of Theorem 2.3.2, f is applied to unrelated arguments (which are disjoint parts of the input). This makes the proof relatively easy, but also makes the construction very inefficient. Instead, in the construction presented in the proof of the current theorem, we apply the one-way permutation f to related arguments. The first idea that comes to mind is to apply f iteratively many times, each time to the value resulting from the previous application. This will not help if easy instances for the inverting algorithm continue to be mapped, by f, to themselves. We cannot just hope that this will not happen. So the second idea is to use randomization between successive applications of f. It is important that we use only a small amount of randomization, since the "randomization" will be encoded into the argument of the constructed function. The randomization between successive applications of f takes the form of a random step on an expander graph. Hence a few words about these graphs and random walks on them are in order.

A graph $G = (V, E)$ is called an (n, d, c)-*expander* if it has n vertices (i.e., $|V| = n$), every vertex in V has degree d (i.e., G is d-regular), and G has the following *expansion property* (with *expansion factor* $c > 0$): For every subset $S \subset V$, if $|S| \leq \frac{n}{2}$, then $|N(S)| \geq (1 + c) \cdot |S|$, where $N(S)$ denotes the set of neighbors of vertices in S (i.e., $N(S) \stackrel{\text{def}}{=} \{u \in V : \exists v \in S \text{ s.t. } (u, v) \in E\}$).[16] By *explicitly constructed* (d, c)-*expanders* we mean a family of graphs $\{G_n\}_{n \in \mathbb{N}}$ such that each G_n is a $(2^n, d, c)$-expander and such that there exists a polynomial-time algorithm that on input a description of a vertex in an expander outputs the list of its neighbors, where vertices in G_n are represented by binary strings of length n. We stress that the constants $d \in \mathbb{N}$ and $c > 0$, as well as the algorithm, are fixed for all graphs in the family. Such expander families do exist. By a *random walk* on a graph we mean the sequence of vertices visited by starting at a uniformly chosen vertex and randomly selecting at each step one of the neighboring vertices of the current vertex, with uniform probability distribution. The expanding property implies (via a non-trivial proof) that the vertices along random walks on an expander have surprisingly strong "random properties." In particular, for every subset of constant density within the vertex set and every l, the probability that no vertex along an $O(l)$-step-long random walk will hit the subset is at most 2^{-l} (i.e., as would have been the case if we had chosen $O(l)$ vertices independently), where the constant in the O-notation depends only on the expansion factor of the graph.

We remind the reader that we are interested in successively applying the permutation f, while interleaving randomization steps between successive applications. Hence, before applying permutation f to the result of the previous application, we take one random step on an expander. Namely, we associate the domain of the given

---

[16] We use a somewhat non-standard definition. The standard definition of expansion with factor $c > 0$ is that for every such S (i.e., $S \subset V$ and $|S| \leq \frac{n}{2}$), it holds that $|N'(S)| \geq c \cdot |S|$, where $N'(S)$ denotes the vertices in $V \setminus S$ that have neighbors in S (i.e., $N'(S) \stackrel{\text{def}}{=} \{u \in V \setminus S : \exists v \in S \text{ s.t. } (u, v) \in E\}$). Every (n, d, c)-expander under the standard definition can be easily transformed into an $(n, d + 1, c)$-expander under our definition (e.g., by adding self-loops).

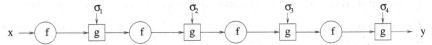

Figure 2.3: The essence of Construction 2.6.3.

one-way permutation with the vertex set of the expander. Our construction alternately applies the given one-way permutation f and randomly moves from the vertex just reached to one of its neighbors. A key observation is that the composition of an expander with any permutation on its vertices yields an expander (with the same expansion properties). Combining the properties of random walks on expanders and a "reducibility" argument, the following construction is used to amplify the one-wayness of the given permutation in an efficient manner. (We warn that Theorem 2.6.2 is not proved by direct application of the following construction; see Section 2.6.2.)

Construction 2.6.3: *Let $\{G_n\}_{n\in\mathbb{N}}$ be a family of d-regular graphs, so that G_n has vertex set $\{0, 1\}^n$ and self-loops at every vertex. Consider a labeling of the edges incident to each vertex (using the labels $1, 2, \ldots, d$). Define $g_l(x)$ to be the vertex reachable from vertex x by following the edge labeled l. Let $f : \{0, 1\}^* \to \{0, 1\}^*$ be a 1-1 length-preserving function, and let λ denote the empty sequence (over $\{1, 2, \ldots, d\}$). Then for every $k \geq 0$, $x \in \{0, 1\}^n$ and $\sigma_1, \sigma_2, \ldots, \sigma_k \in \{1, 2, \ldots, d\}$, define $F(x, \lambda) = x$ and*

$$F(x, \sigma_1\sigma_2\cdots\sigma_k) = \sigma_1, F(g_{\sigma_1}(f(x)), \sigma_2, \ldots, \sigma_k)$$

That is,

$$F(x, \sigma_1\sigma_2\cdots\sigma_k) = \sigma_1, \sigma_2, \ldots, \sigma_k, y$$

where $$y = g_{\sigma_k}(f(\cdots(g_{\sigma_2}(f(g_{\sigma_1}(f(x)))))\cdots))$$

For every $k : \mathbb{N} \to \mathbb{N}$, define $F_k(\alpha) \overset{\text{def}}{=} F(x, \sigma_1, \ldots, \sigma_t)$, where α is parsed into $(x, \sigma_1, \ldots, \sigma_t)$, so that $t = k(|x|)$ and $\sigma_i \in \{1, 2, \ldots, d\}$.

Clearly, F_k is 1-1 and length-preserving. The process in which y is obtained from x is depicted in Figure 2.3 (for $k = 4$): A circle marked f denotes application of the one-way permutation f, whereas a box marked g denotes taking a step on the expander (in the direction specified by the auxiliary input σ_i).

2.6.2. Analysis

The "hardness-amplification" property of Construction 2.6.3 is stated in the following proposition.

Proposition 2.6.4: *Let $\{G_n\}$, $f : \{0, 1\}^* \to \{0, 1\}^*$, $k : \mathbb{N} \to \mathbb{N}$, and F_k be as in Construction 2.6.3. Let $d \in \mathbb{N}$, $c > 0$, and ℓ be constants, and let $\alpha : \mathbb{N} \to \mathbb{R}$ and $T : \mathbb{N} \to \mathbb{N}$ be functions such that the following conditions hold:*

——— **81** ———

1. *The family of graphs $\{G_n\}_{n\in\mathbb{N}}$ is an explicitly constructed family of (d, c)-expanders.*

2. *The permutation f is polynomial-time-computable as well as $\alpha'(\cdot)$-one-way with respect to time $T : \mathbb{N} \to \mathbb{N}$, where $\alpha'(n) = \alpha(n) + 2^{-n}$.*

3. *The function $\alpha : \mathbb{N} \to \mathbb{R}$ is polynomial-time-computable.*

4. $\ell \geq \frac{4+c^2}{c^2} \cdot d.$

Then the permutation F_k is polynomial-time-computable, and for every polynomial-time-computable $\varepsilon : \mathbb{N} \to \mathbb{R}$, the permutation F_k is $((1 - \varepsilon(\cdot))\beta(\cdot))$-one-way with respect to time $T' : \mathbb{N} \to \mathbb{N}$, where

$$\beta(n + k(n) \cdot \log_2 d) \stackrel{\text{def}}{=} 1 - \left(1 - \frac{\alpha(n)}{2}\right)^{k(n)/\ell}$$

$$T'(n + k(n) \cdot \log_2 d) \stackrel{\text{def}}{=} \frac{(\varepsilon(n) \cdot \alpha(n))^2}{O(n + k(n))^3} \cdot T(n)$$

For $k(n) = 3\ell \cdot n$ and $\alpha(n) = 1/\text{poly}(n)$, we get $\beta(O(n)) = 1 - (1 - 0.5 \cdot \alpha(n))^{3n}$ and $T'(O(n)) = \text{poly}(\varepsilon(n)/n) \cdot T(n)$. In particular, for $\alpha(n) = o(1/n)$ we have $\beta(O(n)) \approx 1.5n \cdot \alpha(n)$, for $\alpha(n) \leq 1/2n$ we have $\beta(O(n)) > 1.02n \cdot \alpha(n)$, and for constant α we have $\beta(O(n)) > 1 - 2^{-\Omega(n)}$.

Proof of Theorem 2.6.2: Theorem 2.6.2 follows by applying Proposition 2.6.2 $\delta + 1$ times, where δ is the degree of the polynomial $p(\cdot)$ (specified in the hypothesis that f is $\frac{1}{p(\cdot)}$-one-way). In all applications of the proposition, we use $k(n) \stackrel{\text{def}}{=} 3\ell n$. In the first δ applications we use $\varepsilon(n) = 0.01$. For $i \leq \delta$, the function resulting from the ith application of the proposition is $\frac{1}{2n^{\delta-i}}$-one-way. In particular, after δ applications, the resulting function is $\frac{1}{2}$-one-way. (It seems that the notion of $\frac{1}{2}$-one-wayness is worthy of special attention and deserves a name such as *mostly one-way*.) In the last (i.e., $\delta + 1$) application we use $\varepsilon(n) = \epsilon(n)$. The function resulting from the last (i.e., $\delta + 1$) application of the proposition satisfies the statement of Theorem 2.6.2. ∎

Overview of the Proof of Proposition 2.6.4. The proposition itself is proved by combining two different types of arguments, the main parts of which are stated in Lemmata 2.6.5 and 2.6.6, below. Lemma 2.6.5 is a purely combinatorial lemma regarding the behavior of random walks on expander graphs. Lemma 2.6.6 presupposes such behavior (of random walks on the graphs $\{G_{f,n}\}$, defined below) and uses it in order to establish Proposition 2.6.4. The proof of Lemma 2.6.6 is by a reducibility argument, which generalizes the proof of Theorem 2.3.2. We start with the combinatorics.

The Combinatorics. First note that we are not interested in random walks on G_n, but rather in random walks on the graph $G_{f,n} \stackrel{\text{def}}{=} (\{0, 1\}^n, E_{f,n})$ obtained from $G_n = (\{0, 1\}^n, E_n)$ by letting $E_{f,n} \stackrel{\text{def}}{=} \{(u, v) : (f(u), v) \in E_n\}$. The first observation is that $G_{f,n}$ preserves the expansion property of G_n, since f is a permutation over $\{0, 1\}^n$.

(In general, for any graph $G = (V, E)$, if $f : V \to V$ is 1-1, then $G_f = (V, E_f)$, defined analogously, preserves the expansion property of G.[17]) The next combinatorial step consists of showing that, for c and d as in the proposition, the ratio of the two largest eigenvalues (in absolute value) of the adjacency matrix of each G_n is bounded away from 1. That is, for some $\rho < 1$ and all n, this eigenvalue ratio for G_n is at most ρ. (This is shown using the known relation between the expansion constant of a regular graph and the eigenvalue ratio of its adjacency matrix; specifically, $\rho \le 1 - \frac{c^2}{(4+c^2) \cdot d}$.) The next observation is that in the graph $G^\ell_{f,n} = (\{0, 1\}^n, P_\ell)$ obtained from $G_{f,n}$ by letting P_ℓ equal the set of ℓ-edge-long paths in $G_{f,n}$, the eigenvalue ratio is at most ρ^ℓ. By the hypothesis regarding ℓ and the bound on ρ, it follows that $\rho^\ell < \frac{1}{2}$. The main combinatorial step is captured by the following lemma.[18]

Lemma 2.6.5 (Random Walk Lemma): *Let G be a regular graph having an adjacency matrix for which the ratio of the absolute values of the first and second eigenvalues is smaller than $\frac{1}{2}$. Let S be a subset of measure μ of the graph's vertices. Then a random walk of length t on G will hit S with probability at least $1 - (1 - 0.5 \cdot \mu)^t$.*

Proof Idea: Because it is of little relevance to the topic of this book, we provide only a rough idea of what is involved in this proof. The proof refers to the stochastic matrix obtained from the adjacency matrix of G by division with G's degree, and it views probability distributions over the graph's vertex set as linear combinations of the (orthogonal) eigenvectors of this matrix. The ratio of eigenvalues in the new matrix is as in the adjacency matrix of G. Furthermore, the largest eigenvalue is 1, and the eigenvector associated with it is the uniform distribution.

Going step-by-step along the random walk, we bound from above the probability mass assigned to random walks that do not pass through the set S. At each step, the component of the current distribution that is in the direction of the first eigenvector loses a factor μ of its weight (where this loss is due to the fraction of the paths that enter S in the current step). Using the bound on the second eigenvalue, it can be shown that in each step the L_2-norm of the other components is decreased by a factor of 2 (so that the residual distribution is "pushed" toward the direction of the first eigenvector). Intuitively, the event *passing through the set S* acts as a sieve on the residual distribution, but this sieve is effective only when the residual distribution is close to uniform, which is being preserved by the next random step on the expander.

[17]That is, we let $E_f \overset{\text{def}}{=} \{(u, v) : (f(u), v) \in E\}$ and denote $N(S) \overset{\text{def}}{=} \{v \in V : \exists u \in S \text{ s.t. } (u, v) \in E\}$ and $N_f(S) \overset{\text{def}}{=} \{v \in V : \exists u \in S \text{ s.t. } (u, v) \in E_f\}$. Then $N_f(S) = \{v \in V : \exists f(u) \in f(S) \text{ s.t. } (f(u), v) \in E\} = N(f(S))$, where $f(S) \overset{\text{def}}{=} \{f(u) : u \in S\}$. Using the 1-1 property of f, we have $|f(S)| = |S|$, and the claim follows (i.e., if G has expansion factor c, then so does G_f).

[18]Below, a random walk of length t means a sequence of t vertices generated as follows. First, a start vertex is selected uniformly in the vertex set. For $i = 2, \dots, t$, the ith vertex is selected uniformly among the neighbors of the $i - 1$ vertex. We stress that if a vertex has a self-loop, then it is considered a neighbor of itself.

Next we provide a (sketch of a) formal analysis that closely follows the foregoing intuition. Unfortunately, this simple analysis only establishes a weaker bound than the one claimed. This weaker bound does not suffice for our purposes, since it is meaningful only for $\mu \geq \frac{1}{4}$ (whereas we also need to relate to much smaller values of μ, specifically, $1/\mu$, being poly-logarithmic in the size of the graph).

Proof sketch for a weaker bound: Let us denote by M the stochastic matrix representing a random step on the graph $G = (V, E)$, and let ρ denote a bound on the absolute value of the second largest eigenvalue of M (where the largest eigenvalue is 1). Let P be a 0-1 "sieving matrix" that has 1-entries only on its diagonal and furthermore only in entries (i, i) that correspond to $i \notin S$. We represent (residual) probability distributions, over V, by vectors. For such a vector $\vec{v}$, the vector $M\vec{v}$ represents the distribution obtained from the distribution $\vec{v}$ by taking one random step on the graph G, and $P\vec{v}$ is the (residual) distribution obtained from $\vec{v}$ by setting to zero all entries that correspond to vertices in S. We represent the uniform distribution over V by the vector $\vec{\pi}$ (in which each entry equals $1/|V|$) and observe that $M\vec{\pi} = \vec{\pi}$ (since the uniform distribution is the eigenvector associated with the eigenvalue 1).

One key observation is that the probability that a random t-step walk does not pass through S equals the sum of the elements of the (non-negative) vector $(PM)^{t-1}P\vec{\pi} = (PM)^t\vec{\pi}$. Since the vector $(PM)^t\vec{\pi}$ is non-negative, we can evaluate its L_1-norm instead, which in turn is bounded from above by $\sqrt{|V|} \cdot \|(PM)^t\vec{\pi}\|$, where $\|\cdot\|$ denotes the Euclidean norm (i.e., L_2-norm). Later, we shall prove that for every vector $\vec{z}$ it holds that $\|PM\vec{z}\| \leq ((1 - \mu) + \rho^2)^{1/2} \cdot \|\vec{z}\|$, and we obtain

$$\|(PM)^t\vec{\pi}\| \leq ((1 - \mu) + \rho^2)^{t/2} \cdot \|\vec{\pi}\| = ((1 - \mu) + \rho^2)^{t/2} \cdot \sqrt{|V| \cdot \frac{1}{|V|^2}}$$

It follows that the probability that a random t-step walk does not pass through S is at most $((1 - \mu) + \rho^2)^{t/2}$, which for $\mu \geq 2\rho^2$ (e.g., $\mu \geq 1/2$ and $\rho \leq 1/2$) yields an upper bound of $(1 - 0.5 \cdot \mu)^{t/2}$.

In order to prove that $\|PM\vec{z}\| \leq ((1 - \mu) + \rho^2)^{1/2} \cdot \|\vec{z}\|$, we write $\vec{z} = \vec{z}_1 + \vec{z}_2$ such that $\vec{z}_1$ is the component of $\vec{z}$ that is in the direction of the first eigenvector (i.e., $\vec{\pi}$), and $\vec{z}_2$ is the component that is orthogonal to it. Using $M\vec{\pi} = \vec{\pi}$, $\|P\vec{\pi}\| = \sqrt{1 - \mu} \cdot \|\vec{\pi}\|$, $\|M\vec{z}_2\| \leq \rho \cdot \|\vec{z}_2\|$, and $\|P\vec{v}\| \leq \|\vec{v}\|$ (for every $\vec{v}$), we have

$$\|PM(\vec{z}_1 + \vec{z}_2)\| \leq \|PM\vec{z}_1\| + \|PM\vec{z}_2\|$$
$$\leq \sqrt{1 - \mu} \cdot \|\vec{z}_1\| + \rho \cdot \|\vec{z}_2\|$$
$$\leq \sqrt{(1 - \mu) + \rho^2} \cdot \sqrt{\|\vec{z}_1\|^2 + \|\vec{z}_2\|^2}$$
$$= ((1 - \mu) + \rho^2)^{1/2} \cdot \|\vec{z}_1 + \vec{z}_2\|$$

where the last inequality uses the Cauchy-Schwarz inequality (i.e., $\sum_i a_i \cdot b_i \leq (\sum_i a_i^2)^{1/2} \cdot (\sum_i b_i^2)^{1/2}$), and the last equality uses the fact that $\vec{z}_1$ and $\vec{z}_2$ are orthogonal.

We comment that the lower bound claimed in the lemma can be generalized to $1 - (1 - \mu + \mu \cdot \rho)^t$, where ρ is an upper bound on the eigenvalue ratio. ■

The Algorithmics. The second lemma (stated next) is analogous to the essence of the proof of Theorem 2.3.2 (i.e., the simple amplification). However, there are two key differences between the two proofs:

1. In the proof of Theorem 2.3.2, we used a trivial combinatorial statement regarding the number of k-sequences over $\{0, 1\}^n$ that each has an element in some set S (i.e., the probability that such a uniformly chosen k-sequence has no element in the set S is $(1 - 2^{-n} \cdot |S|)^k$). Here we use a generic hypothesis regarding the relationship between the density of S and the fraction of k-sequences of a certain type that pass through it. That is, here we consider only k-sequences that result from a k-step walk on a fixed regular graph.

2. More importantly, the proof of Theorem 2.3.2 refers to inverting the original function f on a sequence of (independently distributed) instances, whereas here we refer to inverting successive applications of f (interleaved with g_σ-moves) on a single instance (and the sequence in question is the one of intermediate results).

Thus the proof that follows is more complex than the proof of Theorem 2.3.2. The following lemma will be used, with $\beta(n + k(n) \log_2 d) = 1 - (1 - 0.5 \cdot \alpha(n))^{k(n)/\ell}$, as provided by the earlier combinatorial argument.

Lemma 2.6.6 (Reducibility Lemma): *Let d, $\{G_n = (\{0, 1\}^n, E_n)\}$, $f : \{0, 1\}^*$ $\to \{0, 1\}^*$, $k : \mathbb{N} \to \mathbb{N}$, and F_k be as in Construction 2.6.3.*

- *Let $G_{f,n} \stackrel{\text{def}}{=} (\{0, 1\}^n, E_{f,n})$, where $E_{f,n} \stackrel{\text{def}}{=} \{(u, v) : (f(u), v) \in E_n\}$.*
- *Let $\alpha, \alpha', \beta : \mathbb{N} \to [0, 1]$, and $k : \mathbb{N} \to \mathbb{N}$ be such that $\beta(n + k(n) \log_2 d) > \alpha(n)$ and $\alpha'(n) \geq \alpha(n) + 2^{-n}$.*

Suppose that $G_{f,n}$ satisfies the following random-path property:

- *For every measure-$\alpha(n)$ subset S of $G_{f,n}$'s nodes, at least a fraction $\beta(n + k(n) \cdot \log_2 d)$ of the paths of length $k(n)$ will pass through a node in S.*

Suppose that f is $\alpha'(\cdot)$-one-way with respect to time $T(\cdot)$. Then for every polynomial-time-computable $\varepsilon : \mathbb{N} \to \mathbb{R}$, the function F_k is $(1 - \varepsilon(\cdot))\beta(\cdot)$-one-way with respect to time $T' : \mathbb{N} \to \mathbb{N}$, where $T'(n + k(n) \log_2 d) \stackrel{\text{def}}{=} \frac{\varepsilon(n)^2 \alpha(n)^2}{O(n+k(n))^3} \cdot T(n)$.

Note that the lemma is of no interest in case $\beta(n + k(n) \log_2 d) \leq \alpha(n)$.

Proof Sketch: The proof, as suggested by the name of the lemma, is by a reducibility argument. This argument is similar in flavor to the one used in the proof of Theorem 2.3.2. Assume, to the contradiction, that for $m \stackrel{\text{def}}{=} n + k(n) \log_2 d$, the permutation F_k can be inverted on $F_k(U_m)$ in time $T'(\cdot)$ with success probability at least

$$1 - (1 - \varepsilon(m)) \cdot \beta(m) = 1 - \beta(m) + \varepsilon(m)\beta(m)$$

Modify the inverting algorithm so that it inverts F_k with overwhelming proba-
bility on a $1 - \beta(m) + \varepsilon'(m)$ fraction of the inputs of length m, where $\varepsilon'(m) =$
$\varepsilon(m)\beta(m)/2$. (This can be done by first observing that the inverting algorithm must
invert at least a $1 - \beta(m) + \varepsilon'(m)$ fraction of the inputs with probability at least
$\varepsilon'(m)$ and then increasing its success on such inputs by $m/\varepsilon'(m)$ independent tries.)
Denote the resulting algorithm, which has running time $(2m \cdot T'(m))/(\varepsilon(m)\beta(m))$,
by A. Note that inputs to A correspond to $k(n)$-long paths on the graph G_n.
Consider the set, denoted I_n, of paths (x, p) such that A inverts $F_k(x, p)$ with
overwhelming probability (e.g., probability at least $1 - 2^{-n}$).

In the sequel, we use the shorthand $k \stackrel{\text{def}}{=} k(n)$, $m \stackrel{\text{def}}{=} n + k \log_2 d$, $\varepsilon \stackrel{\text{def}}{=} \varepsilon(m)$,
$\varepsilon' \stackrel{\text{def}}{=} \varepsilon'(m)$, $\beta \stackrel{\text{def}}{=} \beta(m)$, $\alpha \stackrel{\text{def}}{=} \alpha(n)$, and $I \stackrel{\text{def}}{=} I_n$. Recall that $|I| \geq (1 - \beta + \varepsilon') \cdot 2^m$.
Let P_v be the set of all k-long paths that pass through v, and let I_v be the subset
of I containing paths that pass through v (i.e., $I_v = I \cap P_v$). Define v as *good*
if $|I_v|/|P_v| \geq \varepsilon'/k$ (and *bad* otherwise). Intuitively, a vertex v is called good
if at least a ε'/k fraction of the paths going through it can be inverted by A.
Let $I' = I \setminus \cup_{v \text{ bad}} I_v$; namely, I' contains all "invertible" paths that pass solely
through good nodes. Clearly, we have the following:

Claim 2.6.6.1: The density of I' in the set of all paths is greater than $1 - \beta$.

Proof: Denote by $\mu(S) = |S|/|P|$ the density of the set S in the set of all paths.
Then

$$\mu(I') = \mu(I) - \mu(\cup_{v \text{ bad}} I_v)$$
$$\geq (1 - \beta + \varepsilon') - \sum_{v \text{ bad}} \mu(I_v)$$
$$> 1 - \beta + \varepsilon' - \sum_v \frac{\varepsilon'}{k} \cdot \mu(P_v)$$
$$\geq 1 - \beta$$

where the last inequality is due to the fact that each path in P contributes to at
most k of the P_v's. $\square$

Using the random-path property, we have the following:

Claim 2.6.6.2: The density of good nodes is greater than $1 - \alpha$.

Proof: Otherwise, let S be the set of bad nodes, and suppose that $|S| \geq \alpha \cdot 2^n$.
By the random-path property, since S has measure (at least) α, the fraction of
paths that pass through vertices of S is at least β. That is, the fraction of paths
that pass through a bad vertex is at least β. But I' does not contain paths that pass
through bad vertices, and so I' can contain at most a $1 - \beta$ fraction of all paths,
in contradiction to Claim 2.6.6.1. $\square$

The following algorithm for inverting f is quite natural. The algorithm uses as
subroutine an algorithm, denoted A, for inverting F_k. Inverting f on y is done by
placing y on a random point along a randomly selected path $\bar{p}$, taking a walk from

y according to the suffix of $\bar{p}$, and asking A for the pre-image of the resulting pair under F_k.

Algorithm for inverting f: On input y, repeat $\frac{2nk}{\varepsilon\beta}$ times:

1. Select randomly $i \in \{1, 2, \ldots, k\}$ and $\sigma_1, \sigma_2, \ldots, \sigma_k \in \{1, 2, \ldots, d\}$.
2. Compute $y' = F(g_{\sigma_i}(y), \sigma_{i+1} \ldots \sigma_k)$.
3. Invoke A to obtain $x' \leftarrow A(\sigma_1\sigma_2, \ldots, \sigma_k, y')$.
4. Compute $x = F(x', \sigma_1 \ldots \sigma_{i-1})$.
5. If $f(x) = y$, then halt and output x.

Analysis of the inverting algorithm (for a good x): Since x is good, a random path going through it (selected as before) corresponds to an "invertible path" with probability at least $\varepsilon'/k = \varepsilon\beta/2k$. If such a good path is selected, then we obtain the inverse of $f(x)$ with overwhelming probability. The algorithm for inverting f repeats the process sufficiently many times to guarantee overwhelming probability of selecting an "invertible path."

By Claim 2.6.6.2, the good x's constitute at least a $1 - \alpha$ fraction of all n-bit strings. Thus, the success probability of our inverting algorithm on input $f(U_n)$ is at least

$$(1 - \alpha(n)) \cdot (1 - 2^{-n}) > 1 - \alpha(n) - 2^{-n} \geq 1 - \alpha'(n)$$

The running time of our inverting algorithm is

$$\frac{2nk(n)}{\varepsilon(m)\beta(m)} \cdot \frac{2m \cdot T'(m)}{\varepsilon(m)\beta(m)} = \frac{4nmk(n)}{\varepsilon(m)^2\beta(m)^2} \cdot T'(m) \leq T(n)$$

where the last inequality uses $\beta(m) \geq \alpha(n)$. Hence, the existence of an algorithm inverting F_k in time $T'(\cdot)$ with probability at least $1 - (1 - \varepsilon(\cdot))\beta(\cdot)$ implies the existence of an algorithm inverting f in time $T(\cdot)$ with probability at least $1 - \alpha'(\cdot)$. The latter constitutes a contradiction to the hypothesis of the lemma, and hence the lemma follows. ∎

Finishing the Proof of Proposition 2.6.4. When Lemma 2.6.5 is applied to the graph $G_{f,n}^\ell$, it follows that, for every set $S \subseteq V$ of measure $\alpha(n)$, a random walk of length t on $G_{f,n}^\ell$ hits S with probability at least $1 - (1 - 0.5 \cdot \alpha(n))^t$. Recall that edges in $G_{f,n}^\ell$ represent ℓ-edge paths in $G_{f,n}$, and so the vertices visited in a k-step walk on $G_{f,n}$ are a subset of those visited in a corresponding (k/ℓ)-step walk on $G_{f,n}^\ell$. It follows that a random walk of length $k(n)$ on $G_{f,n}$ hits S with probability at least $1 - (1 - 0.5 \cdot \alpha(n))^{k(n)/\ell}$. Applying Lemma 2.6.6, with $\alpha'(n) = \alpha(n) + 2^{-n}$ and $\beta(n + k(n) \cdot \log_2 d) = 1 - (1 - 0.5 \cdot \alpha(n))^{k(n)/\ell}$, we conclude that if f is $\alpha'(n)$-one-way with respect to time $T(\cdot)$, then F_k is $((1 - \varepsilon(\cdot))\beta(\cdot))$-one-way with respect to time $T'(\cdot)$, where β and T' are as in Proposition 2.6.4. This completes the proof.

An Alternative Analysis. Our analysis of Construction 2.6.3 is conducted using the eigenvalue ratio of expander graphs, rather than their natural combinatorial definition (in terms of expansion properties). Because the transformation between the two formulation is not tight, we lose by stating our results in terms of expansion properties. Hence, for a tighter analysis, we replace Condition 1 of Proposition 2.6.4 by the requirement that *for some $\rho < 1$, each graph in the explicitly constructible family $\{G_n\}$ has an eigenvalue ratio of at most ρ*, and we replace Condition 4 by $\ell \geq \max(1, \lceil \log_\rho(1/2) \rceil)$. The modified proposition is proved as the original one, except that here we observe that the eigenvalue ratio of $\{G_{f,n}\}$ is smaller than or equal to the eigenvalue ratio of $\{G_n\}$.[19] The modified proposition allows to use an explicitly constructible family $\{G_n\}$ having degree 18 and eigenvalue ratio below $\frac{1}{2}$, which in turn allows us to set $\ell = 1$. Thus, for $k(n) = 3n$ and every polynomial-time-computable $\varepsilon : \mathbb{N} \to \mathbb{R}$, the permutation F_k is $((1 - \varepsilon(\cdot))\beta(\cdot))$-one-way with respect to time $T' : \mathbb{N} \to \mathbb{N}$, where

$$\beta(15n) \approx 1 - \left(1 - \frac{\alpha(n)}{2}\right)^{3n}$$

$$T'(15n) \approx \frac{(\varepsilon(n) \cdot \alpha(n))^2}{O(n)^3} \cdot T(n).$$

In particular, for $\alpha(n) \leq 1/2n$ we have $\beta(15n) > 1.02n \cdot \alpha(n)$, whereas for constant α we have $\beta(15n) > 1 - 2^{-\Omega(n)}$. Regarding the example mentioned at the beginning of this section, using $n = 1000$ and $k \approx 960$ it follows that *if f is hard to invert in practice on 1% of the strings of length 1000, then F_k is hard to invert in practice on 99% of the strings of length 5000*.

2.7. Miscellaneous

We stress that the aforementioned relationships among the various forms of one-way functions are the only ones that are known to hold. Specifically:

- Weak one-way functions (resp., permutations (resp., with trapdoor)) can be transformed into strong one-way functions (resp., permutations (resp., with trapdoor)). The other direction is trivial.

- Non-uniform hardness implies uniform hardness, but not the other way around.

- Trapdoor permutations are special cases of one-way permutations, which in turn are special cases of one-way functions. We do not know if it is possible to transform arbitrary one-way functions into one-way permutations or the latter into trapdoor permutations.[20]

[19] Letting M be as in the proof of Lemma 2.6.5, and letting R be a matrix representing the mapping $v \mapsto f(v)$, observe that the first eigenvalue and eigenvector of MR are exactly as those of M (i.e., 1 and a uniform vector, respectively). Furthermore, the subspace orthogonal to the uniform vector is preserved by R, and so this subspace must contain all the other eigenvectors of MR (whereas each vector in this subspace is a linear combination of the other eigenvectors of M). Let $\vec{e}$ be some orthogonal-to-uniform eigenvector of MR, and let ρ' be the eigenvalue corresponding to it. Then $\rho' \cdot \|\vec{e}\| = \|MR\vec{e}\| \leq \rho \cdot \|R\vec{e}\| \leq \rho \cdot \|\vec{e}\|$, where $\|S\vec{v}\| \leq \|\vec{v}\|$ holds for every stochastic matrix S (and in particular for the matrix R).

[20] We mention that trapdoor functions (in which given the trapdoor, one can retrieve some pre-image) can be constructed from arbitrary one-way functions (cf. [18]), but the number of pre-images of each image of the constructed function is exponential.

Evidence to the contrary has been presented ([140] and [133], respectively, where it is shown that "black-box" reductions are unlikely to provide such transformations).

- Collections of claw-free function (resp., permutation) pairs yield collections of one-way functions (resp., permutations), but the other direction is not known.

2.7.1. Historical Notes

The notions of a one-way function and a trapdoor permutation originate from the seminal paper of Diffie and Hellman [63]. Weak one-way functions were introduced by Yao [210]. The RSA function was introduced by Rivest, Shamir, and Adleman [191], whereas squaring modulo a composite was suggested and studied by Rabin [187]. Other authors have suggested basing one-way functions on the believed intractability of decoding random linear codes [29, 108] and on the subset-sum problem [132].

The equivalence of the existence of weak and strong one-way functions (i.e., Theorem 2.3.2) is implicit in Yao's work [210], with the first proof appearing in [91]. The efficient amplification of one-way functions presented in Section 2.6 is taken from Goldreich et al. [104], which in turn uses a technical tool originating in [4] (see also [55, 135]). The existence of universal one-way functions is stated in Levin's work [150].

The concept of hard-core predicates originates from the work of Blum and Micali [36]. They also proved that a particular predicate constitutes a hard-core for the "DLP function" (i.e., exponentiation in a finite field), provided that the latter function is one-way. Consequently, Yao showed how to transform any one-way function into a hard-core predicate (i.e., the result is not stated in [210], but is rather due to oral presentations of that work). A proof first appeared in Levin's work [150] (see details in [114]). However, Yao's construction, which is analogous to the construction used in the proof of Theorem 2.3.2, is of little practical value.

The fact that the inner product mod 2 is a hard-core for any one-way function (of the form $g(x, r) = (f(x), r)$) was proved by Goldreich and Levin [110]. The proof presented in this book, which follows ideas originating in [5], was discovered independently by Leonid Levin and Charles Rackoff. The improvement captured by Proposition 2.5.4 is due to Levin [151].

Theorem 2.5.6 (hard-core functions of logarithmically many bits based on any one-way function) is also due to [110]. The Computational XOR Lemma (Lemma 2.5.8) is due to [208], but the proof presented here is due to Leonid Levin. (An alternative construction of hard-core functions is presented in [117].)

Hard-core predicates (and functions) for specific collections of permutations have been suggested [36, 141, 5, 208]. Specifically, Alexi et al. [5] proved that the intractability of factoring yields hard-core predicates for permutations induced by squaring modulo a composite number. A simpler and tighter proof has subsequently been found [82].

2.7.2. Suggestions for Further Reading

Our exposition of the RSA and Rabin functions is quite sparse in details. In particular, the computational problems of generating uniformly distributed "certified primes" and of "primality checking" deserve much more attention. A probabilistic polynomial-time algorithm for generating uniformly distributed primes together with corresponding certificates of primality has been presented by Bach [9]. The certificate produced by this algorithm for a prime P consists of the prime factorization of $P - 1$, together with certificates for primality of these factors. This recursive form of certificates for primality originates in Pratt's proof [184] that the set of primes is in $\mathcal{NP}$. However, the foregoing procedure is not very practical. Instead, when using the RSA (or Rabin) function in practice, one is likely to prefer an algorithm that generates integers at random and checks them for primality using fast primality checkers, such as the algorithms presented in [203, 185]. One should note, however, that these algorithms do not produce certificates for primality and that with some (small) parameterized probability they may assert that a composite number is a prime. Probabilistic polynomial-time algorithms (yet not practical ones) that, given a prime, produce a certificate for primality have been presented [121, 1].

The common belief that the RSA, Rabin, and DLP functions are one-way is based on the failure of researchers to come up with probabilistic polynomial-time algorithms for factoring and discrete logarithms. (It is debatable whether this record of failure should be traced back a couple of centuries or "only" a few decades.) For a survey of the best algorithms known for the factoring and discrete-logarithm problems, the reader is directed to Odlyzko's surveys ([178] and [179], respectively).

The subset-sum problem is known to be easy in two special cases. One case is that in which the input sequence is constructed based on a simple "hidden sequence." For example, Merkle and Hellman [163] suggested the construction of an instance of the subset-sum problem based on a "hidden super-increasing sequence" as follows. Let $s_1, \ldots, s_n, s_{n+1} \overset{\text{def}}{=} M$ be a sequence satisfying $s_i > \sum_{j=1}^{i-1} s_j$, for $i = 2, \ldots, n+1$. Such a sequence is called *super-increasing*. For w relatively prime to M, consider the instance of the subset-sum problem consisting of $(x_1, \ldots, x_n)$ and $\sum_{i \in I} x_i$, where $x_i \overset{\text{def}}{=} w \cdot s_i \bmod M$ and $I \subseteq \{1, \ldots, n\}$. Clearly, knowledge of both w and M allows one to easily solve the subset-sum problem for the foregoing instance (e.g., simply retrieve the super-increasing sequence and iteratively determine if $i \in I$ for $i = n, n-1, \ldots, 1$). The hope was that when w and M were not given, solving the subset-sum problem would be hard (even for instances generated based on a super-increasing sequence). (That would have led to a trapdoor one-way function.) Unfortunately, that hope was not realized. Shamir presented an efficient algorithm for solving the subset-sum problem for instances with a hidden super-increasing sequence [197]. Another case for which the subset-sum problem is known to be easy is the case of *low-density* instances. In these instances, the lengths of the elements in binary representations are considerably larger than the numbers of elements (i.e., $|x_1| = \cdots = |x_n| = (1 + \varepsilon)n$ for some constant $\varepsilon > 0$). For further details, consult the work of Lagarias and Odlyzko [145] and the later survey of Brickell and Odlyzko [43].

Two computational problems that are seemingly related to the subset-sum problem are the decoding of random linear codes and the finding of closest vectors in integer lattices. In all three cases the problem is to find a linear combination of given elements such that the sum equals or is close to a target value. However, the similarity is superficial, because the arithmetic is different in the three cases. In the case of the subset sum, we refer to *addition over integers*; in the case of linear codes, we have *addition in vector spaces over a finite field* (typically of two elements); and in the case of integer lattices, *the addition is of real vectors* (or of rational or integer vectors). We mention that the decoding of random linear codes is a long-standing open problem in coding theory [207]. Regarding the complexity of lattice problems, there seems to be a huge gap between the theoretical upper bounds [148] and the performance in practice [195].

We refer the reader to a fascinating result by Ajtai [3] (cf. [101]): If certain computational problems regarding integer lattices are hard *in the worst case*, then one-way functions exist. This result is unique in translating possible worst-case hardness into average-case hardness.

In view of the general efficient transformation of one-way functions to hard-core predicates presented in Section 2.5, we did not present proofs that certain natural predicates are hard-cores for specific popular candidates for one-way functions. Details on hard-core predicates for the RSA and Rabin functions are available [82; cf. 5], as are details on hard-core predicates for various "DLP functions" [141; cf. 36].

Tradition attributes to Yao a proof of the existence of hard-core predicates based on any one-way function. The alleged proof proceeds in two steps. First, one proves the existence of a mild form of a hard-core predicate; specifically, given a one-way function f, one construct a one-way function f' and a polynomial-time-computable predicate b' such that any probabilistic polynomial-time predictor given $f'(U_n)$ *fails* to guess $b'(U_n)$ with probability *at least* $1/2n$ (e.g., let $f'(x, i) = (f(x), i)$ and $b'(x, i)$ be the ith bit of x). The second step, which is the main one and is called *Yao's XOR Lemma*, is to prove that taking many independent copies of such a "mild hard-core predicate" and XORing them together will yield a hard-core predicate. That is, for $t = |w_1|^2 = \cdots = |w_t|^2$, we let $b''(w_1, \ldots, w_t) = \oplus_{i=1}^{t} b'(w_i)$ and $f''(w_1, \ldots, w_t) = (f'(w_1), \ldots, f'(w_t))$ and prove that b'' is a hard-core of f''. Yao's XOR Lemma has found other applications in complexity theory [114, 134].

The theory of average-case complexity, initiated by Levin [149], is somewhat related to the notion of one-way functions. Surveys of this theory are available [24, 96]. Loosely speaking, the difference is that in our context hard (on the average) instances can easily be solved by the (efficient) "generator" of those instances, whereas in Levin's work the instances are hard (on the average) to solve even for the "generator." However, the notion of average-case reducibility introduced by Levin is also relevant in our context.

Further details about expander graphs and random walks on them are available from [6, 167]. In particular, Lemma 2.6.5 is a special case of Kahale's Corollary 6.1 [139]. Explicit constructions of expander graphs have been published [85, 154], as has the specific construction mentioned at the end of Section 2.6 [154].

2.7.3. Open Problems

As discussed in Section 2.1, $\mathcal{NP} \setminus \mathcal{BPP} \neq \emptyset$ is a necessary condition for the existence of one-way functions. However, $\mathcal{NP} \setminus \mathcal{BPP} \neq \emptyset$ is not known to imply any practical consequences (i.e., it may be that hard instances exist but occur very rarely with respect to any simple distribution). Any progress in showing that $\mathcal{NP} \setminus \mathcal{BPP} \neq \emptyset$ implies some form of average-case hardness, and that the latter implies the existence of one-way functions would be of great interest.

Turning to relatively less ambitious goals, we mention two open problems that pertain to extending the results of the type presented in this chapter. We believe that a resolution for either of these problems will require the discovery of new important paradigms. Firstly, in a continuation of the efficient amplification of one-way permutations (presented in Section 2.6), we seek an analogous transformation that can be applied to *arbitrary* (weak) one-way functions. Currently, we know of such transformations only for special types of functions (e.g., regular ones [104]). We believe that providing an efficient amplification of arbitrary one-way functions is a very important open problem. It may also be instrumental for more efficient constructions of pseudorandom generators based on arbitrary one-way functions (see Section 3.5).

An open problem of more acute practical importance is to try to present hard-core *functions* of larger range for the RSA and Rabin functions. Specifically, assuming that squaring mod N is one-way, is the function that returns the first half of x a hard-core of squaring mod N? Some support for an affirmative answer has been provided [130]. An affirmative answer would allow us to construct extremely efficient pseudorandom generators and public-key encryption schemes based on the conjectured intractability of the factoring problem.

2.7.4. Exercises

Exercise 1: *Closing the gap between the motivating discussion and the definition of one-way functions:* We say that a function $h : \{0, 1\}^* \rightarrow \{0, 1\}^*$ is *hard on the average but easy with auxiliary input* if there exists a probabilistic polynomial-time algorithm G such that

1. there exists a polynomial-time algorithm A such that $A(x, y) = h(x)$ for every (x, y) in the range of G (i.e., for every (x, y) such that (x, y) is a possible output of $G(1^n)$ for some input 1^n), and
2. for every probabilistic polynomial-time algorithm A' every positive polynomial $p(\cdot)$, and all sufficiently large n's,

$$\Pr[A'(X_n) = h(X_n)] < \frac{1}{p(n)}$$

where $(X_n, Y_n) \stackrel{\text{def}}{=} G(1^n)$ is a random variable assigned the output of G.
Prove that if there exist functions that are "hard on the average but easy with auxiliary input," then one-way functions exist.

Guideline: Define a function mapping the coins used by G to its first output.

Exercise 2: *One-way functions and the $\mathcal{P}$-versus-$\mathcal{NP}$ question (Part 1):* Prove that the existence of one-way functions implies $\mathcal{P} \neq \mathcal{NP}$.

Guideline: For any polynomial-time-computable function f, define a set $L_f \in \mathcal{NP}$ such that if $L_f \in \mathcal{P}$, then there exists a polynomial-time algorithm for inverting f.

Exercise 3: *One-way functions and the $\mathcal{P}$-versus-$\mathcal{NP}$ question (Part 2):* Assuming that $\mathcal{P} \neq \mathcal{NP}$, construct a function f such that the following three claims hold:
1. Function f is polynomial-time-computable.
2. There is no polynomial-time algorithm that always inverts f (i.e., successfully inverts f on every y in the range of f).
3. Function f is not one-way. Furthermore, there exists a polynomial-time algorithm that inverts f with exponentially small failure probability, where the probability space is (as usual) uniform over all possible choices of input (i.e., $f(x)$) and the internal coin tosses for the algorithm.
Guideline: Consider the function f_{sat} defined so that $f_{sat}(\phi, \tau) = (\phi, 1)$ if τ is a satisfying assignment to propositional formulae ϕ, and $f_{sat}(\phi, \tau) = (\phi, 0)$ otherwise. Modify this function so that it is easy to invert in most instances, yet inverting f_{sat} is reducible to inverting its modification. (Hint: The modified function f' coincides with f_{sat} on a negligible fraction of the domain of f' and is easy to invert on the rest of the domain.)

Exercise 4: Suppose that f is a one-way function and that for some function $\ell : \mathbb{N} \rightarrow \mathbb{N}$ the following conditions hold:
1. $|f(x)| = \ell(|x|)$ for all x's;
2. $\ell(n) = \ell(m)$ only if $n = m$ (i.e., ℓ is 1-1);
3. $\ell(n) \geq n$ for all n's.
Show that given $f(x)$, one can generate $1^{|x|}$, in time polynomial in $|x|$.
Guideline: The foregoing conditions guarantee that $|x| \leq |f(x)|$ and that $|x|$ is uniquely determined by $|f(x)| = |f(1^{|x|})|$.

Exercise 5: Let f be a strongly one-way function. Prove that for every probabilistic polynomial-time algorithm A and for every positive polynomial $p(\cdot)$, the set

$$B_{A, p} \stackrel{\text{def}}{=} \left\{ x : \Pr\left[A(f(x)) \in f^{-1}(f(x)) \right] \geq \frac{1}{p(|x|)} \right\}$$

has negligible density in the set of all strings (i.e., for every polynomial $q(\cdot)$ and all sufficiently large n, it holds that $\frac{|B_{A, p} \cap \{0,1\}^n|}{2^n} < \frac{1}{q(n)}$.

Exercise 6: *Another definition of non-uniformly one-way functions:* Consider the definition resulting from Definition 2.2.6 by allowing the circuits to be probabilistic (i.e., have an auxiliary input that is uniformly selected). Prove that the resulting new definition is equivalent to the original one.

Exercise 7: *Addition is easily reversible:* We associate bit strings with positive integers in some natural manner (e.g., the n-bit-long string $\sigma_{n-1} \cdots \sigma_0$ is associated with the integer $2^n + \sum_{i=0}^{n-1} \sigma_i \cdot 2^i$):
1. Define $f_{add} : \{0, 1\}^* \rightarrow \{0, 1\}^*$ such that $f_{add}(xy) = x + y$, where $|x| = |y|$. Prove that f_{add} is not a one-way function (not even in the weak sense).
2. Redefine $f_{add} : \{0, 1\}^* \rightarrow \{0, 1\}^*$ such that $f_{add}(xy) = \text{prime}(x) + \text{prime}(y)$, where $|x| = |y|$ and $\text{prime}(z)$ is the smallest prime that is larger than z. Prove that f_{add} is not a one-way function.

As a warm-up, prove that $f_{XOR}(xy) = x \oplus y$, where $|x| = |y|$, is not one-way.

Guideline (Part 2): Do not try to capitalize on the possibility that prime(N) is too large (e.g., larger than $N + \text{poly}(\log N)$). It is unlikely that such a (number-theoretic) result can be proved. Furthermore, it is generally believed that there exists a constant c such that for all integer $N \geq 2$, it holds that prime(N) $< N + (\log_2 N)^c$. Hence, it is likely that f_{add} is polynomial-time-computable. The point is that it can be shown to be easily invertible.

Exercise 8: *One-way functions based on hardness of factoring:* Throughout this exercise, assume that it is infeasible to factor composite numbers that are the products of two primes of polynomially related lengths. That is, for every probabilistic polynomial-time algorithm A, for every positive polynomial p, for all sufficiently large n's, and for every $\sqrt{n} < m < n^2$,

$$\Pr[A(P_m \cdot Q_n) = P_m] < \frac{1}{p(n)}$$

where P_m and Q_n are uniformly and independently distributed primes of length m and n, respectively. (Recall the density-of-primes theorem, which guarantees that at least a $1/n$ fraction of the n-bit integers are primes [7].)

1. Let $f_{mult}(x, y) = x \cdot y$, where $|x| = |y|$.
   (a) (Easy) Prove that f_{mult} is weakly one-way.
   (b) (Hard) Prove that f_{mult} is strongly one-way.
      Guideline: Use the fact that, with overwhelmingly high probability, when uniformly selecting an n-bit-long integer and considering the product of all its prime factors that are smaller than $2^{\sqrt{n}}$, this product is smaller than $2^{n/3}$. Next, argue that if f_{mult} can be inverted with non-negligible probability, then with non-negligible probability this happens when each of the two parts of the pre-image has a prime factor of size at least $2^{\sqrt{n}}$. At this point, a reducibility argument can be applied. (The number-theoretic fact used earlier can be proved by relying on known results regarding the distribution of smooth numbers; see [47] for the latter.)

2. Let $f_{mmult}(x_1, \ldots, x_{n^2}) = \prod_{i=1}^{n^2}$, where $|x_i| = n$ for all i's. Prove that f_{mmult} is strongly one-way.
   Guideline: Show how to use an algorithm that inverts f_{mmult} with non-negligible probability in order to factor the products of two n-bit primes. Remember the need to feed the former algorithm with a distribution as in the hypothesis (or sufficiently close to it).

Exercise 9 (suggested by Bao Feng): Refute the following conjecture:

For every (length-preserving) one-way function f, the function $f'(x) \stackrel{\text{def}}{=} f(x) \oplus x$ is also one-way.

Guideline: Let g be a (length-preserving) one-way function, and consider f defined on pairs of strings of the same length, so that $f(y, z) \stackrel{\text{def}}{=} (g(y) \oplus z, z)$.

Exercise 10: Prove that *one-way functions cannot have polynomial-size ranges.* Namely, prove that if f is (even weakly) one-way, then for every polynomial $p(\cdot)$ and all sufficiently large n's, it holds that $|\{f(x) : x \in \{0, 1\}^n\}| > p(n)$.

Guideline: Suppose that $|\{f(x) : x \in \{0, 1\}^n\}| \leq p(n)$. To invert f on $y = f(U_n)$, with success probability $1/p(n)$, it suffices to select uniformly $r \in \{0, 1\}^n$ and hope that $f(r) = y$. To invert f on $y = f(U_n)$ with success probability $1 - \varepsilon(n)$, we select uniformly many such r_i's, with the hope that y is "heavy" and that all "heavy" f-images are hit by some $f(r_i)$. (Extra hint: y' is heavy if $\Pr[f(U_n) = y'] \geq \frac{\varepsilon(n)}{2p(n)}$.)

Exercise 11: Prove that length-preserving *one-way functions cannot have polynomially bounded cycles.* Namely, for every function f, define $\mathrm{cyc}_f(x)$ to be the smallest *positive* integer i such that $f^i(x) = x$, where $f^{i+1}(x) = f(f^i(x))$ and $f^0(x) = x$. Prove that if f is (even weakly) one-way, then for every polynomial $p(\cdot)$ and all sufficiently large n's, the expected value of $\mathrm{cyc}_f(U_n)$ is greater than $p(n)$, where U_n is a random variable uniformly distributed over $\{0, 1\}^n$.

> **Guideline:** Note that if $\mathrm{E}\mathrm{cyc}_f(U_n)] > p(n)$, then for every polynomial q, it holds that $\Pr[\mathrm{cyc}_f(U_n) > q(n) \cdot p(n)] < 1/q(n)$. Why is the length-preserving condition needed?

Exercise 12: Assuming the existence of one-way functions (resp., permutations), construct one-way functions (resp., permutations) in which there are no sub-exponential cycles. That is, let $\mathrm{cyc}_f(x)$ be defined as in Exercise 11; then the constructed f should satisfy $\mathrm{cyc}_f(x) \geq 2^{|x|/2}$ for all x's.

> **Guideline:** Given a one-way function (resp., permutation) f', construct $f(x', x'') \overset{\text{def}}{=} (f'(x'), h(x''))$ for some suitable h and $|x'| = |x''|$. What is a suitable h?

Exercise 13: *One-way function with a "fixed point":* Prove that if one-way functions exist, then there exists a one-way function f such that $f(0^n) = 0^n$ for every n. Do the same for one-way permutations.

> **Guideline:** The first part is trivial. For the second part, using any one-way permutation f', let $f(x, y) = (f'(x), y)$ if $y \in \{0, 1\}^{|x|} \setminus \{0\}^{|x|}$, and $f(x, 0^{|x|}) = (x, 0^{|x|})$ otherwise.

Exercise 14: Let $\{(a_n, b_n) : n \in \mathbb{N}\}$ be recognizable in (deterministic) polynomial time, where $a_n, b_n \in \{0, 1\}^n$. Prove that if one-way functions exist, then there exists a one-way function f such that $f(a_n) = b_n$ for every n. Do the same for one-way permutations.

> **Guideline:** The first part is trivial. For the second part, consider any one-way permutation f', and suppose $f'(a_n) \neq b_n$. Construct a one-way permutation f as required by switching two values of f'.

Exercise 15: *On the improbability of strengthening Theorem 2.3.2 (Part 1):* Suppose that the definition of a weak one-way function is further weakened so that it is required that every probabilistic polynomial-time algorithm fails to invert the function with noticeable probability. That is, the order of quantifiers in Definition 2.2.2 is reversed (we now have "for every algorithm there exists a polynomial" rather than "there exists a polynomial such that for every algorithm"). Demonstrate the difficulty of extending the proof of Theorem 2.3.2 to this case.

> **Guideline:** Suppose that there exists a family of algorithms, one per each polynomial $p(\cdot)$, such that an algorithm with time bound $p(n)$ fails to invert the function with probability $1/p(n)$. Demonstrate the plausibility of such a family.

Exercise 16: *On the improbability of strengthening Theorem 2.3.2 (Part 2)* (due to Steven Rudich): Suppose that the definition of a strong one-way function is further strengthened such that it is required that *every* probabilistic polynomial-time algorithm fails to invert the function with some *specified* negligible probability (e.g., $2^{-\sqrt{n}}$). Demonstrate the difficulty of extending the proof of Theorem 2.3.2 to this case.

> **Guideline:** Suppose that we construct the strong one-way function g as in the original proof. Further suppose that there exists an inverting algorithm A that inverts the function g on $g(U_n)$ with probability $\varepsilon(n)$. Show that any inverting algorithm for the weakly one-way function f that uses algorithm A as a black box must invoke it at least $\frac{1}{\text{poly}(n) \cdot \varepsilon(n)}$ times.

Exercise 17: *Advanced topic: distributionally one-way functions* [131]: We say that a polynomial-time-computable function $f : \{0, 1\}^* \to \{0, 1\}^*$ is **distributionally one-way** if there exists a positive polynomial p such that for every probabilistic polynomial-time algorithm A and all sufficiently large n's, the statistical difference between $(U_n, f(U_n))$ and $(A(1^n, f(U_n)), f(U_n))$ is greater than $1/p(n)$. (That is, the inverting task is to provide a uniformly distributed pre-image rather than an arbitrary one, and failure is measured in terms of the deviation of A's output from this distribution.)

1. Prove that if f is weakly one-way (as in Definition 2.2.2), then it is distributionally one-way.
2. Prove that if there exist distributionally one-way functions, then there exist one-way functions.

> **Guideline (Part 2):** Use hashing ideas as in Section 3.5. Specifically, given a distributionally one-way function f, consider the function $F(x, i, h) = (f(x), h_i(x), i, h)$, where $x \in \{0, 1\}^n$, $i \in \{1, \ldots, n\}$, $h : \{0, 1\}^n \to \{0, 1\}^n$ is a hashing function, and $h_i(x)$ denotes the i-bit-long prefix of $h(x)$. Prove that F is weakly one-way.

> **Guideline (Part 2, extra help):** Suppose, to the contrary, that F can be inverted on at least a $1 - \varepsilon(n) > 1 - (2n)^{-1}$ fraction of the inputs (x, i, h), where $|x| = n$. Then for any $\ell : \mathbb{N} \to \mathbb{N}$, the function F can be inverted on at least a $1 - n\varepsilon(n)$ fraction of the inputs $(x, \lfloor \log_2 | f^{-1}(f(x))| \rfloor + \ell(n), h)$. Given $y = f(x)$, we generate a random pre-image of y under f as follows. First, for $\ell(n) = O(\log n)$, we find an i such that $i = \lfloor \log_2 | f^{-1}(f(x))| \rfloor + \ell(n) \pm O(1)$. (This is done by trying to invert F on (y, i, r, h), where h and $r \in \{0, 1\}^i$ are uniformly chosen, and choosing i if a pre-image is found with probability approximately $2^{-\ell(n)}$.) Next, using this i, we output a pre-image of (y, i, r, h) under F, where (again) h and $r \in \{0, 1\}^i$ are uniformly chosen. (In case inversion fails, we try again.) Show that the output distribution of this algorithm deviates from the desired distribution by at most $O(2^{\ell(n)} + 2^{2\ell(n) + 2\log_2 n}) \cdot \varepsilon(n))$, and so the claim follows.

Exercise 18: *One-way functions and collections of one-way functions:*

1. Given any collection of one-way functions (I, D, F), represent it as a single one-way function.
2. Given any one-way function f, represent it as a collection of one-way functions. (Remark: This direction is quite trivial.)

Exercise 19: *A convention for collections of one-way functions:* Show that without loss of generality, algorithms I and D of a collection (of one-way functions) can be modified so that each of them uses a number of coins that exactly equals the input length.

> **Guideline:** Apply padding.

Exercise 20: *Justification for a convention concerning one-way collections:* Show that giving the index of the function to the inverting algorithm is essential for a meaningful definition of a collection of one-way functions.

  Guideline: Consider a collection $\{ f_i : \{0, 1\}^{|i|} \rightarrow \{0, 1\}^{|i|} \}$, where $f_i(x) = x \oplus i$.

Exercise 21: *Rabin's collection and factoring:* Show that the Rabin collection is one-way if and only if the factoring of integers that are the products of two primes of equal binary expansions is intractable in a strong sense (i.e., every efficient algorithm succeeds with negligible probability).

  Guideline: See Appendix A.

Exercise 22: *Claw-free collections imply one-way functions:* Let (I, D, F) be a claw-free collection of functions (see Section 2.4.5). Prove that for every $\sigma \in \{0, 1\}$, the triplet (I, D, F_σ), where $F_\sigma(i, x) \overset{\text{def}}{=} F(\sigma, i, x)$, is a collection of strong one-way functions. Repeat the exercise, replacing the word "functions" with "permutations."

Exercise 23: *More on the inadequacy of graph isomorphism as a basis for one-way functions:* In continuation of the discussion in Section 2.4.6, consider another suggestion to base one-way functions on the conjectured difficulty of the Graph Isomorphism problem. This time we present a collection of functions defined by the algorithmic triplet (I_{GI}, D_{GI}, F_{GI}). On input 1^n, algorithm I_{GI} selects uniformly a $d(n)$-regular graph on n vertices (i.e., each of the n vertices in the graph has degree $d(n)$). On input a graph on n vertices, algorithm D_{GI} randomly selects a permutation in the symmetric group of n elements (i.e., the set of permutations of n elements). On input an (n-vertex) graph G and an (n-element) permutation π, algorithm F_{GI} returns $f_G(\pi) \overset{\text{def}}{=} \pi G$.

1. Present a polynomial-time implementation of I_{GI}.
2. In light of the known algorithms for the Graph Isomorphism problem, which values of $d(n)$ should definitely be avoided?
3. Using a known algorithm, prove that the foregoing collection does not have a one-way property, no matter which function $d(\cdot)$ one uses.

  Guideline: A search of the relevant literature is indeed required for Items 2 and 3. Specifically, for certain values of $d(n)$, there exists a polynomial-time algorithm for deciding isomorphism. Furthermore, for proving 3, it suffices to have an algorithm that runs fast on randomly selected pairs of d-regular graphs.

Exercise 24: Assuming the existence of one-way functions, prove that there exists a one-way function f such that *no* single bit of the pre-image constitutes a hard-core predicate.

  Guideline: Given a one-way function f, construct a function g such that $g(x, I) \overset{\text{def}}{=} (f(x_I), x_I, I)$, where $I \subseteq \{1, 2, \ldots |x|\}$, and x_S denotes the string resulting by taking only the bits of x with positions in the set S (i.e., $x_{\{i_1, \ldots, i_s\}} \overset{\text{def}}{=} x_{i_1} \cdots x_{i_s}$, where $x = x_1 \cdots x_{|x|}$). How well can you predict each bit? To obtain more "dramatic" predictability, consider $g(x, I_1, \ldots, I_t) \overset{\text{def}}{=} (f(x_{\cap_{j=1}^t I_j}), x_{\cup_{j=1}^t I_j}, I_1, \ldots, I_t)$. What value of t (as a function of $|x|$) should be used?

———— 97 ————

Exercise 25: *A hard-core predicate for a 1-1 function implies that the function is one-way:* Let f be a 1-1 function (you may assume for simplicity that it is length-preserving), and suppose that b is a hard-core for f.

1. Prove that if f is polynomial-time-computable, then it is strongly one-way.
2. Prove that (regardless of whether or not f is polynomial-time-computable) the function f must be at least "weakly hard to invert"; that is, for some positive polynomial p, every probabilistic polynomial-time algorithm A must satisfy $\Pr[A(f(U_n)) \neq U_n] > 1/p(n)$ for all sufficiently large n's. Furthermore, prove that for every positive polynomial p, every probabilistic polynomial-time algorithm A must satisfy $\Pr[A(f(U_n)) = U_n] < \frac{1}{2} + \frac{1}{p(n)}$ for all sufficiently large n's.

   Guideline: Use the inverting algorithm for predicting the hard-core. Distinguish the case in which you can check that the inverting algorithm is correct (i.e., in Item 1) from the case in which you cannot do so (i.e., in Item 2).

Exercise 26: *An unbiased hard-core predicate* (suggested by Erez Petrank): Assuming the existence of one-way functions, prove the existence of hard-core predicates (for such functions) that are unbiased (i.e., the predicate b satisfies $\Pr[b(U_n) = 1] = \frac{1}{2}$).

   Guideline: Slightly modify the predicate defined in Theorem 2.5.2 (i.e., you need to modify it only on all-zero x). Alternatively, convert any hard-core b for a function f into $b'(x, \sigma) = \sigma \oplus b(x)$ for $f'(x, \sigma) = (f(x), \sigma)$.

Exercise 27: *Universal hard-core predicate:* A polynomial-time-computable predicate $b : \{0, 1\}^* \to \{0, 1\}$ is called a *universal hard-core predicate* if for every one-way function f, the predicate b is a hard-core of f. Note that the predicate presented in Theorem 2.5.2 is "almost universal" (i.e., for every one-way function f, that predicate is a hard-core of $f'(x, r) = (f(x), r)$, where $|x| = |r|$). Prove that there exists no universal hard-core predicate.

   Guideline: Let b be a candidate universal hard-core predicate, and let f be an arbitrary one-way function. Then define the (one-way) function $f'(x) = (f(x), b(x))$.

Exercise 28: *Theorem 2.5.2, an alternative perspective* (suggested by Russell Impagliazzo, Madhu Sudan, and Luca Trevisan): The hard-core predicate of Theorem 2.5.2 can be viewed as $b(x, i)$ equaling the ith bit in the Hadamard code of x, where the Hadamard code is the most redundant (non-repeating) linear code (i.e., a string $x \in \{0, 1\}^n$ is mapped to the values obtained from all possible 2^n linear combinations of its bits). Let $H(x)$ denote the codeword associated with x by the Hadamard code. The argument presented in the proof of Theorem 2.5.2 actually provides a "list-decoding" algorithm for the Hadamard code. Specifically, given oracle access to the bits of a string $y \in \{0, 1\}^{2^n}$ and a parameter $\varepsilon > 0$, we recover, within poly(n/ε) time, all strings $x \in \{0, 1\}^n$ such that $H(x)$ and y differ on at most $(\frac{1}{2} - \varepsilon) \cdot 2^n$ locations.

1. Verify the foregoing claim, that is, that a "list-decoding" algorithm (for the Hadamard code) with the stated features is implicit in the proof of Theorem 2.5.2.
2. Let C be an error-correcting code mapping n-bit strings to $\ell(n)$-bit strings. What requirements should C satisfy so that $b(x, i)$, defined as the ith bit in $C(x)$, would constitute a hard-core predicate of $f'(x, i) = (f(x), i)$ for every one-way function f.

Guideline: Note that we should support any ε of the form $1/\text{poly}(n)$, and remember that b has to be polynomial-time-computable. Also note that $|i| = \text{poly}(|x|)$. Why?

3. Using a list-decoding algorithm for Reed-Solomon codes [203], present such a hard-core predicate. Specifically, you should be able to have $|i| = \ell(|x|)$ for any "nice" super-logarithmic function $\ell : \mathbb{N} \to \mathbb{N}$ (e.g., $\ell(n) = (\log_2 n)^2$ will do).

Exercise 29: In contrast to the last item of Exercise 28, prove that if $b(x, y)$ is a hard-core for every one-way function of the form $f'(x, y) = (f(x), y)$, then $|y|$ must be greater than the logarithm of $|x|$.

Guideline: Extend the argument of Exercise 27 using the fact that if $|y| = O(\log|x|)$, then $y = 0^{|y|}$ occurs with probability $1/\text{poly}(|x|)$.

Exercise 30: *Abstracting the proof of Theorem 2.5.2*: Suppose you are given oracle access to an arbitrary predicate $P_x : \{0, 1\}^{|x|} \to \{0, 1\}$ satisfying

$$\Pr[P_x(U_{|x|}) = b(x, U_{|x|})] \geq \frac{1}{2} + \varepsilon$$

1. Present a probabilistic oracle machine that runs for $\text{poly}(|x|)/\varepsilon^2$ steps and, given oracle access to any such P_x, outputs a list of strings that with probability at least $\frac{1}{2}$ contains x.

2. Let M be an oracle machine that for any oracle P_x, as before, outputs a list of strings that with probability at least $\frac{1}{2}$ contains x. Prove that M must make $\min(2^{\Omega(n)}, \Omega(n/\varepsilon^2))$ steps.
   Guideline (Part 1): Let $n = |x|$, and assume that $\varepsilon \geq 2^{-n}$. Implicit in the proof of Theorem 2.5.2 is a machine that runs for $\text{poly}(n)/\varepsilon^2$ steps and outputs a single string that with probability at least $\varepsilon^2/\text{poly}(n)$ equals x. This yields a machine running in time $\text{poly}(n)/\varepsilon^4$ and outputting a list as desired. A machine running in time $\text{poly}(n)/\varepsilon^2$ and outputting a list as desired is implicit in the proof of Proposition 2.5.4.
   Guideline (Part 2): Consider a probabilistic oracle (or process) defined as follows. First, x is selected uniformly in $\{0, 1\}^n$ and fixed for the rest of the process. Next, each time a query q is made (regardless of whether it is made for the first time or not), the oracle answers $b(x, q)$ with probability $\frac{1}{2} + \varepsilon$, and answers $1 - b(x, q)$ otherwise. Show that the amount of information about x obtained by each query is $O(\varepsilon^2)$. On the other hand, a list of ℓ strings containing x has at least $n - \log_2 \ell$ bits of information about x. Use the obvious fact that the length of the list output by M and the number of queries that M makes are both bounded above by the running time of M.

Exercise 31: *An alternative definition of hard-core functions*: Let $h : \{0, 1\}^* \to \{0, 1\}^*$ and $l : \mathbb{N} \to \mathbb{N}$ satisfy $|h(x)| = l(|x|)$ for all $x \in \{0, 1\}^*$. We say that h **is hard to approximate from** f if for every probabilistic polynomial-time algorithm A, every positive polynomial p, and all sufficiently large n's, it holds that

$$\Pr[A(f(X_n)) = h(X_n)] < 2^{-l(n)} + \frac{1}{p(n)} \tag{2.16}$$

where X_n is uniformly distributed over $\{0, 1\}^n$.

1. Prove that *for* $l : \mathbb{N} \to \mathbb{N}$ *satisfying* $l(n) = O(\log n)$ and a polynomial-time-computable $h : \{0, 1\}^* \to \{0, 1\}^*$, the function h is a hard-core of f if and only if h is hard to approximate from f.

2. Show that one direction in Part 1 does not hold in general (i.e., for super-logarithmically growing l).

Comment: This exercise is related to Section 3.3.5.

Guideline (mainly for Part 1): Assuming that there exists an algorithm A that violates Eq. (2.16), construct an algorithm D' as in Definition 2.5.5 such that $D'(y, \alpha) = 1$ if and only if $A(y) = \alpha$. Show that the distinguishing gap of D' is at least $s(n) - 2^{-l(n)}$, where $s(\cdot)$ represents the success probability of A. On the other hand, assuming that there exists an algorithm D' violating the condition in Definition 2.5.5, construct an algorithm A that violates Eq. (2.16). Specifically, suppose, without loss of generality, that $\Pr[D'(f(X_n), h(X_n)) = 1] = \Pr[D'(f(X_n), R_{l(n)}) = 1] + \varepsilon(n)$, where $\varepsilon(n) > \frac{1}{p(n)}$. Then, on input y, algorithm A uniformly selects $r \in \{0, 1\}^{l(n)}$ and $r' \in (\{0, 1\}^{l(n)} \setminus \{r\})$, invokes D', and outputs r if $D'(y, r) = 1$, and r' otherwise. Show that the success probability of D' is at least $\frac{\varepsilon(n)}{2^{l(n)} - 1}$.

CHAPTER 3

Pseudorandom Generators

In this chapter we discuss pseudorandom generators. Loosely speaking, these are efficient deterministic programs that expand short, randomly selected seeds into much longer "pseudorandom" bit sequences (see illustration in Figure 3.1). Pseudorandom sequences are defined as computationally indistinguishable from truly random sequences by efficient algorithms. Hence the notion of computational indistinguishability (i.e., indistinguishability by efficient procedures) plays a pivotal role in our discussion. Furthermore, the notion of computational indistinguishability plays a key role also in subsequent chapters, in particular in the discussions of secure encryption, zero-knowledge proofs, and cryptographic protocols.

The theory of pseudorandomness is also applied to functions, resulting in the notion of pseudorandom functions, which is a useful tool for many cryptographic applications.

In addition to definitions of pseudorandom distributions, pseudorandom generators, and pseudorandom functions, this chapter contains constructions of pseudorandom generators (and pseudorandom functions) based on various types of one-way functions. In particular, very simple and efficient pseudorandom generators are constructed based on the existence of one-way permutations. We highlight the *hybrid technique*, which plays a central role in many of the proofs. (For the first use and further discussion of this technique, see Section 3.2.3.)

Organization. Basic discussions, definitions, and constructions of pseudorandom generators appear in Sections 3.1–3.4: We start with a motivating discussion (Section 3.1), proceed with a general definition of computational indistinguishability (Section 3.2), next present and discuss definitions of pseudorandom generators (Section 3.3), and finally present some simple constructions (Section 3.4). More general constructions are discussed in Section 3.5. Pseudorandom functions are defined and constructed (based on any pseudorandom generator) in Section 3.6. Pseudorandom permutations are discussed in Section 3.7.

Teaching Tip. The *hybrid technique*, first used to show that computational indistinguishability is preserved under multiple samples (Section 3.2.3), plays an important

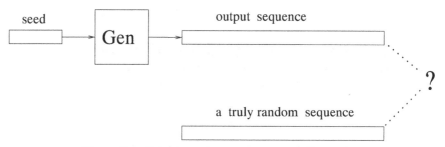

Figure 3.1: Pseudorandom generators: an illustration.

role in many of the proofs that refer to computational indistinguishability. Thus, in case you choose to skip this specific proof, do incorporate a discussion of the hybrid technique in the first place you use it.

3.1. Motivating Discussion

The nature of randomness has puzzled thinkers for centuries. We believe that the notion of computation, and in particular that of efficient computation, provides a good basis for understanding the nature of randomness.

3.1.1. Computational Approaches to Randomness

One computational approach to randomness was initiated by Solomonov and Kolmogorov in the early 1960s (and rediscovered by Chaitin in the early 1970s). This approach is "ontological" in nature. Loosely speaking, a string s is considered *Kolmogorov-random* if its length (i.e., $|s|$) equals the length of the shortest program producing s. This shortest program can be considered the "simplest" "explanation" for the phenomenon described by the string s. Hence the string s is considered Kolmogorov-random if it does not possess a "simple" explanation (i.e., an explanation that is substantially shorter than $|s|$). We stress that one cannot determine whether or not a given string is Kolmogorov-random (and, more generally, Kolmogorov complexity is a function that cannot be computed). Furthermore, this approach seems to have no application to the issue of "pseudorandom generators."

An alternative computational approach to randomness is presented in the rest of this chapter. This approach was initiated in the early 1980s. In contrast to the approach of Kolmogorov, this new approach is behavioristic in nature. Instead of considering the "explanation" for a phenomenon, we consider the phenomenon's effect on the environment. Loosely speaking, a string is considered *pseudorandom* if no efficient observer can distinguish it from a uniformly chosen string of the same length. The underlying postulate is that objects that cannot be differentiated by efficient procedures are considered equivalent, although they may be very different in nature (e.g., can have fundamentally different (Kolmogorov) complexities). Furthermore, the new approach naturally leads to the concept of a pseudorandom generator, which is a fundamental concept with lots of practical applications (particularly in the field of cryptography).

3.1.2. A Rigorous Approach to Pseudorandom Generators

The approach to pseudorandom generators presented in this book stands in contrast to the heuristic approach that is still common in discussions concerning "pseudorandom generators" that are being used in real computers. The heuristic approach considers "pseudorandom generators" as programs that produce bit sequences that can "pass" *some specific* statistical tests. The choices of statistical tests to which these programs are subjected are quite arbitrary and lack any systematic foundation. Furthermore, it is possible to construct efficient statistical tests that will foil the "pseudorandom generators" commonly used in practice (and in particular will distinguish their output from a uniformly chosen string of equal length). Consequently, before using a "pseudorandom generator" in a new application that requires "random" sequences, extensive tests have to be conducted in order to determine whether or not the behavior of the application when using the "pseudorandom generator" will be the same as its behavior when using a "true source of randomness." Any modification of the application will require a new comparison of the "pseudorandom generator" against the "random source," because the non-randomness of the "pseudorandom generator" may adversely affect the modified application (even if it did not affect the original application). Things become even worse with respect to cryptographic applications, because in such cases an application is fully determined only after the adversary is fixed. That is, one cannot *test* the effect of the "pseudorandom generator" on the performance of a yet-unspecified adversary, and it is unreasonable to assume that the adversary is going to employ a specific strategy known to the designer. Thus, using such a "pseudorandom generator" for cryptographic purposes is highly risky.

In contrast, the concept of pseudorandom generators presented herein is a robust one: By definition, these pseudorandom generators produce sequences that look random to any efficient observer. It follows that the output of a pseudorandom generator can be used instead of "random sequences" in any efficient application requiring such (i.e., "random") sequences. In particular, no efficient adversary can capitalize on the replacement of "truly random sequences" by pseudorandom ones.

3.2. Computational Indistinguishability

As stated earlier, the concept of computational indistinguishability is the basis for our definition of pseudorandomness. Thus, we start with a general definition and discussion of this fundamental concept.

The concept of efficient computation leads naturally to a new kind of equivalence between objects: *Objects are considered to be computationally equivalent if they cannot be differentiated by any efficient procedure.* We note that considering *indistinguishable objects* as equivalent is one of the basic paradigms of both science and real-life situations. Hence, we believe that the notion of computational indistinguishability is a very natural one.

3.2.1. Definition

The notion of computational indistinguishability is formulated in a way that is standard in the field of computational complexity: by considering objects as infinite sequences of strings. Hence, the sequences $\{x_n\}_{n \in N}$ and $\{y_n\}_{n \in N}$ are said to be computationally indistinguishable if no efficient procedure can tell them apart. In other words, no efficient algorithm D can accept infinitely many x_n's while rejecting their y counterparts (i.e., for every efficient algorithm D and all sufficiently large n's, it holds that D accepts x_n iff D accepts y_n). Objects that are computationally indistinguishable in this sense can be considered equivalent as far as any practical purpose is concerned (because practical purposes are captured by efficient algorithms, and they cannot distinguish these objects).

The foregoing discussion extends naturally to the probabilistic setting. Furthermore, as we shall see, this extension yields very useful consequences. Loosely speaking, two distributions are called computationally indistinguishable if no efficient algorithm can tell them apart. Given an efficient algorithm D, we consider the probability that D accepts (e.g., outputs 1 on input) a string taken from the first distribution. Likewise, we consider the probability that D accepts a string taken from the second distribution. If these two probabilities are close, we say that D does not distinguish the two distributions. Again, the formulation of this discussion is with respect to two infinite sequences of distributions (rather than with respect to two fixed distributions). Such sequences are called probability ensembles.

> **Definition 3.2.1 (Probability Ensemble):** *Let I be a countable index set. An* **ensemble indexed by** *I is a sequence of random variables indexed by I. Namely, any $X = \{X_i\}_{i \in I}$, where each X_i is a random variable, is an ensemble indexed by I.*

We shall use either $\mathbb{N}$ or a subset of $\{0, 1\}^*$ as the index set. Typically in our applications, an ensemble of the form $X = \{X_n\}_{n \in N}$ has each X_n ranging over strings of length poly(n), whereas an ensemble of the form $X = \{X_w\}_{w \in \{0,1\}^*}$ will have each X_w ranging over strings of length poly($|w|$). In the rest of this chapter we shall deal with ensembles indexed by $\mathbb{N}$, whereas in other chapters (e.g., in the definition of secure encryption and zero-knowledge) we shall deal with ensembles indexed by strings. To avoid confusion, we shall present variants of the definition of computational indistinguishability for each of these two cases. The two formulations can be unified if one associates the natural numbers with their unary representations (i.e., associate $\mathbb{N}$ and $\{1^n : n \in \mathbb{N}\}$).

> **Definition 3.2.2 (Polynomial-Time Indistinguishability):**
>
> *1.* Variant for ensembles indexed by $\mathbb{N}$: *Two ensembles, $X \stackrel{\text{def}}{=} \{X_n\}_{n \in \mathbb{N}}$ and $Y \stackrel{\text{def}}{=} \{Y_n\}_{n \in \mathbb{N}}$, are* **indistinguishable in polynomial time** *if for every probabilistic polynomial-time algorithm D, every positive polynomial $p(\cdot)$, and all*

sufficiently large n's,

$$|\Pr[D(X_n, 1^n)=1] - \Pr[D(Y_n, 1^n)=1]| < \frac{1}{p(n)}$$

2. Variant for ensembles indexed by a set of strings S: *Two ensembles,* $X \stackrel{\text{def}}{=} \{X_w\}_{w \in S}$ *and* $Y \stackrel{\text{def}}{=} \{Y_w\}_{w \in S}$, *are* **indistinguishable in polynomial time** *if for every probabilistic polynomial-time algorithm D, every positive polynomial p(·), and all sufficiently long* $w \in S$,

$$|\Pr[D(X_w, w)=1] - \Pr[D(Y_w, w)=1]| < \frac{1}{p(|w|)}$$

We often say computational indistinguishability *instead of indistinguishability in polynomial time.*

The probabilities in the foregoing definition are taken over the corresponding random variables X_i (or Y_i) and the internal coin tosses of algorithm D (which is allowed to be a probabilistic algorithm). The second variant of this definition will play a key role in subsequent chapters, and further discussion of it is postponed to those places. In the rest of this chapter, we refer to only the first variant of the foregoing definition. The string 1^n is given as auxiliary input to algorithm D in order to make the first variant consistent with the second one. We comment that *in typical cases*, the length of X_n (resp., Y_n) and n are polynomially related (i.e., $|X_n| < \text{poly}(n)$ and $n < \text{poly}(|X_n|)$) and furthermore can be computed one from the other in $\text{poly}(n)$ time. In such cases, *giving 1^n as auxiliary input is redundant.* Indeed, throughout this chapter we typically omit this auxiliary input and assume that n can be efficiently determined from X_n.

The following mental experiment may be instructive. For each $\alpha \in \{0, 1\}^*$, consider the probability, hereafter denoted $d(\alpha)$, that algorithm D outputs 1 on input α. Consider the expectation of d taken over each of the two ensembles: That is, let $d_X(n) = \mathsf{E}[d(X_n)]$ and $d_Y(n) = \mathsf{E}[d(Y_n)]$. Then X and Y are said to be indistinguishable by D if the difference (function) $\delta(n) \stackrel{\text{def}}{=} |d_X(n) - d_Y(n)|$ is negligible in n. Recall that a function $\mu : \mathbb{N} \to [0, 1]$ is called *negligible* if for every positive polynomial p and all sufficiently large n's, $\mu(n) < 1/p(n)$.

A couple of examples may help to clarify the definition. Consider an algorithm D_1 that, obliviously of the input, flips a (0–1-valued) coin and outputs its outcome. Clearly, on every input, algorithm D_1 outputs 1 with probability exactly $\frac{1}{2}$ and hence does not distinguish any pair of ensembles. Next, consider an algorithm D_2 that outputs 1 if and only if the input string contains more zeros than ones. Because D_2 can be implemented in polynomial time, it follows that if X and Y are polynomial-time-indistinguishable, then the difference $|\Pr[\text{wt}(X_n) < \frac{n}{2}] - \Pr[\text{wt}(Y_n) < \frac{n}{2}]|$ is negligible (in n), where $\text{wt}(\alpha)$ denotes the number of ones in the string α. Similarly, polynomial-time-indistinguishable ensembles must exhibit the same "profile" (up to negligible error) with respect to any "string statistics" that can be computed in polynomial time. However, it is not required that polynomial-time-indistinguishable ensembles have similar "profiles" with respect to quantities that cannot be computed in polynomial time (e.g., Kolmogorov complexity, or the function presented immediately after Proposition 3.2.3).

3.2.2. Relation to Statistical Closeness

Computational indistinguishability is a coarsening of a traditional notion from probability theory. We call two ensembles $X \stackrel{\text{def}}{=} \{X_n\}_{n\in\mathbb{N}}$ and $Y \stackrel{\text{def}}{=} \{Y_n\}_{n\in\mathbb{N}}$ *statistically close* if their statistical difference is negligible, where the *statistical difference* (also known as *variation distance*) between X and Y is defined as the function

$$\Delta(n) \stackrel{\text{def}}{=} \frac{1}{2} \cdot \sum_{\alpha} |\Pr[X_n = \alpha] - \Pr[Y_n = \alpha]| \tag{3.1}$$

Clearly, if the ensembles X and Y are statistically close, then they are also polynomial-time-indistinguishable (see Exercise 6). The converse, however, is not true. In particular:

Proposition 3.2.3: *There exists an ensemble* $X = \{X_n\}_{n\in\mathbb{N}}$ *such that* X *is not statistically close to the uniform ensemble* $U \stackrel{\text{def}}{=} \{U_n\}_{n\in\mathbb{N}}$, *and yet* X *and* U *are polynomial-time-indistinguishable. Furthermore,* X_n *assigns all its probability mass to at most* $2^{n/2}$ *strings (of length n).*

Recall that U_n is uniformly distributed over strings of length n. Although X and U are polynomial-time-indistinguishable, one can define a function $f : \{0,1\}^* \to \{0,1\}$ such that f has average 1 over X while having average almost 0 over U (e.g., $f(x) = 1$ if and only if $\Pr[X=x] > 0$). Hence, X and U have different "profiles" with respect to the function f, yet it is (necessarily) impossible to compute f in polynomial time.

Proof: We claim that for all sufficiently large n, there exists a random variable X_n, distributed over some set of at most $2^{n/2}$ strings (each of length n), such that for every circuit C_n of size (i.e., number of gates) $2^{n/8}$, it holds that

$$|\Pr[C_n(U_n)=1] - \Pr[C_n(X_n)=1]| < 2^{-n/8} \tag{3.2}$$

The proposition follows from this claim, because polynomial-time-distinguishers (even probabilistic ones; see Exercise 10 (Part 1)) yield polynomial-size circuits with at least as large a distinguishing gap.

The foregoing claim is proved using a probabilistic argument. That is, we actually show that most distributions of a certain class can "fool" all circuits of size $2^{n/8}$. Specifically, we show that if we select uniformly a multi-set of $2^{n/2}$ strings in $\{0,1\}^n$ and let X_n be uniform over this multi-set, then Eq. (3.2) holds with overwhelmingly high probability (over the choices of the multi-set).

Let C_n be some fixed circuit with n inputs, and let $p_n \stackrel{\text{def}}{=} \Pr[C_n(U_n)=1]$. We select, independently and uniformly, $2^{n/2}$ strings, denoted $s_1, \ldots, s_{2^{n/2}}$, in $\{0,1\}^n$. We define random variables ζ_i's such that $\zeta_i = C_n(s_i)$; that is, these random variables depend on the random choices of the corresponding s_i's. Using the Chernoff bound, we get that

$$\Pr\left[\left|p_n - \frac{1}{2^{n/2}} \cdot \sum_{i=1}^{2^{n/2}} \zeta_i\right| \geq 2^{-n/8}\right] \leq 2e^{-2\cdot2^{n/2}\cdot(2^{-n/8})^2} < 2^{-2^{n/4}} \tag{3.3}$$

Because there are at most $2^{2^{n/4}}$ different circuits of size (number of gates) $2^{n/8}$, it follows that there exists a sequence $s_1, \ldots, s_{2^{n/2}} \in \{0, 1\}^n$ such that for every circuit C_n of size $2^{n/8}$ it holds that

$$\left| \Pr[C_n(U_n) = 1] - \frac{\sum_{i=1}^{2^{n/2}} C_n(s_i)}{2^{n/2}} \right| < 2^{-n/8}$$

Fixing such a sequence of s_i's, and letting X_n be distributed uniformly over the elements in the sequence, the claim follows. ∎

High-Level Comment. Proposition 3.2.3 presents a pair of ensembles that are computationally indistinguishable, although they are statistically far apart. One of the two ensembles is not constructible in polynomial time (see Definition 3.2.5). Interestingly, a pair of polynomial-time-constructible ensembles that are both computationally indistinguishable and have a noticeable statistical difference can exist only if pseudorandom generators exist. Jumping ahead, we note that this necessary condition is also sufficient. (The latter observation follows from the fact that pseudorandom generators give rise to a polynomial-time-constructible ensemble that is computationally indistinguishable from the uniform ensemble and yet statistically far from it.)

Low-Level Comment. A closer examination of the foregoing proof reveals that all but a negligible fraction of the sequences of length $2^{n/2}$ can be used to define the random variable X_n. Specifically, the second inequality in Eq. (3.3) is a gross overestimate, and an upper bound of $2^{-2^{\Omega(n)}} \cdot 2^{-2^{n/4}}$ actually holds. Observing that most sequences contain no repetitions, we can fix such a sequence. Consequently, X_n will be uniform over the $2^{n/2}$ distinct elements of the sequence.

3.2.3. Indistinguishability by Repeated Experiments

By Definition 3.2.2, two ensembles are considered computationally indistinguishable if no efficient procedure can tell them apart based on a single sample. We now show that for "efficiently constructible" ensembles, computational indistinguishability (based on a single sample) implies computational indistinguishability based on multiple samples. We start by presenting definitions of "indistinguishability by multiple samples" and "efficiently constructible ensembles."

Definition 3.2.4 (Indistinguishability by Repeated Sampling): *Two ensembles, $X \stackrel{\text{def}}{=} \{X_n\}_{n \in \mathbb{N}}$ and $Y \stackrel{\text{def}}{=} \{Y_n\}_{n \in \mathbb{N}}$, are **indistinguishable by polynomial-time sampling** if for every probabilistic polynomial-time algorithm D, every two positive polynomials $m(\cdot)$ and $p(\cdot)$, and all sufficiently large n's,*

$$\left| \Pr\left[D\left(X_n^{(1)}, \ldots, X_n^{(m(n))} \right) = 1 \right] - \Pr\left[D\left(Y_n^{(1)}, \ldots, Y_n^{(m(n))} \right) = 1 \right] \right| < \frac{1}{p(n)}$$

where $X_n^{(1)}$ through $X_n^{(m(n))}$ and $Y_n^{(1)}$ through $Y_n^{(m(n))}$ are independent random variables, with each $X_n^{(i)}$ identical to X_n and each $Y_n^{(i)}$ identical to Y_n.

Definition 3.2.5 (Efficiently Constructible Ensembles): *An ensemble* $X \stackrel{\text{def}}{=}$ $\{X_n\}_{n \in \mathbb{N}}$ *is said to be* **polynomial-time-constructible** *if there exists a proba-bilistic polynomial-time algorithm S such that for every n, the random variables* $S(1^n)$ *and* X_n *are identically distributed.*

Theorem 3.2.6: *Let* $X \stackrel{\text{def}}{=} \{X_n\}_{n \in \mathbb{N}}$ *and* $Y \stackrel{\text{def}}{=} \{Y_n\}_{n \in \mathbb{N}}$ *be two polynomial-time-constructible ensembles, and suppose that X and Y are indistinguishable in polynomial time (as in Definition 3.2.2). Then X and Y are indistinguishable by polynomial-time sampling (as in Definition 3.2.4).*

An alternative formulation of Theorem 3.2.6 proceeds as follows. For every ensemble $Z \stackrel{\text{def}}{=} \{Z_n\}_{n \in \mathbb{N}}$ and every polynomial $m(\cdot)$, define the $m(\cdot)$-*product* of Z as the ensemble $\{(Z_n^{(1)}, \ldots, Z_n^{(m(n))})\}_{n \in \mathbb{N}}$, where the $Z_n^{(i)}$'s are independent copies of Z_n. Theorem 3.2.6 asserts that *if the ensembles X and Y are polynomial-time-indistinguishable and each is polynomial-time-constructible, then for every polynomial $m(\cdot)$ the $m(\cdot)$-product of X and the $m(\cdot)$-product of Y are polynomial-time-indistinguishable.*

The information-theoretic analogue of the foregoing theorem is quite obvious: If two ensembles are statistically close, then their polynomial-products are statistically close (see Exercise 7). Adapting the proof to the computational setting requires, as usual, a reducibility argument. This argument uses, for the first time in this book, the *hybrid technique*. The hybrid technique plays a central role in demonstrating the computational indistinguishability of complex ensembles, constructed on the basis of simpler (computationally indistinguishable) ensembles. Subsequent applications of the hybrid technique will involve more technicalities. Hence the reader is urged not to skip the following proof.

Proof: The proof is by a reducibility argument. We show that the existence of an efficient algorithm that distinguishes the ensembles X and Y using several samples implies the existence of an efficient algorithm that distinguishes the ensembles X and Y using a single sample. The implication is proved using the following argument, which will later be called a "hybrid argument."

Suppose, to the contrary, that there is a probabilistic polynomial-time algorithm D, as well as polynomials $m(\cdot)$ and $p(\cdot)$, such that for infinitely many n's it holds that

$$\Delta(n) \stackrel{\text{def}}{=} \left| \Pr\left[D\left(X_n^{(1)}, \ldots, X_n^{(m)}\right) = 1\right] - \Pr\left[D\left(Y_n^{(1)}, \ldots, Y_n^{(m)}\right) = 1\right] \right| \qquad (3.4)$$
$$> \frac{1}{p(n)}$$

where $m \stackrel{\text{def}}{=} m(n)$, and the $X_n^{(i)}$'s and $Y_n^{(i)}$'s are as in Definition 3.2.4. In the sequel, we shall derive a contradiction by presenting a probabilistic polynomial-time algorithm D' that distinguishes the ensembles X and Y (in the sense of Definition 3.2.2).

For every k, with $0 \le k \le m$, we define the *hybrid* random variable H_n^k as a (m-long) sequence consisting of k independent copies of X_n followed by $m - k$

independent copies of Y_n. Namely,

$$H_n^k \stackrel{\text{def}}{=} (X_n^{(1)}, \ldots, X_n^{(k)}, Y_n^{(k+1)}, \ldots, Y_n^{(m)})$$

where $X_n^{(1)}$ through $X_n^{(k)}$ and $Y_n^{(k+1)}$ through $Y_n^{(m)}$ are independent random variables, with each $X_n^{(i)}$ identical to X_n and each $Y_n^{(i)}$ identical to Y_n. Clearly, $H_n^m = (X_n^{(1)}, \ldots, X_n^{(m)})$, whereas $H_n^0 = (Y_n^{(1)}, \ldots, Y_n^{(m)})$.

By our hypothesis, algorithm D can distinguish the extreme hybrids (i.e., H_n^0 and H_n^m). Because the total number of hybrids is polynomial in n, a non-negligible gap between (the "accepting" probability of D on) the extreme hybrids translates into a non-negligible gap between (the "accepting" probability of D on) a pair of neighboring hybrids. It follows that D, although not "designed to work on general hybrids," can distinguish a pair of neighboring hybrids. The punch line is that algorithm D can be easily modified into an algorithm D' that distinguishes X and Y. Details follow.

We construct an algorithm D' that uses algorithm D as a subroutine. On input α (supposedly in the range of either X_n or Y_n), algorithm D' proceeds as follows. Algorithm D' first selects k uniformly in the set $\{0, 1, \ldots, m-1\}$. Using the efficient sampling algorithm for the ensemble X, algorithm D' generates k independent samples of X_n. These samples are denoted $x^1, \ldots, x^k$. Likewise, using the efficient sampling algorithm for the ensemble Y, algorithm D' generates $m - k - 1$ independent samples of Y_n, denoted $y^{k+2}, \ldots, y^m$. Finally, algorithm D' invokes algorithm D and halts with output $D(x^1, \ldots, x^k, \alpha, y^{k+2}, \ldots, y^m)$.

Clearly, D' can be implemented in probabilistic polynomial time. It is also easy to verify the following claims.

Claim 3.2.6.1:

$$\Pr[D'(X_n) = 1] = \frac{1}{m} \sum_{k=0}^{m-1} \Pr[D(H_n^{k+1}) = 1]$$

and

$$\Pr[D'(Y_n) = 1] = \frac{1}{m} \sum_{k=0}^{m-1} \Pr[D(H_n^{k}) = 1]$$

Proof: By construction of algorithm D', we have

$$D'(\alpha) = D(X_n^{(1)}, \ldots, X_n^{(k)}, \alpha, Y_n^{(k+2)}, \ldots, Y_n^{(m)})$$

where k is uniformly distributed in $\{0, 1, \ldots, m-1\}$. Using the definition of the hybrids H_n^k, the claim follows. $\square$

Claim 3.2.6.2: For $\Delta(n)$ as in Eq. (3.4),

$$|\Pr[D'(X_n) = 1] - \Pr[D'(Y_n) = 1]| = \frac{\Delta(n)}{m(n)}$$

Proof: Using Claim 3.2.6.1 for the first equality, we get

$$|\Pr[D'(X_n)=1]-\Pr[D'(Y_n)=1]| = \frac{1}{m}\cdot\left|\sum_{k=0}^{m-1}\Pr[D(H_n^{k+1})=1]-\Pr[D(H_n^k)=1]\right|$$

$$= \frac{1}{m}\cdot\left|\Pr[D(H_n^m)=1]-\Pr[D(H_n^0)=1]\right|$$

$$= \frac{\Delta(n)}{m}$$

where the last equality follows by recalling that $H_n^m = (X_n^{(1)},\ldots,X_n^{(m)})$ and $H_n^0 = (Y_n^{(1)},\ldots,Y_n^{(m)})$ and using the definition of $\Delta(n)$. $\square$

Since by our hypothesis $\Delta(n)>\frac{1}{p(n)}$ for infinitely many n's, it follows that the probabilistic polynomial-time algorithm D' distinguishes X and Y in contradiction to the hypothesis of the theorem. Hence, the theorem follows. ∎

The Hybrid Technique: A Digest

It is worthwhile to give some thought to the *hybrid technique* (used for the first time in the preceding proof). The hybrid technique constitutes a special type of a "reducibility argument" in which the computational indistinguishability of *complex* ensembles is proved using the computational indistinguishability of *basic* ensembles. The actual reduction is in the other direction: Efficiently distinguishing the basic ensembles is reduced to efficiently distinguishing the complex ensembles, and *hybrid* distributions are used in the reduction in an essential way. The following properties of the construction of the hybrids play an important role in the argument:

1. *Extreme hybrids collide with the complex ensembles*: This property is essential because what we want to prove (i.e., indistinguishability of the complex ensembles) relates to the complex ensembles.

2. *Neighboring hybrids are easily related to the basic ensembles*: This property is essential because what we know (i.e., indistinguishability of the basic ensembles) relates to the basic ensembles. We need to be able to translate our knowledge (i.e., computational indistinguishability) of the basic ensembles to knowledge (i.e., computational indistinguishability) of any pair of neighboring hybrids. Typically it is required to efficiently transform strings in the range of a basic distribution into strings in the range of a hybrid, so that the transformation maps the first basic distribution to one hybrid and the second basic distribution to the neighboring hybrid. (In the proof of Theorem 3.2.6, the hypothesis that both X and Y are polynomial-time-constructible is instrumental for such an efficient transformation.)

3. *The number of hybrids is small* (i.e., polynomial): This property is essential in order to deduce the computational indistinguishability of extreme hybrids from the computational indistinguishability of each pair of neighboring hybrids. Typically, the provable "distinguishability gap" is inversely proportional to the number of hybrids.

We remark that during the course of a hybrid argument a distinguishing algorithm referring to the complex ensembles is being analyzed and even executed on arbitrary hybrids. The reader may be annoyed by the fact that the algorithm "was not designed to work on such hybrids" (but rather only on the extreme hybrids). However, *an algorithm is an algorithm*: Once it exists, we can apply it to any input of our choice and analyze its performance on arbitrary input distributions.

Advanced Comment on the Non-triviality of Theorem 3.2.6: Additional indication of the non-triviality of Theorem 3.2.6 is provided by the fact that the conclusion may fail in case the individual ensembles are *not both* efficiently constructible. Indeed, the hypothesis that both ensembles are efficiently constructible plays a central role in the proof of Theorem 3.2.6. Contrast this fact with the fact that an information-theoretic analogue of Theorem 3.2.6 asserts that for *any* two ensembles, statistical closeness implies statistical closeness of multiple samples.

3.2.4.* Indistinguishability by Circuits

A stronger notion of computational indistinguishability is the notion of computational indistinguishability by non-uniform families of polynomial-size circuits. This notion will be used in subsequent chapters.

Definition 3.2.7 (Indistinguishability by Polynomial-Size Circuits):

1. Variant for ensembles indexed by $\mathbb{N}$: *Two ensembles, $X \stackrel{\text{def}}{=} \{X_n\}_{n\in\mathbb{N}}$ and $Y \stackrel{\text{def}}{=} \{Y_n\}_{n\in\mathbb{N}}$, are* **indistinguishable by polynomial-size circuits** *if for every family $\{C_n\}_{n\in\mathbb{N}}$ of polynomial-size circuits, every positive polynomial $p(\cdot)$, and all sufficiently large n's,*

$$|\Pr[C_n(X_n)=1] - \Pr[C_n(Y_n)=1]| < \frac{1}{p(n)}$$

2. Variant for ensembles indexed by a set of strings S: *Two ensembles, $X \stackrel{\text{def}}{=} \{X_w\}_{w\in S}$ and $Y \stackrel{\text{def}}{=} \{Y_w\}_{w\in S}$, are* **indistinguishable by polynomial-size circuits** *if for every family $\{C_n\}_{n\in\mathbb{N}}$ of polynomial-size circuits, every positive polynomial $p(\cdot)$, and all sufficiently long w's,*

$$\left|\Pr\left[C_{|w|}(X_w)=1\right] - \Pr\left[C_{|w|}(Y_w)=1\right]\right| < \frac{1}{p(|w|)}$$

We comment that the variant for ensembles indexed by S is equivalent to the following (seemingly stronger) condition:

For every polynomial $s(\cdot)$, every collection $\{C_w\}_{w\in S}$ of circuits such that C_w has size at most $s(|w|)$, every positive polynomial $p(\cdot)$, and all sufficiently long w's,

$$|\Pr[C_w(X_w)=1] - \Pr[C_w(Y_w)=1]| < \frac{1}{p(|w|)} \qquad (3.5)$$

We show that the second requirement is not stronger than the requirement in the definition: That is, we show that if the second requirement is not satisfied, then neither is the first. Suppose that for some polynomials s and p there exist infinitely many w's violating Eq. (3.5). Then there exists an infinite set N such that for every $n \in N$, there exists a string $w_n \in \{0, 1\}^n$ violating Eq. (3.5). Letting $C'_n \stackrel{\text{def}}{=} C_{w_n}$, we obtain a contradiction to the requirement of the definition.

We note that allowing probabilistic circuits in the preceding definition does not increase its power (see Exercise 8). Consequently, in accordance with our meta-theorem (see Section 1.3.3), indistinguishability by polynomial-size circuits (as per Definition 3.2.7) implies indistinguishability by probabilistic polynomial-time machines (as per Definition 3.2.2); see Exercise 10. The converse is false (see Exercise 10). Finally, we note that indistinguishability by polynomial-size circuits is preserved under repeated experiments, even if both ensembles are not efficiently constructible (see Exercise 9).

3.2.5. Pseudorandom Ensembles

One special, yet important, case of computationally indistinguishable pairs of ensembles is the case in which one of the ensembles is uniform. Ensembles that are computationally indistinguishable from a uniform ensemble are called pseudorandom. Recall that U_m denotes a random variable uniformly distributed over the set of strings of length m. The ensemble $\{U_n\}_{n \in \mathbb{N}}$ is called the *standard uniform ensemble*. Yet, it will also be convenient to call *uniform* those ensembles of the form $\{U_{l(n)}\}_{n \in \mathbb{N}}$, where $l : \mathbb{N} \to \mathbb{N}$.

> **Definition 3.2.8 (Pseudorandom Ensembles):** *The ensemble* $X = \{X_n\}_{n \in \mathbb{N}}$ *is called* **pseudorandom** *if there exists a uniform ensemble* $U = \{U_{l(n)}\}_{n \in \mathbb{N}}$ *such that* X *and* U *are indistinguishable in polynomial time.*

We stress that $|X_n|$ is not necessarily n (whereas $|U_m| = m$). In fact, for polynomial-time-computable $l : \mathbb{N} \to \mathbb{N}$ and $X = \{X_n\}_{n \in \mathbb{N}}$ as in Definition 3.2.8, with very high probability, $|X_n|$ equals $l(n)$.

In the foregoing definition, as well as in the rest of this book, pseudorandomness is shorthand for *pseudorandomness with respect to polynomial time*.

3.3. Definitions of Pseudorandom Generators

A pseudorandom ensemble, as defined here, can be used instead of a uniform ensemble in any efficient application, with, at most, negligible degradation in performance (otherwise the efficient application can be transformed into an efficient distinguisher of the supposedly pseudorandom ensemble from the uniform one). Such a replacement is useful only if we can generate pseudorandom ensembles at a lower cost than that required to generate the corresponding uniform ensemble. The cost of generating an ensemble has several aspects. Standard cost considerations include the time and space complexities. However, in the context of randomized algorithms, and in particular in the context of generating probability ensembles, a major cost consideration is the quantity and quality of the random source used by the algorithm. In particular, in many applications (and especially in cryptography) *it is desirable to generate pseudorandom ensembles using as little true randomness as possible.* This leads to the definition of a pseudorandom generator.

3.3.1. Standard Definition of Pseudorandom Generators

Definition 3.3.1 (Pseudorandom Generator, Standard Definition): A pseudo-random generator *is a deterministic polynomial-time algorithm G satisfying the following two conditions:*

1. Expansion: *There exists a function $l : \mathbb{N} \to \mathbb{N}$ such that $l(n) > n$ for all $n \in \mathbb{N}$, and $|G(s)| = l(|s|)$ for all $s \in \{0, 1\}^*$.*

2. Pseudorandomness: *The ensemble $\{G(U_n)\}_{n \in \mathbb{N}}$ is pseudorandom.*

The function l is called the expansion factor *of G.*

The input s to the generator is called its *seed*. The expansion condition requires that the algorithm G map n-bit-long seeds into $l(n)$-bit-long strings, with $l(n) > n$. The pseudorandomness condition requires that the output distribution induced by applying algorithm G to a uniformly chosen seed be polynomial-time-indistinguishable from a uniform distribution, although it is *not* statistically close to uniform. Specifically, using Exercise 5 (for the first equality), we can bound the statistical difference between $G(U_n)$ and $U_{l(n)}$ as follows:

$$\frac{1}{2} \cdot \sum_x \left| \Pr[U_{l(n)} = x] - \Pr[G(U_n) = x] \right| = \max_S \left\{ \Pr[U_{l(n)} \in S] - \Pr[G(U_n) \in S] \right\}$$

$$\geq \Pr\left[U_{l(n)} \notin \{G(s) : s \in \{0, 1\}^n\}\right]$$

$$\geq \left(2^{l(n)} - 2^n\right) \cdot 2^{-l(n)}$$

$$= 1 - 2^{-(l(n)-n)} \geq \frac{1}{2}$$

where the last inequality uses $l(n) \geq n + 1$. Note that for $l(n) \geq 2n$, the statistical difference is at least $1 - 2^{-n}$.

The foregoing definition is quite permissive regarding the expansion factor $l : \mathbb{N} \to \mathbb{N}$. It asserts only that $l(n) \geq n + 1$ and $l(n) \leq \text{poly}(n)$. (It also follows that $l(n)$ is computed in time polynomial in n; e.g., by computing $|G(1^n)|$.) Clearly, a pseudorandom generator with expansion factor $l(n) = n + 1$ is of little value in practice, since it offers no *significant* saving in coin tosses. Fortunately, as shown in the next subsection, even pseudorandom generators with such a small expansion factor can be used to construct pseudorandom generators with any polynomial expansion factor. Hence, for every two expansion factors $l_1 : \mathbb{N} \to \mathbb{N}$ and $l_2 : \mathbb{N} \to \mathbb{N}$ that can be computed in $\text{poly}(n)$ time, there exists a pseudorandom generator with expansion factor l_1 if and only if there exists a pseudorandom generator with expansion factor l_2. This statement is proved by using any pseudorandom generator with expansion factor $l_1(n) \overset{\text{def}}{=} n + 1$ to construct, for every polynomial $p(\cdot)$, a pseudorandom generator with expansion factor $p(n)$. Note that a pseudorandom generator with expansion factor $l_1(n) \overset{\text{def}}{=} n + 1$ can be derived from any pseudorandom generator.

Each pseudorandom generator, as defined earlier, will have a predetermined expansion function. In Section 3.3.3 we shall consider "variable-output pseudorandom generators" that, given a random seed, will produce an infinite sequence of bits such that every polynomially long prefix of it will be pseudorandom.

3.3.2. Increasing the Expansion Factor

Given a pseudorandom generator G_1 with expansion factor $l_1(n) = n + 1$, we construct a pseudorandom generator G with arbitrary polynomial expansion factor as follows.

Construction 3.3.2: *Let G_1 be a deterministic polynomial-time algorithm mapping strings of length n into strings of length $n + 1$, and let $p(\cdot)$ be a polynomial. Define $G(s) = \sigma_1 \cdots \sigma_{p(|s|)}$, where $s_0 \overset{\text{def}}{=} s$, the bit σ_i is the first bit of $G_1(s_{i-1})$, and s_i is the $|s|$-bit-long suffix of $G_1(s_{i-1})$ for every $1 \leq i \leq p(|s|)$. That is, on input s, algorithm G proceeds as follows:*

> *Let $s_0 = s$ and $n = |s|$.*
> *For $i = 1$ to $p(n)$, do*
>
> $\quad \sigma_i s_i \leftarrow G_1(s_{i-1}), \;\; \text{where } \sigma_i \in \{0, 1\} \text{ and } |s_i| = |s_{i-1}|.$
>
> *Output $\sigma_1 \sigma_2 \cdots \sigma_{p(|s|)}.$*

The construction is depicted in Figure 3.2: On input s, algorithm G applies G_1 for $p(|s|)$ times, each time on a new seed. Applying G_1 to the current seed yields a new seed (for the next iteration) as well as one *extra bit* (which is being output immediately). The seed in the first iteration is s itself. The seed in the ith iteration is the $|s|$-bit-long suffix of the string obtained from G_1 in the previous iteration. Algorithm G outputs the concatenation of the "extra bits" obtained in the $p(|s|)$ iterations. Clearly, G is polynomial-time-computable and expands inputs of length n into output strings of length $p(n)$.

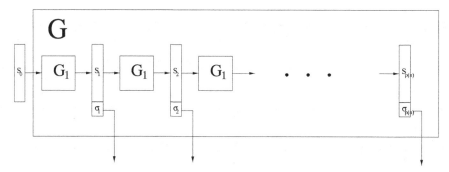

Figure 3.2: Construction 3.3.2, as operating on seed $s_0 \in \{0, 1\}^n$.

Theorem 3.3.3: *Let G_1, $p(\cdot)$, and G be as in Construction 3.3.2 such that $p(n) > n$. If G_1 is a pseudorandom generator, then so is G.*

Intuitively, the pseudorandomness of G follows from that of G_1 by replacing each application of G_1 by a random process that on input a uniformly distributed n-bit-long string will output a uniformly distributed $(n + 1)$-bit-long string. Loosely speaking, the indistinguishability of a single application of the random process from a single application of G_1 implies that polynomially many applications of the random process are indistinguishable from polynomially many applications of G_1. The actual proof uses the hybrid technique.

Proof: Suppose, to the contrary, that G is not a pseudorandom generator. It follows that the ensembles $\{G(U_n)\}_{n \in \mathbb{N}}$ and $\{U_{p(n)}\}_{n \in \mathbb{N}}$ are not polynomial-time-indistinguishable. We shall show that it follows that the ensembles $\{G_1(U_n)\}_{n \in \mathbb{N}}$ and $\{U_{n+1}\}_{n \in \mathbb{N}}$ are not polynomial-time-indistinguishable, in contradiction to the hypothesis that G_1 is a pseudorandom generator with expansion factor $l_1(n) = n + 1$. The implication is proved using the hybrid technique.

For every k, with $0 \leq k \leq p(n)$, we define a hybrid H_n^k to be the concatenation of a uniformly chosen k-bit-long string and the $(p(n) - k)$-bit-long prefix of $G(U_n)$. Denoting by $\mathtt{pref}_j(\alpha)$ the j-bit-long prefix of the strings α, where $j \leq |\alpha|$, and by $x \cdot y$ the concatenation of the strings x and y, we have

$$H_n^k \stackrel{\text{def}}{=} U_k^{(1)} \cdot \mathtt{pref}_{p(n)-k}\left(G\left(U_n^{(2)}\right)\right) \tag{3.6}$$

where $U_k^{(1)}$ and $U_n^{(2)}$ are independent random variables (the first uniformly distributed over $\{0, 1\}^k$, and the second uniformly distributed over $\{0, 1\}^n$).

A different way of viewing the hybrid H_n^k is depicted in Figure 3.3: Starting with Construction 3.3.2, we pick s_k uniformly in $\{0, 1\}^n$ and $\sigma_1 \cdots \sigma_k$ uniformly in $\{0, 1\}^k$, and for $i = k + 1, \ldots, p(n)$ we obtain $\sigma_i s_i = G_1(s_{i-1})$ as in the construction.

At this point it is clear that H_n^0 equals $G(U_n)$, whereas $H_n^{p(n)}$ equals $U_{p(n)}$. It follows that if an algorithm D can distinguish the extreme hybrids, then D can also distinguish two neighboring hybrids (since the total number of hybrids is polynomial in n, and a non-negligible gap between the extreme hybrids translates into a non-negligible gap between some neighboring hybrids). The punch line

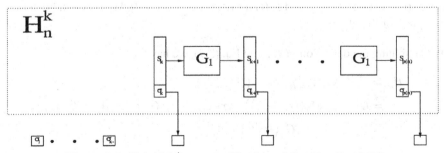

Figure 3.3: Hybrid H_n^k as a modification of Construction 3.3.2

is that, using the structure of neighboring hybrids, algorithm D can be easily modified to distinguish the ensembles $\{G_1(U_n)\}_{n\in\mathbb{N}}$ and $\{U_{n+1}\}_{n\in\mathbb{N}}$.

The core of the argument is the way in which the distinguishability of neighboring hybrids relates to the distinguishability of $G_1(U_n)$ from U_{n+1}. As stated, this relation stems from the structure of neighboring hybrids. Let us take a closer look at the hybrids H_n^k and H_n^{k+1} for some $0 \le k \le p(n) - 1$. Another piece of notation is useful: We let $\mathtt{suff}_j(\alpha)$ denote the j-bit-long suffix of the string α, where $j \le |\alpha|$. First observe (see justification later) that for every $x \in \{0, 1\}^n$,

$$\mathtt{pref}_{j+1}(G(x)) = \mathtt{pref}_1(G_1(x)) \cdot \mathtt{pref}_j(G(\mathtt{suff}_n(G_1(x)))) \qquad (3.7)$$

Thus (further justification follows),

$$\begin{aligned} H_n^k &= U_k^{(1)} \cdot \mathtt{pref}_{(p(n)-k-1)+1}(G(U_n^{(2)})) \\ &\equiv U_k^{(1)} \cdot \mathtt{pref}_1(G_1(U_n^{(2)})) \cdot \mathtt{pref}_{p(n)-k-1}(G(\mathtt{suff}_n(G_1(U_n^{(2)})))) \\ H_n^{k+1} &= U_{k+1}^{(1)} \cdot \mathtt{pref}_{p(n)-(k+1)}(G(U_n^{(2)})) \\ &\equiv U_k^{(1)} \cdot \mathtt{pref}_1(U_{n+1}^{(3)}) \cdot \mathtt{pref}_{p(n)-k-1}(G(\mathtt{suff}_n(U_{n+1}^{(3)}))) \end{aligned}$$

Thus, the ability to distinguish H_n^k and H_n^{k+1} translates to the ability to distinguish $G_1(U_n^{(2)})$ from $U_{n+1}^{(3)}$: On input $\alpha \in \{0, 1\}^{n+1}$, we uniformly select $r \in \{0, 1\}^k$ and apply the "hybrid distinguisher" to $r \cdot \mathtt{pref}_1(\alpha) \cdot \mathtt{pref}_{p(n)-k-1}(G(\mathtt{suff}_n(\alpha)))$. Details follow.

First let us restate and further justify the equalities stated previously. We start with notation capturing the operator mentioned a few lines earlier. For every $k \in \{0, 1, \ldots, p(n) - 1\}$ and $\alpha \in \{0, 1\}^{n+1}$, let

$$f_{p(n)-k}(\alpha) \stackrel{\text{def}}{=} \mathtt{pref}_1(\alpha) \cdot \mathtt{pref}_{p(n)-k-1}(G(\mathtt{suff}_n(\alpha))) \in \{0, 1\}^{p(n)-k} \qquad (3.8)$$

Claim 3.3.3.1 ($G_1(U_n)$ and U_{n+1} versus H_n^k and H_n^{k+1}):

1. H_n^k is distributed identically to $U_k^{(1)} \cdot f_{p(n)-k}(G_1(U_n^{(2)}))$.

2. H_n^{k+1} is distributed identically to $U_k^{(1)} \cdot f_{p(n)-k}(U_{n+1}^{(3)})$.

Proof: Consider any $x \in \{0, 1\}^n$, and let $\sigma = \mathtt{pref}_1(G_1(x))$ and $y = \mathtt{suff}_n(G_1(x))$ (i.e., $\sigma y = G_1(x)$). Then, by construction of G, we have $G(x) = \sigma \cdot \mathtt{pref}_{p(n)-1}(G(y))$. This justifies Eq. (3.7); that is, $\mathtt{pref}_{j+1}(G(x)) = \mathtt{pref}_1(G_1(x)) \cdot \mathtt{pref}_j(G(\mathtt{suff}_n(G_1(x))))$ for every $j \ge 0$. We now establish the two parts of the claim:

1. Combining the definition of H_n^k and Eq. (3.7), we have

$$\begin{aligned} H_n^k &= U_k^{(1)} \cdot \mathtt{pref}_{(p(n)-k-1)+1}(G(U_n^{(2)})) \\ &= U_k^{(1)} \cdot \mathtt{pref}_1(G_1(U_n^{(2)})) \cdot \mathtt{pref}_{p(n)-k-1}(G(\mathtt{suff}_n(G_1(U_n^{(2)})))) \\ &= U_k^{(1)} \cdot f_{p(n)-k}(G_1(U_n^{(2)})) \end{aligned}$$

which establishes the first part.

_____ **116** _____

2. For the second part, combining the definition of H_n^{k+1} and Eq. (3.7), we have

$$
\begin{aligned}
H_n^{k+1} &= U_{k+1}^{(1)} \cdot \mathtt{pref}_{p(n)-(k+1)}\left(G\left(U_n^{(2)}\right)\right) \\
&\equiv U_k^{(1')} \cdot U_1^{(1'')} \cdot \mathtt{pref}_{p(n)-k-1}\left(G\left(\mathtt{suff}_n\left(U_{n+1}^{(2)}\right)\right)\right) \\
&\equiv U_k^{(1')} \cdot \mathtt{pref}_1\left(U_{n+1}^{(2)}\right) \cdot \mathtt{pref}_{p(n)-k-1}\left(G\left(\mathtt{suff}_n\left(U_{n+1}^{(2)}\right)\right)\right) \\
&= U_k^{(1')} \cdot f_{p(n)-k}\left(U_{n+1}^{(2)}\right)
\end{aligned}
$$

Thus, both parts are established. $\square$

Hence, distinguishing $G_1(U_n)$ from U_{n+1} is reduced to distinguishing the neighboring hybrids (i.e., H_n^k and H_n^{k+1}) by applying $f_{p(n)-k}$ to the input, padding the outcome (in the front) by a uniformly chosen string of length k, and applying the hybrid-distinguisher to the resulting string. Further details follow.

We assume, contrary to the theorem, that G is not a pseudorandom generator. Suppose that D is a probabilistic polynomial-time algorithm such that for some polynomial $q(\cdot)$ and for infinitely many n's, it holds that

$$
\Delta(n) \overset{\text{def}}{=} \left|\Pr[D(G(U_n)) = 1] - \Pr\left[D\left(U_{p(n)}\right) = 1\right]\right| > \frac{1}{q(n)}
$$

We derive a contradiction by constructing a probabilistic polynomial-time algorithm D' that distinguishes $G_1(U_n)$ from U_{n+1}.

Algorithm D' uses algorithm D as a subroutine. On input $\alpha \in \{0, 1\}^{n+1}$, algorithm D' operates as follows. First, D' selects an integer k uniformly in the set $\{0, 1, \ldots, p(n) - 1\}$, next it selects β uniformly in $\{0, 1\}^k$, and finally it halts with output $D(\beta \cdot f_{p(n)-k}(\alpha))$, where $f_{p(n)-k}$ is as defined in Eq. (3.8).

Clearly, D' can be implemented in probabilistic polynomial time (in particular, $f_{p(n)-k}$ is implemented by combining the algorithm for computing G with trivial string operations). It is left to analyze the performance of D' on each of the distributions $G_1(U_n)$ and U_{n+1}.

Claim 3.3.3.2:

$$
\Pr[D'(G_1(U_n)) = 1] = \frac{1}{p(n)} \sum_{k=0}^{p(n)-1} \Pr\left[D\left(H_n^k\right) = 1\right]
$$

and

$$
\Pr[D'(U_{n+1}) = 1] = \frac{1}{p(n)} \sum_{k=0}^{p(n)-1} \Pr\left[D\left(H_n^{k+1}\right) = 1\right]
$$

Proof: By construction of D', we get, for every $\alpha \in \{0, 1\}^{n+1}$,

$$
\Pr[D'(\alpha) = 1] = \frac{1}{p(n)} \sum_{k=0}^{p(n)-1} \Pr\left[D\left(U_k \cdot f_{p(n)-k}(\alpha)\right) = 1\right]
$$

Using Claim 3.3.3.1, our claim follows. $\square$

Let $d^k(n)$ denote the probability that D outputs 1 on input taken from the hybrid H_n^k (i.e., $d^k(n) \stackrel{\text{def}}{=} \Pr[D(H_n^k) = 1]$). Recall that H_n^0 equals $G(U_n)$, whereas $H_n^{p(n)}$ equals $U_{p(n)}$. Hence, $d^0(n) = \Pr[D(G(U_n)) = 1], d^{p(n)}(n) = \Pr[D(U_{p(n)}) = 1]$, and $\Delta(n) = |d^0(n) - d^{p(n)}(n)|$. Combining these facts with Claim 3.3.3.2, we get

$$|\Pr[D'(G_1(U_n)) = 1] - \Pr[D'(U_{n+1}) = 1]|$$

$$= \frac{1}{p(n)} \cdot \left| \left(\sum_{k=0}^{p(n)-1} d^k(n) \right) - \left(\sum_{k=0}^{p(n)-1} d^{k+1}(n) \right) \right|$$

$$= \frac{|d^0(n) - d^{p(n)}(n)|}{p(n)}$$

$$= \frac{\Delta(n)}{p(n)}$$

Recall that by our (contradiction) hypothesis, $\Delta(n) > \frac{1}{q(n)}$ for infinitely many n's. Contradiction to the pseudorandomness of G_1 follows. ∎

3.3.3.* Variable-Output Pseudorandom Generators

Pseudorandom generators, as defined earlier (i.e., in Definition 3.3.1), provide a predetermined amount of expansion. That is, once the generator is fixed and the seed is fixed, the length of the pseudorandom sequence that the generator provides is also determined. A more flexible definition, provided next, allows one to produce a pseudorandom sequence "on the fly." That is, for any fixed seed, an infinite sequence is being defined such that the following two conditions hold:

1. One can produce any prefix of this sequence in time polynomial in the seed and the length of the prefix.

2. For a uniformly chosen n-bit-long seed, any poly(n)-bit prefix of corresponding output sequence is pseudorandom.

In other words:

Definition 3.3.4 (Variable-Output Pseudorandom Generator): A variable-output pseudorandom generator *is a deterministic polynomial-time algorithm G satisfying the following two conditions:*

1. *Variable output: For all $s \in \{0, 1\}^*$ and $t \in \mathbb{N}$, it holds that $|G(s, 1^t)| = t$ and $G(s, 1^t)$ is a prefix of $G(s, 1^{t+1})$.*

2. *Pseudorandomness: For every polynomial p, the ensemble $\{G(U_n, 1^{p(n)})\}_{n \in \mathbb{N}}$ is pseudorandom.*

By a minor modification of Construction 3.3.2, we have the following:

Theorem 3.3.5: *If pseudorandom generators exist, then there exists a variable-output pseudorandom generator.*

In a similar manner, one can modify all constructions presented in Section 3.4 to obtain variable-output pseudorandom generators. In fact, in all constructions one can maintain a hidden state that allows production of the next bit in the sequence in time polynomial in the length of the seed, regardless of the number of bits generated thus far. This leads to the notion of an on-line generator, as defined and studied in Exercise 21.

3.3.4. The Applicability of Pseudorandom Generators

Pseudorandom generators have the remarkable property of being efficient "amplifiers/expanders of randomness." Using very little randomness (in the form of a randomly chosen seed) they produce very long sequences that look random with respect to any efficient observer. Hence, the output of a pseudorandom generator can be used instead of a "truly random sequence" in any efficient application requiring such (i.e., "random") sequences, the reason being that such an application can be viewed as a distinguisher. In other words, if some efficient algorithm suffers non-negligible degradation in performance when replacing the random sequences it uses by a pseudorandom sequence, then this algorithm can be easily modified into a distinguisher that will contradict the pseudorandomness of the latter sequences.

The generality of the notion of a pseudorandom generator is of great importance in practice. Once we are guaranteed that an algorithm is a pseudorandom generator, we can use it in every efficient application requiring "random sequences," without testing the performance of the generator in the specific new application.

The benefits of pseudorandom generators in cryptography are innumerable (and only the most important ones will be presented in the subsequent chapters). The reason that pseudorandom generators are so useful in cryptography is that the implementation of all cryptographic tasks requires a lot of "high-quality randomness." Thus the process of producing, exchanging, and sharing large amounts of "high-quality random bits" at low cost is of primary importance. Pseudorandom generators allow us to produce (resp., exchange and/or share) poly(n) pseudorandom bits at the cost of producing (resp., exchanging and/or sharing) only n random bits!

3.3.5. Pseudorandomness and Unpredictability

A key property of pseudorandom sequences that is used to justify the use of such sequences in some cryptographic applications is the unpredictability of a sequence. Loosely speaking, a sequence is *unpredictable* if no efficient algorithm, given a prefix of the sequence, can guess its next bit with a non-negligible advantage over $\frac{1}{2}$. Namely:

Definition 3.3.6 (Unpredictability): *An ensemble $\{X_n\}_{n\in\mathbb{N}}$ is called **unpredictable in polynomial time** if for every probabilistic polynomial-time algorithm A, every positive polynomial $p(\cdot)$, and all sufficiently large n's,*

$$\Pr\left[A\left(1^{|X_n|}, X_n\right) = \text{next}_A(X_n)\right] < \frac{1}{2} + \frac{1}{p(n)}$$

where $\text{next}_A(x)$ returns the $i + 1$ bit of x if on input $(1^{|x|}, x)$ algorithm A reads *only $i < |x|$ of the bits of x, and returns a uniformly chosen bit otherwise (i.e., in case A reads the entire string x).*

The role of the input $1^{|x|}$ given with x is to allow the algorithm to determine the length of x (and operate in time polynomial in that length) before reading x. In case A reads all of x, it must guess a perfectly random bit and certainly cannot succeed with probability higher than $\frac{1}{2}$. (Alternatively, one may disallow A to read all its input; see Exercise 20.) The interesting case is, of course, when A chooses not to read the entire input, but rather tries to guess the $i + 1$ bit of x based on the first i bits of x. An ensemble is called unpredictable in polynomial time if no probabilistic polynomial-time algorithm can succeed in the latter task with probability non-negligibly higher than $\frac{1}{2}$.

Intuitively, pseudorandom ensembles are unpredictable in polynomial time (since so are all uniform ensembles). It turns out that the converse holds as well. Namely, only pseudorandom ensembles are unpredictable in polynomial time.

Theorem 3.3.7 (Pseudorandomness versus Unpredictability): *An ensemble $\{X_n\}_{n\in\mathbb{N}}$ is pseudorandom if and only if it is unpredictable in polynomial time.*

Proof for the "Only-if" Direction: The proof that pseudorandomness implies unpredictability indeed follows the intuition mentioned earlier. Because the ensemble $X \stackrel{\text{def}}{=} \{X_n\}_{n\in\mathbb{N}}$ is pseudorandom, it is polynomial-time-indistinguishable from some uniform ensemble. Clearly, the uniform ensemble is unpredictable in polynomial time; in fact, it is unpredictable regardless of the time bounds imposed on the predicting algorithm. Thus, the ensemble X must also be polynomial-time-unpredictable, or else we could distinguish the ensemble X from the uniform ensemble in polynomial time (in contradiction to the hypothesis). Details follow.

For simplicity (and without loss of generality), suppose that the ensemble $X = \{X_n\}_{n\in\mathbb{N}}$ satisfies $|X_n| = n$ and thus is polynomial-time-indistinguishable from the standard uniform ensemble $\{U_n\}_{n\in\mathbb{N}}$. Suppose, toward the contradiction, that $\{X_n\}_{n\in\mathbb{N}}$ is predictable in polynomial time by an algorithm A; that is, for some polynomial p and infinitely many n's,

$$\Pr[A(1^n, X_n) = \text{next}_A(X_n)] \geq \frac{1}{2} + \frac{1}{p(n)}$$

Then A can be easily transformed into a distinguisher, denoted D, operating as follows. On input y, the distinguisher invokes A on input $(1^{|y|}, y)$ and records the number of bits that A has actually read, as well as A's prediction for the next bit. In case the prediction is correct, D outputs 1, and otherwise it outputs 0. Clearly,

$$\Pr[D(X_n) = 1] = \Pr[A(1^n, X_n) = \text{next}_A(X_n)]$$
$$\geq \frac{1}{2} + \frac{1}{p(n)}$$

whereas

$$Pr[D(U_n){=}1] = Pr[A(1^n, U_n) = next_A(U_n)]$$
$$\leq \frac{1}{2}$$

Thus, $Pr[D(X_n){=}1] - Pr[D(U_n){=}1] \geq 1/p(n)$, and we reach a contradiction to the hypothesis that $\{X_n\}_{n\in\mathbb{N}}$ is pseudorandom. The "only-if" direction follows. ■

Proof for the "Opposite" Direction: The proof for the opposite direction (i.e., unpredictability implies pseudorandomness) is more complex. In fact, the intuition in this case is less clear. One motivation is provided by the information-theoretic analogue: The only sequence of 0-1 random variables that cannot be predicted (when discarding computational issues) is the one in which the random variables are independent and uniformly distributed over $\{0, 1\}$. In the current case, the computational analogue again holds, but proving it is (again) more complex. The proof combines the use of the hybrid technique and a *special case* of the very statement being proved. Loosely speaking, the special case refers to two ensembles $Y \overset{\text{def}}{=} \{Y_n\}_{n\in\mathbb{N}}$ and $Y' \overset{\text{def}}{=} \{Y'_n\}_{n\in\mathbb{N}}$, where Y'_n is derived from Y_n by omitting the last bit of Y_n. The claim is that if Y' is pseudorandom and Y is unpredictable in polynomial time, then Y is pseudorandom. By this claim, if the i-bit-long prefix of X_n is pseudorandom and the $(i + 1)$-bit-long prefix of X_n is polynomial-time-unpredictable, then the latter is also pseudorandom. We next work this intuition into a rigorous proof.

Suppose, toward the contradiction, that $X = \{X_n\}_{n\in\mathbb{N}}$ is not pseudorandom. Again, for simplicity (and without loss of generality), we assume that $|X_n| = n$. Thus there exists a probabilistic polynomial-time algorithm D that distinguishes X from the standard uniform ensemble $\{U_n\}_{n\in\mathbb{N}}$; that is, for some polynomial p and infinitely many n's,

$$|Pr[D(X_n){=}1] - Pr[D(U_n){=}1]| \geq \frac{1}{p(n)} \tag{3.9}$$

Assume, without loss of generality, that for infinitely many n's,

$$Pr[D(X_n){=}1] - Pr[D(U_n){=}1] \geq \frac{1}{p(n)} \tag{3.10}$$

Justification for the dropping of absolute value: Let S be the infinite set of n's for which Eq. (3.9) holds. Then S must contain either an infinite subset of n's for which $Pr[D(X_n){=}1] - Pr[D(U_n){=}1]$ is positive or an infinite subset for which it is negative. Without loss of generality, we assume that the former holds. Otherwise, we modify D by flipping its output.

For each n satisfying Eq. (3.10), we define $n + 1$ hybrids. The ith hybrid ($i = 0, 1, \ldots, n$), denoted H_n^i, consists of the i-bit-long prefix of X_n followed by the $(n - i)$-bit-long suffix of U_n. The foregoing hypothesis implies that there exists

———— **121** ————

a pair of neighboring hybrids that are polynomial-time-distinguishable. Actually, this holds, on the average, for a "random" pair of neighboring hybrids:

Claim 3.3.7.1: For each n satisfying Eq. (3.10),

$$\frac{1}{n} \cdot \sum_{i=0}^{n-1} \left(\Pr[D(H_n^{i+1}) = 1] - \Pr[D(H_n^i) = 1] \right) \geq \frac{1}{p(n) \cdot n}$$

Proof: The proof is immediate by Eq. (3.10) and the definition of the hybrids. In particular, we use the fact that $H_n^n \equiv X_n$ and $H_n^0 \equiv U_n$. $\square$

Claim 3.3.7.1 suggests a natural algorithm for predicting the next bit of $\{X_n\}_{n \in \mathbb{N}}$. The algorithm, denoted A, selects i uniformly in $\{0, 1, \ldots, n-1\}$, reads i bits from X_n, and invokes D on the n-bit string that results by concatenating these i bits with $n - i$ uniformly chosen bits. If D responds with 1, then A's prediction is set to the value of the first among these $n - i$ random bits; otherwise it is set to the complementary value. The reasoning is as follows. If the first among the $n - i$ random bits happens to equal the $i + 1$ bit of X_n, then A is invoked on input distributed identically to H_n^{i+1}. On the other hand, if the first among the $n - i$ random bits happens to equal the complementary value (of the $i + 1$ bit of X_n), then A is invoked on input distributed identically to a distribution Z that is even more clearly distinguishable from H_n^{i+1} than is H_n^i (i.e., H_n^i equals Z with probability $\frac{1}{2}$, and H_n^{i+1} otherwise). Details follow.

We start with a more precise description of algorithm A. On input 1^n and $x = x_1 \cdots x_n$, algorithm A proceeds as follows:

1. Select i uniformly in $\{0, 1, \ldots, n-1\}$.

2. Select $r_{i+1}, \ldots, r_n$ independently and uniformly in $\{0, 1\}$.

3. If $D(x_1 \cdots x_i r_{i+1} \cdots r_n) = 1$, then output r_{i+1}, and otherwise output $1 - r_{i+1}$.

Claim 3.3.7.2: For each n satisfying Eq. (3.10),

$$\Pr[A(1^n, X_n) = \text{next}_A(X_n)] \geq \frac{1}{2} + \frac{1}{p(n) \cdot n}$$

Proof: Let us denote by X^j the jth bit of X_n, and by $R^{i+1}, \ldots, R^n$ a sequence of $n - i$ independent random variables each uniformly distributed over $\{0, 1\}$. Using the definition of A and the fact that $\Pr[X^{i+1} = R^{i+1}] = \frac{1}{2}$, we have

$$s_A(n) \stackrel{\text{def}}{=} \Pr[A(1^n, X_n) = \text{next}_A(X_n)]$$

$$= \frac{1}{n} \cdot \sum_{i=0}^{n-1} (\Pr[D(X^1 \cdots X^i R^{i+1} \cdots R^n) = 1 \ \& \ R^{i+1} = X^{i+1}]$$

$$+ \Pr[D(X^1 \cdots X^i R^{i+1} \cdots R^n) = 0 \ \& \ 1 - R^{i+1} = X^{i+1}])$$

$$= \frac{1}{2n} \cdot \sum_{i=0}^{n-1} (\Pr[D(X^1 \cdots X^i X^{i+1} R^{i+2} \cdots R^n) = 1]$$

$$+ 1 - \Pr[D(X^1 \cdots X^i \overline{X}^{i+1} R^{i+2} \cdots R^n) = 1])$$

—— **122** ——

where $\overline{X}^{i+1} \overset{\text{def}}{=} 1 - X^{i+1}$. Using the fact that H_n^i is distributed identically to the distribution obtained by taking $H_n^{i+1} = X^1 \cdots X^i X^{i+1} R^{i+2} \cdots R^n$ with probability $\frac{1}{2}$, and $Z \overset{\text{def}}{=} X^1 \cdots X^i \overline{X}^{i+1} R^{i+2} \cdots R^n$ otherwise, we obtain

$$\Pr[D(H_n^i)=1] = \frac{\Pr[D(H_n^{i+1})=1] + \Pr[D(Z)=1]}{2}$$

which implies $\Pr[D(Z)=1] = 2\Pr[D(H_n^i)=1] - \Pr[D(H_n^{i+1})=1]$. Thus, using Claim 3.3.7.1 in the last step, we get

$$
\begin{aligned}
s_A(n) &= \frac{1}{2} + \frac{1}{2n} \cdot \sum_{i=0}^{n-1} \left(\Pr[D(H_n^{i+1})=1] - \Pr[D(Z)=1] \right) \\
&= \frac{1}{2} + \frac{1}{2n} \cdot \sum_{i=0}^{n-1} \left(\Pr[D(H_n^{i+1})=1] \right. \\
&\qquad \left. - \left(2\Pr[D(H_n^i)=1] - \Pr[D(H_n^{i+1})=1] \right) \right) \\
&= \frac{1}{2} + \frac{1}{n} \cdot \sum_{i=0}^{n-1} \left(\Pr[D(H_n^{i+1})=1] - \Pr[D(H_n^i)=1] \right) \\
&\geq \frac{1}{2} + \frac{1}{p(n) \cdot n}
\end{aligned}
$$

and the claim follows. $\square$

Because A is a probabilistic polynomial-time algorithm, Claim 3.3.7.2 contradicts the hypothesis that $\{X_n\}_{n \in \mathbb{N}}$ is polynomial-time-unpredictable, and so the opposite direction of the theorem also follows. ∎

Comment. Unfolding the argument for the "opposite direction," we note that all the hybrids considered in it are in fact polynomial-time-indistinguishable, and hence they are all pseudorandom. The argument actually shows that if the i-bit prefix of H_n^{i+1} is pseudorandom and the $(i + 1)$-bit prefix of H_n^{i+1} is unpredictable (which is the same as saying that H_n^{i+1} is unpredictable), then the $(i + 1)$-bit prefix of H_n^{i+1} is pseudorandom. This coincides with the motivating discussion presented at the beginning of the proof for the "opposite direction."

3.3.6. Pseudorandom Generators Imply One-Way Functions

Up to this point we have avoided the question of whether or not pseudorandom generators exist at all. Before saying anything positive, we remark that a necessary condition to the existence of pseudorandom generators is the existence of one-way function. Jumping ahead, we mention that this necessary condition is also sufficient: Hence, pseudorandom generators exist if and only if one-way functions exist. At this point we shall prove only that the existence of pseudorandom generators implies the existence of one-way function. Namely:

Proposition 3.3.8: *Let G be a pseudorandom generator with expansion factor $l(n) = 2n$. Then the function $f : \{0, 1\}^* \to \{0, 1\}^*$ defined by letting $f(x, y) \overset{\text{def}}{=} G(x)$, for every $|x| = |y|$ is a strongly one-way function.*

Proof: Clearly, f is polynomial-time-computable. It is left to show that each probabilistic polynomial-time algorithm can invert f with only negligible success probability. We use a reducibility argument. Suppose, on the contrary, that A is a probabilistic polynomial-time algorithm that for infinitely many n's inverts f on $f(U_{2n})$ with success probability at least $\frac{1}{\text{poly}(n)}$. We shall construct a probabilistic polynomial-time algorithm D that distinguishes U_{2n} and $G(U_n)$ on these n's, reaching a contradiction.

The distinguisher D uses the inverting algorithm A as a subroutine. On input $\alpha \in \{0, 1\}^*$, algorithm D uses A in order to try to get a pre-image of α under f. Algorithm D then checks whether or not the string it obtained from A is indeed a pre-image and halts outputting 1 in case it is (otherwise it outputs 0). Namely, algorithm D computes $\beta \leftarrow A(\alpha)$ and outputs 1 if $f(\beta) = \alpha$, and 0 otherwise (i.e., $D(\alpha) = 1$ iff $f(A(\alpha)) = \alpha$).

By our hypothesis, for some polynomial $p(\cdot)$ and infinitely many n's,

$$\Pr[f(A(f(U_{2n}))) = f(U_{2n})] > \frac{1}{p(n)}$$

By f's construction, the random variable $f(U_{2n})$ equals $G(U_n)$, and therefore $\Pr[D(G(U_n)) = 1] = \Pr[f(A(G(U_n))) = G(U_n)] > \frac{1}{p(n)}$. On the other hand, by f's construction, at most 2^n different $2n$-bit-long strings (i.e., those in the support of $G(U_n)$) have pre-images under f. Hence, $\Pr[D(U_{2n}) = 1] = \Pr[f(A(U_{2n})) = U_{2n}] \leq 2^{-n}$. It follows that for infinitely many n's,

$$\Pr[D(G(U_n)) = 1] - \Pr[D(U_{2n}) = 1] > \frac{1}{p(n)} - \frac{1}{2^n} > \frac{1}{2p(n)}$$

which contradicts the pseudorandomness of G. ∎

3.4. Constructions Based on One-Way Permutations

In this section we present constructions of pseudorandom generators based on one-way permutations. The first construction has a more abstract flavor, as it uses a single length-preserving 1-1 one-way function (i.e., a single one-way permutation). The second construction utilizes the same underlying ideas to present pseudorandom generators based on collections of one-way permutations.

3.4.1. Construction Based on a Single Permutation

We provide two alternative presentations of the same pseudorandom generator. In the first presentation, we provide a pseudorandom generator expanding n-bit-long seeds into $(n + 1)$-bit-long strings, which combined with Construction 3.3.2 yields a pseudorandom generator expanding n-bit-long seeds into $p(n)$-bit-long strings for every polynomial p. The alternative construction is obtained by unfolding this combination. The resulting construction is appealing per se, and more importantly it serves as a good warm-up for the construction of pseudorandom generators based on collections of one-way permutations (presented in Section 3.4.2).

3.4.1.1. The Preferred Presentation

By Theorem 3.3.3 (in Section 3.3.2), it suffices to present a pseudorandom generator expanding n-bit-long seeds into $(n + 1)$-bit-long strings. Assuming that one-way permutations (i.e., 1-1 length-preserving functions) exist, such pseudorandom generators can be constructed easily. We remind the reader that the existence of a one-way permutation implies the existence of a one-way permutation with a corresponding hard-core predicate (see Theorem 2.5.2). Thus, it suffices to prove the following, where $x \cdot y$ denotes the concatenation of the strings x and y.

> **Theorem 3.4.1:** *Let f be a length-preserving 1-1 (strongly one-way) function, and let b be a hard-core predicate for f. Then the algorithm G, defined by $G(s) \stackrel{\text{def}}{=} f(s) \cdot b(s)$, is a pseudorandom generator.*

Clearly, G is polynomial-time-computable, and $|G(s)| = |f(s)| + |b(s)| = |s| + 1$. Intuitively, the ensemble $\{f(U_n) \cdot b(U_n)\}_{n \in \mathbb{N}}$ is pseudorandom, because otherwise $b(U_n)$ could be efficiently predicted from $f(U_n)$ (in contradiction to the hypothesis). The proof merely formalizes this intuition.

Actually, we present two alternative proofs. The first proof invokes Theorem 3.3.7 (which asserts that polynomial-time unpredictability implies pseudorandomness) and thus is confined to show that the ensemble $\{G(U_n)\}_{n \in \mathbb{N}}$ is unpredictable in polynomial time. The second proof directly establishes the pseudorandomness of the ensemble $\{G(U_n)\}_{n \in \mathbb{N}}$, but does so by using one of the ideas that appeared in the proof of Theorem 3.3.7.

> **First Proof of Theorem 3.4.1:** By Theorem 3.3.7 (specifically, the fact that polynomial-time unpredictability implies pseudorandomness), it suffices to show that the ensemble $\{G(U_n) = f(U_n) \cdot b(U_n)\}_{n \in \mathbb{N}}$ is unpredictable in polynomial time.
>
> Because f is 1-1 and length-preserving, the random variable $f(U_n)$ is uniformly distributed in $\{0, 1\}^n$. Thus, none of the first n bits in $f(U_n) \cdot b(U_n)$ can be predicted better than with probability $\frac{1}{2}$, regardless of computation time (since these bits are independently and uniformly distributed in $\{0, 1\}$). What can be predicted (and actually determined) in exponential time is the $n + 1$ bit of $f(U_n) \cdot b(U_n)$ (i.e., the bit $b(U_n)$). However, by the hypothesis that b is a hard-core of f, this bit (i.e., $b(U_n)$) cannot be predicted from the n-bit prefix (i.e., $f(U_n)$) in polynomial time. A more rigorous argument follows.
>
> We use a reducibility argument. Suppose, contrary to our claim, that there exists an efficient algorithm A that on input $(1^{n+1}, G(U_n))$ reads a prefix of $G(U_n)$ and

predicts the next bit, denoted $\text{next}_A(G(U_n))$, with probability that is non-negligibly higher than $\frac{1}{2}$. That is, for some positive polynomial p and infinitely many n's,

$$\Pr[A(1^{n+1}, G(U_n)) = \text{next}_A(G(U_n))] > \frac{1}{2} + \frac{1}{p(n)} \tag{3.11}$$

We first claim that, without loss of generality, algorithm A always tries to guess the last (i.e., $n + 1$) bit of $G(U_n)$. This is justified by observing that the success probability for any algorithm in guessing any other bit of $G(U_n)$ is bounded above by $\frac{1}{2}$. On the other hand, a success probability of $\frac{1}{2}$ in guessing any bit (and in particular the last bit of $G(U_n)$) can be easily achieved by a random unbiased coin toss.

Rigorous justification of the preceding claim: Given an algorithm A as before, we consider a modified algorithm A' that operates as follows. On input $(1^{n+1}, \alpha)$, where $\alpha \in \{0, 1\}^{n+1}$, algorithm A' emulates the execution of A, while always reading the first n bits of α and never reading the last bit of α. In the course of the emulation, exactly one of the following three cases will arise:

1. In case A tries to predict one of the first n bits of α, algorithm A' outputs a uniformly selected bit.

2. In case A tries to predict the last bit of α, algorithm A' outputs the prediction obtained from A.

3. In case A tries to read all bits of α, algorithm A' outputs a uniformly selected bit. (We stress that A' never reads the last bit of α.)

Note that the success probability for A in Cases 1 and 3 is at most $\frac{1}{2}$ (and is exactly $\frac{1}{2}$ if A outputs a bit). The actions taken by A' in these cases guarantee success probability of $\frac{1}{2}$ (in guessing the last bit of α). Thus, the success probability for A' is no less than that for A. (In the rest of the argument, we identify A' with A.)

Next, we use algorithm A to predict $b(U_n)$ from $f(U_n)$. Recall that $G(x) = f(x) \cdot b(x)$, where $x \in \{0, 1\}^n$. Thus, by the foregoing claim, on input $(1^{n+1}, f(x) \cdot b(x))$, algorithm A always tries to guess $b(x)$ after reading $f(x)$ (and without ever reading $b(x)$). Thus, A is actually predicting $b(U_n)$ from $f(U_n)$. Again, a minor modification is required in order to make the last statement rigorous: We consider an algorithm A'' that on input $y = f(x)$, where $x \in \{0, 1\}^n$, invokes A on input $(1^{n+1}, y \, 0)$ and outputs whatever A does. Because A never reads the last bit of its input, its actions are independent of the value of that bit (i.e., $A(1^{n+1}, y0) \equiv A(1^{n+1}, y1)$). Combining this fact with the fact that A always tries to predict the last bit of its input (and thus $\text{next}_A(y \cdot \sigma) = \sigma$), we get

$$\Pr[A''(f(U_n)) = b(U_n)] = \Pr[A(1^{n+1}, f(U_n) \cdot 0) = b(U_n)]$$
$$= \Pr[A(1^{n+1}, f(U_n) \cdot b(U_n)) = b(U_n)]$$
$$= \Pr[A(1^{n+1}, f(U_n) \cdot b(U_n)) = \text{next}_A(f(U_n) \cdot b(U_n))]$$

Combining this with Eq. (3.11), we obtain $\Pr[A''(f(U_n)) = b(U_n)] \geq \frac{1}{2} + \frac{1}{p(n)}$ for infinitely many n's, in contradiction to the hypothesis that b is a hard-core of f. The theorem follows. ∎

Second Proof of Theorem 3.4.1: Recall that $G(U_n) = f(U_n) \cdot b(U_n)$ and that our goal is to prove that the ensembles $\{G(U_n)\}_{n \in \mathbb{N}}$ and $\{U_{n+1}\}_{n \in \mathbb{N}}$ are polynomial-time-indistinguishable. We first note that the n-bit-long prefix of $f(U_n) \cdot b(U_n)$ is uniformly distributed in $\{0, 1\}^n$. Thus, letting $\overline{b}(x) \overset{\text{def}}{=} 1 - b(x)$, all that we need to prove is that the ensembles $E^{(1)} \overset{\text{def}}{=} \{f(U_n) \cdot b(U_n)\}_{n \in \mathbb{N}}$ and $E^{(2)} \overset{\text{def}}{=} \{f(U_n) \cdot \overline{b}(U_n)\}_{n \in \mathbb{N}}$ are polynomial-time-indistinguishable (since $\{U_{n+1}\}_{n \in \mathbb{N}}$ is distributed identically to the ensemble obtained by taking $E^{(1)}$ with probability $\frac{1}{2}$, and $E^{(2)}$ otherwise).

Further justification of the foregoing claim: First, note that $E^{(1)}$ is identical to $\{G(U_n)\}_{n \in \mathbb{N}}$. Next note that $\{U_{n+1}\}_{n \in \mathbb{N}}$ is distributed identically to the ensemble $\{f(U_n) \cdot U_1\}_{n \in \mathbb{N}}$, where U_n and U_1 are independently random variables. Thinking of U_1 as being uniformly distributed in $\{b(U_n), \overline{b}(U_n)\}$, we observe that $f(U_n) \cdot U_1$ is distributed identically to the distribution obtained by taking $E_n^{(1)} \overset{\text{def}}{=} f(U_n) \cdot b(U_n)$ with probability $\frac{1}{2}$, and $E_n^{(2)} \overset{\text{def}}{=} f(U_n) \cdot \overline{b}(U_n)$ otherwise. Thus, for every algorithm D,

$$\Pr[D(U_{n+1}) = 1] = \Pr[D(f(U_n) \cdot U_1) = 1]$$
$$= \frac{1}{2} \cdot \Pr\left[D\left(E_n^{(1)}\right) = 1\right] + \frac{1}{2} \cdot \Pr\left[D\left(E_n^{(2)}\right) = 1\right]$$

It follows that

$$\Pr[D(G(U_n)) = 1] - \Pr[D(U_{n+1}) = 1]$$
$$= \Pr\left[D\left(E_n^{(1)}\right) = 1\right] - \left(\frac{1}{2} \cdot \Pr\left[D\left(E_n^{(1)}\right) = 1\right] + \frac{1}{2} \cdot \Pr\left[D\left(E_n^{(2)}\right) = 1\right]\right)$$
$$= \frac{1}{2} \cdot \left(\Pr\left[D\left(E_n^{(1)}\right) = 1\right] - \Pr\left[D\left(E_n^{(2)}\right) = 1\right]\right)$$

Thus, in order to show that an algorithm D does not distinguish the ensembles $\{G(U_n)\}_{n \in \mathbb{N}}$ and $\{U_{n+1}\}_{n \in \mathbb{N}}$, it suffices to show that D does not distinguish the ensembles $E^{(1)}$ and $E^{(2)}$.

We now prove that the ensembles $E^{(1)} = \{f(U_n) \cdot b(U_n)\}_{n \in \mathbb{N}}$ and $E^{(2)} = \{f(U_n) \cdot \overline{b}(U_n)\}_{n \in \mathbb{N}}$ are polynomial-time-indistinguishable. We do so by simplifying the argument presented in the proof of Theorem 3.3.7. That is, using any algorithm (denoted D) that distinguishes $E^{(1)}$ and $E^{(2)}$, we construct a predictor (denoted A) of $b(U_n)$ based on $f(U_n)$. We assume, to the contradiction and without loss of generality, that for some polynomial p and infinitely many n's,

$$\Pr[D(f(U_n) \cdot b(U_n)) = 1] - \Pr[D(f(U_n) \cdot \overline{b}(U_n)) = 1] > \frac{1}{p(n)} \qquad (3.12)$$

Using D as a subroutine, we construct an algorithm A as follows. On input of $y = f(x)$, algorithm A proceeds as follows:

1. Select σ uniformly in $\{0, 1\}$.

2. If $D(y \cdot \sigma) = 1$, then output σ, and otherwise output $1 - \sigma$.

Then, letting U_1 be independent of U_n (where U_1 represents the choice of σ in Step 1 of algorithm A), we have

$$\Pr[A(f(U_n)) = b(U_n)]$$
$$= \Pr[D(f(U_n) \cdot U_1) = 1 \ \& \ U_1 = b(U_n)]$$
$$\quad + \Pr[D(f(U_n) \cdot U_1) = 0 \ \& \ 1 - U_1 = b(U_n)]$$
$$= \Pr[D(f(U_n) \cdot b(U_n)) = 1 \ \& \ U_1 = b(U_n)]$$
$$\quad + \Pr[D(f(U_n) \cdot \overline{b}(U_n)) = 0 \ \& \ U_1 = \overline{b}(U_n)]$$
$$= \frac{1}{2} \cdot \Pr[D(f(U_n) \cdot b(U_n)) = 1] + \frac{1}{2} \cdot (1 - \Pr[D(f(U_n) \cdot \overline{b}(U_n)) = 1])$$
$$= \frac{1}{2} + \frac{1}{2} \cdot (\Pr[D(f(U_n) \cdot b(U_n)) = 1] - \Pr[D(f(U_n) \cdot \overline{b}(U_n)) = 1])$$
$$> \frac{1}{2} + \frac{1}{2p(n)}$$

where the inequality is due to Eq. (3.12.) But this contradicts the theorem's hypothesis by which b is a hard-core of f. ∎

3.4.1.2. An Alternative Presentation

Combining Theorems 3.3.3 and 3.4.1, we obtain, for any polynomial stretch function p, a pseudorandom generator stretching n-bit-long seeds into $p(n)$-bit-long pseudorandom sequences. Unfolding this combination we get the following construction:

Construction 3.4.2: *Let $f : \{0, 1\}^* \to \{0, 1\}^*$ be a 1-1 length-preserving and polynomial-time-computable function. Let $b : \{0, 1\}^* \to \{0, 1\}$ be a polynomial-time-computable predicate, and let $p(\cdot)$ be an arbitrary polynomial satisfying $p(n) > n$. Define $G(s) = \sigma_1 \cdots \sigma_{p(|s|)}$, where $s_0 \stackrel{\text{def}}{=} s$, and for every $1 \le j \le p(|s|)$ it holds that $\sigma_j = b(s_{j-1})$ and $s_j = f(s_{j-1})$. That is,*

> *Let $s_0 = s$ and $n = |s|$.*
> *For $j = 1$ to $p(n)$, do*
>
> $\quad \sigma_j \gets b(s_{j-1})$ *and* $s_j \gets f(s_{j-1})$.
>
> *Output $\sigma_1 \sigma_2 \cdots \sigma_{p(n)}$.*

The construction is depicted in Figure 3.4. Note that σ_j is easily computed from s_{j-1}, but if b is a hard-core of f, then $\sigma_j = b(s_{j-1})$ is "hard to approximate" from $s_j = f(s_{j-1})$. The pseudorandomness property of algorithm G depends on the fact that G does not output the intermediate s_j's. (By examining the following proof, the reader can easily verify that outputting the last element, namely, $s_{p(n)}$, does not hurt the pseudorandomness property; cf. Proposition 3.4.6.)

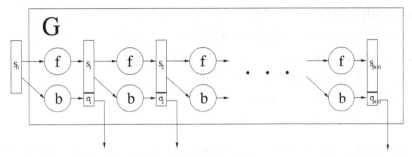

Figure 3.4: Construction 3.4.2, as operating on seed $s_0 \in \{0, 1\}^n$.

Proposition 3.4.3: *Let f, b, and G be as in Construction 3.4.2. If b is a hard-core of f, then G is a pseudorandom generator.*

Proof: Consider the generator G' obtained by reversing the order of the bits in the output of G. That is, if $G(s) = \sigma_1 \sigma_2 \cdots \sigma_{p(|s|)}$, then $G'(s) = \sigma_{p(|s|)} \cdots \sigma_2 \sigma_1$. We first observe that the ensemble $\{G(U_n)\}_{n \in \mathbb{N}}$ is pseudorandom if and only if the ensemble $\{G'(U_n)\}_{n \in \mathbb{N}}$ is pseudorandom. Using Theorem 3.3.7, it suffices to show that the ensemble $\{G'(U_n)\}_{n \in \mathbb{N}}$ is unpredictable in polynomial time. This is shown by generalizing the argument used in the first proof of Theorem 3.4.1. Toward this goal, it is instructive to notice that

$$G'(s) = b\left(f^{p(|s|)-1}(s)\right) \cdot b\left(f^{p(|s|)-2}(s)\right) \cdots b(s)$$

where $f^0(s) = s$ and $f^{i+1}(s) = f^i(f(s))$. That is, the jth bit in $G'(s)$, which equals the $p(|s|) - j + 1$ bit in $G(s)$, equals $b(f^{p(|s|)-j}(s))$.

Intuitively, the proof of unpredictability proceeds as follows. Suppose, toward the contradiction, that for some $j < t \stackrel{\text{def}}{=} p(n)$, given the j-bit-long prefix of $G'(U_n)$, an algorithm A' can predict the $j + 1$ bit of $G'(U_n)$. That is, given $b(f^{t-1}(s)) \cdots b(f^{t-j}(s))$, algorithm A' predicts $b(f^{t-(j+1)}(s))$, where s is uniformly distributed in $\{0, 1\}^n$. Then for x uniformly distributed in $\{0, 1\}^n$, given $y = f(x)$, one can predict $b(x)$ by invoking A' on input $b(f^{j-1}(y)) \cdots b(y) = b(f^j(x)) \cdots b(f(x))$, which in turn is polynomial-time-computable from $y = f(x)$. In the analysis, we use the hypothesis that f induces a permutation over $\{0, 1\}^n$, and we associate x with $f^{t-(j+1)}(s)$. Details follow.

Suppose, toward the contradiction, that there exists a probabilistic polynomial-time algorithm A' and a polynomial p' such that for infinitely many n's,

$$\Pr\left[A'(1^{p(n)}, G'(U_n)) = \text{next}_{A'}(G'(U_n))\right] > \frac{1}{2} + \frac{1}{p'(n)} \tag{3.13}$$

Then we derive a contradiction by constructing an algorithm A'' that, given $f(U_n)$, predicts $b(U_n)$ with probability that is non-negligibly higher than $\frac{1}{2}$. Algorithm A'' operates as follows, on input $y \in \{0, 1\}^n$, where $t \stackrel{\text{def}}{=} p(n)$:

1. Uniformly select $j \in \{0, \ldots, t - 1\}$.
2. Compute $\alpha \leftarrow b(f^{j-1}(y)) \cdots b(y)$. (Note that $|\alpha| = j$.)

3. Uniformly select $\beta \in \{0, 1\}^{t-j}$.

4. Invoke A' on input $(1^t, \alpha\beta)$ and record the following values:

    (a) in variable ℓ, the length of the prefix of $\alpha\beta$ read by A',

    (b) in variable τ, the output of A'.

5. If $\ell = j$, then halt with output τ.

6. Otherwise (i.e., $\ell \neq j$), output a uniformly selected bit.

Clearly, A'' is implementable in probabilistic polynomial time. We now analyze the success probability of A'' in predicting $b(U_n)$ when given $f(U_n)$. A key observation is that on input $f(U_n)$, for each possible value assigned to j in Step 1 the value of α (as determined in Step 2 of A') is distributed identically to the j-bit-long prefix of the distribution $G'(U_n)$. This is due to the fact that f induces a permutation over $\{0, 1\}^n$, and so $b(f^{j-1}(U_n)) \cdots b(U_n)$ is distributed identically to $b(f^{t-1}(U_n)) \cdots b(f^{t-j}(U_n))$. We use the following notations and observations:

- Let R_j be a randomized process that, given y, outputs $b(f^{j-1}(y)) \cdots b(y) \cdot r$, where r is uniformly distributed in $\{0, 1\}^{t-j}$.

  Note that on input y, after selecting j in Step 1, algorithm A'' invokes A' on input $(1^t, R_j(y))$. By the foregoing ("key") observation, the j-bit-long prefix of $R_j(f(U_n))$ is distributed identically to the j-bit-long prefix of $G'(U_n)$. Also note that $b(f^{j-1}(f(U_n))) \cdots b(f(U_n)) \cdot b(U_n)$ is distributed identically to the $(j+1)$-bit-long prefix of $G'(U_n)$ and that the former is obtained by concatenating the j-bit-long prefix of $R_j(f(U_n))$ with $b(U_n)$.

- Let $L_{A'}(\gamma)$ be a random variable representing the length of the prefix of $\gamma \in \{0, 1\}^t$ read by A' on input $(1^t, \gamma)$.

  Note that the behavior of A' on input $(1^t, \gamma)$ depends only on the $L_{A'}(\gamma)$ first bits of γ (and is independent of the $t - L_{A'}(\gamma)$ last bits of γ). On the other hand, $\text{next}_{A'}(\gamma)$ equals the $L_{A'}(\gamma) + 1$ bit of γ.

- Let J be a random variable representing the random choice made in Step 1, and let U_1 represent the random choice made in Step 6. Recall that U_1 is uniformly distributed in $\{0, 1\}$, independently of anything else.

  Note that if $L_{A'}(\gamma) = J$, then A'' outputs the value $A'(1^t, \gamma)$, and otherwise A'' outputs U_1.

Using all the foregoing, we get

$$\Pr[A''(f(U_n)) = b(U_n)]$$
$$= \Pr[A'(1^t, R_J(f(U_n))) = b(U_n) \ \& \ L_{A'}(R_J(f(U_n))) = J]$$
$$+ \Pr[U_1 = b(U_n) \ \& \ L_{A'}(R_J(f(U_n))) \neq J]$$
$$= \Pr[A'(1^t, G'(U_n)) = \text{next}_{A'}(G'(U_n)) \ \& \ J = L_{A'}(G'(U_n))]$$
$$+ \Pr[J \neq L_{A'}(G'(U_n))] \cdot \frac{1}{2}$$

where we use the fact that when $L_{A'}(R_J(f(U_n))) = J$, the behavior of A' depends only on the J-bit-long prefix of $R_J(f(U_n))$, which in turn is distributed identically to the J-bit-long prefix of $G'(U_n)$. Next, we use the following additional observations:

- The event $A'(1^t, G'(U_n)) = \text{next}_{A'}(G'(U_n))$ is independent of J. Thus,

$$\Pr[A'(1^t, G'(U_n)) = \text{next}_{A'}(G'(U_n)) \ \& \ J = L_{A'}(G'(U_n))]$$
$$= \Pr[J = L_{A'}(G'(U_n))] \cdot \Pr[A'(1^t, G'(U_n)) = \text{next}_{A'}(G'(U_n))]$$

- We can assume, without loss of generality, that A' never reads its entire input (because the success probability of an arbitrary A' can be easily met by a modified A' that does not read its last input bit; see Exercise 20). It follows that $L_{A'}(G'(U_n)) \in \{0, \ldots, t-1\}$, and so $\Pr[J = L_{A'}(G'(U_n))] = \frac{1}{t}$.

Combining all the preceding with Eq. (3.13) (and $t = p(n)$), we get

$$\Pr[A''(f(U_n)) = b(U_n)] = \frac{1}{t} \cdot \Pr[A'(1^t, G'(U_n)) = \text{next}_{A'}(G'(U_n))] + \frac{t-1}{t} \cdot \frac{1}{2}$$
$$\geq \frac{1}{p(n)} \cdot \left(\frac{1}{2} + \frac{1}{p'(n)}\right) + \left(1 - \frac{1}{p(n)}\right) \cdot \frac{1}{2}$$
$$= \frac{1}{2} + \frac{1}{p(n) \cdot p'(n)}$$

for infinitely many n's, in contradiction to the hypothesis that b is a hard-core of f. $\blacksquare$

3.4.2. Construction Based on Collections of Permutations

We now apply the ideas underlying Construction 3.4.2 in order to present constructions of pseudorandom generators based on collections of one-way permutations. The following generic construction is readily instantiated using popular candidate collections of one-way permutations; see details following the abstract presentation.

3.4.2.1. An Abstract Presentation

Let (I, D, F) be a triplet of algorithms defining a collection of one-way permutations (see Section 2.4.2) such that $D(i)$ is uniformly distributed over the domain of f_i for every i in the range of I. Let q be a polynomial bounding the number of coins used by algorithms I and D (as a function of the input length).[1] For $r \in \{0, 1\}^{q(n)}$, let us denote by $I(1^n, r) \in \{0, 1\}^n$ the output of algorithm I on input 1^n and coin tosses r. Likewise, $D(i, s)$ denotes the output of algorithm D on input i and coin tosses $s \in \{0, 1\}^{q(n)}$. We remind the reader that Theorem 2.5.2 (existence of hard-core predicates) applies also to collections of one-way permutations.

> **Construction 3.4.4:** *Let (I, D, F) be a triplet of algorithms defining a collection of one-way permutations, and let B be a hard-core predicate for this collection. Let $p(\cdot)$ be an arbitrary polynomial. For $n \in \mathbb{N}$ and $r, s \in \{0, 1\}^{q(n)}$, define $G(r, s) =$*

---

[1] In many cases, the polynomial q is actually linear. In fact, one can modify any collection of one-way permutations so that $q(n) = n$; see Exercise 19 in Chapter 2.

$\sigma_1 \cdots \sigma_{p(n)}$, where $i \overset{\text{def}}{=} I(1^n, r)$, $s_0 \overset{\text{def}}{=} D(i, s)$, and for every $1 \leq j \leq p(|s|)$ it holds that $\sigma_j = B(i, s_{j-1})$ and $s_j = f_i(s_{j-1})$. That is, on input a seed $(r, s) \in \{0, 1\}^{q(n)} \times \{0, 1\}^{q(n)}$, algorithm G operates as follows, where $F(i, x) = f_i(x)$:

Set $i \leftarrow I(1^n, r)$ and $s_0 \leftarrow D(i, s)$.

For $j = 1$ to $p(n)$, do

$\sigma_j \leftarrow B(i, s_{j-1})$ and $s_j \leftarrow F(i, s_{j-1})$.

Output $\sigma_1 \sigma_2 \cdots \sigma_{p(n)}$.

On input seed (r, s), algorithm G first uses r to determine a permutation f_i over D_i (i.e., $i \leftarrow I(1^n, r)$). Second, algorithm G uses s to determine a "starting point" s_0 uniformly distributed in D_i. The essential part of algorithm G is the repeated application of the function f_i to the starting point s_0 and the outputting of a hard-core predicate for each resulting element. This part mimics Construction 3.4.2, while replacing the single permutation f with the permutation f_i determined earlier. The expansion property of algorithm G depends on the choice of the polynomial $p(\cdot)$. Namely, the polynomial $p(\cdot)$ should be larger than twice the polynomial $q(\cdot)$.

Theorem 3.4.5: *Let (I, D, F), B, $q(\cdot)$, $p(\cdot)$, and G be as in Construction 3.4.4, and suppose that $p(n) > 2q(n)$ for all n's. Further suppose that for every i in the range of algorithm I, the random variable $D(i)$ is uniformly distributed over the set D_i. Then G is a pseudorandom generator.*

Theorem 3.4.5 is an immediate corollary of the following proposition.

Proposition 3.4.6: *Let n and t be integers. For every i in the range of $I(1^n)$ and every x in D_i, define*

$$G_i^t(x) = B(i, x) \cdot B(i, f_i(x)) \cdots B(i, f_i^{t-1}(x))$$

where $f_i^0(x) = x$ and $f_i^{j+1}(x) = f_i^j(f_i(x))$ for any $j \geq 0$. Let (I, D, F) and B be as in Theorem 3.4.5, with I_n a random variable representing $I(1^n)$ and $X_n = D(I_n)$ a random variable uniformly distributed in D_{I_n}. Then for every polynomial $p(\cdot)$, the ensembles

$$\left\{ \left(I_n, G_{I_n}^{p(n)}(X_n), f_{I_n}^{p(n)}(X_n) \right) \right\}_{n \in \mathbb{N}} \quad \text{and} \quad \left\{ \left(I_n, U_{p(n)}, f_{I_n}^{p(n)}(X_n) \right) \right\}_{n \in \mathbb{N}}$$

are polynomial-time-indistinguishable.

Hence the distinguishing algorithm gets, in addition to the $p(n)$-bit-long sequence to be examined, the index i chosen by G (in the first step of G's computation) and the last domain element (i.e., $f_i^{p(n)}(X_n)$) computed by G. Even with this extra information it is infeasible to distinguish $G_{I_n}^{p(n)}(X_n) \equiv G(U_{2q(n)})$ from $U_{p(n)}$. We note that providing the distinguishing algorithm with $f_i^{p(n)}(X_n)$ only makes the proposition stronger and that this stronger form is not required for proving Theorem 3.4.5. However, the stronger form will be used in Chapter 5.

Proof Outline: The proof is analogous to the proof of Proposition 3.4.3. Specifically, we let $\bar{G}_i^t(x) = B(i, f_i^{t-1}(x)) \cdots B(i, x)$ (the reverse of $G_i^t(x)$) and prove
that even when given I_n and $f_{I_n}^{p(n)}(X_n)$ as auxiliary inputs, the sequence
$\bar{G}_{I_n}^{p(n)}(X_n)$ is unpredictable in polynomial time. This is done by a reducibility
argument: An algorithm predicting the next bit of $\bar{G}_{I_n}^{p(n)}(X_n)$, given also I_n and
$f_{I_n}^{p(n)}(X_n)$, is used to construct an algorithm for predicting $B(I_n, X_n)$ from I_n and
$f_{I_n}(X_n)$, which contradicts the hypothesis by which B is a hard-core predicate
for the collection (I, D, F). The extra hypothesis by which $D(i)$ is uniformly
distributed over D_i is used in order to establish that the distributions $D(i)$ and
$f_i^j(D(i))$ are identical[2] for every $j < t$. The reader should be able to complete
the argument. ∎

Generalization. Proposition 3.4.6 and Theorem 3.4.5 remain valid even if one relaxes
the condition concerning the distribution of $D(i)$ and requires only that $D(i)$ be sta-
tistically close (as a function in $|i|$) to the uniform distribution over D_i. Similarly, one
can relax the condition regarding I so that the foregoing holds for all but a negligible
measure of the i's generated by $I(1^n)$ (rather than for all such i's).

3.4.2.2. Concrete Instantiations

As an immediate application of Construction 3.4.4, we derive pseudorandom generators
based on either of the following assumptions:

- *The intractability of the discrete-logarithm problem*: Specifically, we assume that the
  DLP collection, as presented in Section 2.4.3, is one-way. The generator is based on the
  fact that, under the foregoing assumption, the following problem is intractable: Given a
  prime P, a primitive element G in the multiplicative group mod P, and an element Y
  in this group, guess whether or not there exists $0 \le x \le P/2$ such that $Y \equiv G^x$ mod P.
  In other words, the latter predicate, denoted B_P, constitutes a hard-core for the DLP
  collection.

  The generator uses the seed in order to select a prime P, a primitive element G
  in the multiplicative group mod P, and an element Y of the group. It outputs the
  sequence

$$B_P(Y), B_P(G^Y \bmod P), B_P\left(G^{G^Y \bmod P} \bmod P\right), \ldots$$

  That is, the function being iterated is $Z \mapsto G^Z \bmod P$.

- *The difficulty of inverting RSA*: Specifically, we assume that the RSA collection, as presented in Section 2.4.3, is one-way. The generator is based on the fact that under this
  assumption, the least significant bit (denoted lsb) constitutes a hard-core for the RSA
  collection.

  The generator uses the seed in order to select a pair of primes (P, Q), an integer
  e relatively prime to $\phi(N) = (P - 1) \cdot (Q - 1)$, and an element X in the multiplicative

---

[2] We comment that weaker hypotheses can in fact suffice for that purpose. Alternatively, one can postulate that
the function f_i is hard to invert on the distribution $f_i^j(D(i))$ for every $j < t$.

group mod $N \stackrel{\text{def}}{=} P \cdot Q$. It outputs the sequence

$$\text{lsb}(X), \text{lsb}(X^e \bmod N), \text{lsb}(X^{e^2 \bmod \phi(N)} \bmod N), \text{lsb}(X^{e^3 \bmod \phi(N)} \bmod N), \ldots$$

That is, the function being iterated is $Z \mapsto Z^e \bmod N$.

- *The intractability of factoring Blum integers*: Specifically, we assume that given a product of two large primes, each congruent to 3 (mod 4), it is infeasible to retrieve these primes. The generator is based on the fact that (under this assumption) the least significant bit constitutes a hard-core predicate for the modular squaring function. We also use the fact that for such moduli (called Blum integers), modular squaring induces a permutation over the quadratic residues.

  The generator uses the seed in order to select a pair of primes (P, Q), each congruent to 3 (mod 4), and an element X in the multiplicative group mod $N \stackrel{\text{def}}{=} P \cdot Q$. It outputs the sequence

$$\text{lsb}(X), \text{lsb}(X^2 \bmod N), \text{lsb}(X^{2^2 \bmod \phi(N)} \bmod N), \text{lsb}(X^{2^3 \bmod \phi(N)} \bmod N), \ldots$$

  That is, the function being iterated is $Z \mapsto Z^2 \bmod N$.

All these suggestions rely on a randomized algorithm for selecting random primes. Thus, regarding the random bits such an algorithm uses, the fewer the better. Obvious algorithms for generating n-bit-long random primes utilize $O(n^3)$ random bits (see Appendix A). We comment that there are procedures that are more randomness-efficient for generating an n-bit-long prime, utilizing only $O(n)$ random bits.

3.4.3.* Using Hard-Core Functions Rather than Predicates

Construction 3.4.2 (resp., Construction 3.4.4) can be easily generalized to one-way permutations (resp., collections of one-way permutations) having hard-core functions, rather than hard-core predicates. The advantage in such constructions is that the number of bits output by the generator per each application of the one-way permutation is larger (i.e., greater than 1). We assume familiarity with Section 2.5.3, where hard-core functions are defined. Next, we present only the generalization of Construction 3.4.4.

Construction 3.4.7: *Let (I, D, F) be as in Construction 3.4.4, and suppose that H is a corresponding hard-core function. Let $p(\cdot)$ be an arbitrary polynomial. For $n \in \mathbb{N}$ and $r, s \in \{0, 1\}^{q(n)}$, define $G(r, s) = \alpha_1 \cdots \alpha_{p(n)}$, where $i \stackrel{\text{def}}{=} I(1^n, r)$, $s_0 \stackrel{\text{def}}{=} D(i, s)$, and for every $1 \leq j \leq p(|s|)$ it holds that $\alpha_j = H(i, s_{j-1})$ and $s_j = f_i(s_{j-1})$.*

For a hard-core function H, we denote by $\ell_H(n)$ the logarithm to base 2 of the size of the range of $H(i, \cdot)$ for i produced by $I(1^n)$. Any hard-core predicate can be viewed as a hard-core function H with $\ell_H(n) = 1$. Recall that any one-way function can be modified to have a hard-core function H with $\ell_H(n) = O(\log n)$ (see Theorem 2.5.6). Also, assuming that the RSA collection is one-way, the $O(\log n)$ least significant bits constitute a hard-core function (with $\ell_H(n) = O(\log n)$). The same holds for the Rabin collection.

Theorem 3.4.8: *Let (I, D, F), H, $q(\cdot)$, $p(\cdot)$, and G be as in Construction 3.4.7, and suppose that $p(n) \cdot \ell_H(n) > 2q(n)$ for all n's. Further suppose that for every i in the range of algorithm I, the random variable $D(i)$ is uniformly distributed over the set D_i. Then G is a pseudorandom generator.*

The proof, which is via a natural generalization of the proof of Theorem 3.4.5, is omitted. Again, the theorem holds even if the distinguishing algorithm gets, in addition to the $p(n) \cdot \ell_H(n)$-bit-long sequence to be examined, the index i chosen by G (in the first step of G's computation) and the last domain element (i.e., $f_i^{p(n)}(s_0)$) computed by G. Even with this extra information it is infeasible to distinguish between $G(U_{2q(n)})$ and $U_{p(n) \cdot \ell_H(n)}$.

The generator of Construction 3.4.7 outputs $\ell_H(n)$ bits per each application of the one-way collection, where H is the corresponding hard-core function. Thus, if one could prove the existence of a hard-core function H with $\ell_H(n) = \Omega(n)$ for the Rabin collection, then a very efficient pseudorandom generator would follow (producing $\Omega(n)$ bits per each modular squaring with respect to an n-bit modulus).

3.5.* Constructions Based on One-Way Functions

It is known that one-way functions exist if and only if pseudorandom generators exist. However, the currently known construction, which transforms arbitrary one-way functions into pseudorandom generators, is impractical. Furthermore, the proof that this construction indeed yields pseudorandom generators is very complex and unsuitable for a book of this nature. Instead, we confine ourselves to a presentation of some of the ideas underlying this construction, as well as some partial results. (We believe that these ideas may be useful elsewhere.)

3.5.1. Using 1-1 One-Way Functions

Recall that if f is a 1-1 length-preserving one-way function and b is a corresponding hard-core predicate, then $G(s) \overset{\text{def}}{=} f(s) \cdot b(s)$ constitutes a pseudorandom generator, where $x \cdot y$ denotes the concatenation of the strings x and y. Let us relax the condition imposed on f and assume that f is a 1-1 one-way function (but is not necessarily length-preserving). Without loss of generality, we can assume that there exists a polynomial $p(\cdot)$ such that $|f(x)| = p(|x|)$ for all x's. In case f is not length-preserving, it follows that $p(n) > n$. At first glance, one might think that we could only benefit in such a case, because f by itself has an expanding property. But on second thought, one should realize that the benefit is not clear, because the expanded strings may not "look random." In particular, it may be the case that the first bit of $f(x)$ is zero for all x's. Furthermore, it may be the case that the first $|f(x)| - |x|$ bits of $f(x)$ are all zero for all x's. In general, $f(U_n)$ may be easy to distinguish from $U_{p(n)}$ (otherwise f itself would constitute a pseudorandom generator). Hence, in the general case, we need to get rid of the expansion property of f because it is not accompanied by a "pseudorandom" property. In general, we need to shrink $f(U_n)$ back to a length of approximately n so that the shrunk result will induce a uniform distribution. The question is how to *efficiently* carry out this shrinking process.

Suppose that there exists an efficiently computable function h such that $f_h(x) \overset{\text{def}}{=} h(f(x))$ is length-preserving and 1-1. In such a case we can let $G(s) \overset{\text{def}}{=} h(f(s)) \cdot b(s)$, where b is a hard-core predicate for f, and get a pseudorandom generator. The pseudorandomness of G follows from the observation that if b is a hard-core for f, it is also a hard-core for f_h (since an algorithm guessing $b(x)$ from $h(f(x))$ can be easily modified so that it guesses $b(x)$ from $f(x)$, by applying h first). The problem is that we "know nothing about the structure" of f and hence are not guaranteed that such an h exists. An important observation is that a uniformly selected "hashing" function will have approximately the desired properties. Hence, hashing functions play a central role in the construction, and consequently we need to discuss these functions first.

3.5.1.1. Hashing Functions

Let S_n^m be a set of strings representing functions mapping n-bit strings to m-bit strings. For simplicity we assume that $S_n^m = \{0, 1\}^{l(n,m)}$ for some function l. In the sequel, we freely associate the strings in S_n^m with the functions that they represent. Let H_n^m be a random variable uniformly distributed over the set S_n^m. We call S_n^m a *hashing family* (or a *family of hashing functions*) if it satisfies the following three conditions:

1. S_n^m *is a pairwise-independent family of mappings*: For every $x \neq y \in \{0, 1\}^n$, the random variables $H_n^m(x)$ and $H_n^m(y)$ are independent and uniformly distributed in $\{0, 1\}^m$.

2. S_n^m *has succinct representation*: $S_n^m = \{0, 1\}^{\text{poly}(n,m)}$.

3. S_n^m *can be efficiently evaluated*: There exists a polynomial-time algorithm that on input a representation of a function h (in S_n^m) and a string $x \in \{0, 1\}^n$ returns $h(x)$.

We stress that hashing families as defined here carry no hardness requirement and exist independently of any intractability assumption.[3] One widely used hashing family is the set of affine transformations mapping n-dimensional binary vectors to m-dimensional ones (i.e., transformations effected by multiplying the n-dimensional vector by an n-by-m binary matrix and adding an m-dimensional vector to the result). A hashing family with more succinct representation is obtained by considering only the transformations effected by Toeplitz matrices (i.e., matrices that are invariant along the diagonals). For further details, see Exercise 22.

The following lemma concerning hashing functions is central to our analysis (as well as to many applications of hashing functions in complexity theory). Loosely speaking, the lemma asserts that if a random variable X_n does not assign too much probability mass to any single string, then most h's in a hashing family will have $h(X_n)$ distributed almost uniformly. Specifically, when using a hashing family S_n^m, as earlier, we shall consider only random variables X_n satisfying $\Pr[X_n = x] \ll 2^{-m}$, for every $x \in \{0, 1\}^n$.

---

[3] In contrast, notions such as collision-free hashing and universal one-way hashing have a hardness requirement and exist only if one-way functions exist. (Collision-free hashing and universal one-way hashing will be defined and discussed in Chapter 6, which will appear in Volume 2.)

Lemma 3.5.1: *Let $m < n$ be integers, S_n^m be a hashing family, and b and δ be two reals such that $m \le b \le n$ and $\delta \ge 2^{-\frac{b-m}{2}}$. Suppose that X_n is a random variable distributed over $\{0, 1\}^n$ such that for every x, it holds that $\Pr[X_n = x] \le 2^{-b}$. Then for every $\alpha \in \{0, 1\}^m$ and for all but at most a $2^{-(b-m)}\delta^{-2}$ fraction of the h's in S_n^m, it holds that*

$$\Pr[h(X_n) = \alpha] \in (1 \pm \delta) \cdot 2^{-m}$$

The average value of $\Pr[h(X_n) = \alpha]$, when averaging over all h's, equals 2^{-m}. Hence the lemma upper-bounds the fraction of h's that deviate from the average value. Specifically, a function h not satisfying $\Pr[h(X_n) = \alpha] \in (1 \pm \delta) \cdot 2^{-m}$ is called *bad* (for α and the random variable X_n). The lemma asserts that the fraction of bad functions is at most $2^{-(b-m)}\delta^{-2}$. Typically we shall use $\delta \stackrel{\text{def}}{=} 2^{-\frac{b-m}{3}} \ll 1$ (making the deviation from average equal the fraction of bad h's). Another useful choice is $\delta \ge 1$ (which yields an even smaller fraction of bad h's, yet here non-badness implies only that $\Pr[h(X_n) = \alpha] \le (1 + \delta) \cdot 2^{-m}$, since $\Pr[h(X_n) = \alpha] \ge 0$ always holds).

Proof: Fix an arbitrary random variable X_n satisfying the conditions of the lemma and an arbitrary $\alpha \in \{0, 1\}^m$. Denote $w_x \stackrel{\text{def}}{=} \Pr[X_n = x]$. For every h, we have

$$\Pr[h(X_n) = \alpha] = \sum_x w_x \zeta_x(h)$$

where $\zeta_x(h)$ equals 1 if $h(x) = \alpha$, and 0 otherwise. Hence, we are interested in the probability, taken over all possible choices of h, that $|2^{-m} - \sum_x w_x \zeta_x(h)| > \delta 2^{-m}$. Looking at the ζ_x's as random variables defined over the random variable H_n^m, it is left to show that

$$\Pr\left[\left|2^{-m} - \sum_x w_x \zeta_x\right| > \delta \cdot 2^{-m}\right] < \frac{2^{-(b-m)}}{\delta^2}$$

This is proved by applying Chebyshev's inequality, using the following facts:

1. The ζ_x's are pairwise independent, and $\text{Var}(\zeta_x) < 2^{-m}$ (since $\zeta_x = 1$ with probability 2^{-m}, and $\zeta_x = 0$ otherwise).
2. $w_x \le 2^{-b}$ (by the hypothesis), and $\sum_x w_x = 1$.

Namely,

$$\Pr\left[\left|2^{-m} - \sum_x w_x \zeta_x\right| > \delta \cdot 2^{-m}\right] \le \frac{\text{Var}\left[\sum_x w_x \zeta_x\right]}{(\delta \cdot 2^{-m})^2}$$

$$= \frac{\sum_x w_x^2 \cdot \text{Var}(\zeta_x)}{\delta^2 \cdot 2^{-2m}}$$

$$< \frac{2^{-m} 2^{-b}}{\delta^2 \cdot 2^{-2m}}$$

The lemma follows. ∎

3.5.1.2. The Basic Construction

Using any 1-1 one-way function and any hashing family, we can take a major step toward constructing a pseudorandom generator.

Construction 3.5.2: *Let* $f : \{0, 1\}^* \to \{0, 1\}^*$ *be a function satisfying* $|f(x)| = p(|x|)$ *for some polynomial* $p(\cdot)$ *and all x's. For any integer function* $l : \mathbb{N} \to \mathbb{N}$, *let* $g : \{0, 1\}^* \to \{0, 1\}^*$ *be a function satisfying* $|g(x)| = l(|x|) + 1$, *and let* $S_{p(n)}^{n-l(n)}$ *be a hashing family. For every* $x \in \{0, 1\}^n$ *and* $h \in S_{p(n)}^{n-l(n)}$, *define*

$$G(x, h) \stackrel{\text{def}}{=} (h(f(x)), h, g(x))$$

Clearly, $|G(x, h)| = (|x| - l(|x|)) + |h| + (l(|x|) + 1) = |x| + |h| + 1$. Thus, G satisfies the expanding requirement. The next proposition provides an upper bound on the distinguishability between the output of G and a uniform ensemble (alas, this upper bound is negligible only if $l : \mathbb{N} \to \mathbb{N}$ is super-logarithmic).

Proposition 3.5.3: *Let* f, l, g, *and* G *be as before. Suppose that* f *is 1-1 and that* g *is a hard-core function of* f. *Then for every probabilistic polynomial-time algorithm* A, *every positive polynomial* $p(\cdot)$, *and all sufficiently large n's,*

$$|\Pr[A(G(U_n, U_k)) = 1] - \Pr[A(U_{n+k+1}) = 1]| < 2 \cdot 2^{-\frac{l(n)}{3}} + \frac{1}{p(n)}$$

where k *is the length of the representation of the hashing functions in* $S_{p(n)}^{n-l(n)}$.

Recall that by Exercises 22 and 23 we can use $k = O(n)$. In particular, the foregoing proposition holds for functions $l(\cdot)$ of the form $l(n) \stackrel{\text{def}}{=} c \log_2 n$, where $c > 0$ is a constant. For such functions l, every one-way function (can be easily modified into a function that) has a hard-core g as required in the proposition's hypothesis (see Section 2.5.3). Hence, we get very close to constructing a pseudorandom generator (see later).

Proof Sketch: Let $H_{p(n)}^{n-l(n)}$ denote a random variable uniformly distributed over $S_{p(n)}^{n-l(n)}$. We first note that

$$G(U_{n+k}) \equiv \left(H_{p(n)}^{n-l(n)}(f(U_n)), H_{p(n)}^{n-l(n)}, g(U_n) \right)$$
$$U_{n+k+1} \equiv \left(U_{n-l(n)}, H_{p(n)}^{n-l(n)}, U_{l(n)+1} \right)$$

We consider the hybrid distribution $(H_{p(n)}^{n-l(n)}(f(U_n)), H_{p(n)}^{n-l(n)}, U_{l(n)+1})$. The proposition is a direct consequence of the following two claims.

Claim 3.5.3.1: The ensembles

$$\left\{ \left(H_{p(n)}^{n-l(n)}(f(U_n)), H_{p(n)}^{n-l(n)}, g(U_n) \right) \right\}_{n \in \mathbb{N}}$$

and

$$\left\{\left(H_{p(n)}^{n-l(n)}(f(U_n)),\ H_{p(n)}^{n-l(n)},\ U_{l(n)+1}\right)\right\}_{n\in\mathbb{N}}$$

are polynomial-time-indistinguishable.

Proof Idea: Use a reducibility argument. If the claim does not hold, then contradiction of the hypothesis that g is a hard-core of f is derived. Specifically, given an algorithm D that violates the claim, we construct an algorithm D' that, on input (y, z), uniformly selects $h \in S_{p(n)}^{n-l(n)}$ and outputs $D(h(y), h, z)$. Then D' distinguishes between $\{(f(U_n), g(U_n))\}_{n\in\mathbb{N}}$ and $\{(f(U_n), U_{l(n)+1})\}_{n\in\mathbb{N}}$. $\square$

Claim 3.5.3.2: The statistical difference between the random variables

$$\left(H_{p(n)}^{n-l(n)}(f(U_n)),\ H_{p(n)}^{n-l(n)},\ U_{l(n)+1}\right)$$

and

$$\left(U_{n-l(n)},\ H_{p(n)}^{n-l(n)},\ U_{l(n)+1}\right)$$

is bounded by $2 \cdot 2^{-l(n)/3}$.

Proof Idea: Use the hypothesis that $S_{p(n)}^{n-l(n)}$ is a hashing family, and apply Lemma 3.5.1. Specifically, use $\delta = 2^{-l(n)/3}$, note that $\Pr[f(U_n)=y] \le 2^{-n}$ for every y, and count separately the contributions of bad and non-bad h's to the statistical difference between $(H_{p(n)}^{n-l(n)}(f(U_n)),\ H_{p(n)}^{n-l(n)})$ and $(U_{n-l(n)},\ H_{p(n)}^{n-l(n)})$. $\square$

Because the statistical difference is a bound on the ability of algorithms to distinguish, the proposition follows. ∎

Extension. Proposition 3.5.3 can be extended to the case in which the function f is polynomial-to-1 (instead of 1-to-1). Specifically, let f satisfy $|f^{-1}(f(x))| < q(|x|)$ for some polynomial $q(\cdot)$ and all sufficiently long x's. The modified proposition asserts that *for every probabilistic polynomial-time algorithm A, every polynomial $p(\cdot)$, and all sufficiently large n's,*

$$\left|\Pr[A(G(U_n, U_k)) = 1] - \Pr[A(U_{n+k+1}) = 1]\right| < 2 \cdot 2^{-\frac{l(n)-\log_2 q(n)}{3}} + \frac{1}{p(n)}$$

where k is as in Proposition 3.5.3.

3.5.1.3. Obtaining Pseudorandom Generators

With Proposition 3.5.3 proved, we consider the possibility of applying it in order to construct pseudorandom generators. We stress that applying Proposition 3.5.3 with length function $l(\cdot)$ requires having a hard-core function g for f, with $|g(x)| = l(|x|)+1$. By Theorem 2.5.6 (in Section 2.5.3), such hard-core functions exist essentially for all one-way functions, provided that $l(\cdot)$ is logarithmic. (Actually, Theorem 2.5.6 asserts that such hard-cores exist for a modification of any one-way function, where the modified function preserves the 1-1 property of the original function.) Hence, combining

Theorem 2.5.6 and Proposition 3.5.3 and using a logarithmic length function, we get very close to constructing a pseudorandom generator. In particular, for every polynomial $p(\cdot)$, using $l(n) \stackrel{\text{def}}{=} 3\log_2 p(n)$, we can construct a deterministic polynomial-time algorithm expanding $O(n)$-bit-long seeds into $(O(n)+1)$-bit-long strings such that no polynomial-time algorithm can distinguish the output strings from uniformly chosen ones with probability greater than $\frac{1}{p(n)}$ (except for finitely many n's). Yet this does not imply that the output is pseudorandom (i.e., that the distinguishing gap is smaller than *any* polynomial fraction). An additional idea is needed (because we cannot use $l(\cdot)$ larger than any logarithmic function). In the sequel, we shall present two alternative ways of obtaining a pseudorandom generator from Construction 3.5.2.

The First Alternative. As a prelude to the actual construction, we use Construction 3.3.2 (in Section 3.3.2) in order to increase the expansion factors for the algorithms arising from Construction 3.5.2. In particular, for every $i \in \mathbb{N}$, we construct a deterministic polynomial-time algorithm, denoted G_i, expanding n-bit-long seeds into n^3-bit-long strings such that no polynomial-time algorithm can distinguish the output strings from uniformly chosen ones with probability greater than $\frac{1}{n^i}$ (except for finitely many n's). Denote these algorithms by $G_1, G_2, \ldots$. We now construct a pseudorandom generator G by letting

$$G(s) \stackrel{\text{def}}{=} G_1(s_1) \oplus G_2(s_2) \oplus \cdots \oplus G_{m(|s|)}\big(s_{m(|s|)}\big)$$

where $\oplus$ denotes bit-by-bit XOR of strings, $s_1 s_2 \cdots s_{m(|s|)} = s$, $|s_i| = \frac{|s|}{m(|s|)} \pm 1$, and $m(n) \stackrel{\text{def}}{=} \sqrt[3]{n}$.[4] Clearly, $|G(s)| \approx (\frac{|s|}{m(|s|)})^3 = |s|^2$. The pseudorandomness of G follows by a reducibility argument. Specifically, if for some i and infinitely many n's, some polynomial-time algorithm can distinguish $G(U_n)$ from U_{n^2} with probability greater than $\frac{1}{n^{2i/3}}$, then we can distinguish $G_i(U_{n/m(n)})$ from $U_{(n/m(n))^3}$ (in polynomial time) with probability greater than $\frac{1}{n^{2i/3}} = \frac{1}{(n/m(n))^i}$, in contradiction to the hypothesis regarding G_i.

The Second Alternative. Here we apply Construction 3.5.2 to the function $\overline{f}$ defined by

$$\overline{f}(x_1, \ldots, x_n) \stackrel{\text{def}}{=} f(x_1) \cdots f(x_n)$$

where $|x_1| = \cdots = |x_n| = n$. The benefit in applying Construction 3.5.2 to the function $\overline{f}$ is that we can use $l(n^2) \stackrel{\text{def}}{=} n - 1$, and hence Proposition 3.5.3 indicates that G is a pseudorandom generator. All that is left is to show that $\overline{f}$ has a hard-core function that maps n^2-bit strings into n-bit strings. Assuming that b is a hard-core predicate of the function f, we can construct such a hard-core function for $\overline{f}$. Specifically:

Construction 3.5.4: *Let $f : \{0,1\}^* \to \{0,1\}^*$ and $b : \{0,1\}^* \to \{0,1\}$. Define*

$$\overline{f}(x_1, \ldots, x_n) \stackrel{\text{def}}{=} f(x_1) \cdots f(x_n)$$
$$\overline{g}(x_1, \ldots, x_n) \stackrel{\text{def}}{=} b(x_1) \cdots b(x_n)$$

where $|x_1| = \cdots = |x_n| = n$.

---

[4] The choice of the function $m : \mathbb{N} \to \mathbb{N}$ is rather arbitrary; any unbounded function $m : \mathbb{N} \to \mathbb{N}$ satisfying $m(n) < n^{2/3}$ will do.

Proposition 3.5.5: *Let f and b be as in Construction 3.5.4. If b is a hard-core predicate of f, then $\overline{g}$ is a hard-core function of $\overline{f}$.*

Proof Idea: Use the hybrid technique. The ith hybrid is

$$\left(f(U_n^{(1)}), \ldots, f(U_n^{(n)}), b(U_n^{(1)}), \ldots, b(U_n^{(i)}), U_1^{(i+1)}, \ldots, U_1^{(n)}\right)$$

Indeed, the nth hybrid equals $(\overline{f}(U_{n^2}), \overline{g}(U_{n^2}))$, whereas the 0th hybrid equals $(\overline{f}(U_{n^2}), U_n)$. Next, show how to transform an algorithm that distinguishes neighboring hybrids into one predicting $b(U_n)$ from $f(U_n)$. Specifically, this transformation is analogous to a construction used in the proof of the "opposite direction" for Theorem 3.3.7 and in the second proof of Theorem 3.4.1. ∎

Conclusion. Using either of the preceding two alternatives, we get the following:

Theorem 3.5.6: *If there exist 1-1 one-way functions, then pseudorandom generators exist as well.*

The entire argument can be extended to the case in which the function f is polynomial-to-1 (instead of 1-to-1). Specifically, let f satisfy $|f^{-1}f(x)| < q(|x|)$ for some polynomial $q(\cdot)$ and all sufficiently long x's. We claim that if f is one-way, then (either of the preceding alternatives yields that) pseudorandom generators exist. Proving the latter statement using the first alternative is quite straightforward, given the extension of Proposition 3.5.3 (stated at the end of Section 3.5.1.2). For proving the statement using the second alternative, apply Construction 3.5.2 to the function $\overline{f}$, with $l(n^2) \stackrel{\text{def}}{=} n - 1 + n \cdot \log_2 q(n)$. This requires showing that $\overline{f}$ has a hard-core function that maps n^2-bit strings into $(n \cdot (1 + \log_2 q(n)))$-bit strings. Assuming that g is a hard-core function of the function f, with $|g(x)| = 1 + \log_2 q(|x|)$, we can construct such a hard-core function for $\overline{f}$. Specifically,

$$\overline{g}(x_1, \ldots, x_n) \stackrel{\text{def}}{=} g(x_1) \cdots g(x_n)$$

where $|x_1| = \cdots = |x_n| = n$.

3.5.2. Using Regular One-Way Functions

The validity of Proposition 3.5.3 relies heavily on the fact that if f is 1-1, then $f(U_n)$ maintains the "entropy" of U_n in a strong sense (i.e., $\Pr[f(U_n) = \alpha] \leq 2^{-n}$ for every α). In this case, it is possible to shrink $f(U_n)$ (to $n - l(n)$ bits) and get almost uniform distribution over $\{0, 1\}^{n-l(n)}$. As stressed earlier, the condition can be relaxed to requiring that f be polynomial-to-1 (instead of 1-to-1). In such a case, only logarithmic loss of "entropy" occurs, and such a loss can be compensated by an appropriate increase in the range of the hard-core function. We stress that hard-core functions of logarithmic length (i.e., satisfying $|g(x)| = O(\log |x|)$) can be constructed for any one-way function. However, in general, the function f may not be polynomial-to-1, and in particular it can map exponentially many pre-images to the same image. If that is the case, then applying f to U_n will yield a great loss in "entropy" that cannot be compensated by using the foregoing methods. For example, if $f(x, y) \stackrel{\text{def}}{=} f'(x)0^{|y|}$ for $|x| = |y|$ then $\Pr[f(U_n) = \alpha] \geq 2^{-\frac{|\alpha|}{2}}$ for some α's. In this case, achieving uniform distribution from $f(U_n)$ requires shrinking it to length approximately $n/2$. In general, we cannot compensate for these lost bits (using the foregoing methods), because f may not have a hard-core with such a huge range (i.e., a hard-core g satisfying $|g(\alpha)| > \frac{|\alpha|}{2}$). Hence, in this case, a new idea is needed and indeed is presented next.

The idea is that in case f maps different pre-images into the same image y, we can augment y by the index of the pre-image in the set $f^{-1}(y)$, *without damaging the hardness-to-invert of f*. Namely, we define $F(x) \stackrel{\text{def}}{=} f(x) \cdot \text{idx}_f(x)$, where $\text{idx}_f(x)$ denotes the index (say by lexicographic order) of x in the set $\{x' : f(x') = f(x)\}$. We claim that inverting F is not substantially easier than inverting f. This claim can be proved by a reducibility argument. Given an algorithm for inverting F, we can invert f as follows. On input y (supposedly in the range of $f(U_n)$), we first select m uniformly in $\{1, \ldots, n\}$, next select i uniformly in $\{1, \ldots, 2^m\}$, and finally try to invert F on (y, i). When analyzing this algorithm, consider the case $i = \lceil \log_2 |f^{-1}(y)| \rceil$.

The suggested function F *does preserve the hardness-to-invert of f*. The problem is that F *does not preserve the easy-to-compute property of f*. In particular, for general f, it is not clear how to compute $\text{idx}_f(x)$; the best we can say is that this task can be performed in exponential time (and polynomial *space*). Again, hashing functions come to the rescue. Suppose, for example, that f is 2^m-to-1 on strings of length n. Then we can let $\text{idx}_f(x) = (H_n^m, H_n^m(x))$, obtaining "probabilistic indexing" of the set of pre-images. We stress that applying this idea requires having a good estimate for the size of the set of pre-images (of a given image). That is, given x, it should be easy to compute $|f^{-1}(f(x))|$. A simple case where such an estimate is handy is the case of regular functions.

Definition 3.5.7 (Regular Functions): *A function $f : \{0, 1\}^* \to \{0, 1\}^*$ is called* **regular** *if there exists an integer function $m : \mathbb{N} \to \mathbb{N}$ such that for all sufficiently long $x \in \{0, 1\}^*$, it holds that*

$$|\{y : f(x) = f(y) \wedge |x| = |y|\}| = 2^{m(|x|)}$$

For simplicity, the reader can further assume that there exists an algorithm that on input n computes $m(n)$ in poly(n) time. As we shall see at the end of this subsection, one can do without this assumption. For the sake of simplicity (of notation), we assume in the sequel that if $f(x) = f(y)$, then $|x| = |y|$.

Construction 3.5.8: *Let $f : \{0, 1\}^* \to \{0, 1\}^*$ be a regular function, with $m(|x|) = \log_2 |f^{-1}(f(x))|$ for some integer function $m(\cdot)$. Let $l : \mathbb{N} \to \mathbb{N}$ be an integer function, and $S_n^{m(n)-l(n)}$ a hashing family. For every $x \in \{0, 1\}^n$ and $h \in S_n^{m(n)-l(n)}$, define*

$$F(x, h) \stackrel{\text{def}}{=} (f(x), h(x), h)$$

If f can be computed in polynomial time and $m(n)$ can be computed from n in poly(n) time, then F can be computed in polynomial time. We now show that if f is a regular

——— 142 ———

one-way function, then F is "hard to invert." Furthermore, if $l(\cdot)$ is logarithmic, then F is "almost 1-1."

Proposition 3.5.9: *Let f, m, l, and F be as in Construction 3.5.8. Suppose that there exists an algorithm that on input n computes $m(n)$ in $\mathrm{poly}(n)$ time. Then:*

1. *F is "almost" 1-1:*

$$\Pr\left[\left|F^{-1}F\left(U_n, H_n^{m(n)-l(n)}\right)\right| > 2^{l(n)+1}\right] < O\left(n \cdot 2^{-l(n)/4}\right)$$

(Recall that H_n^k denotes a random variable uniformly distributed over S_n^k.)

2. *F "preserves" the one-wayness of f:*
   If f is strongly (resp., weakly) one-way, then so is F.

Proof Sketch: Part 1 is proved by applying Lemma 3.5.1, using the hypothesis that $S_n^{m(n)-l(n)}$ is a hashing family. Specifically, Lemma 3.5.1 implies that for every α and all but a $2^{-l(n)}$ fraction of $h \in S_n^{m(n)-l(n)}$, it holds that $\Pr[h(U_n) = \alpha] \leq 2^{-m(n)+l(n)+1}$. Thus, for every α, it holds that $\Pr[|F^{-1}(\alpha, H_n^{m(n)-l(n)})| > 2^{l(n)+1}] < 2^{-l(n)}$. Letting $B \overset{\text{def}}{=} \{(\alpha, h) : |F^{-1}(\alpha, h)| > 2^{l(n)+1}\}$, we have $\Pr[(U_{m(n)-l(n)}, H_n^{m(n)-l(n)}) \in B] < 2^{-l(n)}$. Using Claim 3.5.9.1 (given later), it follows that $\Pr[(H_n^{m(n)-l(n)}(U_n), H_n^{m(n)-l(n)}) \in B] < O(m(n) \cdot 2^{-l(n)})^{1/4}$, as required in Part 1.

Part 2 is proved using a reducibility argument. Assuming, to the contradiction, that there exists an efficient algorithm A that inverts F with unallowable success probability, we construct an efficient algorithm A' that inverts f with unallowable success probability (reaching contradiction). For the sake of concreteness, we consider the case in which f is strongly one-way and assume, to the contradiction, that algorithm A inverts F on $F(U_n, H_n^{m(n)-l(n)})$ with success probability $\varepsilon(n)$, such that $\varepsilon(n) > \frac{1}{\mathrm{poly}(n)}$ for infinitely many n's. Following is a description of A'.

On input y (supposedly in the range of $f(U_n)$), algorithm A' selects uniformly $h \in S_n^{m(n)-l(n)}$ and $\alpha \in \{0, 1\}^{m(n)-l(n)}$ and initiates A on input (y, α, h). Algorithm A' sets x to be the n-bit-long prefix of $A(y, \alpha, h)$ and outputs x.

Clearly, algorithm A' runs in polynomial time. We now evaluate the success probability of A'. For every possible input y to algorithm A', we consider a random variable X_n uniformly distributed in $f^{-1}(y)$ (i.e., $\Pr[X_n = \alpha] = 2^{-m(n)}$ if $\alpha \in f^{-1}(y)$, and $\Pr[X_n = \alpha] = 0$ otherwise). Let $\delta(y)$ denote the success probability of algorithm A on input $(y, H_n^k(X_n), H_n^k)$, where $n \overset{\text{def}}{=} |y|$ and $k \overset{\text{def}}{=} m(n) - l(n)$. That is,

$$\delta(y) \overset{\text{def}}{=} \Pr\left[A\left(y, H_n^k(X_n), H_n^k\right) \in F^{-1}\left(y, H_n^k(X_n), H_n^k\right)\right] \tag{3.14}$$

By the contradiction hypothesis (and the definition of $\delta(y)$), it holds that $\mathrm{E}[\delta(f(U_n))] = \varepsilon(n)$, and $\Pr[\delta(f(U_n)) > \frac{\varepsilon(n)}{2}] > \frac{\varepsilon(n)}{2}$ follows. We fix an arbitrary $y \in \{0, 1\}^n$ such that $\delta(y) > \frac{\varepsilon(n)}{2}$. We prove the following technical claim.

Claim 3.5.9.1: Let $k \leq n$ be natural numbers, and let $X_n \in \{0, 1\}^n$ be a random variable satisfying $\Pr[X_n = x] \leq 2^{-k}$ for all $x \in \{0, 1\}^n$. Suppose that B is a set of pairs, and

$$\delta \stackrel{\text{def}}{=} \Pr\left[\left(H_n^k(X_n), H_n^k\right) \in B\right]$$

Then

$$\Pr\left[(U_k, H_n^k) \in B\right] > \frac{\delta^4}{O(k)}$$

Using the definition of A' and applying Claim 3.5.9.1 to Eq. (3.14), it follows that the probability that A' inverts f on y equals

$$\Pr\left[A\left(y, U_k, H_n^k\right) \in F^{-1}\left(y, U_k, H_n^k\right)\right] > \frac{\delta(y)^4}{O(k)} > \frac{\delta(y)^4}{O(n)} \tag{3.15}$$

Thus,

$$\Pr[A'(f(U_n)) \in f^{-1}(f(U_n))]$$
$$\geq \Pr\left[\delta(f(U_n)) > \frac{\varepsilon(n)}{2}\right] \cdot \Pr\left[A'(f(U_n)) \in f^{-1}(f(U_n)) \,\middle|\, \delta(f(U_n)) > \frac{\varepsilon(n)}{2}\right]$$
$$> \frac{\varepsilon(n)}{2} \cdot \frac{(\varepsilon(y)/2)^4}{O(n)}$$

We reach a contradiction (to the hypothesis that f is strongly one-way), and the proposition follows.[5] All that is left is to prove Claim 3.5.9.1. The proof, which follows, is rather technical. ∎

We stress that the fact that $m(n)$ can be computed from n does not play an essential role in the reducibility argument (as it is possible to try all possible values of $m(n)$).

Claim 3.5.9.1 is of interest for its own sake. However, its proof provides no significant insights and can be skipped without significant damage (especially by readers who are more interested in cryptography than in "probabilistic analysis").

Proof of Claim 3.5.9.1: We first use Lemma 3.5.1 to show that only a "tiny" fraction of the hashing functions in S_n^k can map a "large" probability mass into "small" subsets. Once this is done, the claim is proved by dismissing those few bad functions and relating the two probabilities, appearing in the statement of the claim, conditioned on the function not being bad. Details follow.

We begin by bounding the fraction of the hashing functions that map a "large" probability mass into "small" subsets. We say that a function $h \in S_n^k$ is (T, Ψ)-*expanding* if there exists a set $R \subset \{0, 1\}^k$ of cardinality $\Psi \cdot 2^k$ such that $\Pr[h(X_n) \in R] \geq (T + 1) \cdot \Psi$.

---

[5] In case f is weakly one-way, the argument is slightly modified. Specifically, suppose that for some positive polynomial, any probabilistic polynomial-time algorithm that tries to invert f on $f(U_n)$ fails with probability at least $1/p(n)$. We claim that any probabilistic polynomial-time algorithm that tries to invert F on $F(U_n, H_n^k)$ fails with probability at least $1/4p(n)$. Suppose, toward the contradiction, that there exists a probabilistic polynomial-time algorithm that inverts F on $F(U_n, H_n^k)$ with probability at least $1 - \varepsilon(n)$, where $\varepsilon(n) \leq 1/4p(n)$. Then, for $\delta(\cdot)$, as before, it holds that $E[\delta(f(U_n))] = 1 - \varepsilon(n)$, and $\Pr[\delta(f(U_n)) \geq 1 - 2p(n)\varepsilon(n)] \geq 1 - \frac{1}{2p(n)}$ follows. Using $\varepsilon(n) \leq 1/4p(n)$, we infer that for at least a $1 - \frac{1}{2p(n)}$ fraction of the n-bit-long strings x, it holds that $\delta(f(x)) \geq \frac{1}{2}$. Applying Claim 3.5.9.1, it follows that (for these x's) the probability that A' inverts f on $f(x)$ is $\Omega(1/n)$. Considering an algorithm that iterates A' for $O(n^2)$ times, we obtain a probabilistic polynomial-time algorithm that inverts f on $f(U_n)$ with success probability at least $(1 - \frac{1}{2p(n)}) \cdot (1 - 2^{-n}) > 1 - \frac{1}{p(n)}$, in contradiction to our hypothesis concerning f.

That is, h maps to some small set (of density Ψ) a probability mass $T + 1$ times the density of the set (i.e., h maps a relatively large probability mass to this set). Our first goal is to prove that for some constant $c > 0$, at most $\frac{3}{4}$ of the h's are $(\frac{c \cdot k}{\delta^2}, \frac{\delta^3}{3c \cdot k})$-expanding. In other words, only $\frac{3}{4}$ of the functions map to some set of density $\frac{\delta^3}{3c \cdot k}$ a probability mass of more than $(\frac{c \cdot k}{\delta^2} + 1) \cdot \frac{\delta^3}{3c \cdot k} \approx \frac{\delta}{3}$.

We start with a related question. We say that $\alpha \in \{0, 1\}^k$ is t-overweighted by the function h if $\Pr[h(X_n) = \alpha] \geq (t + 1) \cdot 2^{-k}$. A function $h \in S_n^k$ is called (t, ρ)-overweighting if there exists a set $R \subset \{0, 1\}^k$ of cardinality $\rho 2^k$ such that each $\alpha \in R$ is t-overweighted by h. (Clearly, if h is (t, ρ)-overweighting, then it is also (t, ρ)-expanding, but the converse is not necessarily true.) We first show that at most a $\frac{1}{t^2 \rho}$ fraction of the h's are (t, ρ)-overweighting. The proof is in two steps:

1. Recall that $\Pr[X_n = x] \leq 2^{-k}$ for every x. Using Lemma 3.5.1, it follows that each $\alpha \in \{0, 1\}^k$ is t-overweighted by at most a t^{-2} fraction of the h's.

2. Consider a bipartite graph having (t, ρ)-overweighting functions on one side and k-bit-long strings on the other side such that $(h, \alpha) \in S_n^k \times \{0, 1\}^k$ is an edge in this graph if and only if α is t-overweighted by h. In this graph, each of the (t, ρ)-overweighting functions has degree at least $\rho \cdot 2^k$, whereas each image α has degree at most $t^{-2} \cdot |S_n^k|$. Thus, the number of (t, ρ)-overweighting functions is at most $\frac{2^k \cdot (t^{-2} \cdot |S_n^k|)}{\rho \cdot 2^k} = \frac{1}{t^2 \rho} \cdot |S_n^k|$.

We now relate the expansion and overweighting properties, showing that upper bounds on the number of overweighting functions yield upper bounds on the number of expanding functions (which is the non-trivial direction). Specifically, we prove the following:

Subclaim: For $T \geq 4$, if h is (T, Ψ)-expanding, then there exists an integer $i \in \{1, \ldots, k + 2\}$ such that h is $(T \cdot 2^{i-3}, \frac{\Psi}{k \cdot 2^{i+1}})$-overweighting.

The subclaim is proved as follows: Let R be a set of cardinality $\Psi \cdot 2^k$ such that $\Pr[h(X_n) \in R] \geq (T + 1) \cdot \Psi$. For $i = 1, \ldots, k + 3$, let $R_i \subseteq R$ denote the subset of points in R that are $(2^{i-3} \cdot T)$-overweighted by h. (Indeed, $R_{k+3} = \emptyset$.) Suppose, contrary to the claim, that $|R_i| < \frac{\Psi}{k \cdot 2^{i+1}} \cdot 2^k$ for every $i \in \{1, \ldots, k + 2\}$. Then for $T \geq 4$ and $k \geq 1$,

$$\Pr[h(X_n) \in R] = \Pr[h(X_n) \in (R \setminus R_1)] + \Pr\left[h(X_n) \in \bigcup_{i=1}^{k+2}(R_i \setminus R_{i+1})\right]$$

$$\leq \left(\frac{T}{4} + 1\right) \cdot \Psi + \sum_{i=1}^{k+2} (2^{(i+1)-3} \cdot T + 1) \cdot \frac{|R_i \setminus R_{i+1}|}{2^k}$$

$$< \left(\frac{T}{4} + 1\right) \cdot \Psi + \sum_{i=1}^{k+2}(2^{i-2} \cdot T + 1) \cdot \frac{\Psi}{k \cdot 2^{i+1}}$$

$$\leq (T + 1) \cdot \Psi$$

which contradicts the hypothesis regarding R.

Using this subclaim (for any $T \geq 4$ and $\Psi > 0$), the fraction of the h's that are (T, Ψ)-expanding is bounded above by

$$\sum_{i=1}^{k} \frac{1}{(T \cdot 2^{i-3})^2 \cdot \frac{\Psi}{k \cdot 2^{i+1}}} < \frac{128k}{T^2 \cdot \Psi}$$

where the ith term in the sum is an upper bound on the fraction of the h's that are $(T \cdot 2^{i-3}, \frac{\Psi}{k \cdot 2^{i+1}})$-overweighting. For $c = 1536$, setting $T = \frac{ck}{\delta^2}$ and $\Psi = \frac{\delta^3}{3ck}$, we conclude that at most a $\frac{128k}{(ck/\delta^2)^2 \cdot (\delta^3/3ck)} = \frac{\delta}{4}$ fraction of the h's are $(\frac{ck}{\delta^2}, \frac{\delta^3}{3ck})$-expanding.

Having established an upper bound on suitably expanding functions, we now turn to the actual claim. Specifically, we call h *honest* if it is *not* $(\frac{1536k}{\delta^2}, \frac{\delta^3}{4608k})$-expanding. There are two important facts about honest functions:

Fact 1: All but at most a $\frac{\delta}{4}$ fraction of the h's are honest.

Fact 2: If h is honest and $\Pr[h(X_n) \in R] \geq \frac{\delta}{2}$, then $\Pr[U_k \in R] \geq \frac{\delta^3}{4608k}$. (Suppose that h is honest and $\Pr[U_k \in R] \leq \frac{\delta^3}{4608k}$ holds. Then $\Pr[h(X_n) \in R] < (\frac{1536k}{\delta^2} + 1) \cdot \frac{\delta^3}{4608k} = \frac{\delta}{3} + \frac{\delta^3}{4608k} < \frac{\delta}{2}$.)

Concentrating on the honest h's, we now evaluate the probability that (α, h) hits B when α is uniformly chosen. We call h *good* if $\Pr[(h(X_n), h) \in B] \geq \frac{\delta}{2}$. Using the Markov inequality (and the definition of δ), we get the following:

Fact 3: The probability that H_n^k is good is at least $\frac{\delta}{2}$.

Denote by P (for "perfect") the set of h's that are both good and honest. Combining Facts 1 and 3, we have the following:

Fact 4: $\Pr[H_n^k \in P] \geq \frac{\delta}{2} - \frac{\delta}{4} = \frac{\delta}{4}$.

Let $B_h \stackrel{\text{def}}{=} \{\alpha : (\alpha, h) \in B\}$. Clearly, for every $h \in P$ we have $\Pr[h(X_n) \in B_h] \geq \frac{\delta}{2}$ (since h is good), and $\Pr[U_k \in B_h] \geq \frac{\delta^3}{4608k}$ (since h is honest and the hypothesis of Fact 2 applies to B_h). Thus:

Fact 5: For every $h \in P$, it holds that $\Pr[(U_k, h) \in B] \geq \frac{\delta^3}{4608k}$.

Combining Facts 4 and 5, we have

$$\Pr\left[(U_k, H_n^k) \in B\right] \geq \Pr\left[(U_k, H_n^k) \in B \mid H_n^k \in P\right] \cdot \Pr\left[H_n^k \in P\right]$$
$$\geq \frac{\delta^3}{4608k} \cdot \frac{\delta}{4}$$

and the claim follows. $\square$

Applying Proposition 3.5.9

It is possible to apply Construction 3.5.2 to the function resulting from Construction 3.5.8 and have the statement of Proposition 3.5.3 still hold, with minor modifications. Specifically, the modified bound (analogous to Proposition 3.5.3) is $2^{-\Omega(l(n))} + \frac{1}{p(n)}$ (instead of $2 \cdot 2^{-\frac{l(n)}{3}} + \frac{1}{p(n)}$) for every positive polynomial p. The argument leading to Theorem 3.5.6 remains valid as well. Furthermore, we can even waive the requirement that $m(n)$ can be computed (since we can construct functions F_m for every possible value of $m(n)$). Finally, we note that the entire argument holds even if the definition of regular functions is relaxed as follows.

Definition 3.5.10 (Regular Functions, Revised Definition): *A function* f: $\{0, 1\}^* \to \{0, 1\}^*$ *is called* **regular** *if there exists an integer function* m':

$\mathbb{N} \to \mathbb{N}$ and a polynomial $q(\cdot)$ such that for all sufficiently long $x \in \{0, 1\}^*$, it holds that

$$2^{m'(|x|)} \leq |\{y : f(x) = f(y)\}| \leq q(|x|) \cdot 2^{m'(|x|)}$$

When using these (relaxed) regular functions in Construction 3.5.8, set $m(n) \overset{\text{def}}{=} m'(n)$. The resulting function F will have a slightly weaker "almost" 1-1 property. Namely,

$$\Pr\left[\left|F^{-1}(F(U_n, H_n^{m(n)-l(n)}))\right| > q(n) \cdot 2^{l(n)+1}\right] < 2^{-\Omega(l(n))}$$

The application of Construction 3.5.2 will be modified accordingly. We get the following:

Theorem 3.5.11: *If there exist regular one-way functions, then pseudorandom generators exist as well.*

3.5.3. Going Beyond Regular One-Way Functions

The proof of Proposition 3.5.9 relies heavily on the fact that the one-way function f is regular (at least in the weak sense). Alternatively, Construction 3.5.8 needs to be modified so that different hashing families are associated with different $x \in \{0, 1\}^n$. Furthermore, the argument leading to Theorem 3.5.6 cannot be repeated unless it is easy to compute the cardinality of set $f^{-1}(f(x))$ given x. Note that this time we cannot construct functions F_m for every possible value of $\lceil \log_2 |f^{-1}(y)| \rceil$, because none of the functions may satisfy the statement of Proposition 3.5.9. Again, a new idea is needed.

A key observation is that although the value of $\log_2 |f^{-1}(f(x))|$ may vary for different $x \in \{0, 1\}^n$, the value $m(n) \overset{\text{def}}{=} \mathsf{E}(\log_2 |f^{-1}(f(U_n))|)$ is unique. Furthermore, the function $\overline{f}$ defined by

$$\overline{f}(x_1, \ldots, x_{n^2}) \overset{\text{def}}{=} f(x_1), \ldots, f(x_{n^2})$$

where $|x_1| = \cdots = |x_{n^2}| = n$, has the property that all but a negligible fraction of the domain resides in pre-image sets, with the logarithm of their cardinality not deviating too much from the expected value. Specifically, let $\overline{m}(n^3) \overset{\text{def}}{=} \mathsf{E}(\log_2 |\overline{f}^{-1}(\overline{f}(U_{n^3}))|)$. Clearly, $\overline{m}(n^3) = n^2 \cdot m(n)$. Using the Chernoff bound, we get

$$\Pr[|\overline{m}(n^3) - \log_2 |\overline{f}^{-1}(\overline{f}(U_{n^3}))|| > n^2] < 2^{-n}$$

Suppose we apply Construction 3.5.8 to $\overline{f}$, setting $l(n^3) \overset{\text{def}}{=} n^2$. Denote the resulting function by $\overline{F}$. Suppose we apply Construction 3.5.2 to $\overline{F}$, this time setting $l(n^3) \overset{\text{def}}{=} 2n^2 - 1$. Using the ideas presented in the proofs of Propositions 3.5.3 and 3.5.9, we can show that if the function mapping n^3 bits to $l(n^3) + 1$ bits used in Construction 3.5.2 is a hard-core of $\overline{F}$, then the resulting algorithm constitutes a pseudorandom generator. Yet, we are left with the problem of constructing a huge hard-core function $\overline{G}$ for the function $\overline{F}$. Specifically, $|\overline{G}(x)|$ has to equal $2|x|^{\frac{2}{3}}$ for all x's. A natural idea is to define $\overline{G}$ analogously to the way $\overline{g}$ is defined in Construction 3.5.4. Unfortunately, we do not know how to prove the validity of this construction (when applied to $\overline{F}$), and a much more complicated construction is required. This construction does use all the

—— **147** ——

foregoing ideas in conjunction with additional ideas not presented here. The proof of the validity of this construction is even more complex and is not suitable for a book of this nature. Thus we merely state the result obtained.

Theorem 3.5.12: *If there exist one-way functions, then pseudorandom generators exist as well.*

We conclude by mentioning that a non-uniform complexity analogue of Theorem 3.5.12 holds, and in fact is considerably easier to establish:

Theorem 3.5.13: *Suppose there exist non-uniformly one-way functions (as per Definition 2.2.6). Then there exist pseudorandom generators. Furthermore, the output ensemble of these generators is indistinguishable from the uniform ensemble by polynomial-size circuits (as per Definition 3.2.7).*

3.6. Pseudorandom Functions

In this section we present definitions and constructions for pseudorandom functions (using any pseudorandom generator as a building block). Pseudorandom functions will be instrumental for some constructions to be presented in Chapters 5 and 6 of Volume 2.

Motivation. Recall that pseudorandom generators enable us to generate, exchange, and share a large number of pseudorandom values at the cost of a much smaller number of random bits. Specifically, $\text{poly}(n)$ pseudorandom bits can be generated, exchanged, and shared at the cost of n (uniformly chosen bits). Because any efficient application uses only a polynomial number of random values, providing access to polynomially many pseudorandom entries might seem sufficient for any such application. But that conclusion is too hasty, because it assumes implicitly that these entries (i.e., the addresses to be accessed) are fixed beforehand. In some natural applications, one may need to access addresses that are determined "dynamically" by the application. For example, we may want to assign random values to ($\text{poly}(n)$-many) n-bit-long strings, produced throughout the application, so that these values can be retrieved at a later time. Using pseudorandom generators, that task can be achieved at the cost of generating n random bits and storing $\text{poly}(n)$-many values. The challenge, met in this section, is to carry out that task at the cost of generating only n random bits *and storing only n bits*. The key to the solution is the notion of pseudorandom functions. Intuitively, a pseudorandom function shared by a group of users gives them a function that appears random to adversaries (outside of the group).

3.6.1. Definitions

Loosely speaking, pseudorandom functions are functions that cannot be distinguished from truly random functions by any efficient procedure that can get the values of the functions at arguments of its choice. Hence, the distinguishing procedure may query the function being examined at various points, depending possibly on previous answers obtained, and yet cannot tell whether the answers were supplied by a function taken from the pseudorandom ensemble (of functions) or by one from the uniform ensemble (of functions). Indeed, to formalize the notion of pseudorandom functions, we need to consider ensembles of functions. For the sake of simplicity, we shall consider ensembles of length-preserving functions, and in the following the reader is encouraged to further simplify the discussion by setting $\ell(n) = n$. Generalizations are discussed in Section 3.6.4.

Definition 3.6.1 (Function Ensembles): *Let $\ell : \mathbb{N} \to \mathbb{N}$ (e.g., $\ell(n) = n$). An* **ℓ-bit function ensemble** *is a sequence $F = \{F_n\}_{n \in \mathbb{N}}$ of random variables such that the random variable F_n assumes values in the set of functions mapping $\ell(n)$-bit-long strings to $\ell(n)$-bit-long strings. The* **uniform ℓ-bit function ensemble,** *denoted $H = \{H_n\}_{n \in \mathbb{N}}$, has H_n uniformly distributed over the set of all functions mapping $\ell(n)$-bit-long strings to $\ell(n)$-bit-long strings.*

To formalize the notion of pseudorandom functions, we use (probabilistic polynomial-time) *oracle machines* (see Section 1.3.5). We stress that our use of the term "oracle machine" is almost identical to the standard usage. One minor deviation is that the oracle machines we consider have a length-preserving function as oracle, rather than a Boolean function (as is more standard in complexity theory). Furthermore, we assume that on input 1^n, the oracle machine makes queries of only length $\ell(n)$. These conventions are not really essential (they merely simplify the exposition a little). We let M^f denote the execution of the oracle machine M when given access to the oracle f.

Definition 3.6.2 (Pseudorandom Function Ensembles): *An ℓ-bit function ensemble $F = \{F_n\}_{n \in \mathbb{N}}$ is called* **pseudorandom** *if for every probabilistic polynomial-time oracle machine M, every polynomial $p(\cdot)$, and all sufficiently large n's,*

$$\left| \Pr\left[M^{F_n}(1^n) = 1 \right] - \Pr\left[M^{H_n}(1^n) = 1 \right] \right| < \frac{1}{p(n)}$$

where $H = \{H_n\}_{n \in \mathbb{N}}$ is the uniform ℓ-bit function ensemble.

Using techniques similar to those presented in the proof of Proposition 3.2.3 (in Section 3.2.2), we can demonstrate the existence of pseudorandom function ensembles that are not statistically close to the uniform one. However, to be of practical use, we require that the pseudorandom functions can be efficiently computed. That is, functions in the ensemble should have succinct representations that support both selecting them and evaluating them. These aspects are captured by the following definition, in which I is an algorithm selecting representations of functions (which are associated to the functions themselves by the mapping ϕ).

Definition 3.6.3 (Efficiently Computable Function Ensembles): *An ℓ-bit function ensemble $F = \{F_n\}_{n \in \mathbb{N}}$ is called* **efficiently computable** *if the following two conditions hold:*

1. Efficient indexing: *There exists a probabilistic polynomial-time algorithm I and a mapping from strings to functions, ϕ, such that $\phi(I(1^n))$ and F_n are identically distributed.*

   We denote by f_i the function assigned to the string i (i.e., $f_i \overset{\text{def}}{=} \phi(i)$).

2. Efficient evaluation: *There exists a polynomial-time algorithm V such that $V(i, x) = f_i(x)$ for every i in the range of $I(1^n)$ and $x \in \{0, 1\}^{\ell(n)}$.*

In particular, functions in an efficiently computable function ensemble have relatively succinct representations (i.e., of polynomial (in n) rather than exponential (in n) length). It follows that efficiently computable function ensembles can have only exponentially many functions (out of the double-exponentially many possible functions, assuming $\ell(n) = n$).

Another point worth stressing is that efficiently computable pseudorandom functions can be efficiently evaluated at given points *provided that the function description is given as well*. However, if the function (or its description) is *not* known, then the value of the function at a given point cannot be approximated, even in a very liberal sense and even if the values of the function at other points are given.

Terminology. In the rest of this book we consider only efficiently computable pseudorandom function ensembles. Hence, whenever we talk of pseudorandom functions, we actually mean functions chosen at random from an efficiently computable pseudorandom function ensemble.

Observe that, without loss of generality, the sequence of coin tosses used by the indexing algorithm in Definition 3.6.3 can serve as the function's description. Combining this observation with Definition 3.6.2, we obtain the following alternative definition of efficiently computable pseudorandom functions:

Definition 3.6.4 (Efficiently Computable Pseudorandom Function Ensembles, Alternative Formulation): *An* **efficiently computable pseudorandom function ensemble** (pseudorandom function) *is a set of finite functions*

$$\left\{ f_s : \{0, 1\}^{\ell(|s|)} \to \{0, 1\}^{\ell(|s|)} \right\}_{s \in \{0,1\}^*}$$

where $\ell : \mathbb{N} \to \mathbb{N}$ and the following two conditions hold:

1. Efficient evaluation: *There exists a polynomial-time algorithm that on input s and $x \in \{0, 1\}^{\ell(|s|)}$ returns $f_s(x)$.*

2. Pseudorandomness: *The function ensemble $F = \{F_n\}_{n \in \mathbb{N}}$, defined so that F_n is uniformly distributed over the multi-set $\{f_s\}_{s \in \{0,1\}^n}$, is pseudorandom.*

We comment that more general notions of pseudorandom functions can be defined and constructed analogously; see Section 3.6.4.

3.6.2. Construction

Using any pseudorandom generator, we can construct a pseudorandom function ensemble (for $\ell(n) = n$) that is efficiently computable.

Construction 3.6.5: *Let G be a deterministic algorithm that expands inputs of length n into strings of length 2n. We denote by $G_0(s)$ the $|s|$-bit-long prefix of $G(s)$, and by $G_1(s)$ the $|s|$-bit-long suffix of $G(s)$ (i.e., $G(s) = G_0(s)G_1(s)$). For every $s \in \{0, 1\}^n$, we define a function $f_s : \{0, 1\}^n \to \{0, 1\}^n$ such that for every $\sigma_1, \ldots, \sigma_n \in \{0, 1\}$,*

$$f_s(\sigma_1\sigma_2\cdots\sigma_n) \overset{\text{def}}{=} G_{\sigma_n}(\cdots(G_{\sigma_2}(G_{\sigma_1}(s)))\cdots)$$

That is, on input s and $x = \sigma_1\sigma_2\cdots\sigma_n$, the value $f_s(x)$ is computed as follows:

> *Let $y = s$.*
> *For $i = 1$ to n, do*
>
> $\quad\quad y \leftarrow G_{\sigma_i}(y)$.
>
> *Output y.*

Let F_n be a random variable defined by uniformly selecting $s \in \{0, 1\}^n$ and setting $F_n = f_s$. Finally, let $F = \{F_n\}_{n\in\mathbb{N}}$ be our function ensemble.

Pictorially (see Figure 3.5), the function f_s is defined by n-step walks down a full binary tree of depth n having labels at the vertices. The root of the tree, hereafter referred to as the level-0 vertex of the tree, is labeled by the string s. If an internal vertex is labeled r, then its left child is labeled $G_0(r)$, whereas its right child is labeled $G_1(r)$. The value of

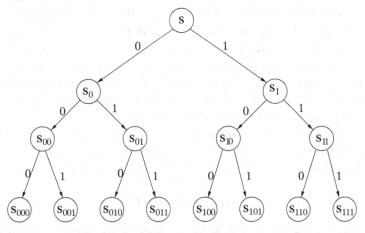

We let $s_\lambda = s$ and $s_{\alpha\sigma} = G_\sigma(s_\alpha)$. The value of $f_s(\sigma_1\sigma_2\cdots\sigma_n) = s_{\sigma_1\sigma_2\cdots\sigma_n}$ is obtained at the leaf reachable from the root (labeled s) by following the path $\sigma_1\sigma_2\cdots\sigma_n$.

For example, $f_s(001) = s_{001} = G_1(s_{00}) = G_1(G_0(s_0)) = G_1(G_0(G_0(s)))$.

Figure 3.5: Construction 3.6.5, for $n=3$

$f_s(x)$ is the string residing in the leaf reachable from the root by a path corresponding to the string x. The random variable F_n is assigned labeled trees corresponding to all possible 2^n labelings of the root, with uniform probability distribution.

A function operating on n-bit strings in the ensemble just constructed can be specified by n bits. Hence, selecting, exchanging, and storing such a function can be implemented at the cost of selecting, exchanging, and storing a single n-bit string.

Theorem 3.6.6: *Let G and F be as in Construction 3.6.5, and suppose that G is a pseudorandom generator. Then F is an efficiently computable ensemble of pseudorandom functions.*

Combining Theorems 3.5.12 and 3.6.6, we immediately get the following:

Corollary 3.6.7: *If there exist one-way functions, then pseudorandom functions exist as well.*

Also, combining Theorem 3.6.6 with the observation that for $\ell(n) > \log_2 n$, any pseudorandom function (as in Definition 3.6.4) gives rise to a pseudorandom generator (see Exercise 28), we obtain the following:

Corollary 3.6.8: *Pseudorandom functions (for super-logarithmic ℓ) exist if and only if pseudorandom generators exist.*

Proof of Theorem 3.6.6: Clearly, the ensemble F is efficiently computable. To prove that F is pseudorandom, we use the hybrid technique. The kth hybrid will be assigned a function that results from uniformly selecting labels for the vertices of the kth (highest) level of the tree and computing the labels for lower levels as in Construction 3.6.5. The 0 hybrid will correspond to the random variable F_n (since a uniformly chosen label is assigned to the root), whereas the n hybrid will correspond to the uniform random variable H_n (since a uniformly chosen label is assigned to each leaf). It will be shown that an efficient oracle machine distinguishing neighboring hybrids can be transformed into an algorithm that distinguishes polynomially many samples of $G(U_n)$ from polynomially many samples of U_{2n}. Using Theorem 3.2.6, we derive a contradiction to the hypothesis (that G is a pseudorandom generator). Details follows.

For every k, with $0 \le k \le n$, we define a hybrid distribution H_n^k, assigned as values functions $f : \{0, 1\}^n \to \{0, 1\}^n$, as follows. For every $s_1, s_2, \ldots, s_{2^k} \in \{0, 1\}^n$, we define a function $f_{s_1, \ldots, s_{2^k}} : \{0, 1\}^n \to \{0, 1\}^n$ such that

$$f_{s_1, \ldots, s_{2^k}}(\sigma_1 \sigma_2 \cdots \sigma_n) \overset{\text{def}}{=} G_{\sigma_n}\left(\cdots \left(G_{\sigma_{k+2}}\left(G_{\sigma_{k+1}}\left(s_{\text{idx}(\sigma_k \cdots \sigma_1)} \right) \right) \right) \cdots \right)$$

where $\text{idx}(\alpha)$ is the index of α in the standard lexicographic order of binary strings of length $|\alpha|$. Namely, $f_{s_1, \ldots, s_{2^k}}(x)$ is computed by first using the k-bit-long prefix of x to determine one of the s_j's and then using the $(n - k)$-bit-long suffix of x to determine which of the functions G_0 and G_1 to apply at each of the remaining stages (of Construction 3.6.5). The random variable H_n^k is uniformly distributed over the $(2^n)^{2^k}$ possible functions (corresponding to all possible choices of $s_1, s_2, \ldots, s_{2^k} \in \{0, 1\}^n$). Namely,

$$H_n^k \stackrel{\text{def}}{=} f_{U_n^{(1)}, \ldots, U_n^{(2^k)}}$$

where $U_n^{(j)}$'s are independent random variables, each uniformly distributed over $\{0, 1\}^n$.

At this point it is clear that H_n^0 is identical with F_n, whereas H_n^n is identical to H_n. Again, as is usual in the hybrid technique, the ability to distinguish the extreme hybrids yields the ability to distinguish a pair of neighboring hybrids. This ability is further transformed so that contradiction to the pseudorandomness of G is reached. Further details follow.

We assume, in contradiction to the theorem, that the function ensemble F is not pseudorandom. It follows that there exists a probabilistic polynomial-time oracle machine M and a polynomial $p(\cdot)$ such that for infinitely many n's,

$$\Delta(n) \stackrel{\text{def}}{=} \left| \Pr\left[M^{F_n}(1^n) = 1\right] - \Pr\left[M^{H_n}(1^n) = 1\right] \right| > \frac{1}{p(n)}$$

Let $t(\cdot)$ be a polynomial bounding the running time of $M(1^n)$ (such a polynomial exists because M is a polynomial-time machine). It follows that on input 1^n, the oracle machine M makes at most $t(n)$ queries (since the number of queries is clearly bounded by the running time). Using the machine M, we construct an algorithm D that distinguishes the $t(\cdot)$-product of the ensemble $\{G(U_n)\}_{n \in \mathbb{N}}$ from the $t(\cdot)$-product of the ensemble $\{U_{2n}\}_{n \in \mathbb{N}}$ as follows.

Algorithm D: On input $\alpha_1, \ldots, \alpha_t \in \{0, 1\}^{2n}$ (with $t = t(n)$), algorithm D proceeds as follows. First, D selects uniformly $k \in \{0, 1, \ldots, n - 1\}$. This random choice, hereafter called the *checkpoint*, is the only random choice made by D itself. Next, algorithm D invokes the oracle machine M (on input 1^n) and answers M's queries as follows. The first query of machine M, denoted q_1, is answered by

$$G_{\sigma_n}\left(\cdots \left(G_{\sigma_{k+2}}\left(P_{\sigma_{k+1}}(\alpha_1)\right)\right) \cdots\right)$$

where $q_1 = \sigma_1 \cdots \sigma_n$, ($\alpha_1$ is the first input string) and $P_0(\alpha)$ (resp., $P_1(\alpha)$) denotes the n-bit prefix of α (resp., the n-bit suffix of α). In addition, algorithm D records this query (i.e., q_1). Each subsequent query is answered by first checking to see if its k-bit-long prefix equals the k-bit-long prefix of a previous query. In case the k-bit-long prefix of the current query, denoted q_i, is different from the k-bit-long prefixes of all previous queries, we associate this prefix with a new input string (i.e., α_i). Namely, we answer query q_i by

$$G_{\sigma_n}\left(\cdots \left(G_{\sigma_{k+2}}\left(P_{\sigma_{k+1}}(\alpha_i)\right)\right) \cdots\right)$$

where $q_i = \sigma_1 \cdots \sigma_n$. In addition, algorithm D records the current query (i.e., q_i). The other possibility is that the k-bit-long prefix of the ith query equals the k-bit-long prefix of some previous query. Let j be the smallest integer such that the k-bit-long prefix of the ith query equals the k-bit-long prefix of the jth query (by hypothesis, $j < i$). Then we record the current query (i.e., q_i), but answer it using the string associated with query q_j (i.e., the input string α_j). Namely, we answer query q_i by

$$G_{\sigma_n}\big(\cdots\big(G_{\sigma_{k+2}}\big(P_{\sigma_{k+1}}(\alpha_j)\big)\big)\cdots\big)$$

where $q_i = \sigma_1 \cdots \sigma_n$. Finally, when machine M halts, algorithm D halts as well and outputs the same output as M.

Pictorially, algorithm D answers the first query by first placing the two halves of α_1 in the corresponding children of the tree's vertex reached by following the path from the root corresponding to $\sigma_1 \cdots \sigma_k$. The labels of all vertices in the subtree corresponding to $\sigma_1 \cdots \sigma_k$ are determined by the labels of these two children (as in the construction of F). Subsequent queries are answered by following the corresponding paths from the root. In case the path does not pass through a $(k + 1)$-level vertex that already has a label, we assign this vertex and its sibling a new string (taken from the input). For the sake of simplicity, in case the path of the ith query requires a new string, we use the ith input string (rather than the first input string not used thus far). In case the path of a new query passes through a $(k + 1)$-level vertex that has already been labeled, we use this label to compute the labels of subsequent vertices along this path (and in particular the label of the leaf). We stress that the algorithm *does not* compute the labels of *all* vertices in a subtree corresponding to $\sigma_1 \cdots \sigma_k$ (although these labels are determined by the label of the vertex corresponding to $\sigma_1 \cdots \sigma_k$), but rather computes only the labels of vertices along the paths corresponding to the queries.

Clearly, algorithm D can be implemented in polynomial time. It is left to evaluate its performance. The key observation is the correspondence between D's actions on checkpoint k and the hybrids k and $k + 1$:

- When the inputs are taken from the $t(n)$-product of U_{2n} (and algorithm D chooses k as the checkpoint), the invoked machine M behaves exactly as on the $k + 1$ hybrid. This is so because D places halves of truly random $2n$-bit-long strings at level $k + 1$ (which is the same as placing truly random n-bit-long strings at level $k + 1$).
- On the other hand, when the inputs are taken from the $t(n)$-product of $G(U_n)$ (and algorithm D chooses k as the checkpoint), then M behaves exactly as on the kth hybrid. Indeed, D does not place the (unknown to it) corresponding seeds (generating these pseudorandom strings) at level k; but putting the two halves of the pseudorandom strings at level $k + 1$ has exactly the same effect.

Thus:

Claim 3.6.6.1: Let n be an integer, and $t \overset{\text{def}}{=} t(n)$. Let K be a random variable describing the random choice of checkpoint by algorithm D (on input a t-long sequence of $2n$-bit-long strings). Then for every $k \in \{0, 1, \ldots, n - 1\}$,

$$\Pr\big[D\big(G\big(U_n^{(1)}\big), \ldots, G\big(U_n^{(t)}\big)\big) = 1 \mid K = k\big] = \Pr\big[M^{H_n^k}(1^n) = 1\big]$$
$$\Pr\big[D\big(U_{2n}^{(1)}, \ldots, U_{2n}^{(t)}\big) = 1 \mid K = k\big] = \Pr\big[M^{H_n^{k+1}}(1^n) = 1\big]$$

where the $U_n^{(i)}$'s and $U_{2n}^{(j)}$'s are independent random variables uniformly distributed over $\{0, 1\}^n$ and $\{0, 1\}^{2n}$, respectively.

Claim 3.6.6.1 is quite obvious; yet a rigorous proof is more complex than one might realize at first glance, the reason being that M's queries may depend on previous answers it has received, and hence the correspondence between the inputs of D and possible values assigned to the hybrids is less obvious than it seems. To illustrate the difficulty, consider an N-bit string that is selected by a pair of interactive processes that proceed in N iterations. At each iteration, the first process chooses a new location (i.e., an unused $i \in \{1, \ldots, N\}$) based on the entire history of the interaction, and the second process sets the value of this bit (i.e., the ith bit) by flipping an unbiased coin. It is intuitively clear that the resulting string is uniformly distributed; still, a proof is required (since randomized processes are subtle entities that often lead to mistakes). In our setting, the situation is slightly more involved. The process of determining the string is terminated after $T < N$ iterations, and statements are made regarding the resulting string that is only partially determined. Consequently, the situation is slightly confusing, and we feel that a detailed argument is required. However, the argument provides no additional insights and can be skipped without significant damage (especially by readers who are more interested in cryptography than in "probabilistic analysis").

Proof of Claim 3.6.6.1: We start by sketching a proof of the claim for the extremely simple case in which M's queries are the first t strings (of length n) in lexicographic order. Let us further assume, for simplicity, that on input $\alpha_1, \ldots, \alpha_t$, algorithm D happens to choose checkpoint k such that $t = 2^{k+1}$. In this case the oracle machine M is invoked on input 1^n and access to the function $f_{s_1, \ldots, s_{2^{k+1}}}$, where $s_{2j-1+\sigma} = P_\sigma(\alpha_j)$ for every $j \leq 2^k$ and $\sigma \in \{0, 1\}$. Thus, if the inputs to D are uniformly selected in $\{0, 1\}^{2n}$, then M is invoked with access to the $k + 1$ hybrid random variable (since in this case the s_j's are independent and uniformly distributed in $\{0, 1\}^n$). On the other hand, if the inputs to D are distributed as $G(U_n)$, then M is invoked with access to the kth hybrid random variable (since in this case $f_{s_1, \ldots, s_{2^{k+1}}} = f_{r_1, \ldots, r_{2^k}}$, where the r_j's are seeds corresponding to the α_j's).

For the general case, we consider an alternative way of defining the random variable H_n^m for every $0 \leq m \leq n$. This alternative way is somewhat similar to the way in which D answers the queries of the oracle machine M. (We use the symbol m instead of k, since m *does not* necessarily equal the checkpoint (denoted k) chosen by algorithm D.) This way of defining H_n^m consists of the interleaving of two random processes, which together first select at random a function $g : \{0, 1\}^m \to \{0, 1\}^n$ that is later used to determine a function $f : \{0, 1\}^n \to \{0, 1\}^n$. The first random process, denoted ρ, is an arbitrary process ("given to us from the outside") that specifies points in the domain of g. (The process ρ corresponds to the queries of M, whereas the second process corresponds to the way A answers these queries.) The second process, denoted ψ, assigns uniformly selected n-bit-long strings to every new point specified by ρ, thus defining the value of g at this point. We stress that in case ρ specifies an old point (i.e., a point for which g is already defined), then the second process does nothing (i.e., the value of g at this point is left unchanged). The process ρ may depend on the history of the two processes and in particular on the values chosen for the previous points. When ρ terminates, the second process (i.e., ψ) selects random values for the remaining undefined points (in case such exist). We stress that the second process (i.e., ψ) is fixed for all possible choices of a ("first") process ρ. The rest of this paragraph

——— **155** ———

gives a detailed description of the interleaving of the two random processes (*and can be skipped*). We consider a randomized process ρ mapping sequences of n-bit strings (representing the history) to single m-bit strings. We stress that ρ is *not* necessarily memoryless (and hence may "remember" its previous random choices). Namely, for every fixed sequence $v_1, \ldots, v_i \in \{0, 1\}^n$, the random variable $\rho(v_1, \ldots, v_i)$ is (arbitrarily) distributed over $\{0, 1\}^m \cup \{\bot\}$, where $\bot$ is a special symbol denoting termination. A "random" function $g : \{0, 1\}^m \to \{0, 1\}^n$ is defined by iterating the process ρ with the random process ψ defined next. Process ψ starts with g that is undefined on every point in its domain. At the ith iteration, ψ lets $p_i \overset{\text{def}}{=} \rho(v_1, \ldots, v_{i-1})$ and, assuming $p_i \neq \bot$, sets $v_i \overset{\text{def}}{=} v_j$ if $p_i = p_j$ for some $j < i$, and lets v_i be uniformly distributed in $\{0, 1\}^n$ otherwise. In the latter case (i.e., p_i is new, and hence g is not yet defined on p_i), ψ sets $g(p_i) \overset{\text{def}}{=} v_i$ (in fact, $g(p_i) = g(p_j) = v_j = v_i$ also in case $p_i = p_j$ for some $j < i$). When ρ terminates (i.e., $\rho(v_1, \ldots, v_T) = \bot$ for some T), process ψ completes the function g (if necessary) by choosing independently and uniformly in $\{0, 1\}^n$ values for the points at which g is still undefined. (Alternatively, we can augment the process ρ so that it terminates only after specifying all possible m-bit strings.)

Once a function $g : \{0, 1\}^m \to \{0, 1\}^n$ is totally defined, we define a function $f^g : \{0, 1\}^n \to \{0, 1\}^n$ by

$$f^g(\sigma_1 \sigma_2 \cdots \sigma_n) \overset{\text{def}}{=} G_{\sigma_n}\left(\cdots \left(G_{\sigma_{m+2}} \left(G_{\sigma_{m+1}} (g(\sigma_m \cdots \sigma_1)) \right) \right) \cdots \right)$$

The reader can easily verify that f^g equals $f_{g(0^m), \ldots, g(1^m)}$ (as defined in the hybrid construction earlier). Also, one can easily verify that the preceding random process (i.e., the interleaving of ψ with any ρ) yields a function g that is uniformly distributed over the set of all possible functions mapping m-bit strings to n-bit strings. It follows that the previously described random process yields a result (i.e., a function) that is distributed identically to the random variable H_n^m.

Suppose now that the checkpoint chosen by D equals k and that D's inputs are independently and uniformly selected in $\{0, 1\}^{2n}$. In this case the way in which D answers M's queries can be viewed as placing independently and uniformly selected n-bit strings as the labels of the $(k + 1)$-level vertices. It follows that the way in which D answers M's queries corresponds to the previously described process with $m = k + 1$ (with M playing the role of ρ and A playing the role of ψ). Hence, in this case, M is invoked with access to the $k + 1$ hybrid random variable.

Suppose, on the other hand, that (again the checkpoint chosen by D equals k and that) D's inputs are independently selected so that each is distributed identically to $G(U_n)$. In this case the way in which D answers M's queries can be viewed as placing independently and uniformly selected n-bit strings as the labels of the k-level vertices. It follows that the way in which D answers M's queries corresponds to the previously described process with $m = k$. Hence, in this case M is invoked with access to the kth hybrid random variable. $\square$

Combining Claim 3.6.6.1 and $\Delta(n) = \Pr[M^{H_n^0}(1^n) = 1] - \Pr[M^{H_n^k}(1^n) = 1]$, it follows that

$$\Pr\left[D\left(G(U_n^{(1)}), \ldots, G(U_n^{(t)})\right) = 1\right] - \Pr\left[D\left(U_{2n}^{(1)}, \ldots, U_{2n}^{(t)}\right) = 1\right]$$

$$= \left(\frac{1}{n} \sum_{k=0}^{n-1} \Pr\left[M^{H_n^k}(1^n) = 1\right]\right) - \left(\frac{1}{n} \sum_{k=0}^{n-1} \Pr\left[M^{H_n^{k+1}}(1^n) = 1\right]\right)$$

$$= \frac{\Delta(n)}{n}$$

which, by the contradiction hypothesis, is greater than $\frac{1}{n \cdot p(n)}$ for infinitely many n's. So it follows that D (which is a probabilistic polynomial-time algorithm) distinguishes polynomially many samples of $G(U_n)$ from polynomially many samples of U_{2n}. Using Theorem 3.2.6, we derive a contradiction to the hypothesis (of the current theorem) that G is a pseudorandom generator, and the current theorem follows. ∎

3.6.3. Applications: A General Methodology

Sharing a pseudorandom function allows parties to determine random-looking values depending on their current views of the environment (which need not be known a priori). To appreciate the potential of this tool, one should realize that sharing a pseudorandom function is essentially as good as being able to agree, on the fly, on the association of random values to (on-line) given values, where the latter are taken from a huge set of possible values. We stress that this agreement is achieved without communication and synchronization: Whenever some party needs to associate a random value to a given value $v \in \{0, 1\}^n$, it will associate to v the same random value $r_v \in \{0, 1\}^n$.

As an illustrative example, consider the problem of *identifying friend or foe*, in which members of a club sharing some secret wish to be able to identify one another as belonging to the club. A possible solution is for the club members to share a secret function, defined over a huge domain, and prove their membership in the club by answering a random challenge presented to them, with the value of the secret function evaluated at the challenge. We claim that using a pseudorandom function in the role of the secret function guarantees that it will be infeasible for an adversary to pass as a member, even after conducting polynomially many interactions with members in which the adversary may ask them to reply to challenges of its choice. To prove this claim, consider what happens when the secret function is a truly random one. (We stress that this is merely a mental experiment, since it is infeasible to share such a huge random object.) In such a case, the random function's values at new points (corresponding to new challenges that the adversary should answer) are uncorrelated to its values at any other points (corresponding to answers the adversary has obtained by challenging legitimate members). Thus, the adversary will fail in such an imaginary situation. It follows that the adversary must also fail in the actual situation (in which the secret function is selected from a pseudorandom ensemble), or else we derive a distinguisher of pseudorandom functions from truly random ones.

In general, the following two-step methodology is useful in many cases:

1. Design your scheme assuming that all legitimate users share a random function, $f : \{0, 1\}^n \rightarrow \{0, 1\}^n$. (The adversaries may be able to obtain, from the legitimate users, the values of f on arguments of their choice, but will not have direct access to f itself.[6]) This step culminates in proving the security of the scheme, assuming that f is indeed uniformly chosen among all possible such functions, while ignoring the question of how such an f can be selected and handled.

---

[6] This is different from the *Random Oracle Model*, where the adversary has *direct* access to a random oracle (that is later "implemented" by a function, the description of which is also given to the adversary).

2. Construct a real scheme by replacing the random function by a pseudorandom function. Namely, the legitimate users will share a random/secret seed specifying such a pseudorandom function, whereas the adversaries will not know the seed. As before, the adversaries can, at most, obtain (from the legitimate users) the values of the function at arguments of their choice. Finally, conclude that the real scheme (as presented here) is secure (since otherwise one could distinguish a pseudorandom function from a truly random one).

We stress that this methodology can be applied only if the legitimate users can share random/secret information not known to the adversary (e.g., as is the case in private-key encryption schemes).[7]

3.6.4.* Generalizations

We present generalizations of the notion of a pseudorandom function, first to the case where the function is not length-preserving, and then to the case where the function is defined over the set of all strings. These generalizations offer greater flexibility in using pseudorandom functions in applications.

3.6.4.1. Functions That Are Not Length-Preserving

Departing from Definition 3.6.4, we present the following generalization of the notion of a pseudorandom function ensemble.

Definition 3.6.9 (Pseudorandom Function Ensembles, Generalization): *Let* $d, r : \mathbb{N} \to \mathbb{N}$. *We say that*

$$\left\{ f_s : \{0, 1\}^{d(|s|)} \to \{0, 1\}^{r(|s|)} \right\}_{s \in \{0,1\}^*}$$

is an **efficiently computable generalized pseudorandom function ensemble** (generalized pseudorandom function) *if the following two conditions hold:*

1. Efficient evaluation: *There exists a polynomial-time algorithm that on input s and* $x \in \{0, 1\}^{d(|s|)}$ *returns* $f_s(x)$.

2. Pseudorandomness: *For every probabilistic polynomial-time oracle machine M, every polynomial* $p(\cdot)$, *and all sufficiently large n's,*

$$\left| \Pr\left[M^{F_n}(1^n)=1\right] - \Pr\left[M^{H_n}(1^n)=1\right] \right| < \frac{1}{p(n)}$$

where F_n *is a random variable uniformly distributed over the multi-set* $\{f_s\}_{s \in \{0,1\}^n}$, *and* H_n *is uniformly distributed among all functions mapping* $d(n)$-bit-long strings *to* $r(n)$-bit-long strings.

---

[7] In contrast, the *Random Oracle Methodology* refers to a situation in which the adversary is also given the description of the function, which replaces the random oracle to which it has *direct* access (as discussed in footnote 6). We warn that, in contrast to the methodology presented here, the Random Oracle Methodology is a heuristic. See further discussion in Section 3.8.2.

Clearly, $r : \mathbb{N} \to \mathbb{N}$ must be upper-bounded by a polynomial. Definition 3.6.4 is obtained as a special case (of Definition 3.6.9) by letting the functions d and r equal the function ℓ. Similarly to Construction 3.6.5, for any $d, r : \mathbb{N} \to \mathbb{N}$, where $r(n)$ is computable in poly(n) time from n, we can construct general pseudorandom functions using any pseudorandom generator. Specifically:

Construction 3.6.10: *Let G, G_0, and G_1 be as in Construction 3.6.5. Let $d, r : \mathbb{N} \to \mathbb{N}$, and let G' be a deterministic algorithm mapping n-bit-long inputs into $r(n)$-bit outputs. Then for every $s \in \{0, 1\}^n$, we define a function f_s: $\{0, 1\}^{d(n)} \to \{0, 1\}^{r(n)}$ such that for every $\sigma_1, \dots, \sigma_{d(n)} \in \{0, 1\}$,*

$$f_s(\sigma_1 \sigma_2 \cdots \sigma_{d(n)}) \overset{\text{def}}{=} G'(G_{\sigma_{d(n)}}(\cdots (G_{\sigma_2}(G_{\sigma_1}(s))) \cdots))$$

Construction 3.6.5 is regained from Construction 3.6.10 by letting $d(n) = r(n) = n$ and using the identity function in the role of G'. By extending the proof of Theorem 3.6.6, we obtain the following:

Theorem 3.6.11: *Let G, G', and the f_s's be as in Construction 3.6.10, and suppose that G is a pseudorandom generator. Further suppose that G' is polynomial-time-computable and that the ensemble $\{G'(U_n)\}_{n \in \mathbb{N}}$ is pseudorandom,[8] as defined in Definition 3.2.8. Then $\{f_s\}_{s \in \{0,1\}^*}$ is an efficiently computable ensemble of generalized pseudorandom functions.*

Proof: In case G' is the identity transformation (and $r(n) = n$), the proof is almost identical to the proof of Theorem 3.6.6. To deal with the general case, we use a hybrid argument. Specifically, we use a *single* intermediate *hybrid* (i.e., a single hybrid of the function ensemble $\{f_s\}$ and a truly random function): For every n, we consider the (random) function $g : \{0, 1\}^{d(n)} \to \{0, 1\}^{r(n)}$ defined by letting $g(x) = G'(h'(x))$, where h' is uniformly selected among all functions mapping $d(n)$-bit-long strings to n-bit strings. The theorem follows by showing that this hybrid ensemble is indistinguishable from both the uniform function ensemble and the function ensemble of Construction 3.6.10.

In the following, we denote by H_n (resp., H_n') a random variable uniformly distributed over the set of all functions mapping $d(n)$-bit-long strings to $r(n)$-bit-long (resp., n-bit-long) strings. Recall that the hybrid distribution, denoted $G' \circ H_n'$, is obtained by functional composition of the fixed function G' and the random function distribution H_n'. As usual, F_n denotes a random variable uniformly distributed over the multi-set $\{f_s\}_{s \in \{0,1\}^n}$.

Claim 3.6.11.1: For every probabilistic polynomial-time oracle machine M, every polynomial $p(\cdot)$, and all sufficiently large n's,

$$\left| \Pr[M^{G' \circ H_n'}(1^n) = 1] - \Pr[M^{H_n}(1^n) = 1] \right| < \frac{1}{p(n)}$$

---

[8] In case $r(n) > n$ (for all n's), what we require is that G' be a pseudorandom generator. But otherwise this cannot be required, since G' is not expanding. Still, the other features of a pseudorandom generator (i.e., efficient computability and pseudorandomness of the output) are always required here.

Proof Sketch: Intuitively, oracle access to $G' \circ H'_n$ is equivalent to being given multiple independent samples from the distribution $G'(U_n)$, whereas oracle access to H_n is equivalent to being given multiple independent samples from the distribution $U_{r(n)}$. Using the pseudorandomness of $\{G'(U_n)\}_{n \in \mathbb{N}}$, the claim follows.

In the actual proof, we transform the oracle machine M into an ordinary machine M' that gets a sequence of samples and emulates an execution of M while using its input sequence in order to emulate some related oracle for M. Specifically, on input $\alpha_1, \ldots, \alpha_T$, machine M' invokes M, and answers its ith distinct query with α_i. (Without loss of generality, we can assume that M never issues the same query twice.)

1. Indeed, on input a sequence of samples from distribution $G'(U_n)$, machine M' emulates an execution of $M^{G' \circ H'_n}(1^n)$.

   (The key observation is that the responses of oracle $G' \circ H'_n$ to a sequence $q_1, \ldots, q_t$ of distinct queries are $G'(s_{q_1}), \ldots, G'(s_{q_t})$, where the s_{q_i}'s are uniformly and independently distributed in $\{0, 1\}^n$.)

2. On the other hand, on input a sequence of samples from distribution $U_{r(n)}$, machine M' emulates an execution of $M^{H_n}(1^n)$.

   (The key observation is that the responses of oracle H_n to a sequence $q_1, \ldots, q_t$ of distinct queries are uniformly and independently distributed in $\{0, 1\}^{r(n)}$.)

Thus, if M violates the statement of the claim, then M' violates the pseudorandomness of $\{G'(U_n)\}_{n \in \mathbb{N}}$, in contradiction to the theorem's hypothesis. $\square$

Claim 3.6.11.2: For every probabilistic polynomial-time oracle machine M, every polynomial $p(\cdot)$, and all sufficiently large n's,

$$\left| \Pr\left[M^{G' \circ H'_n}(1^n) = 1 \right] - \Pr\left[M^{F_n}(1^n) = 1 \right] \right| < \frac{1}{p(n)}$$

Proof Sketch: Any function f_s (as defined in Construction 3.6.10) can be written as $f_s(x) = G'(f'_s(x))$, where f'_s is defined by

$$f'_s(\sigma_1 \sigma_2 \cdots \sigma_{d(n)}) \overset{\text{def}}{=} G_{\sigma_{d(n)}}\left(\cdots \left(G_{\sigma_2}(G_{\sigma_1}(s)) \right) \cdots \right) \tag{3.16}$$

We have already established that $\{f'_s\}$ is a generalized pseudorandom function ensemble (i.e., f'_s corresponds to the case where G' is the identity), and so by incorporating G' in the distinguisher, the claim follows.

In the actual proof, we transform the oracle machine M into an oracle machine M' that emulates M while using its own oracle in order to emulate some related oracle for M. Specifically, when M issues a query q, machine M' forwards q to its own oracle, applies G' to the answer that it receives, and forwards the result to M.

1. Indeed, when given oracle access to h', machine M' emulates an execution of $M^{G' \circ h'}(1^n)$ (the reason being that, in this case, M' responds to query q (made by

M) with $G'(h'(q)) = (G' \circ h')(q)$). Thus, when given oracle access to H'_n, machine M' emulates an execution of $M^{G' \circ H'_n}(1^n)$.

2. On the other hand, when given oracle access to f'_s, machine M' emulates an execution of $M^{f_s}(1^n)$ (the reason being that, in this case, M' responds to query q (made by M) with $G'(f'_s(q)) = f_s(q)$). Thus, for uniformly selected $s \in \{0, 1\}^n$, when given oracle access to f'_s, machine M' emulates an execution of $M^{F_n}(1^n)$.

Thus, if M violates the statement of the claim, then M' violates the pseudorandomness of $\{f'_s\}$, which contradicts what we have already established. $\square$

Combining Claims 3.6.11.1 and 3.6.11.2, the theorem follows. ∎

Comment. One major component of the proof of Theorem 3.6.11 is proving the following proposition:

Let $\{f'_s : \{0, 1\}^{d(|s|)} \to \{0, 1\}^{|s|}\}_{s \in \{0,1\}^*}$ be a generalized pseudorandom function ensemble, and let G' be as in the theorem's hypothesis. Then the generalized function ensemble $\{f_s : \{0, 1\}^{d(|s|)} \to \{0, 1\}^{r(|s|)}\}_{s \in \{0,1\}^*}$, defined by $f_s(x) \stackrel{\text{def}}{=} G'(f'_s(x))$, is pseudorandom.

The proof of Claim 3.6.11.2 actually establishes this proposition and then applies it to $\{f'_s\}_{s \in \{0,1\}^*}$ as defined in Eq. (3.16).

3.6.4.2. Functions Defined on All Strings

Thus far we have considered only function ensembles in which each function is finite (i.e., maps a finite domain to a finite range). Using such functions requires a priori knowledge of an upper bound on the length of the inputs to which the function is to be applied. (Shorter inputs can always be encoded as inputs of some longer and predetermined length.) However, it is preferable not to require such a priori knowledge of the upper bound (e.g., since such a requirement may rule out some applications). It is thus useful to have a more flexible notion of a pseudorandom-function ensemble, allowing application of individual functions to inputs of varying lengths not known a priori. Such ensembles are defined and constructed next.

Definition 3.6.12 (Pseudorandom Function Ensembles with Unbounded Inputs): *Let $r : \mathbb{N} \to \mathbb{N}$. We say that*

$$\{f_s : \{0, 1\}^* \to \{0, 1\}^{r(|s|)}\}_{s \in \{0,1\}^*}$$

*is an **efficiently computable unbounded-input pseudorandom function ensemble** (unbounded-input pseudorandom function) if the following two conditions hold:*

1. Efficient evaluation: *There exists a polynomial-time algorithm that on input s and $x \in \{0, 1\}^*$ returns $f_s(x)$.*

2. Pseudorandomness: *For every probabilistic polynomial-time oracle machine M, every polynomial $p(\cdot)$, and all sufficiently large n's,*

$$\left| \Pr\left[M^{F_n}(1^n) = 1\right] - \Pr\left[M^{H_n}(1^n) = 1\right] \right| < \frac{1}{p(n)}$$

where F_n is a random variable uniformly distributed over the multi-set $\{f_s\}_{s \in \{0,1\}^n}$, and H_n is uniformly distributed[9] among all functions mapping arbitrary long strings to $r(n)$-bit-long strings.

A few comments regarding Definition 3.6.12 are in order. First, note that the fact that the length of the input to f_s is not known a priori raises no problems in Item 1, since the running time of the evaluating algorithm may depend (polynomially) on the length of the input to f_s. Regarding Item 2, because M has a-priori-bounded (polynomial) running time, that upper-bounds the length of the queries made to the oracle. The latter fact resolves a technical problem that arises in the earlier definition (see footnote 9). In typical applications, one uses $r(n) = n$ (or $r(n)$ that is polynomially related to n). Another special case of interest is the case where $r \equiv 1$, that is, the case of pseudorandom Boolean functions.

Similarly to Constructions 3.6.5 and 3.6.10, for any $r : \mathbb{N} \to \mathbb{N}$ such that $r(n)$ is computable in poly(n) time from n, we can construct unbounded-input pseudorandom functions using any pseudorandom generator. Specifically:

Construction 3.6.13: *Let G be a deterministic algorithm expanding inputs of length n into strings of length $2n + r(n)$. We denote by $G_0(s)$ the $|s|$-bit-long prefix of $G(s)$, by $G_1(s)$ the next $|s|$ bits in $G(s)$, and by $G_2(s)$ the $r(|s|)$-bit-long suffix of $G(s)$ (i.e., $G(s) = G_0(s)G_1(s)G_2(s)$). Then for every $s \in \{0,1\}^n$, we define a function $f_s : \{0,1\}^* \to \{0,1\}^{r(n)}$ such that for every non-negative integer d and every $\sigma_1, \ldots, \sigma_d \in \{0,1\}$,*

$$f_s(\sigma_1 \sigma_2 \cdots \sigma_d) \stackrel{\text{def}}{=} G_2\big(G_{\sigma_d}\big(\cdots \big(G_{\sigma_2}\big(G_{\sigma_1}(s)\big)\big)\cdots\big)\big)$$

Pictorially, the function f_s is defined by walks down an infinite ternary tree having labels at the vertices. Internal vertices have $|s|$-bit-long labels, and leaves have $r(|s|)$-bit-long labels. The root of the tree, hereafter referred to as the level-0 vertex of the tree, is labeled by the string s. If an internal vertex is labeled s', then its leftmost child is labeled $G_0(s')$, its middle child is labeled $G_1(s')$, and its rightmost child is labeled $G_2(s')$. The first two children of each internal vertex are internal vertices, whereas the rightmost child of an internal vertex is a leaf. The value of $f_s(\sigma_1 \cdots \sigma_d)$ is the string residing in the leaf reachable from the root by "following the path $\sigma_1, \ldots, \sigma_d, 2$," when the root is labeled by s. Again, by extending the proof of Theorem 3.6.6, we obtain the following:

---

[9] Since the running time of M is a priori bounded by some polynomial, it follows that for some polynomial d and all n's, it holds that, on input 1^n, machine M makes only queries of length at most $d(n)$. Thus, H_n can be defined as the uniform distribution over all functions mapping strings of length up to $d(n)$ to $r(n)$-bit-long strings. This resolves the technical problem of what is meant by a uniform distribution over an infinite set (i.e., the set of all functions mapping arbitrary long bit strings to $r(n)$-bit-long strings).

Theorem 3.6.14: *Let G and the f_s's be as in Construction 3.6.13, and suppose that G is a pseudorandom generator. Then $\{f_s\}_{s \in \{0,1\}^*}$ is an efficiently computable ensemble of unbounded-input pseudorandom functions.*

Proof Sketch: We follow the proof method of Theorem 3.6.6. That is, we use the hybrid technique, where the kth hybrid will be assigned a function that results from uniformly selecting labels for the vertices of the highest $k + 1$ levels of the tree, and computing the labels for lower levels as in Construction 3.6.13. Specifically, the kth hybrid is defined as equal to the function $f_{s_1,\ldots,s_{3k}} : \{0, 1\}^* \to \{0, 1\}^{r(n)}$, defined next, where $s_1, \ldots, s_{3k} \in \{0, 1\}^{2n+r(n)}$ are uniformly and independently distributed.

$$f_{s_1,\ldots,s_{3k}}(\sigma_1 \sigma_2 \cdots \sigma_d)$$

$$\stackrel{\text{def}}{=} \begin{cases} P_2\big(s_{\mathrm{idx}(2^{k-d} \cdot \sigma_d \cdots \sigma_1)}\big) & \text{if } d \le k \\ G_2\big(G_{\sigma_d}\big(\cdots \big(G_{\sigma_{k+2}}\big(G_{\sigma_{k+1}}\big(s_{\mathrm{idx}(\sigma_k \cdots \sigma_1)}\big)\big)\big) \cdots \big)\big) & \text{otherwise} \end{cases}$$

where $\mathrm{idx}(\alpha)$ is the index of α in the standard lexicographic order of ternary strings of length $|\alpha|$, and $P_2(\beta)$ is the $r(n)$-bit-long suffix of β.

Note that (unlike the proof of Theorem 3.6.6) for every n there are infinitely many hybrids, because here k can be any non-negative integer (rather than $k \in \{0, 1, \ldots, n\}$ as in the proof of Theorem 3.6.6). Still, because we consider an (arbitrary) probabilistic *polynomial-time* distinguisher denoted M, there exists a polynomial d such that on input 1^n the oracle machine M makes only queries of length at most $d(n) - 1$. Thus, giving M oracle access to the $d(n)$ hybrid is equivalent to giving M oracle access to the uniform random variable H_n (where H_n is as in Definition 3.6.12), because a uniformly chosen label is assigned to each i-level leaf for $i \le d(n)$. On the other hand, the 0 hybrid corresponds to the random variable F_n (where F_n is as in Definition 3.6.12), because a uniformly chosen label is assigned to the root. Thus, if M can distinguish $\{F_n\}$ from $\{H_n\}$, then it can distinguish a (random) pair of neighboring hybrids (i.e., the $k - 1$ and k hybrids, where k is uniformly selected in $\{1, \ldots, d(n)\}$). As in the proof of Theorem 3.6.6, the latter assertion can be shown to violate the pseudorandomness of G. Specifically, we can distinguish multiple independent samples taken from the distribution $U_{2n+r(n)}$ and multiple independent samples taken from the distribution $G(U_n)$: Given a sequence of $(2n + r(n))$-bit-long strings, we use these strings in order to label vertices in the highest $k + 1$ levels of the tree (by breaking each string into three parts and using those parts as labels for the three children of some $(i - 1)$-level node, for $i \le k$). In case the strings are taken from $U_{2n+r(n)}$, we emulate the k hybrid, whereas in case the strings are taken from $G(U_n)$, we emulate the $k - 1$ hybrid. The theorem follows. $\square$

Comment. Unbounded-input (and generalized) pseudorandom functions can be constructed directly from (ordinary) pseudorandom functions; see Section 3.8.2.

3.7.* Pseudorandom Permutations

In this section we present definitions and constructions for pseudorandom permutations. Clearly, pseudorandom permutations (over huge domains) can be used instead of pseudorandom functions in any efficient application, yet pseudorandom permutations offer the extra advantage of having unique pre-images. This extra advantage can sometimes be useful, but less than what one might expect (e.g., it is not used in the rest of this book, not even in the chapter on encryption schemes, for reasons explained there).

We show how to construct pseudorandom permutations using pseudorandom functions as building blocks, in a manner identical to the high-level structure of the DES. Hence, the proof presented in this section can be viewed as supporting the DES's methodology of converting "random-looking" functions into "random-looking" permutations.[10]

3.7.1. Definitions

We start with the definition of pseudorandom permutations. Loosely speaking, a pseudorandom ensemble of permutations is defined analogously to a pseudorandom ensemble of functions. Namely:

Definition 3.7.1 (Permutation Ensembles): *A* **permutation ensemble** *is a sequence* $P = \{P_n\}_{n \in \mathbb{N}}$ *of random variables such that the random variable* P_n *assumes values in the set of permutations mapping n-bit-long strings to n-bit-long strings. The* **uniform permutation ensemble,** *denoted* $K = \{K_n\}_{n \in \mathbb{N}}$, *has* K_n *uniformly distributed over the set of all permutations mapping n-bit-long strings to n-bit-long strings.*

Every permutation ensemble is a function ensemble. Hence the definition of an *efficiently computable* permutation ensemble is obvious (i.e., it is derived from the definition of an efficiently computable function ensemble). Pseudorandom permutations are defined as computationally indistinguishable from the uniform *permutation* ensemble.

Definition 3.7.2 (Pseudorandom Permutation Ensembles): *A permutation ensemble* $P = \{P_n\}_{n \in \mathbb{N}}$ *is called* **pseudorandom** *if for every probabilistic polynomial-time oracle machine M, every polynomial* $p(\cdot)$, *and all sufficiently large n's,*

$$\left| \Pr\left[M^{P_n}(1^n)=1\right] - \Pr\left[M^{K_n}(1^n)=1\right] \right| < \frac{1}{p(n)}$$

where $K = \{K_n\}_{n \in \mathbb{N}}$ *is the uniform permutation ensemble.*

The fact that P is a pseudorandom permutation ensemble, rather than just a pseudorandom function ensemble, cannot be detected in poly(n) time by an observer given

---

[10]The fact that in the DES this methodology is applied to functions that are NOT "random-looking" is not of concern here.

oracle access to P_n. This fact stems from the observation that the uniform permutation ensemble is polynomial-time-indistinguishable from the uniform function ensemble. Namely:

Proposition 3.7.3: *The uniform permutation ensemble (i.e., $K = \{K_n\}_{n\in\mathbb{N}}$) constitutes a pseudorandom function ensemble.*

Proof Sketch: Recall that $\{H_n\}_{n\in\mathbb{N}}$ denotes the uniform function ensemble. The probability that when given access to oracle H_n a machine will detect a collision in the oracle function is bounded by $t^2 \cdot 2^{-n}$, where t denotes the number of queries made by the machine. Conditioned on not finding such a collision, the answers of H_n are indistinguishable from those of K_n. Finally, using the fact that a polynomial-time machine can ask at most polynomially many queries, the proposition follows. ∎

Hence, the use of pseudorandom permutations instead of pseudorandom functions has reasons beyond the question of whether or not a computationally restricted observer can detect the difference. Typically, the reason is that one wants to be guaranteed of the *uniqueness* of pre-images. A natural strengthening of this requirement is that given the description of the permutation, *the* (unique) *pre-image can be efficiently found*.

Definition 3.7.4 (Efficiently Computable and Invertible Permutation Ensembles): *A permutation ensemble $P = \{P_n\}_{n\in\mathbb{N}}$ is called **efficiently computable and invertible** if the following three conditions hold:*

1. Efficient indexing: *There exists a probabilistic polynomial-time algorithm I and a mapping from strings to permutation, ϕ, such that $\phi(I(1^n))$ and P_n are identically distributed.*

2. Efficient evaluation: *There exists a probabilistic polynomial-time algorithm V such that $V(i, x) = f_i(x)$, where (as in Definition 3.6.3) $f_i \overset{\text{def}}{=} \phi(i)$.*

3. Efficient inversion: *There exists a probabilistic polynomial-time algorithm N such that $N(i, x) = f_i^{-1}(x)$ (i.e., $f_i(N(i, x)) = x$).*

Items 1 and 2 are guaranteed by the definition of an efficiently computable permutation ensemble. The additional requirement is stated in Item 3. In some settings it makes sense to augment the definition of a pseudorandom ensemble by requiring that the ensemble cannot be distinguished from the uniform one even when the observer gets access to two oracles: one for the permutation and the other for its inverse. Thus, we consider augmented oracle machines that can make queries to two oracles; the two-oracle model can be emulated by the standard (single) oracle model by combining the two oracles f_1 and f_2 into one oracle f defined by $f(i, q) = f_i(q)$.

Definition 3.7.5 (Strong Pseudorandom Permutations): *A permutation ensemble $P = \{P_n\}_{n\in\mathbb{N}}$ is called **strongly pseudorandom** if for every probabilistic* *polynomial-time oracle machine M, every polynomial p(·), and all sufficiently large n's,*

$$\left|\Pr\left[M^{P_n, P_n^{-1}}(1^n)=1\right] - \Pr\left[M^{K_n, K_n^{-1}}(1^n)=1\right]\right| < \frac{1}{p(n)}$$

where $M^{f,g}$ denotes the execution of machine M when given access to the oracles f and g.

3.7.2. Construction

The construction of pseudorandom permutations uses pseudorandom functions as building blocks, in a manner identical to the high-level structure of the DES (see Figure 3.6). Namely:

Construction 3.7.6: *Let $f : \{0, 1\}^n \to \{0, 1\}^n$. For every $x, y \in \{0, 1\}^n$, we define*

$$\mathrm{DES}_f(x, y) \stackrel{\mathrm{def}}{=} (y, x \oplus f(y))$$

where $x \oplus y$ denotes the bit-by-bit XOR of the binary strings x and y. Likewise, for $f_1, \ldots, f_t : \{0, 1\}^n \to \{0, 1\}^n$, we define

$$\mathrm{DES}_{f_t,\ldots,f_1}(x, y) \stackrel{\mathrm{def}}{=} \mathrm{DES}_{f_t,\ldots,f_2}(\mathrm{DES}_{f_1}(x, y))$$

For every function ensemble $F = \{F_n\}_{n \in \mathbb{N}}$ and every function $t : \mathbb{N} \to \mathbb{N}$, we define the function ensemble $\{\mathrm{DES}_{F_n}^{t(n)}\}_{n \in \mathbb{N}}$ by letting $\mathrm{DES}_{F_n}^{t(n)} \stackrel{\mathrm{def}}{=} \mathrm{DES}_{F_n^{(t)},\ldots,F_n^{(1)}}$, where $t = t(n)$ and the $F_n^{(i)}$'s are independent copies of the random variable F_n.

Theorem 3.7.7: *Let F_n, $t(\cdot)$, and $\mathrm{DES}_{F_n}^{t(n)}$ be as in Construction 3.7.6. Suppose that $\{F_n\}_{n \in \mathbb{N}}$ is efficiently computable and that on input n one can compute $t(n)$ in $\mathrm{poly}(n)$ time. Then for every polynomial-time-computable function $t(\cdot)$, the ensemble $\{\mathrm{DES}_{F_n}^{t(n)}\}_{n \in \mathbb{N}}$ is an efficiently computable and invertible permutation*

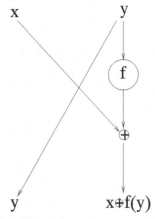

Figure 3.6: The high-level structure of the DES.

ensemble. Furthermore, if $F = \{F_n\}_{n\in\mathbb{N}}$ is a pseudorandom function ensemble, then the ensemble $\{DES^3_{F_n}\}_{n\in\mathbb{N}}$ is pseudorandom and the ensemble $\{DES^4_{F_n}\}_{n\in\mathbb{N}}$ is strongly pseudorandom.

Clearly, the ensemble $\{DES'^{(n)}_{F_n}\}_{n\in\mathbb{N}}$ is efficiently computable. The fact that it is a permutation ensemble, and furthermore one with an efficient inverting algorithm, follows from the observation that $DES_{zero, f, zero}$ is the inverse of DES_f, where $zero(z) \stackrel{\text{def}}{=} 0^{|z|}$ for all $z \in \{0, 1\}^n$. That is, for every $x, y \in \{0, 1\}^n$, $DES_{zero}(x, y) = (y, x)$, and

$$DES_{zero, f, zero}(DES_f(x, y)) = DES_{zero, f, zero}(y, x \oplus f(y))$$
$$= DES_{zero, f}(x \oplus f(y), y)$$
$$= DES_{zero}(y, (x \oplus f(y)) \oplus f(y))$$
$$= (x, y)$$

To prove the pseudorandomness of $\{DES^3_{F_n}\}_{n\in\mathbb{N}}$ (resp., strong pseudorandomness of $\{DES^4_{F_n}\}_{n\in\mathbb{N}}$) it suffices to prove the pseudorandomness of $\{DES^3_{H_n}\}_{n\in\mathbb{N}}$ (resp., strong pseudorandomness of $\{DES^4_{H_n}\}_{n\in\mathbb{N}}$). The reason is that if, say, $\{DES^4_{H_n}\}_{n\in\mathbb{N}}$ is pseudorandom, while $\{DES^3_{F_n}\}_{n\in\mathbb{N}}$ is not, then one can derive a contradiction to the pseudorandomness of the function ensemble F (i.e., distinguish F from the uniform function ensemble H; see Exercise 35). Hence, Theorem 3.7.7 follows from Proposition 3.7.8.

Proposition 3.7.8: $\{DES^3_{H_n}\}_{n\in\mathbb{N}}$ *is pseudorandom, whereas* $\{DES^4_{H_n}\}_{n\in\mathbb{N}}$ *is strongly pseudorandom.*

Proof Sketch: We start by proving that $\{DES^3_{H_n}\}_{n\in\mathbb{N}}$ is pseudorandom. Let $P_{2n} \stackrel{\text{def}}{=} \{DES^3_{H_n}\}_{n\in\mathbb{N}}$, and let K_{2n} be the random variable uniformly distributed over all possible permutations acting on $\{0, 1\}^{2n}$. We prove that for every oracle machine M that on input 1^n asks at most m queries, it holds that

$$\left| \Pr[M^{P_{2n}}(1^n)=1] - \Pr[M^{K_{2n}}(1^n)=1] \right| \leq \frac{2m^2}{2^n} \tag{3.17}$$

Let $q_i = (L^0_i, R^0_i)$, with $|L^0_i|=|R^0_i|=n$, be a random variable representing the ith query of M when given access to oracle P_{2n}. Recall that $P_{2n} = DES_{H^{(3)}_n, H^{(2)}_n, H^{(1)}_n}$, where the $H^{(j)}_n$'s are three independent random variables, each uniformly distributed over the functions acting on $\{0, 1\}^n$. Let $R^{k+1}_i \stackrel{\text{def}}{=} L^k_i \oplus H^{(k+1)}_n(R^k_i)$ and $L^{k+1}_i \stackrel{\text{def}}{=} R^k_i$ for $k = 0, 1, 2$. That is,

$$(L^{k+1}_i, R^{k+1}_i) = (R^k_i, L^k_i \oplus H^{(k+1)}_n(R^k_i))$$

We assume, without loss of generality, that M never asks the same query twice. We define a random variable ζ_m representing the event that there exist $i < j \leq m$ and $k \in \{1, 2\}$ such that $R^k_i = R^k_j$ (namely, on input 1^n and access to oracle P_{2n}, two of the m first queries of M satisfy the relation $R^k_i = R^k_j$). We use the following two claims.

Claim 3.7.8.1: For every $m \geq 1$, conditioned on $\neg \zeta_m$, the R_i^3's are uniformly and independently distributed over $\{0, 1\}^n$, and the L_j^3's are uniformly distributed over the n-bit strings not assigned to previous L_j^3's. Namely, for every $\alpha_1, \ldots, \alpha_m \in \{0, 1\}^n$,

$$\Pr\left[\wedge_{i=1}^m \left(R_i^3 = \alpha_i\right) \mid \neg \zeta_m\right] = \left(\frac{1}{2^n}\right)^m \qquad (3.18)$$

whereas for every *distinct* $\beta_1, \ldots, \beta_m \in \{0, 1\}^n$,

$$\Pr\left[\wedge_{i=1}^m \left(L_i^3 = \beta_i\right) \mid \neg \zeta_m\right] = \prod_{i=1}^m \frac{1}{2^n - i + 1} \qquad (3.19)$$

Proof Idea: Eq. (3.18) follows from the observation that the R_i^3's are determined by applying the random function $H_n^{(3)}$ to different arguments (i.e., the R_i^2's), where the distinctness of the R_i^2's is implied by $\neg \zeta_m$. Similarly, the $L_i^3 = R_i^3$'s are determined by applying the random function $H_n^{(2)}$ to different arguments (i.e., the R_i^1's), and $\neg \zeta_m$ also conditions the results (i.e., the R_i^2's) to be different. Thus, Eq. (3.19) also holds. $\square$

Claim 3.7.8.2: For every $m \geq 1$,

$$\Pr[\zeta_{m+1} \mid \neg \zeta_m] \leq \frac{2m}{2^n}$$

Proof Idea: Fixing any $i \leq m$, we consider the probability that $R_{m+1}^1 = R_i^1$. There are two cases:

1. If $R_i^0 = R_{m+1}^0$, then certainly (since $(L_i^0, R_i^0) \neq (L_{m+1}^0, R_{m+1}^0)$) we have

$$R_i^1 = L_i^0 \oplus H_n^{(1)}(R_i^0) = L_i^0 \oplus H_n^{(1)}(R_{m+1}^0) \neq L_{m+1}^0 \oplus H_n^{(1)}(R_{m+1}^0) = R_{m+1}^1$$

2. On the other hand, if $R_i^0 \neq R_{m+1}^0$, then

$$\Pr\left[R_i^1 = R_{m+1}^1\right] = \Pr\left[H_n^{(1)}(R_i^0) \oplus H_n^{(1)}(R_{m+1}^0) = L_i^0 \oplus L_{m+1}^0\right] = 2^{-n}$$

where the last equality holds because the random function $H_n^{(1)}$ is applied to different arguments (i.e., R_i^0 and R_{m+1}^0).

Thus, in both cases, $\Pr[R_i^1 = R_{m+1}^1] \leq 2^{-n}$. In similarity to the foregoing Case 2, conditioned on $R_i^1 \neq R_{m+1}^1$, we have

$$\Pr\left[R_i^2 = R_{m+1}^2\right] = \Pr\left[H_n^{(2)}(R_i^1) \oplus H_n^{(2)}(R_{m+1}^1) = R_i^0 \oplus R_{m+1}^0\right] = 2^{-n}$$

Thus, for every $i \leq m$,

$$\Pr\left[R_i^1 = R_{m+1}^1 \vee R_i^2 = R_{m+1}^2\right] \leq \Pr\left[R_i^1 = R_{m+1}^1\right] + \Pr\left[R_i^2 = R_{m+1}^2 \mid R_i^1 \neq R_{m+1}^1\right]$$
$$\leq 2 \cdot 2^{-n}$$

and the claim follows. $\square$

Using $\Pr[\zeta_m] \leq \Pr[\zeta_{m-1}] + \Pr[\zeta_m \mid \neg \zeta_{m-1}]$ and Claim 3.7.8.2, it follows, by induction on m, that $\Pr[\zeta_m] < \frac{m^2}{2^n}$. By Claim 3.7.8.1, conditioned on $\neg \zeta_m$, the answers of P_{2n} have left halves that are uniformly chosen among all n-bit strings not appearing as left halves in previous answers, whereas the right halves are uniformly distributed among all n-bit strings. On the other hand, the answers of K_{2n} are uniformly distributed among all $2n$-bit strings not appearing as previous answers. Hence, the statistical difference between the distributions of answers in the two cases (i.e., answers by P_{2n} or by K_{2n}) is bounded above by $\frac{m^2}{2^n} + \binom{m}{2} \cdot 2^{-n} < \frac{2m^2}{2^n}$, and Eq. (3.17) follows.

The proof that $\{DES^4_{H_n}\}_{n \in \mathbb{N}}$ is strongly pseudorandom is more complex, yet uses essentially the same ideas.[11] In particular, the event corresponding to ζ_m is the disjunction of four types of events. Events of the first type are of the form $R^k_i = R^k_j$ for $k \in \{2, 3\}$, where $q_i = (L^0_i, R^0_i)$ and $q_j = (L^0_j, R^0_j)$ are queries of the forward direction. Similarly, events of the second type are of the form $R^k_i = R^k_j$ for $k \in \{2, 1\}$, where $q_i = (L^4_i, R^4_i)$ and $q_j = (L^4_j, R^4_j)$ are queries of the backward direction. Events of the third type are of the form $R^k_i = R^k_j$ for $k \in \{2, 3\}$, where $q_i = (L^0_i, R^0_i)$ is of the forward direction, $q_j = (L^4_j, R^4_j)$ is of the backward direction, and $j < i$. Similarly, events of the fourth type are of the form $R^k_i = R^k_j$ for $k \in \{2, 1\}$, where $q_i = (L^4_i, R^4_i)$ is of the backward direction, $q_j = (L^0_j, R^0_j)$ is of the forward direction, and $j < i$. As before, one bounds the probability of event ζ_m and bounds the statistical distance between answers by K_{2n} and answers by $\{DES^4_{H_n}\}_{n \in \mathbb{N}}$ given that ζ_m is false. ∎

3.8. Miscellaneous

3.8.1. Historical Notes

The notion of computationally indistinguishable ensembles was first presented by Goldwasser and Micali (in the context of encryption schemes) [123]. In the general setting, the notion first appeared in Yao's work, which was also the origin of the definition of pseudorandomness [210]. Yao also observed that pseudorandom ensembles could be very far from uniform, yet our proof of Proposition 3.2.3 is taken from [107].

Pseudorandom generators were introduced by Blum and Micali [36], who defined such generators as producing sequences that are unpredictable. Blum and Micali proved that such pseudorandom generators do exist assuming the intractability of the discrete-logarithm problem. Furthermore, they presented a general paradigm for constructing pseudorandom generators that has been used explicitly or implicitly in all subsequent developments. Other suggestions for pseudorandom generators by Goldwasser et al. [126] and Blum et al. [32] soon followed. Consequently, Yao proved that the existence of any one-way *permutation* implies the existence of pseudorandom generators [210]. Yao was the first to define pseudorandom generators as producing sequences that are computationally indistinguishable from uniform sequences. He also proved

---

[11] Here we assume that the machine avoids queries to which it knows the answers. That is, not only does it not make the same query twice, but also if it makes the forward (resp., backward) query q and receives the answer a, then it does not make a backward (resp., forward) query a.

that this definition of pseudorandom generators is equivalent to the definition of Blum and Micali [36].

Generalizations of Yao's result, by which one-way *permutations* imply pseudorandom generators, were published by Levin [150] and by Goldreich, Krawczyk, and Luby [108], culminating with the result of Håstad, Impagliazzo, Levin, and Luby [129] asserting that pseudorandom generators exist if and only if one-way *functions* exist. The constructions presented in Section 3.5 follow those ideas [108, 129]. These constructions make extensive use of universal$_2$ hashing functions, which were introduced by Carter and Wegman [49] and were first used in complexity theory by Sipser [201].

Simple pseudorandom generators based on specific intractability assumptions are presented in [36, 32, 5, 208, 141]. In particular, [5] presents pseudorandom generators based on the intractability of factoring, whereas [141] presents pseudorandom generators based on the intractability of various discrete-logarithm problems (see Section 2.4.3.4). In both cases, the main technical step is the construction of hard-core predicates for the corresponding collections of one-way permutations.

Pseudorandom functions were introduced and investigated by Goldreich, Goldwasser, and Micali [102]. In particular, the construction of pseudorandom functions based on pseudorandom generators is taken from [102]. First applications of pseudorandom functions were given in [103, 89, 90], and the list of applications has been rapidly growing since.

Pseudorandom permutations were defined and constructed by Luby and Rackoff [156], and our presentation follows their work.

The hybrid method originated from the work of Goldwasser and Micali [123]. The terminology was suggested by Leonid Levin.

3.8.2. Suggestions for Further Reading

A wider perspective on pseudorandomness is offered by Goldreich [97]. It surveys various notions of pseudorandom generators, viewing the one discussed in this chapter as an archetypical instantiation of a general paradigm. The general paradigm amounts to considering as pseudorandom those distributions that cannot be distinguished from the uniform distribution by certain types of resource-bounded distinguishers. The complexity of the generator itself, as well as its stretch function, can vary as well (rather than being polynomial-time and polynomially bounded, respectively, as here). Starting with the general paradigm, Chapter 3 of [97] surveys the archetypical case of pseudorandom generators (considered here), as well as generators withstanding space-bounded distinguishers, the de-randomization of complexity classes such as $\mathcal{BPP}$, and various special-purpose generators. (Readers interested in Kolmogorov complexity are referred elsewhere [152].)

Proposition 3.2.3 presents a pair of ensembles that are computationally indistinguishable, although they are statistically far apart. This is shown without making any intractability assumptions, but one of the two ensembles is not constructible in polynomial time. This situation is unavoidable, because the existence of a pair of polynomial-time-constructible ensembles having such properties (i.e., being computationally indistinguishable and yet statistically far apart) implies the existence of one-way functions [93]. Other abstract results regarding the notion of computational indistinguishability appear in [111, 119].

Combining Theorem 2.5.6 and Construction 3.4.7, we obtain a generic (black-box) construction of a pseudorandom generator based on any one-way permutation that outputs a logarithmic number of bits per each application of the one-way permutation. Elsewhere [88] it is shown that as far as generic (black-box) constructions go, this is the best performance (i.e., number of output bits per an application of the one-way permutation) that one can expect.

Section 3.5 falls short of presenting the construction of Håstad et al. [129], not to mention proving its validity. Unfortunately, the proof of this fundamental theorem, asserting that pseudorandom generators exist if one-way functions exist, is too complicated to fit into this book. The interested reader is thus referred to the original paper [129].

Alternative constructions of pseudorandom functions were given in [172]. Constructions of unbounded-input (and generalized) pseudorandom functions based on (ordinary) pseudorandom functions are discussed in [14].

An alternative presentation of the construction of pseudorandom permutations (based on pseudorandom functions) can be found in [173]. That alternative distills the real structure of the proof and provides related results.

Pseudorandom generators and functions have many applications to cryptography; some of them will be presented in Volume 2 of this book (e.g., signatures and encryption).

Using Sources of Imperfect Randomness. Pseudorandom generators and functions enable us to expand randomness (or pseudorandomness), but they do not allow us to "generate randomness (or pseudorandomness) deterministically." In fact, we cannot expect to have an efficient deterministic program that generates pseudorandom objects (because the very same program may be employed by the distinguisher). In order to employ a pseudorandom generator (or function), we need to start with a random seed, and the question is where to obtain it. The answer is that this random seed (or something that appears so) can be obtained by sampling some physical phenomena. Indeed, such samples may not be uniformly distributed over the set of strings (of a specific length), yet if they contain enough entropy, then almost perfect randomness can be (efficiently) extracted from them. Methods for such randomness extraction will be discussed in the third volume of this book.

The Random Oracle Methodology. In contrast to the methodology discussed in Section 3.6.3, the *Random Oracle Model* refers to a setting in which the adversary has *direct* access to a random oracle (that is later "implemented" by a function, the description of which is given also to the adversary). The *Random Oracle Methodology* [80, 21] consists of first designing an *ideal* system in which all parties (including the adversary) have oracle access to a truly random function, and then replacing the random oracle by a "good cryptographic hashing function," providing all parties (including the adversary) the succinct description of this function. Recall that, in contrast, the methodology of Section 3.6.3 refers to a situation in which the adversary does not have direct oracle access to the random function and does not obtain the description of the pseudorandom function used in the latter implementation. We warn that, in contrast to the methodology presented in Section 3.6.3, the Random Oracle Methodology is heuristic. In particular, there exist encryption and signature schemes that are secure in the Random Oracle Model, but *do not* have *any* secure implementation by a function ensemble [46].

3.8.3. Open Problems

Although Håstad et al. [129] showed how to construct pseudorandom generators given any one-way *function*, their construction is not practical, the reason being that the "quality" of the generator on seeds of length n is related to the hardness of inverting the given function on inputs of length less than $\sqrt{n}$. We believe that presenting an efficient transformation of arbitrary one-way functions to pseudorandom generators is one of the most important open problems in this area and that doing so may require the discovery of new important paradigms.

An open problem of more acute practical importance is to present even more efficient pseudorandom generators based on the intractability of specific computational problems like integer factorization. For further details, see Sections 3.4.3 and 2.7.3.

3.8.4. Exercises

Exercise 1: *Computational indistinguishability, trivial variations:* Prove that the following trivial variations on Definition 3.2.2 are equivalent to it. In all versions we consider the ensembles $X \overset{\text{def}}{=} \{X_n\}_{n \in \mathbb{N}}$ and $Y \overset{\text{def}}{=} \{Y_n\}_{n \in \mathbb{N}}$.

1. Ensembles X and Y are *indistinguishable1 in polynomial time* if for every probabilistic polynomial-time algorithm D, every positive polynomial $p(\cdot)$, and all sufficiently large n's,

$$|\Pr[D(X_n, 1^n) = 1] - \Pr[D(Y_n, 1^n) = 1]| \leq \frac{1}{p(n)}$$

That is, the strict inequality is replaced by $\leq$.

2. Ensembles X and Y are *indistinguishable2 in polynomial time* if for every probabilistic polynomial-time algorithm D, every positive polynomial $p(\cdot)$, and all sufficiently large n's,

$$\Pr[D(X_n, 1^n) = 1] - \Pr[D(Y_n, 1^n) = 1] < \frac{1}{p(n)}$$

That is, the absolute value is dropped.

3. Suppose that $|X_n| = |Y_n| = n$. Ensembles X and Y are *indistinguishable3 in polynomial time* if for every probabilistic polynomial-time algorithm D, every positive polynomial $p(\cdot)$, and all sufficiently large n's,

$$|\Pr[D(X_n) = 1] - \Pr[D(Y_n) = 1]| < \frac{1}{p(n)}$$

That is, the auxiliary input 1^n is omitted.

Exercise 2: *Computational indistinguishability is preserved by efficient algorithms*: Let $\{X_n\}_{n\in\mathbb{N}}$ and $\{Y_n\}_{n\in\mathbb{N}}$ be two ensembles that are polynomial-time-indistinguishable.
1. For any probabilistic polynomial-time algorithm A, prove that the ensembles $\{A(X_n)\}_{n\in\mathbb{N}}$ and $\{A(Y_n)\}_{n\in\mathbb{N}}$ are polynomial-time-indistinguishable.
2. Show that if A is not polynomial-time, then $\{A(X_n)\}_{n\in\mathbb{N}}$ and $\{A(Y_n)\}_{n\in\mathbb{N}}$ are *not* necessarily polynomial-time-indistinguishable.

Exercise 3: *Statistical closeness is preserved by any function*: Let $\{X_n\}_{n\in\mathbb{N}}$ and $\{Y_n\}_{n\in\mathbb{N}}$ be two ensembles that are statistically close, and let $f:\{0,1\}^* \to \{0,1\}^*$ be a function. Prove that the ensembles $\{f(X_n)\}_{n\in\mathbb{N}}$ and $\{f(Y_n)\}_{n\in\mathbb{N}}$ are statistically close.

Exercise 4: Prove that for every $L \in \mathcal{BPP}$ and every pair of polynomial-time-indistinguishable ensembles $\{X_n\}_{n\in\mathbb{N}}$ and $\{Y_n\}_{n\in\mathbb{N}}$, it holds that the function

$$\Delta_L(n) \overset{\text{def}}{=} |\Pr[X_n \in L] - \Pr[Y_n \in L]|$$

is negligible in n.

It is tempting to think that the converse holds as well, but we do not know whether or not it does; note that $\{X_n\}$ and $\{Y_n\}$ can be distinguished by a probabilistic algorithm, but not by a deterministic one. In such a case, which language should we define? For example, suppose that A is a probabilistic polynomial-time algorithm, and let $L \overset{\text{def}}{=} \{x : \Pr[A(x) = 1] \geq \frac{1}{2}\}$. Then L is not necessarily in $\mathcal{BPP}$. (Exercise 5 shows that in the non-computational setting both the foregoing and its converse are true.)

Exercise 5: *An equivalent formulation of statistical closeness*: Prove that two ensembles, $\{X_n\}_{n\in\mathbb{N}}$ and $\{Y_n\}_{n\in\mathbb{N}}$, are statistically close if and only if for every set $S \subseteq \{0,1\}^*$,

$$\Delta_S(n) \overset{\text{def}}{=} |\Pr[X_n \in S] - \Pr[Y_n \in S]|$$

is negligible in n.
   Guideline: Show that the statistical difference between X_n and Y_n, as defined in Eq. (3.1), equals $\max_S\{\Delta_S(n)\}$.

Exercise 6: *Statistical closeness implies computational indistinguishability*: Prove that if two ensembles are statistically close, then they are polynomial-time-indistinguishable.
   Guideline: Use the result of Exercise 5, and define for every function $f:\{0,1\}^* \to \{0,1\}$ a set $S_f \overset{\text{def}}{=} \{x : f(x)=1\}$.

Exercise 7: *An information-theoretic analogue of Theorem 3.2.6*: Prove that if two ensembles are statistically close, then their polynomial products must be statistically close.
   Guideline: Show that the statistical difference between the m-products of two distributions is bounded by m times the distance between the individual distributions.

Exercise 8: *Computational indistinguishability by circuits, probabilism versus determinism*: Let $\{X_n\}_{n\in\mathbb{N}}$ and $\{Y_n\}_{n\in\mathbb{N}}$ be two ensembles, and let $C \overset{\text{def}}{=} \{C_n\}_{n\in\mathbb{N}}$ be a family of probabilistic polynomial-size circuits. Prove that there exists a family of (deterministic)

— **173** —

polynomial-size circuits $D \overset{\text{def}}{=} \{D_n\}_{n \in \mathbb{N}}$ such that for every n,

$$\Delta_D(n) \geq \Delta_C(n)$$

where

$$\Delta_D(n) \overset{\text{def}}{=} |\Pr[D_n(X_n) = 1] - \Pr[D_n(Y_n) = 1]|$$
$$\Delta_C(n) \overset{\text{def}}{=} |\Pr[C_n(X_n) = 1] - \Pr[C_n(Y_n) = 1]|$$

Exercise 9: *Computational indistinguishability by circuits, single sample versus several samples*: Prove that $X = \{X_n\}_{n \in \mathbb{N}}$ and $Y = \{Y_n\}_{n \in \mathbb{N}}$ are indistinguishable by polynomial-size circuits (as per Definition 3.2.7) if and only if their $m(\cdot)$-products are indistinguishable by polynomial-size circuits, for every polynomial $m(\cdot)$. We stress that X and Y need not be polynomial-time-constructible.

  Guideline: A "good choice" of $x^1, \ldots, x^k$ and $y^{k+2}, \ldots, y^m$ can be "hard-wired" into the circuit.

Exercise 10: *Computational indistinguishability, circuits versus algorithms*:
1. (*Easy*) Suppose that the ensembles $X = \{X_n\}_{n \in \mathbb{N}}$ and $Y = \{Y_n\}_{n \in \mathbb{N}}$ are indistinguishable by polynomial-size circuits. Prove that they are computationally indistinguishable (by probabilistic polynomial-time algorithms).

  Guideline: Use Exercise 8.
2. (*Hard*) Show that there exist ensembles that are computationally indistinguishable (by probabilistic polynomial-time algorithms), but are distinguishable by polynomial-size circuits.

  Guideline (Part 2): Given any function $f : \{0, 1\}^* \to [0, 1]$, prove the existence of an ensemble $X = \{X_n\}_{n \in \mathbb{N}}$ such that each X_n has support of size at most 2 and yet $\Pr[f(X_n) = 1] = \Pr[f(U_n) = 1]$, where U_n is uniformly distributed over $\{0, 1\}^n$. Generalize the argument so that given t such functions, $f_1, \ldots, f_t : \{0, 1\}^* \to [0, 1]$, each X_n has support of size at most $t + 1$ and yet $\Pr[f_i(X_n) = 1] = \Pr[f_i(U_n) = 1]$ for each $i = 1, \ldots, t$. (Extra hint: Consider the t-dimensional vectors $(f_1(x), \ldots, f_t(x))$ for each $x \in \{0, 1\}^n$ and think of convex hulls.) A standard diagonalization argument will finish the job. (In case you did not get it, consult [111].)

Exercise 11: Prove that the existence of a pair of polynomial-time-constructible ensembles that are computationally indistinguishable and are not statistically close implies the existence of one-way functions.

  Guideline: We seek a simpler proof than one presented earlier [93], where it was proved that the hypothesis implies the existence of pseudorandom generators. Still, the main idea of that proof should be applied: Taking sufficiently many independent copies of each ensemble, construct two computationally indistinguishable ensembles that are "almost disjoint" (i.e., have statistical difference at least $1 - 2^{-n}$). Next, assuming for a moment that the ensembles are disjoint (i.e., have statistical difference 1), prove the conclusion of this exercise (by using a variant of the proof of Proposition 3.3.8). Finally, deal with the general case by using an analogous argument in order to show that the hypothesis implies the existence of a "distributionally one-way function" as in Exercise 17 of Chapter 2.

Exercise 12: Prove that pseudorandom generators do not assign noticeable probability mass to any string. That is, if G is a pseudorandom generator, then for every positive polynomial p and all sufficiently large n and α, $\Pr[G(U_n) = \alpha] < 1/p(n)$.

Exercise 13: *Do pseudorandom generators induce* 1-1 *mappings?* That is, if G is a pseudorandom generator, is it the case that the mapping $G : \{0, 1\}^n \to \{0, 1\}^{l(n)}$ is 1-1?
1. Show that if pseudorandom generators exist, then there exist pseudorandom generators G such that the mapping $G : \{0, 1\}^n \to \{0, 1\}^{l(n)}$ is not 1-1.
2. Show that if one-way permutations exist, then there exist pseudorandom generators G such that the mapping $G : \{0, 1\}^n \to \{0, 1\}^{l(n)}$ is 1-1.

Exercise 14: Let G be a pseudorandom generator, and let h be a polynomial-time-computable permutation (over strings of the same length). Prove that G' and G'' defined by $G'(s) \stackrel{\text{def}}{=} h(G(s))$ and $G''(s) \stackrel{\text{def}}{=} G(h(s))$ are both pseudorandom generators.

Exercise 15: Suppose that G is a pseudorandom generator, and consider the following modifications to it:
1. $G'(s) \stackrel{\text{def}}{=} 0^{|G(s)|}$ if the number of 1's in s is exactly $|s|/2$, and $G'(s) \stackrel{\text{def}}{=} G(s)$ otherwise.
2. $G''(s) \stackrel{\text{def}}{=} 0^{|G(s)|}$ if the number of 1's in s is exactly $|s|/3$, and $G''(s) \stackrel{\text{def}}{=} G(s)$ otherwise.
Which of these is a pseudorandom generator?

Exercise 16: Analogously to Exercise 9 in Chapter 2, refute the following conjecture:

For every pseudorandom generator G, the function $G'(s) \stackrel{\text{def}}{=} G(s) \oplus s0^{|G(s)|-|s|}$ is also a pseudorandom generator.

Guideline: Let g be a pseudorandom generator, and consider G defined on pairs of strings of the same length such that $G(r, s) = (r, g(s))$.

Exercise 17: *A more general definition of a pseudorandom generator:* The following definition deviates from the standard one by refraining from the length-regular requirement regarding the generator (i.e., it is not required that $|G(x)| = |G(y)|$ for all $|x| = |y|$). A *general pseudorandom generator* is a deterministic polynomial-time algorithm G satisfying the following two conditions:

Expansion: For every $s \in \{0, 1\}^*$, it holds that $|G(s)| > |s|$.

Pseudorandomness (as in Definition 3.3.1): The ensemble $\{G(U_n)\}_{n \in \mathbb{N}}$ is pseudorandom.

Prove the following statements:
1. If there exists a general pseudorandom generator, then there exists a standard one.
2. Let G be a general pseudorandom generator, and let $l : \mathbb{N} \to \mathbb{N}$ be such that $\{G(U_n)\}_{n \in \mathbb{N}}$ is polynomial-time-indistinguishable from $\{U_{l(n)}\}_{n \in \mathbb{N}}$.
   (a) Prove that $l(n) > n$ holds for all but finitely many n's.
   (b) Prove that the probability that $G(U_n)$ has length not equal to $l(n)$ is negligible (in n).
   Guideline (Part 2b): The difficult case is when $l(n)$ is not computable in poly(n) time from n (otherwise, one can simply compare the length of the tested string to $l(n)$). In the

general case, first prove that there exists a function $l' : \mathbb{N} \to \mathbb{N}$ such that the probability that $|G(U_n)| \neq l'(n)$ is negligible (in n). (Hint: Otherwise, one could distinguish polynomial products of $G(U_n)$ from polynomial products of $U_{l(n)}$.) Next prove that $l'(n) = l(n)$ by considering a distinguisher that on input 1^n and a string to be tested, α, first samples $G(U_n)$ and compares its length to $|\alpha|$.

Exercise 18: Consider a modification of Construction 3.3.2, where $s_i \sigma_i = G_1(s_{i-1})$ is used instead of $\sigma_i s_i = G_1(s_{i-1})$. Provide a *simple* proof that the resulting algorithm is also pseudorandom.

    Guideline: Do not modify the proof of Theorem 3.3.3, but rather modify G_1 itself.

Exercise 19: *Alternative construction of pseudorandom generator with large expansion factor*: Let G_1 be a pseudorandom generator with expansion factor $l(n) = n+1$, and let $p(\cdot)$ be a polynomial. Define $G(s)$ to be the result of applying G_1 iteratively $p(|s|)$ times on s (i.e., $G(s) \overset{\text{def}}{=} G_1^{p(|s|)}(s)$, where $G_1^0(s) \overset{\text{def}}{=} s$ and $G_1^{i+1} \overset{\text{def}}{=} G_1(G_1^i(s))$).

    Prove that G is a pseudorandom generator.

    What are the advantages of using Construction 3.3.2?

Exercise 20: *An alternative definition of unpredictable ensembles*: Consider a modification to Definition 3.3.6 in which the quantification is over only (probabilistic polynomial-time) algorithms that never read the entire input. That is, in every execution of such an algorithm A, on input $(1^{|x|}, x)$, algorithm A reads at most $|x| - 1$ bits of x. Prove that the modified definition is equivalent to the original one.

    Guideline: Since the scope of the modified definition is smaller that the scope of the original one, we need only show how to convert an arbitrary probabilistic polynomial-time algorithm A into one that never reads the entire input and still has at least the same success probability in predicting the next bit. This can be done by emulating A without ever reading the last input bit, so that whenever A tries to read the last input bit, we halt with a uniformly selected output bit. (Otherwise, we faithfully emulate A.) Note that in case A reads its last input bit, its output-prediction bit is correct with probability $\frac{1}{2}$ (by the fictitious definition of next$_A$ in this case; see Definition 3.3.6). This success probability is met by our modified algorithm that outputs a uniformly selected bit as a guess of the last input bit.

Exercise 21: *On-line pseudorandom generator*: Recall that variable-output pseudorandom generators (see Section 3.3.3) are deterministic polynomial-time programs that when given a random seed will produce an infinite sequence of bits such that every polynomially long prefix of it will be pseudorandom. On-line pseudorandom generators are a special case of variable-output pseudorandom generators in which a hidden state is maintained and updated so as to allow generation of the next output bit in time polynomial in the length of the seed, regardless of the number of bits generated thus far. On-line pseudorandom generators are defined through their *next-step function* that maps the current state of the generator to a pair consisting of an output bit and a next state. That is, a polynomial-time algorithm g mapping n-bit-long strings to $(n+1)$-bit-long strings is called a *next-step function of an on-line pseudorandom generator* if for every polynomial p the ensemble $\{G_n^p\}_{n \in \mathbb{N}}$ is pseudorandom, where G_n^p is defined by the following random process:

Uniformly select $s_0 \in \{0, 1\}^n$.

For $i = 1$ to $p(n)$, do $\sigma_i \cdot s_i \leftarrow g(s_{i-1})$, where $\sigma_i \in \{0, 1\}$ (and $s_i \in \{0, 1\}^n$).

Output $\sigma_1 \sigma_2 \cdots \sigma_{p(n)}$.

That is, s_0 is the initial (random) state of the on-line pseudorandom generator, and s_i is its state after outputting i bits. (Indeed, the definition of this ensemble is similar to Construction 3.3.2.)

1. Prove that if G is an ordinary pseudorandom generator with expansion function $\ell(n) = n + 1$, then it also constitutes a next-step function of an on-line pseudorandom generator.

   Guideline: Use the similarity mentioned earlier.

2. Show that the converse does not necessarily hold; that is, if g is the next-step function of an on-line pseudorandom generator, then it is not necessarily a pseudorandom generator.

   Guideline: Given a next-step function g', consider the next-step function $g(s \cdot r) = g'(s) \cdot 0^{|r|}$ for (say) $|r| = |s|$.

3. Still, show that given any (next-step function g of an) on-line pseudorandom generator, one can easily construct a pseudorandom generator.

   Guideline: Just activate the on-line generator enough times.

This definition of (a next-step function of) an on-line pseudorandom generator guarantees that the current state of the generator does not grow in size/length with the number of bits generated. We next consider a somewhat relaxed definition that allows moderate growth in the size/length of the current state. For example, consider a relaxed definition of an on-line pseudorandom generator that allows (polynomial-time-computable) next-step functions g that map m-bit-long strings to $(m + O(1))$-bit-long strings. (The distribution considered is again defined by selecting s_0 uniformly in $\{0, 1\}^n$, letting $\sigma_i \cdot s_i = g(s_{i-1})$, where $\sigma_i \in \{0, 1\}$, and outputting $\sigma_1 \sigma_2 \cdots \sigma_{p(n)}$; however, here $|s_{p(n)}| \neq |s_0|$, unless $|g(s)| = |s| + 1$ as before.)

- Show that using the relaxed definition of an on-line pseudorandom generator does not guarantee that each next output bit will be generated in time polynomial in the length of the seed (i.e., regardless of the number of bits generated thus far).
- Show that the foregoing Item 3 still holds.
- Let g be the next-step function of a relaxed on-line pseudorandom generator, and let $T_g(m)$ denote the complexity of computing g on inputs of length m. Provide an upper bound on the complexity of producing $t(n)$ bits out of an n-bit seed in the relaxed on-line pseudorandom generator based on g. Compare this bound to the one obtained for a non-relaxed on-line pseudorandom generator.
- How much can we allow the current state to grow at each step so as to maintain polynomial-time operation when outputting polynomially many bits?

Exercise 22: *Constructions of hashing families:* We associate ℓ-dimensional binary vectors with ℓ-bit-long strings.

1. Consider the set S_n^m of functions mapping n-bit-long strings into m-bit strings. A function $h_{A,b}$ in S_n^m is represented by a pair (A, b), where A is an n-by-m binary matrix and b is an m-dimensional binary vector. The n-dimensional binary vector x is mapped by the function $h_{A,b}$ to the m-dimensional binary vector resulting from multiplying x by A and adding the vector b to the resulting vector (i.e., $h_{A,b}(x) = xA + b$). Prove that S_n^m so defined constitutes a hashing family (as defined in Section 3.5.1.1).

2. Repeat Item 1 when the n-by-m matrices are restricted to be Toeplitz matrices. An n-by-m Toeplitz matrix $T = \{T_{i,j}\}$ satisfies $T_{i,j} = T_{i+1,j+1}$ for all i, j.

Note that binary n-by-m Toeplitz matrices can be represented by strings of length $n + m - 1$, whereas representing arbitrary n-by-m binary matrices requires strings of length $n \cdot m$.

> **Guideline:** For every $x \neq x'$ in $\{0, 1\}^n$ and every $v, v' \in \{0, 1\}^m$, show that the number of functions $h \in S_n^m$ that satisfy $h(x) = v$ and $h(x') = v'$ is independent of v and v'. For example, in Part 1, each such function is associated with a pair (A, b), and we consider the pairs satisfying the system of equations $xA + b = v$ and $x'A + b = v'$ (or, equivalently, $xA + b = v$ and $(x - x')A = v - v'$), where x, x', v, and v' are fixed and the entries of A and b are the unknowns.

Exercise 23: *Another construction of hashing families*: Here we use an efficiently manipulated representation of the finite field $GF(2^n)$. This requires an irreducible polynomial of degree n over the two-element field $GF(2)$. For specific values of n, a good representation exists: Specifically, for $n = 2 \cdot 3^e$ (with e integer), the polynomial $x^n + x^{n/2} + 1$ is irreducible over $GF(2)$ [153, Thm. 1.1.28].

For $m \leq n$, consider the set S_n^m of functions mapping n-bit-long strings into m-bit strings as follows. A function $h_{a,b}$ in S_n^m is represented by two elements $a, b \in GF(2^n)$, and for every $x \in GF(2^n)$, the value of $h_{a,b}(x)$ equals the m-bit prefix in an n-bit representation of $ax + b$, where the arithmetic is of the field $GF(2^n)$.

1. Prove that S_n^m so defined constitutes a hashing family.

2. Prove that all but an exponentially vanishing fraction of the functions in S_n^m are regular (i.e., 2^{n-m}-to-1).

> **Guideline:** For Part 1, use the fact that for every $x \neq x'$ and every $v, v' \in GF(2^n)$, there exists a single pair (a, b) such that $ax + b = v$ and $ax' + b = v'$. For Part 2, use the fact that for every $a \neq 0$ and b, the mapping $x \mapsto ax + b$ is 1-1.

Exercise 24: *Another hashing lemma*: Let m, n, S_n^m, b, X_n, and δ be as in Lemma 3.5.1. Prove that for every set $S \subseteq \{0, 1\}^m$ and for all but at most a $2^{-(b-m+\log_2 |S|)} \cdot \delta^{-2}$ fraction of the h's in S_n^m, it holds that

$$\Pr[h(X_n) \in S] \in (1 \pm \delta) \cdot \frac{|S|}{2^m}$$

> **Guideline:** Follow the proof of Lemma 3.5.1, defining $\zeta_x(h) = 1$ if $h(x) \in S$, and 0 otherwise.

Exercise 25: *Yet another hashing lemma*: Let m, n, and S_n^m be as before, and let $B \subseteq \{0, 1\}^n$ and $S \subseteq \{0, 1\}^m$ be sets. Prove that for all but at most a $\frac{2^m}{|B| \cdot |S|} \cdot \delta^{-2}$ fraction of the h's in S_n^m, it holds that

$$|\{x \in B : h(x) \in S\}| \in (1 \pm \delta) \cdot \frac{|S|}{2^m} \cdot |B|$$

> **Guideline:** Define a random variable X_n that is uniformly distributed over B.

Exercise 26: *Failure of an alternative construction of pseudorandom functions*: Consider a construction of a function ensemble where the functions in F_n are defined as follows. For every $s \in \{0, 1\}^n$, the function f_s is defined such that

$$f_s(x) \stackrel{\text{def}}{=} G_{\sigma_n}(\cdots(G_{\sigma_2}(G_{\sigma_1}(x)))\cdots)$$

where $s = \sigma_1 \cdots \sigma_n$ and G_σ is as in Construction 3.6.5. Namely, the roles of x and s in Construction 3.6.5 are switched (i.e., the root of the tree is labeled by x, and the value of f_s on x is obtained by following the path corresponding to the index s). Prove that the resulting function ensemble is not necessarily pseudorandom (even if G is a pseudorandom generator).

Guideline: Show, first, that if pseudorandom generators exist, then there exists a pseudorandom generator G satisfying $G(0^n) = 0^{2n}$.

Exercise 27: *Pseudorandom generators with direct access:* A *direct-access pseudorandom generator* is a deterministic polynomial-time algorithm G for which no probabilistic polynomial-time oracle machine can distinguish the following two cases:
1. New queries of the oracle machine are answered by independent flips of an unbiased coin. (Repeating the same query twice yields the same answer.)
2. First, a random "seed" s of length n is uniformly chosen. Next, each query q is answered by $G(s, q)$.

The bit $G(s, i)$ can be thought of as the ith bit in a bit sequence corresponding to the seed s, where i is represented in binary.

- Prove that the existence of (ordinary) pseudorandom generators implies the existence of pseudorandom generators with direct access.
    Guideline: A pseudorandom generator with direct access is essentially a pseudorandom function ensemble.
- Show that modifying this definition, so that only unary queries are allowed, will yield an alternative definition of a relaxed on-line pseudorandom generator (as defined in Exercise 21).
    Guideline: Given a next-step function g of a relaxed on-line pseudorandom generator, we obtain a generator G supporting "direct access" to a polynomially long sequence by letting $G(s, 1^i)$ be the ith bit produced by the relaxed on-line generator on initial state s. Conversely, given such a "unary direct-access" machine G, we obtain a next-step function g by letting $g(s, 1^i) = (G(s, 1^{i+1}), (s, 1^{i+1}))$. (That is, the ith state is $(s, 1^i)$, where $s \equiv (s, \lambda)$ is the initial state.)
- Evaluate the advantage of direct-access pseudorandom generators over on-line pseudorandom generators *even in settings requiring direct access only to bits of a polynomially long pseudorandom sequence.*

Exercise 28: Consider pseudorandom function ensembles as defined in Definition 3.6.4, with respect to a length function $\ell : \mathbb{N} \to \mathbb{N}$.
1. Show that for $\ell(n) > \log_2 n$, any such pseudorandom function gives rise to a pseudorandom generator. In fact, it suffices to have $\ell(n)^{\ell(n)} > n$.
2. For $\ell(n)^{\ell(n)} \leq n$, present a construction of a pseudorandom function ensembles with length $\ell : \mathbb{N} \to \mathbb{N}$, without relying on any assumptions.

Exercise 29: Let $\{f'_s : \{0, 1\}^{d(|s|)} \to \{0, 1\}^{|s|}\}_{s \in \{0,1\}^*}$ be a generalized pseudorandom function ensemble, and suppose that G' is polynomial-time-computable and that the ensemble $\{G'(U_n)\}_{n\in\mathbb{N}}$ is pseudorandom, as defined in Definition 3.2.8. (If G' is a pseudorandom generator, then it satisfies both conditions, but the converse is not true.)

Prove that the generalized function ensemble $\{f_s : \{0, 1\}^{d(|s|)} \rightarrow \{0, 1\}^{r(|s|)}\}_{s\in\{0,1\}^*}$, defined by $f_s(x) \overset{\text{def}}{=} G'(f'_s(x))$, is pseudorandom.

Guideline: See proof of Theorem 3.6.11.

Exercise 30: *Speeding up pseudorandom function constructions* (suggested by Leonid Levin): For some $d, r : \mathbb{N} \rightarrow \mathbb{N}$, consider a generalized pseudorandom function ensemble

$$F \overset{\text{def}}{=} \{f_s : \{0, 1\}^{d(|s|)} \rightarrow \{0, 1\}^{r(|s|)}\}_{s\in\{0,1\}^*}$$

as in Definition 3.6.9. Let Primes$_m$ denote the set of primes in the interval $(2^{m-1}, 2^m)$. For any $d' : \mathbb{N} \rightarrow \mathbb{N}$, consider a new function ensemble,

$$F' \overset{\text{def}}{=} \{f'_{s,p} : \{0, 1\}^{d'(|s|)} \rightarrow \{0, 1\}^{r(|s|)}\}_{s\in\{0,1\}^*, p\in\text{Primes}_{d(|s|)}}$$

such that $f'_{s,p}(x) \overset{\text{def}}{=} f_s(x \bmod p)$, where $\{0, 1\}^{d'(|s|)}$ and $\{0, 1\}^{d(|s|)}$ are associated with $\{0, \ldots, 2^{d'(|s|)} - 1\}$ and $\{0, \ldots, 2^{d(|s|)} - 1\}$, respectively.

The point is that the functions in F' are computable in time related to the time-complexity of F. Whenever $d'(n) \gg d(n)$ (e.g., $d'(n) = n^2$ and $d(n) = \log_n^2 n$), this yields a speedup in the time-complexity of F' (when compared with Construction 3.6.10).

1. Prove that if $d(n) = \omega(\log n)$, then F' is pseudorandom.

2. Show that, on the other hand, if $d(n) = O(\log n)$ (and $d'(n) > d(n)$), then F' is not pseudorandom.

Note that, in general, the "pseudorandomness" of F' (as quantified with respect to the running time sufficient to see evidence that F' is not random) depends on $d : \mathbb{N} \rightarrow \mathbb{N}$. Specifically, evidence that F' is not random can be found in time exponential in d.

Guideline (Part 2): Going over all possible p's, try to gather evidence that the target function indeed uses reduction modulo p. (Hint: For fixed p, any two distinct $x, y \in \{0, 1\}^{d'(|s|)}$ such that $x \equiv y \pmod p$ yield such evidence.)

Guideline (Part 1): Consider applying the foregoing construction to the uniform function ensemble H, rather than to the pseudorandom ensemble F. The main issue is to show that the resulting ensemble H' is pseudorandom. (F' is indistinguishable from H', or else we can distinguish F from H.)

Guideline (Part 1, extra hints): We refer to the function ensemble $H' = \{H'_n\}_{n\in\mathbb{N}}$, where H'_n is defined by uniformly selecting a function $h : \{0, 1\}^{d(n)} \rightarrow \{0, 1\}^{r(n)}$ and $p \in \text{Prime}_{d(n)}$ and letting $H'_n = h'_p$ such that $h'_p(x) = h(x \bmod p)$. If the distinct queries $x_1, \ldots, x_t \in \{0, 1\}^{d'(n)}$ have distinct residues mod p, then the answers obtained from h'_p are independently and uniformly distributed in $\{0, 1\}^{r(n)}$. Thus, essentially, we need to lower-bound the probability of the former event for a uniformly selected $p \in \text{Prime}_{d(n)}$. We upper-bound the probability of the complementary event (i.e., $\exists i \neq j$ s.t. $x_i \equiv x_j \pmod p$). For distinct $x, y \in \{0, 1\}^{d'(n)}$, it holds that $x \equiv y \pmod p$ iff p divides $x - y$. At this stage the argument is simplified by the fact that p is prime:[12] The probability that a uniformly

---

[12] What if the construction were to be modified so that p was uniformly selected among all integers in $\{2^{d(n)-1}, \ldots, 2^{d(n)} - 1\}$?

chosen $d(n)$-bit-long prime divides a $d'(n)$-bit-long integer is at most $\frac{d'(n)/d(n)}{|\text{Prime}_{d(n)}|}$, which is $\Theta(d'(n) \cdot 2^{-d(n)})$.

Exercise 31: *An alternative construction for Exercise 30:* Let F and let d' be as in Exercise 30, and let $S_{d'(n)}^{d(n)}$ be a hashing family (as defined in Section 3.5.1.1). For every $s \in \{0, 1\}^*$ and $h \in S_{d'(|s|)}^{d(|s|)}$, define $f'_{s,h}$ such that $f'_{s,h}(x) = f_s(h(x))$, and let

$$F' \stackrel{\text{def}}{=} \{ f'_{s,h} : \{0, 1\}^{d'(|s|)} \to \{0, 1\}^{r(|s|)} \}_{s \in \{0,1\}^*, h \in S_{d'(|s|)}^{d(|s|)}}$$

(This construction requires longer seeds than the one in Exercise 30; however, one can use much smaller families of functions that approximate the desired features.)
1. Prove that if $d(n) = \omega(\log n)$, then F' is pseudorandom.
2. On the other hand, show that if $d(n) = O(\log n)$ and $r(n) > d(n)$, then F' is not pseudo-random.

Guideline (Part 2): For any distinct $x, y \in \{0, 1\}^{d'(n)}$ and a uniformly selected function mapping $d'(n)$-bit-long strings to $r(n)$-bit-long string, the probability that x and y are mapped to the same image is $2^{-r(n)}$. However, the probability that x and y are mapped to the same image under a uniformly selected $f'_{s,h}$ is lower-bounded by $\Pr[h(x) = h(y)] = 2^{-d(n)}$.

Exercise 32: *An alternative definition of pseudorandom functions:* For the sake of sim-plicity, this exercise is stated in terms of ensembles of Boolean functions (analogously to Definition 3.6.9, with $d(n) = n$ and $r(n) = 1$). That is, we consider a Boolean-function ensemble $\{ f_s : \{0, 1\}^{|s|} \to \{0, 1\} \}_{s \in \{0,1\}^*}$ and let F_n be uniformly distributed over the multi-set $\{ f_s \}_{s \in \{0,1\}^n}$. We say that the function ensemble $\{F_n\}_{n \in \mathbb{N}}$ is *unpredictable* if for every probabilistic polynomial-time oracle machine M, for every polynomial $p(\cdot)$, and for all sufficiently large n's,

$$\Pr\left[\text{corr}^{F_n}(M^{F_n}(1^n))\right] < \frac{1}{2} + \frac{1}{p(n)}$$

where $M^{F_n}(1^n)$ assumes values of the form $(x, \sigma) \in \{0, 1\}^n \times \{0, 1\}$ such that x is *not* a query appearing in the computation $M^{F_n}(1^n)$, and $\text{corr}^f(x, \sigma)$ is defined as the predicate "$f(x) = \sigma$". Intuitively, after getting the values of f on points of its choice, the machine M outputs a new point (i.e., x) along with a guess (i.e., σ) for the value of f on this point. The value of $\text{corr}^f(x, \sigma)$ represents whether or not M is correct in its guess.

Assuming that $F = \{F_n\}_{n \in \mathbb{N}}$ is efficiently computable, prove that F is pseudorandom if and only if F is unpredictable.

Guideline: The proof is analogous to the proof of Theorem 3.3.7

Exercise 33: *A mistaken "alternative" definition of pseudorandom functions:* Again, we consider ensembles of Boolean functions, as in Exercise 32. Consider the following definition of *weak unpredictability* of function ensembles. The predicting oracle machine M is given a uniformly chosen $x \in \{0, 1\}^n$ as input and should output a guess for $f(x)$, after querying the oracle f on polynomially many other (than x) points of its choice. We require that for every probabilistic polynomial-time oracle machine M that *does not* query the oracle on its own input, for every polynomial $p(\cdot)$, and for all sufficiently large n's,

$$\Pr[M^{F_n}(U_n) = F_n(U_n)] < \frac{1}{2} + \frac{1}{p(n)}$$

That is, unlike the formulation of Exercise 32, the predicting machine cannot select the point for which it has to predict the value of the function (but rather this point is random and is given as input).

1. Show that any pseudorandom function ensemble is weakly unpredictable.
2. Assuming that pseudorandom function ensembles exist, show that there exists a function ensemble that is weakly unpredictable, although it is not pseudorandom.

This exercise contradicts a flawed claim (which appeared in earlier versions of this manuscript). The flaw was pointed out by Omer Reingold.

> **Guideline:** For Part 1, show that unpredictability, as defined in Exercise 32, implies weak unpredictability. Alternatively, provide a direct proof (as in Exercise 32). For Part 2, modify a pseudorandom function ensemble so that each f in the range of F_n satisfies $f(0^n) = 0$.

Exercise 34: *An unsuccessful attempt to strengthen the notion of weak unpredictability of function ensembles so that it is equivalent to pseudorandomness of functions:* In continuation of Exercise 33, suppose that we strengthen the requirement by allowing the input x to be chosen from any polynomial-time-constructible ensemble. Namely, here we say that a function ensemble $F = \{F_n\}_{n \in \mathbb{N}}$ is *weakly2 unpredictable* if for every probabilistic polynomial-time oracle machine M that *does not* query the oracle on its own input, for every polynomial-time-constructible ensemble $\{X_n\}_{n \in \mathbb{N}}$, where X_n ranges over $\{0, 1\}^n$, for every polynomial $p(\cdot)$, and for all sufficiently large n's,

$$\Pr[M^{F_n}(X_n) = F_n(X_n)] < \frac{1}{2} + \frac{1}{p(n)}$$

Again, show that this definition is a necessary but insufficient condition for pseudorandom function ensembles.

> **Guideline:** Modify the function ensemble so that each f in the range of F_n satisfies $f(f(a^1) f(a^2) \cdots f(a^n)) = 0$, where $a^1, \ldots, a^n \in \{0, 1\}^n$ are some easy-to-compute strings (e.g., $a^i = 0^{i-1}10^{n-i}$).

Exercise 35: Let $t : \mathbb{N} \to \mathbb{N}$ be such that on input n, one can compute $t(n)$ in poly(n) time. Let $\{F_n\}_{n \in \mathbb{N}}$ and $\{H_n\}_{n \in \mathbb{N}}$ be two function ensembles that are indistinguishable by any probabilistic polynomial-time oracle machine. Prove that the permutation ensembles $\{\text{DES}_{F_n}^{t(n)}\}_{n \in \mathbb{N}}$ and $\{\text{DES}_{H_n}^{t(n)}\}_{n \in \mathbb{N}}$ (defined as in Section 3.7.2) are indistinguishable by any probabilistic polynomial-time oracle machine. Furthermore, this holds even when the oracle machine is given access both to the permutation and to its inverse (as in Definition 3.7.5).

> **Guideline:** Use a hybrid argument to bridge between the $t(n)$ independent copies of F_n and the $t(n)$ independent copies of H_n. The ith hybrid is $\text{DES}_{F_n^{(t(n))}, \ldots, F_n^{(i+1)}, H_n^{(i)}, \ldots, H_n^{(1)}}$. Note that oracle access to the permutation $\text{DES}_{F_n^{(t(n))}, \ldots, F_n^{(i+2)}, g, H_n^{(i)}, \ldots, H_n^{(1)}}$ (as well as to its inverse) can be emulated by using oracle access to the function g.

Exercise 36: Let F_n and $\text{DES}_{F_n}^t$ be as in Construction 3.7.6. Prove that regardless of the choice of the ensemble $F = \{F_n\}_{n \in \mathbb{N}}$, the ensemble $\text{DES}_{F_n}^2$ is *not* pseudorandom.

Guideline: Start by showing that the ensemble $DES^1_{F_n}$ is *not* pseudorandom (a single query suffices here). Use two related queries in order to distinguish $DES^2_{F_n}$ from a random permutation.

Exercise 37 (Suggested by Luca Trevisan): Assuming the existence of pseudorandom function ensembles, prove that there exists a pseudorandom permutation ensemble that is *not* strongly pseudorandom.

Guideline: First construct a pseudorandom permutation ensemble with seed length smaller than or equal to the logarithm of domain size. Next modify it so that the seed is mapped to a fixed point (e.g., the all-zero string) and so that the modified ensemble remains one of permutations.

Exercise 38: In similarity to Exercise 36, prove that the ensemble $DES^3_{F_n}$ is *not strongly* pseudorandom.

Guideline: This requires more thought and probably more than a couple of queries. You should definitely use queries to both oracles.

CHAPTER 4

Zero-Knowledge Proof Systems

In this chapter we discuss zero-knowledge (ZK) proof systems. Loosely speaking, such proof systems have the remarkable property of being convincing *and* yielding nothing (beyond the validity of the assertion). In other words, receiving a zero-knowledge proof that an assertion holds is equivalent to being told by a trusted party that the assertion holds (see illustration in Figure 4.1). The main result presented in this chapter is a method for constructing zero-knowledge proof systems for every language in $\mathcal{NP}$. This method can be implemented using any bit-commitment scheme, which in turn can be implemented using any pseudorandom generator. The importance of this method stems from its generality, which is the key to its many applications. Specifically, almost all statements one may wish to prove in practice can be encoded as claims concerning membership in languages in $\mathcal{NP}$. In addition, we discuss more advanced aspects of the concept of zero-knowledge and their effects on the applicability of this concept.

Organization. The basic material is presented in Sections 4.1 through 4.4. In particular, we start with motivation (Section 4.1), next we define and exemplify the notions of interactive proofs (Section 4.2) and of zero-knowledge (Section 4.3), and finally

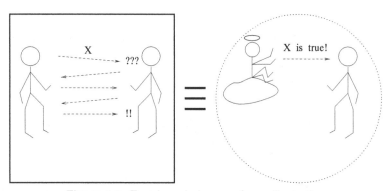

Figure 4.1: Zero-knowledge proofs: an illustration.

Section 4.5:	*Negative results*
Section 4.6:	*Witness indistinguishability* and *witness hiding*
Section 4.7:	*Proofs of knowledge*
Section 4.8:	*Computationally sound proofs* (*arguments*)
Section 4.9:	*Constant-round* zero-knowledge systems
Section 4.10:	*Non-interactive zero-knowledge* proofs
Section 4.11:	*Multi-prover* zero-knowledge proofs

Figure 4.2: The advanced sections of this chapter.

we present a zero-knowledge proof system for every language in $\mathcal{NP}$ (Section 4.4). Sections dedicated to advanced topics follow (see Figure 4.2). Unless stated differently (in the following list and in Figure 4.3), each of these advanced sections can be read independently of the others.

- In Section 4.5 we present some *negative results* regarding zero-knowledge proofs. These results demonstrate the "optimality" of the results in Section 4.4 and motivate the variants presented in Sections 4.6 and 4.8.

- In Section 4.6 we present a major relaxation of zero-knowledge and prove that it is closed under parallel composition (which is not the case, in general, for zero-knowledge). Here we refer to a notion called *witness indistinguishability*, which is related to *witness hiding* (also defined and discussed).

- In Section 4.7 we define and discuss (zero-knowledge) *proofs of knowledge*.

- In Section 4.8 we discuss a relaxation of interactive proofs, termed *computationally sound proofs* (or *arguments*).

- In Section 4.9 we present two constructions of *constant-round* zero-knowledge systems. The first is an interactive proof system, whereas the second is an argument system. Section 4.8.2 (discussing perfectly hiding commitment schemes) is a prerequisite for the first construction, whereas Sections 4.8, 4.7, and 4.6 constitute a prerequisite for the second.

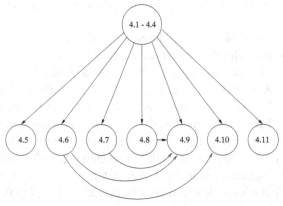

Figure 4.3: The dependence structure of this chapter.

_____ **185** _____

- In Section 4.10 we discuss *non-interactive zero-knowledge* proofs. The notion of witness indistinguishability (defined in Section 4.6) is a prerequisite for the results presented in Section 4.10.3.1.

- In Section 4.11 we discuss *multi-prover* proof systems.

We conclude, as usual, with a miscellaneous section (Section 4.12).

Teaching Tip. The interactive proof system for Graph Non-Isomorphism (presented in Section 4.2) and the zero-knowledge proof of Graph Isomorphism (presented in Section 4.3) are merely illustrative examples. Thus, one should avoid analyzing those examples in detail.

4.1. Zero-Knowledge Proofs: Motivation

An archetypical cryptographic problem consists of providing mutually distrustful parties with a means of disclosing (predetermined) "pieces of information." It refers to settings in which parties posses secrets, and they wish to reveal parts of these secrets. The secrets are fully or partially determined by some publicly known information, and so it makes sense to talk about revealing the correct value of the secret. The question is how to allow verification of newly revealed parts of the secret without disclosing other parts of the secret. To clarify the issue, let us consider a specific example.

> Suppose that all users in a system keep backups of their entire file systems, encrypted using their secret keys, in publicly accessible storage media. Suppose that at some point, one user, called Alice, wishes to reveal to another user, called Bob, the cleartext of some record in one of her files (which appears in her backup). A trivial "solution" is for Alice simply to send the (cleartext) record to Bob. The problem with this "solution" is that Bob has no way of verifying that Alice has really sent him the true record (as appearing encrypted in her public backup), rather than just sending him an arbitrary record. Alice could prove that she sent the correct record simply by revealing to Bob her secret key. However, doing so would reveal to Bob the contents of all her files, which is certainly something that Alice does not want. The question is whether or not Alice can convince Bob that she has indeed revealed the correct record without yielding any additional "knowledge."
>
> An analogous problem can be phrased formally as follows. Let f be a one-way *permutation* and b a hard-core predicate with respect to f. Suppose that one party, A, has a string x, whereas another party, denoted B, has only $f(x)$. Furthermore, suppose that A wishes to reveal $b(x)$ to party B, without yielding any further information. The trivial "solution" is to let A send $b(x)$ to B, but, as explained earlier, B will have no way of verifying that A has really sent the correct bit (and not its complement). Party A could indeed prove that it has sent the correct bit (i.e., $b(x)$) by sending x as well, but revealing x to B would be much more than what A originally had in mind. Again, the question is whether or not A can convince B that it has indeed revealed the correct bit (i.e., $b(x)$), without yielding any additional "knowledge."

In general, the question is whether or not *it is possible to prove a statement without yielding anything beyond its validity.* Such proofs, whenever they exist, are called *zero-knowledge*, and they play a central role in the construction of "cryptographic" protocols.

Loosely speaking, *zero-knowledge proofs are proofs that yield nothing* (i.e., "no knowledge") *beyond the validity of the assertion.* In the rest of this introductory section, we discuss the notion of a "proof" and a possible meaning of the phrase "yield nothing (i.e., no knowledge) beyond something."

4.1.1. The Notion of a Proof

> *A proof is whatever convinces me.*
> Shimon Even, answering a student's question
> in his graph-algorithms class (1978)

We discuss the notion of a proof with the intention of uncovering some of its underlying aspects.

4.1.1.1. A Static Object versus an Interactive Process

Traditionally in mathematics, a "proof" is a *fixed* sequence consisting of statements that either are self-evident or are derived from previous statements via self-evident rules. Actually, it is more accurate to replace the phrase "self-evident" with the phrase "commonly agreed." In fact, in the formal study of proofs (i.e., logic), the commonly agreed statements are called *axioms*, whereas the commonly agreed rules are referred to as *derivation rules*. We wish to stress two properties of mathematical proofs:

1. Proofs are viewed as fixed objects.

2. Proofs are considered at least as fundamental as their consequences (i.e., the theorems).

However, in other areas of human activity, the notion of a "proof" has a much wider interpretation. In particular, a proof is not a fixed object, but rather a process by which the validity of an assertion is established. For example, withstanding cross-examination in court can yield what can be considered a proof in law, and failure to provide an adequate answer to a rival's claim is considered a proof in philosophical, political, and sometimes even technical discussions. In addition, in many real-life situations, proofs are considered secondary (in importance) to their consequences.

To summarize, in "canonical" mathematics, proofs have a static nature (e.g., they are "written"), whereas in real-life situations proofs have a dynamic nature (i.e., they are established via an interaction). A dynamic interpretation of the notion of a proof is more appropriate to our setting, in which proofs are used as tools (i.e., sub-protocols) inside "cryptographic" protocols. Furthermore, a dynamic interpretation (at least in a weak sense) is essential to the non-triviality of the notion of a zero-knowledge proof.

4.1.1.2. Prover and Verifier

The notion of a prover is implicit in all discussions of proofs, be it in mathematics or in real-life situations: The prover is the (sometimes hidden or transcendental) entity providing the proof. In contrast, the notion of a verifier tends to be more explicit in such discussions, which typically emphasize the *verification process*, or in other words the role of the verifier. Both in mathematics and in real-life situations, proofs are defined in terms of the verification procedure. The verification procedure is considered to be relatively simple, and the burden is placed on the party/person supplying the proof (i.e., the prover).

The asymmetry between the complexity of the verification task and the complexity of the theorem-proving task is captured by the complexity class $\mathcal{NP}$, which can be viewed as a class of proof systems. Each language $L \in \mathcal{NP}$ has an efficient verification procedure for proofs of statements of the form "$x \in L$." Recall that each $L \in \mathcal{NP}$ is characterized by a polynomial-time-recognizable relation R_L such that

$$L = \{x : \exists y \text{ s.t. } (x, y) \in R_L\}$$

and $(x, y) \in R_L$ only if $|y| \leq \text{poly}(|x|)$. Hence, the verification procedure for membership claims of the form "$x \in L$" consists of applying the (polynomial-time) algorithm for recognizing R_L to the claim (encoded by) x and a prospective proof, denoted y. Any y satisfying $(x, y) \in R_L$ is considered a *proof* of membership of $x \in L$. Thus, correct statements (i.e., $x \in L$) and only these have proofs in this proof system. Note that the verification procedure is "easy" (i.e., polynomial-time), whereas coming up with proofs may be "difficult" (if indeed $\mathcal{NP}$ is not contained in $\mathcal{BPP}$).

It is worthwhile to note the "distrustful attitude" toward the prover that underlies any proof system. If the verifier trusts the prover, then no proof is needed. Hence, whenever discussing a proof system, one considers a setting in which the verifier is not trusting the prover and furthermore is skeptical of anything the prover says.

4.1.1.3. Completeness and Soundness

Two fundamental properties of a proof system (i.e., a verification procedure) are its *soundness* (or *validity*) and *completeness*. The soundness property asserts that the verification procedure cannot be "tricked" into accepting false statements. In other words, *soundness* captures the verifier's ability to protect itself from being convinced of false statements (no matter what the prover does in order to fool the verifier). On the other hand, *completeness* captures the ability of some prover to convince the verifier of true statements (belonging to some predetermined set of true statements). Note that both properties are essential to the very notion of a proof system.

We remark here that not every set of true statements has a "reasonable" proof system in which each of those statements can be proved (while no false statement can be "proved"). This fundamental fact is given precise meaning in results such as *Gödel's Incompleteness Theorem* and *Turing's* theorem regarding the *undecidability of the Halting Problem*. We stress that in this chapter we confine ourselves to the class of sets (of valid statements) that do have "efficient proof systems." In fact, Section 4.2 is devoted to discussing and formulating the concept of "efficient proof systems." Jumping ahead, we hint that the efficiency of a proof system will be associated with the efficiency of its verification procedure.

4.1.2. Gaining Knowledge

Recall that we have motivated zero-knowledge proofs as proofs by which the verifier gains "no knowledge" (beyond the validity of the assertion). The reader may rightfully wonder what knowledge is and what a gain in knowledge is. When discussing zero-knowledge proofs, we avoid the first question (which is quite complex) and treat the second question directly. Namely, *without* presenting a definition of knowledge, we present a generic case in which it is certainly justified to say that no knowledge is gained. Fortunately, this approach seems to suffice as far as cryptography is concerned.

To motivate the definition of zero-knowledge, consider a conversation between two parties, Alice and Bob. Assume first that this conversation is unidirectional; specifically, Alice only talks, and Bob only listens. Clearly, we can say that Alice gains no knowledge from the conversation. On the other hand, Bob may or may not gain knowledge from the conversation (depending on what Alice says). For example, if all that Alice says is "$1 + 1 = 2$," then clearly Bob gains no knowledge from the conversation, because he already knows that fact. If, on the other hand, Alice reveals to Bob a proof that $\mathcal{P} \neq \mathcal{NP}$, then he certainly gains knowledge from the conversation.

To give a better flavor of the definition, we now consider a conversation between Alice and Bob in which Bob asks Alice questions about a large graph (that is known to both of them). Consider first the case in which Bob asks Alice whether or not the graph[1] is Eulerian. Clearly, Bob gains no knowledge from Alice's answer, because he could easily have determined the answer by himself (by running a linear-time decision procedure[2]). On the other hand, if Bob asks Alice whether or not the graph is Hamiltonian, and Alice (somehow) answers this question, then we cannot say that Bob has gained no knowledge (because we do not know of an efficient procedure by which Bob could have determined the answer by himself, and assuming $\mathcal{P} \neq \mathcal{NP}$, no such efficient procedure exists). Hence, we say that Bob *has gained knowledge* from the interaction if his *computational ability*, concerning the publicly known graph, *has increased* (i.e., if after the interaction he can easily compute something that he could not have efficiently computed before the interaction). On the other hand, if whatever Bob can efficiently compute about the graph *after interacting* with Alice he can also efficiently compute *by himself* (from the graph), then we say that Bob *has gained no knowledge* from the interaction. That is, Bob gains knowledge only if he receives the result of a computation that is infeasible for him. The question of how Alice could conduct this infeasible computation (e.g., answer Bob's question of whether or not the graph is Hamiltonian) has been ignored thus far. Jumping ahead, we remark that Alice may be a mere abstraction or may be in possession of additional hints that enable her to efficiently conduct computations that are otherwise infeasible (and in particular are infeasible for Bob, who does not have these hints).

---

[1] See Footnote 13.

[2] For example, by relying on Euler's theorem, which asserts that a graph is Eulerian if and only if it is connected and all its vertices have even degrees.

Knowledge versus Information

We wish to stress that *knowledge* (as discussed here) is very different from *information* (in the sense of information theory). Two major aspects of the difference are as follows:

1. *Knowledge* is related to computational difficulty, whereas *information* is not. In the foregoing examples, there is a difference between the knowledge revealed in the case in which Alice answers questions of the form "Is the graph Eulerian?" and the case in which she answers questions of the form "Is the graph Hamiltonian?" From an information-theory point of view there is no difference between the two cases (i.e., in each case the answer is determined by the question, and so Bob gets no information).

2. *Knowledge* relates mainly to publicly known objects, whereas *information* relates mainly to objects on which only partial information is publicly known. Consider the case in which Alice answers each question by flipping an unbiased coin and telling Bob the outcome. From an information-theoretic point of view, Bob gets from Alice information concerning an event. However, we say that Bob gains no knowledge from Alice, because he could toss coins by himself.

4.2. Interactive Proof Systems

In this section we introduce the notion of an interactive proof system and present a non-trivial example of such a system (specifically to claims of the form "the following two graphs are *not* isomorphic"). The presentation is directed toward the introduction of zero-knowledge interactive proofs. Interactive proof systems are interesting for their own sake and have important complexity-theoretic applications.[3]

4.2.1. Definition

The definition of an interactive proof system refers explicitly to the two computational tasks related to a proof system: "producing" a proof and verifying the validity of a proof. These tasks are performed by two different parties, called the *prover* and the *verifier*, which interact with one another. In some cases, the interaction may be very simple and, in particular, unidirectional (i.e., the prover sends a text, called the proof, to the verifier). In general, the interaction may be more complex and may take the form of the verifier interrogating the prover. We start by defining such an interrogation process.

4.2.1.1. Interaction

Interaction between two parties is defined in the natural manner. The only point worth noting is that the interaction is parameterized by a common input (given to both parties). In the context of interactive proof systems, the common input represents the statement to be proved. We first define the notion of an interactive machine and next the notion

---

[3]See the suggestions for further reading at the end of the chapter.

of interaction between two such machines. The reader may skip to Section 4.2.1.2, which introduces some important conventions (regarding interactive machines), with little loss (if any).

Definition 4.2.1 (An Interactive Machine):

- *An* **interactive Turing machine** (ITM) *is a (deterministic) multi-tape Turing machine. The tapes are a read-only* input tape, *a read-only* random tape, *a read-and-write* work tape, *a write-only* output tape, *a pair of* communication tapes, *and a read-and-write* switch tape *consisting of a single cell. One communication tape is read-only, and the other is write-only.*
- *Each ITM is associated a single bit $\sigma \in \{0, 1\}$, called its* **identity**. *An ITM is said to be* active, *in a configuration, if the content of its switch tape equals the machine's identity. Otherwise the machine is said to be* idle. *While being idle, the state of the machine, the locations of its heads on the various tapes, and the contents of the writable tapes of the ITM are not modified.*
- *The content of the input tape is called* **input**, *the content of the random tape is called* random input, *and the content of the output tape at termination is called* **output**. *The content written on the write-only communication tape during a (time) period in which the machine is active is called the* **message sent** *at that period. Likewise, the content read from the read-only communication tape during an active period is called the* **message received** *(at that period).*

   (Without loss of generality, the machine movements on both communication tapes are in only one direction, e.g., from left to right.)

This definition, taken by itself, seems quite non-intuitive. In particular, one may say that once being idle, the machine will never become active again. One may also wonder as to what is the point of distinguishing the read-only communication tape from the input tape (and respectively distinguishing the write-only communication tape from the output tape). The point is that we are never going to consider a single interactive machine, but rather a pair of machines combined together such that some of their tapes coincide. Intuitively, the messages sent by one interactive machine are received by a second machine that shares its communication tapes (so that the read-only communication tape of one machine coincides with the write-only tape of the other machine). The active machine may become idle by changing the content of the shared switch tape, and when it does so, the other machine (having opposite identity) will become active. The computation of such a pair of machines consists of the machines alternately sending messages to one another, based on their initial (common) input, their (distinct) random inputs, and the messages each machine has received thus far.

Definition 4.2.2 (Joint Computation of Two ITMs):

- *Two interactive machines are said to be* **linked** *if they have opposite identities, their input tapes coincide, their switch tapes coincide, and the read-only communication tape of one machine coincides with the write-only communication tape of the other machine, and vice versa. We stress that the other tapes of both machines (i.e., the random tape, the work tape, and the output tape) are distinct.*

—— **191** ——

- *The **joint computation** of a linked pair of ITMs, on a common input x, is a sequence of pairs representing the local configurations of both machines. That is, each pair consists of two strings, each representing the local configuration of one of the machines. In each such pair of local configurations, one machine (not necessarily the same one) is active, while the other machine is idle. The first pair in the sequence consists of initial configurations corresponding to the common input x, with the content of the switch tape set to zero.*
- *If one machine halts while the switch tape still holds its identity, then we say that both machines have halted. The **outputs** of both machines are determined at that time.*

At this point, the reader may object to this definition, saying that the individual machines are deprived of individual local inputs (whereas they are given individual and unshared random tapes). This restriction is removed in Section 4.2.4, and in fact allowing individual local inputs (in addition to the common shared input) is quite important (at least as far as practical purposes are concerned). Yet, for a first presentation of interactive proofs, as well as for demonstrating the power of this concept, we prefer the foregoing simpler definition. On the other hand, the convention of individual random tapes is essential to the power of interactive proofs (see Exercise 4).

4.2.1.2. Conventions Regarding Interactive Machines

Typically, we consider executions in which the content of the random tape of each machine is uniformly and independently chosen (among all infinite bit sequences). The convention of having an infinite sequence of internal coin tosses should not bother the reader, because during a finite computation only a finite prefix is read (and matters). The content of each of these random tapes can be viewed as internal coin tosses of the corresponding machine (as in the definition of ordinary probabilistic machines presented in Chapter 1). Hence, interactive machines are in fact probabilistic.

Notation. Let A and B be a linked pair of ITMs, and suppose that all possible interactions of A and B on each common input terminate in a finite number of steps. We denote by $\langle A, B \rangle(x)$ the random variable representing the (local) output of B when interacting with machine A on common input x, when the random input to each machine is uniformly and independently chosen. (Indeed, this definition is asymmetric, since it considers only B's output.)

Another important convention is to consider the time-complexity of an interactive machine as a function of only its input's length.

> **Definition 4.2.3 (The Complexity of an Interactive Machine):** *We say that an interactive machine A has **time-complexity** $t : \mathbb{N} \to \mathbb{N}$ if for every interactive machine B and every string x, it holds that when interacting with machine B, on common input x, machine A always (i.e., regardless of the content of its random tape and B's random tape) halts within $t(|x|)$ steps. In particular, we say that A is **polynomial-time** if there exists a polynomial p such that A has time-complexity p.*

We stress that the time-complexity, so defined, is independent of the content of the messages that machine A receives. In other words, it is an upper bound that holds for all possible incoming messages (as well as all internal coin tosses). In particular, an interactive machine with time-complexity $t(\cdot)$ may read, on input x, only a prefix of total length $t(|x|)$ of the messages sent to it.

4.2.1.3. Proof Systems

In general, proof systems are defined in terms of the verification procedure (which can be viewed as one entity, called the verifier). A "proof" for a specific claim is always considered as coming from the outside (which can be viewed as another entity, called the prover). The verification procedure itself does not generate "proofs," but merely verifies their validity. Interactive proof systems are intended to capture whatever can be efficiently verified via interaction with the outside. In general, the interaction with the outside can be very complex and may consist of many message exchanges, as long as the total time spent by the verifier is polynomial (in the common input).

Our choice to consider probabilistic polynomial-time verifiers is justified by the association of efficient procedures with probabilistic polynomial-time algorithms. Furthermore, the verifier's verdict of whether to accept or reject the claim is probabilistic, and a bounded error probability is allowed. (Jumping ahead, we mention that the error can be decreased to be negligible by repeating the verification procedure sufficiently many times.)

Loosely speaking, we require that the prover be able to convince the verifier of the validity of true statements, while nobody can fool the verifier into believing false statements. Both conditions are given a probabilistic interpretation: It is required that the verifier accept valid statements with "high" probability, whereas the probability that it will accept a false statement is "low" (regardless of the machine with which the verifier interacts). In the following definition, the verifier's output is interpreted as its decision on whether to accept or reject the common input. Output 1 is interpreted as "accept," whereas output 0 is interpreted as "reject."

Definition 4.2.4 (Interactive Proof System): *A pair of interactive machines (P, V) is called an* **interactive proof system for a language** *L if machine V is polynomial-time and the following two conditions hold:*

- Completeness: *For every $x \in L$,*

$$\Pr[\langle P, V \rangle(x) = 1] \geq \frac{2}{3}$$

- Soundness: *For every $x \notin L$ and every interactive machine B,*

$$\Pr[\langle B, V \rangle(x) = 1] \leq \frac{1}{3}$$

Some remarks are in order. We first stress that the soundness condition refers to all potential "provers," whereas the completeness condition refers only to the prescribed prover P. Second, the verifier is required to be a (probabilistic) polynomial-time machine, but no resource bounds are placed on the computing power of the prover (in either completeness or soundness conditions). Third, as in the case of $\mathcal{BPP}$, the error probability in the foregoing definition can be made exponentially small by repeating the interaction (polynomially) many times.

Every language in $\mathcal{NP}$ has an interactive proof system. Specifically, let $L \in \mathcal{NP}$, and let R_L be a witness relation associated with the language L (i.e., R_L is recognizable in polynomial time, and L equals the set $\{x : \exists y \text{ s.t. } |y| = \text{poly}(|x|) \wedge (x, y) \in R_L\}$). Then an interactive proof for the language L consists of a prover that on input $x \in L$ sends a witness y (as before), and a verifier that upon receiving y (on common input x) outputs 1 if $|y| = \text{poly}(|x|)$ and $(x, y) \in R_L$ (and outputs 0 otherwise). Clearly, when interacting with the prescribed prover, this verifier will always accept inputs in the language. On the other hand, no matter what a cheating "prover" does, this verifier will never accept inputs not in the language. We point out that in this specific proof system, both parties are deterministic (i.e., make no use of their random tapes). It is easy to see that only languages in $\mathcal{NP}$ have interactive proof systems in which both parties are deterministic (see Exercise 2).

In other words, $\mathcal{NP}$ can be viewed as a class of interactive proof systems in which the interaction is unidirectional (i.e., from the prover to the verifier) and the verifier is deterministic (and never errs). In general interactive proofs, *both* restrictions are waived: The interaction is bidirectional, and the verifier is probabilistic (and may err, with some small probability). Both bidirectional interaction and randomization seem essential to the power of interactive proof systems (see Exercise 2).

Definition 4.2.5 (The Class $\mathcal{IP}$): *The class $\mathcal{IP}$ consists of all languages having interactive proof systems.*

By the foregoing discussion, $\mathcal{NP} \subseteq \mathcal{IP}$. Because languages in $\mathcal{BPP}$ can be viewed as each having a verifier that decides on membership without any interaction, it follows that $\mathcal{BPP} \cup \mathcal{NP} \subseteq \mathcal{IP}$. We remind the reader that it is not known whether or not $\mathcal{BPP} \subseteq \mathcal{NP}$.

We next show that the definition of the class $\mathcal{IP}$ remains invariant if we replace the (constant) bounds in the completeness and soundness conditions with two functions $c, s : \mathbb{N} \to [0, 1]$ satisfying $c(n) < 1 - 2^{-\text{poly}(n)}$, $s(n) > 2^{-\text{poly}(n)}$, and $c(n) > s(n) + \frac{1}{\text{poly}(n)}$. Namely, we consider the following generalization of Definition 4.2.4.

Definition 4.2.6 (Generalized Interactive Proof): *Let $c, s : \mathbb{N} \to \mathbb{R}$ be functions satisfying $c(n) > s(n) + \frac{1}{p(n)}$ for some polynomial $p(\cdot)$. An interactive pair (P, V) is called a (generalized) interactive proof system for the language L, with* **completeness bound** $c(\cdot)$ *and* **soundness bound** $s(\cdot)$, *if*

- (modified) completeness: *for every $x \in L$,*

$$\Pr[\langle P, V \rangle(x) = 1] \geq c(|x|)$$

- (modified) soundness: *for every $x \notin L$ and every interactive machine B,*

$$\Pr[\langle B, V \rangle(x) = 1] \leq s(|x|)$$

The function g$(\cdot)$ *defined as* g$(n) \stackrel{\text{def}}{=}$ c(n) − s(n) *is called the* acceptance gap *of* (P, V), *and the function* e$(\cdot)$, *defined as* e$(n) \stackrel{\text{def}}{=}$ max$\{1$ − c(n), s$(n)\}$, *is called the* error probability *of* (P, V). *In particular,* s *is the* soundness error *of* (P, V), *and* 1 − c *is its* completeness error.

We stress that c is a lower bound, whereas s is an upper bound.

Proposition 4.2.7: *The following three conditions are equivalent:*

1. $L \in \mathcal{IP}$. *Namely, there exists an interactive proof system, with completeness bound* $\frac{2}{3}$ *and soundness bound* $\frac{1}{3}$, *for the language* L.

2. L *has very strong interactive proof systems: For every polynomial* $p(\cdot)$, *there exists an interactive proof system for the language* L, *with error probability bounded above by* $2^{-p(\cdot)}$.

3. L *has a very weak interactive proof: There exists a polynomial* $p(\cdot)$ *and a generalized interactive proof system for the language* L, *with acceptance gap bounded below by* $1/p(\cdot)$. *Furthermore, completeness and soundness bounds for this system, namely, the values* c(n) *and* s(n), *can be computed in time polynomial in* n.

Clearly, either of the first two items implies the third one (including the requirement for efficiently computable bounds). The ability to efficiently compute completeness and soundness bounds is used in proving the opposite (non-trivial) direction. The proof is left as an exercise (i.e., Exercise 1).

4.2.2. An Example (Graph Non-Isomorphism in $\mathcal{IP}$)

All examples of interactive proof systems presented thus far have been degenerate (e.g., the interaction, if any, has been unidirectional). We now present an example of a non-degenerate interactive proof system. Furthermore, we present an interactive proof system for a language *not known to be in* $\mathcal{BPP} \cup \mathcal{NP}$. Specifically, the language is the set of *pairs of non-isomorphic graphs*, denoted GNI. The idea underlying this proof system is presented through the following story:

> Petra von Kant claims that Goldstar[4] beer in large bottles tastes different than Goldstar beer in small bottles. Virgil does not believe her. To prove her claim, Petra and Virgil repeat the following process a number of times sufficient to convince Virgil beyond reasonable doubt.
>
> Virgil selects at random either a large bottle or a small one and pours some beer into a tasting glass, without Petra seeing which bottle he uses. Virgil then hands Petra the glass and asks her to tell which of the bottles he has used.
>
> If Petra never errs in her answers, then Virgil is convinced of the validity of her claim. (In fact, he should be convinced even if she answers correctly with probability substantially larger than 50%, because if the beer tastes the same

---

[4]Goldstar is an Israeli beer, available in 330-ml and 500-ml bottles. Actually, the story traces back to Athena's claim regarding jars of nectar, which was contested by Zeus himself. Unfortunately, Ovid does not tell the outcome of their interaction.

regardless of the bottle, then there would be no way for Petra to guess correctly with probability higher than 50% which bottle was used.)

We now get back to the formal exposition. Let us first define the language in focus: Two graphs,[5] $G_1 = (V_1, E_1)$ and $G_2 = (V_2, E_2)$, are called *isomorphic* if there exists a 1-1 and onto mapping, π, from the vertex set V_1 to the vertex set V_2 such that $(u, v) \in E_1$ if and only if $(\pi(v), \pi(u)) \in E_2$. The mapping π, if it exists, is called an *isomorphism* between the graphs. The set of pairs of non-isomorphic graphs is denoted by GNI.

Construction 4.2.8 (An Interactive Proof System for Graph Non-Isomorphism):

- **Common input:** *A pair of two graphs, $G_1 = (V_1, E_1)$ and $G_2 = (V_2, E_2)$. Suppose, without loss of generality, that $V_1 = \{1, 2, \ldots, |V_1|\}$, and similarly for V_2.*
- **Verifier's first step (V1):** *The verifier selects at random one of the two input graphs and sends to the prover a random isomorphic copy of this graph. Namely, the verifier selects uniformly $\sigma \in \{1, 2\}$ and a random permutation π from the set of permutations over the vertex set V_σ. The verifier constructs a graph with vertex set V_σ and edge set*

$$F \overset{\text{def}}{=} \{(\pi(u), \pi(v)) : (u, v) \in E_\sigma\}$$

  and sends (V_σ, F) to the prover.
- **Motivating remark:** *If the input graphs are non-isomorphic, as the prover claims, then the prover should be able to distinguish (not necessarily by an efficient procedure) isomorphic copies of one graph from isomorphic copies of the other graph. However, if the input graphs are isomorphic, then a random isomorphic copy of one graph will be distributed identically to a random isomorphic copy of the other graph.*
- **Prover's first step (P1):** *Upon receiving a graph $G' = (V', E')$ from the verifier, the prover finds $\tau \in \{1, 2\}$ such that the graph G' is isomorphic to the input graph G_τ. (If both $\tau = 1$ and $r = 2$ satisfy the condition, then τ is selected arbitrarily. In case no $\tau \in \{1, 2\}$ satisfies the condition, τ is set to 0.) The prover sends τ to the verifier.*
- **Verifier's second step (V2):** *If the message τ received from the prover equals σ (chosen in Step V1), then the verifier outputs 1 (i.e., accepts the common input). Otherwise the verifier outputs 0 (i.e., rejects the common input).*

This verifier program is easily implemented in probabilistic polynomial time. We do not know of a probabilistic polynomial-time implementation of the prover's program, but this is not required. We shall now show that the foregoing pair of interactive machines constitutes an interactive proof system (in the general sense) for the language GNI (Graph Non-Isomorphism).

Proposition 4.2.9: *The language GNI is in the class $\mathcal{IP}$. Furthermore, the programs specified in Construction 4.2.8 constitute a generalized interactive proof system for GNI, with completeness bound 1 and soundness bound $\frac{1}{2}$. Namely:*

[5]See footnote 13.

1. *If G_1 and G_2 are not isomorphic (i.e., $(G_1, G_2) \in GNI$), then the verifier always accepts (when interacting with the prover).*

2. *If G_1 and G_2 are isomorphic (i.e., $(G_1, G_2) \notin GNI$), then no matter with what machine the verifier interacts, it rejects the input with probability at least $\frac{1}{2}$.*

Proof: Clearly, if G_1 and G_2 are not isomorphic, then no graph can be isomorphic to both G_1 and G_2. It follows that there exists a unique τ such that the graph G' (received by the prover in Step P1) is isomorphic to the input graph G_τ. Hence, τ found by the prover in Step P1 always equals σ chosen in Step V1. Part 1 follows.

On the other hand, if G_1 and G_2 are isomorphic, then the graph G' is isomorphic to both input graphs. Furthermore, we shall show that in this case the graph G' yields no information about σ, and consequently no machine can (on input G_1, G_2 and G') set τ such that it will equal σ with probability greater than $\frac{1}{2}$. Details follow.

Let π be a permutation on the vertex set of a graph $G = (V, E)$. We denote by $\pi(G)$ the graph with vertex set V and edge set $\{(\pi(u), \pi(v)) : (u, v) \in E\}$. Let ξ be a random variable uniformly distributed over $\{1, 2\}$, and let Π be a random variable uniformly distributed over the set of permutations on V. We stress that these two random variables are independent. We are interested in the distribution of the random variable $\Pi(G_\xi)$. We are going to show that although $\Pi(G_\xi)$ is determined by the random variables Π and ξ, the random variables ξ and $\Pi(G_\xi)$ are statistically independent. In fact, we show the following:

Claim 4.2.9.1: If the graphs G_1 and G_2 are isomorphic, then for every graph G' that is isomorphic to G_1 (and G_2), it holds that

$$\Pr[\xi = 1 \mid \Pi(G_\xi) = G'] = \Pr[\xi = 2 \mid \Pi(G_\xi) = G'] = \frac{1}{2}$$

Proof: We first claim that the sets $S_1 \overset{\text{def}}{=} \{\pi : \pi(G_1) = G'\}$ and $S_2 \overset{\text{def}}{=} \{\pi : \pi(G_2) = G'\}$ are of the same cardinality. This follows from the observation that there is a 1-1 and onto correspondence between the set S_1 and the set S_2 (the correspondence is given by the isomorphism between the graphs G_1 and G_2). Hence,

$$\Pr[\Pi(G_\xi) = G' \mid \xi = 1] = \Pr[\Pi(G_1) = G']$$
$$= \Pr[\Pi \in S_1]$$
$$= \Pr[\Pi \in S_2]$$
$$= \Pr[\Pi(G_\xi) = G' \mid \xi = 2]$$

Using Bayes' rule, the claim follows. $\square$

Intuitively, Claim 4.2.9.1 says that for every pair (G_1, G_2) of isomorphic graphs, the random variable $\Pi(G_\xi)$ yields no information on ξ, and so no prover can fool the verifier into accepting with probability greater than $\frac{1}{2}$. Specifically, we let R be an arbitrary randomized process (representing a possible cheating-prover strategy that depends on (G_1, G_2)) that given the verifier's message in Step V1 tries to guess the value of ξ. Then, $R(\Pi(G_\xi)) = \xi$ represents the event in which the verifier accepts, and we have

$$\Pr[R(\Pi(G_\xi)) = \xi] = \sum_{G'} \Pr[\Pi(G_\xi) = G'] \cdot \Pr[R(G') = \xi \mid \Pi(G_\xi) = G']$$

Using Claim 4.2.9.1 for the third equality, we have (for any G' in the support of $\Pi(G_\xi)$):

$$
\begin{aligned}
\Pr[R(G') = \xi \mid \Pi(G_\xi) = G'] &= \sum_v \Pr[R(G') = v \,\&\, \xi = v \mid \Pi(G_\xi) = G'] \\
&= \sum_v \Pr[R(G') = v] \cdot \Pr[\xi = v \mid \Pi(G_\xi) = G'] \\
&= \sum_{v \in \{1,2\}} \Pr[R(G') = v] \cdot \Pr[\xi = v] \\
&= \frac{\Pr[R(G') \in \{1, 2\}]}{2} \\
&\leq \frac{1}{2}
\end{aligned}
$$

with equality in case R always outputs an element in the set $\{1, 2\}$. Part 2 of the proposition follows. ∎

Remarks Concerning Construction 4.2.8. In the proof system of Construction 4.2.8, the verifier *always* accepts inputs *in* the language (i.e., the completeness error equals zero). The fact that $GNI \in \mathcal{IP}$, whereas it is not known whether or not $GNI \in \mathcal{NP}$, is an indication of the power of interaction and randomness in the context of theorem-proving. Finally, we note that it is essential that the prover not know the outcome of the verifier's internal coin tosses. For a wider perspective on these issues, see the following advanced subsection.

4.2.3.* The Structure of the Class $\mathcal{IP}$

In continuation to the foregoing remarks, we briefly discuss several aspects regarding the "proving power" of interactive proof systems.

1. *The completeness and soundness bounds*: All interactive proof systems presented in this book happen to have *perfect completeness*; that is, the verifier *always* accepts inputs IN the language (i.e., the completeness error equals zero). In fact, one can *transform* any interactive proof system into an interactive proof system (for the same language) in which the verifier always accepts inputs in the language.

   On the other hand, as shown in Exercise 5, only languages in $\mathcal{NP}$ have interactive proof systems in which the verifier *always rejects* inputs NOT IN the language (i.e., having soundness error equal to zero).

2. *The privacy of the verifier's coins:Arthur-Merlin proofs* (a.k.a. *public-coin proof systems*) are a special case of interactive proofs, where the verifier must send the outcome of any coin it tosses (and thus need not send any other information). As stated earlier, the

proof system of Construction 4.2.8 is *not* of the public-coin type. Yet one can *transform* any interactive proof system into a *public-coin* interactive proof system (for the same language), while preserving perfect completeness.

3. *Which languages have interactive proof systems?* (We have ignored this natural question until now.) It turns out that every language in $\mathcal{PSPACE}$ has an interactive proof system. In fact,

$$\mathcal{IP} \text{ equals } \mathcal{PSPACE}$$

We comment that $\mathcal{PSPACE}$ is believed to be much larger than $\mathcal{NP}$; in particular, co$\mathcal{NP} \subseteq \mathcal{PSPACE}$, whereas it is commonly believed that co$\mathcal{NP} \neq \mathcal{NP}$. Also, because $\mathcal{PSPACE}$ is closed under complementation, so is $\mathcal{IP}$.

4. *Constant-round interactive proofs*: Construction 4.2.8 constitutes a constant-round protocol (i.e., a constant number of messages are sent). In contrast, in the generic interactive proof system for $\mathcal{PSPACE}$, the number of communication rounds is polynomially related to the input length. We comment that co$\mathcal{NP}$ is believed NOT to have *constant-round* interactive proofs.

We mention that any language having a *constant-round* interactive proof system also has a public-coin interactive proof system in which only two messages are sent: The latter consists of a random challenge from the verifier that is answered by the prover. In general, for any function $r : \mathbb{N} \to \mathbb{N}$, any $2r$-round proof system can be transformed into an r-round proof system (for the same language).

4.2.4. Augmentation of the Model

For purposes that will become more clear in Sections 4.3 and 4.4, we augment the basic definition of an interactive proof system by allowing each of the parties to have a private input (in addition to the common input). Loosely speaking, these inputs are used to capture additional information available to each of the parties. Specifically, when using interactive proof systems as sub-protocols inside larger protocols, the private inputs are associated with the local configurations of the machines before entering the sub-protocol. In particular, the private input of the prover may contain information that enables an efficient implementation of the prover's task.

Definition 4.2.10 (Interactive Proof Systems, Revisited):

1. An interactive machine *is defined as in Definition 4.2.1, except that the machine has an additional read-only tape called* **the auxiliary-input tape***. The content of this tape is called* **auxiliary input***.*

2. The complexity of such an interactive machine is still measured as a function of the (common) input length. Namely, the interactive machine A has time-complexity $t : \mathbb{N} \to \mathbb{N}$ *if for every interactive machine B and every string x, it holds that when interacting with machine B, on common input x, machine A always (i.e., regardless of the content of its random tape and its auxiliary-input tape, as well as the content of B's tapes) halts within $t(|x|)$ steps.*

3. *We denote by* $\langle A(y), B(z)\rangle(x)$ *the random variable representing the (local) output of B when interacting with machine A on common input x, when the random input to each machine is uniformly and independently chosen, and A (resp., B) has auxiliary input y (resp., z).*

4. *A pair of interactive machines* (P, V) *is called an* interactive proof system for a language *L if machine V is polynomial-time and the following two conditions hold:*

   - Completeness: *For every* $x \in L$, *there exists a string y such that for every* $z \in \{0, 1\}^*$,

   $$\Pr\left[\langle P(y), V(z)\rangle(x) = 1\right] \geq \frac{2}{3}$$

   - Soundness: *For every* $x \notin L$, *every interactive machine B, and every* $y, z \in \{0, 1\}^*$,

   $$\Pr\left[\langle B(y), V(z)\rangle(x) = 1\right] \leq \frac{1}{3}$$

We stress that when saying that an interactive machine is polynomial-time, we mean that its running time is polynomial in the length of the common input. Consequently, it is not guaranteed that such a machine has enough time to read its entire auxiliary input.

Teaching Tip. The augmented model of interactive proofs is first used in this book in Section 4.3.3, where the notion of zero-knowledge is extended to account for a priori information that the verifier may have. One may thus prefer to present Definition 4.2.10 after presenting the basic definitions of zero-knowledge, that is, postpone Definition 4.2.10 to Section 4.3.3. (However, conceptually speaking, Definition 4.2.10 does belong to the current section.)

4.3. Zero-Knowledge Proofs: Definitions

In this section we introduce the notion of a zero-knowledge interactive proof system and present a non-trivial example of such a system (specifically, to claims of the form "the following two graphs are isomorphic").

4.3.1. Perfect and Computational Zero-Knowledge

Loosely speaking, we say that an interactive proof system (P, V) for a language L is zero-knowledge if whatever can be efficiently computed after interacting with P on input $x \in L$ can also be efficiently computed from x (without any interaction). We stress that this holds with respect to any efficient way of interacting with P, not necessarily the way defined by the verifier program V. Actually, zero-knowledge is a property of the prescribed prover P. It captures P's robustness against attempts to gain knowledge by interacting with it. A straightforward way of capturing the informal discussion follows.

Let (P, V) be an interactive proof system for some language L. We say that (P, V), or actually P, is *perfect zero-knowledge* if for every probabilistic polynomial-time interactive machine V^* there exists an (*ordinary*) probabilistic polynomial-time algorithm M^* such that for every $x \in L$ the following two random variables are identically distributed:

- $\langle P, V^* \rangle(x)$ (i.e., the output of the interactive machine V^* after interacting with the interactive machine P on common input x)
- $M^*(x)$ (i.e., the output of machine M^* on input x)

Machine M^* is called a *simulator* for the interaction of V^* with P.

We stress that we require that *for every* V^* interacting with P, not merely for V, there exists a ("perfect") simulator M^*. This simulator, although not having access to the interactive machine P, is able to simulate the interaction of V^* with P. The fact that such simulators exist means that V^* does not gain any knowledge from P (since the same output could be generated without any access to P).

The Simulation Paradigm

The foregoing discussion follows a general definitional paradigm that is also used in other chapters of this book (specifically, in Volume 2). The *simulation paradigm* postulates that whatever a party can do by itself cannot be considered a gain from interaction with the outside. The validity of this paradigm is evident, provided we bear in mind that by "doing" we mean "efficiently doing" something (and more so if the complexity of "doing it alone" is tightly related to the complexity of "doing it after interaction with the outside").[6] Admittedly, failure to provide a simulation of an interaction with the outside does NOT necessarily mean that this interaction results in some "real gain" (in some intuitive sense). Yet what matters is that any "real gain" can NOT occur whenever we are able to present a simulation. In summary, the approach underlying the simulation paradigm may be overly cautious, but it is certainly valid. (Furthermore, to say the least, it seems much harder to provide a robust definition of "real gain.")

Trivial Cases. Note that every language in $\mathcal{BPP}$ has a perfect zero-knowledge proof system in which the prover does nothing (and the verifier checks by itself whether to accept or reject the common input). To demonstrate the zero-knowledge property of this "dummy prover," one can present for every verifier V^* a simulator M^* that is essentially identical to V^* (except that the communication tapes of V^*, which are never used, are considered as ordinary work tapes of M^*).

4.3.1.1. Perfect Zero-Knowledge

Unfortunately, the preceding formulation of (perfect) zero-knowledge is slightly too strict (at least as far as we know).[7] We relax the formulation by allowing the simulator to fail, with bounded probability, to produce an interaction.

---

[6] See the discussion of knowledge tightness in Section 4.4.4.2.

[7] That is, we do not know of any non-trivial case in which that requirement is satisfied. In contrast, non-trivial cases satisfying the relaxed definition given next are known, and we actually present one (i.e., a perfect zero-knowledge proof for Graph Isomorphism).

Definition 4.3.1 (Perfect Zero-Knowledge): *Let (P, V) be an interactive proof system for some language L. We say that (P, V) is* **perfect zero-knowledge** *if for every probabilistic polynomial-time interactive machine V^* there exists a probabilistic polynomial-time algorithm M^* such that for every $x \in L$ the following two conditions hold:*

1. *With probability at most $\frac{1}{2}$, on input x, machine M^* outputs a special symbol denoted $\perp$ (i.e., $\Pr[M^*(x) = \perp] \leq \frac{1}{2}$).*

2. *Let $m^*(x)$ be a random variable describing the distribution of $M^*(x)$ conditioned on $M^*(x) \neq \perp$ (i.e., $\Pr[m^*(x) = \alpha] = \Pr[M^*(x) = \alpha \mid M^*(x) \neq \perp]$ for every $\alpha \in \{0, 1\}^*$). Then the following random variables are identically distributed:*

   - *$\langle P, V^* \rangle(x)$ (i.e., the output of the interactive machine V^* after interacting with the interactive machine P on common input x)*
   - *$m^*(x)$ (i.e., the output of machine M^* on input x, conditioned on not being $\perp$)*

Machine M^* is called a **perfect simulator** *for the interaction of V^* with P.*

Condition 1 can be replaced by a stronger condition requiring that M^* output the special symbol (i.e., $\perp$) only with negligible probability. For example, one can require that (on input x) machine M^* will output $\perp$ with probability bounded above by $2^{-p(|x|)}$, for any polynomial $p(\cdot)$; see Exercise 6. Consequently, the statistical difference between the random variables $\langle P, V^* \rangle(x)$ and $M^*(x)$ can be made negligible (in $|x|$); see Exercise 8. Hence, whatever the verifier efficiently computes after interacting with the prover can be efficiently computed (with only an extremely small error) by the simulator (and hence by the verifier himself).

4.3.1.2. Computational Zero-Knowledge

Following the spirit of Chapter 3, we observe that for practical purposes there is no need to be able to "perfectly simulate" the output of V^* after it interacts with P. Instead, it suffices to generate a probability distribution that is computationally indistinguishable from the output of V^* after it interacts with P. The relaxation is consistent with our original requirement that "whatever can be efficiently computed after interacting with P on input $x \in L$ can also be efficiently computed from x (without any interaction)," the reason being that we consider computationally indistinguishable ensembles as being the same. Before presenting the relaxed definition of general zero-knowledge, we recall the definition of computationally indistinguishable ensembles (see Item 2 in Definition 3.2.2). Here we consider ensembles indexed by strings from a language L. We say that the ensembles $\{R_x\}_{x \in L}$ and $\{S_x\}_{x \in L}$ are **computationally indistinguishable** if for every probabilistic polynomial-time algorithm D, for every polynomial $p(\cdot)$, and for all sufficiently long $x \in L$, it holds that

$$|\Pr[D(x, R_x) = 1] - \Pr[D(x, S_x) = 1]| < \frac{1}{p(|x|)}$$

Definition 4.3.2 (Computational Zero-Knowledge): *Let (P, V) be an interactive proof system for some language L. We say that (P, V) is **computational zero-knowledge** (or just **zero-knowledge**) if for every probabilistic polynomial-time interactive machine V^* there exists a probabilistic polynomial-time algorithm M^* such that the following two ensembles are computationally indistinguishable:*

- *$\{\langle P, V^* \rangle (x)\}_{x \in L}$ (i.e., the output of the interactive machine V^* after it interacts with the interactive machine P on common input x)*
- *$\{M^*(x)\}_{x \in L}$ (i.e., the output of machine M^* on input x)*

Machine M^* is called a simulator *for the interaction of V^* with P.*

The reader can easily verify (see Exercise 9) that allowing the simulator to output the special symbol $\perp$ (with probability bounded above by, say, $\frac{1}{2}$) and considering the conditional output distribution (as done in Definition 4.3.1) does not add to the power of Definition 4.3.2.

The Scope of Zero-Knowledge. We stress that both definitions of zero-knowledge apply to interactive proof systems in the general sense (i.e., having any noticeable gap between the acceptance probabilities for inputs inside and outside the language). In fact, the definitions of zero-knowledge apply to any pair of interactive machines (actually to each interactive machine): Namely, we can say that the interactive machine A is *zero-knowledge on L* if whatever can be efficiently computed after the interaction with A on common input $x \in L$ can also be efficiently computed from x itself.

4.3.1.3. An Alternative Formulation of Zero-Knowledge

An alternative formulation of zero-knowledge considers the verifier's view of the interaction with the prover, rather than only the output of the verifier after such an interaction. By the "verifier's view of the interaction" we mean the entire sequence of the local configurations of the verifier during an interaction (execution) with the prover. Clearly, it suffices to consider only the content of the random tape of the verifier and the sequence of messages that the verifier has received from the prover during the execution (since the entire sequence of local configurations and the final output are determined by those objects).

Definition 4.3.3 (Zero-Knowledge, Alternative Formulation): *Let (P, V), L, and V^* be as in Definition 4.3.2. We denote by $\text{view}_{V^*}^P(x)$ a random variable describing the content of the random tape of V^* and the messages V^* receives from P during a joint computation on common input x. We say that (P, V) is **zero-knowledge** if for every probabilistic polynomial-time interactive machine V^* there exists a probabilistic polynomial-time algorithm M^* such that the ensembles $\{\text{view}_{V^*}^P(x)\}_{x \in L}$ and $\{M^*(x)\}_{x \in L}$ are computationally indistinguishable.*

A few remarks are in order. First, note that Definition 4.3.3 is obtained from Definition 4.3.2 by replacing $\langle P, V^* \rangle (x)$ with $\text{view}_{V^*}^P(x)$. The simulator M^* used in

Definition 4.3.3 is related to but not equal to the simulator used in Definition 4.3.2 (yet this fact is not reflected in the text of those definitions). Clearly, $\langle P, V^* \rangle(x)$ can be computed in (deterministic) polynomial time from $\text{view}^P_{V^*}(x)$ for each V^*. Although that is not always true for the opposite direction, Definition 4.3.3 is equivalent to Definition 4.3.2 (by virtue of the universal quantification on the V^*'s; see Exercise 10). The latter fact justifies the use of Definition 4.3.3, which is more convenient to work with, although it seems less natural than Definition 4.3.2. An analogous alternative formulation of perfect zero-knowledge can be obtained from Definition 4.3.1 and is clearly equivalent to it.

4.3.1.4.* Almost-Perfect (Statistical) Zero-Knowledge

A less drastic (than computational zero-knowledge) relaxation of the notion of perfect zero-knowledge is the following:

> **Definition 4.3.4 (Almost-Perfect (Statistical) Zero-Knowledge):** *Let (P, V) be an interactive proof system for some language L. We say that (P, V) is **almost-perfect zero-knowledge** (or **statistical zero-knowledge**) if for every probabilistic polynomial-time interactive machine V^* there exists a probabilistic polynomial-time algorithm M^* such that the following two ensembles are statistically close as functions of $|x|$:*
>
> - *$\{\langle P, V^* \rangle(x)\}_{x \in L}$ (i.e., the output of the interactive machine V^* after it interacts with the interactive machine P on common input x)*
> - *$\{M^*(x)\}_{x \in L}$ (i.e., the output of machine M^* on input x).*
>
> *That is, the statistical difference between $\langle P, V^* \rangle(x)$ and $M^*(x)$ is negligible in terms of $|x|$.*

As in the case of computational zero-knowledge, allowing the simulator to output the symbol $\perp$ (with probability bounded above by, say, $\frac{1}{2}$) and considering the conditional output distribution (as done in Definition 4.3.1) does not add to the power of Definition 4.3.4; see Exercise 8. It is also easy to show that perfect zero-knowledge implies almost-perfect zero-knowledge, which in turn implies computational zero-knowledge.

The three definitions (i.e., perfect, almost-perfect, and computational zero-knowledge) correspond to a natural three-stage hierarchy of interpretations of the notion of "close" pairs of probability ensembles. (In all three cases, the pairs of ensembles being postulated as being close are $\{\langle P, V^* \rangle(x)\}_{x \in L}$ and $\{M^*(x)\}_{x \in L}$.)

1. The most stringent interpretation of closeness is the requirement that the two ensembles be identically distributed. This is the requirement in the case of perfect zero-knowledge.

2. A slightly more relaxed interpretation of closeness is that the two ensembles be statistically indistinguishable (or statistically close). This is the requirement in the case of almost-perfect (or statistical) zero-knowledge.

3. A much more relaxed interpretation of closeness, which suffices for all practical purposes, is that the two ensembles be computationally indistinguishable. This is the requirement in the case of computational zero-knowledge.

4.3.1.5.* Complexity Classes Based on Zero-Knowledge

The various definitions of zero-knowledge give rise to natural complexity classes:

Definition 4.3.5 (Class of Languages Having Zero-Knowledge Proofs): *We denote by* $\mathcal{ZK}$ (*also* $\mathcal{CZK}$) *the class of languages having* (computational) *zero-knowledge interactive proof systems. Likewise,* $\mathcal{PZK}$ (*resp.,* $\mathcal{SZK}$) *denotes the class of languages having* perfect (*resp.,* statistical) *zero-knowledge interactive proof systems.*

Clearly,

$$\mathcal{BPP} \subseteq \mathcal{PZK} \subseteq \mathcal{SZK} \subseteq \mathcal{CZK} \subseteq \mathcal{IP}$$

Assuming the existence of (non-uniformly) one-way functions, the last inclusion is an equality (i.e., $\mathcal{CZK} = \mathcal{IP}$); see Proposition 4.4.5 and Theorems 3.5.12 and 4.4.12. On the other hand, we believe that the first and third inclusions are strict (as equalities in either case contradict widely believed complexity assumptions). Thus, our belief is that

$$\mathcal{BPP} \subset \mathcal{PZK} \subseteq \mathcal{SZK} \subset \mathcal{CZK} = \mathcal{IP}$$

The relationship of $\mathcal{PZK}$ to $\mathcal{SZK}$ remains an open problem (with no evidence either way).

4.3.1.6.* Expected Polynomial-Time Simulators

The formulation of perfect zero-knowledge presented in Definition 4.3.1 is different from the definition used in some early publications in the literature. The original definition requires that the simulator *always* output a legal transcript (which has to be distributed identically to the real interaction), yet it allows the simulator to run in *expected* polynomial time rather than in strictly polynomial time. We stress that the expectation is taken over the coin tosses of the simulator (whereas the input to the simulator is fixed). This yields the following:

Definition 4.3.6 (Perfect Zero-Knowledge, Liberal Formulation): *We say that* (P, V) *is* **perfect zero-knowledge in the liberal sense** *if for every probabilistic polynomial-time interactive machine* V^* *there exists an* expected *polynomial-time algorithm* M^* *such that for every* $x \in L$ *the random variables* $\langle P, V^* \rangle(x)$ *and* $M^*(x)$ *are identically distributed.*

We stress that by *probabilistic polynomial time* we mean a strict bound on the running time in all possible executions, whereas by *expected polynomial time* we allow non-polynomial-time executions but require that the running time be "polynomial on the average." Clearly, Definition 4.3.1 implies Definition 4.3.6 (see Exercise 7). Interestingly, there exist interactive proofs that are perfect zero-knowledge with respect to the liberal definition but are not known to be perfect zero-knowledge with respect to Definition 4.3.1. We point out that the naive way of transforming an expected probabilistic polynomial-time algorithm to one that runs in strict polynomial time is not suitable for the current context.[8]

We prefer to adopt Definition 4.3.1, rather than Definition 4.3.6, because we want to avoid the notion of expected polynomial time. The main reason for our desire to avoid the latter notion is that the correspondence between average polynomial time and efficient computations is more controversial than the widely accepted association of strict polynomial time with efficient computations. Furthermore, the notion of expected polynomial time is more subtle than one realizes at first glance:

> The naive interpretation of expected polynomial time is having an *average* running time that is *bounded by a polynomial* in the input length. This definition of expected polynomial time is unsatisfactory because it is *not closed under reductions* and is (too) *machine-dependent*. Both aggravating phenomena follow from the fact that a function can have an average (say over $\{0, 1\}^n$) that is bounded by a polynomial (in n) and yet squaring the function will yield a function that is not bounded by a polynomial (in n). For example, the function $f(x) \stackrel{\text{def}}{=} 2^{|x|}$ if $x \in \{0\}^*$, and $f(x) \stackrel{\text{def}}{=} |x|^2$ otherwise, satisfies $\mathsf{E}[f(U_n)] < n^2 + 1$, but $\mathsf{E}[f(U_n)^2] > 2^n$.
>
> Hence, a better interpretation of expected polynomial time is having a running time that is *bounded by a polynomial in a function that has an average linear growth rate*. That is, using the naive definition of linear on the average, we say that f is *polynomial on the average* if there exist a polynomial p and a linear-on-the-average function ℓ such that $f(x) \leq p(\ell(x))$ for all sufficiently long x's. Note that if f is polynomial on the average, then so is f^2.

An analogous discussion applies to computational zero-knowledge. More specifically, Definition 4.3.2 requires that the simulator work in polynomial time, whereas a more liberal notion would allow it to work in *expected* polynomial time.

We comment that for the sake of elegance it is customary to modify the definitions that allow *expected* polynomial-time simulators by requiring that such simulators also exist for the interaction of *expected* polynomial-time verifiers with the prover.

4.3.1.7.* Honest-Verifier Zero-Knowledge

We briefly discuss a weak notion of zero-knowledge. The notion, called *honest-verifier zero-knowledge*, requires simulatability of the view of only the *prescribed* (or *honest*) verifier, rather than simulatability of the view of *any possible* (probabilistic polynomial-time) verifier. Although this notion does not suffice for typical cryptographic applications, it is interesting for at least a couple of reasons: First, this weak notion of zero-knowledge is highly non-trivial and fascinating by itself. Second, public-coin

---

[8]The naive transformation truncates runs of the algorithm (in our case, the simulator) that take more than t times the expected number of steps. (Such a truncated run is said to produce some fixed output.) The statistical difference between the output distribution of the original algorithm and the output distribution of the modified algorithm is at most $1/t$. The problem is that t must be bounded by a fixed polynomial in the running time, and so the statistical difference is not negligible. To see that the analysis of this naive transformation is tight, consider its effect on the following algorithm: On input 1^n, the algorithm first selects uniformly $r \in \{0, 1\}^n$, next takes 2^i idle steps, where i is the length of the longest all-zero prefix of r, and finally runs $S(1^n)$, where S is an arbitrary (strict) probabilistic polynomial-time algorithm.

protocols that are zero-knowledge with respect to the honest verifier can be transformed into similar protocols that are zero-knowledge in general. We stress that in the current context (of the single prescribed verifier) the formulations of *output simulatability* (as in Definition 4.3.2) and *view simulatability* (as in Definition 4.3.3) are NOT equivalent, and it is important to use the latter.[9]

Definition 4.3.7 (Zero-Knowledge with Respect to an Honest Verifier): *Let* (P, V), *L, and* $\text{view}_V^P(x)$ *be as in Definition 4.3.3. We say that* (P, V) *is* **honest-verifier zero-knowledge** *if there exists a probabilistic polynomial-time algorithm M such that the ensembles* $\{\text{view}_V^P(x)\}_{x\in L}$ *and* $\{M(x)\}_{x\in L}$ *are computationally indistinguishable.*

The preceding definition refers to computational zero-knowledge and is a restriction of Definition 4.3.3. Versions for perfect and statistical zero-knowledge are defined analogously.

4.3.2. An Example (Graph Isomorphism in $\mathcal{PZK}$)

As mentioned earlier, every language in $\mathcal{BPP}$ has a trivial (i.e., degenerate) zero-knowledge proof system. We now present an example of a non-degenerate zero-knowledge proof system. Furthermore, we present a zero-knowledge proof system for a language not known to be in $\mathcal{BPP}$. Specifically, the language is the set of *pairs of isomorphic graphs*, denoted GI (see definition in Section 4.2). Again, the idea underlying this proof system is presented through a story:

> In this story, Petra von Kant claims that there is a footpath between the north gate and the south gate of her labyrinth (i.e., a path going inside the labyrinth). Virgil does not believe her. Petra is willing to prove her claim to Virgil, but does not want to provide him any additional knowledge (and, in particular, not to assist him to find an inside path from the north gate to the south gate). To prove her claim, Petra and Virgil repeat the following process a number of times sufficient to convince Virgil beyond reasonable doubt.
>
> Petra miraculously transports Virgil to a random place in her labyrinth. Then Virgil asks to be shown the way to either the north gate or the south gate. His choice is supposed to be random, but he may try to cheat. Petra then chooses a (sufficiently long) random walk from their current location to the desired destination and guides Virgil along that walk.
>
> Clearly, if the labyrinth has a path as claimed (and Petra knows her way in the labyrinth), then Virgil will be convinced of the validity of her claim. If, on the other hand, the labyrinth has no such path, then at each iteration, with probability at least 50%, Virgil will detect that Petra is lying. Finally, Virgil will gain no knowledge from the guided tour, the reason being that he can simulate a guided

---

[9]Note that for any interactive proof of perfect completeness, the output of the honest verifier is trivially simulatable (by an algorithm that always outputs 1). In contrast, many of the negative results presented in Section 4.5 also apply to zero-knowledge with respect to an honest verifier, as defined next. For example, only languages in $\mathcal{BPP}$ have *unidirectional* proof systems that are zero-knowledge with respect to an honest verifier.

tour by himself, as follows: First, he selects north or south (as he does in the real guided tour) and goes to the suitable gate (from outside the labyrinth). Next, he takes a random walk from the gate to inside the labyrinth while unrolling a spool of thread behind him, and finally he traces the thread back to the gate. (A sufficiently long random walk whose length equals the length of the tour guided by Petra will guarantee that Virgil will visit a random place in the labyrinth, and the way back will look like a random walk from the location at the end of his thread to the chosen gate.)

We now get back to the formal exposition.

Construction 4.3.8 (A Perfect Zero-Knowledge Proof for Graph Isomorphism):

- **Common input:** *A pair of two graphs, $G_1 = (V_1, E_1)$ and $G_2 = (V_2, E_2)$. Let ϕ be an isomorphism between the input graphs; namely, ϕ is a 1-1 and onto mapping of the vertex set V_1 to the vertex set V_2 such that $(u, v) \in E_1$ if and only if $(\phi(v), \phi(u)) \in E_2$.*
- **Prover's first step (P1):** *The prover selects a random isomorphic copy of G_2 and sends it to the verifier. Namely, the prover selects at random, with uniform probability distribution, a permutation π from the set of permutations over the vertex set V_2 and constructs a graph with vertex set V_2 and edge set*

$$F \overset{\text{def}}{=} \{(\pi(u), \pi(v)) : (u, v) \in E_2\}$$

The prover sends (V_2, F) to the verifier.
- **Motivating remark:** *If the input graphs are isomorphic, as the prover claims, then the graph sent in Step P1 is isomorphic to both input graphs. However, if the input graphs are not isomorphic, then no graph can be isomorphic to both of them.*
- **Verifier's first step (V1):** *Upon receiving a graph $G' = (V', E')$ from the prover, the verifier asks the prover to show an isomorphism between G' and one of the input graphs, chosen at random by the verifier. Namely, the verifier uniformly selects $\sigma \in \{1, 2\}$ and sends it to the prover (who is supposed to answer with an isomorphism between G_σ and G').*
- **Prover's second step (P2):** *If the message σ received from the verifier equals 2, then the prover sends π to the verifier. Otherwise (i.e., $\sigma \neq 2$), the prover sends $\pi \circ \phi$ (i.e., the composition of π on ϕ, defined as $\pi \circ \phi(v) \overset{\text{def}}{=} \pi(\phi(v))$) to the verifier. (Remark: The prover treats any $\sigma \neq 2$ as $\sigma = 1$.)*
- **Verifier's second step (V2):** *If the message, denoted ψ, received from the prover is an isomorphism between G_σ and G', then the verifier outputs 1; otherwise it outputs 0.*

Let us denote the prover's program by P_{GI}.

The verifier program just presented is easily implemented in probabilistic polynomial time. In case the prover is given an isomorphism between the input graphs as auxiliary input, the prover's program can also be implemented in probabilistic polynomial time. We now show that this pair of interactive machines constitutes a *zero-knowledge* interactive proof system (in the general sense) for the language GI (Graph Isomorphism).

Proposition 4.3.9: *The language GI has a perfect zero-knowledge interactive proof system. Furthermore, the programs specified in Construction 4.3.8 satisfy the following:*

1. *If G_1 and G_2 are isomorphic (i.e., $(G_1, G_2) \in GI$), then the verifier always accepts (when interacting with P_{GI}).*

2. *If G_1 and G_2 are not isomorphic (i.e., $(G_1, G_2) \notin GI$), then no matter with which machine the verifier interacts, it will reject the input with probability at least $\frac{1}{2}$.*

3. *The prover (i.e., P_{GI}) is perfect zero-knowledge. Namely, for every probabilistic polynomial-time interactive machine V^*, there exists a probabilistic polynomial-time algorithm M^* outputting $\perp$ with probability at most $\frac{1}{2}$, so that for every $x \stackrel{\text{def}}{=} (G_1, G_2) \in GI$, the following two random variables are identically distributed:*

   - *$\text{view}_{V^*}^{P_{GI}}(x)$ (i.e., the view of V^* after interacting with P_{GI}, on common input x)*
   - *$m^*(x)$ (i.e., the output of machine M^*, on input x, conditioned on not being $\perp$).*

A zero-knowledge interactive proof system for GI with error probability 2^{-k} (only in the soundness condition) can be derived by executing the foregoing protocol, *sequentially*, k times. We stress that in each repetition of the protocol, both the (prescribed) prover and verifier must use "fresh" coin tosses that are independent of the coin tosses used in prior repetitions of the protocol. For further discussion, see Section 4.3.4. We remark that k *parallel* executions will also decrease the error in the soundness condition to 2^{-k}, but the resulting interactive proof is not known to be zero-knowledge in the case in which k grows faster than logarithmic in the input length. In fact, we believe that such an interactive proof is *not* zero-knowledge. For further discussion, see Section 4.5.

We stress that it is not known whether or not $GI \in \mathcal{BPP}$. Hence, Proposition 4.3.9 asserts the existence of a perfect zero-knowledge proof for a language not known to be in $\mathcal{BPP}$.

Proof: We first show that these programs indeed constitute a (general) interactive proof system for GI. Clearly, if the input graphs G_1 and G_2 are isomorphic, then the graph G' constructed in Step P1 will be isomorphic to both of them. Hence, if each party follows its prescribed program, then the verifier will always accept (i.e., output 1). Part 1 follows. On the other hand, if G_1 and G_2 are not isomorphic, then no graph can be isomorphic to both G_1 and G_2. It follows that no matter how the (possibly cheating) prover constructs G', there exists $\sigma \in \{1, 2\}$ such that G' and G_σ are *not* isomorphic. Hence, if the verifier follows its program, then it will reject (i.e., output 0) with probability at least $\frac{1}{2}$. Part 2 follows.

It remains to show that P_{GI} is indeed perfect zero-knowledge on GI. This is indeed the difficult part of the entire proof. It is easy to simulate the output of the verifier specified in Construction 4.3.8 (since its output is identically 1 for inputs in the language GI). Also, it is not hard to simulate the output of a verifier that follows the program specified in Construction 4.3.8, except that at termination it will output the entire transcript of its interaction with P_{GI} (see Exercise 12). The difficult part is to simulate the output of an efficient verifier that deviates arbitrarily from the specified program.

We shall use here the alternative formulation of (perfect) zero-knowledge and show how to simulate V^*'s view of the interaction with P_{GI} for every probabilistic polynomial-time interactive machine V^*. As mentioned earlier, it is not hard to simulate the verifier's view of the interaction with P_{GI} when the verifier follows the specified program. However, we need to simulate the view of the verifier in the general case (in which it uses an arbitrary polynomial-time interactive program). Following is an overview of our simulation (i.e., of our construction of a simulator M^* for each V^*).

The simulator M^* incorporates the code of the interactive program V^*. On input (G_1, G_2), the simulator M^* first selects at random one of the input graphs (i.e., either G_1 or G_2) and generates a random isomorphic copy, denoted G'', of this input graph. In doing so, the simulator behaves differently from P_{GI}, but the graph generated (i.e., G'') is distributed identically to the message sent in Step P1 of the interactive proof. Say that the simulator has generated G'' by randomly permuting G_1. Now, if V^* asks to see the isomorphism between G_1 and G'', then the simulator can indeed answer correctly, and in doing so it completes a simulation of the verifier's view of the interaction with P_{GI}. However, if V^* asks to see the isomorphism between G_2 and G'', then the simulator (which, unlike P_{GI}, does not "know" ϕ) has no way to answer correctly, and we let it halt with output $\perp$. We stress that the simulator "has no way of knowing" whether V^* will ask to see an isomorphism to G_1 or to G_2. The point is that the simulator can try one of the possibilities at random, and if it is lucky (which happens with probability exactly $\frac{1}{2}$), then it can output a distribution that will be identical to the view of V^* when interacting with P_{GI} (on common input (G_1, G_2)). A key fact (see Claim 4.3.9.1, following) is that the distribution of G'' is stochastically independent of the simulator's choice of which of the two input graphs to use, and so V^* cannot affect the probability that the simulator will be lucky. A detailed description of the simulator follows.

Simulator M^*. On input $x \stackrel{\text{def}}{=} (G_1, G_2)$, simulator M^* proceeds as follows:

1. *Setting the random tape of V^**: Let $q(\cdot)$ denote a polynomial bounding the running time of V^*. The simulator M^* starts by uniformly selecting a string $r \in \{0, 1\}^{q(|x|)}$ to be used as the content of the random tape of V^*. (Alternatively, one could produce coins for V^* "on the fly," that is, during Step 3, which follows.)

2. *Simulating the prover's first step* (P1): The simulator M^* selects at random, with uniform probability distribution, a "bit" $\tau \in \{1, 2\}$ and a permutation ψ from the set of permutations over the vertex set V_τ. It then constructs a graph with vertex set V_τ and edge set

$$F \stackrel{\text{def}}{=} \{(\psi(u), \psi(v)) : (u, v) \in E_\tau\},$$

and sets $G'' \stackrel{\text{def}}{=} (V_\tau, F)$.

3. *Simulating the verifier's first step* (V1): The simulator M^* initiates an execution of V^* by placing x on V^*'s common-input tape, placing r (selected in Step 1) on V^*'s random tape, and placing G'' (constructed in Step 2) on V^*'s incoming-message tape. After executing a polynomial number of steps of V^*, the simulator can read

the outgoing message of V^*, denoted σ. To simplify the rest of the description, we *normalize* σ by setting $\sigma = 1$ if $\sigma \neq 2$ (and leave σ unchanged if $\sigma = 2$).

4. *Simulating the prover's second step* (P2): If $\sigma = \tau$, then the simulator halts with output (x, r, G'', ψ).

5. *Failure of the simulation:* Otherwise (i.e., $\sigma \neq \tau$), the simulator halts with output $\perp$.

Using the hypothesis that V^* is polynomial-time, it follows that so is the simulator M^*. It is left to show that M^* outputs $\perp$ with probability at most $\frac{1}{2}$ and that, conditioned on not outputting $\perp$, the simulator's output is distributed as the verifier's view in a "real interaction with P_{GI}." The following claim is the key to the proof of both claims.

Claim 4.3.9.1: Suppose that the graphs G_1 and G_2 are isomorphic. Let ξ be a random variable uniformly distributed in $\{1, 2\}$, and let Π be a random variable uniformly distributed over the set of permutations over V_ξ. Then for every graph G'' that is isomorphic to G_1 (and G_2), it holds that

$$\Pr[\xi = 1 \mid \Pi(G_\xi) = G''] = \Pr[\xi = 2 \mid \Pi(G_\xi) = G''] = \frac{1}{2}$$

where, as in Claim 4.2.9.1, $\pi(G)$ denotes the graph obtained from the graph G by relabeling its nodes using the permutation π.

Claim 4.3.9.1 is identical to Claim 4.2.9.1 (used to demonstrate that Construction 4.2.8 constitutes an interactive proof for GNI).[10] As in the rest of the proof of Proposition 4.2.9, it follows that any random process with output in $\{1, 2\}$, given $\Pi(G_\xi)$, outputs ξ with probability exactly $\frac{1}{2}$. Hence, given G'' (constructed by the simulator in Step 2), the verifier's program yields (normalized) σ, so that $\sigma \neq \tau$ with probability exactly $\frac{1}{2}$. We conclude that the simulator outputs $\perp$ with probability $\frac{1}{2}$. It remains to prove that, conditioned on not outputting $\perp$, the simulator's output is identical to "V^*'s view of real interactions." Namely:

Claim 4.3.9.2: Let $x = (G_1, G_2) \in GI$. Then for every string r, graph H, and permutation ψ, it holds that

$$\Pr\left[\text{view}_{V^*}^{P_{GI}}(x) = (x, r, H, \psi)\right] = \Pr[M^*(x) = (x, r, H, \psi) \mid M^*(x) \neq \perp]$$

Proof: Let $m^*(x)$ describe $M^*(x)$ conditioned on its not being $\perp$. We first observe that both $m^*(x)$ and $\text{view}_{V^*}^{P_{GI}}(x)$ are distributed over quadruples of the form $(x, r, \cdot, \cdot)$, with uniformly distributed $r \in \{0, 1\}^{q(|x|)}$. Let $v(x, r)$ be a random variable describing the last two elements of $\text{view}_{V^*}^{P_{GI}}(x)$ conditioned on the second element equaling r. Similarly, let $\mu(x, r)$ describe the last two elements of $m^*(x)$ (conditioned on the second element equaling r). We need to show that $v(x, r)$

---

[10] In Construction 4.2.8, the graph $\Pi(G_\xi)$ was presented to the prover, and Claim 4.2.9.1 was used to establish the soundness of the proof system (i.e., analyze what happens in case $(G_1, G_2) \notin GNI$, which means $(G_1, G_2) \in GI$). Here the graph $\Pi(G_\xi)$ is presented to the verifier, and the claim is used to establish the zero-knowledge property (and so also refers to $(G_1, G_2) \in GI$).

and $\mu(x, r)$ are identically distributed for every x and r. Observe that once r is fixed, the message sent by V^*, on common input x, random tape r, and incoming message H, is uniquely defined. Let us denote this message by $v^*(x, r, H)$. We show that both $v(x, r)$ and $\mu(x, r)$ are uniformly distributed over the set

$$C_{x,r} \stackrel{\text{def}}{=} \{(H, \psi) : H = \psi(G_{v^*(x,r,H)})\}$$

where (again) $\psi(G)$ denotes the graph obtained from G by relabeling the vertices using the permutation ψ (i.e., if $G = (V, E)$, then $\psi(G) = (V, F)$, so that $(u, v) \in E$ iff $(\psi(u), \psi(v)) \in F$). The proof of this statement is rather tedious and is unrelated to the subjects of this book (and hence can be skipped with no damage).

The proof is slightly non-trivial because it relates (at least implicitly) to the automorphism group of the graph G_2 (i.e., the set of permutations π for which $\pi(G_2)$ is identical with G_2, not just isomorphic to G_2). For simplicity, consider first the special case in which the automorphism group of G_2 consists of merely the identity permutation (i.e., $G_2 = \pi(G_2)$ if and only if π is the identity permutation). In this case, $(H, \psi) \in C_{x,r}$ if and only if H is isomorphic to (both G_1 and) G_2 and ψ is the (unique) isomorphism between H and $G_{v^*(x,r,H)}$. Hence, $C_{x,r}$ contains exactly $|V_2|!$ pairs, each containing a different graph H as the first element. In the general case, $(H, \psi) \in C_{x,r}$ if and only if H is isomorphic to (both G_1 and) G_2 and ψ is an isomorphism between H and $G_{v^*(x,r,H)}$. We stress that $v^*(x, r, H)$ is the same in all pairs containing H. Let $\text{aut}(G_2)$ denote the size of the automorphism group of G_2. Then each H (isomorphic to G_2) appears in exactly $\text{aut}(G_2)$ pairs of $C_{x,r}$, and each such pair contains a different isomorphism between H and $G_{v^*(x,r,H)}$. The number of different H's that are isomorphic to G_2 is $|V_2|!/\text{aut}(G_2)$, and so $|C_{x,r}| = |V_2|!$ also in the general case.

We first consider the random variable $\mu(x, r)$ (describing the suffix of $m^*(x)$). Recall that $\mu(x, r)$ is defined by the following two-step random process. In the *first* step, one selects uniformly a pair (τ, ψ), over the set of pairs ($\{1, 2\} \times$ permutation), and sets $H = \psi(G_\tau)$. In the *second* step, one outputs (i.e., sets $\mu(x, r)$ to) $(\psi(G_\tau), \psi)$ if $v^*(x, r, H) = \tau$ (and ignores the (τ, ψ) pair otherwise). Hence, each graph H (isomorphic to G_2) is generated, at the first step, by exactly $\text{aut}(G_2)$ different $(1, \cdot)$-pairs (i.e., the pairs $(1, \psi)$ satisfying $H = \psi(G_1)$) and by exactly $\text{aut}(G_2)$ different $(2, \cdot)$-pairs (i.e., the pairs $(2, \psi)$ satisfying $H = \psi(G_2)$). All these $2 \cdot \text{aut}(G_2)$ pairs yield the same graph H and hence lead to the same value of $v^*(x, r, H)$. It follows that out of the $2 \cdot \text{aut}(G_2)$ pairs of the form (τ, ψ) that yield the graph $H = \psi(G_\tau)$, only the $\text{aut}(G_2)$ pairs satisfying $\tau = v^*(x, r, H)$ lead to an output. Hence, for each H (that is isomorphic to G_2), the probability that $\mu(x, r) = (H, \cdot)$ equals $\text{aut}(G_2)/(|V_2|!)$. Furthermore, for each H (that is isomorphic to G_2),

$$\Pr[\mu(x, r) = (H, \psi)] = \begin{cases} \frac{1}{|V_2|!} & \text{if} \quad H = \psi(G_{v^*(x,r,H)}) \\ 0 & \text{otherwise} \end{cases}$$

Hence $\mu(x, r)$ is uniformly distributed over $C_{x,r}$.

We now consider the random variable $v(x, r)$ (describing the suffix of the verifier's view in a "real interaction" with the prover). Recall that $v(x, r)$ is defined by selecting uniformly a permutation π (over the set V_2) and setting $v(x, r) = (\pi(G_2), \pi)$ if $v^*(x, r, \pi(G_2)) = 2$, and $v(x, r) = (\pi(G_2), \pi \circ \phi)$ otherwise, where ϕ is the isomorphism between G_1 and G_2. Clearly, for each H (that is isomorphic to G_2), the probability that $v(x, r) = (H, \cdot)$ equals $\text{aut}(G_2)/(|V_2|!)$. Furthermore, for each H (that is isomorphic to G_2),

$$\Pr[v(x,r) = (H, \psi)] = \begin{cases} \frac{1}{|V_2|!} & \text{if } \quad \psi = \pi \circ \phi^{2-v^*(x,r,H)} \\ 0 & \text{otherwise} \end{cases}$$

Observing that $H = \psi(G_{v^*(x,r,H)})$ if and only if $\psi = \pi \circ \phi^{2-v^*(x,r,H)}$, we conclude that $\mu(x,r)$ and $v(x,r)$ are identically distributed.

The claim follows. $\square$

This completes the proof of Part 3 of the proposition. ∎

4.3.3. Zero-Knowledge with Respect to Auxiliary Inputs

The definitions of zero-knowledge presented earlier fall short of what is required in practical applications, and consequently a minor modification should be used. We recall that these definitions guarantee that whatever can be efficiently computed after interaction with the prover on any *common input* can be efficiently computed *from the input itself*. However, in typical applications (e.g., when an interactive proof is used as a sub-protocol inside a larger protocol) the verifier interacting with the prover on common input x may have some additional a priori information, encoded by a string z, that may assist it in its attempts to "extract knowledge" from the prover. This danger may become even more acute in the likely case in which z is related to x. (For example, consider the protocol of Construction 4.3.8 and the case where the verifier has a priori information concerning an isomorphism between the input graphs.) What is typically required is that whatever can be efficiently computed from x and z after interaction with the prover on any common input x can be efficiently computed from x and z (without any interaction with the prover). This requirement is formulated next using the augmented notion of interactive proofs presented in Definition 4.2.10.

Definition 4.3.10 (Zero-Knowledge, Revisited): *Let (P, V) be an interactive proof for a language L (as in Definition 4.2.10). Denote by $P_L(x)$ the set of strings y satisfying the completeness condition with respect to $x \in L$ (i.e., $\Pr[\langle P(y), V(z)\rangle(x) = 1] \geq \frac{2}{3}$ for every $z \in \{0, 1\}^*$). We say that (P, V) is **zero-knowledge with respect to auxiliary input** (or is **auxiliary-input zero-knowledge**) if for every probabilistic polynomial-time interactive machine V^* there exists a probabilistic algorithm M^*, running in time polynomial in the length of its first input, such that the following two ensembles are computationally indistinguishable (when the distinguishing gap is considered as a function of $|x|$):*

- *$\{\langle P(y_x), V^*(z)\rangle(x)\}_{x \in L, z \in \{0,1\}^*}$ for arbitrary $y_x \in P_L(x)$*
- *$\{M^*(x, z)\}_{x \in L, z \in \{0,1\}^*}$*

Namely, for every probabilistic algorithm D with running time polynomial in the length of the first input, for every polynomial $p(\cdot)$, and for all sufficiently long $x \in L$, all $y \in P_L(x)$, and $z \in \{0, 1\}^*$, it holds that

$$|\Pr[D(x, z, \langle P(y), V^*(z)\rangle(x)) = 1] - \Pr[D(x, z, M^*(x, z)) = 1]| < \frac{1}{p(|x|)}$$

In this definition, y represents a priori information to the prover, whereas z represents a priori information to the verifier. Both y and z may depend on the common input x; for example, if y facilitates the proving task, then y must depend on x (e.g., in case y is an $\mathcal{NP}$-witness for $x \in L \in \mathcal{NP}$). We stress that the local inputs (i.e., y and z) may not be known, even in part, to the other party. We also stress that the auxiliary input z (but not y) is also given to the distinguishing algorithm (which can be thought of as an extension of the verifier).

Recall that by Definition 4.2.10, saying that the interactive machine V^* is probabilistic polynomial-time means that its running time is bounded by a polynomial in the length of the common input. Hence, the verifier program, the simulator, and the distinguishing algorithm all run in time polynomial in the length of x (and not in time polynomial in the total length of all their inputs). This convention is essential in many respects (unless one explicitly bounds the length of the auxiliary input by a polynomial in the length of x; see Exercise 11). For example, having allowed the distinguishing algorithm to run in time proportional to the length of the auxiliary input would have collapsed computational zero-knowledge to perfect zero-knowledge (e.g., by considering verifiers that run in time polynomial in the common input, yet have huge auxiliary inputs of length exponential in the common input).

Definition 4.3.10 refers to computational zero-knowledge. A formulation of perfect zero-knowledge with respect to auxiliary input is straightforward. We remark that the perfect zero-knowledge proof for Graph Isomorphism, presented in Construction 4.3.8, is in fact perfect zero-knowledge with respect to auxiliary input. This fact follows easily by a minor augmentation to the simulator constructed in the proof of Proposition 4.3.9 (i.e., when invoking the verifier, the simulator should provide it the auxiliary input that is given to the simulator). In general, a demonstration of zero-knowledge can be extended to yield zero-knowledge with respect to auxiliary input whenever the simulator used in the original demonstration works by invoking the verifier's program as a black box (see Definition 4.5.10 in Section 4.5.4). All simulators presented in this book have this property.

Advanced Comment: Implicit Non-Uniformity in Definition 4.3.10

The non-uniform nature of Definition 4.3.10 is captured by the fact that the distinguisher gets an auxiliary input. It is true that this auxiliary input is also given to both the verifier program and the simulator; however, if the auxiliary input is sufficiently long, then only the distinguisher can make use of its suffix (since the distinguisher may be determined after the polynomial-time bound of the simulator is fixed). It follows that the simulator guaranteed in Definition 4.3.10 produces output that is indistinguishable from the real interactions also by non-uniform polynomial-size circuits (see Definition 3.2.7). Namely, for every (even non-uniform) polynomial-size circuit family $\{C_n\}_{n \in \mathbb{N}}$, every polynomial $p(\cdot)$, all sufficiently large n's, all $x \in L \cap \{0, 1\}^n$, all $y \in P_L(x)$, and $z \in \{0, 1\}^*$,

$$|\Pr[C_n(x, z, \langle P(y), V^*(z)\rangle(x)) = 1] - \Pr[C_n(x, z, M^*(x, z)) = 1]| < \frac{1}{p(|x|)}$$

Following is a sketch of the proof of this claim. We assume, to the contrary, that there exists a polynomial-size circuit family $\{C_n\}_{n\in\mathbb{N}}$ such that for infinitely many n's there exist triples (x, y, z) for which C_n has a non-negligible distinguishing gap. We derive a contradiction by incorporating the description of C_n together with the auxiliary input z into a longer auxiliary input, denoted z'. This is done in such a way that both V^* and M^* have insufficient time to reach the description of C_n. For example, let $q(\cdot)$ be a polynomial bounding the running times of both V^* and M^*. Assume, without loss of generality, that $|z| \leq q(n)$ (or else the rest of z, which is unreadable by both V^* and M^*, can be ignored). Then we let z' be the string that results by padding z with blanks to a total length of $q(n)$ and appending the description of the circuit C_n at its end (i.e., z is a prefix of z'). Clearly, $M^*(x, z') = M^*(x, z)$ and $\langle P(y), V^*(z')\rangle(x) = \langle P(y), V^*(z)\rangle(x)$. On the other hand, by using a universal circuit-evaluating algorithm, we get a probabilistic polynomial-time algorithm D such that $D(x, z', \alpha) = C_n(x, z, \alpha)$, and contradiction (to the hypothesis that M^* produces output that is probabilistic polynomial-time-indistinguishable from the output of (P, V^*)) follows.

We mention that Definition 4.3.2 itself has some non-uniform flavor, since it requires indistinguishability for all but finitely many x's. In contrast, a fully uniform analogue of the definition would require only that it be infeasible to find x's on which the simulation would fail (with respect to some probabilistic polynomial-time distinguisher). That is, a fully uniform definition of zero-knowledge requires only that it be infeasible to find x's on which a verifier can gain knowledge (and not that such instances do not exist at all). See further discussion in Section 4.4.2.4.

Advanced Comment: Why Not Go for a Fully Non-Uniform Formulation?

An oversimplified version of Definition 4.3.10 allows the verifier to be modeled by a (non-uniform) family of (polynomial-size) circuits, and allows the same for the simulator. The non-uniform circuits are supposed to account for auxiliary inputs, and so these are typically omitted from such an oversimplified version. For example, one may require the following:

> For every polynomial-size circuit family $\{V_n\}_{n\in\mathbb{N}}$ (representing a possible verifier strategy machine) there exists a polynomial-size circuit family $\{M_n\}_{n\in\mathbb{N}}$ (representing a simulator) such that the ensembles $\{\langle P, V_{|x|}\rangle(x)\}_{x\in L}$ and $\{M_{|x|}(x)\}_{x\in L}$ are indistinguishable by polynomial-size circuits.

However, the impression that non-uniform circuits account for auxiliary inputs is wrong, and in general we find such oversimplified versions unsatisfactory. First, these versions do not guarantee an "effective" transformation of verifiers to simulators. Indeed, such a transformation is not required in Definition 4.3.10 either, but there the objects (i.e., machines) are of fixed size, whereas here we deal with infinite objects (i.e., circuit families). Thus, the level of "security" offered by the oversimplified definition is unsatisfactory. Second, the oversimplified version does not guarantee a relation between the size of the non-uniform part of the verifier and the corresponding part of the simulator, whereas in Definition 4.3.10 the only non-uniform part is the auxiliary input, which remains unchanged. Both issues arise when trying to prove a sequential-composition theorem for a non-constant number of iterations of zero-knowledge proof systems. Finally, we note that the oversimplified version does *not* imply the basic version (i.e., Definition 4.3.2); consider, for example, a prover that on common input x sends some hard-to-compute poly($|x|$)-bit-long string that depends only on $|x|$ (e.g., the prime-factorization of all integers in the interval $[2^{|x|} + 1, \ldots, 2^{|x|} + |x|^3]$).

4.3.4. Sequential Composition of Zero-Knowledge Proofs

An intuitive requirement that a definition of zero-knowledge proofs must satisfy is that zero-knowledge proofs should be closed under sequential composition. Namely, if we execute one zero-knowledge proof after another, then the composed execution must be zero-knowledge. The same should remain valid even if we execute polynomially many proofs one after the other. Indeed, as will be shown shortly, the revised definition of zero-knowledge (i.e., Definition 4.3.10) satisfies this requirement. Interestingly, zero-knowledge proofs as defined in Definition 4.3.2 are not closed under sequential composition, and this fact is indeed another indication of the necessity of augmenting this definition (as done in Definition 4.3.10).

In addition to its conceptual importance, the sequential-composition lemma is an important tool in the design of zero-knowledge proof systems. Typically, such a proof system consists of many repetitions of an atomic zero-knowledge proof. Loosely speaking, the atomic proof provides *some* (but not much) statistical evidence for the validity of the claim. By repeating the atomic proof sufficiently many times, the confidence in the validity of the claim is increased. More precisely, the atomic proof offers a gap between the acceptance probabilities for strings in the language and strings outside the language. For example, in Construction 4.3.8, pairs of isomorphic graphs (i.e., inputs in GI) are accepted with probability 1, whereas pairs of non-isomorphic graphs (i.e., inputs not in GI) are accepted with probability at most $\frac{1}{2}$. By repeating the atomic proof, the gap between the two probabilities is further increased. For example, repeating the proof of Construction 4.3.8 k times will yield a new interactive proof in which inputs in GI are still accepted with probability 1, whereas inputs not in GI are accepted with probability at most $\frac{1}{2^k}$. The sequential-composition lemma guarantees that if the atomic-proof system is zero-knowledge, then so is the proof system resulting from repeating the atomic proof polynomially many times.

Before we state the sequential-composition lemma, we remind the reader that the zero-knowledge property of an interactive proof is actually a property of the prover. Also, the prover is required to be zero-knowledge only on inputs in the language. Finally, we stress that when talking about zero-knowledge with respect to auxiliary input, we refer to all possible auxiliary inputs for the verifier.

Lemma 4.3.11 (Sequential-Composition Lemma): *Let P be an interactive machine (i.e., a prover) that is zero-knowledge with respect to auxiliary input on some language L. Suppose that the last message sent by P, on input x, bears a special end-of-proof symbol. Let $Q(\cdot)$ be a polynomial, and let P_Q be an interactive machine that, on common input x, proceeds in $Q(|x|)$ phases, each of them consisting of running P on common input x. (We stress that in case P is probabilistic, the interactive machine P_Q uses independent coin tosses for* *each of the $Q(|x|)$ phases.) Then P_Q is zero-knowledge (with respect to auxiliary input) on L. Furthermore, if P is perfect zero-knowledge (with respect to auxiliary input), then so is P_Q.*

The convention concerning the end-of-proof symbol is introduced for technical purposes (and is redundant in all known proof systems, and furthermore whenever the number of messages sent during the execution is easily computed from the common input). Clearly, every machine P can be easily modified so that its last message will bear an appropriate symbol (as assumed earlier), and doing so will preserve the zero-knowledge properties of P (as well as the completeness and soundness conditions).

The lemma ignores other aspects of repeating an interactive proof several times, specifically, the effect on the gap between the acceptance probabilities for inputs inside and outside of the language. The latter aspect of repeating an interactive proof system is discussed in Section 4.2.1.3 (see also Exercise 1).

Proof: Let V^* be an *arbitrary* probabilistic polynomial-time interactive machine interacting with the composed prover P_Q. Our task is to construct a (polynomial-time) simulator M^* that will simulate the real interactions of V^* with P_Q. Following is a very high level description of the simulation. The key idea is to simulate the real interaction on common input x in $Q(|x|)$ phases corresponding to the phases of the operation of P_Q. Each phase of the operation of P_Q is simulated using the simulator guaranteed for the atomic prover P. The information accumulated by the verifier in each phase is passed to the next phase using the auxiliary input.

(In the following exposition, we ignore the auxiliary input to the prover. This merely simplifies our notation. That is, instead of writing $P(y)$ and $P_Q(y)$, where y is the prover's auxiliary input, we write P and P_Q.)

The first step in carrying out this plan is to partition the execution of an arbitrary interactive machine V^* into phases. The partition may not exist in the code of the program V^*, and yet it can be imposed on the executions of this program. This is done using the phase structure *of the prescribed prover* P_Q, which in turn is induced by the end-of-proof symbols. Hence, we claim that no matter how V^* operates, the interaction of V^* with P_Q on common input x can be captured by $Q(|x|)$ successive interactions of a related machine, denoted V^{**}, with P. Namely:

Claim 4.3.11.1: There exists a probabilistic polynomial-time V^{**} such that for every common input x and auxiliary input z, it holds that

$$\langle P_Q, V^*(z) \rangle (x) = Z^{(Q(|x|))}$$

where $Z^{(0)} \overset{\text{def}}{=} z$ and

$$Z^{(i+1)} \overset{\text{def}}{=} \langle P, V^{**}(Z^{(i)}) \rangle (x) \quad \text{for } i = 0, \ldots, Q(|x|) - 1$$

Namely, $Z^{(Q(|x|))}$ is a random variable describing the output of V^{**} after $Q(|x|)$ successive interactions with P, on common input x, where the auxiliary input of V^{**} in the $i + 1$ interaction equals the output of V^{**} after the ith interaction (i.e., $Z^{(i)}$).

—— **217** ——

Proof: Intuitively, V^{**} captures the functionality of V^* during each single phase. By the *functionality of V^* during a phase* we mean the way V^* transforms the content of its work tapes at the beginning of the phase to their content at the end of the phase, as well as the way V^* determines the messages it sends during this phase. Indeed, this transformation depends on the messages received during the current phase. We stress that we can effect this transformation without "reverse-engineering" (the code of) V^*, but rather by emulating its execution while monitoring all its tapes. Details follow.

In order to facilitate this process, we first modify V^* so that all its "essential" activities refer only to its work tapes. Machine V^* can be slightly modified so that it starts its execution by reading the common input, the random input, and the auxiliary input into special regions in its work tape and never accesses the aforementioned read-only tapes again. Likewise, V^* is modified so that it starts each active period[11] (see Definition 4.2.2) by reading the current incoming message from the communication tape to a special region in the work tape (and never accesses the incoming-message tape again during this period). Actually, this description should be modified so that V^* copies only a polynomially long (in the common input) prefix of each of these tapes, the polynomial being the one bounding the running time of (the original) V^*.

(Formally speaking, given an arbitrary V^*, we construct a machine W^* that emulates V^* in a way that satisfies the foregoing conditions; that is, W^* will satisfy these conditions even if V^* does not. Machine W^* will have several extra work tapes that will be designated as the common-input, random-input, auxiliary-input, and incoming-communication tapes of V^*. Machine W^* will start by copying its own common input, random input, and auxiliary input to the corresponding designated tapes. Likewise, W^* will start each active period by copying the current incoming message from its own communication tape to the corresponding designated tape (i.e., the incoming-communication tape of V^*). After completing these copying activities, W^* just emulates the execution of V^*. Clearly, W^* satisfies the requirements postulated. Thus, formally speaking, whenever we later refer to V^*, we mean W^*.)

Consider an interaction of $V^*(z)$ with P_Q, on common input x. By the foregoing modification, the interaction consists of $Q(|x|)$ phases, so that, except in the first phase, machine V^* never accesses its common-input, random-input, and auxiliary-input tapes. (In the first phase, machine V^* starts by copying the content of these tapes into its work tapes and never accesses the former tapes again.) Likewise, when executing the current phase, machine V^* does not try to read messages of *previous* phases from its incoming-communication tape (yet it may read these "old" messages from storage in its work tapes). Considering the content of the *work tapes of V^** at the end of *each* of the $Q(|x|)$ phases (of interaction with P_Q) naturally leads us to the construction of V^{**}.

We are now finally ready present the construction of V^{**}: On common input x and auxiliary input z', machine V^{**} starts by copying z' into the work tape of

---

[11] Recall that an *active period* during an execution of an interactive machine M consists of the steps M takes from the time the last message is received up to the time at which M completes sending its response message.

V^*. Next, machine V^{**} emulates a *single phase* of the interaction of V^* with P_Q (on input x), starting with the foregoing contents of the work tape of V^* (instead of starting with an empty work tape). The emulated machine V^* regards the communication tapes of machine V^{**} as its own communication tapes. When V^* completes the interaction in the current phase, machine V^{**} terminates by outputting the current contents of the work tape of V^*. Thus, when z' equals a possible content of the work tape of V^* after $i \geq 1$ phases, the emulated V^* behaves as in the $i + 1$ phase, and the output of V^{**} is distributed as the content of the work tape of V^* after $i + 1$ phases. Actually, the foregoing description should be slightly modified to deal with the first phase in the interaction with P_Q (i.e., the case $i = 0$ ignored earlier). Specifically, V^{**} copies z' into the work tape of V^* only if z' encodes the content of the work tape of V^* (we assume, without loss of generality, that the content of the work tape of V^* is encoded differently from the encoding of an auxiliary input for V^*). In case z' encodes an auxiliary input to V^*, machine V^{**} invokes V^* on an empty work tape, and V^* regards the readable tapes of V^{**} (i.e., common-input tape, random-input tape, and auxiliary-input tape) as its own. Observe that $Z^{(1)} \overset{\text{def}}{=} \langle P, V^{**}(z) \rangle (x)$ describes the content of the work tape of V^* after the first phase (in the interaction with P_Q on common input x and auxiliary input z). Likewise, for every $i = 2, \ldots, Q(|x|)$, the random variable $Z^{(i)} \overset{\text{def}}{=} \langle P, V^{**}(Z^{(i-1)}) \rangle (x)$ describes the content of the work tape of V^* after i phases. The claim follows. $\square$

Because V^{**} is a polynomial-time interactive machine (with auxiliary input) interacting with P, it follows by the lemma's hypothesis that there exists a probabilistic machine that simulates these interactions in time polynomial in the length of the first input. Let M^{**} denote this simulator.[12] Then for every probabilistic polynomial-time (in x) algorithm D, every polynomial $p(\cdot)$, all sufficiently long $x \in L$, and all $z \in \{0, 1\}^*$, we have

$$|\Pr[D(x, z, \langle P, V^{**}(z) \rangle (x)) = 1] - \Pr[D(x, z, M^{**}(x, z)) = 1]| < \frac{1}{p(|x|)}$$

(4.1)

We are now ready to present the construction of a simulator M^* that simulates the "real" output of V^* after interaction with P_Q. We can assume, without loss of generality, that the output of V^* equals the content of its work tapes at the end of the interaction (since the output of V^* is probabilistic polynomial-time-computable from the content of its work tapes at that time). Machine M^* uses the simulator M^{**} (as a black box).

The simulator M^*: On input (x, z), machine M^* sets $z^{(0)} = z$ and proceeds in $Q(|x|)$ phases. In the ith phase, machine M^* computes $z^{(i)}$ by running machine

---

[12] Recall that in the case of perfect zero-knowledge (see Definition 4.3.1) machine M^{**} may halt with no real output (but rather with output $\perp$). However, by sufficiently many repetitions, we can make the probability of this event exponentially vanishing. In the rest of the exposition, we assume for simplicity that M^{**} always halts with output.

M^{**} on input $(x, z^{(i-1)})$. After $Q(|x|)$ phases are completed, machine M^* stops outputting $z^{(Q(|x|))}$.

Clearly, machine M^*, as constructed here, runs in time polynomial in its first input. It is left to show that machine M^* indeed produces output that is computationally indistinguishable from the output of V^* (after interacting with P_Q). Namely:

Claim 4.3.11.2: For every probabilistic algorithm D with running time polynomial in its first input, every polynomial $p(\cdot)$, all sufficiently long $x \in L$, and all $z \in \{0, 1\}^*$, we have

$$|\Pr[D(x, z, \langle P_Q, V^*(z) \rangle(x)) = 1] - \Pr[D(x, z, M^*(x, z)) = 1]| < \frac{1}{p(|x|)}$$

Furthermore, if P is perfect zero-knowledge, then $\langle P_Q, V^*(z) \rangle(x)$ and $M^*(x, z)$ are identically distributed.

Proof sketch: We use a hybrid argument (see Chapter 3). In particular, we define the following $Q(|x|) + 1$ hybrids. The ith hybrid, $0 \le i \le Q(|x|)$, corresponds to the following random process. We first let V^{**} interact with P for i phases, starting with common input x and auxiliary input z, and denote by $Z^{(i)}$ the output of V^{**} after the ith phase. We next repeatedly iterate M^{**} for the remaining $Q(|x|) - i$ phases. In both cases, we use the output of the previous phase as auxiliary input to the new phase. Formally, the hybrid $H^{(i)}$ is defined as follows:

$$H^{(i)}(x, z) \overset{\text{def}}{=} M^{**}_{Q(|x|)-i}(x, Z^{(i)})$$

where the $Z^{(j)}$'s are as defined in Claim 4.3.11.1, and where

$$M^{**}_0(x, z') \overset{\text{def}}{=} z' \quad \text{and} \quad M^{**}_k(x, z') \overset{\text{def}}{=} M^{**}_{k-1}(x, M^{**}(x, z'))$$
$$\text{for } k = 1, \dots, Q(|x|) - i$$

By Claim 4.3.11.1, the $Q(|x|)$ hybrid (i.e., $H^{(Q(|x|))}(x, z) = Z^{(Q(|x|))}$) equals $\langle P_Q, V^*(z) \rangle(x)$. On the other hand, recalling the construction of M^*, we see that the zero hybrid (i.e., $H^{(0)}(x, z) = M^{**}_{Q(|x|)}(x, z)$) equals $M^*(x, z)$. Hence, all that is required to complete the proof is to show that all pairs of two adjacent hybrids are computationally indistinguishable (as this will imply that the extreme hybrids, $H^{(Q(|x|))}$ and $H^{(0)}$, are also indistinguishable). To this end, we rewrite the i and $i - 1$ hybrids as follows:

$$H^{(i)}(x, z) = M^{**}_{Q(|x|)-i}(x, Z^{(i)})$$
$$= M^{**}_{Q(|x|)-i}(x, \langle P, V^{**}(Z^{(i-1)}) \rangle(x))$$
$$H^{(i-1)}(x, z) = M^{**}_{Q(|x|)-(i-1)}(x, Z^{(i-1)})$$
$$= M^{**}_{Q(|x|)-i}(x, M^{**}(x, Z^{(i-1)}))$$

where $Z^{(i-1)}$ is as defined in Claim 4.3.11.1.

Using an averaging argument, it follows that if an algorithm D distinguishes the hybrids $H^{(i)}(x, z)$ and $H^{(i-1)}(x, z)$, then there exists a z' (in the support of $Z^{(i-1)}$) such that algorithm D distinguishes the random variables $M^{**}_{Q(|x|)-i}(x, \langle P, V^{**}(z')\rangle(x))$ and $M^{**}_{Q(|x|)-i}(x, M^{**}(x, z'))$ at least as well. (In all cases, D is also given x and z.) Using algorithms M^{**} and D, we get a new algorithm D', with running time polynomially related to the former algorithms, that distinguishes the random variables $(x, z, i, z', \langle P, V^{**}(z')\rangle(x))$ and $(x, z, i, z',$ $M^{**}(x, z'))$ at least as well. Specifically, on input $(x, (z, i, z'), \alpha)$ (where α is taken either from $\langle P, V^{**}(z')\rangle(x)$ or from $M^{**}(x, z')$), algorithm D' invokes D on input $(x, z, M^{**}_{Q(|x|)-i}(x, \alpha))$ and outputs whatever D does. Clearly,

$$|\Pr[D'(x, (z, i, z'), \langle P, V^{**}(z')\rangle(x)) = 1] - \Pr[D'(x, (z, i, z'), M^{**}(x, z')) = 1]|$$
$$\geq |\Pr[D(x, z, H^{(i)}(x, z)) = 1] - \Pr[D(x, z, H^{(i-1)}(x, z)) = 1]|$$

Note that D' uses additional input (x, z, i, z'), whereas it distinguishes $\langle P, V^{**}(z')\rangle(x)$ from $M^{**}(x, z')$. This does not fit the definition of a distinguisher for (auxiliary-input) zero-knowledge, as the latter is to be given only (x, z') and the string to be distinguished. In other words, we have actually constructed a non-uniform $D' = D'_{i,z}$ that, depending on i and z, distinguishes $\langle P, V^{**}(z')\rangle(x)$ from $M^{**}(x, z')$. Still, in the case of perfect zero-knowledge, letting D be an arbitrary function (rather than an efficient algorithm), this suffices for contradicting the hypothesis that M^{**} perfectly simulates (P, V^{**}). For the case of computational zero-knowledge, we use the fact that the definition of auxiliary-input zero-knowledge implies robustness against non-uniform (polynomial-size) distinguishers, and we note that $D'_{i,z}$ falls into this category (provided that D also does). Thus, in both cases, contradiction (to the hypothesis that M^{**} simulates (P, V^{**})) follows. □

Further details concerning the proof of Claim 4.3.11.2: At this stage (assuming the reader has gone through Chapter 3), the reader should be able to transform the foregoing proof sketch into a detailed proof. The main thing that is missing is the detail concerning the way in which an algorithm contradicting the hypothesis that M^{**} is a simulator for (P, V^{**}) is derived from an algorithm contradicting the statement of Claim 4.3.11.2. These details are presented next.

We assume, to the contradiction, that there exists a probabilistic polynomial-time algorithm D and a polynomial $p(\cdot)$ such that for infinitely many $x \in L$, there exists $z \in \{0, 1\}^*$ such that

$$|\Pr[D(x, z, \langle P_Q, V^*(z)\rangle(x)) = 1] - \Pr[D(x, z, M^*(x, z)) = 1]| > \frac{1}{p(|x|)}$$

It follows that for every such x and z, there exists an $i \in \{1, \ldots, Q(|x|)\}$ such that

$$\left|\Pr\left[D(x, z, H^{(i)}(x, z)) = 1\right] - \Pr\left[D(x, z, H^{(i-1)}(x, z)) = 1\right]\right| > \frac{1}{Q(|x|) \cdot p(|x|)}$$

where the hybrid $H^{(j)}$'s are as defined earlier. Denote $\varepsilon(n) \overset{\text{def}}{=} 1/(Q(n) \cdot p(n))$. Combining, as before, the definitions of the i and $i - 1$ hybrids with an averaging argument, it follows that for each such x, z, and i, there exists a z' such that

$$\left| \Pr\left[D\left(x, z, M^{**}_{Q(|x|)-i}(x, \langle P, V^{**}(z')\rangle(x))\right) = 1\right] \right.$$
$$\left. - \Pr\left[D\left(x, z, M^{**}_{Q(|x|)-i}(x, M^{**}(x, z'))\right) = 1\right] \right| > \varepsilon(|x|)$$

This almost leads to the desired contradiction. Namely, the random variables $(x, z', \langle P, V^{**}(z')\rangle(x))$ and $(x, z', M^{**}(x, z'))$ can be distinguished using the algorithms D and M^{**}, *provided we "know" i and z.* But how do we get to "know" i and z? The problem is resolved using the fact, pointed out earlier, that the output of M^{**} should be indistinguishable from the interactions of V^{**} with P even with respect to non-uniform polynomial-size circuits. Thus, in order to derive a contradiction, it suffices to construct a non-uniform distinguisher that incorporates i and z in its description. Alternatively, we can incorporate i and z in a new auxiliary input, denoted z'', so that z' is a prefix of z'', but z'' looks the same as z' to both V^* and M^*. Next we shall follow the latter alternative.

Let T denote a polynomial upper bound on the time-complexity of both V^* and M^*. Note that for every z' determined for a pair (x, z), as before, it must hold that $|z'| \le T(|x|)$ (since z' is a possible record of a partial computation of $M^*(x, z)$). Let $z'' = (z' \flat^{T(|x|)-|z'|}, i, z)$, where i and z are as before (and $\flat$ denotes the blank symbol of the work tape). We construct a probabilistic polynomial-time algorithm D' that distinguishes $(x, z'', \langle P, V^{**}(z'')\rangle(x))$ and $(x, z'', M^{**}(x, z''))$ for the aforementioned (x, z, i, z')-tuples. On input (x, z'', α) (where α supposedly is in either $\langle P, V^{**}(z'')\rangle(x) = \langle P, V^{**}(z')\rangle(x)$ or $M^{**}(x, z'') = M^{**}(x, z')$), algorithm D' first extracts i and z from z''. Next, it uses M^{**} to compute $\beta = M^{**}_{Q(|x|)-i}(x, \alpha)$. Finally, D' halts with output $D(x, z, \beta)$. Using the fact that V^{**} and M^{**} cannot distinguish the auxiliary inputs z' and z'', we have

$$|\Pr[D'(x, z'', \langle P, V^{**}(z'')\rangle(x)) = 1] - \Pr[D'(x, z'', M^{**}(x, z'')) = 1]|$$
$$= |\Pr[D'(x, z'', \langle P, V^{**}(z')\rangle(x)) = 1] - \Pr[D'(x, z'', M^{**}(x, z')) = 1]|$$
$$= \left| \Pr\left[D\left(x, z, M_{Q(|x|)-i}(x, \langle P, V^{**}(z')\rangle(x))\right) = 1\right] \right.$$
$$\left. - \Pr\left[D\left(x, z, M_{Q(|x|)-i}(x, M^{**}(x, z'))\right) = 1\right] \right|$$
$$> \varepsilon(|x|)$$

Contradiction (to the hypothesis that M^{**} is a simulator for (P, V^{**})) follows. $\square$

The lemma follows. ∎

And What About Parallel Composition?

Unfortunately, we cannot prove that zero-knowledge (even with respect to auxiliary input) is preserved under parallel composition. Furthermore, there exist (auxiliary-input) zero-knowledge proofs that when played twice in parallel do yield knowledge (to a "cheating verifier"). For further details, see Section 4.5.4.

The fact that zero-knowledge is not preserved under parallel composition of protocols is indeed bad news. One might even say that this fact is a conceptually annoying phenomenon. We disagree with that assessment. Our feeling is that the behavior of protocols and "games" under parallel composition is, in general (i.e., not only in the context of zero-knowledge), a much more complex issue than their behavior under sequential composition: in fact, in several other cases (e.g., computationally sound proofs, proofs of knowledge, and multi-prover proof systems; see Sections 4.8, 4.7, and 4.11, respectively), parallel composition lags behind sequential composition. Furthermore, the only advantage of parallel composition over sequential composition is in efficiency. Hence, we do not consider the non-closure under parallel composition to be a fundamental weakness of the formulation of zero-knowledge. Yet the "non-closure" of zero-knowledge motivates the search for alternative (related) notions that are preserved under parallel composition. (Such notions may be either weaker or stronger than the formulation of zero-knowledge.) For further details, the reader is referred to Sections 4.9 and 4.6.

4.4. Zero-Knowledge Proofs for $\mathcal{NP}$

This section presents the main thrust of this chapter, namely, a method for constructing zero-knowledge proofs for *every* language in $\mathcal{NP}$. The importance of this method stems from its generality, which is the key to its many applications. Specifically, almost all statements one might wish to prove in practice can be encoded as claims concerning membership in languages in $\mathcal{NP}$. In particular, the construction of zero-knowledge proofs for such statements provides a tool for "forcing" parties to properly execute any given protocol.

The method for constructing zero-knowledge proofs for $\mathcal{NP}$ languages makes essential use of the concept of *bit commitment*. Hence, we start with a presentation of the latter concept. (A reader who wishes to have more of the flavor of this application of commitment schemes before studying them is encouraged to read Section 4.4.2.1 first.)

4.4.1. Commitment Schemes

Commitment schemes are basic ingredients in many cryptographic protocols. They are used to enable a party to commit itself to a value while keeping it secret. In a later stage the commitment is "opened," and it is guaranteed that the "opening" can yield only a single value determined in the committing phase. Commitment schemes are the digital analogues of non-transparent sealed envelopes. By putting a note in such an envelope, a party commits itself to the content of the note while keeping the content secret.

4.4.1.1. Definition

Loosely speaking, a commitment scheme is an efficient *two-phase* two-party protocol through which one party, called the *sender*, can commit itself to a *value* such that the following two conflicting requirements are satisfied.

1. *Secrecy* (or *hiding*): At the end of the first phase, the other party, called the *receiver*, does not gain any knowledge of the sender's value. This requirement has to be satisfied even if the receiver tries to cheat.

2. *Unambiguity* (or *binding*): Given the transcript of the interaction in the first phase, there exists at most one value that the receiver can later (i.e., in the second phase) accept as a legal "opening" of the commitment. This requirement has to be satisfied even if the sender tries to cheat.

In addition, one should require that the protocol be *viable*, in the sense that if both parties follow it, then at the end of the second phase the receiver gets the value committed to by the sender. The first phase is called the *commit phase*, and the second phase is called the *reveal phase*. We are requiring that the commit phase yield no knowledge (at least no knowledge of the sender's value) to the receiver, whereas the commit phase does "bind" the sender to a unique value (in the sense that in the reveal phase the receiver can accept only this value). We stress that the protocol is efficient in the sense that the predetermined programs of both parties can be implemented in probabilistic polynomial time. Without loss of generality, the reveal phase may consist of merely letting the sender send, to the receiver, the original value and the sequence of random coin tosses that it has used during the commit phase. The receiver will accept the value if and only if the supplied information matches its transcript of the interaction in the commit phase. The latter convention leads to the following definition (which refers explicitly only to the commit phase).

Definition 4.4.1 (Bit-Commitment Scheme): *A* **bit-commitment scheme** *is a pair of probabilistic polynomial-time interactive machines, denoted* (S, R) *(for* sender *and* receiver*), satisfying the following:*

- Input specification: *The* common input *is an integer n presented in unary (serving as the security parameter).*
  The private input *to the sender is a bit, denoted* v.
- Secrecy (or hiding): *The receiver (even when deviating arbitrarily from the protocol) cannot distinguish a commitment to 0 from a commitment to 1. Namely, for every probabilistic polynomial-time machine R^* interacting with S, the probability ensembles describing the output of R^* in the two cases, namely $\{\langle S(0), R^* \rangle (1^n)\}_{n \in \mathbb{N}}$ and $\{\langle S(1), R^* \rangle (1^n)\}_{n \in \mathbb{N}}$, are computationally indistinguishable.*
- Unambiguity (or binding): *Preliminaries to the requirement:*

  1. *A receiver's view of an interaction with the sender, denoted $(r, \overline{m})$, consists of the random coins used by the receiver (r) and the sequence of messages received from the sender $(\overline{m})$.*

  2. *Let $\sigma \in \{0, 1\}$. We say that a receiver's view (of such interaction), $(r, \overline{m})$, is a* **possible σ-commitment** *if there exists a string s such that $\overline{m}$ describes the messages received by R when R uses local coins r and interacts with machine S that uses local coins s and has input $(\sigma, 1^n)$.*

     (Using the notation of Definition 4.3.3, we say that $(r, \overline{m})$ is a possible σ-commitment if $(r, \overline{m}) = \text{view}_{R(1^n, r)}^{S(\sigma, 1^n, s)}$.)

3. *We say that the receiver's view* $(r, \overline{m})$ *is* **ambiguous** *if it is both a possible 0-commitment and a possible 1-commitment.*

The unambiguity requirement *asserts that for all but a negligible fraction of the coin tosses of the receiver there exists no sequence of messages (from the sender) that together with these coin tosses forms an ambiguous receiver view. Namely, for all but a negligible fraction of the* $r \in \{0, 1\}^{\text{poly}(n)}$ *there is no* $\overline{m}$ *such that* $(r, \overline{m})$ *is ambiguous.*

The secrecy requirement is a computational one. On the other hand, the *unambiguity requirement* has an information-theoretic flavor (i.e., it does not refer to computational powers) and is sometimes referred to as *perfect* (or *absolute*). Thus, a commitment scheme as in Definition 4.4.1 is sometimes referred to as *computationally hiding* and *perfectly binding*. A dual definition, requiring information-theoretic secrecy and computational infeasibility of creating ambiguities, is presented in Section 4.8.2. (The latter is referred to as *perfectly hiding* and *computationally binding*.)

Canonical Reveal Phase. The secrecy requirement refers explicitly to the situation at the end of the commit phase. On the other hand, we stress that the unambiguity requirement implicitly assumes that the reveal phase takes the following form:

1. The sender sends to the receiver its initial private input v and the random coins s it has used in the commit phase.

2. The receiver verifies that v and s (together with the coins (r) used by R in the commit phase) indeed yield the messages that R has received in the commit phase. Verification is done in polynomial time (by running the programs S and R).

Note that the viability requirement (i.e., asserting that if both parties follow the protocol, then at the end of the reveal phase the receiver gets v) is implicitly satisfied by this convention.

4.4.1.2. Construction Based on Any One-Way Permutation

Some public-key encryption scheme can be used as a commitment scheme. This can be done by having the sender generate a pair of keys and use the public key together with the encryption of a value as its commitment to the value. In order to satisfy the unambiguity requirement, the underlying public-key scheme needs to satisfy additional requirements (i.e., the set of legitimate public keys should be efficiently recognizable, and an encryption relative to legitimate public keys should have a unique decryption). In any case, public-key encryption schemes have additional properties not required of commitment schemes, and their existence seems to require stronger intractability assumptions. (Thus, we consider the aforementioned approach to be "conceptually wrong.") An alternative construction, presented next, uses any *one-way permutation*. Specifically, we use a one-way permutation, denoted f, and a hard-core predicate for it, denoted b (see Section 2.5). In fact, we can use any 1-1 one-way function.

Construction 4.4.2 (Simple Bit Commitment): *Let* $f : \{0, 1\}^* \to \{0, 1\}^*$ *be a function, and let* $b : \{0, 1\}^* \to \{0, 1\}$ *be a predicate.*

1. Commit phase: *To commit to value $v \in \{0, 1\}$ (using security parameter n), the sender uniformly selects $s \in \{0, 1\}^n$ and sends the pair $(f(s), b(s) \oplus v)$ to the receiver.*

2. (Canonical) reveal phase: *In the reveal phase, the sender reveals the bit v and the string s used in the commit phase. The receiver accepts the value v if $f(s) = \alpha$ and $b(s) \oplus v = \sigma$, where (α, σ) is the receiver's view of the commit phase.*

Proposition 4.4.3: *Let $f : \{0, 1\}^* \rightarrow \{0, 1\}^*$ be a 1-1 one-way function, and let $b : \{0, 1\}^* \rightarrow \{0, 1\}$ be a hard-core predicate of f. Then the protocol presented in Construction 4.4.2 constitutes a bit-commitment scheme.*

Proof: The secrecy requirement follows directly from the fact that b is a hard-core of f. The unambiguity requirement follows from the 1-1 property of f. In fact, there exists *no* ambiguous receiver view. Namely, for each possible receiver view (α, σ), there is a unique $s \in \{0, 1\}^{|\alpha|}$ such that $f(s) = \alpha$, and hence a unique $v \in \{0, 1\}$ such that $b(s) \oplus v = \sigma$. ∎

4.4.1.3. Construction Based on Any One-Way Function

We now present a construction of a bit-commitment scheme that is based on the weakest assumption possible: the existence of one-way functions. Proving that the assumption is indeed minimal is left as an exercise (i.e., Exercise 13). On the other hand, by the results in Chapter 3 (specifically, Theorems 3.3.3 and 3.5.12), the existence of one-way functions implies the existence of pseudorandom generators expanding n-bit strings into $3n$-bit strings. We shall use such a pseudorandom generator in the construction presented next.

We start by motivating the construction. Let G be a pseudorandom generator satisfying $|G(s)| = 3 \cdot |s|$. Assume that G has the property that the sets $\{G(s) : s \in \{0, 1\}^n\}$ and $\{G(s) \oplus 1^{3n} : s \in \{0, 1\}^n\}$ are disjoint, where $\alpha \oplus \beta$ denotes the bit-by-bit XOR of the strings α and β. Then the sender can commit itself to the bit v by uniformly selecting $s \in \{0, 1\}^n$ and sending the message $G(s) \oplus v^{3n}$ (v^k denotes the all-v k-bit-long string). Unfortunately, the foregoing assumption cannot be justified in general, and a slightly more complex variant is required. The key observation is that for most strings $r \in \{0, 1\}^{3n}$ the sets $\{G(s) : s \in \{0, 1\}^n\}$ and $\{G(s) \oplus r : s \in \{0, 1\}^n\}$ are disjoint. Such a string r is called *good*. This observation suggests the following protocol: The receiver uniformly selects $r \in \{0, 1\}^{3n}$, hoping that it is good, and sends r to the sender. Having received r, the sender commits to the bit v by uniformly selecting $s \in \{0, 1\}^n$ and sending the message $G(s)$ if $v = 0$, and $G(s) \oplus r$ otherwise.

Construction 4.4.4 (Bit Commitment under General Assumptions): *Let $G : \{0, 1\}^* \rightarrow \{0, 1\}^*$ be a function such that $|G(s)| = 3 \cdot |s|$ for all $s \in \{0, 1\}^*$.*

1. Commit phase:

   - *To receive a commitment to a bit (using security parameter n), the receiver uniformly selects $r \in \{0, 1\}^{3n}$ and sends it to the sender.*

- Upon receiving the message r (from the receiver), the sender commits to value $v \in \{0, 1\}$ by uniformly selecting $s \in \{0, 1\}^n$ and sending $G(s)$ if $v = 0$, and $G(s) \oplus r$ otherwise.

2. (Canonical) reveal phase: In the reveal phase, the sender reveals the string s used in the commit phase. The receiver accepts the value 0 if $G(s) = \alpha$ and accepts the value 1 if $G(s) \oplus r = \alpha$, where (r, α) is the receiver's view of the commit phase.

Such a definition of the (canonical) reveal phase allows the receiver to accept both values, but we shall show that that happens very rarely (if at all).

Proposition 4.4.5: If G is a pseudorandom generator, then the protocol presented in Construction 4.4.4 constitutes a bit-commitment scheme.

Proof: The secrecy requirement follows the fact that G is a pseudorandom generator. Specifically, let U_k denote the random variable uniformly distributed on strings of length k. Then for every $r \in \{0, 1\}^{3n}$, the random variables U_{3n} and $U_{3n} \oplus r$ are identically distributed. Hence, if it is feasible to find an $r \in \{0, 1\}^{3n}$ such that $G(U_n)$ and $G(U_n) \oplus r$ are computationally distinguishable, then either U_{3n} and $G(U_n)$ are computationally distinguishable or $U_{3n} \oplus r$ and $G(U_n) \oplus r$ are computationally distinguishable. In either case, contradiction to the pseudorandomness of G follows.

We now turn to the unambiguity requirement. Following the motivating discussion, we call $r \in \{0, 1\}^{3n}$ *good* if the sets $\{G(s) : s \in \{0, 1\}^n\}$ and $\{G(s) \oplus r : s \in \{0, 1\}^n\}$ are disjoint. We say that $r \in \{0, 1\}^{3n}$ *yields a collision between the seeds* s_1 *and* s_2 if $G(s_1) = G(s_2) \oplus r$. Clearly, r is good if it does not yield a collision between any pair of seeds. On the other hand, there is at most one string r that yields a collision between a given pair of seeds (s_1, s_2); that is, $r = G(s_1) \oplus G(s_2)$. Because there are at most $\binom{2^n}{2} < 2^{2n}$ possible pairs of seeds, fewer than 2^{2n} strings will yield collisions between pairs of seeds, and so all the other $3n$-bit-long strings are good. It follows that with probability at least $1 - 2^{2n-3n}$ the receiver selects a good string, in which case its view (r, α) is unambiguous (since if r is good and $G(s_1) = \alpha$ holds for some s_1, then $G(s_2) \neq \alpha \oplus r$ must hold for all s_2's). The unambiguity requirement follows. ■

4.4.1.4. Extensions

The definition and the constructions of bit-commitment schemes are easily extended to general commitment schemes, enabling the sender to commit to a string rather than to a single bit. Actually, for the purposes of the rest of this section, we need a commitment scheme by which one can commit to a ternary value. Extending the definition and the constructions to deal with this special case is even more straightforward.

In the rest of this section we shall need commitment schemes with a seemingly stronger secrecy requirement than defined earlier. Specifically, instead of requiring secrecy with respect to all polynomial-time machines, we require secrecy with respect to all (not necessarily uniform) families of polynomial-size circuits. Assuming the existence of non-uniformly one-way functions (see Definition 2.2.6 in Section 2.2), commitment schemes with non-uniform secrecy can be constructed, using the same construction as in the uniform case. Thus, we have the following:

Theorem 4.4.6: *Suppose there exist non-uniformly one-way functions (as in Definition 2.2.6). Then there exists a bit-commitment scheme (as in Definition 4.4.1) for which the secrecy condition also holds with respect to polynomial-size circuits.*

4.4.2. Zero-Knowledge Proof of Graph Coloring

Presenting a zero-knowledge proof system for one $\mathcal{NP}$-complete language implies the existence of a zero-knowledge proof system for every language in $\mathcal{NP}$. This intuitively appealing statement does require a proof, which we postpone to a later stage. In the current section we present a zero-knowledge proof system for one $\mathcal{NP}$-complete language, specifically Graph 3-Colorability. This choice is indeed arbitrary.

The language *Graph 3-Coloring*, denoted $G3C$, consists of all simple (finite) graphs (i.e., no parallel edges or self-loops)[13] that can be *vertex-colored* using three colors such that no two adjacent vertices are given the same color. Formally, a graph $G = (V, E)$ is *3-colorable* if there exists a mapping $\phi : V \to \{1, 2, 3\}$ such that $\phi(u) \neq \phi(v)$ for every $(u, v) \in E$.

4.4.2.1. Motivating Discussion

The idea underlying the zero-knowledge proof system for $G3C$ is to break the proof of the claim that a graph is 3-colorable into polynomially many *pieces* arranged in *templates* so that each template by itself will yield no knowledge and yet all the templates put together will guarantee the validity of the main claim. Suppose that the prover generates such pieces of information, places each of them in a separate sealed and non-transparent envelope, and allows the verifier to open and inspect the pieces participating in one of the templates. Then certainly the verifier gains no knowledge in the process, yet its confidence in the validity of the claim (that the graph is 3-colorable) increases. A concrete implementation of this abstract idea follows.

To prove that the graph $G = (V, E)$ is 3-colorable, the prover generates a random 3-coloring of the graph, denoted ϕ (actually a random relabeling of a fixed coloring will do). The color of each single vertex constitutes a piece of information concerning the 3-coloring. The set of templates corresponds to the set of edges (i.e., each pair $(\phi(u), \phi(v))$, where $(u, v) \in E$, constitutes a template to the claim that G is 3-colorable). Each single template (being merely a random pair of distinct elements in $\{1, 2, 3\}$) will yield no knowledge. However, if all the templates are OK (i.e., each contains a pair of distinct elements in $\{1, 2, 3\}$), then the graph must be 3-colorable. Consequently, graphs that

---

[13]A simple finite graph is a pair (V, E), where V is a finite set and E is a set of 2-subsets of V; that is, $E \subseteq \{e \subseteq V : |e| = 2\}$. The elements of V are called **vertices**, and the elements of E are called **edges**. Although each edge is an unordered pair of two elements in V, we use the ordered-pair notation $(u, v) \in E$ rather than the notation $\{u, v\} \in E$. For $e = (u, v) \in E$, we say that u and v are the endpoints of e and that u is adjacent to v.

are not 3-colorable must contain at least one bad template and hence will be rejected with noticeable probability. Following is an abstract description of the resulting zero-knowledge interactive proof system for $G3C$.

- *Common input:* A simple graph $G = (V, E)$.

- *Prover's first step:* Let ψ be a 3-coloring of G. The prover selects a random permutation π over $\{1, 2, 3\}$ and sets $\phi(v) \overset{\text{def}}{=} \pi(\psi(v))$ for each $v \in V$. Hence, the prover forms a random relabeling of the 3-coloring ψ. The prover sends the verifier a sequence of $|V|$ locked and non-transparent boxes such that the vth box contains the value $\phi(v)$.

- *Verifier's first step:* The verifier uniformly selects an edge $(u, v) \in E$ and sends it to the prover.

- *Motivating remark:* The verifier asks to inspect the colors of vertices u and v.

- *Prover's second step:* The prover sends to the verifier the keys to boxes u and v.

- *Verifier's second step:* The verifier opens boxes u and v and accepts if and only if they contain two different elements in $\{1, 2, 3\}$.

Clearly, if the input graph is 3-colorable, then the prover can cause the verifier to always accept. On the other hand, if the input graph is not 3-colorable, then any content placed in the boxes must be invalid on at least one edge, and consequently the verifier will reject with probability at least $1/|E|$. Hence, the foregoing protocol exhibits a noticeable gap in the acceptance probabilities between the case of inputs in $G3C$ and the case of inputs not in $G3C$. The zero-knowledge property follows easily in this abstract setting, because one can simulate the real interaction by placing a random pair of different colors in the boxes indicated by the verifier. We stress that this simple argument will not be possible in the digital implementation, because the boxes are not totally unaffected by their contents (but rather are affected, yet in an indistinguishable manner). Finally, we remark that confidence in the validity of the claim (that the input graph is 3-colorable) can be increased by sequentially applying the foregoing proof sufficiently many times. (In fact, if the boxes are perfect, as assumed, then one can also use parallel repetitions; however, the boxes are not perfect in the digital implementation presented next.)

4.4.2.2. The Interactive Proof

We now turn to the digital implementation of the abstract protocol. In this implementation the boxes are implemented by a commitment scheme. Namely, for each box, we invoke an *independent* execution of the commitment scheme. This will enable us to execute the reveal phase for only some of the commitments, a property that is crucial to our scheme. For simplicity of exposition, we use the simple commitment scheme presented in Construction 4.4.2 (or, more generally, any *one-way-interaction* commitment scheme). We denote by $C_s(\sigma)$ the commitment of the sender, using coins s, to the (ternary) value σ.

Construction 4.4.7 (A Zero-Knowledge Proof for Graph 3-Coloring):

- Common input: *A simple (3-colorable) graph* $G = (V, E)$. *Let* $n \overset{\text{def}}{=} |V|$ *and* $V = \{1, \ldots, n\}$.

- Auxiliary input to the prover: *A 3-coloring of G, denoted ψ.*
- Prover's first step (P1): *The prover selects a random permutation π over $\{1, 2, 3\}$ and sets $\phi(v) \stackrel{\text{def}}{=} \pi(\psi(v))$ for each $v \in V$. The prover uses the commitment scheme to commit itself to the color of each of the vertices. Namely, the prover uniformly and independently selects $s_1, \ldots, s_n \in \{0, 1\}^n$, computes $c_i = C_{s_i}(\phi(i))$ for each $i \in V$, and sends $c_1, \ldots, c_n$ to the verifier.*
- Verifier's first step (V1): *The verifier uniformly selects an edge $(u, v) \in E$ and sends it to the prover.*
- Prover's second step (P2): *Without loss of generality, we can assume that the message received from the verifier is an edge, denoted (u, v). (Otherwise, the prover sets (u, v) to be some predetermined edge of G.) The prover uses the (canonical) reveal phase of the commitment scheme in order to reveal the colors of vertices u and v to the verifier. Namely, the prover sends $(s_u, \phi(u))$ and $(s_v, \phi(v))$ to the verifier.*
- Verifier's second step (V2): *The verifier checks whether or not the values corresponding to commitments u and v were revealed correctly and whether or not these values are different. Namely, upon receiving (s, σ) and (s', τ), the verifier checks whether or not $c_u = C_s(\sigma)$, $c_v = C_{s'}(\tau)$, and $\sigma \neq \tau$ (and both σ and τ are in $\{1, 2, 3\}$). If all conditions hold, then the verifier accepts. Otherwise it rejects.*

Let us denote this prover's program by P_{G3C}.

We stress that the program of the verifier and that of the prover can be implemented in probabilistic polynomial time. In the case of the prover's program, this property is made possible by use of the *auxiliary input* to the prover. As we shall later see, the foregoing protocol constitutes a weak interactive proof for $G3C$. As usual, the confidence can be increased (i.e., the error probability can be decreased) by sufficiently many successive applications. However, the mere existence of an interactive proof for $G3C$ is obvious (since $G3C \in \mathcal{NP}$). The punch line is that this protocol is zero-knowledge (also with respect to auxiliary input). Using the sequential-composition-lemma (Lemma 4.3.11), it follows that polynomially many sequential applications of this protocol will preserve the zero-knowledge property.

> **Proposition 4.4.8:** *Suppose that the commitment scheme used in Construction 4.4.7 satisfies the (non-uniform) secrecy and the unambiguity requirements. Then Construction 4.4.7 constitutes an auxiliary-input zero-knowledge (generalized) interactive proof for $G3C$.*

For further discussion of Construction 4.4.7, see Section 4.4.2.4.

4.4.2.3. The Simulator: Proof of Proposition 4.4.8

We first prove that Construction 4.4.7 constitutes a weak interactive proof for $G3C$. Assume first that the input graph is indeed 3-colorable. Then if the prover follows the specified program, the verifier will always accept (i.e., accept with probability 1). On the other hand, if the input graph is not 3-colorable, then no matter what the prover does, the n commitments sent in Step P1 cannot correspond to a 3-coloring of the graph (since such coloring does not exist). We stress that the unique correspondence of commitments to values is guaranteed by the unambiguity property of the commitment scheme. It follows that there must exist an edge $(u, v) \in E$ such that c_u and c_v, sent in Step P1, are not commitments to two *different* elements of $\{1, 2, 3\}$. Hence, no matter how the prover behaves, the verifier will reject with probability at least $1/|E|$. Therefore, there is a noticeable (in the input length) gap between the acceptance probabilities in the case in which the input is in $G3C$ and in the case in which it is not.

We shall now show that P_{G3C}, the prover program specified in Construction 4.4.7, is indeed zero-knowledge for $G3C$. The claim is proved without reference to auxiliary-input (to the verifier), but an extension of the argument to auxiliary-input zero-knowledge is straightforward. Again, we use the alternative formulation of zero-knowledge (i.e., Definition 4.3.3) and show how to simulate V^*'s view of the interaction with P_{G3C} for every probabilistic polynomial-time interactive machine V^*. As in the case of the Graph Isomorphism proof system (i.e., Construction 4.3.8), it is easy to simulate the verifier's view of the interaction with P_{G3C}, *provided that* the verifier follows the specified program. However, we need to simulate the view of the verifier in the general case (in which the verifier uses an *arbitrary* polynomial-time interactive program). Following is an overview of our simulation (i.e., of our construction of a simulator M^* for an arbitrary V^*).

The simulator M^* incorporates the code of the interactive program V^*. On input a graph $G = (V, E)$, the simulator M^* (not having access to a 3-coloring of G) first uniformly and independently selects n values $e_1, \ldots, e_n \in \{1, 2, 3\}$ and constructs a commitment to each of them. (These e_i's constitute a "pseudo-coloring" of the graph in which the endpoints of each edge will be colored differently with probability $\frac{2}{3}$.) In doing so, the simulator behaves very differently from P_{G3C}, but nevertheless the sequence of commitments thus generated is computationally indistinguishable from the sequence of commitments to a valid 3-coloring sent by P_{G3C} in Step P1. If V^*, when given the commitments generated by the simulator, asks to inspect an edge (u, v) such that $e_u \neq e_v$, then the simulator can indeed answer correctly, and in doing so it completes a simulation of the verifier's view of the interaction with P_{G3C}. However, if V^* asks to inspect an edge (u, v) such that $e_u = e_v$, then the simulator has no way to answer correctly, and we let it halt with output $\perp$. We stress that we do not assume that the simulator "knows" a priori which edge the verifier V^* will ask to inspect. The validity of the simulator stems from a different source. If the verifier's request were oblivious of the prover's commitment, then with probability $\frac{2}{3}$ the verifier would have asked to inspect an edge that was properly colored. Using the secrecy property of the commitment scheme, it follows that the verifier's request is "almost oblivious" of the values in the commitments. The zero-knowledge claim follows (yet, with some effort). Further details follow. We start with a detailed description of the simulator.

Simulator M^*. On input a graph $G = (V, E)$, where $n = |V|$, the simulator M^* proceeds as follows:

1. *Setting the random tape of V^*:* Let $q(\cdot)$ denote a polynomial bounding the running time of V^*. The simulator M^* starts by uniformly selecting a string $r \in \{0, 1\}^{q(n)}$ to be used as the content of the local random tape of V^*.

2. *Simulating the prover's first step* (P1): The simulator M^* uniformly and independently selects n values $e_1, \ldots, e_n \in \{1, 2, 3\}$ and n random strings $s_1, \ldots, s_n \in \{0, 1\}^n$ to be used for committing to these values. The simulator computes, for each $i \in V$, a commitment $d_i = C_{s_i}(e_i)$.

3. *Simulating the verifier's first step* (V1): The simulator M^* initiates an execution of V^* by placing G on V^*'s common-input tape, placing r (selected in Step 1) on V^*'s local random tape, and placing the sequence $(d_1, \ldots, d_n)$ (constructed in Step 2) on V^*'s incoming-message tape. After executing a polynomial number of steps of V^*, the simulator can read the outgoing message of V^*, denoted m. Again, we assume without loss of generality that $m \in E$ and let $(u, v) = m$. (Actually, $m \notin E$ is treated as in Step P2 of P_{G3C}; namely, (u, v) is set to be some predetermined edge of G.)

4. *Simulating the prover's second step* (P2): If $e_u \neq e_v$, then the simulator halts with output $(G, r, (d_1, \ldots, d_n), (s_u, e_u, s_v, e_v))$.

5. *Failure of the simulation:* Otherwise (i.e., $e_u = e_v$), the simulator halts with output $\bot$.

Using the hypothesis that V^* is polynomial-time, it follows that so is the simulator M^*. It is left to show that M^* outputs $\bot$ with probability at most $\frac{1}{2}$ and that, conditioned on not outputting $\bot$, the simulator's output is computationally indistinguishable from the verifier's view in a "real interaction with P_{G3C}." The proposition will follow by running the simulator n times and outputting the first output different from $\bot$. We now turn to proving the two claims.

Claim 4.4.8.1: For every sufficiently large graph $G = (V, E)$, the probability that $M^*(G) = \bot$ is bounded above by $\frac{1}{2}$.

(Actually, a stronger claim can be proved: For every polynomial p and all sufficiently large graphs $G = (V, E)$, the probability that $M^*(G) = \bot$ is bounded above by $\frac{1}{3} + \frac{1}{p(|V|)}$.)

Proof: Let us denote by $p_{u,v}(G, r, (e_1, \ldots, e_n))$ the probability, taken over all the choices of $s_1, \ldots, s_n \in \{0, 1\}^n$, that V^*, on input G, random coins r, and prover message $(C_{s_1}(e_1), \ldots, C_{s_n}(e_n))$, replies with the message (u, v). We assume, for simplicity, that V^* always answers with an edge of G (since otherwise its message is treated as if it were an edge of G). We first claim that for every sufficiently large graph $G = (V, E)$, every $r \in \{0, 1\}^{q(n)}$, every edge $(u, v) \in E$, and every two sequences $\alpha, \beta \in \{1, 2, 3\}^n$, it holds that

$$|p_{u,v}(G, r, \alpha) - p_{u,v}(G, r, \beta)| \leq \frac{1}{2|E|} \qquad (4.2)$$

Actually, we can prove the following sub-claim.

Request Obliviousness Sub-Claim: For every polynomial $p(\cdot)$, every sufficiently large graph $G = (V, E)$, every $r \in \{0, 1\}^{q(n)}$, every edge $(u, v) \in E$, and

$$\underline{\qquad} \mathbf{232} \underline{\qquad}$$

every two sequences $\alpha, \beta \in \{1, 2, 3\}^n$, it holds that

$$|p_{u,v}(G, r, \alpha) - p_{u,v}(G, r, \beta)| \leq \frac{1}{p(n)}$$

The Request Obliviousness Sub-Claim is proved using the non-uniform secrecy of the commitment scheme. The reader should be able to fill out the details of such a proof at this stage. (Nevertheless, a proof of the sub-claim follows.)

Proof of the Request Obliviousness Sub-Claim: Assume, on the contrary, that there exists a polynomial $p(\cdot)$ and an infinite sequence of integers such that for each integer n (in the sequence) there exists an n-vertex graph $G_n = (V_n, E_n)$, a string $r_n \in \{0, 1\}^{q(n)}$, an edge $(u_n, v_n) \in E_n$, and two sequences $\alpha_n, \beta_n \in \{1, 2, 3\}^n$ such that

$$\left|p_{u_n,v_n}(G_n, r_n, \alpha_n) - p_{u_n,v_n}(G_n, r_n, \beta_n)\right| > \frac{1}{p(n)}$$

We construct a circuit family $\{A_n\}$ by letting A_n incorporate the interactive machine V^*, the graph G_n, and $r_n, u_n, v_n, \alpha_n, \beta_n$, all being as in the contradiction hypothesis. On input y (supposedly a sequence of commitments to either α_n or β_n), circuit A_n runs V^* (on input G_n, coins r_n, and prover's message y) and outputs 1 if and only if V^* replies with (u_n, v_n). Clearly, $\{A_n\}$ is a (non-uniform) family of polynomial-size circuits. The key observation is that A_n distinguishes commitments to α_n from commitments to β_n, since

$$\Pr\left[A_n\left(C_{U_n^{(1)}}(e_1), \ldots, C_{U_n^{(n)}}(e_n)\right) = 1\right] = p_{u_n,v_n}(G_n, r_n, (e_1, \ldots, e_n))$$

where the $U_n^{(i)}$'s denote, as usual, independent random variables uniformly distributed over $\{0, 1\}^n$. Contradiction to the (non-uniform) secrecy of the commitment scheme follows by a standard hybrid argument (which relates the indistinguishability of sequences of commitments to the indistinguishability of single commitments).

Returning to the proof of Claim 4.4.8.1, we now use this sub-claim to upper-bound the probability that the simulator outputs $\perp$. The intuition is simple: Because the requests of V^* are almost oblivious of the values to which the simulator has committed itself, it is unlikely that V^* will request to inspect an illegally colored edge more often than it would if it had made the request without looking at the commitment. Thus, V^* asks to inspect an illegally colored edge with probability approximately $\frac{1}{3}$, and so $\Pr[M^*(G) = \perp] \approx \frac{1}{3}$. A more rigorous (but straightforward) analysis follows.

Let $M_r^*(G)$ denote the output of machine M^* on input G, conditioned on the event that it chooses the string r in Step 1. We remind the reader that $M_r^*(G) = \perp$ only in the case in which the verifier, on input G, random tape r, and a commitment to some pseudo-coloring $(e_1, \ldots, e_n)$, asks to inspect an edge (u, v) that is illegally colored (i.e., $e_u = e_v$). Let $E_{(e_1,\ldots,e_n)}$ denote the set of edges $(u, v) \in E$ that are illegally colored (i.e., satisfy $e_u = e_v$) with respect to $(e_1, \ldots, e_n)$. Then, fixing an arbitrary r and considering all possible choices of $\bar{e} = (e_1, \ldots, e_n) \in \{1, 2, 3\}^n$, we have

$$\Pr[M_r^*(G) = \perp] = \sum_{\bar{e} \in \{1,2,3\}^n} \frac{1}{3^n} \cdot \sum_{(u,v) \in E_{\bar{e}}} p_{u,v}(G, r, \bar{e})$$

— 233 —

(Recall that $p_{u,v}(G, r, \bar{e})$ denotes the probability that the verifier will ask to inspect (u, v) when given a sequence of random commitments to the values $\bar{e}$.) Define $B_{u,v}$ to be the set of n-tuples $(e_1, \ldots, e_n) \in \{1, 2, 3\}^n$ satisfying $e_u = e_v$. Clearly, $|B_{u,v}| = 3^{n-1}$, and

$$\{(\bar{e}, (u, v)) : \bar{e} \in \{1, 2, 3\}^n \ \& \ (u, v) \in E_{\bar{e}}\} = \{(\bar{e}, (u, v)) : \bar{e} \in \{1, 2, 3\}^n \ \& \ e_u = e_v\}$$
$$= \{(\bar{e}, (u, v)) : (u, v) \in E \ \& \ \bar{e} \in B_{u,v}\}$$

By straightforward calculation we get

$$\Pr[M_r^*(G) = \perp] = \frac{1}{3^n} \cdot \sum_{\bar{e} \in \{1,2,3\}^n} \sum_{(u,v) \in E_{\bar{e}}} p_{u,v}(G, r, \bar{e})$$

$$= \frac{1}{3^n} \cdot \sum_{(u,v) \in E} \sum_{\bar{e} \in B_{u,v}} p_{u,v}(G, r, \bar{e})$$

$$\leq \frac{1}{3^n} \cdot \sum_{(u,v) \in E} |B_{u,v}| \cdot \left(p_{u,v}(G, r, (1, \ldots, 1)) + \frac{1}{2|E|} \right)$$

$$= \frac{1}{6} + \frac{1}{3} \cdot \sum_{(u,v) \in E} p_{u,v}(G, r, (1, \ldots, 1))$$

$$= \frac{1}{6} + \frac{1}{3}$$

where the inequality is due to Eq. (4.2). The claim follows. $\square$

For simplicity, we assume in the sequel that on common input $G \in G3C$ the prover gets the *lexicographically first* 3-coloring of G as auxiliary input. This enables us to omit the auxiliary input to P_{G3C} (which is now implicit in the common input) from the notation. The argument is easily extended to the general case where P_{G3C} gets an arbitrary 3-coloring of G as auxiliary input.

Claim 4.4.8.2: The ensemble consisting of the output of M^* on input $G = (V, E) \in G3C$, conditioned on it not being $\perp$, is computationally indistinguishable from the ensemble $\{\text{view}_{V^*}^{P_{G3C}}(G)\}_{G \in G3C}$. Namely, for every probabilistic polynomial-time algorithm A, every polynomial $p(\cdot)$, and all sufficiently large graphs $G = (V, E)$,

$$\left| \Pr[A(M^*(G)) = 1 \mid M^*(G) \neq \perp] - \Pr\left[A\left(\text{view}_{V^*}^{P_{G3C}}(G)\right) = 1\right] \right| < \frac{1}{p(|V|)}$$

We stress that these ensembles are very different (i.e., the statistical distance between them is very close to the maximum possible), and yet they are computationally indistinguishable. Actually, we can prove that these ensembles are indistinguishable also by (non-uniform) families of polynomial-size circuits. At first glance it seems that Claim 4.4.8.2 follows easily from the secrecy property of the commitment scheme. Indeed, Claim 4.4.8.2 is proved using the secrecy property of the commitment scheme, but the proof is more complex than one might anticipate at first glance. The difficulty lies in the fact that the foregoing ensembles consist not only of commitments to values but also of openings of *some*

---

234 ———

of the values. Furthermore, the choice of which commitments are to be opened depends on the entire sequence of commitments. (We take advantage of the fact that the number of such openings is a constant.)

Proof: Let $m^*(G)$ denote the distribution of $M^*(G)$ conditioned on $M^*(G) \neq \perp$. For any algorithm A, we denote the distinguishing gap of A, regarding the ensembles in the claim, by $\varepsilon_A(G)$; that is,

$$\varepsilon_A(G) \stackrel{\text{def}}{=} \left| \Pr[A(m^*(G)) = 1] - \Pr\left[A\left(\text{view}_{V^*}^{P_{G3C}}(G)\right) = 1\right] \right| \qquad (4.3)$$

Our goal is to prove that for every probabilistic polynomial-time algorithm A, the value of $\varepsilon_A(G)$ is negligible as a function of the number of vertices in G. Recall that for $G = (V, E)$ both $m^*(G)$ and $\text{view}_{V^*}^{P_{G3C}}(G)$ are sequences of the form $(r, (\alpha_1, \ldots, \alpha_{|V|}), (u, v), (s_u, \sigma_u, s_v, \sigma_v))$, where $r \in \{0, 1\}^{q(|V|)}$, $(u, v) \in E$, $\sigma_u \neq \sigma_v \in \{1, 2, 3\}$, $\alpha_u = C_{s_u}(\sigma_u)$, and $\alpha_v = C_{s_v}(\sigma_v)$. In both cases, the pair (u, v) is called the *verifier's request*.

Given a graph $G = (V, E)$, we define for each edge $(u, v) \in E$ two random variables describing, respectively, the output of M^* and the view of V^* in a real interaction in the case in which the verifier's request equals (u, v). Specifically:

- $\mu_{u,v}(G)$ describes $M^*(G)$ (equivalently, $m^*(G)$) conditioned on $M^*(G)$ (equivalently, $m^*(G)$) having the verifier's request equal to (u, v).
- $\nu_{u,v}(G)$ describes $\text{view}_{V^*}^{P_{G3C}}(G)$ conditioned on $\text{view}_{V^*}^{P_{G3C}}(G)$ having the verifier's request equal to (u, v).

Let $p_{u,v}(G)$ denote the probability that $m^*(G)$ has the verifier's request equal to (u, v). Similarly, let $q_{u,v}(G)$ denote the probability that $\text{view}_{V^*}^{P_{G3C}}(G)$ has the verifier's request equal to (u, v).

Assume, contrary to the claim, that the ensembles mentioned in the claim are computationally distinguishable. Then one of the following cases must occur.

Case 1: There is a non-negligible difference between the probabilistic profile of the request of V^* when interacting with P_{G3C} and that of the verifier's request in the output represented by $m^*(G)$. Formally, there exists a polynomial $p(\cdot)$ and an infinite sequence of integers such that for each integer n (in the sequence) there exists an n-vertex graph $G_n = (V_n, E_n)$ and an edge $(u_n, v_n) \in E_n$ such that

$$\left| p_{u_n, v_n}(G_n) - q_{u_n, v_n}(G_n) \right| > \frac{1}{p(n)}$$

Otherwise, for every polynomial p', all but finitely many G's, and all edges (u, v) in such $G = (V, E)$, it holds that

$$|p_{u,v}(G) - q_{u,v}(G)| \leq \frac{1}{p'(|V|)} \qquad (4.4)$$

Case 2: An algorithm distinguishing the foregoing ensembles also does so conditioned on V^* making a particular request. Furthermore, this request occurs with non-negligible probability that is about the same for both ensembles. Formally, there exists a probabilistic polynomial-time algorithm A, a polynomial $p(\cdot)$, and an infinite sequence of integers such that for each integer n (in the sequence) there exists an n-vertex graph $G_n = (V_n, E_n)$ and an edge $(u_n, v_n) \in E_n$ such that the following conditions hold:

- $q_{u_n, v_n}(G_n) > \frac{1}{p(n)}$
- $|p_{u_n, v_n}(G_n) - q_{u_n, v_n}(G_n)| < \frac{1}{3 \cdot p(n)^2}$
- $|\Pr[A(\mu_{u_n, v_n}(G_n)) = 1] - \Pr[A(\nu_{u_n, v_n}(G_n)) = 1]| > \frac{1}{p(n)}$

The fact that if Case 1 does not hold, then Case 2 does hold follows by breaking the probability space according to the edge being revealed. The obvious details follow:

Consider an algorithm A that distinguishes the simulator's output from the real interaction for infinitely many graphs $G = (V, E)$, where the distinguishing gap is a reciprocal of a polynomial in the size of G; i.e., $\varepsilon_A(G) > 1/\text{poly}(|V|)$. Let $\text{req}_{u,v}(\alpha)$ denote the event that *in transcript α, the verifier's request equals (u, v)*. Then there must be an edge (u, v) in G such that

$$\left| \Pr[A(m^*(G)) = 1 \ \& \ \text{req}_{u,v}(m^*(G))] \right.$$
$$\left. - \Pr\left[A\left(\text{view}_{V^*}^{P_{G3C}}(G)\right) = 1 \ \& \ \text{req}_{u,v}\left(\text{view}_{V^*}^{P_{G3C}}(G)\right)\right] \right| \geq \frac{\varepsilon_A(G)}{|E|}$$

Note that

$$p_{u,v}(G) = \Pr[\text{req}_{u,v}(m^*(G))]$$
$$q_{u,v}(G) = \Pr\left[\text{req}_{u,v}\left(\text{view}_{V^*}^{P_{G3C}}(G)\right)\right]$$
$$\Pr[A(\mu_{u,v}(G)) = 1] = \Pr[A(m^*(G)) = 1 \mid \text{req}_{u,v}(m^*(G))]$$
$$\Pr[A(\nu_{u,v}(G)) = 1] = \Pr\left[A\left(\text{view}_{V^*}^{P_{G3C}}(G)\right) = 1 \mid \text{req}_{u,v}\left(\text{view}_{V^*}^{P_{G3C}}(G)\right)\right]$$

Thus, omitting G from some of the notations, we have

$$|p_{u,v} \cdot \Pr[A(\mu_{u,v}(G)) = 1] - q_{u,v} \cdot \Pr[A(\nu_{u,v}(G)) = 1]| \geq \frac{\varepsilon_A(G)}{|E|}$$

Setting $p(|V|) \stackrel{\text{def}}{=} \frac{2|E|}{\varepsilon_A(G)}$ (i.e., so that $\frac{\varepsilon_A(G)}{|E|} = \frac{2}{p(|V|)}$) and using Eq. (4.4) (with $p' = 3p^2$), we get $|p_{u,v} - q_{u,v}| < \frac{1}{3p(|V|)^2}$ and

$$|q_{u,v} \cdot \Pr[A(\mu_{u,v}(G)) = 1] - q_{u,v} \cdot \Pr[A(\nu_{u,v}(G)) = 1]| > \frac{1}{p(|V|)}$$

for all but finitely many of these G's. Thus, both $q_{u,v} > 1/p(|V|)$ and

$$|\Pr[A(\mu_{u,v}(G)) = 1] - \Pr[A(\nu_{u,v}(G)) = 1]| > 1/p(|V|)$$

follow.

Case 1 can immediately be discarded because it leads easily to contradiction (to the non-uniform secrecy of the commitment scheme): The idea is to use the Request Obliviousness Sub-Claim appearing in the proof of Claim 4.4.8.1. Details are omitted. We are thus left with Case 2.

We are now going to show that Case 2 also leads to contradiction. To this end we shall construct a circuit family that will distinguish commitments to different sequences of values. Interestingly, neither of these sequences will equal the sequence of commitments generated either by the prover or by the simulator. Following is an overview of the construction. The nth circuit gets a sequence of $3n$ commitments and produces from it a sequence of n commitments (part of which is a subsequence of the input). When the input sequence to the circuit is taken from one distribution, the circuit generates a subsequence corresponding to the sequence of commitments generated by the prover. Likewise, when the input sequence (to the circuit) is taken from the other distribution, the circuit will generate a subsequence corresponding to the sequence of commitments generated by the simulator. We stress that the circuit does so without knowing from which distribution the input is taken. After generating an n-long sequence, the circuit feeds it to V^*, and depending on V^*'s behavior the circuit may feed part of the sequence to algorithm A (mentioned in Case 2). Following is a detailed description of the circuit family.

Let us denote by ψ_n the (lexicographically first) 3-coloring of $G_n = (V_n, E_n)$ used by the prover, where $V_n = \{1, \ldots, n\}$. We construct a circuit family, denoted $\{A_n\}$, by letting A_n incorporate the interactive machine V^*, the "distinguishing" algorithm A, the graph G_n, the 3-coloring ψ_n, and the edge (u_n, v_n), all being as guaranteed in Case 2. The input to circuit A_n will be a sequence of commitments to $3n$ values, each in $\{1, 2, 3\}$. The circuit will distinguish commitments to a uniformly chosen $3n$-long sequence from commitments to the fixed sequence $1^n 2^n 3^n$ (i.e., the sequence consisting of n 1-values, followed by n 2-values, followed by n 3-values). Following is a description of the operation of A_n. In this description, for $e \in \{1, 2, 3\}$, we denote by $C(e)$ the random variable obtained by uniformly selecting $s \in \{0, 1\}^n$ and outputting $C_s(e)$. We extend this notation to sequences over $\{1, 2, 3\}$ (i.e., $C(e_1, \ldots, e_t) = C(e_1), \ldots, C(e_t)$, where independent randomization is used in each commitment).

Operation of A_n: On input $y = (y_1, \ldots, y_{3n})$ (where each y_i supposedly is a commitment to an element of $\{1, 2, 3\}$), the circuit A_n proceeds as follows:

- A_n first selects uniformly a permutation π over $\{1, 2, 3\}$ and computes $\phi(i) = \pi(\psi_n(i))$ for each $i \in V_n$.

   Note that $(\phi(u_n), \phi(v_n))$ is uniformly distributed among the six possible pairs of distinct elements of $\{1, 2, 3\}$.
- For each $i \in V_n \setminus \{u_n, v_n\}$, the circuit sets $c_i = y_{\phi(i) \cdot n - n + i}$ (i.e., $c_i = y_i$ if $\phi(i) = 1$, $c_i = y_{n+i}$ if $\phi(i) = 2$, and $c_i = y_{2n+i}$ if $\phi(i) = 3$).

   Note that each y_j is used at most once and that $2n + 2$ of the y_j's are not used at all.
- The circuit uniformly selects $s_{u_n}, s_{v_n} \in \{0, 1\}^n$ and sets $c_{u_n} = C_{s_{u_n}}(\phi(u_n))$ and $c_{v_n} = C_{s_{v_n}}(\phi(v_n))$.

   In case y is taken from the distribution $C(1^n 2^n 3^n)$, the sequence $c_1, \ldots, c_n$ just formed is distributed exactly as the sequence of commitments sent by the prover in Step P1. On the other hand, suppose that y is uniformly distributed among all possible commitments to all possible $3n$-long sequences (i.e., y is formed by uniformly selecting $\alpha \in \{1, 2, 3\}^{3n}$ and outputting $C(\alpha)$). Then the sequence $c_1, \ldots, c_n$ just formed is distributed exactly as the sequence of commitments formed by the simulator in Step 2, conditioned on vertices u_n and v_n being assigned different colors.

- The circuit initiates an execution of V^* by placing G_n on V^*'s common-input tape, placing a uniformly selected $r \in \{0, 1\}^{q(n)}$ on V^*'s local random tape, and placing the sequence $(c_1, \ldots, c_n)$ on V^*'s incoming-message tape. The circuit reads the outgoing message of V^*, denoted m.
- If $m \neq (u_n, v_n)$, then the circuit outputs 0.
- Otherwise (i.e., $m = (u_n, v_n)$), the circuit invokes algorithm A and outputs

$$A\left(G_n, r, (c_1, \ldots, c_n), \left(s_{u_n}, \phi(u_n), s_{v_n}, \phi(v_n)\right)\right)$$

Clearly, the size of A_n is polynomial in n. We now evaluate the distinguishing ability of A_n. Let us first consider the probability that circuit A_n will output 1 on input a random commitment to the sequence $1^n 2^n 3^n$. The reader can easily verify that the sequence $(c_1, \ldots, c_n)$ constructed by circuit A_n is distributed identically to the sequence sent by the prover in Step P1. Hence, recalling some of the notations introduced earlier, we get

$$\Pr[A_n(C(1^n 2^n 3^n)) = 1] = q_{u_n, v_n}(G_n) \cdot \Pr\left[A\left(v_{u_n, v_n}(G_n)\right) = 1\right]$$

On the other hand, we consider the probability that circuit A_n will output 1 on input a random commitment to a uniformly chosen $3n$-long sequence over $\{1, 2, 3\}$. The reader can easily verify that the sequence $(c_1, \ldots, c_n)$ constructed by circuit A_n is distributed identically to the sequence $(d_1, \ldots, d_n)$ generated by the simulator in Step 2, conditioned on $e_{u_n} \neq e_{v_n}$. (Recall that $d_i = C(e_i)$.) Letting T_{3n} denote a random variable uniformly distributed over $\{1, 2, 3\}^{3n}$, we get

$$\Pr[A_n(C(T_{3n})) = 1] = p'_{u_n, v_n}(G_n) \cdot \Pr\left[A\left(\mu_{u_n, v_n}(G_n)\right) = 1\right]$$

where $p'_{u_n, v_n}(G_n)$ denotes the probability that in Step 3 of the simulation the verifier will answer with (u_n, v_n), conditioned on $e_{u_n} \neq e_{v_n}$. Using the fact that the proof of Claim 4.4.8.1 actually establishes that $|\Pr[M^*(G_n) \neq \perp] - \frac{2}{3}|$ is negligible in n, it follows that $|p'_{u_n, v_n}(G_n) - p_{u_n, v_n}(G_n)| < \frac{1}{3 \cdot p(n)^2}$ for all but at most finitely many G_n's.

Justification for the last assertion: Note that $p'_{u_n, v_n}(G_n)$ and $p_{u_n, v_n}(G_n)$ refer to the same event (i.e., V^*'s request equals (u_n, v_n)), but under a different conditional space (i.e., either $e_{u_n} \neq e_{v_n}$ or $M^*(G_n) \neq \perp$). In fact, it is instructive to consider in both cases the event that V^*'s request equals (u_n, v_n) and $e_{u_n} \neq e_{v_n}$. Denoting the latter event by X, we have[14]

---

[14] For further justification of the following equations, let X' denote the event that V^*'s request equals (u_n, v_n), and observe that X is the conjunction of X' and $e_{u_n} \neq e_{v_n}$. Then:

- By definition, $p'_{u_n, v_n}(G_n) = \Pr[X' | e_{u_n} \neq e_{v_n}]$, which equals $\Pr[X' \& e_{u_n} \neq e_{v_n}]/\Pr[e_{u_n} \neq e_{v_n}] = \Pr[X]/\Pr[e_{u_n} \neq e_{v_n}]$.
- By definition, $p_{u_n, v_n}(G_n) = \Pr[X' | M^*(G_n) \neq \perp]$. Note that the conjunction of $M^*(G_n) \neq \perp$ and X' implies $e_{u_n} \neq e_{v_n}$, and so the former conjunction implies X. On the other hand, X implies $M^*(G_n) \neq \perp$. It follows that $\Pr[M^*(G_n) \neq \perp] \cdot \Pr[X' | M^*(G_n) \neq \perp] = \Pr[X' \& M^*(G_n) \neq \perp] = \Pr[X \& M^*(G_n) \neq \perp] = \Pr[X]$. We conclude that $p_{u_n, v_n}(G_n) = \Pr[X]/\Pr[M^*(G_n) \neq \perp]$.

- $p'_{u_n,v_n}(G_n) = \Pr[X|e_{u_n} \neq e_{v_n}] = \Pr[X]/\Pr[e_{u_n} \neq e_{v_n}]$
- $p_{u_n,v_n}(G_n) = \Pr[X|M^*(G_n) \neq \bot] = \Pr[X]/\Pr[M^*(G_n) \neq \bot]$

Using $\Pr[e_{u_n} \neq e_{v_n}] = \frac{2}{3} \approx \Pr[M^*(G_n) \neq \bot]$, where $\approx$ denotes equality up to a negligible (in n) quantity, it follows that $|p'_{u_n,v_n}(G_n) - p_{u_n,v_n}(G_n)|$ is negligible (in n).

Using the conditions of case 2, and omitting G_n from the notation, it follows that

$$\left| p'_{u_n,v_n} - q_{u_n,v_n} \right| \leq \left| p'_{u_n,v_n} - p_{u_n,v_n} \right| + \left| p_{u_n,v_n} - q_{u_n,v_n} \right| < \frac{2}{3 \cdot p(n)^2}$$

Combining the foregoing, we get

$$
\begin{aligned}
&\left| \Pr[A_n(C(1^n 2^n 3^n)) = 1] - \Pr[A_n(C(T_{3n})) = 1] \right| \\
&= \left| q_{u_n,v_n} \cdot \Pr[A(\nu_{u_n,v_n}) = 1] - p'_{u_n,v_n} \cdot \Pr[A(\mu_{u_n,v_n}) = 1] \right| \\
&\geq q_{u_n,v_n} \cdot \left| \Pr[A(\nu_{u_n,v_n}) = 1] - \Pr[A(\mu_{u_n,v_n}) = 1] \right| - \left| p'_{u_n,v_n} - q_{u_n,v_n} \right| \\
&> \frac{1}{p(n)} \cdot \frac{1}{p(n)} - \frac{2}{3 \cdot p(n)^2} = \frac{1}{3 \cdot p(n)^2}
\end{aligned}
$$

Hence, the circuit family $\{A_n\}$ distinguishes commitments to $\{1^n 2^n 3^n\}$ from commitments to $\{T_{3n}\}$. Combining an averaging argument with a hybrid argument, we conclude that there exists a polynomial-size circuit family that distinguishes commitments. This contradicts the non-uniform secrecy of the commitment scheme.

Having reached contradiction in both cases, Claim 4.4.8.2 follows. $\square$

Combining Claims 4.4.8.1 and 4.4.8.2 (and using Exercise 9), the zero-knowledge property of P_{G3C} follows. This completes the proof of the proposition. $\blacksquare$

4.4.2.4. Concluding Remarks

Construction 4.4.7 has been presented using a unidirectional commitment scheme. A fundamental property of such schemes is that their secrecy is preserved in case (polynomially) many instances are invoked simultaneously. The proof of Proposition 4.4.8 indeed took advantage on this property. We remark that Construction 4.4.4 also possesses this simultaneous secrecy property (although it is not unidirectional), and hence the proof of Proposition 4.4.8 can be carried out if the commitment scheme used is the one of Construction 4.4.4 (see Exercise 15). We recall that this latter construction constitutes a commitment scheme if and only if such schemes exist at all (since Construction 4.4.4 is based on any one-way function, and the existence of one-way functions is implied by the existence of commitment schemes).

Proposition 4.4.8 assumes the existence of a *non-uniformly* secure commitment scheme. The proof of the proposition makes essential use of the non-uniform security by incorporating instances in which the zero-knowledge property fails into circuits that contradict the security hypothesis. We stress that the sequence of "bad" instances is not necessarily constructible by efficient (uniform) machines. In other words, the zero-knowledge requirement has some non-uniform flavor. A *uniform analogue of zero-knowledge* would require only that it be infeasible to find instances in which a verifier gains knowledge (and not that such instances do not exist at all). Using a *uniformly* secure commitment scheme, Construction 4.4.7 can be shown to be *uniformly* zero-knowledge.

By itself, Construction 4.4.7 has little practical value, since it offers a very moderate acceptance gap (between inputs from inside and outside of the language). Yet, repeating the protocol, on common input $G = (V, E)$, for $k \cdot |E|$ times (and letting the verifier accept only if all iterations are acceptance) will yield an interactive proof for $G3C$ with error probability bounded by e^{-k}, where $e \approx 2.718$ is the natural-logarithm base. Namely, on common input $G \in G3C$, the verifier always accepts, whereas on common input $G \notin G3C$, the verifier accepts with probability bounded above by e^{-k} (no matter what the prover does). We stress that by virtue of the sequential-composition lemma (Lemma 4.3.11), if these iterations are performed sequentially, then the resulting (strong) interactive proof is zero-knowledge as well. Setting k to be any super-logarithmic function of $|G|$ (e.g., $k = |G|$), the error probability of the resulting interactive proof is negligible. We remark that it is unlikely that the interactive proof that results by performing these $k \cdot |E|$ iterations in parallel is zero-knowledge; see Section 4.5.4.

An important property of Construction 4.4.7 is that the prescribed prover (i.e., P_{G3C}) can be implemented in probabilistic polynomial time, provided that it is given as auxiliary input a 3-coloring of the common-input graph. As we shall see, this property is essential for application of Construction 4.4.7 to the design of cryptographic protocols.

As mentioned earlier, the choice of $G3C$ as a "bootstrapping" $\mathcal{NP}$-complete language is totally arbitrary. It is quite easy to design analogous zero-knowledge proofs for other popular $\mathcal{NP}$-complete languages using the underlying ideas presented in Section 4.4.2.1 (i.e., the *motivating discussion*).

4.4.3. The General Result and Some Applications

The theoretical and practical importance of a zero-knowledge proof for Graph 3-Coloring (e.g., Construction 4.4.7) follows from the fact that it can be applied to prove, in zero-knowledge, any statement having a short proof that can be efficiently verified. More precisely, a zero-knowledge proof system for a specific $\mathcal{NP}$-complete language (e.g., Construction 4.4.7) can be used to present zero-knowledge proof systems for every language in $\mathcal{NP}$.

Before presenting zero-knowledge proof systems for every language in $\mathcal{NP}$, let us recall some conventions and facts concerning $\mathcal{NP}$. We first recall that every language $L \in \mathcal{NP}$ is *characterized* by a binary relation R satisfying the following properties:

- There exists a polynomial $p(\cdot)$ such that for every $(x, y) \in R$, it holds that $|y| \le p(|x|)$.
- There exists a polynomial-time algorithm for deciding membership in R.
- $L = \{x : \exists w \text{ s.t. } (x, w) \in R\}$.

  (Such a w is called a witness for the membership of $x \in L$.)

Actually, each language in $\mathcal{NP}$ can be characterized by infinitely many such relations. Yet for each $L \in \mathcal{NP}$, we fix and consider one characterizing relation, denoted R_L. Because $G3C$ is $\mathcal{NP}$-complete, we know that L is polynomial-time-reducible (i.e.,

Karp-reducible) to $G3C$. Namely, there exists a polynomial-time-computable function f such that $x \in L$ if and only if $f(x) \in G3C$. Last, we observe that the standard reduction of L to $G3C$, denoted f_L, has the following additional property:

- There exists a polynomial-time-computable function, denoted g_L, such that for every $(x, w) \in R_L$, it holds that $g_L(x, w)$ is a 3-coloring of $f_L(x)$.

We stress that this additional property is not required by the standard definition of a Karp reduction. Yet it can be easily verified (see Exercise 16) that the standard reduction f_L (i.e., the composition of the generic reduction of L to SAT, the standard reductions of SAT to $3SAT$, and the standard reduction of $3SAT$ to $G3C$) does have such a corresponding g_L. Using these conventions, we are ready to "reduce" the construction of zero-knowledge proofs for $\mathcal{NP}$ to a zero-knowledge proof system for $G3C$.

Construction 4.4.9 (A Zero-Knowledge Proof for a Language $L \in \mathcal{NP}$):

- Common input: *A string x (supposedly in L).*
- Auxiliary input to the prover: *A witness, w, for the membership of $x \in L$ (i.e., a string w such that $(x, w) \in R_L$).*
- Local pre-computation: *Each party computes $G \overset{\text{def}}{=} f_L(x)$. The prover computes $\psi \overset{\text{def}}{=} g_L(x, w)$.*
- Invoking a zero-knowledge proof for $G3C$: *The parties invoke a zero-knowledge proof on common input G. The prover enters this proof with auxiliary input ψ.*

Clearly, if the prescribed prover in the $G3C$ proof system can be implemented in probabilistic polynomial time when given an $\mathcal{NP}$-witness (i.e., a 3-coloring) as auxiliary input, then the same holds for the prover in Construction 4.4.9.

Proposition 4.4.10: *Suppose that the sub-protocol used in the last step of Construction 4.4.9 is indeed an auxiliary-input zero-knowledge proof for $G3C$. Then Construction 4.4.9 constitutes an auxiliary-input zero-knowledge proof for L.*

Proof: The fact that Construction 4.4.9 constitutes an interactive proof for L is immediate from the validity of the reduction (and the fact that it uses an interactive proof for $G3C$). At first glance it seems that the zero-knowledge property of Construction 4.4.9 follows just as easily. There is, however, a minor issue that one should not ignore: The verifier in the zero-knowledge proof for $G3C$ invoked in Construction 4.4.9 possesses not only the common-input graph G but also the original common input x that reduces to G. This extra information might have helped this verifier to extract knowledge in the $G3C$ interactive proof if it were not the case that this proof system is also zero-knowledge with respect to the auxiliary input. Details follow.

Suppose we need to simulate the interaction of a machine V^* with the prover of Construction 4.4.9, on common input x. Without loss of generality, we can assume that machine V^* invokes an interactive machine V^{**} that interacts with the prover of the $G3C$ interactive proof, on common input $G = f_L(x)$, and has auxiliary input x. Using the hypothesis that the $G3C$ interactive proof is auxiliary-input zero-knowledge, it follows that there exists a simulator M^{**} that on input (G, x) simulates the interaction of V^{**} with the $G3C$ prover (on common input G and the verifier's auxiliary input x). Hence the simulator for Construction 4.4.9, denoted M^*, operates as follows: On input x, the simulator M^* computes $G \overset{\text{def}}{=} f_L(x)$ and outputs $M^{**}(G, x)$. The proposition follows. ∎

An alternative way of resolving the minor difficulty addressed earlier is to observe that the function f_L (i.e., the one induced by the standard reductions) can be inverted in polynomial time (see Exercise 17). In any case, we immediately get the following:

Theorem 4.4.11: *Suppose that there exists a commitment scheme satisfying the (non-uniform) secrecy and unambiguity requirements. Then every language in $\mathcal{NP}$ has an auxiliary-input zero-knowledge proof system. Furthermore, the pre-scribed prover in this system can be implemented in probabilistic polynomial time provided it gets the corresponding $\mathcal{NP}$-witness as auxiliary input.*

We remind the reader that the condition of the theorem is satisfied if (and only if) there exist (non-uniformly) one-way functions: See Theorem 3.5.12 (asserting that one-way functions imply pseudorandom generators), Proposition 4.4.5 (asserting that pseudorandom generators imply commitment schemes), and Exercise 13 (asserting that commitment schemes imply one-way functions).

Applications: An Example

A typical application of Theorem 4.4.11 is to enable one party to prove some property of its secret without revealing the secret. For concreteness, consider a party, denoted S, that makes a commitment to another party, denoted R. Suppose that at a later stage, party S is willing to reveal partial information about the committed value but is not willing to reveal all of it. For example, party S may want to reveal a single bit indicating whether or not the committed value is larger than some value specified by R. If party S sends only this bit, party R cannot know if the bit sent is indeed the correct one. Using a zero-knowledge proof allows S to convince R of the correctness of the revealed bit without yielding any additional knowledge. The existence of such a zero-knowledge proof follows from Theorem 4.4.11 and the fact that the statement to be proved is of $\mathcal{NP}$ type (and that S knows the corresponding $\mathcal{NP}$-witness).

> A reader who is not fully convinced of the validity of the foregoing claims (i.e., regarding the applicability of Theorem 4.4.11) may want to formalize the story as follows: Let v denote the value to which S commits, let s denote the randomness it uses in the commitment phase, and let $c \overset{\text{def}}{=} C_s(v)$ be the resulting commitment (relative to the commitment scheme C). Suppose that S wants to prove to R that c is a commitment to a value greater than u. So what S wants to prove (in zero-knowledge) is that *there exist v and s such that $c = C_s(v)$ and $v > u$*, where c and u are known to R. Indeed, this is an $\mathcal{NP}$-type statement, and S knows the corresponding $\mathcal{NP}$-witness (i.e., (v, s)), since it has picked v and s by itself.

Formally, we define a language

$$L \stackrel{\text{def}}{=} \{(c, u) : \exists v, s \text{ s.t. } c = C_s(v) \text{ and } v > u\}$$

Clearly, the language L is in $\mathcal{NP}$, and the $\mathcal{NP}$-witness for $(c, u) \in L$ is a pair (v, s), as shown. Hence, Theorem 4.4.11 can be applied.

Additional examples are presented in Exercise 18. Other applications will appear in Volume 2.

We stress that because it is a general (and in some sense generic) result, the construction underlying Theorem 4.4.11 cannot be expected to provide a practical solution (especially in simple cases). Theorem 4.4.11 should be viewed as a plausibility argument: It asserts that there is a wide class of cryptographic problems (that amount to proving the consistency of a secret-dependent action with respect to some public information) that are solvable in principle. Thus, when faced with such a problem *in practice*, one can infer that a solution does exist. This is merely a first step, to be followed by the search for a practical solution.

Zero-Knowledge for Any Language in $\mathcal{IP}$

Interestingly, the result of Theorem 4.4.11 can be extended "to the maximum," in the sense that under the same conditions every language having an interactive proof system also has a zero-knowledge interactive proof system. Namely:

Theorem 4.4.12: *Suppose that there exists a commitment scheme satisfying the (non-uniform) secrecy and unambiguity requirements. Then every language in $\mathcal{IP}$ has a zero-knowledge proof system.*

We believe that this extension (of Theorem 4.4.11 to Theorem 4.4.12) does not have much practical significance. Theorem 4.4.12 is proved by first converting the interactive proof for L into a public-coin interactive proof with perfect completeness (see Section 4.2.3). In the latter proof system, the verifier is supposed to send random strings (regardless of the prover's previous messages) and decide whether or not to accept by applying some polynomial-time predicate to the full transcript of the communication. Thus, we can modify this proof system by letting the new prover send commitments to the messages sent by the original (public-coin-system) prover, rather than sending these messages in the clear. Once this "encrypted" interaction is completed, the prover proves in zero-knowledge that the original verifier would have accepted the hidden transcript (this is an $\mathcal{NP}$ statement). Thus, Theorem 4.4.12 is proved by applying Theorem 4.4.11.

4.4.4. Second-Level Considerations

When presenting zero-knowledge proof systems for every language in $\mathcal{NP}$, we made no attempt to present the most efficient construction possible. Our main concern was to present a proof that is as simple to explain as possible. However, once we know that zero-knowledge proofs for $\mathcal{NP}$ exist, it is natural to ask how efficient they can be. More importantly, we introduce and discuss a more refined measure of the "actual security" of a zero-knowledge proof, called knowledge tightness.

In order to establish common ground for comparing zero-knowledge proofs, we have to specify a desired measure of error probability for these proofs. An instructive choice, used in the sequel, is to consider the complexity of zero-knowledge proofs with error probability 2^{-k}, where k is a parameter that may depend on the length of the common input. Another issue to bear in mind when comparing zero-knowledge proofs concerns the assumptions under which they are valid. Throughout this entire subsection we stick to the assumption used thus far (i.e., the existence of one-way functions).

4.4.4.1. Standard Efficiency Measures

Natural and standard efficiency measures to be considered are as follows:

- The *communication complexity of the proof*. The most important communication measure is the *round complexity* (i.e., the number of message exchanges). The total number of bits exchanged in the interaction is also an important consideration.

- The *computational complexity of the proof* (specifically, the number of elementary steps taken by each of the parties).

Communication complexity seems more important than computational complexity as long as the trade-off between them is "reasonable."

To demonstrate these measures, we consider the zero-knowledge proof for $G3C$ presented in Construction 4.4.7. Recall that this proof system has a very moderate acceptance gap, specifically $1/|E|$, on common input graph $G = (V, E)$. Thus, Construction 4.4.7 has to be applied sequentially $k \cdot |E|$ times in order to result in a zero-knowledge proof with error probability e^{-k}, where $e \approx 2.718$ is the natural-logarithm base. Hence, the round complexity of the resulting zero-knowledge proof is $O(k \cdot |E|)$, the bit complexity is $O(k \cdot |E| \cdot |V|^2)$, and the computational complexity is $O(k \cdot |E| \cdot \text{poly}(|V|))$, where the polynomial $\text{poly}(\cdot)$ depends on the commitment scheme in use.

Much more efficient zero-knowledge proof systems can be custom-made for specific languages in $\mathcal{NP}$. Furthermore, even if one adopts the approach of reducing the construction of zero-knowledge proof systems for $\mathcal{NP}$ languages to the construction of a zero-knowledge proof system for a single $\mathcal{NP}$-complete language, efficiency improvements can be achieved. For example, using Exercise 20, one can present zero-knowledge proofs for the Hamiltonian-cycle problem (again with error 2^{-k}) having round complexity $O(k)$, bit complexity $O(k \cdot |V|^{2+\varepsilon})$, and computational complexity $O(k \cdot |V|^{2+O(\varepsilon)})$, where $\varepsilon > 0$ is a constant depending on the desired security of the commitment scheme (in Construction 4.4.7 and in Exercise 20 we chose $\varepsilon = 1$). Note that complexities depending on the instance size are affected by reductions among problems, and hence a fair comparison is obtained by considering the complexities for the generic problem (i.e., Bounded Halting).

The round complexity of a protocol is a very important efficiency consideration, and it is desirable to reduce it as much as possible. In particular, it is desirable to have zero-knowledge proofs with constant numbers of rounds and negligible error probability. This goal is pursued in Section 4.9.

4.4.4.2. Knowledge Tightness

The foregoing efficiency measures are generic in the sense that they are applicable to any protocol (independent of whether or not it is zero-knowledge). Because security and efficiency often are convertible from one to the other (especially in this context), one should consider refined measures of efficiency only in conjunction with a refined measure of security.

In contrast to the generic (efficiency) measures, we consider a (security) measure specific to zero-knowledge, called *knowledge tightness*. Intuitively, knowledge tightness is a refinement of zero-knowledge that is aimed at measuring the "actual security" of the proof system, namely, how much harder the verifier needs to work, when not interacting with the prover, in order to compute something that it can compute after interacting with the prover. Thus, knowledge tightness is the ratio between the (expected) running time of the simulator and the running time of the verifier in the real interaction simulated by the simulator. Note that the simulators presented thus far, as well as all known simulators, operate by repeated random trials, and hence an instructive measure of tightness should consider their expected running times (assuming they never err, i.e., never output the special $\perp$ symbol), rather than the worst case. (Alternatively, one can consider the running time of a simulator that outputs $\perp$ with probability at most $\frac{1}{2}$.)

> **Definition 4.4.13 (Knowledge Tightness):** *Let $t : \mathbb{N} \to \mathbb{N}$ be a function. We say that a zero-knowledge proof for language L has **knowledge tightness** $t(\cdot)$ if there exists a polynomial $p(\cdot)$ such that for every probabilistic polynomial-time verifier V^* there exists a simulator M^* (as in Definition 4.3.2) such that for all sufficiently long $x \in L$ we have*
>
> $$\frac{\text{Time}_{M^*}(x) - p(|x|)}{\text{Time}_{V^*}(x)} \le t(|x|)$$
>
> *where $\text{Time}_{M^*}(x)$ denotes the expected running time of M^* on input x, and $\text{Time}_{V^*}(x)$ denotes the running time of V^* on common input x.*

We assume a model of computation that allows one machine to emulate another machine at the cost of only the running time of the latter machine. The purpose of polynomial $p(\cdot)$ in the foregoing definition is to take care of generic overhead created by the simulation (this is important only in case the verifier V^* is extremely fast). We remark that the definition of zero-knowledge does not guarantee that the knowledge tightness is polynomial. Yet all known zero-knowledge proofs, and, more generally, all zero-knowledge properties demonstrated using a single simulator with black-box access to V^*, have polynomial knowledge tightness. In particular, Construction 4.3.8 (like the construction in Exercise 20) has knowledge tightness 2, whereas Construction 4.4.7 has knowledge tightness approximately $\frac{3}{2}$. We believe that knowledge tightness is a very important efficiency consideration and that it is desirable to have it be a constant.

We comment that the notion of knowledge tightness is also instructive in reconciling statements like the following:

1. Executing Construction 4.4.7 $O(\log n)$ times in parallel, where n is the number of vertices in the graph, results in a zero-knowledge proof system.

2. Executing Construction 4.4.7 more than $O(\log n)$ times (say $O((\log n) \cdot (\log \log n))$) times) in parallel is not known to result in a zero-knowledge proof system. (Furthermore, it is unlikely that the resulting proof system can be shown to be zero-knowledge; see Section 4.5.4.2.)

The gap between these conflicting statements seems less dramatic once one realizes that executing Construction 4.4.7 $k(n) = O(\log n)$ times in parallel results in a zero-knowledge proof system of knowledge tightness approximately $(3/2)^{k(n)}$. (See Exercise 19.)

4.5.* Negative Results

In this section we review some negative results concerning zero-knowledge. These results indicate that some of the shortcomings of the results and constructions presented in previous sections are unavoidable. Most importantly, Theorem 4.4.11 asserts the existence of (computational) zero-knowledge interactive proof systems for $\mathcal{NP}$, assuming that one-way functions exist. Three questions arise naturally:

1. *Unconditional results*: Can one prove the existence of (computational) zero-knowledge proof systems for $\mathcal{NP}$ without making any assumptions?

2. *Perfect zero-knowledge*: Can one present perfect zero-knowledge proof systems for $\mathcal{NP}$ even under some reasonable assumptions?

3. *The role of randomness and interaction*: For example, can one present error-free zero-knowledge proof systems for $\mathcal{NP}$?

The answers to all these questions seem to be negative.

Another important question concerning zero-knowledge proofs is their preservation under parallel composition. We shall show that, *in general*, zero-knowledge is not preserved under parallel composition (i.e., there exists a pair of zero-knowledge protocols that when executed in parallel will leak knowledge, in a strong sense). Furthermore, we shall consider some natural proof systems, obtained via parallel composition of zero-knowledge proofs (e.g., the one of Construction 4.4.7), and indicate that it is unlikely that the resulting composed proofs can be proved to be zero-knowledge.

Organization. We start by reviewing some results regarding the essential roles of both randomness and interaction in Theorem 4.4.11 (i.e., the existence of zero-knowledge proofs for $\mathcal{NP}$). For these results we also present the relatively simple proof ideas (see Section 4.5.1). Next, in Section 4.5.2, we claim that the existence of zero-knowledge proofs for $\mathcal{NP}$ implies some form of average-case one-way hardness, and so the assumption in Theorem 4.4.11 cannot be totally eliminated. In Section 4.5.3 we consider perfect zero-knowledge proof systems, and in Section 4.5.4, the composition of zero-knowledge protocols.

Jumping ahead, we mention that all the results presented in this section, except Theorem 4.5.8 (i.e., the limitation of perfect zero-knowledge proofs), apply also to zero-knowledge arguments as defined and discussed in Section 4.8.

4.5.1. On the Importance of Interaction and Randomness

We call a proof system *trivial* if it is a proof system for a language in $\mathcal{BPP}$. Because languages in $\mathcal{BPP}$ can be decided by the verifier without any interaction with the prover, such proof systems are of no use (at least as far as cryptography is concerned).

On the Triviality of Unidirectional Zero-Knowledge Proofs. A *unidirectional* proof system is one in which a single message is sent (i.e., from the prover to the verifier). We show that such proof systems, which constitute a special class of interactive proofs that includes $\mathcal{NP}$-type proofs as special cases, are too restricted to allow non-trivial zero-knowledge proofs.

Theorem 4.5.1: *Suppose that L has a unidirectional zero-knowledge proof system. Then $L \in \mathcal{BPP}$.*

Proof Idea: Given a simulator M for the view of the honest verifier in this system (as guaranteed by Definition 4.3.3), we construct a decision procedure for L. On input x, we invoke $M(x)$ and obtain (w, r), where w supposedly is a message sent by the prover and $r \in \{0, 1\}^\ell$ supposedly is the random tape of the verifier. We uniformly select $r' \in \{0, 1\}^\ell$ and decide as the true verifier would have decided upon receiving the message w and using r' as the content of its random tape. The hypothesis that M is a good simulator is used in the analysis of the case $x \in L$, whereas the soundness of the proof system (and the fact that r' is selected independently of w) is used for the case $x \notin L$. ∎

On the Essential Role of the Verifier's Randomness. We next show that randomization on the verifier's part is necessary for the non-triviality of zero-knowledge proof systems. It follows that a non-zero error probability is essential to the non-triviality of zero-knowledge proof systems, because otherwise the verifier could always set its random tape to be all zeros. (In fact, we can directly prove that a non-zero soundness error is essential to the non-triviality of zero-knowledge proof systems and derive Theorem 4.5.2 as a special case.[15])

Theorem 4.5.2: *Suppose that L has a zero-knowledge proof system in which the verifier program is deterministic. Then $L \in \mathcal{BPP}$.*

---

[15] Again, given a simulator M for the view of the honest verifier in this system, we construct a decision procedure for L. On input x, we invoke $M(x)$ and accept if and only if the output corresponds to a transcript that the honest verifier would have accepted. The hypothesis that M is a good simulator is used in the analysis of the case $x \in L$, whereas the *perfect* soundness of the proof system is used for the case $x \notin L$. Theorem 4.5.2 follows because deterministic verifiers necessarily have zero soundness error.

Proof Idea: Because the verifier is deterministic, the prover can fully determine each of its future messages. Thus the proof system can be converted into an equivalent one in which the prover simply sends to the verifier the full transcript of an execution in the original proof system. Observe that the completeness, soundness, and zero-knowledge properties of the original proof system are preserved and that the resulting proof system is unidirectional. We conclude by applying Theorem 4.5.1. ∎

On the Essential Role of the Prover's Randomness. Finally, we show that randomization on the prover's part is also necessary for the non-triviality of zero-knowledge proof systems.

Theorem 4.5.3: *Suppose that L has an* auxiliary-input *zero-knowledge proof system in which the prover program is deterministic. Then $L \in \mathcal{BPP}$.*

Note that the hypothesis (i.e., the type of zero-knowledge requirement) is stronger here. (Computationally unbounded deterministic provers may suffice for the non-triviality of the bare definition of zero-knowledge (i.e., Definition 4.3.2).)

Proof Idea: Suppose, without loss of generality, that the verifier is the party sending the first message in this proof system. We consider a cheating verifier that given an auxiliary input $z_1, \ldots, z_t$ sends z_i as its ith message. The remaining messages of this verifier are determined arbitrarily. We first observe that because the prover is deterministic, in a real interaction the first $i \leq t$ responses of the prover are determined by $z_1, \ldots, z_i$. Thus, that must be essentially the case in the simulation. We construct a decision procedure for L by emulating the interaction of the prescribed prover with the prescribed verifier on common input equal to the input to the procedure, denoted x. Toward this end, we uniformly select and fix a random tape, denoted r, for the verifier. The emulation proceeds in iterations corresponding to the prover's messages. To obtain the prover's next message, we first determine the next verifier message (by running the program of the prescribed verifier on input x, coins r, and incoming messages as recorded thus far). Next, we invoke the simulator on input $(x, (z_1, \ldots, z_i))$, where $z_1, \ldots, z_i$ are the verifier's messages determined thus far, and so we obtain and record the prover's ith message. Our final decision is determined by the verifier's decision. ∎

4.5.2. Limitations of Unconditional Results

Recall that Theorem 4.4.12 asserts the existence of zero-knowledge proofs for all languages in $\mathcal{IP}$, *provided that non-uniformly one-way functions exist.* In this subsection we consider the question of whether or not this sufficient condition is also necessary. The following results seem to provide some (yet, weak) indication in that direction. Specifically, the existence of zero-knowledge proof systems for languages outside of $\mathcal{BPP}$ implies (very weak) forms of one-wayness. In a dual way, the existence of zero-knowledge proof systems for languages that are hard to approximate (in some average-case sense) implies the existence of one-way functions (but not of non-uniformly one-way functions). In the rest of this subsection we merely provide precise statements of these results.

Non-Triviality of ZK Implies Weak Forms of One-Wayness. By the non-triviality of zero-knowledge we mean the existence of zero-knowledge proof systems for languages outside of $\mathcal{BPP}$ (as the latter have trivial zero-knowledge systems in which the prover does nothing). Let us clarify what we mean by "weak forms of one-wayness." Our starting point is the definition of a collection of one-way functions (i.e., Definition 2.4.3). Recall that these are collections of functions, indexed by some $\overline{I} \subseteq \{0, 1\}^*$, that are easy to sample and evaluate but *typically* hard to invert. That is, a typical function f_i (for $i \in \overline{I}$) is hard to invert on a typical image. Here we require only that there exist functions in the collection that are hard to invert on a typical image.

> **Definition 4.5.4 (Collection of Functions with One-Way Instances):** *A collection of functions* $\{f_i : D_i \to \{0, 1\}^*\}_{i \in \overline{I}}$ *is said to* **have one-way instances** *if there exist three probabilistic polynomial-time algorithms I, D, and F such that the following two conditions hold:*
>
> 1. **Easy to sample and compute:** *As in Definition 2.4.3.*
> 2. **Some functions are hard to invert:** *For every probabilistic polynomial-time algorithm A', every polynomial $p(\cdot)$, and infinitely many $i \in \overline{I}$,*
>
> $$\Pr\left[A'(i, f_i(X_i)) \in f_i^{-1}(f_i(X_i))\right] < \frac{1}{p(|i|)}$$
>
> *where $X_i = D(i)$.*

Actually, because the hardness condition does not refer to the distribution induced by I, we can omit I from the definition and refer only to the index set $\overline{I}$. Such a collection contains infinitely many functions that are hard to invert, but there may be no efficient way of selecting such a function (and thus the collection is of no real value). Still, we stress that the hardness condition has an average-case flavor; each of these infinitely many functions is hard to invert in a strong probabilistic sense, not merely in the worst case.

> **Theorem 4.5.5:** *If there exist zero-knowledge proofs for languages outside of $\mathcal{BPP}$, then there exist collections of functions with one-way instances.*

We remark that the mere assumption that $\mathcal{BPP} \subset \mathcal{IP}$ is not known to imply any form of (average) one-wayness. Even the existence of a language in $\mathcal{NP}$ that is not in $\mathcal{BPP}$ does not imply any form of average-case hardness; it merely implies the existence of a function that is easy to compute but hard to invert *in the worst case* (see Section 2.1).

ZK for "Hard" Languages Yields One-Way Functions. Our notion of hard languages is the following:

> **Definition 4.5.6:** *We say that a language L is **hard to approximate** if there exists a probabilistic polynomial-time algorithm S such that for every probabilistic polynomial-time algorithm A, every polynomial p(·), and all sufficiently large n's,*
>
> $$\Pr[A(X_n) = \chi_L(X_n)] < \frac{1}{2} + \frac{1}{p(n)}$$
>
> *where $X_n \stackrel{\text{def}}{=} S(1^n)$, and χ_L is the characteristic function of the language L (i.e., $\chi_L(x) = 1$ if $x \in L$, and $\chi_L(x) = 0$ otherwise).*

For example, if f is a one-way permutation and b is a hard-core predicate for f, then the language $L_f \stackrel{\text{def}}{=} \{x \in \{0, 1\}^* : b(f^{-1}(x)) = 1\} \in \mathcal{NP}$ is hard to approximate (under the uniform distribution).

> **Theorem 4.5.7:** *If there exist zero-knowledge proofs for languages that are hard to approximate, then there exist one-way functions.*

We stress that the mere existence of languages that are hard to approximate is not known to imply the existence of one-way functions (see Section 2.1).

4.5.3. Limitations of Statistical ZK Proofs

A theorem bounding the class of languages possessing *perfect* zero-knowledge proof systems follows. In fact, the bound refers even to *statistical* (i.e., *almost-perfect*) zero-knowledge proof systems (see Section 4.3.1.4). We start with some background. By $\mathcal{AM}$ we denote the class of languages having interactive proofs that proceed as follows. First the verifier sends a random string to the prover, next the prover answers with some string, and finally the verifier decides whether to accept or reject based on a deterministic computation (depending on the common input and the two strings). It is believed that $\text{co}\mathcal{NP}$ is not contained in $\mathcal{AM}$ (or, equivalently, $\mathcal{NP}$ is not contained in $\text{co}\mathcal{AM}$). Additional support for this belief is provided by the fact that $\text{co}\mathcal{NP} \subseteq \mathcal{AM}$ implies the collapse of the Polynomial-Time Hierarchy. In any case, the result we wish to mention is the following:

> **Theorem 4.5.8:** *If there exists a statistical (almost-perfect) zero-knowledge proof system for a language L, then $L \in \text{co}\mathcal{AM}$. (In fact, $L \in \text{co}\mathcal{AM} \cap \mathcal{AM}$.)*

The theorem remains valid under several relaxations of statistical zero-knowledge (e.g., allowing the simulator to run in expected polynomial-time). Hence, if some $\mathcal{NP}$-complete language has a statistical zero-knowledge proof system, then $\text{co}\mathcal{NP} \subseteq \mathcal{AM}$, which is unlikely.

We stress that Theorem 4.5.8 *does not* apply to perfect (or statistical) zero-knowledge *arguments*, defined and discussed in Section 4.8. Hence, there is no conflict between Theorem 4.5.8 and the fact that under some reasonable complexity assumptions, perfect zero-knowledge arguments do exist for every language in $\mathcal{NP}$.

4.5.4. Zero-Knowledge and Parallel Composition

We present two negative results regarding parallel composition of zero-knowledge protocols. These results are very different in terms of their conceptual standing: The first result asserts the failure (in general) of the *parallel-composition conjecture* (i.e., the conjecture that running *any* two zero-knowledge protocols in parallel will result in a zero-knowledge protocol), but says nothing about specific natural candidates. The second result refers to a class of interactive proofs that contains several interesting and natural examples, and it asserts that the members of this class cannot be proved zero-knowledge using a general paradigm (known by the name "black-box simulation"). The relation of the second result to this subsection follows from the fact that some of the members in this class are obtained by parallel composition of natural zero-knowledge proofs. We mention that it is hard to conceive an alternative way of demonstrating the zero-knowledge property of protocols (other than by providing a black-box simulator).

We stress that by "parallel composition" we mean playing several copies of the protocol in parallel, where the prescribed (honest) parties execute each copy independently of the other copies. Specifically, if a party is required to toss coins in a certain round, then it will toss independent coins for each of the copies.

4.5.4.1. Failure of the Parallel-Composition Conjecture

As a warning about trusting unsound intuitions, we mention that for several years (following the introduction of zero-knowledge proofs) some researchers insisted that the following must be true:

> **Parallel-Composition Conjecture:** *Let P_1 and P_2 be two zero-knowledge provers. Then the prover that results from running both of them in parallel is also zero-knowledge.*

However, the parallel-composition conjecture is simply wrong.

> **Proposition 4.5.9:** *There exist two provers, P_1 and P_2, such that each is zero-knowledge, and yet the prover that results from running both of them in parallel yields knowledge (e.g., a cheating verifier can extract from this prover a solution to a problem that is not solvable in polynomial time). Furthermore, the foregoing holds even if the zero-knowledge property of each of the P_i's can be demonstrated with a simulator that uses the verifier as a black box (as in Definition 4.5.10).*

> **Proof Idea:** Consider a prover, denoted P_1, that sends "knowledge" to the verifier if and only if the verifier can answer some randomly chosen *hard question* (i.e., we stress that the question is chosen by P_1). Answers to such hard questions

look pseudorandom, yet P_1 (which is not computationally bounded) can verify their correctness. Now consider a second (computationally unbounded) prover, denoted P_2, that answers these hard questions. Each of these provers (by itself) is zero-knowledge: P_1 is zero-knowledge because it is unlikely that any probabilistic polynomial-time verifier can answer its questions, whereas P_2 is zero-knowledge because its answers can be simulated by random strings. Yet, once they are played in parallel, a cheating verifier can answer the question of P_1 by sending it to P_2 and using the answer obtained from P_2 to gain knowledge from P_1. To turn this idea into a proof we need to construct a hard problem with the previously postulated properties. ∎

The foregoing proposition refutes the parallel-composition conjecture by means of exponential-time provers. Assuming the existence of one-way functions, the parallel-composition conjecture can also be refuted for probabilistic polynomial-time provers (with auxiliary inputs). For example, consider the following two provers P_1 and P_2, which make use of proofs of knowledge (see Section 4.7). Let C be a bit-commitment scheme (which we know to exist provided that one-way functions exist). On common input $C(1^n, \sigma)$, where $\sigma \in \{0, 1\}$, prover P_1 proves to the verifier, in zero-knowledge, that it knows σ. (To this end the prover is given as auxiliary input the coins used in the commitment.) In contrast, on common input $C(1^n, \sigma)$, prover P_2 asks the verifier to prove that it knows σ, and if P_2 is convinced, then it sends σ to the verifier. This verifier employs the same proof-of-knowledge system used by the prover P_1. Clearly, each prover is zero-knowledge, and yet their parallel composition is not.

Similarly, using stronger intractability assumptions, one can also refute the parallel-composition conjecture with respect to almost-perfect zero-knowledge (rather than with respect to computational zero-knowledge). (Here we let the provers use a perfect zero-knowledge, computationally sound proof of knowledge; see Section 4.8.)

4.5.4.2. Problems Occurring with "Natural" Candidates

By definition, to show that a prover is zero-knowledge, one has to present, for each prospective verifier V^*, a corresponding simulator M^* (which simulates the interaction of V^* with the prover). However, all known demonstrations of zero-knowledge proceed by presenting one "universal" simulator that uses any prospective verifier V^* as a black box. In fact, these demonstrations use as a black box (or oracle) the next-message function determined by the verifier program (i.e., V^*), its auxiliary input, and its random input. (This property of the simulators is implicit in our constructions of the simulators in previous sections.) We remark that it is hard to conceive an alternative way of demonstrating the zero-knowledge property (because a non-black-box usage of a verifier seems to require some "reverse engineering" of its code). This difficulty is greatly amplified in the context of auxiliary-input zero-knowledge.

Definition 4.5.10 (Black-Box Zero-Knowledge):

- Next-message function: *Let B be an interactive Turing machine, and let x, z, and r be strings representing a common input, an auxiliary input, and a random* input, respectively. Consider the function $B_{x,z,r}(\cdot)$ describing the messages sent by machine B such that $B_{x,z,r}(\overline{m})$ denotes the message sent by B on common input x, auxiliary input z, random input r, and sequence of incoming messages $\overline{m}$. For simplicity, we assume that the output of B appears as its last message.

- Black-box simulator: We say that a probabilistic polynomial-time oracle machine M is a **black-box simulator** for the prover P and the language L if for every polynomial-time interactive machine B, every probabilistic polynomial-time oracle machine D, every polynomial $p(\cdot)$, all sufficiently large $x \in L$, and every $z, r \in \{0, 1\}^*$,

$$\left| \Pr\left[D^{B_{x,z,r}}(\langle P, B_r(z)\rangle(x)) = 1 \right] - \Pr\left[D^{B_{x,z,r}}\left(M^{B_{x,z,r}}(x) \right) = 1 \right] \right| < \frac{1}{p(|x|)}$$

where $B_r(z)$ denotes the interaction of machine B with auxiliary input z and random input r.
- We say that P is **black-box zero-knowledge** if it has a black-box simulator.

Essentially, the definition says that a black-box simulator mimics the interaction of prover P with any polynomial-time verifier B relative to any auxiliary input (i.e., z) that B may get and any random input (i.e., r) that B may choose. The simulator does so (efficiently) merely by using oracle calls to $B_{x,z,r}$ (which specifies the next message that B sends on input x, auxiliary input z, and random input r). The simulation is indistinguishable from the true interaction even if the distinguishing algorithm (i.e., D) is given access to the oracle $B_{x,z,r}$. An equivalent formulation is presented in Exercise 21. Clearly, if P is black-box zero-knowledge, then it is zero-knowledge with respect to auxiliary input (and has polynomially bounded knowledge tightness, see Definition 4.4.13).

Theorem 4.5.11: *Suppose that* (P, V) *is an interactive proof system with negligible error probability* for the language L. Further suppose that (P, V) has the following properties:

- Constant round: *There exists an integer k such that for every* $x \in L$, *on input x the prover P sends at most k messages.*
- Public coins: *The messages sent by the verifier V are predetermined consecutive segments of its random tape.*
- Black-box zero-knowledge: *The prover P has a black-box simulator (over the language L).*

Then $L \in \mathcal{BPP}$.

The theorem also holds for computationally sound zero-knowledge proof systems defined and discussed in Section 4.8.

We remark that both Construction 4.3.8 (zero-knowledge proof for Graph Isomorphism) and Construction 4.4.7 (zero-knowledge proof for Graph Colorability) are constant-round, use public coins, and are black-box zero-knowledge (for the corresponding language). However, they *do not* have negligible error probability. Yet, repeating each of these constructions polynomially many times *in parallel* yields an interactive proof, with negligible error probability, for the corresponding language.[16] Clearly the resulting proof systems are constant-round and use public coins. Hence, unless the corresponding languages are in $\mathcal{BPP}$, these resulting proof systems *are not* black-box zero-knowledge.

Theorem 4.5.11 is sometimes interpreted as pointing to an inherent limitation of interactive proofs with public coins (also known as *Arthur-Merlin* games). Such proofs cannot be both *round-efficient* (i.e., have constant number of rounds and negligible error) and black-box zero-knowledge (unless they are trivially so, i.e., the language is in $\mathcal{BPP}$). In other words, *when constructing round-efficient zero-knowledge proof systems* (for languages not in $\mathcal{BPP}$), *one should use "private coins"* (i.e., let the verifier send messages depending upon, but not revealing, its coin tosses). This is indeed the approach taken in Section 4.9.

4.6.* Witness Indistinguishability and Hiding

In light of the non-closure of zero-knowledge under parallel composition (see Section 4.5.4), alternative "privacy" criteria that are preserved under parallel composition are of practical and theoretical importance. Two notions, called witness indistinguishability and witness hiding, that refer to the "privacy" of interactive proof systems (of languages in $\mathcal{NP}$) are presented in this section. Both notions seem weaker than zero-knowledge, yet they suffice for some specific applications.

We remark that witness indistinguishability and witness hiding, like zero-knowledge, are properties of the prover (and, more generally, of any interactive machine).

4.6.1. Definitions

In this section we confine ourselves to proof systems for languages in $\mathcal{NP}$. Recall that a *witness relation* for a language $L \in \mathcal{NP}$ is a binary relation R_L that is polynomially bounded (i.e., $(x, y) \in R_L$ implies $|y| \leq \mathrm{poly}(|x|)$), is polynomial-time-recognizable and characterizes L by

$$L = \{x : \exists y \text{ s.t. } (x, y) \in R_L\}$$

For $x \in L$, any y satisfying $(x, y) \in R_L$ is called a *witness* (for the membership $x \in L$). We let $R_L(x)$ denote the set of witnesses for the membership $x \in L$; that is, $R_L(x) \overset{\text{def}}{=} \{y : (x, y) \in R_L\}$.

---

[16]In fact, a super-logarithmic number of repetitions will suffice in the case of Construction 4.3.8, as well as for a modified version of Construction 4.4.7. The modified proof system invokes Construction 4.4.7 on the graph resulting from the input graph by applying a special polynomial-time reduction that is guaranteed by the so-called PCP theorem. Specifically, this reduction reduces $G3C$ to itself, so that non-members of $G3C$ are mapped into graphs for which every three-way partition of the vertex set has at least a constant fraction of violating edges (i.e., edges with both endpoints on the same side of the partition). Let $\varepsilon > 0$ be the constant guaranteed by the PCP theorem. Then the resulting proof system has perfect completeness and soundness error at most $1 - \varepsilon$, and so a super-logarithmic number of repetitions will yield negligible error probability.

4.6.1.1. Witness Indistinguishability

Loosely speaking, an interactive proof for a language $L \in \mathcal{NP}$ is *witness-independent* (resp., *witness-indistinguishable*) if the verifier's view of the interaction with the prover is statistically independent (resp., "computationally independent") of the auxiliary input of the prover. Actually, we shall specialize the requirement to the case in which the auxiliary input constitutes an $\mathcal{NP}$-witness to the common input; namely, for a witness relation R_L of the language $L \in \mathcal{NP}$, we consider only interactions on common input $x \in L$, where the prover is given an auxiliary input in $R_L(x)$. By saying that the view is *computationally independent* of the witness, we mean that for every two choices of auxiliary inputs, the resulting views are computationally indistinguishable. Analogously to the discussion in Section 4.3, we obtain equivalent definitions by considering the verifier's view of the interaction with the prover or the verifier's output after such an interaction. In the actual definition, we adopt the latter (i.e., "output") formulation and use the notation of Definition 4.3.10.

Definition 4.6.1 (Witness Indistinguishability/Independence): *Let* (P, V), $L \in \mathcal{NP}$ *and* V^* *be as in Definition 4.3.10, and let* R_L *be a fixed witness relation for the language* L. *We say that* (P, V) *is* **witness-indistinguishable for** R_L *if for every probabilistic polynomial-time interactive machine* V^* *and every two sequences* $W^1 = \{w_x^1\}_{x \in L}$ *and* $W^2 = \{w_x^2\}_{x \in L}$, *such that* $w_x^1, w_x^2 \in R_L(x)$, *the following two ensembles are computationally indistinguishable:*

- $\{\langle P(w_x^1), V^*(z) \rangle(x)\}_{x \in L, z \in \{0,1\}^*}$
- $\{\langle P(w_x^2), V^*(z) \rangle(x)\}_{x \in L, z \in \{0,1\}^*}$

Namely, for every probabilistic polynomial-time algorithm D, *every polynomial* $p(\cdot)$, *all sufficiently long* $x \in L$, *and all* $z \in \{0, 1\}^*$, *it holds that*

$$\left| \Pr\left[D\left(x, z, \langle P(w_x^1), V^*(z) \rangle(x)\right) = 1 \right] \right.$$
$$\left. - \Pr\left[D\left(x, z, \langle P(w_x^2), V^*(z) \rangle(x)\right) = 1 \right] \right| < \frac{1}{p(|x|)}$$

We say that (P, V) *is* **witness-independent for** R_L *if the foregoing ensembles are identically distributed. Namely, for every* $x \in L$, *every* $w_x^1, w_x^2 \in R_L(x)$, *and* $z \in \{0, 1\}^*$, *the random variables* $\langle P(w_x^1), V^*(z) \rangle(x)$ *and* $\langle P(w_x^2), V^*(z) \rangle(x)$ *are identically distributed.*

In particular, z may equal (w_x^1, w_x^2). A few additional comments are in order:

- Proof systems in which the prover ignores its auxiliary input are (trivially) witness-independent. In particular, exponential-time provers can afford to ignore their auxiliary input (without any decrease in the probability that they will convince the verifier) and so can be trivially witness-independent. Yet probabilistic polynomial-time provers cannot afford to ignore their auxiliary input (since otherwise they become useless). Hence, for probabilistic polynomial-time provers (for languages outside $\mathcal{BPP}$), the witness-indistinguishability requirement may be non-trivial.

- Any zero-knowledge proof system for a language in $\mathcal{NP}$ is witness-indistinguishable (since the the distribution corresponding to each witness can be approximated by the same simulator; see details later). Likewise, perfect zero-knowledge proofs are witness-independent.

- On the other hand, witness indistinguishability does NOT imply zero-knowledge. In particular, any proof system for a language having unique witnesses is trivially witness-indistinguishable, but may not be zero-knowledge. For example, for a one-way permutation f, consider the ("unnatural") witness relation $\{(f(w), w) : w \in \{0, 1\}^*\}$, characterizing the set of all strings, and a prover that on common input $f(w)$ and auxiliary input w sends w to the verifier.

- It is relatively easy to see that witness indistinguishability and witness independence are preserved under sequential composition. In the next subsection, we show that they are also preserved under parallel composition.

An Augmented Notion. An augmented notion of witness indistinguishability requires that whenever the common inputs to the proof system are computationally indistinguishable, so are the corresponding views of the verifier. That is, we augment Definition 4.6.1 as follows:

> **Definition 4.6.2 (Strong Witness Indistinguishability):** *Let (P, V) and all other notation be as in Definition 4.6.1. We say that (P, V) is **strongly witness-indistinguishable** for R_L if for every probabilistic polynomial-time interactive machine V^* and for every two probability ensembles $\{(X_n^1, Y_n^1, Z_n^1)\}_{n\in\mathbb{N}}$ and $\{(X_n^2, Y_n^2, Z_n^2)\}_{n\in\mathbb{N}}$, such that each (X_n^i, Y_n^i, Z_n^i) ranges over $(R_L \times \{0, 1\}^*) \cap (\{0, 1\}^n \times \{0, 1\}^* \times \{0, 1\}^*)$, the following holds:*
>
> *If $\{(X_n^1, Z_n^1)\}_{n\in\mathbb{N}}$ and $\{(X_n^2, Z_n^2)\}_{n\in\mathbb{N}}$ are computationally indistinguishable, then so are $\{\langle P(Y_n^1), V^*(Z_n^1)\rangle(X_n^1)\}_{n\in\mathbb{N}}$ and $\{\langle P(Y_n^2), V^*(Z_n^2)\rangle(X_n^2)\}_{n\in\mathbb{N}}$.*

We stress that $\{(X_n^1, Y_n^1, Z_n^1)\}_{n\in\mathbb{N}}$ and $\{(X_n^2, Y_n^2, Z_n^2)\}_{n\in\mathbb{N}}$ are not required to be computationally indistinguishable; such a requirement would trivialize the definition at least as far as probabilistic polynomial-time provers are concerned. Definition 4.6.1 can be obtained from Definition 4.6.2 by considering the special case in which X_n^1 and X_n^2 are identically distributed (and observing that no computational requirement was placed on the $\{(X_n^i, Y_n^i, Z_n^i)\}_{n\in\mathbb{N}}$'s). On the other hand, assuming that one-way permutations exist, witness indistinguishability does *not* imply strong witness indistinguishability (see Exercise 25). Still, one can easily show that any zero-knowledge proof system for a language in $\mathcal{NP}$ is strongly witness-indistinguishable.

> **Proposition 4.6.3:** *Let (P, V) be an auxiliary-input zero-knowledge proof system for a language $L \in \mathcal{NP}$. Then (P, V) is strongly witness-indistinguishable.*

> **Proof Idea:** Using the simulator M^*, guaranteed for V^*, we obtain that $E^i \stackrel{\text{def}}{=} \{\langle P(Y_n^i), V^*(Z_n^i)\rangle(X_n^i)\}_{n\in\mathbb{N}}$ and $S^i \stackrel{\text{def}}{=} \{M^*(X_n^i, Z_n^i)\}_{n\in\mathbb{N}}$ are computationally indistinguishable for both i's. Thus, if E^1 and E^2 are not computationally

indistinguishable, then S^1 and S^2 are not computationally indistinguishable. Incorporating M^* into the distinguisher, it follows that $\{(X_n^1, Z_n^1)\}_{n\in\mathbb{N}}$ and $\{(X_n^2, Z_n^2)\}_{n\in\mathbb{N}}$ are not computationally indistinguishable either. ∎

4.6.1.2. Witness-Hiding

We now turn to the notion of witness-hiding. Intuitively, a proof system for a language in $\mathcal{NP}$ is witness-hiding if after interacting with the prover it is still infeasible for the verifier to find an $\mathcal{NP}$-witness for the common input. Clearly, such a requirement can hold only if it is infeasible to find witnesses from scratch. Because each $\mathcal{NP}$ language has instances for which witness-finding is easy, we must consider the task of witness-finding for specially selected hard instances. This leads to the following definitions.

Definition 4.6.4 (Distribution of Hard Instances): *Let $L \in \mathcal{NP}$, and let R_L be a witness relation for L. Let $X \stackrel{\text{def}}{=} \{X_n\}_{n\in\mathbb{N}}$ be a probability ensemble such that X_n ranges over $L \cap \{0,1\}^n$. We say that X is **hard for** R_L if for every probabilistic polynomial-time* (witness-finding) *algorithm F, every polynomial $p(\cdot)$, all sufficiently large n's, and all $z \in \{0,1\}^{\text{poly}(n)}$,*

$$\Pr[F(X_n, z) \in R_L(X_n)] < \frac{1}{p(n)}$$

For example, if f is a (length-preserving and non-uniformly) one-way function, then the probability ensemble $\{f(U_n)\}_{n\in\mathbb{N}}$ is hard for the witness relation $\{(f(w), w) : w \in \{0,1\}^*\}$, where U_n is uniform over $\{0,1\}^n$.

Definition 4.6.5 (Witness-Hiding): *Let (P, V), $L \in \mathcal{NP}$, and R_L be as in the foregoing definitions. Let $X = \{X_n\}_{n\in\mathbb{N}}$ be a hard-instance ensemble for R_L. We say that (P, V) is **witness-hiding for** the relation R_L **under** the instance ensemble X if for every probabilistic polynomial-time machine V^*, every polynomial $p(\cdot)$, all sufficiently large n's, and all $z \in \{0,1\}^*$,*

$$\Pr[\langle P(Y_n), V^*(z)\rangle(X_n) \in R_L(X_n)] < \frac{1}{p(n)}$$

where Y_n is arbitrarily distributed over $R_L(X_n)$.

We remark that the relationship between the two privacy criteria (i.e., witness indistinguishability and witness-hiding) is not obvious. Yet zero-knowledge proofs (for $\mathcal{NP}$) are also witness-hiding (for any corresponding witness relation and any hard distribution). We mention a couple of extensions of Definition 4.6.5:

1. One can say that (P, V) is *universally witness-hiding for R_L* if the proof system (P, V) is witness-hiding for R_L under every ensemble of hard instances for R_L. (Alternatively, one can require only that (P, V) be witness-hiding for R_L under every *efficiently constructible*[17] ensemble of hard instances for R_L.)

---

[17] See Definition 3.2.5.

2. Variants of the foregoing definitions, in which the auxiliary input z is replaced by a distribution Z_n that may depend on X_n, are of interest too. Here we consider ensembles $\{(X_n, Z_n)\}_{n\in\mathbb{N}}$, where X_n ranges over $L \cap \{0, 1\}^n$. Such an ensemble is *hard for R_L* if for every probabilistic polynomial-time algorithm F, the probability that $F(X_n, Z_n) \in R_L(X_n)$ is negligible. The system (P, V) is *witness-hiding for R_L under* $\{(X_n, Z_n)\}_{n\in\mathbb{N}}$ if for every probabilistic polynomial-time verifier V^*, the probability that $\langle P(Y_n), V^*(Z_n)\rangle(X_n) \in R_L(X_n)$ is negligible.

4.6.2. Parallel Composition

In contrast to zero-knowledge proof systems, witness-indistinguishable proofs offer some robustness under parallel composition. Specifically, parallel composition of witness-indistinguishable proof systems results in a witness-indistinguishable system, *provided that the original prover is probabilistic polynomial-time.*

Lemma 4.6.6 (Parallel-Composition Lemma for Witness Indistinguishability): *Let $L \in \mathcal{NP}$ and R_L be as in Definition 4.6.1, and suppose that P is probabilistic polynomial-time and (P, V) is witness-indistinguishable (resp., witness-independent) for R_L. Let $Q(\cdot)$ be a polynomial, and let P_Q denote a program that on common input $x_1, \ldots, x_{Q(n)} \in \{0, 1\}^n$ and auxiliary input $w_1, \ldots, w_{Q(n)} \in \{0, 1\}^*$ invokes P in parallel $Q(n)$ times, so that in the ith copy P is invoked on common input x_i and auxiliary input w_i. Then P_Q is witness-indistinguishable (resp., witness-independent) for*

$$R_L^Q \stackrel{\text{def}}{=} \{(\overline{x}, \overline{w}) : \forall i, (x_i, w_i) \in R_L\}$$

where $\overline{x} = (x_1, \ldots, x_m)$ and $\overline{w} = (w_1, \ldots, w_m)$, so that $m = Q(n)$ and $|x_i| = n$ for each i.

Proof Sketch: Both the computational and information-theoretic versions follow by a hybrid argument. We concentrate on the computational version. To avoid cumbersome notation, we consider a generic n for which the claim of the lemma fails. (By contradiction, there must be infinitely many such n's, and a precise argument will actually handle all these n's together.) Namely, suppose that by using a verifier program V_Q^* it is feasible to distinguish the witnesses $\overline{w}^1 = (w_1^1, \ldots, w_m^1)$ and $\overline{w}^2 = (w_1^2, \ldots, w_m^2)$ used by P_Q in an interaction on common input $\overline{x} \in L^m$. Then for some i, the program V_Q^* also distinguishes the hybrid witnesses $\overline{h}^{(i)} = (w_1^1, \ldots, w_i^1, w_{i+1}^2, \ldots, w_m^2)$ and $\overline{h}^{(i+1)} = (w_1^1, \ldots, w_{i+1}^1, w_{i+2}^2, \ldots, w_m^2)$. Rewrite $\overline{h}^{(i)} = (w_1, \ldots, w_i, w_{i+1}^2, w_{i+2}, \ldots, w_m)$ and $\overline{h}^{(i+1)} = (w_1, \ldots, w_i, w_{i+1}^1, w_{i+2}, \ldots, w_m)$, where $w_j \stackrel{\text{def}}{=} w_j^1$ if $j \le i$, and $w_j \stackrel{\text{def}}{=} w_j^2$ if $j \ge i + 2$. We derive a contradiction by constructing a verifier V^* that distinguishes (the witnesses used by P in) interactions with the original prover P. Details follow.

The program V^* incorporates the programs P and V_Q^* and proceeds by interacting with the actual prover P and simulating $m - 1$ other interactions with (a copy of program) P. The real interaction with P is viewed as the $i + 1$ copy in an interaction of V_Q^* (with P_Q), whereas the simulated interactions are associated with the other copies. Specifically, in addition to the common input x, machine V^* gets the appropriate i and the sequences $\bar{x}$ and $(w_1, \ldots, w_i, w_{i+2}, \ldots, w_m)$ as part of its auxiliary input. For each $j \neq i + 1$, machine V^* will use x_j as common input and w_j as auxiliary input to the jth copy of P. Machine V^* invokes V_Q^* on common input $\bar{x}$ and provides it an interface to a virtual interaction with P_Q. The $i + 1$ component of a message $\bar{\alpha} = (\alpha_1, \ldots, \alpha_m)$ sent by V_Q^* is forwarded to the prover P, and all other components are kept for the simulation of the other copies. When P answers with a message β, machine V^* computes the answers for the other copies of P (by feeding the program P the corresponding auxiliary input and the corresponding sequence of incoming messages). It follows that V^* can distinguish the case in which P uses the witness w_{i+1}^1 from the case in which P uses w_{i+1}^2. ∎

This proof easily extends to the case in which several proof systems are executed concurrently in a totally asynchronous manner (i.e., sequential and parallel executions being two special cases).[18] The proof also extends to strong witness indistinguishability. Thus we have the following:

Lemma 4.6.7 (Parallel Composition for Strong Witness Indistinguishability): *Let $L \in \mathcal{NP}$, R_L, (P, V), Q, R_L^Q, and P_Q be as in Lemma 4.6.6. Then if P is strongly witness-indistinguishable (for R_L), then so is P_Q (for R_L^Q).*

4.6.3. Constructions

In this section we present constructions of witness-indistinguishable and witness-hiding proof systems.

4.6.3.1. Constructions of Witness-Indistinguishable Proofs

Using the parallel-composition lemma (Lemma 4.6.7) and the observation that zero-knowledge proofs are (strongly) witness-indistinguishable, we derive the following:

Theorem 4.6.8: *Assuming the existence of (non-uniformly) one-way functions, every language in $\mathcal{NP}$ has a* constant-round (strongly) *witness-indistinguishable proof system with* negligible *error probability. In fact, the error probability can be made exponentially small.*

We remark that no such result is known for *zero-knowledge* proof systems. Namely, the known proof systems for $\mathcal{NP}$ variously

- are not constant-round (e.g., Construction 4.4.9), or
- have noticeable error probability (e.g., Construction 4.4.7), or

---

[18]That is, executions of polynomially many instances of the proof system are arbitrarily interleaved (in a manner determined by the adversary); see suggestions for further reading in Section 4.12.2.

- require stronger intractability assumptions (see Section 4.9.1), or

- are only computationally sound (see Section 4.9.2).

4.6.3.2. Constructions of Witness-Hiding Proofs

Witness-indistinguishable proof systems are not necessarily witness-hiding. For example, any language with unique witnesses has a proof system that yields the unique witness (and so may fail to be witness-hiding), yet this proof system is trivially witness-independent. On the other hand, for some relations, witness indistinguishability implies witness-hiding, *provided that the prover is probabilistic polynomial-time*. For example:

> **Proposition 4.6.9:** *Let* $\{(f_i^0, f_i^1) : i \in \bar{I}\}$ *be a collection of (non-uniform) claw-free functions, and let*
>
> $$R \stackrel{\text{def}}{=} \{(x, w) : w = (\sigma, r) \wedge x = (i, x') \wedge x' = f_i^\sigma(r)\}$$
>
> *Suppose that P is a probabilistic polynomial-time interactive machine that is witness-indistinguishable for R. Then P is also witness-hiding for R under the distribution generated by setting $i = I(1^n)$ and $x' = f_i^0(D(0, i))$, where I and D are as in Definition 2.4.6.*

By a collection of non-uniform claw-free functions we mean that even non-uniform families of circuits $\{C_n\}$ fail to form claws on input distribution $I(1^n)$, except with negligible probability. We remark that the foregoing proposition does not relate to the purpose of interacting with P (e.g., whether P is proving membership in a language, knowledge of a witness, and so on).

> ***Proof Idea:*** The proposition is proved by contradiction. Suppose that some probabilistic polynomial-time interactive machine V^* finds witnesses after interacting with P. By the witness indistinguishability of P, it follows that V^* is performing equally well regardless of whether the witness used by P is of the form $(0, \cdot)$ or is of the form $(1, \cdot)$. Combining the programs V^* and P with the algorithm D, we derive a claw-forming algorithm (and hence a contradiction). Specifically, the claw-forming algorithm, on input $i \in \bar{I}$, uniformly selects $\sigma \in \{0, 1\}$, randomly generates $r = D(\sigma, i)$, computes $x = (i, f_i^\sigma(r))$, and emulates an interaction of V^* with P on common input x and auxiliary input (σ, r) to P. By the witness indistinguishability of P, the output of V^* is computationally independent of the value of σ. Therefore, if on common input x, machine V^* outputs a witness $w \in R(x)$, then, with probability approximately $\frac{1}{2}$, we have $w = (1 - \sigma, r')$, and a claw is formed (since $f_i^\sigma(r) = f_i^{1-\sigma}(r')$). Finally, observe that we need to analyze the performance of the claw-forming algorithm on input distribution $I(1^n)$, and in this case the common input in the emulation of (P, V^*) is distributed as in the hypothesis of the proposition. ∎

Furthermore, every $\mathcal{NP}$-relation can be "slightly modified" so that, for the modified relation, witness indistinguishability implies witness hiding. Given a relation R, the modified relation, denoted R_2, is defined by

$$R_2 \stackrel{\text{def}}{=} \{((x_1, x_2), w) : |x_1| = |x_2| \wedge \exists i \text{ s.t. } (x_i, w) \in R\} \tag{4.5}$$

Namely, w is a witness under R_2 for the instance (x_1, x_2) if and only if w is a witness under R for either x_1 or x_2.

Proposition 4.6.10: *Let R and R_2 be as before, and let P be a probabilistic polynomial-time interactive machine that is witness-indistinguishable for R_2. Then P is witness-hiding for R_2 under every distribution of pairs of hard instances induced by an efficient algorithm that randomly selects pairs in R. That is:*

Let S be a probabilistic polynomial-time algorithm that on input 1^n outputs $(x, w) \in R$, so that $|x| = n$ and X_n denotes the distribution induced on the first element in the output of $S(1^n)$. Suppose that $\{X_n\}_{n \in \mathbb{N}}$ is an ensemble of hard instances for R. Then P is witness-hiding under the ensemble $\{(X_n^{(1)}, X_n^{(2)})\}_{n \in \mathbb{N}}$, where $X_n^{(1)}$ and $X_n^{(2)}$ denote two independent copies of X_n.

Proof Idea: Let S and $\{X_n\}_{n \in \mathbb{N}}$ be in the hypothesis. Suppose that some interactive machine V^* finds witnesses, with non-negligible probability (under the foregoing distribution), after interacting with P. By the witness indistinguishability of P it follows that V^* is performing equally well regardless of whether the witness w used by P on common input (x_1, x_2) satisfies $(x_1, w) \in R$ or $(x_2, w) \in R$. Combining the programs V^* and P with the algorithm S, we derive an algorithm, denoted F^*, that finds witnesses for R (under the distribution X_n): On input $x \in L$, algorithm F^* generates at random $(x', w') = S(1^{|x|})$ and sets $\overline{x} = (x, x')$ with probability $\frac{1}{2}$, and $\overline{x} = (x', x)$ otherwise. Algorithm F^* emulates an interaction of V^* with P on common input $\overline{x}$ and auxiliary input w' to P, and when V^* outputs a witness w, algorithm F^* checks whether or not $(x, w) \in R$. By the witness indistinguishability of P, the verifier cannot tell the case in which P uses a witness to the first element of $\overline{x}$ from the case in which it uses a witness to the second. Also, by construction of F^*, if the input to F^* is distributed as X_n, then the proof system is emulated on common input $(X_n^{(1)}, X_n^{(2)})$, where $X_n^{(1)}$ and $X_n^{(2)}$ denote two independent copies of X_n. Thus, by the foregoing hypothesis, V^* finds a witness for x with non-negligible probability (taken over the distribution of x and the random choices of F^*). It follows that $\{X_n\}_{n \in \mathbb{N}}$ is not hard for R. ∎

4.6.4. Applications

Applications of the notions presented in this section are scattered in various places in this book. In particular, strong witness-indistinguishable proof systems are used in the construction of constant-round zero-knowledge arguments for $\mathcal{NP}$ (see Section 4.9.2), witness-independent proof systems are used in the zero-knowledge proof for Graph Non-Isomorphism (see Section 4.7.4.3), and witness-hiding proof systems are used for the efficient identification scheme based on factoring (in Section 4.7.5).

4.7.* Proofs of Knowledge

This section addresses the concept of "proofs of knowledge." Loosely speaking, these are proofs in which the prover asserts "knowledge" of some object (e.g., a 3-coloring of a graph) and not merely its existence (e.g., the existence of a 3-coloring of the graph, which in turn implies that the graph is in the language $G3C$). But what is meant by saying that a machine knows something? Indeed, the main thrust of this section is to address this question. Before doing so, we point out that "proofs of knowledge," and in particular zero-knowledge "proofs of knowledge," have many applications to the design of cryptographic schemes and cryptographic protocols. Some of these applications are discussed in Section 4.7.4. Of special interest is the application to identification schemes, which is discussed in Section 4.7.5. Finally, in Section 4.7.6 we introduce the notion of strong proofs of knowledge.

4.7.1. Definition

4.7.1.1. A Motivating Discussion

What does it mean to say that a MACHINE *knows something?* Any standard dictionary suggests several meanings for the verb *to know,* and most meanings are phrased with reference to *awareness*, a notion that is certainly inapplicable in our context. We must look for a *behavioristic* interpretation of the verb *to know*. Indeed, it is reasonable to link knowledge with ability to do something, be it (at the least) the ability to write down whatever one knows. Hence, we shall say that a machine knows a string α if it *can* output the string α. But this seems total nonsense: A machine has a well-defined output – either the output equals α or it does not. *So what can be meant by saying that a machine can do something?* Loosely speaking, it means that the machine can be *easily modified* so that it will do whatever is claimed. More precisely, it means that there exists an *efficient* machine that, using the original machine as a black box, outputs whatever is claimed.

So much for defining the "knowledge of machines." Yet, whatever a machine knows or does not know is "its own business." What can be of interest and reference *to the outside* is the question of what can be deduced about the knowledge of a machine after interacting with it. Hence, we are interested in proofs of knowledge (rather than in mere knowledge).

For the sake of simplicity, let us consider a concrete question: *How can a machine prove that it knows a 3-coloring of a graph?* An obvious way is simply to send the 3-coloring to the verifier. Yet we claim that applying Construction 4.4.7 (i.e., the zero-knowledge proof system for $G3C$) sufficiently many times results in an alternative way of proving knowledge of a 3-coloring of the graph.

Loosely speaking, we say that an interactive machine V constitutes a *verifier for knowledge* of 3-coloring if the probability that the verifier is convinced by a machine P to accept the graph G is inversely proportional to the difficulty of extracting a 3-coloring of G when using machine P as a black box. Namely, the extraction of the 3-coloring is done by an oracle machine, called an *extractor*, that is given access to a function specifying the behavior of P (i.e., the messages it sends in response to particular messages it may receive). We require that the (expected) running time of the extractor, on input G and with access to an oracle specifying P's messages, be inversely related (by a factor polynomial in $|G|$) to the probability that P convinces V to accept G. In case P always convinces V to accept G, the extractor runs in expected polynomial time. The same holds in case P convinces V to accept with noticeable probability. (We stress that the latter special cases do not suffice for a satisfactory definition; see advanced comment in Section 4.7.1.4.)

4.7.1.2. Technical Preliminaries

Let $R \subseteq \{0, 1\}^* \times \{0, 1\}^*$ be a binary relation. Then $R(x) \overset{\text{def}}{=} \{s : (x, s) \in R\}$ and $L_R \overset{\text{def}}{=} \{x : \exists s \text{ s.t. } (x, s) \in R\}$. If $(x, s) \in R$, then we call s a *solution* for x. We say that R is *polynomially bounded* if there exists a polynomial p such that $|s| \leq p(|x|)$ for all $(x, s) \in R$. We say that R is an $\mathcal{NP}$-*relation* if R is polynomially bounded and, in addition, there exists a polynomial-time algorithm for deciding membership in R (indeed, it follows that $L_R \in \mathcal{NP}$). In the sequel, we confine ourselves to polynomially bounded relations. In fact, all the applications presented in this book refer to $\mathcal{NP}$-relations.

We wish to be able to consider in a uniform manner all potential provers, without making distinctions based on their running time, internal structure, and so forth. Yet we observe that these interactive machines can be given auxiliary input that will enable them to "know" and to prove more. Likewise, they may have the good fortune to select a random input that will be more enabling than another. Hence, statements concerning the knowledge of the prover refer not only to the prover's program but also to the specific auxiliary and random inputs it receives. Therefore, we fix an interactive machine as well as all the inputs (i.e., the common input, the auxiliary input, and the random input) to this machine. For such a prover + inputs template, we consider both the acceptance probability (of the verifier) when interacting with this template and the use of this template as an oracle to a "knowledge extractor." This motivates the following definition.

Definition 4.7.1 (Message-Specification Function): *Denote by $P_{x,y,r}(\overline{m})$ the message sent by machine P on common input x, auxiliary input y, and random input r, after receiving messages $\overline{m}$. The function $P_{x,y,r}$ is called the **message-specification function** of machine P with common input x, auxiliary input y, and random input r.*

An oracle machine with access to the function $P_{x,y,r}$ will represent the knowledge of machine P on common input x, auxiliary input y, and random input r. This oracle machine, called the knowledge extractor, will try to find a solution to x (i.e., an $s \in R(x)$). The running time of the extractor will be required to be inversely related to the corresponding acceptance probability (of the verifier when interacting with P on common input x and when P has auxiliary input y and random input r.)

4.7.1.3. Knowledge Verifiers

Now that all the machinery is ready, we present the definition of a system for proofs of knowledge. Actually, the definition is a generalization (to be motivated by the subsequent applications) in which we allow an error parameter specified by the function κ. At first reading, one can set the function κ to be identically zero.

> **Definition 4.7.2 (System for Proofs of Knowledge):** *Let R be a binary relation and* $\kappa : \mathbb{N} \to [0, 1]$. *We say that an interactive function V is a* **knowledge verifier** *for the relation R with* **knowledge error** κ *if the following two conditions hold:*
>
> - Non-triviality: *There exists an interactive machine P such that for every* $(x, y) \in R$ *all possible interactions of V with P on common input x and auxiliary input y are accepting.*
> - Validity (with error κ): *There exists a polynomial* $q(\cdot)$ *and a probabilistic oracle machine K such that for every interactive function P, every* $x \in L_R$, *and every* $y, r \in \{0, 1\}^*$, *machine K satisfies the following condition:*
>
>> *Denote by* $p(x, y, r)$ *the probability that the interactive machine V accepts, on input x, when interacting with the prover specified by* $P_{x,y,r}$. *If* $p(x, y, r) > \kappa(|x|)$, *then, on input x and with access to oracle* $P_{x,y,r}$, *machine K outputs a solution* $s \in R(x)$ *within an expected number of steps bounded by*
>>
>> $$\frac{q(|x|)}{p(x, y, r) - \kappa(|x|)}$$
>
> *The oracle machine K is called a* universal knowledge extractor.

When $\kappa(\cdot)$ *is identically zero, we simply say that V is a* knowledge verifier for the relation R. *An interactive pair* (P, V) *such that V is a knowledge verifier for a relation R and P is a machine satisfying the non-triviality condition (with respect to V and R) is called a* system for proofs of knowledge for the relation R.

An alternative formulation of the validity condition follows. It postulates the existence of a probabilistic oracle machine K (as before). However, instead of requiring $K^{P_{x,y,r}}(x)$ to *always* output a solution within an expected time inversely proportional to $p(x, y, r) - \kappa(|x|)$, the alternative requires $K^{P_{x,y,r}}(x)$ to run in expected *polynomial time* and output a solution with probability at least $p(x, y, r) - \kappa(|x|)$. In fact, we can further relax the alternative formulation by requiring that a solution be output with probability at least $(p(x, y, r) - \kappa(|x|))/\text{poly}(|x|)$.

> **Definition 4.7.3 (Validity with Error κ, Alternative Formulation):** *Let V,* $P_{x,y,r}$ *(with* $x \in L_R$*), and* $p(x, y, r)$ *be as in Definition 4.7.2. We say that V* **satisfies the alternative validity condition with error** κ *if there exists a probabilistic oracle machine K and a positive polynomial q such that on input x and with access to oracle* $P_{x,y,r}$, *machine K runs in expected polynomial time and outputs a solution* $s \in R(x)$ *with probability at least* $(p(x, y, r) - \kappa(|x|))/q(|x|)$.

The two formulations of validity are equivalent in the case of $\mathcal{NP}$-relations. The idea underlying the equivalence is that, in the current context, success probability and expected running time can be converted from one to the other.

Proposition 4.7.4: *Let R be an $\mathcal{NP}$-relation, and let V be an interactive machine. Referring to this relation R, machine V satisfies (with error κ) the validity condition of Definition 4.7.2 if and only if V satisfies (with error κ) the alternative validity condition of Definition 4.7.3.*

Proof Sketch: Suppose that V satisfies the alternative formulation (with error κ), and let K be an adequate extractor and q an adequate polynomial. Using the hypothesis that R is an $\mathcal{NP}$-relation, it follows that when invoking K we can determine whether or not K has succeeded. Thus, we can iteratively invoke K until it succeeds. If K succeeds with probability $s(x, y, r) \geq (p(x, y, r) - \kappa(|x|))/q(|x|)$, then the expected number of invocations is $1/s(x, y, r)$, which is as required in Definition 4.7.2.

Suppose that V satisfies (with error κ) the validity requirement of Definition 4.7.2, and let K be an adequate extractor and q an adequate polynomial (such that K runs in expected time $q(|x|)/(p(x, y, r) - \kappa(|x|))$). Let p be a polynomial bounding the length of solutions for R (i.e., $(x, s) \in R$ implies $|s| \leq p(|x|)$). Then we proceed with up to $p(|x|)$ iterations: In the ith iteration, we emulate the computation of $K^{P_{x,y,r}}(x)$ with time bound $2^{i+1} \cdot q(|x|)$. In case the current iteration yields a solution, we halt outputting this solution. Otherwise, with probability $\frac{1}{2}$, we continue to the next iteration (and with probability $\frac{1}{2}$ we halt with a special failure symbol). In case the last iteration is completed without obtaining a solution, we simply find a solution by exhaustive search (using time $2^{p(|x|)} \cdot \text{poly}(|x|)$). Observe that the ith iteration is executed with probability at most $2^{-(i-1)}$, and so our expected running time is at most

$$\sum_{i=1}^{p(|x|)} 2^{-(i-1)} \cdot (2^{i+1} \cdot q(|x|)) + 2^{-p(|x|)} \cdot (2^{p(|x|)} \cdot \text{poly}(|x|))$$

$$= 4 \cdot p(|x|) \cdot q(|x|) + \text{poly}(|x|)$$

To evaluate the success probability of the new extractor, note that the probability that $K^{P_{x,y,r}}(x)$ will run for more than twice its expected running time (i.e., twice $q(|x|)/(p(x, y, r) - \kappa(|x|))$) is less than $\frac{1}{2}$. Also observe that in iteration $i \stackrel{\text{def}}{=} -\log_2(p(x, y, r) - \kappa(|x|))$ we emulate these many steps (i.e., $2q(|x|)/(p(x, y, r) - \kappa(|x|))$ steps). Thus, the probability that we can extract a solution in one of the first i iterations is at least $\frac{1}{2} \cdot 2^{-(i-1)} = p(x, y, r) - \kappa(|x|)$, as required in the alternative formulation. ∎

Comment. The proof of Proposition 4.7.4 actually establishes that the formulation of Definition 4.7.2 implies the formulation of Definition 4.7.3 with $q \equiv 1$. Thus, the formulation of Definition 4.7.3 with $q \equiv 1$ is equivalent to its general formulation (i.e., with an arbitrary polynomial q). We shall use this fact in the proofs of Propositions 4.7.5 and 4.7.6.

4.7.1.4. Discussion

In view of Proposition 4.7.4, we can freely use either of the two formulations of validity. The formulation of Definition 4.7.2 typically is more convenient when analyzing the effect of a proof of knowledge as a sub-protocol, whereas the formulation of Definition 4.7.3 typically is more convenient when demonstrating that a given system is a proof of knowledge. We mention that variants of Proposition 4.7.4 also hold when R is not an $\mathcal{NP}$-relation (see Exercise 29).

A Reflection. The notion of a proof of knowledge (and, more so, the notion of a knowledge extractor used in formalizing it) is related to the simulation paradigm. This relation is evident in applications in which the knowledge verifier takes some action $\mathcal{A}$ after being convinced that the knowledge prover knows $\mathcal{K}$, where action $\mathcal{A}$ is such that it causes no harm to the knowledge verifier if the knowledge prover indeed knows $\mathcal{K}$. Following the simulation paradigm, our definition asserts that if action $\mathcal{A}$ is taken after the verifier becomes convinced that the prover knows $\mathcal{K}$, then no harm is caused, since in some sense we can simulate a situation in which the prover actually knows $\mathcal{K}$. Indeed, using the knowledge extractor, we can simulate the prover's view of the entire interaction (i.e., the proof process and the action taken afterward by the convinced verifier): In case the prover fails, action $\mathcal{A}$ is not taken, and so the entire interaction is easy to simulate. In case the prover succeeds in convincing the verifier, we extract the relevant knowledge $\mathcal{K}$ and reach a situation in which action $\mathcal{A}$ causes no harm (i.e., $\mathcal{A}$ can be simulated based on $\mathcal{K}$).

About Soundness. In the foregoing definitions, we imposed no requirements regarding what happens when the knowledge verifier for R is invoked on common input not in L_R. The natural requirement is that on input $x \notin L_R$ the verifier will accept with probability at most $\kappa(|x|)$. This holds in many natural cases, but not in the conclusion of Proposition 4.7.6. See further comments in Sections 4.7.3–4.7.6.

An Advanced Comment. A key feature of both formulations of validity is that they handle all possible values of $p(x, y, r)$ in a "uniform" fashion. This is crucial to most applications (e.g., see Section 4.7.4) in which a proof of knowledge is used as a sub-protocol (rather than as the end protocol). Typically, in the former applications (i.e., using a proof of knowledge as a sub-protocol), the knowledge error function is required to be negligible (or even zero). In such cases, we need to deal with all possible values of $p(x, y, r)$ that are not negligible, but we do not know a priori the value of $p(x, y, r)$. We warn that the fact that $p(x, y, r)$ is not negligible (as a function of $|x|$) does *not* mean that it is noticeable (as a function of $|x|$).[19]

---

[19] Recall that a function $\mu : \mathbb{N} \to \mathbb{R}$ is negligible if for every positive polynomial p and all sufficiently large n's, it holds that $\mu(n) < 1/p(n)$, whereas a function $\nu : \mathbb{N} \to \mathbb{R}$ is noticeable if there exists a polynomial p such that for all sufficiently large n's, it holds that $\nu(n) > 1/p(n)$. A function $f : \mathbb{N} \to \mathbb{R}$ may be neither negligible nor noticeable: For example, consider the function f, defined by $f(n) \overset{\text{def}}{=} 2^{-n}$ if n is odd, and $f(n) \overset{\text{def}}{=} n^{-2}$ otherwise.

4.7.2. Reducing the Knowledge Error

The knowledge error can be reduced by sequential repetitions of the proof system. Specifically, the error drops exponentially with the number of repetitions.

Proposition 4.7.5: *Let R be a polynomially bounded relation, and let $t : \mathbb{N} \to \mathbb{N}$ be a polynomially bounded function. Suppose that (P, V) is a system for proof of knowledge for the relation R with knowledge error κ. Then the proof system that results by repeating (P, V) sequentially $t(|x|)$ times on common input x is a system for proof of knowledge for the relation R with knowledge error $\kappa'(n) \stackrel{\text{def}}{=} \kappa(n)^{t(n)}$.*

Proof Sketch: Let (P', V') denote the protocol obtained by t sequential repetitions of (P, V), as in the proposition. To analyze the validity property of V', we use the formulation of Definition 4.7.3. Given an extractor K_1 for the basic system, we construct an extractor K for the composed system (P', V') as follows. On input x, machine K uniformly selects $i \in \{1, \ldots, t(|x|)\}$, emulates the first $i - 1$ iterations of the basic proof system (P, V), and invokes K_1 with oracle access to the residual prover determined by the transcript of these $i - 1$ iterations. That is, given oracle access to a prover strategy for the composed proof system, we first use it to emulate the first $i - 1$ iterations in (P', V'), resulting in a transcript α. We then define a prover strategy for the basic proof system by considering the way in which the composed-system prover behaves in the ith iteration given that α is the transcript of the first $i - 1$ iterations. Using this (basic-system) prover strategy as oracle, we invoke K_1 in an attempt to extract a solution to x.

It is left to analyze the success probability of extractor K for fixed $x \in L_R$ and y and r as before. Let $t \stackrel{\text{def}}{=} t(|x|)$, $\kappa \stackrel{\text{def}}{=} \kappa(|x|)$, and $\delta \stackrel{\text{def}}{=} p(x, y, r) - \kappa^t$. (We shall omit this fixed (x, y, r) also from the following notations.) Our aim is to show that K extracts a solution for x with probability at least $\delta/\text{poly}(|x|)$. Toward this goal, let us denote by a_{i-1} the probability that the verifier accepts in each of the first $i - 1$ iterations of the composed proof system. For every possible transcript α of the first $i - 1$ iterations, we denote by $p'(\alpha)$ the probability that the verifier accepts in the ith iteration when α describes the transcript of the first $i - 1$ iterations. Note that if K tries to extract a solution after emulating $i - 1$ iterations resulting in transcript α, then its success probability is at least $p'(\alpha) - \kappa$. Let c_i be the expected value of $p'(\alpha)$ when α is selected at random among all $(i - 1)$-iteration transcripts in which the verifier accepts. Then $a_i = a_{i-1} \cdot c_i$, and the probability that K extracts a solution after emulating $i - 1$ iterations is at least $a_{i-1} \cdot (c_i - \kappa)$.

Claim: Either $c_1 - \kappa \geq \delta/t$ or there exists an $i \geq 2$ such that $a_{i-1} \cdot (c_i - \kappa) > \delta/t$.

In both cases we have established an adequate lower bound on the success probability of K; that is, K succeeds with probability at least δ/t^2, where an extra factor of t is to account for the probability that K will select a good i.

Proof: Observe that if $a_1 = c_1 < \kappa + (\delta/t)$, then there must exist an $i \geq 2$ such that $a_{i-1} < \kappa^{i-1} + ((i - 1)\delta/t)$ and $a_i \geq \kappa^i + (i\delta/t)$, since $a_t = \kappa^t + \delta$. Using

—— **267** ——

this i, we have

$$a_{i-1} \cdot (c_i - \kappa) = a_i - a_{i-1} \cdot \kappa$$
$$> \left(\kappa^i + \frac{i\delta}{t} \right) - \left(\kappa^i + \frac{(i-1)\delta}{t} \right)$$
$$= \frac{\delta}{t}$$

The claim follows, and so does the proposition. ∎

What About Parallel Composition? As usual (see Section 4.3.4), the effect of parallel composition is more complex than the effect of sequential composition. Consequently, a result analogous to Proposition 4.7.5 is not known to hold in general. Still, parallel execution of some popular zero-knowledge proofs of knowledge can be shown to reduce the knowledge error exponentially in the number of repetitions; see Exercise 27.

Getting Rid of Tiny Error. For $\mathcal{NP}$-relations, whenever the knowledge error is smaller than the probability of finding a solution by a random guess, one can set the knowledge error to zero.

Proposition 4.7.6: *Let R be an $\mathcal{NP}$-relation, and let $q(\cdot)$ be a polynomial such that $(x, y) \in R$ implies $|y| \leq q(|x|)$. Suppose that (P, V) is a system for proofs of knowledge for the relation R, with knowledge error $\kappa(n) \overset{\text{def}}{=} 2^{-q(n)}$. Then (P, V) is a system for proofs of knowledge for the relation R (with zero knowledge error).*

Proof Sketch: Again, we use the formulation of Definition 4.7.3. Given a knowledge extractor K substantiating the hypothesis, we construct a new knowledge extractor that first invokes K, and in case K fails, it uniformly selects a $q(|x|)$-bit-long string and outputs it if and only if it is a valid solution for x. Let $p(x, y, r)$ be as in Definitions 4.7.2 and 4.7.3, and let $s(x, y, r) \geq p(x, y, r) - \kappa(|x|)$ denote the success probability of $K^{P_{x,y,r}}(x)$. Then the new knowledge extractor succeeds with probability at least

$$s'(x, y, r) \overset{\text{def}}{=} s(x, y, r) + (1 - s(x, y, r)) \cdot 2^{-q(|x|)}$$

The reader can easily verify that $s'(x, y, r) \geq p(x, y, r)/2$ (by separately considering the cases $p(x, y, r) \geq 2 \cdot \kappa(|x|)$ and $p(x, y, r) \leq 2 \cdot \kappa(|x|)$), and the proposition follows. ∎

4.7.3. Zero-Knowledge Proofs of Knowledge for $\mathcal{NP}$

The zero-knowledge proof systems for Graph Isomorphism (i.e., Construction 4.3.8) and for Graph 3-Coloring (i.e., Construction 4.4.7) are in fact proofs of knowledge (with some knowledge error) for the corresponding languages. Specifically, Construction 4.3.8 is a proof of knowledge of an isomorphism with knowledge error $\frac{1}{2}$, whereas

Construction 4.4.7 (when applied on common input $G = (V, E)$) is a proof of knowledge of a 3-coloring with knowledge error $1 - \frac{1}{|E|}$; see Exercise 26. By iterating each construction sufficiently many times, we can get the knowledge error to be exponentially small (see Proposition 4.7.5). In fact, using Proposition 4.7.6, we get proofs of knowledge with zero error. In particular, we have the following:

Theorem 4.7.7: *Assuming the existence of (non-uniformly) one-way functions, every $\mathcal{NP}$-relation has a zero-knowledge system for proofs of knowledge. Furthermore, inputs not in the corresponding language are accepted by the verifier with exponentially vanishing probability.*

4.7.4. Applications

We briefly review some of the applications of (zero-knowledge) proofs of knowledge. Typically, zero-knowledge proofs of knowledge are used for "mutual disclosure" of the same information. Suppose that Alice and Bob both claim that they know something (e.g., a 3-coloring of a common-input graph), but each is doubtful of the other's claim. Employing a zero-knowledge proof of knowledge in both directions is indeed a (conceptually) simple solution to the problem of convincing each other of their knowledge.

Before describing the applications, let us briefly comment on how their security is proved. Typically, a zero-knowledge proof of knowledge is used as a sub-protocol, and rejecting in this sub-protocol means that the verifying party detects cheating. The proof of security for the high-level protocol is by a simulation argument that utilizes the knowledge extractor, but invokes it only in case the verifying party does not detect cheating. Our definition of (the validity condition of) proofs of knowledge guarantees that the simulation will run in expected polynomial time, regardless of the (a priori unknown) probability that the verifying party will accept.

In all applications, the proof of knowledge employed has negligible soundness error (i.e., inputs not in the corresponding language are accepted by the verifier with negligible probability).

4.7.4.1. Non-Oblivious Commitment Schemes

When using a commitment scheme, the receiver is guaranteed that after the commit phase the sender is committed to at most one value (in the sense that it can later "reveal" only this value). Yet the receiver is not guaranteed that the sender "knows" to what value the sender is committed. Such a guarantee can be useful in many settings and can be obtained by using a proof of knowledge. For more details, see Section 4.9.2.

4.7.4.2. Protecting against Chosen Message Attacks

An obvious way of protecting against chosen message attacks on a (public-key) encryption scheme is to augment the ciphertext by a zero-knowledge proof of knowledge of the cleartext. Thus, the benefit (to the adversary) of a chosen message attack is essentially eliminated. However, one should note that the resulting encryption scheme employs bidirectional communication between the sender and the receiver (of the encrypted message). (Definitions and alternative constructions of encryption schemes secure against chosen message attacks will be presented in Chapter 5 of Volume 2.)

4.7.4.3. A Zero-Knowledge Proof System for *GNI*

The interactive proof of Graph Non-Isomorphism (*GNI*) presented in Construction 4.2.8 is not zero-knowledge (unless $GNI \in \mathcal{BPP}$). A cheating verifier can construct an arbitrary graph H and learn whether or not H is isomorphic to the first input graph by sending H as a query to the prover. There is an even more appealing refutation of the claim that Construction 4.2.8 is auxiliary-input zero-knowledge (e.g., the verifier can check whether or not its auxiliary input is isomorphic to one of the common-input graphs). We observe, however, that Construction 4.2.8 "would have been zero-knowledge" if the verifier had always known the answers to its queries (as is the case for an honest verifier). Thus, we can modify Construction 4.2.8 to obtain a zero-knowledge proof for *GNI* by having the verifier prove to the prover that he (i.e., the verifier) knows the answer to his query graph (i.e., that he knows an isomorphism to the appropriate input graph), and the prover answers the query only if she is convinced of this claim. Certainly, the verifier's proof of knowledge should *not* yield the answer (otherwise the prover could use that information in order to cheat, thus foiling the soundness requirement). If the verifier's proof of knowledge is perfect zero-knowledge, then certainly it does not yield the answer. In fact, it suffices that the verifier's proof of knowledge is *witness-independent* (as defined in Section 4.6).

4.7.5. Proofs of Identity (Identification Schemes)

Identification schemes are useful in large distributed systems in which the users are not acquainted with one another. In such distributed systems, one wishes to allow users to authenticate themselves to other users. This goal is achieved by identification schemes, defined next. In the sequel, we shall also see that identification schemes are intimately related to proofs of knowledge. We hint that a person's identity can be linked to his ability to do something and in particular to his ability to prove knowledge of some sort.

4.7.5.1. Definition

Loosely speaking, an identification scheme consists of a *public file* containing *records* for each user and an *identification protocol*. Each (public) record consists of the name (or identity) of a user and auxiliary *identification information* to be used when invoking the identification protocol (as discussed later). The public file is established and maintained by a trusted party that vouches for the authenticity of the records (i.e., that each record has been submitted by the user whose name is specified in it). All users can read the public file at all times. Alternatively, the trusted party can supply each user with a signed copy of its public record. Suppose, now, that Alice wishes to prove to Bob that it is indeed she who is communicating with him. To this end, Alice invokes the identification protocol, with the (public-file) record corresponding to her name as a parameter. Bob verifies that the parameter in use indeed matches Alice's public record and proceeds by executing his role in the protocol. It is required that Alice always be able to convince Bob (that she is indeed Alice), whereas nobody else can fool Bob into believing that she/he is Alice. Furthermore, Carol should not be able to impersonate Alice even after receiving polynomially many proofs of identity from Alice.

The identification information is generated by Alice using a randomized algorithm. Clearly, if the identification information is to be of any use, then Alice must keep secret the random coins she used to generate her record. Furthermore, Alice must use these stored coins during the execution of the identification protocol, but this must be done in a way that will not allow anyone else to impersonate her later.

Conventions. In the following definition, we adopt the formalism and notations of interactive machines with auxiliary input (presented in Definition 4.2.10). We recall that when M is an interactive machine, we denote by $M(y)$ the machine that results by fixing y to be the auxiliary input of machine M. In the following definition, n is the security parameter, and we assume with little loss of generality that the names (i.e., identities) of the users are encoded by strings of length n. If A is a probabilistic algorithm and $x, r \in \{0, 1\}^*$, then $A_r(x)$ denotes the output of algorithm A on input x and random coins r.

Motivation. Algorithm I in the following definition corresponds to the procedure used to generate identification information, and (P, V) corresponds to the identification protocol itself. The interactive machines B' and B'' represent two components of the adversary behavior (i.e., interacting with the user in order to extract its secrets and later trying to impersonate it). On a first reading, the reader can ignore algorithm B' and the random variable T_n (in the security condition). Doing so, however, yields a weaker condition that typically is unsatisfactory.

> **Definition 4.7.8 (Identification Scheme):** *An **identification scheme** consists of a pair (I, Π), where I is a probabilistic polynomial-time algorithm and $\Pi = (P, V)$ is a pair of probabilistic polynomial-time interactive machines satisfying the following conditions:*
>
> - Viability: *For every $n \in \mathbb{N}$, every $\alpha \in \{0, 1\}^n$, and every $s \in \{0, 1\}^{\mathrm{poly}(n)}$,*
>
> $$\Pr\left[\langle P(s), V\rangle(\alpha, I_s(\alpha)) = 1\right] = 1$$
>
> - Security: *For every pair of probabilistic polynomial-time interactive machines B' and B'', every polynomial $p(\cdot)$, all sufficiently large $n \in \mathbb{N}$, every $\alpha \in \{0, 1\}^n$, and every z,*
>
> $$\Pr\left[\langle B''(z, T_n), V\rangle(\alpha, I_{S_n}(\alpha)) = 1\right] < \frac{1}{p(n)}$$
>
> *where S_n is a random variable uniformly distributed over $\{0, 1\}^{\mathrm{poly}(n)}$ and T_n is a random variable describing the output of $B'(z)$ after interacting with $P(S_n)$, on common input $(\alpha, I_{S_n}(\alpha))$, for polynomially many times.*
>
> *Algorithm I is called the **information-generating algorithm**, and the pair (P, V) is called the **identification protocol**.*

Hence, to use the identification scheme, a user, say Alice, whose identity is encoded by the string α, should first uniformly select a secret string s, compute $i \stackrel{\text{def}}{=} I_s(\alpha)$, ask the trusted third party to place the record (α, i) in the public file, and store the string s in a safe place. The viability condition asserts that Alice can convince Bob of her identity by executing the identification protocol: Alice invokes the program P using the stored string s as auxiliary input, and Bob uses the program V and makes sure that the common input is the public record containing α (which is in the public file). Ignoring for a moment the algorithm B' and the random variable T_n, the security condition implies that it is infeasible for a party to impersonate Alice if all that this party has is the public record of Alice and some unrelated auxiliary information (represented by the auxiliary input z). However, such a security condition may not suffice in many applications, since a user wishing to impersonate Alice may ask her first to prove her identity to him/her. The (full) security condition asserts that even if Alice has proved her identity to Carol many times in the past, still it is infeasible for Carol to impersonate Alice. We stress that Carol cannot impersonate Alice to Bob *provided that she cannot interact concurrently with both Alice and* Bob. In case this condition does not hold, nothing is guaranteed (and indeed Carol can easily impersonate Alice by referring Bob's questions to Alice and answering as Alice does).

4.7.5.2. Identification Schemes and Proofs of Knowledge

A natural way to determine a person's identity is to ask him/her to supply a proof of knowledge of a fact that the person is supposed to know. Let us consider a specific (but in fact quite generic) example.

Construction 4.7.9 (Identification Scheme Based on a One-Way Function):
Let f be a function. On input an identity $\alpha \in \{0, 1\}^n$, the information-generating algorithm *uniformly selects a string $s \in \{0, 1\}^n$ and outputs $f(s)$. (The pair $(\alpha, f(s))$ is the public record for the user named α.) The* identification protocol *consists of a proof of knowledge of the inverse of the second element in the public record. Namely, in order to prove its identity, user α proves that it knows a string s such that $f(s) = r$, where (α, r) is a record in the public file. (The proof of knowledge in use is allowed to have negligible knowledge error.)*

Proposition 4.7.10: *If f is a one-way function and the proof of knowledge in use is zero-knowledge, then Construction 4.7.9 constitutes an identification scheme.*

Hence, identification schemes exist if one-way functions exist. Practical identification schemes can be constructed based on specific intractability assumptions. For example, assuming the intractability of factoring, the so-called Fiat-Shamir identification scheme, which is actually a proof of knowledge of a modular square root, follows.

Construction 4.7.11 (The Fiat-Shamir Identification Scheme, Basic Version):
On input an identity $\alpha \in \{0, 1\}^n$, the information-generating algorithm *uniformly selects a composite number N that is the product of two n-bit-long primes and a residue s mod N, and it outputs the pair $(N, s^2 \bmod N)$. (The pair $(\alpha, (N, s^2$*

mod N)) is the public record for user α.) *The identification protocol consists of a proof of knowledge of the corresponding modular square root. Namely, in order to prove its identity, user α proves that it knows a modular square root of $r \stackrel{\text{def}}{=} s^2 \bmod N$, where $(\alpha, (r, N))$ is a record in the public file. (Again, negligible knowledge error is allowed.)*

The proof of knowledge of modular square roots is analogous to the proof system for Graph Isomorphism presented in Construction 4.3.8. Namely, in order to prove knowledge of a square root of $r \equiv s^2 \pmod{N}$, the prover repeats the following steps sufficiently many times:

Construction 4.7.12 (Atomic Proof of Knowledge of Modular Square Root):
This refers to the common input (r, N), where the prescribed prover has auxiliary input s such that $r \equiv s^2 \pmod{N}$:

- *The prover randomly selects a residue g modulo N and sends $h \stackrel{\text{def}}{=} g^2 \bmod N$ to the verifier.*
- *The verifier uniformly selects $\sigma \in \{0, 1\}$ and sends it to the prover.*
- Motivation: *In case $\sigma = 0$, the verifier asks for a square root of $h \bmod N$, whereas in case $\sigma = 1$ the verifier asks for a square root of $h \cdot r \bmod N$. In the sequel, we assume, without loss of generality, that $\sigma \in \{0, 1\}$.*
- *The prover replies with a $\stackrel{\text{def}}{=} g \cdot s^{\sigma} \bmod N$.*
- *The verifier accepts if and only if the messages h and a sent by the prover satisfy $a^2 \equiv h \cdot r^{\sigma} \bmod N$.*

When Construction 4.7.12 is repeated k times, either sequentially or in parallel, the resulting protocol constitutes a proof of knowledge of a modular square root, with knowledge error 2^{-k} (see Exercise 27). In case these repetitions are conducted sequentially, the resulting protocol is zero-knowledge. Yet, for use in Construction 4.7.11, it suffices that the proof of knowledge be *witness-hiding* under the relevant distribution (see Definition 4.6.5), even when polynomially many executions take place concurrently (in an asynchronous manner). Hence the resulting identification scheme has constant-round complexity. We remark that for identification purposes it suffices to perform Construction 4.7.12 super-logarithmically many times. Furthermore, fewer repetitions can also be of value: When applying Construction 4.7.12 for $k = O(\log n)$ times and using the resulting protocol in Construction 4.7.11, we get a scheme (for identification) in which impersonation can occur with probability at most 2^{-k}.

4.7.5.3. Identification Schemes and Proofs of Ability

As hinted earlier, a proof of knowledge of a string (i.e., the ability to output the string) is a special case of a proof of ability to do something. It turns out that identification schemes can also be based on the more general concept of proofs of ability. We avoid defining this concept and confine ourself to two "natural" examples of using a proof of ability as a basis for identification.

It is everyday practice to identify people by their ability to produce their signatures. This practice can be carried into the digital setting. Specifically, the public record of

`Alice` consists of her name and the verification key corresponding to her secret signing key in a predetermined signature scheme. The identification protocol consists of `Alice` signing a random message chosen by the verifier.

A second popular means of identification consists of identifying people by their ability to answer personal questions correctly. A digital analogue of this common practice follows. We use pseudorandom functions (see Section 3.6) and zero-knowledge proofs (of membership in a language). The public record of `Alice` consists of her name and a "commitment" to a randomly selected pseudorandom function (e.g., either via a string-commitment to the index of the function or via a pair consisting of a random domain element and the value of the function at that point). The identification protocol consists of `Alice` returning the value of the function at a random location chosen by the verifier and supplying a zero-knowledge proof that the value returned indeed matches the function appearing in the public record. We remark that the digital implementation offers more security than the everyday practice. In the everyday setting, the verifier is given the list of all possible question-and-answer pairs and is trusted not to try to impersonate the user. Here we have replaced the possession of the correct answers with a zero-knowledge proof that the answer is correct.

4.7.6. Strong Proofs of Knowledge

Definitions 4.7.2 and 4.7.3 rely in a fundamental way on the notion of *expected* running time. Specifically, these definitions refer to the *expected* running time of the knowledge extractor. For reasons discussed in Section 4.3.1.6, we prefer to avoid the notion of *expected* running time whenever possible. Thus, we consider next a more stringent definition in which the knowledge extractor is required to run in *strict* polynomial time, rather than in *expected* time inversely proportional to the acceptance probability (as in Definition 4.7.2). (We also take the opportunity to postulate, in the definition, that instances not in L_R are accepted with negligible probability; this is done by extending the scope of the validity condition also to x's not in L_R.)

4.7.6.1. Definition

Definition 4.7.13 (System of Strong Proofs of Knowledge): *Let R be a binary relation. We say that an interactive function V is a* **strong knowledge verifier** **for the relation** *R if the following two conditions hold:*

- Non-triviality: *As in Definition 4.7.2.*
- Strong validity: *There exists a negligible function* $\mu : \mathbb{N} \to [0, 1]$ *and a pro-babilistic* (strict) polynomial-time *oracle machine K such that for every inter-active function P and every* $x, y, r \in \{0, 1\}^*$, *machine K satisfies the following condition:*

> *Let* $p(x, y, r)$ *and* $P_{x,y,r}$ *be as in Definition 4.7.2. If* $p(x, y, r) > \mu(|x|)$, *then on input x and access to oracle* $P_{x,y,r}$, *machine K outputs a solution* $s \in R(x)$ *with probability at least* $1 - \mu(|x|)$.

The oracle machine K is called a **strong knowledge extractor.**

An interactive pair (P, V) such that V is a strong knowledge verifier for a relation R, and P is a machine satisfying the non-triviality condition (with respect to V and R), is called a **system for strong proofs of knowledge** *for the relation R.*

Our choice of using μ (rather than a different negligible function μ') as an upper bound on the failure probability of the extractor (in the strong validity requirement) is immaterial. Furthermore, for $\mathcal{NP}$-relations, requiring the existence of an extractor that succeeds with noticeable probability is equivalent to requiring the existence of an extractor that fails with exponentially vanishing probability. (That is, in the case of $\mathcal{NP}$-relations, the failure probability can be decreased by successive applications of the extractor.) This *strong validity* requirement is stronger than the validity (with error μ) requirement of Definition 4.7.2, in two ways:

1. The extractor in Definition 4.7.13 runs in (strict) polynomial time, regardless of the value of $p(x, y, r)$, whereas the extractor in Definition 4.7.2 runs in expected time $\mathrm{poly}(n)/(p(x, y, r) - \mu(|x|))$. Note, however, that the extractor in Definition 4.7.13 is allowed to fail with probability at most $\mu(|x|)$, whereas the extractor in Definition 4.7.2 can never fail.

2. The strong validity requirement implies that $x \notin L_R$ is accepted by the verifier with probability at most $\mu(|x|)$, whereas this is not required in Definition 4.7.2. This soundness condition is natural in the context of the current definition that, unlike Definition 4.7.2, always allows for non-zero (but negligible) error probability.

4.7.6.2. An Example: Strong (ZK) Proof of Knowledge of Isomorphism

Sequentially repeating the (zero-knowledge) proof systems for Graph Isomorphism (i.e., Construction 4.3.8) sufficiently many times yields a strong proof of knowledge of isomorphism. The key observation is that each application of the basic proof system (i.e., Construction 4.3.8) results in one of two possible situations, depending on whether the verifier asks to see an isomorphism to the first or second graph. If the prover answers correctly in both cases, then we can retrieve an isomorphism between the input graphs (by composing the isomorphisms provided in the two cases). If the prover fails in both cases, then the verifier will reject regardless of what the prover does from that point on. Specifically, the preceding discussion suggests the following construction of a strong knowledge extractor (where we refer to repeating the basic proof systems n times and set $\mu(n) = 2^{-n}$).

Strong Knowledge Extractor for Graph Isomorphism. On input (G_1, G_2) and access to the prover-strategy oracle P^*, we proceed in n iterations, starting with $i = 1$. Initially, T (the transcript thus far) is empty.

1. Obtain the intermediate graph G' from the prover strategy (i.e., $G' = P^*(T)$).

2. Extract the prover's answers to both possible verifier moves. That is, for $j = 1, 2$, let $\psi_j \leftarrow P^*(T, j)$. We say that ψ_j is *correct* if it is an isomorphism between G_j and G'.

3. If both ψ_j's are correct, then $\phi \leftarrow \psi_2^{-1}\psi_1$ is an isomorphism between G_1 and G_2. In this case we output ϕ and halt.

4. In case ψ_j is correct for a single j, and $i < n$, we let $T \leftarrow (T, j)$ and proceed to the next iteration (i.e., $i \leftarrow i + 1$). Otherwise, we halt, with no output.

It can be easily verified that if this extractor halts with no output in any iteration $i < n$, then the verifier (in the real interaction) accepts with probability zero. Similarly, if the extractor halts with no output in iteration n, then the verifier (in the real interaction) accepts with probability at most 2^{-n}. Thus, whenever $p((G_1, G_2), \cdot, \cdot) > 2^{-n}$, the extractor succeeds in recovering an isomorphism between the two input graphs.

4.7.6.3. Strong (ZK) Proofs of Knowledge for $\mathcal{NP}$-Relations

A similar argument can be applied to some zero-knowledge proof systems for $\mathcal{NP}$. In particular, consider n sequential repetitions of the following basic (zero-knowledge) proof system for the *Hamiltonian-cycle* (HC) problem. We consider directed graphs (and the existence of directed Hamiltonian cycles).

Construction 4.7.14 (Basic Proof System for HC):

- Common input: *a directed graph $G = (V, E)$, with $n \stackrel{\text{def}}{=} |V|$.*
- Auxiliary input to prover: *a directed Hamiltonian cycle, $C \subset E$, in G.*
- Prover's first step (P1): *The prover selects a random permutation π of the vertices V and commits to the entries of the adjacency matrix of the resulting permuted graph. That is, it sends an n-by-n matrix of commitments such that the $(\pi(i), \pi(j))$ entry is a commitment to 1 if $(i, j) \in E$ and is a commitment to 0 otherwise.*
- Verifier's first step (V1): *The verifier uniformly selects $\sigma \in \{0, 1\}$ and sends it to the prover.*
- Motivation: *$\sigma = 0$ means that the verifier asks to check that the matrix of commitments is a legitimate one, whereas $\sigma = 1$ means that the verifier asks to reveal a Hamiltonian cycle in the permuted graph.*
- Prover's second step (P2): *If $\sigma = 0$, then the prover sends π to the verifier along with the revealing (i.e., pre-images) of all commitments. Otherwise, the prover reveals to the verifier only the commitments to entries $(\pi(i), \pi(j))$, with $(i, j) \in C$.*
- Verifier's second step (V2): *If $\sigma = 0$, then the verifier checks that the revealed graph is indeed isomorphic, via π, to G. Otherwise, the verifier simply checks that all revealed values are 1 and that the corresponding entries form a simple n-cycle. (Of course, in both cases, the verifier checks that the revealed values do fit the commitments.) The verifier accepts if and only if the corresponding condition holds.*

We claim that the protocol resulting from sequentially repeating Construction 4.7.14 n times is a (zero-knowledge) strong proof of knowledge of a Hamiltonian cycle; see Exercises 20 and 30. Because a Hamiltonian cycle is $\mathcal{NP}$-complete, we get such proof systems for any language in $\mathcal{NP}$. We mention that the known zero-knowledge strong proofs of knowledge for $\mathcal{NP}$-complete languages are all costly in terms of the round-complexity. Still, we have the following:

Theorem 4.7.15: *Assuming the existence of (non-uniformly) one-way functions, every $\mathcal{NP}$-relation has a zero-knowledge system for* strong *proofs of knowledge.*

4.8.* Computationally Sound Proofs (Arguments)

In this section we consider a relaxation of the notion of an interactive proof system. Specifically, we relax the soundness condition of interactive proof systems. Instead of requiring that it be *impossible* to fool the verifier into accepting false statements (with probability greater than some bound), we require only that it be *infeasible* to do so. We call such protocols *computationally sound proof systems* (or *arguments*). The advantage of computationally sound proof systems is that *perfect* zero-knowledge *computationally sound* proof systems can be constructed, under some reasonable complexity-assumptions, for all languages in $\mathcal{NP}$. Recall that *perfect* zero-knowledge proof systems are unlikely to exist for all languages in $\mathcal{NP}$ (see Section 4.5). Also recall that *computational* zero-knowledge proof systems do exist for all languages in $\mathcal{NP}$, provided that one-way functions exist. Hence, the previously quoted positive results exhibit some kind of a trade-off between the soundness and zero-knowledge properties of the zero-knowledge protocols of $\mathcal{NP}$. (We remark, however, that the perfect zero-knowledge computationally sound proofs for $\mathcal{NP}$ are constructed under stronger complexity-theoretic assumptions than are the ones used for the computational zero-knowledge proofs. It is indeed an interesting research project to try to construct perfect zero-knowledge computationally sound proofs for $\mathcal{NP}$ under weaker assumptions, in particular, assuming only the existence of one-way functions.)

We mention that it seems that computationally sound proof systems can be much more efficient than ordinary proof systems. Specifically, under some plausible complexity assumptions, extremely efficient computationally sound proof systems (i.e., requiring only poly-logarithmic communication and randomness) exist for any language in $\mathcal{NP}$. An analogous result cannot hold for ordinary proof systems unless $\mathcal{NP}$ is contained in deterministic quasi-polynomial time (i.e., $\mathcal{NP} \subseteq \mathrm{Dtime}(2^{\mathrm{polylog}})$).

4.8.1. Definition

The definition of computationally sound proof systems follows naturally from the foregoing discussion. The only issue to consider is that *merely* replacing the soundness condition of Definition 4.2.4 with a *computational-soundness* condition leads to an unnatural definition, since the computational power of the prover in the completeness condition (in Definition 4.2.4) is not restricted. Hence, it is natural to restrict the prover in *both* (the completeness and soundness) conditions to be an efficient one. It is crucial to interpret "efficient" as being probabilistic polynomial-time *given auxiliary input* (otherwise, only languages in $\mathcal{BPP}$ will have such proof systems). Hence, our starting point is Definition 4.2.10 (rather than Definition 4.2.4).

Definition 4.8.1 (Computationally Sound Proof System (Arguments)): *A pair of interactive machines (P, V) is called a* **computationally sound proof system**

(or an argument) **for a language** L *if both machines are polynomial-time* (with auxiliary inputs) *and the following two conditions hold:*

- Completeness: *For every $x \in L$, there exists a string y such that for every string z,*

$$\Pr[\langle P(y), V(z)\rangle(x) = 1] \geq \frac{2}{3}$$

- Computational soundness: *For every polynomial-time interactive machine B, and for all sufficiently long $x \notin L$ and every y and z,*

$$\Pr[\langle B(y), V(z)\rangle(x) = 1] \leq \frac{1}{3}$$

As usual, the error probability (in both the completeness and soundness conditions) can be reduced (from $\frac{1}{3}$) down to as much as $2^{-\text{poly}(|x|)}$ by sequentially repeating the protocol sufficiently many times; see Exercise 31. We mention that *parallel* repetitions may fail to reduce the (computational) soundness error in some cases.

4.8.2. Perfectly Hiding Commitment Schemes

The thrust of the current section is toward a method for constructing *perfect* zero-knowledge *arguments* for every language in $\mathcal{NP}$. This method makes essential use of the concept of a commitment scheme with a *perfect* (or "information-theoretic") secrecy property. Hence, we start with an exposition of such perfectly hiding commitment schemes. We remark that such schemes may also be useful in other settings (e.g., other settings in which the receiver of the commitment is computationally unbounded; see, for example, Section 4.9.1).

The difference between commitment schemes (as defined in Section 4.4.1) and perfectly hiding commitment schemes (defined later) consists in a switch in the scope of the secrecy and unambiguity requirements: In commitment schemes (see Definition 4.4.1), the secrecy requirement is computational (i.e., refers only to probabilistic polynomial-time adversaries), whereas the unambiguity requirement is information-theoretic (and makes no reference to the computational power of the adversary). On the other hand, in perfectly hiding commitment schemes (as defined later), the secrecy requirement is information-theoretic, whereas the unambiguity requirement is computational (i.e., refers only to probabilistic polynomial-time adversaries).

Comments about Terminology. From this point on, we explicitly mention the "perfect" feature of a commitment scheme to which we refer. That is, a commitment scheme as in Definition 4.4.1 will be referred to as *perfectly binding*, whereas a commitment scheme as in Definition 4.8.2 (presented later) will be referred to as *perfectly hiding*. Consequently, when we talk of a commitment scheme without specifying any "perfect" feature, it may be that the scheme is only computationally hiding and computationally binding. We remark that it is impossible to have a commitment scheme that is both perfectly hiding and perfectly binding (see Exercise 32).

—— **278** ——

We stress that the terminology just suggested is inconsistent with the exposition in Section 4.4 (in which schemes such as in Definition 4.4.1 were referred to as "commitment schemes," without the extra qualification of "perfectly binding").[20] Furthermore, the terminology just suggested is inconsistent with significant parts of the literature, in which a variety of terms can be found.[21]

4.8.2.1. Definition

Loosely speaking, a perfectly hiding commitment scheme is an efficient *two-phase* two-party protocol through which the *sender* can commit itself to a *value* such that the following two conflicting requirements are satisfied:

1. *(Perfect) secrecy* (or *hiding*): At the end of the *commit phase*, the *receiver* does not gain any *information* about the sender's value.

2. *Unambiguity* (or *binding*): It is infeasible for the sender to interact with the receiver, so the commit phase is successfully terminated, and yet later it is feasible for the sender to perform the *reveal phase* in two different ways, leading the receiver to accept (as legal "openings") two different values.

Using conventions analogous to those in Section 4.4.1, we state the following definition. Again, S and R are the specified strategies of the commitment's sender and receiver, respectively.

Definition 4.8.2 (Perfectly Hiding Bit-Commitment Scheme): *A* **perfectly hiding bit-commitment scheme** *is a pair of probabilistic polynomial-time interactive machines, denoted (S, R), satisfying the following:*

- Input specification: *The common input is an integer n presented in unary (serving as the security parameter). The private input to the sender is a bit denoted v.*
- Secrecy (hiding): *For every probabilistic (not necessarily polynomial-time) machine R^* interacting with S, the random variables describing the output of R^* in the two cases, namely $\langle S(0), R^* \rangle (1^n)$ and $\langle S(1), R^* \rangle (1^n)$, are identically distributed.*
- Unambiguity (binding): *Preliminaries: For simplicity, $v \in \{0, 1\}$ and $n \in \mathbb{N}$ are implicit in all notations. Fix any probabilistic polynomial-time algorithm F^* and any polynomial $p(\cdot)$.*

  1. *As in Definition 4.4.1, a receiver's view of an interaction with the sender, denoted $(r, \overline{m})$, consists of the random coins used by the receiver (i.e., r) and the sequence of messages received from the sender (i.e., $\overline{m}$). A sender's view of the same interaction, denoted $(s, \overline{m})$, consists of the random coins used by the sender (i.e., s) and the sequence of messages received from the receiver (i.e., $\overline{m}$). A joint view of the interaction is a pair consisting of corresponding receiver and sender views of the same interaction.*

---

[20] The extra qualification was omitted from the terminology of Section 4.4 in order to simplify the basic text.

[21] For example, as in Section 4.4, many works refer to schemes such as in Definition 4.4.1 merely by the term "commitment schemes," and many refer to schemes such as in Definition 4.8.2 by the term "perfect commitment schemes." Furthermore, in some works the term "commitment schemes" means schemes such as in Definition 4.8.2.

2. Let $\sigma \in \{0, 1\}$. We say that a joint view (of an interaction), $((r, \overline{m}), (s, \tilde{m}))$, has **a feasible σ-opening** (with respect to F^* and $p(\cdot)$) if on input $(\overline{m}, (s, \tilde{m}), \sigma)$, algorithm F^* outputs, with probability at least $1/p(n)$, a string s' such that $\overline{m}$ describes the messages received by R when R uses local coins r and interacts with machine S that uses local coins s' and input $(\sigma, 1^n)$.

> (Remark: We stress that s' may, but need not, equal s. The output of algorithm F^* has to satisfy a relation that depends on only part of the input (i.e., the receiver's view $(r, \overline{m})$); the sender's view (i.e., $(s, \tilde{m})$) is supplied to algorithm F^* as additional help.)

3. We say that a joint view is **ambiguous with respect to F^* and** $p(\cdot)$ if it has both a feasible 0-opening and a feasible 1-opening (with respect to F^* and $p(\cdot)$).

The unambiguity (or binding) requirement *asserts that for all but a negligible fraction of the coin tosses of the receiver it is infeasible for the sender to interact with the receiver, so that the resulting joint view is ambiguous with respect to some probabilistic polynomial-time algorithm F^* and some positive polynomial $p(\cdot)$. Namely, for every probabilistic polynomial-time interactive machine S^*, probabilistic polynomial-time algorithm F^*, positive polynomials $p(\cdot)$ and $q(\cdot)$, and all sufficiently large n, the probability that the joint view of the interaction between R and S^*, on common input 1^n, is ambiguous, with respect to F^* and $p(\cdot)$, is smaller than $1/q(n)$.*

In the formulation of the unambiguity requirement, S^* describes the (cheating) sender strategy in the commit phase, whereas F^* describes its strategy in the reveal phase. Hence, it is justified (and in fact necessary) to pass the sender's view of the interaction (between S^* and R) to algorithm F^*. The unambiguity requirement asserts that any efficient strategy S^* will fail to yield a joint view of interaction that can later be (efficiently) opened in two different ways supporting two different values. As usual, events occurring with negligible probability are ignored.

One can consider a relaxation of the secrecy condition in which the probability ensembles $\{\langle S(0), R^*\rangle(1^n)\}_{n\in\mathbb{N}}$ and $\{\langle S(1), R^*\rangle(1^n)\}_{n\in\mathbb{N}}$ are required to be statistically close, rather than identically distributed. We choose not to do so because the currently known constructions achieve the more stringent condition. Furthermore, use of the weaker notion of a perfectly hiding commitment scheme (in Section 4.8.3) yields almost-perfect zero-knowledge arguments rather than perfect zero-knowledge ones.

As in Definition 4.4.1, the secrecy requirement refers explicitly to the situation at the end of the commit phase, whereas the unambiguity requirement implicitly assumes that the reveal phase takes the following canonical form:

1. The sender sends to the receiver its initial private input, v, and the random coins, s, it has used in the commit phase.

2. The receiver verifies that v and s (together with the coins (i.e., r) used by R in the commit phase) indeed yield the messages that R has received in the commit phase. Verification is done in polynomial time (by running the programs S and R).

4.8.2.2. Construction Based on One-Way Permutations

Perfectly hiding commitment schemes can be constructed using any one-way permutation. The known scheme, however, involves a linear (in the security parameter) number of rounds. Hence, it can be used for the purposes of the current section, but not for the construction in Section 4.9.1.

> **Construction 4.8.3 (A Perfectly Hiding Bit Commitment):** *Let f be a permutation, and let $b(x, y)$ denote the inner product* mod 2 *of x and y (i.e., $b(x, y) = \sum_{i=1}^{n} x_i y_i$ mod 2, where $x = x_1 \cdots x_n \in \{0, 1\}^n$ and $y = y_1 \cdots y_n \in \{0, 1\}^n$).*
>
> 1. Commit phase *(using security parameter n):*
>   - (a) (Local computations): *The receiver randomly selects $n - 1$ linearly independent vectors $r^1, \ldots, r^{n-1} \in \{0, 1\}^n$. The sender uniformly selects $s \in \{0, 1\}^n$ and computes $y = f(s)$.*
>   *(Thus far, no message has been exchanged between the parties.)*
>   - (b) (Iterative hashing): *The parties proceed in $n - 1$ rounds. In the i round ($i = 1, \ldots, n - 1$), the receiver sends r^i to the sender, which replies by computing and sending $c^i \stackrel{\text{def}}{=} b(y, r^i)$.*
>   - (c) (The "actual" commitment): *At this point there are exactly two solutions to the system of equations $\{b(y, r^i) = c^i : 1 \le i \le n - 1\}$. (Both parties can easily determine both solutions.)*
>   - *The sender sets $\pi = 1$ if y is the lexicographically first solution (of the two), and $\pi = 0$ otherwise.*
>   - *To commit to a value $v \in \{0, 1\}$, the sender sends $c^n \stackrel{\text{def}}{=} \pi \oplus v$ to the receiver.*
> 2. Canonical reveal phase: *In the reveal phase, the sender reveals v along with the string s randomly selected by it in the commit phase. The receiver accepts the value v if the following two conditions hold, where $((r^1, \ldots, r^{n-1}), (c^1, \ldots, c^n))$ denote the receiver's view of the commit phase:*
>   - $b(f(s), r^i) = c^i$, *for all $1 \le i \le n - 1$.*
>   - *If there exists $y' < f(s)$ (resp., $y' > f(s)$) such that $b(y', r^i) = c^i$ for all $1 \le i \le n - 1$, then $v = c^n$ (resp., $v = c^n \oplus 1$) must hold.*
>
> *That is, the receiver solves the linear system $\{b(y^j, r^i) = c^i\}_{i=1}^{n-1}$, obtaining solutions $y^1 < y^2$, so that $b(y^j, r^i) = c^i$ for $j = 1, 2$ and $i = 1, \ldots, n - 1$. Next, it checks whether or not $f(s) \in \{y^1, y^2\}$ (if the answer is negative, it rejects immediately) and sets π accordingly (i.e., so that $f(s) = y^\pi$). It accepts the value v if and only if $v \equiv c^n + \pi \pmod 2$.*

> **Proposition 4.8.4:** *Suppose that f is a one-way permutation. Then the protocol presented in Construction 4.8.3 constitutes a perfectly hiding bit-commitment scheme.*

It is quite easy to see that Construction 4.8.3 satisfies the secrecy condition. The proof that the unambiguity requirement is satisfied is quite complex and is omitted. The intuition underlying the proof is that it is infeasible to play the iterative hashing so as to reach a situation in which one can invert f on *both* the resulting solutions y^1 and y^2. (We mention that this reasoning fails if one replaces the iterative hashing by an ordinary one; see Exercise 33.)

4.8.2.3. Construction Based on Claw-Free Collections

A perfectly hiding commitment scheme of *constant number of rounds* can be constructed using a seemingly stronger intractability assumption, specifically, the existence of claw-free collections (see Section 2.4.5). This assumption implies the existence of one-way functions, but it is not known if the converse is true. Nevertheless, claw-free collections can be constructed under widely believed assumptions such as the intractability of factoring and DLP. Actually, the construction of perfectly hiding commitment schemes, presented next, uses a claw-free collection with an additional property; specifically, it is assumed that the set of indices of the collection (i.e., the range of algorithm I) can be efficiently recognized (i.e., is in $\mathcal{BPP}$). Such a collection exists under the assumption that DLP is intractable (see Section 2.4.5).

Construction 4.8.5 (A Constant-Round Perfectly Hiding Bit Commitment): *Let (I, D, F) be a triplet of probabilistic polynomial-time algorithms. (Think of I as the index generating algorithm of a claw-free collection $\{(f_i^0, f_i^1) : i \in \overline{I}\}$ and S and F as the corresponding sampling and evaluating algorithms.)*

1. Commit phase: *To receive a commitment to a bit (using security parameter n), the receiver randomly generates $i = I(1^n)$ and sends it to the sender. To commit to value $v \in \{0, 1\}$ (upon receiving the message i from the receiver), the sender checks to see if indeed i is in the range of $I(1^n)$, and if so the sender randomly generates $s = D(v, i)$, computes $c = F(v, i, s)$, and sends c to the receiver. (In case i is not in the range of $I(1^n)$, the sender aborts the protocol, announcing that the receiver is cheating.)*

2. (Almost-canonical) reveal phase: *In the reveal phase, it suffices for the sender to re-veal the string s generated by it in the commit phase. The receiver accepts the value v if $F(v, i, s) = c$, where (i, c) is the receiver's (partial) view of the commit phase.*

Proposition 4.8.6: *Let (I, D, F) be a claw-free collection with a probabilistic polynomial-time-recognizable set of indices. Then the protocol presented in Construction 4.8.5 constitutes a perfectly hiding bit-commitment scheme.*

Proof Sketch: The secrecy requirement follows directly from Property 2 of a claw-free collection (as in Definition 2.4.6) combined with the test $i \in I(1^n)$ conducted by the sender. The unambiguity requirement follows from Property 3 of a claw-free collection (Definition 2.4.6), using a standard reducibility argument. (Note that $F(0, i, s_0) = F(1, i, s_1)$ means that (s_0, s_1) constitute a claw for the permutation pair (f_i^0, f_i^1).) ∎

The rationale for having the sender check to see if the index i indeed belongs to the legitimate index set $\overline{I}$ is that only permutation pairs (f_i^0, f_i^1) with $i \in \overline{I}$ are guaranteed to have identical range distributions. Thus, it actually is not necessary for the sender to check whether or not $i \in \overline{I}$; it suffices for it to check (or be otherwise convinced) that the permutation pair (f_i^0, f_i^1) satisfies the requirement of identical range distributions. Consider, for example, the factoring claw-free collection (presented in Section 2.4.5). This collection *is not known* to have an efficiently recognizable index set. Still, having sent an index N, the receiver can prove in zero-knowledge to the sender that the permutation pair (f_N^0, f_N^1) satisfies the requirement of identical range distributions. What is actually being proved is that half of the square roots of each quadratic residue mod N have Jacobi symbol 1 (relative to N). A (perfect) zero-knowledge proof system for this claim does exist (without assuming anything). In fact, it suffices to use a witness-independent proof system, and such a system having a constant number of rounds does exist (again, without assuming anything). Hence, the factoring claw-free collection can be used to construct a constant-round perfectly hiding commitment scheme, and thus such commitment schemes also exist under the assumption that the factoring of Blum integers is intractable.

4.8.2.4. Non-Uniform Computational Unambiguity

Actually, for the applications to proof/argument systems, both the one following and the one in Section 4.9.1, we need commitment schemes with perfect secrecy and *non-uniform* computational unambiguity. (The reason for this need is analogous to one discussed in the case of the zero-knowledge proof for $\mathcal{NP}$ presented in Section 4.4.) By non-uniform computational unambiguity we mean that the unambiguity condition should also hold for (non-uniform) families of polynomial-size circuits. We stress that the foregoing constructions of perfect commitment schemes possess the non-uniform computational unambiguity, provided that the underlying intractability assumption also holds with respect to non-uniform polynomial-size circuits (e.g., the one-way permutation is hard to invert even by such circuits, and the claw-free collections also foil non-uniform polynomial-size claw-forming circuits).

In order to prevent the terminology from becoming too cumbersome, we omit the attribute "non-uniform" when referring to the perfectly hiding commitment schemes in the description of the two applications mentioned earlier.

4.8.2.5. Commitment Schemes with A Posteriori Secrecy

We conclude the discussion of perfectly hiding commitment schemes by introducing a relaxation of the secrecy requirement. The resulting scheme cannot be used for the purposes of the current section, yet it is useful in different settings discussed later. The advantage of the relaxation is that it allows us to construct such (constant-round perfectly hiding) commitment schemes using any claw-free collection, thus waiving the additional requirement that the index set be efficiently recognizable.

Loosely speaking, we relax the secrecy requirement of perfectly hiding commitment schemes by requiring that it hold only when the receiver follows its prescribed program (denoted R). This seems strange, because we do not really want to assume that the real receiver follows the prescribed program (but rather protect against arbitrary behavior). The point is that a real receiver may disclose its commit-phase coin tosses at a later stage, say even after the reveal phase, and by doing so prove *a posteriori* that (at least in some weak sense) it was following the prescribed program. Actually, the receiver proves only that it has behaved in a manner that is consistent with its program.

Definition 4.8.7 (Commitment Scheme with Perfect A Posteriori Secrecy): *A **bit-commitment scheme with perfect a posteriori secrecy** is defined as in Definition 4.8.2, except that the secrecy requirement is replaced by the following a posteriori secrecy requirement: For every string $r \in \{0, 1\}^{\mathrm{poly}(n)}$, it holds that $\langle S(0), R_r \rangle(1^n)$ and $\langle S(1), R_r \rangle(1^n)$ are statistically close, where R_r denotes the execution of the interactive machine R when using internal coin tosses r.*

Proposition 4.8.8: *Let (I, D, F) be a claw-free collection. Consider a modification of Construction 4.8.5 in which the sender's check of whether or not i is in the range of $I(1^n)$ is omitted (from the commit phase). Then the resulting protocol constitutes a bit-commitment scheme with perfect a posteriori secrecy.*

We stress that in contrast to Proposition 4.8.6, here the claw-free collection need not have an efficiently recognizable index set. Hence, we had to omit the sender's check. Yet the receiver can later prove that the message it sent during the commit phase (i.e., i) is indeed a valid index simply by disclosing the random coins it used in order to generate i (using algorithm I).

Proof Sketch: The a posteriori secrecy requirement follows directly from Property 2 of a claw-free collection (combined with the fact that i is indeed a valid index, since it is generated by invoking I). The unambiguity requirement follows as in Proposition 4.8.6. ∎

A typical application of a commitment scheme with perfect a posteriori secrecy is presented in Section 4.9.1. In that setting the commitment scheme is used inside an interactive proof, with the verifier playing the role of the sender (and the prover playing the role of the receiver). If the verifier a posteriori learns that the prover has been cheating, then the verifier rejects the input. Hence, no damage is caused, in this case, by the fact that the secrecy of the verifier's commitments may have been breached.

4.8.3. Perfect Zero-Knowledge Arguments for $\mathcal{NP}$

Having a perfectly hiding commitment scheme at our disposal, we can construct perfect zero-knowledge arguments for $\mathcal{NP}$ by modifying the construction of (computational) zero-knowledge proofs (for $\mathcal{NP}$) in a totally syntactic manner. We recall that in these proof systems (e.g., Construction 4.4.7 for Graph 3-Colorability) the prover uses a perfectly binding commitment scheme in order to commit itself to many values, some of which it later reveals upon the verifier's request. All that is needed is to replace the perfectly binding commitment scheme used by the prover with a perfectly hiding commitment scheme. We claim that the resulting protocol is a perfect zero-knowledge argument (i.e., computationally sound proof) for the original language.

Proposition 4.8.9: *Consider a modification of Construction 4.4.7 such that the commitment scheme used by the prover is replaced by a perfectly hiding commitment scheme. Then the resulting protocol is a perfect zero-knowledge weak argument for Graph 3-Colorability.*

By a *weak argument* we mean a protocol in which the gap between the completeness and the computational-soundness conditions is noticeable. In our case, the verifier always accepts inputs in $G3C$, whereas no efficient prover can fool him into accepting graphs $G = (V, E)$ not in $G3C$ with probability that is non-negligibly greater than $1 - \frac{1}{|E|}$. Specifically, we shall show that no efficient prover can fool him into accepting graphs $G = (V, E)$ not in $G3C$ with probability greater than $1 - \frac{1}{2|E|}$. Recall that by (sequentially) repeating this protocol polynomially many times the (computational-soundness) error probability can be made negligible.

Proof Sketch: We start by proving that the resulting protocol is perfect zero-knowledge for $G3C$. We use the same simulator as in the proof of Proposition 4.4.8. However, this time analyzing the properties of the simulator is much easier and yields stronger results, the reason being that here the prover's commitment is perfectly hiding, whereas there it is only computationally hiding. Thus, here the prover's commitments are distributed independently of the committed values, and consequently the verifier acts in total oblivion of the values. It follows that the simulator outputs a transcript with probability exactly $\frac{2}{3}$, and for similar reasons this transcript is distributed identically to the real interaction. The perfect zero-knowledge property follows.

The completeness condition is obvious, as in the proof of Proposition 4.4.8. It is left to prove that the protocol satisfies the (weak) computational-soundness requirement. This is indeed the more subtle part of the current proof (in contrast to the proof of Proposition 4.4.8, in which proving soundness is quite easy). The reason is that here the prover's commitment is only computationally binding, whereas there it is perfectly binding. Thus, here we use a reducibility argument to show that a prover's ability to cheat, with too high a probability, on inputs not in $G3C$ translates to an algorithm contradicting the unambiguity of the commitment scheme. Details follow.

We assume, to the contradiction, that there exists a (polynomial-time) cheating prover P^* and an infinite sequence of integers such that for each integer n in this sequence, there exist graphs $G_n = (V_n, E_n) \notin G3C$ and a string y_n such that $P^*(y_n)$ leads the verifier to accept G_n with probability greater than $1 - \frac{1}{2|E_n|}$. Let $k \stackrel{\text{def}}{=} |V_n|$. Let $c_1, \ldots, c_k$ be the sequence of commitments (to the vertex colors) sent by the prover in Step P1. Recall that in the next step, the verifier sends a uniformly chosen edge (of E_n), and the prover must answer by revealing different colors for its endpoint; otherwise the verifier rejects. A straightforward calculation shows that because G_n is not 3-colorable there must exist a vertex for which the prover is able to reveal at least two different colors. Hence, we can construct a polynomial-size circuit incorporating P^*, G_n, and y_n that violates the (non-uniform) unambiguity condition. Contradiction to the hypothesis of the proposition follows, and this completes the proof. ■

Combining Propositions 4.8.4 and 4.8.9, we get the following:

Corollary 4.8.10: *If non-uniformly one-way permutations exist, then every language in $\mathcal{NP}$ has a perfect zero-knowledge argument.*

ZK Proofs versus Perfect ZK Arguments: Which to Prefer?

Propositions 4.4.8 and 4.8.9 exhibit a kind of trade-off between the strength of the soundness and zero-knowledge properties. The protocol of Proposition 4.4.8 offers computational zero-knowledge and "perfect" soundness, whereas the protocol of Proposition 4.8.9 offers perfect zero-knowledge and only computational soundness. We remark that the two results are *not* obtained under the same assumptions: The conclusion of Proposition 4.4.8 is valid as long as one-way functions exist, whereas the conclusion of Proposition 4.8.9 seems to require a (probably) stronger assumption. Yet one may ask which of the two protocols we should prefer, *assuming that they are both valid* (i.e., assuming that the underlying complexity assumptions hold). The answer depends on the setting (i.e., application) in which the protocol is to be used. In particular, one should consider the following issues:

- The relative importance attributed to soundness and zero-knowledge in the specific application. In case of clear priority for one of the two properties, a choice should be made accordingly.

- The computational resources of the various users in the application. One of the users may be known to be in possession of much more substantial computing resources, and it may be desirable to require that he/she not be able to cheat, not even in an information-theoretic sense.

- The soundness requirement refers only to the duration of the execution, whereas in many applications the zero-knowledge property may be of concern for a long time afterward. If that is the case, then perfect zero-knowledge arguments do offer a clear advantage (over zero-knowledge proofs).

4.8.4. Arguments of Poly-Logarithmic Efficiency

A dramatic improvement in the efficiency of zero-knowledge arguments for $\mathcal{NP}$ can be obtained by combining the idea of an authentication tree with results regarding probabilistically checkable proofs (PCPs). In particular, assuming the existence of very strong collision-free hashing functions, one can construct a computationally sound (zero-knowledge) proof for any language in $\mathcal{NP}$, using only poly-logarithmic amounts of communication and randomness. The interesting point in that statement is the mere existence of such extremely efficient arguments, let alone their zero-knowledge property. Hence, we confine ourselves to describing the ideas involved in construct-ing such arguments and do not address the issue of making them zero-knowledge. (We stress that the argument system presented next is *not* zero-knowledge, unless $\mathcal{NP} \subseteq \mathcal{BPP}$.)

By the so-called PCP theorem, every $\mathcal{NP}$ language L can be reduced to $3SAT$, so that non-members of L are mapped into 3CNF formulae for which every truth assignment satisfies at most a $1 - \varepsilon$ fraction of the clauses, where $\varepsilon > 0$ is a universal constant. Let us denote this reduction by f. Now, in order to prove that $x \in L$, it suffices to prove that the formula $f(x)$ is satisfiable. This can be done by supplying a satisfying assignment for $f(x)$. The interesting point is that the verifier need not check that all clauses of $f(x)$ are satisfied by the given assignment. Instead, it can uniformly select only poly-logarithmically many clauses and check that the assignment satisfies all of them. If $x \in L$ (and the prover supplies a satisfying assignment to $f(x)$), then the verifier will always accept. But if $x \notin L$, then no assignment will satisfy more than a $1 - \varepsilon$ fraction of the clauses, and consequently a uniformly chosen clause will not be satisfied with probability at least ε. Hence, checking super-logarithmically many clauses will do.

The preceding paragraph shows that the randomness complexity can be made poly-logarithmic and that the verifier need only inspect a poly-logarithmic number of ran-domly selected values. Specifically, the prover commits to each of the values of the variables in the formula $f(x)$ but is asked to reveal only a few of them. To obtain (total) poly-logarithmic communication complexity, we use a special commitment scheme that allows us to commit to a string of length n such that the commitment phase takes poly-logarithmic communication and individual bits of this string can be revealed (and verified as correct) at poly-logarithmic communication cost. For constructing such a commitment scheme, we use a *collision-free* hashing function. The function maps strings of some length to strings of half that length, so that it is "hard" to find two strings that are mapped by the function to the same image. (The following descrip-tion is slightly inaccurate. What we need is a family of hashing functions such that no small non-uniform circuit, given the description of a function in the family, can form collisions with respect to it.)

Let n denote the length of the input string to which the sender wishes to commit itself, and let k be a parameter (which is later set to be poly-logarithmic in n). Denote by H a collision-free hashing function mapping strings of length $2k$ into strings of length k. The sender partitions its input string into $m \stackrel{\text{def}}{=} \frac{n}{k}$ consecutive blocks, each of length k. Next, the sender constructs a binary tree of depth $\log_2 m$, placing the m blocks in the corresponding leaves of the tree. In each internal node, the sender places the hashing value obtained by applying the function H to the content of the children of this node. The only message sent in the commit phase is the content of the root (sent by the sender to the receiver). By doing so, *unless the sender can form collisions under H*, the sender has "committed" itself to some n-bit-long string. When the receiver wishes to get the value of a specific bit in the string, the sender reveals to the receiver the contents of *both children* of each node along the path from the root to the corresponding leaf. The receiver checks that the values supplied for each node (along the path) match the value obtained by applying H to the values supplied for its two children.

The protocol for arguing that $x \in L$ consists of the prover committing itself to a satisfying assignment for $f(x)$ using the foregoing scheme and the verifier checking individual clauses by asking the prover to reveal the values assigned to the variables in these clauses. The protocol can be shown to be computationally sound provided that it is infeasible to find a distinct pair $\alpha, \beta \in \{0, 1\}^{2k}$ such that $H(\alpha) = H(\beta)$. Specifically, we need to assume that forming collisions under H is not possible in sub-exponential time, namely, that for some $\delta > 0$ forming collisions with probability greater than 2^{-k^δ} must take at least 2^{k^δ} time. In such a case, we set $k = (\log n)^{1+\frac{1}{\delta}}$ and get a computationally sound proof of communication complexity $O(\frac{\log n}{o(1)} \cdot (\log m) \cdot k) = \text{polylog}(n)$. (Weaker lower bounds for the collision-forming task may yield meaningful results by an appropriate setting of the parameter k; for example, the standard assumption that claws cannot be formed in polynomial time allows us to set $k = n^\varepsilon$, for any constant $\varepsilon > 0$, and obtain communication complexity of $n^{\varepsilon+o(1)}$.) We stress that collisions can always be formed in time 2^{2k}, and hence the entire approach fails if the prover is not computationally bounded (and consequently we cannot get (perfectly sound) proof systems this way). Furthermore, one can show that only languages in Dtime(2^{polylog}) have proof systems with poly-logarithmic communication and randomness complexities.

4.9.* Constant-Round Zero-Knowledge Proofs

In this section we consider the problem of constructing *constant-round* zero-knowledge proof systems *with negligible error probability* for all languages in $\mathcal{NP}$. To make the rest of the discussion less cumbersome, we define a proof system to be **round-efficient** if it is *both constant-round and has negligible error probability*. We stress that none of the zero-knowledge proof systems for $\mathcal{NP}$ presented and discussed thus far have been round-efficient (i.e., they either had non-constant numbers of rounds or had non-negligible error probability).

We present two approaches to the construction of round-efficient zero-knowledge proofs for $\mathcal{NP}$:

1. basing the construction of round-efficient zero-knowledge proof systems on constant-round perfectly hiding commitment schemes (as defined in Section 4.8.2)

2. constructing (round-efficient zero-knowledge) *computationally sound* proof systems (as defined in Section 4.8) instead of (round-efficient zero-knowledge) proof systems

The advantage of the second approach is that round-efficient zero-knowledge computationally sound proof systems for $\mathcal{NP}$ can be constructed using any one-way function, whereas it is not known if round-efficient zero-knowledge proof systems for $\mathcal{NP}$ can be constructed under the same general assumption. In particular, we know how to construct constant-round perfectly hiding commitment schemes only by using seemingly stronger assumptions (e.g., the existence of claw-free permutations).

The two approaches have a fundamental idea in common. We start with an abstract exposition of this common idea. Recall that the *basic* zero-knowledge proof for Graph 3-Colorability, presented in Construction 4.4.7, consists of a constant number of rounds. However, this proof system has a non-negligible error probability (in fact, the error probability is very close to 1). In Section 4.4 it was suggested that the error probability be reduced to a negligible value by sequentially applying the proof system sufficiently many times. The problem is that this yields a proof system with a non-constant number of rounds. A natural suggestion is to perform the repetitions of the basic proof in parallel, instead of sequentially. The problem with this "solution" is that it is not known if the resulting proof system is zero-knowledge. Furthermore, it is known that it is not possible to present, as done in the proof of Proposition 4.4.8, a single simulator that uses any possible verifier as a black box (see Section 4.5.4). The source of trouble is that when playing many copies of Construction 4.4.7 in parallel, a cheating verifier can select the edge to be inspected (i.e., Step V1) in each copy, depending on the commitments sent in all copies (i.e., in Step P1). Such behavior of the verifier defeats a simulator analogous to the one presented in the proof of Proposition 4.4.8.

One way to overcome this difficulty is to "switch" the order of Steps P1 and V1. But switching the order of these steps enables the prover to cheat (by sending commitments in which only the "query edges" are colored correctly). Hence, a more refined approach is required. The verifier starts by committing itself to one edge query per each copy (of Construction 4.4.7), then the prover commits itself to the coloring in each copy, and only then does the verifier reveal its queries, after which the rest of the proof proceeds as before. The commitment scheme used by the verifier should prevent the prover from predicting the sequence of edges committed to by the verifier. This is the point where the two approaches differ.

1. The first approach uses a perfectly hiding commitment scheme. The problem with this approach is that such (constant-round) schemes are known to exist only under seemingly stronger assumptions than merely the existence of one-way functions. Yet such schemes do exist under assumptions such as the intractability of factoring integers or the intractability of the discrete-logarithm problem.

2. The second approach bounds the computational resources of prospective cheating provers. Consequently, it suffices to utilize, "against" these provers (as commitment receivers), commitment schemes with computational security. We remark that this approach uses (for the commitments by the prover) a commitment scheme with an extra property. Yet such schemes can be constructed using any one-way function.

Caveat. Both approaches lead to protocols that are zero-knowledge in a liberal sense (i.e., using *expected* polynomial-time simulators as defined in Section 4.3.1.6). It is not known if these protocols (or other round-efficient protocols for $\mathcal{NP}$) can be shown to be zero-knowledge in the strict sense (i.e., using strict probabilistic polynomial-time simulators).

4.9.1. Using Commitment Schemes with Perfect Secrecy

For the sake of clarity, let us start by presenting a detailed description of the constant-round interactive proof (for Graph 3-Colorability, $G3C$) sketched earlier. This interactive proof employs two different commitment schemes. The first scheme is the simple (perfectly binding) commitment scheme presented in Construction 4.4.2. We denote by $C_s(\sigma)$ the commitment of the sender, using coins s, to the (ternary) value

$\sigma \in \{1, 2, 3\}$. The second commitment scheme is a perfectly hiding commitment scheme (see Section 4.8.2). For simplicity, we assume that this scheme has a commit phase in which the receiver sends one message to the sender, which then replies with a single message (e.g., Construction 4.8.5). Let us denote by $P_{m,s}(\alpha)$ the (perfectly hiding) commitment of the sender to the string α, upon receiving message m (from the receiver) and when using coins s.

Construction 4.9.1 (A Round-Efficient Zero-Knowledge Proof for $G3C$):

- Common input: *A simple (3-colorable) graph* $G = (V, E)$. *Let* $n \overset{\text{def}}{=} |V|$, $t \overset{\text{def}}{=} n \cdot |E|$, *and* $V = \{1, \ldots, n\}$.
- Auxiliary input to the prover: *A 3-coloring of G, denoted* ψ.
- Prover's preliminary step (P0): *The prover invokes the commit phase of the perfectly hiding commitment scheme, which results in sending to the verifier a message m.*
- Verifier's preliminary step (V0): *The verifier uniformly and independently selects a sequence of t edges,* $\overline{E} \overset{\text{def}}{=} ((u_1, v_1), \ldots, (u_t, v_t)) \in E^t$, *and sends the prover a random commitment to these edges. Namely, the verifier uniformly selects* $\overline{s} \in \{0, 1\}^{\text{poly}(n)}$ *and sends* $P_{m, \overline{s}}(\overline{E})$ *to the prover.*
- Motivating remark: *At this point the verifier is committed (in a computational sense) to a sequence of t edges. Because this commitment is of perfect secrecy, the prover obtains no information about the edge sequence.*
- Prover's step (P1): *The prover uniformly and independently selects t permutations,* $\pi_1, \ldots, \pi_t$, *over* $\{1, 2, 3\}$ *and sets* $\phi_j(v) \overset{\text{def}}{=} \pi_j(\psi(v))$ *for each* $v \in V$ *and* $1 \le j \le t$. *The prover uses the (perfectly binding, computationally hiding) commitment scheme to commit itself to colors of each of the vertices according to each 3-coloring. Namely, the prover uniformly and independently selects* $s_{1,1}, \ldots, s_{n,t} \in \{0, 1\}^n$, *computes* $c_{i,j} = C_{s_{i,j}}(\phi_j(i))$ *for each* $i \in V$ *and* $1 \le j \le t$, *and sends* $c_{1,1}, \ldots, c_{n,t}$ *to the verifier.*
- Verifier's step (V1): *The verifier performs the (canonical) reveal phase of its commitment, yielding the sequence* $\overline{E} = ((u_1, v_1), \ldots, (u_t, v_t))$. *Namely, the verifier sends* $(\overline{s}, \overline{E})$ *to the prover.*
- Motivating remark: *At this point the entire commitment of the verifier is revealed. The verifier now expects to receive, for each j, the colors assigned by the jth coloring to vertices u_j and v_j (the endpoints of the jth edge in the sequence $\overline{E}$).*
- Prover's step (P2): *The prover checks that the message just received from the verifier is indeed a valid revealing of the commitment made by the verifier at Step V0. Otherwise the prover halts immediately. Let us denote the sequence of t edges, just revealed, by* $(u_1, v_1), \ldots, (u_t, v_t)$. *The prover uses the (canonical) reveal phase of the perfectly binding commitment scheme in order to reveal to the verifier, for each j, the jth coloring of vertices u_j and v_j. Namely, the prover sends to the verifier the sequence of quadruples*

$$\left(s_{u_1, 1}, \phi_1(u_1), s_{v_1, 1}, \phi_1(v_1)\right), \ldots, \left(s_{u_t, t}, \phi_t(u_t), s_{v_t, t}, \phi_t(v_t)\right)$$

- Verifier's step (V2): *The verifier checks whether or not, for each j, the values in the jth quadruple constitute a correct revealing of the commitments $c_{u_j, j}$ and $c_{v_j, j}$ and whether or not the corresponding values are different. Namely, upon receiving*

$(s_1, \sigma_1, s_1', \tau_1)$ through $(s_t, \sigma_t, s_t', \tau_t)$, the verifier checks whether or not for each j it holds that $c_{u_j, j} = C_{s_j}(\sigma_j)$, $c_{v_j, j} = C_{s_j'}(\tau_j)$, and $\sigma_j \neq \tau_j$ (and both σ_j and τ_j are in $\{1, 2, 3\}$). If all conditions hold, then the verifier accepts. Otherwise it rejects.

We first assert that Construction 4.9.1 is indeed an interactive proof for $G3C$. Clearly, the verifier always accepts a common-input in $G3C$. Suppose that the common input graph, $G = (V, E)$, is not in $G3C$. Using the perfect-binding feature of the prover's commitment, we can refer to the values committed to in Step P1 and say that each of the "committed colorings" sent by the prover in Step P1 contains at least one illegally colored edge. Using the perfect secrecy of the commitments sent by the verifier in Step V0, we deduce that at Step P1 the prover has "no idea" which edges the verifier asks to see (i.e., as far as the information available to the prover is concerned, all possibilities are equally likely). Hence, although the prover sends the "coloring commitment" after receiving the "edge commitment," the probability that all the "committed edges" have legally "committed coloring" is at most

$$\left(1 - \frac{1}{|E|}\right)^t \approx e^{-n} < 2^{-n}$$

The (Basic) Simulation Strategy. We now proceed to show that Construction 4.9.1 is indeed zero-knowledge (in the liberal sense allowing *expected* polynomial-time simulators). For every probabilistic polynomial-time interactive machine V^*, we introduce an expected polynomial-time simulator, denoted M^*, that uses V^* as a black box. The simulator starts by selecting and fixing a random tape r for V^* and by emulating the prover's preliminary Step P0, producing a message m. Given the input graph G, the random tape r, and the preliminary (prover) message m, the commitment message of the verifier V^* is determined. Hence, M^* invokes V^* on input G, random tape r, and message m and gets the corresponding commitment message, denoted CM. The simulator proceeds in two steps.

S1. *Extracting the query edges*: M^* generates a sequence of $n \cdot t$ random commitments to dummy values (e.g., all values equal 1) and feeds it to V^*. In case V^* replies by revealing correctly a sequence of t edges, denoted $(u_1, v_1), \ldots, (u_t, v_t)$, the simulator records these edges and proceeds to the next step. In case the reply of V^* is not a valid revealing of the commitment message CM, the simulator halts outputting the current view of V^* (e.g., G, r, m, and the commitments to dummy values).

S2. *Generating an interaction that satisfies the query edges* (an oversimplified exposition): Let $(u_1, v_1), \ldots, (u_t, v_t)$ denote the sequence of edges recorded in Step S1. Machine M^* generates a sequence of $n \cdot t$ commitments, $c_{1,1}, \ldots, c_{n,t}$, such that for each $j = 1, \ldots, t$ it holds that $c_{u_j, j}$ and $c_{v_j, j}$ are random commitments to two different random values in $\{1, 2, 3\}$, and all the other $c_{i,j}$'s are random commitments to dummy values (e.g., all values equal 1). The underlying values are called *pseudo-colorings*. The simulator feeds this sequence of commitments to V^*. If V^* replies by revealing correctly the (previously recorded) sequence of edges, then M^* can complete the simulation of a "real" interaction of V^* (by revealing the colors of the endpoints of these recorded edges). Otherwise, the entire Step S2 is repeated (until success is achieved).

For the sake of simplicity, we ignore the preliminary message m in the rest of the analysis. Furthermore, in the rest of the analysis we ignore the possibility that when invoked in Steps S1 and S2 the verifier reveals two different edge commitments. Loosely speaking, this is justified by the fact that during an expected polynomial-time computation, such an event can occur with only negligible probability (since otherwise it contradicts the computational unambiguity of the commitment scheme used by the verifier).

The Running Time of the Oversimplified Simulator. To illustrate the behavior of the simulator, assume that the program V^* always correctly reveals the commitment made in Step V0. In such a case, the simulator will find out the query edges in Step S1, and using them in Step S2 it will simulate the interaction of V^* with the real prover. Using ideas such as in Section 4.4 one can show that the simulation is computationally indistinguishable from the real interaction. Note that in this case Step S2 of the simulator is performed only once.

Consider now a more complex case in which on each possible sequence of internal coin tosses r, program V^* correctly reveals the commitment made in Step V0 only with probability $\frac{1}{3}$. The probability in this statement is taken over all possible commitments generated to the dummy values (in the simulator Step S1). We first observe that the probability that V^* correctly reveals the commitment made in Step V0, after receiving a random commitment to a sequence of pseudo-colorings (generated by the simulator in Step S2), is approximately $\frac{1}{3}$ (otherwise we derive a contradiction to the computational secrecy of the commitment scheme used by the prover). Hence the simulator reaches Step S2 with probability $\frac{1}{3}$, and each execution of Step S2 is completed successfully with probability $p \approx \frac{1}{3}$. It follows that the expected number of times that Step S2 is executed is $\frac{1}{3} \cdot \frac{1}{p} \approx 1$.

Let us now consider the general case. Let $q(G, r)$ denote the probability that on input graph G and random tape r, *after receiving random commitments to dummy values* (generated in Step S1), program V^* correctly reveals the commitment made in Step V0. Likewise, we denote by $p(G, r)$ the probability that (on input graph G and random tape r) *after receiving a random commitment to a sequence of pseudo-colorings* (generated by the simulator in Step S2), program V^* correctly reveals the commitment made in Step V0. As before, the difference between $q(G, r)$ and $p(G, r)$ is negligible (in terms of the size of the graph G); otherwise one derives a contradiction to the computational secrecy of the prover's commitment scheme. We conclude that the simulator reaches Step S2 with probability $q \overset{\text{def}}{=} q(G, r)$, and each execution of Step S2 is completed successfully with probability $p \overset{\text{def}}{=} p(G, r)$. It follows that the expected number of times that Step S2 is executed is $q \cdot \frac{1}{p}$. Now, here is the bad news: We *cannot* guarantee that $\frac{q}{p}$ is approximately 1 or is even bounded by a polynomial in the input size (e.g., let $p = 2^{-n}$ and $q = 2^{-n/2}$, then the difference between them is negligible, and yet $\frac{q}{p}$ is not bounded by $\text{poly}(n)$). This is why the foregoing description of the simulator is oversimplified and a modification is indeed required.

The Modified Simulator. We make the simulator expected polynomial-time by modifying Step S2 as follows. We add an intermediate Step S1.5, to be performed only if the simulator does not halt in Step S1. The purpose of Step S1.5 is to provide a good estimate of $q(G, r)$. The estimate is computed by repeating Step S1 until a fixed (polynomial-in-$|G|$) number of correct V^* revelations is reached (i.e., the estimate will be the ratio of the number of successes divided by the number of trials). By fixing a sufficiently large polynomial, we can guarantee that with overwhelmingly high probability (i.e., $1 - 2^{-\text{poly}(|G|)}$) the estimate is within a constant factor of $q(G, r)$. It is easily verified that the estimate can be computed within expected time $\text{poly}(|G|)/q(G, r)$. Step S2 of the simulator is modified by adding a bound on the number of times it is performed, and if none of these executions yields a correct V^* revelation, then the simulator outputs a *special empty interaction*. Specifically, Step S2 will be performed at most $\text{poly}(|G|)/\tilde{q}$ times, where $\tilde{q}$ is the estimate for $q(G, r)$ computed in Step S1.5. It follows that the modified simulator has an expected running time bounded by $q(G, r) \cdot \frac{\text{poly}(|G|)}{q(G,r)} = \text{poly}(|G|)$.

It is left to analyze the output distribution of the modified simulator. We confine ourselves to reducing this analysis to the analysis of the output of the original simulator by bounding the probability that the modified simulator outputs a special empty interaction. This probability equals

$$\Delta(G, r) \overset{\text{def}}{=} q(G, r) \cdot (1 - p(G, r))^{\text{poly}(|G|)/q(G,r)}$$

We claim that $\Delta(G, r)$ is a negligible function of $|G|$. Assume, to the contrary, that there exists a polynomial $P(\cdot)$, an infinite sequence of graphs $\{G_n\}$, and an infinite sequence of random tapes $\{r_n\}$ such that $\Delta(G_n, r_n) > 1/P(n)$. It follows that for each such n, we have $q(G_n, r_n) > 1/P(n)$. We consider two cases.

Case 1: For infinitely many n's, it holds that $p(G_n, r_n) \geq q(G_n, r_n)/2$. In such a case we get, for these n's,

$$\Delta(G_n, r_n) \leq (1 - p(G_n, r_n))^{\text{poly}(|G_n|)/q(G_n, r_n)}$$

$$\leq \left(1 - \frac{q(G_n, r_n)}{2}\right)^{\text{poly}(|G_n|)/q(G_n, r_n)}$$

$$< 2^{-\text{poly}(|G_n|)/2}$$

which contradicts our hypothesis that $\Delta(G_n, r_n) > 1/\text{poly}(n)$.

Case 2: For infinitely many n's, it holds that $p(G_n, r_n) < q(G_n, r_n)/2$. It follows that for these n's, we have $|q(G_n, r_n) - p(G_n, r_n)| > \frac{q(G_n, r_n)}{2} > \frac{1}{2P(n)}$, which leads to contradiction of the computational secrecy of the commitment scheme (used by the prover).

Hence, contradiction follows in both cases. ∎

Conclusion. We remark that one can modify Construction 4.9.1 so that weaker forms of perfect commitment schemes can be used. We refer specifically to commitment schemes with perfect a posteriori secrecy (see Section 4.8.2). In such schemes the secrecy is established only a posteriori by the receiver disclosing the coin tosses it used in the commit phase. In our case, the prover plays the role of the receiver, and the verifier plays the role of the sender. It suffices to establish the secrecy property a posteriori, because if secrecy is not established, then the verifier will reject. In such a case no harm has been done, because the secrecy of the perfect commitment scheme is used only to establish the soundness of the interactive proof. Thus, using Proposition 4.8.8, we obtain the following:

Corollary 4.9.2: *If non-uniformly claw-free collections exist, then every language in $\mathcal{NP}$ has a round-efficient zero-knowledge proof system.*

4.9.2. Bounding the Power of Cheating Provers

Construction 4.9.1 yields round-efficient zero-knowledge proof systems for $\mathcal{NP}$, under the assumption that claw-free collections exist. Using the seemingly more general assumption that one-way functions exist, we can modify Construction 4.9.1 so as to obtain zero-knowledge computationally sound proof systems. In the modified protocol, we let the verifier use a commitment scheme with computational secrecy, instead of the commitment scheme with perfect secrecy used in Construction 4.9.1. (Hence, both users commit to their messages using a perfectly binding commitment scheme, which offers only computational secrecy.) Furthermore, the commitment scheme used by the prover must have the extra property that it is infeasible to construct a commitment without "knowing" to what value it commits. Such a commitment scheme is called *non-oblivious*. We start by defining and constructing non-oblivious commitment schemes.

4.9.2.1. Non-Oblivious Commitment Schemes

The non-obliviousness of a commitment scheme is intimately related to the definition of proof of knowledge (see Section 4.7).

Definition 4.9.3 (Non-Oblivious Commitment Schemes): *Let (S, R) be a (perfectly binding) commitment scheme as in Definition 4.4.1. We say that the commitment scheme is **non-oblivious** if the prescribed receiver R constitutes a knowledge verifier that is always convinced by S for the relation*

$$\left\{ ((1^n, r, \overline{m}), (\sigma, s)) : \overline{m} = \text{view}_{R(1^n,r)}^{S(\sigma,1^n,s)} \right\}$$

where, as in Definition 4.4.1, $\text{view}_{R(1^n,r)}^{S(\sigma,1^n,s)}$ denotes the messages received by the interactive machine R, on input 1^n and local coins r, when interacting with machine S (which has input $(\sigma, 1^n)$ and uses coins s).

It follows that the receiver's prescribed program, R, may accept or reject at the end of the commit phase and that this decision is supposed to reflect the sender's ability to later come up with a legal opening of the commitment (i.e., successfully complete the reveal phase). We stress that non-obliviousness relates mainly to cheating senders, because the prescribed sender has no difficulty in later successfully completing the reveal phase (and in fact, during the commit phase, S always convinces the receiver of this ability). Hence, *any* sender program (not merely the prescribed S) that makes the receiver accept can be modified so that at the end of the commit phase it (locally) outputs information enabling the reveal phase (i.e., σ and s). The modified sender runs in expected time that is inversely proportional to the probability that the commit phase is completed successfully.

We remark that in an ordinary commitment scheme, at the end of the commit phase, the receiver does not necessarily "know" whether or not the sender can later successfully conduct the reveal phase. For example, a cheating sender in Construction 4.4.2 can (undetectedly) perform the commit phase without having the ability to later successfully perform the reveal phase (e.g., the sender may simply send a uniformly chosen string). It is guaranteed only that if the sender follows the prescribed program, then the sender can always succeed in the reveal phase. Furthermore, with respect to the scheme presented in Construction 4.4.4, a cheating sender can (undetectedly) perform the commit phase in a way that yields a receiver view that does not have any corresponding legal opening (and hence the reveal phase is doomed to fail); see Exercise 14. Nevertheless, one can prove the following:

Theorem 4.9.4: *If one-way functions exist, then there exist non-oblivious commitment schemes with a constant number of communication rounds. Furthermore, the commitment scheme also preserves the secrecy property when applied (polynomially) many times in parallel.*

The simultaneous secrecy of many copies is crucial to the application in Section 4.9.2.2.

Proof Idea: Recall that (ordinary perfectly binding) commitment schemes can be constructed assuming the existence of one-way functions (see Proposition 4.4.5 and Theorem 3.5.12). Combining such an ordinary commitment scheme with a zero-knowledge proof of knowledge of information allowing a proper decommitment, we get a non-oblivious commitment scheme. (We remark that such proofs do exist under the same assumptions; see Section 4.7.) However, the resulting commitment scheme has an unbounded number of rounds (due to the round complexity of the zero-knowledge proof), whereas we need a bounded-round scheme. We seem to have reached a vicious circle, yet there is a way out: We can use constant-round strong witness-indistinguishable proofs of knowledge, instead of the zero-knowledge proofs (of knowledge). Such proofs do exist under the same assumptions; see Section 4.6 and Exercise 28. The resulting commitment scheme has the additional property that when applied (polynomially) many times in parallel, the secrecy property holds simultaneously in all copies. This fact follows from the parallel-composition lemma for (strong) witness-indistinguishable proofs (see Section 4.6). ∎

4.9.2.2. Modifying Construction 4.9.1

Recall that we are referring to a modification of Construction 4.9.1 in which the verifier uses a perfectly binding commitment scheme (with computational secrecy), instead of the commitment scheme with perfect secrecy used in Construction 4.9.1. In addition, the commitment scheme used by the prover is non-oblivious.

We adopt the analysis of the first approach (i.e., of Section 4.9.1) to suit our current needs. We start with the claim that the modified protocol is a computationally sound proof for $G3C$. Verifying that the modified protocol satisfies the completeness condition is easy, as usual. We remark that the modified protocol does not satisfy the (usual) soundness condition (e.g., a "prover" of exponential computing power can break the verifier's commitment and generate pseudo-colorings that will later fool the verifier into accepting). Nevertheless, one can show that the modified protocol does satisfy the computational-soundness condition (of Definition 4.8.1). Namely, we show that for every polynomial $p(\cdot)$, for every polynomial-time interactive machine B, for all sufficiently large graphs $G \notin G3C$, and for every y and z,

$$\Pr\left[\langle B(y), V_{G3C}(z)\rangle(x) = 1\right] \leq \frac{1}{p(|x|)}$$

where V_{G3C} is the verifier program in the modified protocol.

Using the information-theoretic unambiguity of the commitment scheme employed by the prover, we can talk of a unique color assignment that is induced by the prover's commitments. Using the fact that this commitment scheme is non-oblivious, it follows that the prover can be modified so that in Step P1 it will also output (on its private output tape) the values to which it commits itself at this step. Using this output and relying on the computational secrecy of the verifier's commitment scheme, it follows that the color assignment generated by the prover is almost independent of the verifier's commitment. Hence, the probability that the prover can fool the verifier into accepting an input not in the language is at most negligibly greater than what it would have been if the verifier had asked random queries after the prover made its (color) commitments. The computational soundness of the (modified) protocol follows. (We remark that we do not know if the protocol is computationally sound in the case in which the prover uses a commitment scheme that is not guaranteed to be non-oblivious.[22])

Showing that the (modified) protocol is zero-knowledge is even easier than it was in the first approach (i.e., in Section 4.9.1). The reason is that when demonstrating

---

[22]Specifically, we do not know how to rule out the possibility that after seeing the verifier's commitment of Step V0, the cheating prover could send some strings at Step P1 such that after the verifier revealed its commitments, the prover could open those strings in a suitable way. To illustrate the problem, suppose that two parties wish to toss a coin by using a (perfectly binding) commitment scheme and that the protocol is as follows: First, the first party commits to a bit, then the second party commits to a bit, next the first party reveals its bit, finally the second party reveals its bit, and the result is defined as the XOR of the two revealed bits. Now, by copying the messages of the first party, the second party can force the outcome always to be zero! Note that this problem does *not* arise when the second party uses a non-oblivious commitment scheme. The problem also does *not* arise when the first party commits via a perfectly hiding commitment scheme (and the second party still uses a perfectly binding commitment scheme). (The latter protocol is analogous to the proof system presented in Section 4.9.1.)

zero-knowledge of such protocols, we use the secrecy of the prover's commitment scheme and the unambiguity of the verifier's commitment scheme. Hence, only these properties of the commitment schemes are relevant to the zero-knowledge property of the protocols. Yet the current (modified) protocol uses commitment schemes with relevant properties that are not weaker than the ones of the corresponding commitment schemes used in Construction 4.9.1. Specifically, the prover's commitment scheme in the modified protocol possesses computational secrecy, just like the prover's commitment scheme in Construction 4.9.1. We stress that this commitment, like the simpler commitment used for the prover in Construction 4.9.1, has the simultaneous-secrecy (of many copies) property. Furthermore, the verifier's commitment scheme in the modified protocol possesses "information-theoretic" unambiguity, whereas the verifier's commitment scheme in Construction 4.9.1 is merely computationally unambiguous. Thus, using Theorem 4.9.4, we have the following:

Corollary 4.9.5: *If non-uniformly one-way functions exist, then every language in $\mathcal{NP}$ has a round-efficient zero-knowledge argument.*

4.9.2.3. An Alternative Construction

An alternative way of deriving Corollary 4.9.5 is by modifying Construction 4.4.7 so as to allow easy simulation, and in particular, robustness under parallel composition. A key ingredient in this modification is the notion of commitment schemes with a "trapdoor property." Loosely speaking, the commit phase of such schemes consists of a receiver message followed by a sender message, so that *given the receiver's private coins* one can efficiently generate strings that are computationally indistinguishable from the sender's message and yet later open these strings so as to reveal any value. Note that this does not contradict the computational-binding property, since the latter refers to cheating senders (that do *not* know the receiver's private coins). We refrain from presenting a formal definition and merely sketch how such schemes can be constructed and used.

Constructing a Trapdoor Commitment Scheme Using Any One-Way Function. Let f be a one-way function, and let $R_f \stackrel{\text{def}}{=} \{(f(w), w) : w \in \{0, 1\}^*\}$ be an $\mathcal{NP}$-relation (corresponding to the $\mathcal{NP}$-set Range(f)). On security parameter n, the receiver selects uniformly $r \in \{0, 1\}^n$ and reduces the instance $f(r) \in$ Range(f) to an instance of the Hamiltonian-cycle (HC) problem, using the standard reduction. The resulting graph is sent to the sender that (not knowing a Hamiltonian cycle is in it) is asked to execute Step P1 in Construction 4.7.14 so that it can respond to a Step-V1 message that equals its input bit (to which it wishes to commit). That is, to commit to the bit 0, the sender sends a matrix of commitments to the entries in the adjacency matrix of a random isomorphic copy of the graph, whereas to commit to the bit 1, the sender sends a matrix of commitments to the entries in the adjacency matrix of a random (simple) n-cycle. Hence, the sender behaves analogously to the simulator of Construction 4.7.14. That is repeated, in parallel, for n times, resulting in a constant-round commitment scheme that is computationally hiding (by virtue of the prover's commitments in Step P1 of Construction 4.7.14) and computationally binding (since otherwise the sender recovers r and so inverts f on input $f(r)$). In contrast, knowledge of r allows one to execute the prover's strategy for Step P1 of Construction 4.7.14 and later open the commitment either way. (Note that the standard reduction of Range(f) to HC is augmented by a polynomial-time computable and invertible mapping of pre-images under f to Hamiltonian cycles in the corresponding reduced graphs.)

Using the Trapdoor Commitment Scheme. One way of using the foregoing scheme toward our goals is to use it for the prover's commitment in (Step P1 of) Construction 4.4.7. To this end, we augment the trapdoor commitment scheme so that before the sender sends its actual commitment (i.e., the message corresponding to Step P1 of Construction 4.7.14) we let the receiver prove that it knows a (corresponding) trapdoor (i.e., a sequence of coins that yields the graph it has sent to the sender). This proof of knowledge need only be witness-hiding, and so it can be carried out in a constant number of rounds. The simulator for the foregoing modification of Construction 4.4.7 first uses the corresponding knowledge extractor (to obtain the trapdoor for the prover's commitments) and then takes advantage of the trapdoor feature to generate false commitments that it can later open any way it needs to (so as to answer the verifier's requests).

4.10.* Non-Interactive Zero-Knowledge Proofs

In this section we consider non-interactive zero-knowledge proof systems. The model consists of three entities: a prover, a verifier, and a uniformly selected sequence of bits (which can be thought of as being selected by a trusted third party). Both verifier and prover can read the random sequence, and each can toss additional coins. The interaction consists of a single message sent from the prover to the verifier, who then is left with the decision (whether to accept or not). Non-interactive zero-knowledge proof systems have various applications (e.g., to encryption schemes secure against chosen message attacks and to signature schemes).

We start with basic definitions and constructions allowing us to prove a single assertion of a priori bounded length. Next we extend the treatment to proof systems in which many assertions of various lengths can be proved, as long as the total length of all assertions is a polynomial in a security parameter but the polynomial is *not* a priori known. Jumping ahead, we note that, unlike the basic treatment, the extended treatment allows us to prove assertions of total length much greater than the length of the trusted random string. The relation between the total length of the provable assertions and the length of the trusted random string is analogous to the relation between the total length of messages that can be encrypted (resp., documents that can be signed) and the length of the encryption key (resp., signing key). We stress, however, that even handling the basic case is very challenging in the current context (of non-interactive zero-knowledge proofs).

4.10.1. Basic Definitions

The model of non-interactive proofs seems closer in spirit to the model of $\mathcal{NP}$-proofs than to general interactive proofs. In a sense, the $\mathcal{NP}$-proof model is extended by allowing the prover and verifier to refer to a common random string, as well as toss coins by themselves. Otherwise, as in the case of $\mathcal{NP}$-proofs, the interaction is minimal (i.e., unidirectional: from the prover to the verifier). Thus, in the definition that follows, both the prover and verifier are ordinary probabilistic machines that, in addition to the common input, also get a uniformly distributed (common) *reference string*. We stress that, in addition to the common input and common reference string, both the prover and verifier can toss coins and get auxiliary inputs. However, for the sake of simplicity, we present a definition for the case in which none of these machines gets an auxiliary input (yet they both can toss additional coins). The verifier also gets as input the output produced by the prover.

Definition 4.10.1 (Non-Interactive Proof System): *A pair of probabilistic machines* (P, V) *is called a* **non-interactive proof system for a language** L *if V is polynomial-time and the following two conditions hold:*

- Completeness: *For every $x \in L$,*

$$\Pr[V(x, R, P(x, R)) = 1] \geq \frac{2}{3}$$

  where R is a random variable uniformly distributed in $\{0, 1\}^{\text{poly}(|x|)}$.
- Soundness: *For every $x \notin L$ and every algorithm B,*

$$\Pr[V(x, R, B(x, R)) = 1] \leq \frac{1}{3}$$

  where R is a random variable uniformly distributed in $\{0, 1\}^{\text{poly}(|x|)}$.

The uniformly chosen string R is called the **common reference string**.

As usual, the error probability in both conditions can be reduced (from $\frac{1}{3}$) down to $2^{-\text{poly}(|x|)}$ by repeating the process sufficiently many times (using a sequence of many independently chosen reference strings). In stating the soundness condition, we have deviated from the standard formulation that allows $x \notin L$ to be adversarially selected after R is fixed; the latter "adaptive" formulation of soundness is used in Section 4.10.3.2, and it is easy to transform a system satisfying the foregoing ("non-adaptive") soundness condition into one satisfying the adaptive soundness condition (see Section 4.10.3.2).

Every language in $\mathcal{NP}$ has a non-interactive proof system (in which no randomness is used). However, this $\mathcal{NP}$-proof system is unlikely to be zero-knowledge (see Definition 4.10.2).

The definition of zero-knowledge for the non-interactive model is simplified by the fact that because the verifier cannot affect the prover's actions it suffices to consider the simulatability of the view of a single verifier (i.e., the prescribed one). Actually, we can avoid considering the verifier at all (since its view can be generated from the common reference string and the message sent by the prover).

Definition 4.10.2 (Non-Interactive Zero-Knowledge): *A non-interactive proof system (P, V) for a language L is **zero-knowledge** if there exists a polynomial p and a probabilistic polynomial-time algorithm M such that the ensembles $\{(x, U_{p(|x|)}, P(x, U_{p(|x|)}))\}_{x \in L}$ and $\{M(x)\}_{x \in L}$ are computationally indistinguishable, where U_m is a random variable uniformly distributed over $\{0, 1\}^m$.*

This definition, too, is "non-adaptive" (i.e., the common input cannot depend on the common reference string). An adaptive formulation of zero-knowledge is presented and discussed in Section 4.10.3.2.

Non-Interactive Zero-Knowledge versus Constant-Round Zero-Knowledge. We stress that the non-interactive zero-knowledge model postulates the existence of a uniformly selected reference string available to both prover and verifier. A natural suggestion is to replace this postulate with a two-party protocol for generating a uniformly distributed string of specified length. Such a protocol should be resilient to adversarial behavior by each of the two parties: The output should be uniformly distributed even if one of the parties deviates from the protocol (using any probabilistic polynomial-time strategy). Furthermore, it seems that such a protocol should have a strong simulatability feature, allowing the generation of a random-execution transcript for every given outcome. Specifically, in order to obtain a constant-round zero-knowledge proof system from a non-interactive zero-knowledge proof, one seems to need a constant-round (strongly simulatable) protocol for generating uniformly distributed strings. Such a protocol can be constructed using perfectly hiding commitment schemes. In combination with the results that follow, one can derive an alternative construction of a round-efficient zero-knowledge proof for $\mathcal{NP}$.

4.10.2. Constructions

A fictitious abstraction that nevertheless is very helpful for the design of non-interactive zero-knowledge proof systems is the *hidden-bits model*. In this model the common reference string is uniformly selected as before, but only the prover can see all of it. The "proof" that the prover sends to the verifier consists of two parts; a "certificate" and the specification of some bit positions in the common reference string. The verifier can inspect only the bits of the common reference string residing in the locations that have been specified by the prover. Certainly, in addition, the verifier inspects the common input and the "certificate."

Definition 4.10.3 (Proof Systems in the Hidden-Bits Model): *A pair of probabilistic machines (P, V) is called a **hidden-bits proof system for** L if V is polynomial-time and the following two conditions hold:*

- Completeness: *For every $x \in L$,*

$$\Pr[V(x, R_I, I, \pi) = 1] \geq \frac{2}{3}$$

where $(I, \pi) \overset{\text{def}}{=} P(x, R)$, R is a random variable uniformly distributed in $\{0, 1\}^{\text{poly}(|x|)}$, and R_I is the sub-string of R at positions $I \subseteq \{1, 2, \ldots, \text{poly}(|x|)\}$. That is, $R_I = r_{i_1} \cdots r_{i_t}$, where $R = r_1 \cdots r_t$ and $I = (i_1, \ldots, i_t)$.

- Soundness: *For every $x \notin L$ and every algorithm B,*

$$\Pr[V(x, R_I, I, \pi) = 1] \le \frac{1}{3}$$

where $(I, \pi) \overset{\text{def}}{=} B(x, R)$, R is a random variable uniformly distributed in $\{0, 1\}^{\text{poly}(|x|)}$, and R_I is the sub-string of R at positions $I \subseteq \{1, 2, \ldots, \text{poly}(|x|)\}$.

*In both cases, I is called the set of **revealed bits** and π is called the **certificate**. Zero-knowledge is defined as before, with the exception that we need to simulate $(x, R_I, P(x, R)) = (x, R_I, I, \pi)$ rather than $(x, R, P(x, R))$.*

As stated earlier, we do not suggest the hidden-bits model as a realistic model. The importance of the model stems from two facts. First, it is a "clean" model that facilitates the design of proof systems (in it); second, proof systems in the hidden-bits model can be easily transformed into non-interactive proof systems (i.e., the realistic model). The transformation (which utilizes a one-way permutation f with hard-core b) follows.

Construction 4.10.4 (From Hidden-Bits Proof Systems to Non-Interactive Ones): *Let (P, V) be a hidden-bits proof system for L, and suppose that $f : \{0, 1\}^* \to \{0, 1\}^*$ and $b : \{0, 1\}^* \to \{0, 1\}$ are polynomial-time-computable. Furthermore, let $m = \text{poly}(n)$ denote the length of the common reference string for common inputs of length n, and suppose that f is 1-1 and length-preserving. Following is a specification of a non-interactive system (P', V'):*

- Common input: $x \in \{0, 1\}^n$.
- Common reference string: $s = (s_1, \ldots, s_m)$, where each s_i is in $\{0, 1\}^n$.
- Prover (denoted P'):

    1. computes $r_i = b(f^{-1}(s_i))$ for $i = 1, 2, \ldots, m$,

    2. invokes P to obtain $(I, \pi) = P(x, r_1 \cdots r_m)$,

    3. outputs (I, π, p_I), where $p_I \overset{\text{def}}{=} (f^{-1}(s_{i_1}) \cdots f^{-1}(s_{i_t}))$ for $I = (i_1, \ldots, i_t)$.

- Verifier (denoted V'): *Given the prover's output $(I, \pi, (p_1 \cdots p_t))$, the verifier*

    1. checks that $s_{i_j} = f(p_j)$ for each $i_j \in I$ (in case a mismatch is found, V' halts and rejects),

    2. computes $r_i = b(p_i)$, for $i = 1, \ldots, t$, lets $r = r_1, \ldots, r_t$,

    3. invokes V on (x, r, I, π) and accepts if and only if V accepts.

Proposition 4.10.5: *Let (P, V), L, f, b, and (P', V') be as in Construction 4.10.4. Then (P', V') is a non-interactive proof system for L, provided that $\Pr[b(U_n) = 1] = \frac{1}{2}$. Furthermore, if P is zero-knowledge and b is a hard-core of f, then P' is zero-knowledge too.*

We remark that P' is not perfect zero-knowledge even in case P is. Also, P' cannot be implemented in polynomial-time (even with the help of auxiliary inputs) even if P is (see the following Remark 4.10.6).

> **Proof Sketch:** To see that (P', V') is a non-interactive proof system for L, we note that uniformly chosen $s_i \in \{0, 1\}^n$ induce uniformly distributed bits $r_i \in \{0, 1\}$. This follows from $r_i = b(f^{-1}(s_i))$, the fact that f is 1-1, and the fact that $b(f^{-1}(U_n)) \equiv b(U_n)$ is unbiased. (Note that in case b is a hard-core of f, it is almost unbiased (i.e., $\Pr[b(U_n) = 1] = \frac{1}{2} \pm \mu(n)$, where μ is a negligible function). Thus, saying that b is a hard-core for f essentially suffices.)
>
> To see that P' is zero-knowledge, note that we can convert an efficient simulator for P into an efficient simulator for P'. Specifically, for each revealed bit of value σ, we uniformly select a string $r \in \{0, 1\}^n$ such that $b(r) = \sigma$ and put $f(r)$ in the corresponding position in the common reference string. For each *unrevealed* bit, we uniformly select a string $s \in \{0, 1\}^n$ and put it in the corresponding position in the common reference string. The output of the P' simulator consists of the common reference string generated as before, all the r's generated by the P' simulator for bits revealed by the P simulator, and the output of the P simulator. Using the fact that b is a hard-core of f, it follows that the output of the P' simulator is computationally indistinguishable from the verifier's view (when receiving a proof from P'). ∎

Remark 4.10.6 (Efficient Implementation of P'): As stated earlier, in general, P' cannot be efficiently implemented given black-box access to P. What is needed is the ability (of P') to invert f. On the other hand, for P' to be zero-knowledge, f must be one-way. The obvious solution is to use a family of trapdoor permutations and let the prover know the trapdoor. Furthermore, the family should have the property that its members can be efficiently recognized (i.e., given a description of a function, one can efficiently decide whether or not it is in the family). In other words, P' starts by selecting a permutation f over $\{0, 1\}^n$ such that it knows its trapdoor and proceeds as in Construction 4.10.4, except that it also appends the description of f to the "proof." The verifier acts as in Construction 4.10.4 with respect to the function f specified in the proof. In addition, it checks to see that f is indeed in the family. Both the completeness and the zero-knowledge conditions follow exactly as in the proof of Proposition 4.10.5. For the soundness condition, we need to consider all possible members of the family (without loss of generality, there are at most 2^n such permutations). For each such permutation, the argument is as before, and our claim thus follows by a counting argument (as applied in Section 4.10.3.2).[23] The construction can be extended to arbitrary trapdoor permutations; details omitted.

We now turn to the construction of proof systems in the Hidden-Bits model. Specifically, we are going to construct a proof system for the *Hamiltonian-Cycle (HC)* problem that is $\mathcal{NP}$-complete (and thus get proof systems for any language in $\mathcal{NP}$). We consider

---

[23] Actually, we also need to repeat the (P, V) system $O(n)$ times, so as first to reduce the soundness error to $\frac{1}{3} \cdot 2^{-n}$.

directed graphs (and the existence of directed Hamiltonian cycles). Next, we present a basic zero-knowledge system in which Hamiltonian graphs are accepted with probability 1, whereas non-Hamiltonian graphs on n vertices are rejected with probability $\Omega(n^{-3/2})$. (This system builds on the one presented in Construction 4.7.14.)

Construction 4.10.7 (A Hidden-Bits System for HC):

- Common input: *A directed graph* $G = (V, E)$, *with* $n \stackrel{\text{def}}{=} |V|$.
- Common reference string: *Viewed as an* n^3-*by*-n^3 *Boolean matrix* M, *with each entry being* 1 *with probability* n^{-5}.

  This is implemented by breaking the common reference string into blocks of length $5 \log_2 n$ and setting a matrix entry to 1 if and only if the corresponding block is all 1's.

- Definitions: *A* **permutation matrix** *is a matrix in which each row* (resp., column) *contains a single entry of value* 1. *A* **Hamiltonian matrix** *is a permutation matrix that corresponds to a simple directed cycle going through all rows and columns.* (That is, the corresponding directed graph consists of a single Hamiltonian cycle.)

  An n^3-by-n^3 matrix M is called useful if it contains a generalized n-by-n Hamiltonian sub-matrix and all other $n^6 - n^2$ entries in M are 0. That is, a useful n^3-by-n^3 matrix contains exactly n 1-entries that form a simple n-cycle, $\{(\phi_1(i), \phi_2((i \bmod n) + 1)) : i = 1, \ldots, n\}$, where ϕ_1 and ϕ_2 are 1-1 mappings of $\{1, \ldots, n\}$ to $\{1, \ldots, n^3\}$.

- Prover: *Let* C *be a Hamiltonian cycle in* G, *in case such exists. The prover examines the matrix* M *and acts according to the following two cases:*

  Case 1: M *is useful. Let* H *denote its Hamiltonian* n-by-n *sub-matrix and* C_H *the corresponding Hamiltonian cycle in* H.

  - *The prover reveals all* $(n^6 - n^2)$ *entries in* M *that are not in* H.
  - *The prover finds a* 1-1 *mapping,* π_1, *of* V *to the rows of* H *and a* 1-1 *mapping,* π_2, *of* V *to the columns of* H, *so that the edges of* C *are mapped to the* 1-*entries of* H.

    (Directed pairs of vertices of G, being edges or not, are mapped in the natural manner; that is, (u, v) is mapped to the matrix entry $(\pi_1(u), \pi_2(v))$. The mapping pair (π_1, π_2) is required to be an "isomorphism" of C to C_H.[24] Actually, we should specify one isomorphism among the n possible ones.)

  - *The prover* reveals the $(n^2 - |E|)$ entries corresponding to non-edges of G.

    (The correspondence is by the preceding mappings. That is, entry $(\pi_1(u), \pi_2(v))$ is revealed if and only if $(u, v) \in V \times V \setminus E$.)

---

[24] The minor technicality that prevents us from freely using the term "isomorphism" is that H is not a graph.

- *The prover* outputs *the mapping pair* (π_1, π_2) (as a certificate).

In total, $n^6 - |E|$ entries are revealed, all being 0-entries, and the certificate is (π_1, π_2).

Case 2: M is not useful. *In this case the prover* reveals *all entries of M*.

(No certificate is provided in this case.)

- Verifier: *Given the revealed entries and possibly a certificate, the verifier acts according to the following two cases:*

   Case 1: The prover has not revealed all entries in M. Let (π_1, π_2) be the certificate sent/output by the prover. The verifier checks that all entries in M that do not have pre-images unders (π_1, π_2) in E are revealed and are indeed zero. That is, the verifier accepts if all matrix entries, except for the entries in $\{(\pi_1(u), \pi_2(v)) : (u, v) \in E\}$, are revealed and all revealed bits are 0.

   Case 2: The prover has revealed all of M. In this case the verifier accepts if and only if M is not useful.

The following fact is instrumental for the analysis of Construction 4.10.7.

Fact 4.10.8: $\Pr[M \text{ is useful}] = \Omega(n^{-3/2})$.

Proof Sketch: The expected number of 1-entries in M equals $(n^3)^2 \cdot n^{-5} = n$. Furthermore, with probability $\Theta(1/\sqrt{n})$ the matrix M contains exactly n entries of value 1. Considering any row of M, observe that with probability at most $\binom{n^3}{2} \cdot (n^{-5})^2 < n^{-4}$ this row contains more than a single 1-entry. Thus, with probability at least $1 - 2n^3 \cdot n^{-4} = 1 - O(n^{-1})$ the rows and columns of M each contain at most a single 1-entry. Combining these two facts, it follows that with probability $\Omega(1/\sqrt{n})$ the matrix M contains an n-by-n permutation sub-matrix and all the other entries of M are 0. Now observe that there are $n!$ (n-by-n) permutation matrices, and $(n - 1)!$ of them are Hamiltonian matrices. Thus, conditioned on M containing an n-by-n permutation sub-matrix (and zeros elsewhere), with probability $1/n$ the matrix M is useful. ∎

Proposition 4.10.9: *There exists a* (perfect) *zero-knowledge Hidden-Bits proof system for Graph Hamiltonicity. Furthermore, the prover can be implemented by a polynomial-time machine that gets a Hamiltonian cycle as auxiliary input.*

Proof Sketch: We start by demonstrating a noticeable gap in the acceptance probability for the verifier of Construction 4.10.7. (This gap can be amplified, to meet the requirements, by a polynomial number of repetitions.) First, we claim that if G is Hamiltonian and the prover follows the program, then the verifier accepts, no matter which matrix M appears as the common reference string. The claim follows easily by observing that in Case 1 the mapping pair maps the Hamiltonian cycle of G to the Hamiltonian cycle of H, and because the latter contains the only 1-entries in M, all non-edges of G are mapped to 0-entries of M. (In Case 2 the claim is trivial.) We remark that the prover's actions can be implemented in polynomial time when given a Hamiltonian cycle of G as auxiliary input. Specifically, all that the prover needs to do is to check if M is useful and to find an isomorphism between two given n-vertex cycles.

Next, suppose that G is non-Hamiltonian. By Fact 4.10.8, with probability at least $\Omega(n^{-3/2})$, the matrix M is useful. Fixing any useful matrix M, we show that the verifier rejects G, no matter what the prover does. Clearly, if the prover behaves as in Case 2, then the verifier rejects (since M is useful). Thus we focus on the case in which the prover outputs a pair of matchings (π_1, π_2) (as in Case 1). Let H denote the (unique) n-by-n Hamiltonian sub-matrix of M, and consider the following sub-cases:

1. $\pi_1(V) \times \pi_2(V)$ does not equal H. Because the prover must reveal all entries not in the sub-matrix $\pi_1(V) \times \pi_2(V)$, it follows that it must reveal some row or column of H. But such a row or column must contain a 1-entry, and so the verifier will reject.

2. Otherwise, $\pi_1(V) \times \pi_2(V) = H$. Also, each non-edge of G must be mapped to a 0-entry of H (or else the verifier will reject). It follows that the pre-image of each 1-entry in H must be an edge in G, which implies that G has a Hamiltonian cycle (in contradiction to our hypothesis).

We conclude that in case G is non-Hamiltonian, it is rejected with probability $\Omega(n^{-3/2})$.

Finally, we show that the prover is zero-knowledge. This is done by constructing a simulator that, on input a graph G, randomly selects an n^3-by-n^3 matrix, denoted M, with distribution as in the common reference string (i.e., each entry being 1 with probability n^{-5}). If M is not useful, then the simulator outputs $(G, M, \{1, \ldots, n^3\}^2)$ (i.e., all bits are revealed, with values as in M, and no certificate is given). Otherwise, ignoring this (useful) M, the simulator uniformly selects a pair of 1-1 mappings (π_1, π_2) such that $\pi_i : V \to \{1, \ldots, n^3\}$ for $i = 1, 2$. The simulator outputs $(G, 0^{n^6 - |E|}, I, (\pi_1, \pi_2))$, where $I \stackrel{\text{def}}{=} \{1, \ldots, n^3\}^2 \setminus \{(\pi_1(u), \pi_2(v)) : (u, v) \in E\}$. The reader can easily verify that the output distribution of the simulator is identical to the distribution seen by the verifier. ∎

Using Propositions 4.10.9 and 4.10.5 and Remark 4.10.6, we conclude the following:

Theorem 4.10.10: *Assuming the existence of one-way permutations,*[25] *each language in $\mathcal{NP}$ has a zero-knowledge non-interactive proof system. Furthermore, assuming the existence of families of trapdoor permutations, each language in $\mathcal{NP}$ has a zero-knowledge non-interactive proof system in which the prover can*

---

[25] As usual in this chapter, here and later, we mean constructs for which the hardness requirement also holds with respect to non-uniform (polynomial-size) circuits.

be implemented by a probabilistic polynomial-time machine that gets an $\mathcal{NP}$-witness as auxiliary input.

4.10.3. Extensions

We present the two extensions mentioned at the beginning of this section: First we consider proof systems that preserve zero-knowledge when applied polynomially many times (with the same common reference string), and later we consider proof systems that preserve security when the assertions (i.e., common inputs) are adversarially selected after the common reference string has been fixed.

4.10.3.1. Proving Many Assertions of Varying Lengths

The definitions presented in Section 4.10.1 are restricted in two ways. First, they consider the proving of only one assertion relative to the common reference string, and furthermore the common reference string is allowed to be longer than the assertion (though polynomial in length of the assertion). A stronger definition, provided next, allows the proving of poly(n) assertions, each of poly(n) length, using the same n-bit-long common reference string.

We first note that it suffices to treat the case in which the number of assertions is unbounded but the length of each assertion is a priori bounded. Specifically, for any $\varepsilon > 0$, it suffices to consider the case where poly(n) assertions, each of length n^ε, need to be proved relative to the same n-bit-long common reference string. The reason for this is that we can reduce, in a "zero-knowledge manner," any $\mathcal{NP}$-assertion of length poly(n) into a sequence of poly(n) $\mathcal{NP}$-assertions, each of length n^ε: For example, first we reduce the original (poly(n)-bit-long) $\mathcal{NP}$-assertion to an assertion regarding the 3-colorability of a poly(n)-vertex graph. Next, we use a commitment scheme with commitments of length $n^\varepsilon/2$ in order to commit to the coloring of each vertex. Finally, for each edge, we (invoke the proof system to) prove that the corresponding two commitments are to two different values in $\{1, 2, 3\}$. Note that each such assertion is of an $\mathcal{NP}$ type and refers to a pair of $n^\varepsilon/2$-bit-long strings.

We now turn to the actual definitions. First we note that nothing needs to be changed regarding the definition of non-interactive proof systems (Definition 4.10.1). We still require the ability to be convinced by valid assertions, as well as "protection" from false assertions. Alas, a minor technical difference is that whereas in Definition 4.10.1 we denoted by n the length of the assertion and considered a common reference string of length poly(n), here we let n denote the length of the common reference string used for assertions of length n^ε. We call ε the *fundamental constant* of the proof system. In contrast, the definition of zero-knowledge has to be extended to handle an (a priori) unbounded sequence of proofs. (Recall that U_n denotes a random variable, uniformly distributed over $\{0, 1\}^n$.)

Definition 4.10.11 (Non-Interactive Zero-Knowledge, Unbounded Version):
A non-interactive proof system (P, V), with fundamental constant ε, for a

language L is **unboundedly zero-knowledge** *if for every polynomial p there exists a probabilistic polynomial-time algorithm M such that the following two ensembles are computationally indistinguishable:*

1. $\{((x_1, \ldots, x_{p(n)}), U_n, (P(x_1, U_n), \ldots, P(x_{p(n)}, U_n)))\}_{x_1, \ldots, x_{p(n)} \in L_{n^\varepsilon}}$
2. $\{M(x_1, \ldots, x_{p(n)})\}_{x_1, \ldots, x_{p(n)} \in L_{n^\varepsilon}}$

   where $L_\ell \overset{\text{def}}{=} L \cap \{0, 1\}^\ell$.

We comment that the non-interactive proof systems presented earlier (e.g., Construction 4.10.4) are not unboundedly zero-knowledge; see Exercise 34.

We now turn to the construction of unboundedly zero-knowledge (non-interactive) proof systems. The underlying idea is to facilitate the simulation by potentially proving a fictitious assertion regarding a portion of the common reference string. The assertion that will be potentially proved (about this portion) will have the following properties:

1. The assertion holds for a negligible fraction of the strings of the same length. Thus, adding this potential ability does not significantly affect the soundness condition.

2. Strings satisfying the assertion are computationally indistinguishable from uniformly distributed strings of the same length. Thus, it will be acceptable for the simulator to use such strings, rather than uniformly chosen ones (used in the real proof system).

3. The decision problem for the assertion is in $\mathcal{NP}$. This will allow a reduction to an $\mathcal{NP}$-complete problem.

An immediate assertion, concerning strings, that comes to mind is being produced by a pseudorandom generator. This yields the following construction, where G denotes such a generator.

Construction 4.10.12 (An Unboundedly Zero-Knowledge Non-Interactive Proof System): *Let $G : \{0, 1\}^\ell \to \{0, 1\}^{2\ell}$, let L_1 be an $\mathcal{NP}$-complete language, let L be an arbitrary $\mathcal{NP}$ language, and consider the following $\mathcal{NP}$ language:*

$$L_2 \overset{\text{def}}{=} \{(x, p) : x \in L \bigvee \exists w' \in \{0, 1\}^{|x|} \text{ s.t. } G(w') = p\}$$

Consider a standard reduction of L_2 to L_1, and let q be a polynomial such that 3ℓ-bit-long instances of L_2 are mapped to $q(\ell)$-bit-long instances of L_1. Let (P, V) be an ordinary non-interactive proof system for L_1, and suppose that for some polynomial q' the system (P, V) uses a common reference string of length $q'(\ell)$ for assertions of length $q(\ell)$. Suppose that P takes as auxiliary input an $\mathcal{NP}$-witness for membership in L_1, and let $n = q'(\ell) + 2\ell$. Following is a specification of a non-interactive proof system for $L \in \mathcal{NP}$:

- Common input: $x \in \{0, 1\}^\ell$.
- Common reference string: $r = (p, s)$, where $p \in \{0, 1\}^{2\ell}$ and $s \in \{0, 1\}^{n-2\ell}$.

- Prover:

  1. *Using a standard reduction of L_2 to L_1, the prover reduces $(x, p) \in \{0, 1\}^{\ell+2\ell}$ to $y \in \{0, 1\}^{q(\ell)}$. In addition, when given an $\mathcal{NP}$-witness u for $x \in L$, the prover reduces[26] u to a witness, denoted w, for $y \in L_1$.*

  2. *The prover invokes P on common input y, auxiliary input w, and common reference string s, obtaining output π, which it outputs/sends.*

- Verifier:

  1. *Reduces (x, p) to y using the same standard reduction of L_2 to L_1.*

  2. *Invokes V on common input y, common reference string s, and prover's output π, and decides as V does.*

Note that the reduction maps $(\ell + 2\ell)$-bit-long instances of L_2 to instances of L_1 having length $q(\ell)$. Recall that by the hypothesis, the proof system (P, V) handles L_1 instances of length $q(\ell)$ by using a reference string of length $q'(\ell) = n - 2\ell$, which exactly matches the length of s. Let $\varepsilon > 0$ be a constant satisfying $n^\varepsilon \leq \ell$ (i.e., $(2\ell + q'(\ell))^\varepsilon \leq \ell$). Then we have the following:

Proposition 4.10.13: *Let (P, V) be as before, and let G be a pseudorandom generator. Furthermore, suppose that P is zero-knowledge and that when given an $\mathcal{NP}$-witness as auxiliary input, it can be implemented in probabilistic polynomial time. Then Construction 4.10.12 constitutes an unboundedly zero-knowledge non-interactive proof system for L, with fundamental constant ε. Furthermore, the prover can be implemented by a probabilistic polynomial-time machine that gets an $\mathcal{NP}$-witness as auxiliary input.*

Proof Sketch: The completeness and efficiency claims for the new prover follow immediately from the hypotheses concerning (P, V). The soundness condition follows by observing that the probability that p is in the range of G is at most $2^{-\ell}$ (and relying on the soundness of (P, V)). To prove the zero-knowledge property, we construct a simulator as follows. The simulator uniformly selects $u' \in \{0, 1\}^\ell$ and $s \in \{0, 1\}^{n-2\ell}$, sets $p = G(u')$, and handles each instance $x \in \{0, 1\}^\ell$ in a sequence of L instances as follows: The simulator emulates the prover's program (on input x), except that it uses u' as the $\mathcal{NP}$-witness for $(x, p) \in L_2$. Namely, the simulator reduces $(x, p) \in L_2$ to $y' \in L_1$, along with reducing the $\mathcal{NP}$-witness u' to a witness w' (for y'). Next, the simulator invokes P on common input y', auxiliary input w', and common reference string s. Thus, when given a sequence of instances $\overline{x} = (x_1, \ldots, x_t)$, the simulator outputs $(\overline{x}, (p, s), P_{w'}(y'_1, s), \ldots, P_{w'}(y'_t, s))$, where y_i is the result of applying the reduction to (x_i, p). Note that the efficiency of the simulator relies on the efficient implementation of P (and on the efficiency of G). To prove that the simulator's output is computationally indistinguishable from the verifier's view,

---

[26] We again use the fact that the standard reductions are coupled with an adequate witness-reduction (see Exercise 16).

we combine the following two observations (which also rely on the efficient implementation of P):

1. *The distributions of the common reference string* are indeed very different in the two cases (i.e., real execution versus simulator's output). Yet, by the pseudorandomness of G, this difference is computationally indistinguishable. Thus, the verifier's view in real execution is computationally indistinguishable from its view in the case in which the common reference string is selected exactly as in the simulation (but the prover acts as in Construction 4.10.12).

2. The zero-knowledge property of P implies that P is witness-indistinguishable (as defined in Section 4.6). Thus, one cannot distinguish the case in which P uses a witness for $x \in L$ (as in Construction 4.10.12) from the case in which P uses as witness a seed for the pseudorandom sequence p (as done by the simulator). The same holds when repeating the proving process polynomially many times.

In other words, the zero-knowledge claim is proved by using a hybrid argument, where the (single) intermediate hybrid corresponds to executing the prover strategy (as is) on a pseudorandom reference string as produced by the simulator (rather than on a truly random reference string). These two observations establish that this intermediate hybrid is computationally indistinguishable from both of the extreme hybrids (which are the ensembles we wish to relate). ∎

Using Theorem 4.10.10 and Proposition 4.10.13, we obtain the following:

Theorem 4.10.14: *Assuming the existence of families of trapdoor permutations,[27] each language in $\mathcal{NP}$ has an unboundedly zero-knowledge non-interactive proof system. Furthermore, the prover can be implemented by a probabilistic polynomial-time machine that gets an $\mathcal{NP}$-witness as auxiliary input.*

4.10.3.2. Adaptive Zero-Knowledge

As mentioned in Section 4.10.1, the definitions used thus far are non-adaptive. This refers to both the soundness and the zero-knowledge conditions. (The same applies also to the completeness condition; but because all commonly used schemes have perfect completeness,[28] this issue is of little interest). In the adaptive analogies, the common input is adversarially selected after the common reference string is fixed. The formulation of adaptive soundness is straightforward, and we call the reader's attention to the formulation of adaptive zero-knowledge.

Definition 4.10.15 (Non-Interactive Zero-Knowledge Proofs, Adaptive Version): *Let (P, V) be a non-interactive proof system for a language L (i.e., as in Definition 4.10.1).*

---

[27] See footnote 25.
[28] That is, for every $x \in L$, it actually holds that $\Pr[V(x, R, P(x, R)) = 1] = 1$.

- Adaptive soundness: *We say that (P, V) is **adaptively sound** if for every n and every pair of functions $\Xi : \{0, 1\}^{\text{poly}(n)} \to (\{0, 1\}^n \setminus L)$ and $\Pi : \{0, 1\}^{\text{poly}(n)} \to \{0, 1\}^{\text{poly}(n)}$,*

$$\Pr[V(\Xi(R), R, \Pi(R)) = 1] \leq \frac{1}{3}$$

  where R is a random variable uniformly distributed in $\{0, 1\}^{\text{poly}(n)}$.

- Adaptive zero-knowledge: *We say that (P, V) is **adaptively zero-knowledge** if there exist two probabilistic polynomial-time algorithms M_1 and M_2 such that for every function $\Xi : \{0, 1\}^{\text{poly}(n)} \to (\{0, 1\}^n \cap L)$ the ensembles $\{(R_n, \Xi(R_n), P(\Xi(R_n), R_n))\}_{n \in \mathbb{N}}$, and $\{M^{\Xi}(1^n)\}_{n \in \mathbb{N}}$ are computationally indistinguishable, where R_n is a random variable uniformly distributed in $\{0, 1\}^{\text{poly}(n)}$, and $M^{\Xi}(1^n)$ denotes the output of the following randomized process:*

  1. $(r, s) \leftarrow M_1(1^n)$

  2. $x \leftarrow \Xi(r)$

  3. $\pi \leftarrow M_2(x, s)$

  4. Output (r, x, π)

  (That is, M_1 generates a pair (r, s) consisting of a supposedly common reference string r and auxiliary information s to be used by M_2. The latter, given an adaptively selected input x and the auxiliary information s, generates an alleged proof π. We stress that x can depend on r, but not on s.)

As usual, the error probability (in the adaptive-soundness condition) can be reduced (from $\frac{1}{3}$) down to $2^{-\text{poly}(|x|)}$. Also, any non-interactive proof system (i.e., of non-adaptive soundness) can be transformed into a system that is adaptively sound by merely reducing the error probability and applying the union bound; that is, for every $\Xi : \{0, 1\}^{\text{poly}(n)} \to (\{0, 1\}^n \setminus L)$ and $\Pi : \{0, 1\}^{\text{poly}(n)} \to \{0, 1\}^{\text{poly}(n)}$, we have

$$\Pr[V(\Xi(R), R, \Pi(R)) = 1] \leq \sum_{x \in \{0,1\}^n \setminus L} \Pr[V(x, R, \Pi(R)) = 1]$$

$$\leq 2^n \cdot \max_{x \in \{0,1\}^n \setminus L} \{\Pr[V(x, R, \Pi(R)) = 1]\}$$

In contrast to the foregoing trivial transformation (from non-adaptive to adaptive soundness), we do not know of a simple transformation of non-interactive zero-knowledge proofs into ones that are adaptively zero-knowledge. Fortunately, however, the exposition in Section 4.10.2 extends to the adaptive setting. (The key idea is that the reference string in these proof systems can be generated obliviously of the common input.[29]) We obtain the following:

Theorem 4.10.16: *Assuming the existence of one-way permutations,[30] each language in $\mathcal{NP}$ has a non-interactive proof system that is adaptively*

---

[29] Specifically, this is obvious for the simulator presented in the proof of Proposition 4.10.9. We stress that this simulator determines the values of all hidden bits independently of the common input (i.e., either they form a random unuseful matrix or they are "effectively" all zeros). The simulator for the proof of Proposition 4.10.5 can be easily modified to work for such hidden-bit model simulators.

[30] See footnote 25.

zero-knowledge. Furthermore, assuming the existence of families of trapdoor permutations, the prover strategy in such a proof system can be implemented by a probabilistic polynomial-time machine that gets an $\mathcal{NP}$-witness as auxiliary input.

The "furthermore" statement extends to a model that allows the adaptive selection of polynomially many assertions (i.e., a model that combines the two extensions discussed in this subsection).

4.11.* Multi-Prover Zero-Knowledge Proofs

In this section we consider an extension of the notion of an interactive proof system. Specifically, we consider the interaction of a verifier with more than one prover (say, two provers). The provers can share an a-priori-selected strategy, but it is assumed that they cannot interact with each other during the time period in which they interact with the verifier. Intuitively, the provers can coordinate their strategies prior to, but not during, their interrogation by the verifier. Indeed, the multi-prover model is reminiscent of the common police procedure of isolating suspected collaborators and interrogating each of them separately. We discuss one realistic (digital) setting in which this model is applicable.

The notion of a multi-prover interactive proof plays a fundamental role in complexity theory. That aspect is not addressed here. In the current section we merely address the zero-knowledge aspects of multi-party interactive proofs. Most importantly, the multi-prover model enables the construction of (perfect) zero-knowledge proof systems for $\mathcal{NP}$, *independent of any complexity-theoretic assumptions.*

4.11.1. Definitions

For the sake of simplicity, we consider the two-prover model. We remark that the use of more provers would not offer any essential advantages (and specifically, none that would interest us in this section). Loosely speaking, a two-prover interactive proof system is a three-party protocol in which two parties are provers and the additional party is a verifier. The only interaction allowed in this model is between the verifier and each of the provers individually. In particular, a prover does not "know" the content of the messages sent by the verifier to the other prover. The provers do, however, share a random-input tape that is (as in the one-prover case) "beyond the reach" of the verifier. The two-prover setting is a special case of the *two-partner model* described next.

4.11.1.1. The Two-Partner Model

The two-partner model consists of two *partners* interacting with a third party, called the *solitary*. The two partners can agree on their strategies beforehand, and in particular they can agree on a common uniformly chosen string. Yet once the interaction with the solitary begins, the partners can no longer exchange information. The following definition of such an interaction extends Definitions 4.2.1 and 4.2.2.

Definition 4.11.1 (Two-Partner Model): *The* **two-partner model** *consists of three interactive machines, two called* **partners** *and the third called the* **solitary,** *that are linked and interact as hereby specified:*

- *The input tapes of all three parties coincide, and their content is called the* **common input.**
- *The random tapes of the two partners coincide and are called the* **partners' random tape.** *(The solitary has a separate random tape.)*
- *The solitary has two pairs of communication tapes and two switch tapes, instead of a single pair of communication tapes and a single switch tape (as in Definition 4.2.1).*
- *The two partners have the same identity, and the solitary has an opposite identity (see Definitions 4.2.1 and 4.2.2).*
- *The first (resp., second) switch tape of the solitary coincides with the switch tape of the first (resp., second) partner, and the first (resp., second) read-only communication tape of the solitary coincides with the write-only communication tape of the first (resp., second) partner, and vice versa.*
- *The* **joint computation** *of the three parties, on a common input x, is a sequence of triplets. Each triplet consists of the local configurations of the three machines. The behavior of each partner-solitary pair is as in the definition of the joint computation of a pair of interactive machines.*

We denote by $\langle P_1, P_2, S \rangle(x)$ the output of the solitary S after interacting with the partners P_1 and P_2, on common input x.

4.11.1.2. Two-Prover Interactive Proofs

A two-prover interactive proof system is now defined analogously to the one-prover case (see Definitions 4.2.4 and 4.2.6).

Definition 4.11.2 (Two-Prover Interactive Proof System): *A triplet of interactive machines (P_1, P_2, V) in the two-partner model is called a* **proof system for a language** *L if the machine V (called* verifier*) is probabilistic polynomial-time and the following two conditions hold:*

- Completeness: *For every $x \in L$,*

$$\Pr\left[\langle P_1, P_2, V \rangle(x) = 1\right] \geq \frac{2}{3}$$

- Soundness: *For every $x \notin L$ and every pair of partners (B_1, B_2),*

$$\Pr\left[\langle B_1, B_2, V \rangle(x) = 1\right] \leq \frac{1}{3}$$

As usual, the error probability in both conditions can be reduced (from $\frac{1}{3}$) down to $2^{-\text{poly}(|x|)}$ by *sequentially* repeating the protocol sufficiently many times. Error reduction via *parallel* repetitions is problematic (in general) in this context; see the suggestions for further reading at the end of the chapter.

The notion of zero-knowledge (for multi-prover systems) remains exactly as in the one-prover case. Actually, we make the definition of perfect zero-knowledge more strict by requiring that the simulator never fail (i.e., never outputs the special symbol $\perp$).[31] Namely:

Definition 4.11.3: *We say that a (two-prover) proof system* (P_1, P_2, V) *for a language L is* **perfect zero-knowledge** *if for every probabilistic polynomial-time interactive machine* V^* *there exists a probabilistic polynomial-time algorithm* M^* *such that for every* $x \in L$ *the random variables* $\langle P_1, P_2, V^* \rangle(x)$ *and* $M^*(x)$ *are identically distributed.*

Extension to the auxiliary-input (zero-knowledge) model is straightforward.

4.11.2. Two-Sender Commitment Schemes

The thrust of the current section is toward a method for constructing perfect zero-knowledge two-prover proof systems for every language in $\mathcal{NP}$. This method makes essential use of a commitment scheme *for two senders and one receiver* that possesses information-theoretic secrecy and unambiguity properties (i.e., is perfectly hiding and perfectly binding). We stress that it is impossible to achieve information-theoretic secrecy and unambiguity properties simultaneously in the single-sender model.

4.11.2.1. A Definition

Loosely speaking, a two-sender commitment scheme is an efficient *two-phase* protocol for the two-partner model through which the partners, called *senders*, can commit themselves to a *value* such that the following two conflicting requirements are satisfied:

1. *Secrecy*: At the end of the *commit phase*, the solitary, called the *receiver*, does not gain any *information* about the senders' value.

2. *Unambiguity*: Suppose that the commit phase is successfully completed. Then if later the senders can perform the *reveal phase* such that the receiver accepts the value 0 with probability p, then they cannot perform the *reveal phase* such that the receiver accepts the value 1 with probability substantially greater than $1 - p$. We stress that no interaction is allowed between the senders throughout the *entire* commit and reveal process. (We comment that for every p the senders can always conduct the commit phase such that they can later reveal the value 0 with probability p and the value 1 with probability $1 - p$. See Exercise 35.)

Instead of presenting a general definition, we restrict our attention to the special case of two-sender commitment schemes in which only the first sender (and the receiver) takes part in the commit phase, whereas only the second sender takes part in the (canonical) reveal phase. Furthermore, we assume, without loss of generality, that in the reveal

---

[31] Recall that in Definition 4.3.1, the simulator was allowed to fail (with probability at most $\frac{1}{2}$).

phase the second sender sends the content of the joint random tape (used by the first sender in the commit phase) to the receiver. We stress again that the two senders cannot exchange information between themselves throughout the entire commit and reveal process; thus, in particular, the second sender does not know the messages sent by the receiver to the first sender during the commit phase.

Definition 4.11.4 (Two-Sender Bit Commitment): *A* **two-sender bit-commitment scheme** *is a triplet of probabilistic polynomial-time interactive machines, denoted (S_1, S_2, R), for the two-partner model satisfying the following:*

- Input specification: *The common input is an integer n presented in unary, called the* **security parameter.** *The two partners, called the* **senders,** *have an auxiliary private input $v \in \{0, 1\}$.*
- Secrecy: *The 0-commitment and the 1-commitment are identically distributed. Namely, for every probabilistic (not necessarily polynomial-time) machine R^* interacting with the first sender (i.e., S_1), the random variables $\langle S_1(0), R^* \rangle (1^n)$ and $\langle S_1(1), R^* \rangle (1^n)$ are identically distributed.*
- Unambiguity: *Preliminaries: For simplicity, $v \in \{0, 1\}$ and $n \in \mathbb{N}$ are implicit in all notations.*

1. *As in Definition 4.4.1, a receiver's view of an interaction with the (first) sender, denoted $(r, \overline{m})$, consists of the random coins used by the receiver, denoted r, and the sequence of messages received from the (first) sender, denoted $\overline{m}$.*

2. *Let $\sigma \in \{0, 1\}$. We say that the string s is a* **possible σ-opening** *of the receiver's view $(r, \overline{m})$ if $\overline{m}$ describes the messages received by R when R uses local coins r and interacts with machine S_1, which uses local coins s and input $(\sigma, 1^n)$.*

3. *Let S_1^* be an arbitrary program for the first sender. Let p be a real and $\sigma \in \{0, 1\}$. We say that p is an* **upper bound on the probability of a σ-opening of the receiver's view of the interaction with S_1^*** *if for every random variable X (representing the string sent by the second sender in the reveal phase), which is statistically independent of the receiver's coin tosses, the probability that X is a possible σ-opening of the receiver's view of an interaction with S_1^* is at most p. That is,*

$$\Pr[X \text{ is a } \sigma\text{-opening of } \langle S_1^*, R \rangle (1^n)] \leq p$$

(The probability is taken over the coin tosses of the receiver, the strategy S_1^*, and the random variable X.)

4. *Let S_1^* be as before, and for each $\sigma \in \{0, 1\}$ let p_σ be an upper bound on the probability of a σ-opening of the receiver's view of the interaction with S_1^*. We say that* **the receiver's view of the interaction with S_1^* is unambiguous** *if $p_0 + p_1 \leq 1 + 2^{-n}$.*

The unambiguity *requirement asserts that for every program for the first sender S_1^* the receiver's interaction with S_1^* is unambiguous.*

In the formulation of the unambiguity requirement, the random variables X represent possible strategies of the second sender. Such a strategy may depend on the random input that is shared by the two senders, but is independent of the receiver's random coins (since information on these coins, if any, is only sent to the first sender). The strategies employed by the two senders determine, for each possible coin-tossing of the receiver, a pair of probabilities corresponding to their success in a 0-opening and a 1-opening. (In fact, bounds on these probabilities are determined merely by the strategy of the first sender.) The unambiguity condition asserts that the average of these pairs, taken over all possible receiver's coin tosses, is a pair that sums up to at most $1 + 2^{-n}$. Intuitively, this means that the senders cannot do more harm than deciding at random whether to commit to 0 or to 1. Both the secrecy and unambiguity requirements are information-theoretic (in the sense that no computational restrictions are placed on the adversarial strategies). We stress that we have implicitly assumed that the reveal phase takes the following canonical form:

1. The second sender sends to the receiver the initial private input v and the random coins s used by the first sender in the commit phase.

2. The receiver verifies that v and s (together with the private coins (i.e., r) used by R in the commit phase) indeed yield the messages that R has received in the commit phase. Verification is done in polynomial time (by running the programs S_1 and R).

Consider the pairs (p_0, p_1) assigned to each strategy S_1^* in the unambiguity condition of Definition 4.11.4. We note that the highest possible value of $p_0 + p_1$ is attainable by deterministic strategies for both senders.[32] Thus, it suffices to consider an arbitrary deterministic strategy S_1^* for the first sender and fixed σ-openings, denoted s^σ, for $\sigma \in \{0, 1\}$. The unambiguity condition thus says that for every such S_1^*, s^0, and s^1,

$$\sum_{\sigma \in \{0,1\}} \Pr[s^\sigma \text{ is a } \sigma\text{-opening of } \langle S_1^*, R \rangle(1^n)] \leq 1 + 2^{-n}$$

In fact, for the construction presented next, we shall establish a stronger condition:

Strong unambiguity condition: *For every deterministic strategy S_1^* and every pair of strings (s^0, s^1),*

$$\Pr[\forall \sigma \in \{0, 1\}, \ s^\sigma \text{ is a } \sigma\text{-opening of } \langle S_1^*, R \rangle(1^n)] \leq 2^{-n}$$

(Clearly, if the unambiguity condition is violated, then so is the strong unambiguity condition.)

4.11.2.2. A Construction

By the foregoing conventions, it suffices to explicitly describe the commit phase (in which only the first sender takes part).

---

[32] We use an averaging argument. First note that for every (probabilistic) S_1^* and σ there exists a string s^σ maximizing the probability that any fixed string is a σ-opening of $\langle S_1^*, R \rangle(1^n)$. Thus, the probability that s^σ is a σ-opening of $\langle S_1^*, R \rangle(1^n)$ is an upper bound on the probability that X (as in the definition) is a σ-opening of $\langle S_1^*, R \rangle(1^n)$. Similarly, fixing such a pair (s^0, s^1), we view S_1^* as a distribution over deterministic strategies for the first sender and consider the sum of the two probabilities assigned to each such strategy S_1^{**}. Thus, there exists a deterministic strategy S_1^{**} for which this sum is at least as large as the sum associated with S_1^*.

Construction 4.11.5 (A Two-Sender Bit Commitment):

- Preliminaries: *Let π_0 and π_1 denote two fixed permutations over $\{0, 1, 2\}$ such that π_0 is the identity permutation and π_1 is a permutation consisting of a single transposition, say $(1, 2)$. Namely, $\pi_1(1) = 2$, $\pi_1(2) = 1$, and $\pi_1(0) = 0$.*
- Common input: *The security parameter n (in unary).*
- Sender's input: $\sigma \in \{0, 1\}$.
- A convention: *Suppose that the content of the senders' random tape encodes a uniformly selected $\bar{s} = s_1 \cdots s_n \in \{0, 1, 2\}^n$.*
- Commit phase:

    1. The receiver uniformly selects $\bar{r} = r_1 \cdots r_n \in \{0, 1\}^n$ and sends $\bar{r}$ to the first sender.

    2. For each i, the first sender computes $c_i \stackrel{\text{def}}{=} \pi_{r_i}(s_i) + \sigma \bmod 3$ and sends $c_1 \cdots c_n$ to the receiver.

We remark that the *second* sender could have opened the commitment either way if it had known $\bar{r}$ (sent by the receiver to the *first* sender). The point is that the second sender does not know $\bar{r}$, and this fact drastically limits its ability to cheat.

Proposition 4.11.6: *Construction 4.11.5 constitutes a two-sender bit-commitment scheme.*

Proof: The security property follows by observing that for every choice of $\bar{r} \in \{0, 1\}^n$ the message sent by the first sender is uniformly distributed over $\{0, 1, 2\}^n$.

The (strong) unambiguity property is proved by contradiction. As a motivation, we first consider the execution of the preceding protocol, with n equal to 1, and show that it is impossible for the two senders *always* to be able to open the commitments both ways. Consider any pair, (s^0, s^1), such that s^0 is a possible 0-opening and s^1 is a possible 1-opening, both with respect to the receiver's view. We stress that these s^σ's must match all possible receiver's views (or else the opening does not always succeed). It follows that for each $r \in \{0, 1\}$ both $\pi_r(s^0)$ and $\pi_r(s^1) + 1 \bmod 3$ must fit the message received by the receiver (in the commit phase) in response to message r sent by it. Hence, $\pi_r(s^0) \equiv \pi_r(s^1) + 1$ (mod 3) holds for each $r \in \{0, 1\}$. Contradiction follows because no two $s^0, s^1 \in \{0, 1, 2\}$ can satisfy both $\pi_0(s^0) \equiv \pi_0(s^1) + 1$ (mod 3), and $\pi_1(s^0) \equiv \pi_1(s^1) + 1$ (mod 3), the reason being that the first equality implies $s^0 \equiv s^1 + 1$ (mod 3), which combined with the second equality yields $\pi_1(s^1 + 1 \bmod 3) \equiv \pi_1(s^1) + 1$ (mod 3), whereas for every $s \in \{0, 1, 2\}$ it holds that $\pi_1(s + 1 \bmod 3) \neq \pi_1(s) + 1$ (mod 3).

We now turn to the actual proof of the strong unambiguity property. The arbitrary (deterministic) strategy of the first sender is captured by a function, denoted f, mapping n-bit-long strings into sequences in $\{0, 1, 2\}^n$. Thus, the receiver's view, when using coin sequence $\bar{r} = r_1 \cdots r_n \in \{0, 1\}^n$, consists of $(\bar{r}, f(\bar{r}))$. Let $\bar{s}^0$ and $\bar{s}^1$ denote arbitrary opening attempts (i.e., 0-opening and 1-opening, respectively) of the second sender. Without loss of generality, we can assume that both $\bar{s}^0$ and $\bar{s}^1$ are in $\{0, 1, 2\}^n$ and let $\bar{s}^\sigma = s_1^\sigma \cdots s_n^\sigma$ (with $s_j^\sigma \in \{0, 1, 2\}$). The strong unambiguity property asserts that for a uniformly selected $\bar{r} \in \{0, 1\}^n$ the probability that $\bar{s}^0$ and $\bar{s}^1$ are 0-opening and 1-opening, respectively, of the receiver's view $(\bar{r}, f(\bar{r}))$ is at most 2^{-n}.

Let us denote by R^σ the set of all strings $\bar{r} \in \{0, 1\}^n$ for which the sequence $\bar{s}^\sigma$ is a possible σ-opening of the receiver's view $(\bar{r}, f(\bar{r}))$. Namely,

$$R^\sigma = \{\bar{r} : (\forall i)\ f_i(\bar{r}) \equiv \pi_{r_i}(s_i^\sigma) + \sigma \pmod 3\}$$

where $\bar{r} = r_1 \cdots r_n$, and $f(\bar{r}) = f_1(\bar{r}) \cdots f_n(\bar{r})$. Then the strong unambiguity property asserts that $|R^0 \cap R^1| \leq 2^{-n} \cdot |\{0, 1\}^n|$. That is:

Claim 4.11.6.1: $|R^0 \cap R^1| \leq 1$.

Proof: Suppose, on the contrary, that $\bar{\alpha}, \bar{\beta} \in R^0 \cap R^1$ (and $\bar{\alpha} \neq \bar{\beta}$). Then there exists an i such that $\alpha_i \neq \beta_i$ and, without loss of generality, $\alpha_i = 0$ (and $\beta_i = 1$). By the definition of R^σ it follows that

$$f_i(\bar{\alpha}) \equiv \pi_0(s_i^0) \pmod 3$$
$$f_i(\bar{\alpha}) \equiv \pi_0(s_i^1) + 1 \pmod 3$$
$$f_i(\bar{\beta}) \equiv \pi_1(s_i^0) \pmod 3$$
$$f_i(\bar{\beta}) \equiv \pi_1(s_i^1) + 1 \pmod 3$$

Contradiction follows as in the motivating discussion. That is, using the first two equations and the fact that π_0 is the identity, we have $s_i^1 + 1 \equiv s_i^0 \pmod 3$, and combining this with the last two equations, we have

$$\pi_1(s_i^1 + 1) = \pi_1(s_i^0) \equiv \pi_1(s_i^1) + 1 \pmod 3$$

in contradiction to the (readily verified) fact that $\pi_1(s + 1 \bmod 3) \neq \pi_1(s) + 1$ (mod 3) for every $s \in \{0, 1, 2\}$. $\square$

This completes the proof of the proposition. ∎

Remark 4.11.7 (Parallel Executions). The proof extends to the case in which many instances of the protocol are executed in parallel. In particular, by t parallel executions of Construction 4.11.5, we obtain a two-sender commitment scheme for t-bit-long strings. Note that we are content in asserting that the probability that the verifier's view has two conflicting openings is at most 2^{-n} (or even $t \cdot 2^{-n}$), rather than seeking error reduction (i.e., a probability bound of $2^{-t \cdot n}$).

4.11.3. Perfect Zero-Knowledge for $\mathcal{NP}$

Two-prover perfect zero-knowledge proof systems for any language in $\mathcal{NP}$ follow easily by modifying Construction 4.4.7. The modification consists of replacing the bit-commitment scheme used in Construction 4.4.7 with the two-sender bit-commitment scheme of Construction 4.11.5. Specifically, the modified proof system for Graph Coloring proceeds as follows.

Two-Prover Atomic Proof of Graph Coloring

1. The first prover uses the prover's random tape to determine a permutation of the coloring. In order to commit to each of the resulting colors, the first prover invokes (the commit phase of) a two-sender bit commitment, setting the security parameter to be the number of vertices in the graph. (The first prover plays the role of the first sender, whereas the verifier plays the role of the receiver.)

2. The verifier uniformly selects an edge and sends it to the second prover. In response, the second prover reveals the colors of the endpoints of the required edge by sending the portions of the prover's random tape used in the corresponding instance of the commit phase.

As usual, one can see that the provers can always convince the verifier of valid claims (i.e., the completeness condition holds). Using the unambiguity property of the two-sender commitment scheme (and ignoring the 2^{-n} deviation from the "perfect case"), we can think of the first prover as selecting at random, with *arbitrary* probability distribution, a color assignment to the vertices of the graph. We stress that this claim holds although many instances of the commit protocol are performed concurrently (see Remark 4.11.7). If the graph is not 3-colored, then each of the possible color assignments chosen by the first prover is illegal, and a weak soundness property follows. Yet, by executing this protocol polynomially many times, even in parallel, we derive a protocol satisfying the soundness requirement. We stress that the fact that parallelism is effective here (as means for decreasing error probability) follows from the unambiguity property of the two-sender commitment scheme and *not* from a general "parallel-composition lemma" (which is highly non-trivial in the two-prover setting).

We now turn to the zero-knowledge aspects of this protocol. It turns out that this part is much easier to handle than in all previous cases we have seen. In the construction of the simulator, we take advantage on the fact that the simulator is playing the role of both provers (and hence the unambiguity of the commitment scheme does not apply). Specifically, the simulator, playing the role of both senders, can *easily* open each commitment any way it wants. (Here we take advantage of the specific structure of the commitment scheme of Construction 4.11.5.) Details follow.

Simulation of the Atomic Proof of Graph Coloring

1. The simulator generates random "commitments to nothing." Namely, the simulator invokes the verifier and answers the verifier's messages that belong to the commit phase by a sequence of uniformly chosen strings over $\{0, 1, 2\}$.

2. Upon receiving the query-edge (u, v) from the verifier, the simulator uniformly selects two different colors, ϕ_u and ϕ_v, and opens the corresponding commitments so as to reveal these values. The simulator has no difficulty in doing so, because, unlike the second prover, it knows the messages sent by the verifier in the commit phase. Specifically, given the receiver's view of the commit phase, $(r_1 \cdots r_n, c_1 \cdots c_n)$, a 0-opening (resp.,

1-opening) is computed by setting $s_i = \pi_{r_i}^{-1}(c_i)$ (resp., $s_i = \pi_{r_i}^{-1}(c_i - 1)$) for all i. Note that the receiver's view of the commit phase equals the messages exchanged by the verifier and the first prover, and these were generated in Step 1.

Note that the simulator's messages are distributed identically to the provers' messages in the real interaction. (The only difference is in the way these messages are generated: In the real interaction, the s_i's are selected uniformly in $\{1, 2, 3\}$ and (together with the r_i's and the randomly permuted coloring) determine the c_i's, whereas in the simulation the c_i's are selected uniformly in $\{1, 2, 3\}$ and (together with the r_i's and a random pair in $\{1, 2, 3\}$) determine the revealed s_i's.)

We remark that the entire argument extends easily to the case in which polynomially many instances of the protocol are performed concurrently. Thus, we obtain the following:

Theorem 4.11.8: *Every language in $\mathcal{NP}$ has a perfect zero-knowledge two-prover proof system. Furthermore, this proof system has the following additional properties:*

- *Communication is conducted in a single round: The verifier sends a single message to each of the two provers, which in turn respond with a single message.*
- *The soundness error is exponentially vanishing.*
- *The strategies of the two provers can be implemented by probabilistic polynomial-time machines that get an $\mathcal{NP}$-witness as auxiliary input.*

Efficiency Improvement. A dramatic improvement in the efficiency of two-prover (perfect) zero-knowledge proofs for $\mathcal{NP}$ can be obtained by relying on results regarding probabilistically checkable proofs (PCPs). In particular, such proof systems, with negligible error probability, can be implemented in probabilistic polynomial time, so that the total number of bits exchanged in the interaction is poly-logarithmic.

4.11.4. Applications

Multi-prover interactive proofs are useful only in settings in which the "proving entity" can be "split" into two (or more) parts and its parts kept ignorant of one another during the proving process. In such cases, we get perfect zero-knowledge proofs without having to rely on complexity-theoretic assumptions. In other words, general (widely believed) intractability assumptions are replaced by physical assumptions concerning the specific setting in which the proving process takes place.

One natural application is to the problem of identification and specifically the identification of a *user* at some *station*. In Section 4.7 we discuss how to reduce identification to a zero-knowledge proof of knowledge (for some $\mathcal{NP}$-relation). Here we suggest supplying each user with two smart-cards, implementing the two provers in a two-prover zero-knowledge proof of knowledge. These two smart-cards have to be inserted in two different slots of the station, and this should guarantee that the smart-cards cannot communicate with one another. The station will play the role of the verifier in the zero-knowledge proof of knowledge. This way, the station is perfectly protected against impersonation, whereas the users are perfectly protected against pirate stations that may try to extract knowledge from the smart-cards (so as to enable impersonation by their own agents).

4.12. Miscellaneous

4.12.1. Historical Notes

Interactive proof systems were introduced by Goldwasser, Micali, and Rackoff [124].[33] A restricted form of interactive proof, known by the name *Arthur-Merlin game* (or *public-coin* proof), was introduced in [8] and shown in [128] to be equivalent to general interactive proofs. The interactive proof for Graph Non-Isomorphism is due to Goldreich, Micali, and Wigderson [112]. The amazing theorem-proving power of interactive proofs was subsequently demonstrated in [157, 198], showing interactive proofs for co$\mathcal{NP}$ and (more generally) for $\mathcal{PSPACE}$, respectively.

The concept of zero-knowledge was introduced by Goldwasser, Micali, and Rackoff in the very same paper [124]. That paper also contained a perfect zero-knowledge proof for Quadratic Non-Residuosity. The perfect zero-knowledge proof system for Graph Isomorphism is due to Goldreich, Micali, and Wigderson [112].

The zero-knowledge proof systems for all languages in $\mathcal{NP}$, using any (non-uniform secure) commitment scheme, are also due to Goldreich, Micali, and Wigderson [112].[34] (Zero-knowledge proof systems for all languages in $\mathcal{IP}$ have been presented in [136] and [25].)

The cryptographic applications of zero-knowledge proofs were the very motivation for their introduction in [124]. Zero-knowledge proofs were applied to solve cryptographic problems in [81] and [54]. However, many more applications became possible once it was shown how to construct zero-knowledge proof systems for every language in $\mathcal{NP}$. In particular, general methodologies for the construction of cryptographic protocols have appeared in [112, 113].

The construction of commitment schemes based on one-way permutations can be traced to [31]. The construction of commitment scheme based on pseudorandom generators is due to Naor [170].

Credits for the Advanced Sections

Negative Results. The results demonstrating the necessity of randomness and interaction for zero-knowledge proofs are from [115]. The results providing upper bounds on the complexity of languages with almost-perfect zero-knowledge proofs (i.e., Theorem 4.5.8) are from [83] and [2]. The results indicating that one-way functions are necessary for non-trivial zero-knowledge are from [181]. The negative results

---

[33]Earlier versions of their paper date to early 1983. Yet the paper, having been rejected three times from major conferences, first appeared in public only in 1985, concurrently with the paper of Babai [8].

[34]A weaker result was shown *later* in [41]: It provides an alternative construction of zero-knowledge proof systems for $\mathcal{NP}$, using a *stronger* intractability assumption (specifically, the intractability of the Quadratic Residuosity problem).

concerning parallel composition of zero-knowledge proof systems (i.e., Proposition 4.5.9 and Theorem 4.5.11) are from [106].

Witness Indistinguishability. The notions of witness indistinguishability and witness-hiding, were introduced and developed by Feige and Shamir [78]. Section 4.6 is based on their work.

Proofs of Knowledge. The concept of proofs of knowledge originates from the paper of Goldwasser, Micali, and Rackoff [124]. Early attempts to provide a definition of that concept appear in [75] and [205]; however, those definitions were not fully satisfactory. The issue of defining proofs of knowledge has been extensively investigated by Bellare and Goldreich [17], and we follow their suggestions. The application of zero-knowledge proofs of knowledge to identification schemes was discovered by Feige, Fiat, and Shamir [80, 75]. The Fiat-Shamir identification scheme [80] is based on the zero-knowledge proof for Quadratic Residuosity of Goldwasser, Micali, and Rackoff [124].

Computationally Sound Proof Systems (Arguments). Computationally sound proof systems (i.e., arguments)[35] were introduced by Brassard, Chaum, and Crépeau [40]. Their paper also presents perfect zero-knowledge arguments for $\mathcal{NP}$ based on the intractability of factoring. Naor et al. [171] showed how to construct perfect zero-knowledge arguments for $\mathcal{NP}$ based on any one-way permutation, and Construction 4.8.3 is taken from their paper. The poly-logarithmic-communication argument system for $\mathcal{NP}$ (of Section 4.8.4) is due to Kilian [143].

Constant-Round Zero-Knowledge Protocols. The round-efficient zero-knowledge proof systems for $\mathcal{NP}$, based on any claw-free collection, is taken from [105]. The round-efficient zero-knowledge arguments for $\mathcal{NP}$, based on any one-way function, is due to [77], yet our presentation (which uses some of their ideas) is different. (The alternative construction outlined in Section 4.9.2.3 is much more similar to the construction in [77].)

Non-Interactive Zero-Knowledge Proofs. Non-interactive zero-knowledge proof systems were introduced by Blum, Feldman, and Micali [34]. The constructions presented in Section 4.10 are due to Feige, Lapidot, and Shamir [76]. For further detail on Remark 4.10.6, see [23].

Multi-Prover Zero-Knowledge Proofs. Multi-prover interactive proofs were introduced by Ben-Or, Goldwasser, Kilian, and Wigderson [26]. Their paper also presents a perfect zero-knowledge two-prover proof system for $\mathcal{NP}$. The perfect zero-knowledge two-prover proof for $\mathcal{NP}$ presented in Section 4.11 follows their ideas; however, we explicitly state the properties of the two-sender commitment scheme in use. Consequently, we observe that (sufficiently many) parallel repetitions of this *specific* proof system *will*

---

[35] Unfortunately, there is some confusion regarding terminology in the literature: In some work (particularly [40]), computationally sound proofs (arguments) are negligently referred to as "interactive proofs."

decrease the error probability to a negligible one.[36] (The efficiency improvement, briefly mentioned at the end of Section 4.11.3, is due to [66].)

We mention that multi-prover interactive proof systems are related to probabilistically checkable proof (PCP) systems. The complexity-theoretic aspects of these proof systems have been the focus of much interest. The interested reader is referred to Sections 2.4 and 2.5.2 of [97] (and to the references therein).

4.12.2. Suggestions for Further Reading

A wider perspective on probabilistic proof systems is offered by Goldreich [97]: In particular, Chapter 2 of [97] contains further details on interactive proof systems, an introduction to probabilistically checkable proof (PCP) systems and discussions of other types of probabilistic proof systems. The exposition focuses on the basic definitions and results concerning such systems and emphasizes both the similarities and differences between the various types of probabilistic proofs. Specifically, like zero-knowledge proof systems, all probabilistic proof systems share a common (untraditional) feature: They carry a probability of error. Yet this probability is explicitly bounded and can be reduced by successive applications of the proof system. The gain in allowing this untraditional relaxation is substantial, as demonstrated by three well-known results regarding *interactive proofs*, *zero-knowledge proofs*, and *probabilistic checkable proofs*: In each of these cases, allowing a bounded probability of error makes the system much more powerful and useful than the traditional (errorless) counterparts.

Since their introduction a decade and a half ago, zero-knowledge proofs have been the focus of much research. We refrain from offering a comprehensive list of suggestions for further reading. Instead, we merely point out some works that address obvious gaps in the current chapter.

- A *uniform-complexity treatment* of zero-knowledge is provided in [94]. In particular, it is shown how to use (uniformly) one-way functions to construct interactive proof systems for $\mathcal{NP}$ such that it is infeasible to find instances in which the prover leaks knowledge.

- *Statistical* (a.k.a *almost-perfect*) *zero-knowledge proofs* offer absolute levels of security for both the prover and the verifier; that is, both the zero-knowledge and soundness conditions are satisfied in a strong probabilistic sense rather than in a computational one. The class of problems possessing statistical zero-knowledge proofs, denoted $\mathcal{SZK}$, is quite intriguing (e.g., it contains some hard problems [124, 109], has complete problems [194, 118, 120], and is closed under complementation [180, 194, 118]). The interested reader is directed to Vadhan's thesis [206].

  We mention that some of the techniques developed toward studying $\mathcal{SZK}$ are also applicable in the context of ordinary (computational) zero-knowledge proofs (e.g., the transformation from public-coin proof systems that are zero-knowledge with respect to an honest verifier to similar systems that are zero-knowledge in general [118]).

---

[36]This observation escaped the authors of [146], who, being aware of the problematics of parallel repetitions (of general multi-prover systems), suggested an alternative construction.

- In Section 4.5 we discussed *the problematics of parallel repetition* in the context of zero-knowledge. As mentioned there, parallel repetition is also problematic in the context of computationally sound proofs [19] and in the context of multi-prover proofs [74, 190].

- In continuation of Section 4.9, we mention that round-efficient *perfect* zero-knowledge arguments for $\mathcal{NP}$, based on the intractability of the discrete-logarithm problem, have been published [42].

- In continuation of Section 4.10, we mention that a much *more efficient construction of non-interactive proof systems for $\mathcal{NP}$*, based on the same assumptions as [76], has appeared in [144]. Further strengthenings of non-interactive zero-knowledge have been suggested in [193].

- The paper by Goldwasser, Micali, and Rackoff [124] also contains a suggestion for a general measure of "knowledge" revealed by a prover. For further details on this measure, which is called *knowledge complexity*, see [116] (and the references therein). (Indeed, knowledge-complexity zero coincides with zero-knowledge.)

Finally, we mention recent research taking place regarding the preservation of zero-knowledge in settings such as *concurrent* asynchronous executions [68, 189, 60] and *resettable* executions [47]. It would be unwise to attempt to summarize those research efforts at the current stage.

4.12.3. Open Problems

Our formulation of zero-knowledge (e.g., perfect zero-knowledge as defined in Definition 4.3.1) is different from the standard definition used in the literature (e.g., Definition 4.3.6). The standard definition refers to *expected* polynomial-time machines rather than to strictly (probabilistic) polynomial-time machines. Clearly, Definition 4.3.1 implies Definition 4.3.6 (see Exercise 7), but it is unknown whether or not the converse holds. In particular, the known constant-round zero-knowledge protocols for $\mathcal{NP}$ are known to be zero-knowledge only when allowing *expected* polynomial-time simulators. This state of affairs is quite annoying, and resolving it will be of theoretical and practical importance.

Whereas zero-knowledge proofs for $\mathcal{NP}$ can be constructed based on any (non-uniformly) one-way function (which is the most general assumption used in this book), some other results mentioned earlier require stronger assumptions. Specifically, it would be nice to construct *constant-round* zero-knowledge proofs, *perfect* zero-knowledge arguments, and *non-interactive zero-knowledge* proofs for $\mathcal{NP}$ based on weaker assumptions than the ones currently used.

4.12.4. Exercises

The exercises in this first batch are intended for coverage of the basic material (i.e., Sections 4.1–4.4).

Exercise 1: *Decreasing the error probability in interactive proof systems*: Prove Proposition 4.2.7.

Guideline: Execute the weaker interactive proof sufficiently many times, using independently chosen coin tosses for each execution, and rule by comparing the number of accepting executions to an appropriate threshold. Observe that the bounds on completeness and soundness need to be efficiently computable. Be careful when demonstrating the soundness of the resulting verifier (i.e., do not assume that the cheating prover executes each copy independently of the other copies). We note that the statement remains valid regardless of whether these repetitions are executed sequentially or "in parallel," but demonstrating that the soundness condition is satisfied is much easier in the sequential case.

Exercise 2: *The role of randomization in interactive proofs, Part 1*: Prove that if L has an interactive proof system in which the verifier is deterministic, then $L \in \mathcal{NP}$.

    Guideline: Note that if the verifier is deterministic, then the entire interaction between the prover and the verifier can be determined by the prover.

Exercise 3: *The role of randomization in interactive proofs, Part 2*: Prove that if L has an interactive proof system, then it has one in which the prover is deterministic. Furthermore, prove that for every (probabilistic) interactive machine V, there exists a deterministic interactive machine P such that for every x, the probability $\Pr[\langle P, V \rangle (x) = 1]$ equals the supremum of $\Pr[\langle B, V \rangle (x) = 1]$ taken over all interactive machines B.

    Guideline: For each possible prefix of interaction, the prover can determine a message that maximizes the accepting probability of the verifier V.

Exercise 4: *The role of randomization in interactive proofs, Part 3*: Consider the following (bad) modification to the definition of a pair of linked interactive machines (and interactive proofs). By this modification, also the random tapes of the prover and verifier coincide (i.e., intuitively, both use the same sequence of coin tosses that is known to both of them). We call such proof systems *shared-randomness interactive proofs*. Show that only languages in $\mathcal{MA}$ have a shared-randomness interactive proof system, where a language L is in $\mathcal{MA}$ if there exists a language R_L in $\mathcal{BPP}$ and a polynomial p such that $x \in L$ if and only if there exists $y \in \{0, 1\}^{p(|x|)}$ such that $(x, y) \in R_L$.

    Guideline: First convert a shared-randomness interactive proof system into an interactive proof system (of the original kind) in which the verifier reveals all its coin tosses up-front. Next, use reasoning as in Exercise 2.

Show that $\mathcal{MA}$ actually equals the class of languages having shared-randomness interactive proof systems.

Exercise 5: *The role of error in interactive proofs*: Prove that if L has an interactive proof system in which the verifier never (not even with negligible probability) accepts a string not in the language L, then $L \in \mathcal{NP}$.

    Guideline: Define a relation R_L such that $(x, y) \in R_L$ if y is a full transcript of an interaction leading the verifier to accept the input x. We stress that y contains the verifier's coin tosses and all the messages received from the prover.

Exercise 6: *Simulator error in perfect zero-knowledge simulators, Part 1*: Consider a modification of Definition 4.3.1 in which condition 1 is replaced by requiring that for some function $\beta(\cdot)$, $\Pr[M^*(x) = \bot] < \beta(|x|)$. Assume that $\beta(\cdot)$ is polynomial time-computable. Show that the following hold:

1. If for some polynomial $p_1(\cdot)$ and all sufficiently large n's, $\beta(n) < 1 - (1/p_1(n))$, then the modified definition is equivalent to the original one.
2. If for some polynomial $p_2(\cdot)$ and all sufficiently large n's, $\beta(n) > 2^{-p_2(n)}$, then the modified definition is equivalent to the original one.

Justify the bounds placed on the function $\beta(\cdot)$.

Guideline: Invoke the simulator sufficiently many times.

Exercise 7: *Simulator error in perfect zero-knowledge simulators, Part 2*: Prove that Definition 4.3.1 implies Definition 4.3.6.

Exercise 8: *Perfect versus almost-perfect zero-knowledge*: Prove that every perfect zero-knowledge system is also almost-perfect zero-knowledge. (That is, prove that Definition 4.3.1 implies Definition 4.3.4.)

Guideline: Using Item 2 of Exercise 6, note that the statistical difference between $M^*(x)$ and $m^*(x)$ (i.e., "$M^*(x)$ conditioned that it not be $\perp$") is negligible.

Exercise 9: *Simulator error in computational zero-knowledge simulators*: Consider an alternative to Definition 4.3.2 by which the simulator is allowed to output the symbol $\perp$ (with probability bounded above by, say, $\frac{1}{2}$) and its output distribution is considered conditioned on it not being $\perp$ (as done in Definition 4.3.1). Prove that this alternative definition is equivalent to the original one (i.e., to Definition 4.3.2).

Exercise 10: *An alternative formulation of zero-knowledge, simulating the interaction*: Prove the equivalence of Definitions 4.3.2 and 4.3.3.

Guideline: To show that Definition 4.3.3 implies Definition 4.3.2, observe that the output of every interactive machine can be easily computed from its view of the interaction. To show that Definition 4.3.2 implies Definition 4.3.3, show that for every probabilistic polynomial-time V^* there exists a probabilistic polynomial-time V^{**} such that $\text{view}_{V^*}^{P}(x) = \langle P, V^{**} \rangle (x)$.

Exercise 11: Prove that Definition 4.3.10 is equivalent to a version where the auxiliary input to the verifier is explicitly bounded in length. That is, the alternative zero-knowledge clause reads as follows:

> *for every polynomial ℓ and for every probabilistic polynomial-time interactive machine V^* there exists a probabilistic polynomial-time algorithm M^* such that the following two ensembles are computationally indistinguishable:*
>
> - $\{\langle P(y_x), V^*(z)\rangle(x)\}_{x\in L,\, z\in\{0,1\}^{\ell(|x|)}}$
> - $\{M^*(x, z)\}_{x\in L,\, z\in\{0,1\}^{\ell(|x|)}}$
>
> *where y_x is as in Definition 4.3.10.*

Note that it is immaterial here whether the running time of M^* (as well as the distinguishing gap) is considered as a function of $|x|$ or as a function of $|(x, z)|$.

Exercise 12: Present a *simple* probabilistic polynomial-time algorithm that simulates the view of the interaction of the verifier described in Construction 4.3.8 with the prover defined there. The simulator, on input $x \in GI$, should have output that is distributed identically to $\text{view}_{V_{GI}}^{P_{GI}}(x)$.

Exercise 13: Prove that the existence of bit-commitment schemes implies the existence of one-way functions.

> **Guideline:** Following the notation of Definition 4.4.1, consider the mapping of (v, s, r) to the receiver's view $(r, \overline{m})$. Observe that by the unambiguity requirement, range elements are very unlikely to have inverses with both possible values of v. The mapping is polynomial-time computable, and any algorithm that inverts it with success probability that is not negligible can be used to contradict the secrecy requirement.

Exercise 14: Considering the commitment scheme of Construction 4.4.4, suggest a cheating sender that induces a receiver's view (of the commit phase) that is unlikely to have any possible opening and still is computationally indistinguishable from the receiver's view in interactions with the prescribed sender. That is, present a probabilistic polynomial-time interactive machine S^* such that the following two conditions hold:

1. With overwhelmingly high probability, $\langle S^*(0), R \rangle (1^n)$ is neither a possible 0-commitment nor a possible 1-commitment.
2. The ensembles $\langle S^*(0), R \rangle (1^n)$ and $\langle S(0), R \rangle (1^n)$ are computationally indistinguishable.

> **Guideline:** The sender simply replies with a uniformly chosen string.

Exercise 15: *Using Construction 4.4.4 as a commitment scheme in Construction 4.4.7:* Prove that when the commitment scheme of Construction 4.4.4 is used in the $G3C$ protocol, then the resulting scheme remains zero-knowledge. Consider the modifications required to prove Claim 4.4.8.2.

Exercise 16: *Strong reductions:* Let L_1 and L_2 be two languages in $\mathcal{NP}$, and let R_1 and R_2 be binary relations characterizing L_1 and L_2, respectively. We say that the relation R_1 is *Levin-reducible*[37] to the relation R_2 if there exist two polynomial-time-computable functions f and g such that the following two conditions hold:

Standard requirement: $x \in L_1$ if and only if $f(x) \in L_2$.

Additional requirement: For every $(x, w) \in R_1$, it holds that $(f(x), g(x, w)) \in R_2$.

Prove the following statements:

1. Let $L \in \mathcal{NP}$, and let R_L be the generic relation characterizing L (i.e., fix a non-deterministic machine M_L, and let $(x, w) \in R_L$ if w is an accepting computation of M_L on input x). Let R_{SAT} be the standard relation characterizing SAT (i.e., $(x, w) \in R_{SAT}$ if w is a truth assignment satisfying the CNF formula x). Prove that R_L is Levin-reducible to R_{SAT}.
2. Let R_{SAT} be as before, and let R_{3SAT} be defined analogously for $3SAT$. Prove that R_{SAT} is Levin-reducible to R_{3SAT}.
3. Let R_{3SAT} be as before, and let R_{G3C} be the standard relation characterizing $G3C$ (i.e., $(x, w) \in R_{G3C}$ if w is a 3-coloring of the graph x). Prove that R_{3SAT} is Levin-reducible to R_{G3C}.
4. Levin reductions are transitive.

---

[37] We name this reduction after Levin because it was he who, upon discovering (independently of Cook and Karp) the existence of $\mathcal{NP}$-complete problems, used a stronger definition of a reduction that implies the one here. We assume that the reader is familiar with standard reductions among languages such as Bounded Halting, SAT, and 3SAT (as in [86]).

Exercise 17: Prove the existence of a Karp reduction of any $\mathcal{NP}$ language L to SAT that when considered as a function can be inverted in polynomial time. Same for the reduction of SAT to $3SAT$ and the reduction of $3SAT$ to $G3C$. (In fact, the standard Karp reductions have this property.)

Exercise 18: *Applications of Theorem 4.4.11*: This exercise assumes a basic familiarity with the notions of a public-key encryption scheme and a signature scheme. Assuming the existence of non-uniformly one-way functions, present solutions to the following cryptographic problems:
1. Suppose that party S sends, over a public channel, encrypted data to several parties, $R_1, \ldots, R_t$. Specifically, the data sent to R_i are encrypted using the public encryption key of party R_i. We assume that all parties have access to the ciphertexts sent over the public channel. Suppose that S wants to prove to some other party that it has sent the same data to all R_i's, but it wants to do so without revealing the data.
2. Referring to the same communication setting, consider a party R that has received data encrypted using its own public encryption key. Suppose that these data consist of two parts, and party R wishes to reveal to someone the first part of the data but not the second. Further suppose that the other party wants a proof that R has indeed revealed the correct content of the first part of the data.
3. Suppose that party S wishes to send party R a signature to a publicly known document such that only R receives the signature, but everyone else can verify that such a signature was indeed sent by S. (We assume, again, that all parties share a public channel.)

Exercise 19: *On knowledge tightness*: Prove that the protocol resulting from executing Construction 4.4.7 for $k(n) = O(\log n)$ times in parallel is zero-knowledge. Furthermore, prove that it has knowledge tightness $(3/2)^{k(n)}$ (approximately).

Exercise 20: *More efficient zero-knowledge proofs for $\mathcal{NP}$*: Consider the basic proof system for the Hamiltonian-cycle problem (HC) presented in Construction 4.7.14.
1. Evaluate its acceptance probabilities (i.e., completeness and soundness bounds).
2. Provide a sketch of the proof of the zero-knowledge property (i.e., describe the simulator). Specifically, present a simulator that establishes knowledge tightness of approximately 2. If you are really serious, provide a full proof of the zero-knowledge property.

Exercises for the Advanced Sections. The rest of the exercises refer to the material in the advanced sections (i.e., Sections 4.5–4.11).

Exercise 21: *An alternative formulation of black-box zero-knowledge*: Here we say that a probabilistic polynomial-time oracle machine M is a **black-box simulator** *for the prover P and the language L* if for every (not necessarily uniform) polynomial-size circuit family $\{B_n\}_{n \in \mathbb{N}}$, the ensembles $\{\langle P, B_{|x|}\rangle(x)\}_{x \in L}$ and $\{M^{B_{|x|}}(x)\}_{x \in L}$ are indistinguishable by (non-uniform) polynomial-size circuits. Namely, for every polynomial-size circuit family $\{D_n\}_{n \in \mathbb{N}}$, every polynomial $p(\cdot)$, all sufficiently large n, and $x \in \{0, 1\}^n \cap L$,

$$\left| \Pr[D_n(\langle P, B_n\rangle(x)) = 1] - \Pr[D_n(M^{B_n}(x)) = 1] \right| < \frac{1}{p(n)}$$

Prove that the current formulation is equivalent to the one presented in Definition 4.5.10.

Exercise 22: Prove that the protocol presented in Construction 4.4.7 is indeed a black-box zero-knowledge proof system for $G3C$.

    Guideline: Use the formulation presented in Exercise 21.

Exercise 23: Prove that black-box zero-knowledge is preserved under sequential composition. (Note that this does not follow merely from the fact that auxiliary-input zero-knowledge is preserved under sequential composition.)

    Guideline: Adapt the proof of Lemma 4.3.11.

Exercise 24: *Refuting another parallel-composition conjecture*: Prove that there exists a zero-knowledge prover P such that the prover resulting from running two copies of P in parallel yields knowledge (e.g., a cheating verifier can extract from this prover a solution to a problem that is not solvable in polynomial time).

    Guideline: Let P_1 and P_2 be as in Proposition 4.5.9, and consider the prover P that randomly selects which of the two programs to execute. Alternatively, the choice can be determined by the verifier.

Exercise 25: Assuming that one-way permutations exist, present a witness-indistinguishable proof system (with a probabilistic polynomial-time prover) that is NOT strongly witness-indistinguishable.

    Guideline: Consider a one-way permutation f, a hard-core predicate b of f, and the witness relation $\{(f(w),w):w \in \{0,1\}^*\}$. Consider a prover that on input $f(w)$ (and auxiliary input w) sends w to the verifier, and consider the ensembles $\{X_n^0\}_{n\in\mathbb{N}}$ and $\{X_n^1\}_{n\in\mathbb{N}}$, where X_n^i is uniform on $\{f(w):w \in \{0,1\}^n \,\&\, b(w)=i\}$.

Exercise 26: *Some basic zero-knowledge proofs of knowledge*:
1. Show that Construction 4.3.8 is a proof of knowledge of an isomorphism with knowledge error $\frac{1}{2}$.
2. Show that Construction 4.4.7 (when applied on common input $G = (V, E)$) is a proof of knowledge of a 3-coloring with knowledge error $1 - \frac{1}{|E|}$.

See also Part 1 of Exercise 28.

    Guideline: Observe that in these cases, if the verifier accepts with probability greater than the knowledge error, then it accepts with probability 1. Also observe that the number of possible verifier messages in these proof systems is polynomial in the common input. Thus, the extractor can emulate executions of these systems with all possible verifier messages.

Exercise 27: *Parallel repetitions of some basic proofs of knowledge*: Let $k : \mathbb{N} \to \mathbb{N}$ be polynomially bounded. Consider the proof systems resulting by executing each of the basic systems mentioned in Exercise 26 for k times in parallel.
1. Show that the k parallel execution of Construction 4.3.8 constitutes a proof of knowledge of an isomorphism with knowledge error $2^{-k(\cdot)}$. (Analogously for Construction 4.7.12.)
2. Show that the k parallel execution of Construction 4.4.7 provides a proof of knowledge of a 3-coloring with knowledge error $(1 - (1/|E|))^{-k(|G|)}$.

Note that we make no claim regarding zero-knowledge.

See also Part 2 of Exercise 28.

Guideline: For Part 1, note that any two different transcripts in which the verifier accepts will yield an isomorphism. In Part 2 this simple observation fails. Still, observe that $|E|$ accepting transcripts that differ in any fixed copy of the basic system do yield a 3-coloring.

Exercise 28: *More efficient zero-knowledge proofs of knowledge for $\mathcal{NP}$:* As in Exercise 20, consider the basic proof system for the Hamiltonian-cycle problem (HC) presented in Construction 4.7.14.
1. Prove that the basic proof system is a proof of knowledge of a Hamiltonian cycle with knowledge error $\frac{1}{2}$.
2. Prove that the proof system that results from iterating the basic system k times is a proof of knowledge of a Hamiltonian cycle with knowledge error 2^{-k}. Consider *both* sequential and parallel repetitions.

Exercise 29: *More on the equivalence of Definitions 4.7.2 and 4.7.3:* Suppose that R is polynomially bounded and that the extractor in Definition 4.7.3 outputs either a valid solution or a special failure symbol. Referring to this relation R, show that V satisfies the validity-with-error κ condition of Definition 4.7.2 if and only if V satisfies the alternative validity-with-error κ condition of (the modified) Definition 4.7.3.
    Guideline: Follow the outline of the proof of Proposition 4.7.4, noting that all references to the hypothesis that R is an $\mathcal{NP}$-relation can be replaced by the hypothesis that the extractor in Definition 4.7.3 outputs either a valid solution or a special failure symbol. In particular, in the second direction, omit the exhaustive search that takes place with probability $2^{-\text{poly}(|x|)}$, and use the fact that $p(x, y, r) > \kappa(|x|)$ implies $p(x, y, r) \geq \kappa(|x|) + 2^{-\text{poly}(|x|)}$.

Exercise 30: *Zero-knowledge strong proofs of knowledge for $\mathcal{NP}$:* Consider again the basic proof system for the Hamiltonian-cycle problem (HC) presented in Construction 4.7.14. Prove that the proof system that results from sequentially iterating the basic system sufficiently many times is a strong proof of knowledge of a Hamiltonian cycle. (Recall that it is indeed zero-knowledge.)

Exercise 31: *Error reduction in computationally sound proofs:* Given a computationally sound proof (with error probability $\frac{1}{3}$) for a language L, construct a computationally sound proof with negligible error probability (for L).
    Guideline: Use sequential repetitions. In fact, the error probability can be made exponentially vanishing. Parallel repetitions may fail to reduce computational soundness in some cases (see [19]).

Exercise 32: *Commitment schemes, an impossibility result:* Prove that there exists no two-party protocol that simultaneously satisfies the perfect secrecy requirement of Definition 4.8.2 and the (information-theoretic) unambiguity requirement of Definition 4.4.1.

Exercise 33: *Failure of ordinary hashing in Construction 4.8.3:* Show that in Construction 4.8.3, replacing the iterative hashing by an ordinary one results in a scheme that is NOT binding (not even in a computational sense). That is, using the notation of

Construction 4.8.3, consider replacement of the iterative hashing step with the following step (where b and the r^i's are as in Construction 4.8.3):

- (Ordinary hashing): The receiver sends the message $(r^1, \ldots, r^{n-1})$ to the sender, which replies with the message $(c^1, \ldots, c^{n-1})$, where $c^i \stackrel{\text{def}}{=} b(y, r^i)$, for $i = 1, \ldots, n-1$.

  That is, the prescribed sender computes the c^i's as in Construction 4.8.3, but a cheating sender can determine all c^i's based on all r^i's (rather that determine each c^i based only on $(r^1, \ldots, r^i)$).

Present an efficient strategy that allows the sender to violate the unambiguity condition.

Guideline: Given any one-way permutation f', first construct a one-way permutation f satisfying $f(0^{|x'|}, x') = (0^{|x'|}, x')$ and $f(x', 0^{|x'|}) = (x', 0^{|x'|})$ for every x'. (Hint: First obtain a one-way permutation f'' that satisfies $f''(0^n) = 0^n$ for all n's,[38] and then let $f(0^{|x''|}, x'') \stackrel{\text{def}}{=} (0^{|x''|}, x'')$, $f(x', 0^{|x'|}) \stackrel{\text{def}}{=} (x', 0^{|x'|})$, and $f(x', x'') \stackrel{\text{def}}{=} (f''(x'), f''(x''))$ for $x', x'' \in \{0, 1\}^{|x'|} \setminus \{0\}^{|x'|}$.)

Assuming that the modified protocol is executed with f as constructed here, consider a cheating sender that upon receiving the message $(r^1, \ldots, r^{n-1})$ finds $y^1 \in \{0, 1\}^{n/2}\{0\}^{n/2}$, $y^2 \in \{0\}^{n/2}\{0, 1\}^{n/2}$, and $\bar{c} = (c^1, \ldots, c^{n-1})$ such that the following conditions hold:

1. $c^i = b(y^j, r^i)$ for $i = 1, \ldots, n-1$ and $j = 1, 2$
2. $b(y^j, r^n) \equiv j \pmod 2$ for $j = 1, 2$

(where r^n is the unique vector independent of $r^1, \ldots, r^{n-1}$).

Note that f is invariant under such y^j's, and thus they can serve as valid decommitments.

Finally, prove that such a solution $y^1, y^2, \bar{c}$ always exists and can be found by solving a linear system. (Hint: Consider the linear system $b(x^1 0^{n/2}, r^i) = b(0^{n/2} x^2, r^i)$ for $i = 1, \ldots, n-1$ and $b(x^1 0^{n/2}, r^n) \equiv b(0^{n/2} x^2, r^n) + 1 \pmod 2$. Extra hint: Things may become more clear when writing the conditions in matrix form.)

Exercise 34: *Non-interactive zero-knowledge, bounded versus unbounded:* Show that Construction 4.10.4 is not unboundedly zero-knowledge unless $\mathcal{NP} \subseteq \mathcal{BPP}$.

Guideline: Consider invoking this proof system twice: first on a graph consisting of a simple cycle and then on a graph for which a Hamiltonian cycle is to be found.

Exercise 35: Regarding the definition of a two-sender commitment scheme (Definition 4.11.4), show that for every p there exist senders' strategies such that each resulting receiver view can be 0-opened with probability p and 1-opened with probability $1 - p$.

Guideline: Use the perfect-secrecy requirement and the fact that you can present computationally unbounded senders' strategies.

---

[38] See Exercise 13 in Chapter 2.

Background in Computational Number Theory

The material presented in this appendix is merely the minimum needed for the few examples of specific constructions presented in this book. What we cover here are a few structural and algorithmic facts concerning prime and composite numbers. For a more comprehensive treatment, consult any standard textbook (e.g., [10]).

A.1. Prime Numbers

A *prime* is a natural number that is not divisible by any natural number other than itself and 1. For simplicity, say that 1 is NOT a prime.

For a prime P, the *additive group modulo P*, denoted $\mathbb{Z}_P$, consists of the set $\{0, \ldots, P - 1\}$ and the operation of *addition* mod P. All elements except the identity (i.e., 0) have order P (in this group). The *multiplicative group modulo P*, denoted $\mathbb{Z}_P^*$, consists of the set $\{1, \ldots, P - 1\}$ and the operation of *multiplication* mod P. This group is cyclic too. In fact, at least $1/\log_2 P$ of the elements of the group have order $P - 1$ and are called *primitive*.[1]

A.1.1. Quadratic Residues Modulo a Prime

A *quadratic residue modulo a prime P* is an integer s such that there exists an $r \in \mathbb{Z}_P^*$ satisfying $s \equiv r^2 \pmod{P}$. Thus, in particular, s has to be relatively prime to P. Clearly, if r is a square root of s modulo P, then so is $-r$ (since $(-r)^2 \equiv r^2$). Furthermore, if $x^2 \equiv s \pmod{P}$ has a solution modulo P, then it has exactly two such solutions (as otherwise $r_1 \not\equiv \pm r_2 \pmod{P}$ are both solutions, and $0 \equiv r_1^2 - r_2^2 \equiv (r_1 - r_2)(r_1 + r_2) \pmod{P}$ follows, in contradiction to the primality of P).

The quadratic residues modulo P form a subgroup of the multiplicative group modulo P. The former subgroup contains exactly half of the members of the group.

---

[1] The exact number of primitive elements modulo P depends on the prime factorization of $P - 1 = \prod_{i=1}^{t} P_i^{e_i}$ (see Section A.2): It equals $\prod_{i=1}^{t} ((P_i - 1) \cdot P_i^{e_i - 1})$.

Furthermore, squaring modulo P is a 2-to-1 mapping of the group to the subgroup. In case $P \equiv 3 \pmod 4$, each image of this mapping has one pre-image in the subgroup (i.e., a quadratic residue) and one pre-image that is not in the subgroup (i.e., a non-quadratic residue).[2]

A.1.2. Extracting Square Roots Modulo a Prime

In general, extracting square roots module a prime can be done by using Berlekamp's algorithm [28]. The latter is a randomized algorithm for factoring polynomials modulo a prime. (Note that extracting a square root of s modulo a prime P amounts to solving the equation $x^2 \equiv s \pmod P$, which can be cast as the problem of factoring the polynomial $x^2 - s$ modulo P.)

A more direct approach is possible in the special case in which the prime is congruent to 3 $\pmod 4$, which is the case in most cryptographic applications. In this case we observe that for a quadratic residue $s \equiv x^2 \pmod P$, we have

$$
\begin{aligned}
s^{(P+1)/4} &\equiv x^{(P+1)/2} \pmod P \\
&\equiv x^{(P-1)/2} \cdot x \pmod P \\
&\equiv \pm x \pmod P
\end{aligned}
$$

where in the last equality we use Fermat's little theorem, by which $x^{(P-1)/2} \equiv \pm 1 \pmod P$ for every integer x and prime P. Thus, in this special case, we obtain a square root of s modulo P by raising s to the power $\frac{P+1}{4}$ modulo P. (Note that this square root is a quadratic residue modulo P.)

A.1.3. Primality Testers

The common approach to testing whether or not an integer is a prime is to utilize Rabin's randomized primality tester [185], which is related to a deterministic algorithm due to Miller [166].[3] The alternative of using a somewhat different randomized algorithm, discovered independently by Solovay and Strassen [202], seems less popular. Here we present a third alternative, which seems less well known (and was discovered independently by several researchers, one of them being Manuel Blum). The only number-theoretic facts that we use are as follows:

1. For every *prime* $P > 2$, each quadratic residue mod P has exactly two square roots mod P (and they sum up to P).

2. For every odd and non-integer-power *composite* number N, each quadratic residue mod N has at least four square roots mod N.

---

[2] This follows from the fact that -1 is a non-quadratic residue modulo such primes. In contrast, in case $P \equiv 1$ (mod 4), it holds that -1 is a quadratic residue modulo P. Thus, in case $P \equiv 1 \pmod 4$, for each quadratic residue the two square roots either are both quadratic residues or are both non-quadratic residues.

[3] Miller's algorithm relies on the Extended Riemann Hypothesis (ERH).

Our algorithm uses as a black box an algorithm, denoted SQRT, that given a prime P and a quadratic residue s mod P, returns a square root of s mod P. There is no guarantee as to what the algorithm does in case the input is not of this form (and, in particular, in case P is not a prime).

Algorithm. On input a natural number $N > 2$, do the following:

1. If N is either even or an integer-power, then reject.
2. Uniformly select $r \in \{1, \ldots, N - 1\}$ and set $s \leftarrow r^2$ mod N.
3. Let $r' \leftarrow$ SQRT(N, s). If $r' \equiv \pm r \pmod{N}$, then accept, else reject.

Analysis. By Fact 1, on input a prime number N, the algorithm always accepts (since in this case SQRT$(N, r^2 \text{ mod } N) = \pm r$ for any $r \in \{1, \ldots, N - 1\}$). On the other hand, suppose that N is an odd composite that is not an integer-power. Then, by Fact 2, each quadratic residue s has at least four square roots, and each is equally likely to be chosen at Step 2 (since s yields no information on the specific r). Thus, for every such s, the probability that $\pm$SQRT(N, s) is chosen in Step 2 is at most $\frac{2}{4}$. It follows that on input a composite number, the algorithm rejects with probability at least $\frac{1}{2}$.

Comment. The analysis presupposes that the algorithm SQRT is always correct when fed with a pair (P, s), where P is prime and s is a quadratic residue mod P. Such an algorithm was described for the special case where $P \equiv 3 \pmod{4}$. Thus, whenever the candidate number is congruent to 3 (mod 4), which typically is the case in our applications, this description suffices. For the case $P \equiv 1 \pmod{4}$, we employ the randomized modular square-root-extraction algorithm mentioned earlier and observe that in case SQRT has error probability $\varepsilon < \frac{1}{2}$, our algorithm still distinguishes primes from composites (since on the former it accepts with probability at least $1 - \varepsilon > \frac{1}{2}$, whereas on the latter it accepts with probability at most $\frac{1}{2}$). The statistical difference between the two cases can be amplified by invoking the algorithm several times.

We mention that error-free probabilistic polynomial-time algorithms for testing primality do exist [121, 1], but currently are much slower. (These algorithms output either the correct answer or a special don't know symbol, where the latter is output with probability at most $\frac{1}{2}$.)

A.1.4. On Uniform Selection of Primes

A simple method for uniformly generating a prime number in some interval, say between N and $2N$, consists of repeatedly selecting at random an integer in this interval and testing it for primality. The question, of course, is, *How many times do we need to repeat the procedure before a prime number is found?* This question is intimately related to the *density of primes*, which has been extensively studied in number theory [7]. For our purposes it suffices to assert that in case the sampling interval is sufficiently large (when compared with the size of the integers in it), then the density of primes in it is noticeable (i.e., is a polynomial fraction). Specifically, the density of primes in the interval $[N, 2N]$ is $\Theta(1/\log N)$. Hence, on input N, we can expect to hit a prime in the interval $[N, 2N]$ within $\Theta(\log N)$ trials. Furthermore, with probability at least $1 - (1/N)^2$ we will hit a prime before conducting $\Theta((\log N)^2)$ trials. Hence, for all practical purposes, we can confine ourselves to conducting a number of trials that is polynomial (i.e., n^2) in the length of the prime we want to generate (i.e., $n = \log_2 N$). (We comment that an analogous discussion applies for primes that are congruent to 3 mod 4.)

We remark that there exists a probabilistic polynomial-time algorithm [9] that produces a uniformly selected prime P together with the factorization of $P - 1$. The prime factorization of $P - 1$ can be used to verify that a given residue is a generator of the multiplicative group modulo P: If $g^{P-1} \equiv 1 \pmod{P}$ and $g^N \not\equiv 1 \pmod{P}$ for every N that divides $P - 1$, then g is a generator of the multiplicative group modulo P. (Note that it suffices to check that $g^{P-1} \equiv 1 \pmod{P}$ and $g^{(P-1)/Q} \not\equiv 1 \pmod{P}$ for every prime Q that divides $P - 1$.) We mention that a noticeable fraction of the residues modulo P will be generators of the multiplicative group modulo P.

Finally, we comment that more randomness-efficient procedures for generating an n-bit-long prime do exist and utilize only $O(n)$ random bits.[4]

A.2. Composite Numbers

A natural number (other than 1) that is not a prime is called a *composite*. Such a number N is uniquely represented as a product of prime powers; that is, $N = \prod_{i=1}^{t} P_i^{e_i}$, where the P_i's are distinct primes, the e_i's are natural numbers, and either $t > 1$ or $e_1 > 1$. These P_i's are called the *prime factorization of N*. It is widely believed that given a composite number, it is infeasible to find its prime factorization. Specifically, it is assumed that it is infeasible to find the factorization of a composite number that is the product of two random primes. That is, it is assumed that any probabilistic polynomial-time algorithm, given the product of two uniformly chosen n-bit-long primes, can successfully recover these primes only with negligible probability. Rivest, Shamir, and Adleman [191] have suggested the use of this assumption for the construction of cryptographic schemes. Indeed, they have done so in proposing the RSA function, and their suggestion has turned out to have a vast impact (i.e., being the most popular intractability assumption in use in cryptography).

For a composite N, the *additive group modulo N*, denoted $\mathbb{Z}_N$, consists of the set $\{0, \ldots, N - 1\}$ and the operation of *addition* mod N. All elements that are relatively prime to N have order N (in this group). The *multiplicative group modulo N*, denoted $\mathbb{Z}_N^*$, consists of the set of natural numbers that are smaller than N and relatively prime to it, and the operation is *multiplication* mod N.

---

[4] For example, one can use a generic transformation of [177]. Loosely speaking, the latter transformation takes any polynomial-time linear-space randomized algorithm and returns a similar algorithm that has linear randomness complexity. Note that the selection process described in the preceding text satisfies the premise of the transformation.

A.2.1. Quadratic Residues Modulo a Composite

For simplicity, we focus on odd composite numbers that are not divisible by any strict prime power; that is, we consider numbers of the form $\prod_{i=1}^{t} P_i$, where the P_i's are *distinct odd* primes and $t > 1$.

Let $N = \prod_{i=1}^{t} P_i$ be such a composite number. A *quadratic residue modulo N* is an integer s such that there exists an $r \in \mathbb{Z}_N^*$ satisfying $s \equiv r^2 \pmod{N}$. Using the Chinese Remainder Theorem, one can show that s is a quadratic residue modulo N if and only if it is a quadratic residue modulo each of the P_i's. Suppose that s is a quadratic residue modulo N. Then the equation $x^2 \equiv s \pmod{N}$ has 2^t distinct (integer) solutions modulo N. Again, this can be proved by invoking the Chinese Remainder Theorem: First observe that the system

$$x^2 \equiv s \pmod{P_i} \quad \text{for } i = 1, \ldots, t \tag{A.1}$$

has a solution. Next note that each single equation has two distinct solutions $\pm r_i$ (mod P_i), and finally note that each of the 2^t different combinations yields a distinct-solution to Eq. (A.1) modulo N (i.e., a distinct square root of s modulo N).

The quadratic residues modulo N form a subgroup of the multiplicative group modulo N. The subgroup contains exactly a 2^{-t} fraction of the members of the group. Furthermore, for $N = \prod_{i=1}^{t} P_i$ (as before), squaring modulo N is a 2^t-to-1 mapping of the group to the subgroup. For further discussion of this mapping, in the special case where $t = 2$ and $P_1 \equiv P_2 \equiv 3 \pmod{4}$, see Section A.2.4.

A.2.2. Extracting Square Roots Modulo a Composite

By the preceding discussion (and the effectiveness of the Chinese Remainder Theorem),[5] it follows that given the prime factorization of N, one can efficiently extract square roots modulo N. On the other hand, any algorithm that extracts square roots modulo a composite can be transformed into a factoring algorithm [187]: It suffices to show how an algorithm for extraction of square roots (modulo a composite N) can be used to produce non-trivial divisors of N. The argument is very similar to the one employed in Section A.1.3, the difference being that there the root-extraction algorithm was assumed to work only for extracting square roots modulo a prime (and such efficient algorithms do exist), whereas here we assume that the algorithm works for extracting square roots modulo composites (and such efficient algorithms are assumed not to exist).

Reduction of Factoring to Extracting Modular Square Roots. On input a composite number N, do the following:

1. Uniformly select $r \in \{1, \ldots, N-1\}$.

2. Compute $g \leftarrow \mathrm{GCD}(N, r)$. If $g > 1$, then *output g and halt.*[6]

---

[5]Specifically, the system $x \equiv a_i \pmod{P_i}$ for $i = 1, \ldots, t$ is solved by $\sum_{i=1}^{t} c_i \cdot a_i \bmod \prod_{i=1}^{t} P_i$, where $c_i \stackrel{\text{def}}{=} Q_i \cdot (Q_i^{-1} \bmod P_i)$ and $Q_i \stackrel{\text{def}}{=} \prod_{j \neq i} P_j$.

[6]This step takes place in order to allow us to invoke the root-extraction algorithm only on relatively prime pairs (s, N).

3. Set $s \leftarrow r^2 \bmod N$ and invoke the root-extraction algorithm to obtain r' such that $(r')^2 \equiv s \pmod{N}$.

4. Compute $g \leftarrow \mathrm{GCD}(N, r - r')$. If $g > 1$, then *output* g and halt.

In case the algorithm halts with some output, the output is a non-trivial divisors of N. The prime factorization of N can be obtained by invoking the algorithm recursively on each of the two non-trivial divisors of N.

Analysis. We can assume that r selected in Step 1 is relatively prime to N, or else the GCD of r and N yields the desired divisor. Invoking the root-extraction algorithm, we obtain r' such that $(r')^2 \equiv s \equiv r^2 \pmod{N}$. Because the root-extraction algorithm has no information on r (beyond $r^2 \pmod{N}$) with probability $2/2^t$, we have $r' \equiv \pm r \pmod{N}$. Otherwise, $r' \not\equiv \pm r \pmod{N}$, and still $0 \equiv (r - r')(r + r') \pmod{N}$. Therefore, $r - r'$ (resp., $r + r'$) has a non-trivial GCD with N, which is found in Step 4. Thus, with probability at least $\frac{1}{2}$, we obtain a non-trivial divisor of N.

A.2.3. The Legendre and Jacobi Symbols

The *Legendre symbol* of integer r modulo a prime P, denoted $\mathrm{LS}_P(r)$, is defined as 0 if P divides r, as $+1$ in case r is a quadratic residue modulo P, and as -1 otherwise. Thus, for r that is relatively prime to P, the Legendre symbol of r modulo P indicates whether or not r is a quadratic residue.

The Jacobi symbol of residues modulo a composite N is defined based on the prime factorization of N. Let $\prod_{i=1}^{t} P_i^{e_i}$ denote the prime factorization of N. Then the *Jacobi symbol* of r modulo N, denoted $\mathrm{JS}_N(r)$, is defined as $\prod_{i=1}^{t} \mathrm{LS}_{P_i}(r)^{e_i}$. Although the Jacobi symbol (of r modulo N) is defined in terms of the prime factorization of the modulus, the Jacobi symbol can be computed efficiently *without knowledge of the factorization of the modulus*. That is, there exists a polynomial-time algorithm that given a pair (r, N) computes $\mathrm{JS}_N(r)$. The algorithm proceeds in "GCD-like" manner[7] and utilizes the following facts regarding the Jacobi symbol:

1. $\mathrm{JS}_N(r) = \mathrm{JS}_N(r \bmod N)$

2. $\mathrm{JS}_N(a \cdot b) = \mathrm{JS}_N(a) \cdot \mathrm{JS}_N(b)$, and $\mathrm{JS}_N(1) = 1$

3. $\mathrm{JS}_N(2) = (-1)^{(N^2-1)/8}$ (i.e., $\mathrm{JS}_N(2) = -1$ iff $N \equiv 4 \pm 1 \,(\bmod\ 8)$)

4. $\mathrm{JS}_N(r) = (-1)^{(N-1)(r-1)/4} \cdot \mathrm{JS}_r(N)$ for odd integers N and r

Note that a quadratic residue modulo N must have Jacobi symbol 1, but not all residues of Jacobi symbol 1 are quadratic residues modulo N. (In fact, for $N = \prod_{i=1}^{t} P_i$, as in Section A.2.1, half of the residues with non-zero Jacobi symbols have Jacobi symbol 1, but only a 2^{-t} fraction of these residues are squares modulo N.)[8] The fact that

---

[7]E.g., $\mathrm{JS}_{21}(10) = \mathrm{JS}_{21}(2) \cdot \mathrm{JS}_{21}(5) = (-1)^{55} \cdot (-1)^{20} \cdot \mathrm{JS}_5(21) = -\mathrm{JS}_5(1) = -1$. In general, Fact 2 is used only with $a = 2$ (i.e., $\mathrm{JS}_N(2 \cdot r) = \mathrm{JS}_N(2) \cdot \mathrm{JS}_N(r)$). Also, at the very beginning, one can use $\mathrm{JS}_{2N}(r) = \mathrm{JS}_2(r) \cdot \mathrm{JS}_N(r) = (r \bmod 2) \cdot \mathrm{JS}_N(r)$.

[8]The elements of $\mathbb{Z}_N^*$ having Jacobi symbol 1 form a subgroup of $\mathbb{Z}_N^*$. This subgroup contains exactly half of the members of the group.

the Jacobi symbol can be computed efficiently (without knowledge of the factorization of the modulus) does *not* seem to yield an *efficient* algorithm for determining whether or not a given residue is a square modulo a given composite (of unknown factorization). In fact, it is believed that determining whether or not a given integer is a quadratic residue modulo a given composite (of unknown factorization) is infeasible. Goldwasser and Micali [123] have suggested use of the conjectured intractability of this problem toward the construction of cryptographic schemes, and that suggestion has been followed in numerous works.

A.2.4. Blum Integers and Their Quadratic-Residue Structure

We call $N = P \cdot Q$, where P and Q are primes, a *Blum integer* if $P \equiv Q \equiv 3 \pmod{4}$. For such P (resp., Q), the integer -1 is not a quadratic residue mod P(resp., mod Q), and it follows that -1 is not a quadratic residue modulo N and that -1 has Jacobi symbol 1 mod N.

By earlier discussion, each quadratic residue s modulo N has four square roots, denoted $\pm x$ and $\pm y$, so that $\mathrm{GCD}(N, x \pm y) \in \{P, Q\}$. The important fact about Blum Integers is that exactly one of these square roots is a quadratic residue itself.[9] Consequently, $x \mapsto x^2$ mod N induces a *permutation* on the set of quadratic residues modulo N.

(We comment that some sources use a more general definition of Blum integers, but the preceding special case suffices for our purposes. The term "Blum integers" is commonly used in honor of Manuel Blum, who advocated the use of squaring modulo such numbers as a one-way *permutation*.)

We mention that in case $P \not\equiv Q \pmod{8}$, the Jacobi symbol of 4 modulo $N = P \cdot Q$ is -1. In this case, obtaining a square root of 4 mod N that is a quadratic residue itself allows us to factor N (since such a residue r satisfies $r \not\equiv \pm 2 \pmod{N}$ and $(r - 2) \cdot (r + 2) \equiv 0 \pmod{N}$).

---

[9] Let a and b be such that $a^2 \equiv s \pmod{P}$ and $b^2 \equiv s \pmod{Q}$. Then, either a or $-a$ (but not both) is a quadratic residue mod P, and similarly for b. Suppose, without loss of generality, that a (resp., b) is a quadratic residue mod P (resp., mod Q). The x satisfying $x \equiv a \pmod{P}$ and $x \equiv b \pmod{Q}$ is a square root of s modulo N that is a quadratic residue itself. The other square roots of s modulo N (i.e., $-x$ and $\pm y$, such that $y \equiv a \pmod{P}$ and $y \equiv -b \pmod{Q}$ are not quadratic residues mod N.

Brief Outline of Volume 2

This first volume contains only material on the *basic tools* of modern cryptography, that is, one-way functions, pseudorandomness, and zero-knowledge proofs. These basic tools are used in the construction of the *basic applications* (to be covered in the second volume). The latter will cover encryption, signatures, and general cryptographic protocols. In this appendix we provide brief summaries of the treatments of these basic applications.

B.1. Encryption: Brief Summary

Both private-key and public-key encryption schemes consist of three efficient algorithms: *key generation, encryption*, and *decryption*. The difference between the two types of schemes is reflected in the definition of security: The security of a public-key encryption scheme should also hold when the adversary is given the encryption key, whereas that is not required for private-key encryption schemes. Thus, public-key encryption schemes allow each user to broadcast its encryption key, so that any other user can send it encrypted messages (without needing to first agree on a private encryption key with the receiver). Next we present definitions of security for private-key encryption schemes. The public-key analogies can be easily derived by considering adversaries that get the encryption key as additional input. (For private-key encryption schemes, we can assume, without loss of generality, that the encryption key is identical to the decryption key.)

B.1.1. Definitions

For simplicity, we consider only the encryption of a single message; however, this message can be longer than the key (which rules out information-theoretic secrecy [200]). We present two equivalent definitions of security. The first, called *semantic security*, is a computational analogue of Shannon's definition of *perfect secrecy* [200]. The second definition views secure encryption schemes as those for which it is infeasible to distinguish encryptions of any (known) pair of messages (e.g., the all-zeros message and the all-ones message). The latter definition is technical in nature and is referred to as *indistinguishability of encryptions*.

We stress that the definitions presented here go way beyond saying that it is infeasible to recover the plaintext from the ciphertext. The latter statement is indeed a minimal requirement for a secure encryption scheme, but we claim that it is far too weak a requirement: An encryption scheme typically is used in applications where obtaining specific partial information on the plaintext endangers the security of the application. When designing an application-independent encryption scheme, we do not know which partial information endangers the application and which does not. Furthermore, even if one wants to design an encryption scheme tailored to one's own specific applications, it is rare (to say the least) that one has a precise characterization of all possible partial information that can endanger these applications. Thus, we require that it be *infeasible* to obtain any information about the plaintext from the ciphertext. Furthermore, in most applications the plaintext may not be uniformly distributed, and some a priori information regarding it is available to the adversary. We require that the secrecy of all partial information also be preserved in such a case. That is, even in the presence of a priori information on the plaintext, it is *infeasible* to obtain any (new) information about the plaintext from the ciphertext (beyond what it is feasible to obtain from the a priori information on the plaintext). The definition of semantic security postulates all of this. The equivalent definition of indistinguishability of encryptions is useful in demonstrating the security of candidate constructions, as well as for arguing about their usage as parts of larger protocols.

The Actual Definitions. In both definitions, we consider (feasible) adversaries that obtain, in addition to the ciphertext, auxiliary information that may depend on the potential plaintext (but not on the key). By $E(x)$ we denote the distribution of encryptions of x, when the key is selected at random. To simplify the exposition, let us assume that on security parameter n, the key-generation algorithm produces a key of length n, whereas the scheme is used to encrypt messages of length n^2.

> **Definition B.1.1 (Semantic Security (Following [123])):** *An encryption scheme is **semantically secure** if for every feasible algorithm, A, there exists a feasible algorithm B such that for every two functions $f, h : \{0, 1\}^* \to \{0, 1\}^*$ and all sequences of pairs $(X_n, z_n)_{n \in \mathbb{N}}$, where X_n is a random variable ranging over $\{0, 1\}^{n^2}$ and $|z_n|$ is of feasible (in n) length,*
>
> $$\Pr[A(E(X_n)h(X_n), z_n) = f(X_n)] < \Pr[B(h(X_n), z_n) = f(X_n)] + \mu(n)$$
>
> *where μ is a negligible function. Furthermore, the complexity of B should be related to that of A.*

What Definition B.1.1 says is that a feasible adversary does not gain anything by looking at the ciphertext. That is, whatever information (captured by the function f) it tries to compute about the ciphertext when given a priori information (captured by the function h) can essentially be computed as efficiently from the available a priori information alone. In particular, the ciphertext does not help in (feasibly) computing the least significant bit of the plaintext or any other information regarding the plaintext. This holds for any distribution of plaintexts (captured by the random variable X_n). We now turn to an equivalent definition.

Definition B.1.2 (Indistinguishability of Encryptions (Following [123])): *An encryption scheme has **indistinguishable encryptions** if for every feasible algorithm A and all sequences of triples $(x_n, y_n, z_n)_{n \in \mathbb{N}}$, where $|x_n| = |y_n| = n^2$ and $|z_n|$ is of feasible (in n) length,*

$$|\Pr[A(E(x_n), z_n) = 1] - \Pr[A(E(y_n), z_n) = 1]| < \mu(n)$$

where μ is a negligible function.

In particular, z_n may equal (x_n, y_n). Thus, it is infeasible to distinguish the encryptions of any two fixed messages such as the all-zeros message and the all-ones message.

Theorem B.1.3: *An encryption scheme is semantically secure if and only if it has indistinguishable encryptions.*

Probabilistic Encryption. It is easy to see that a secure public-key encryption scheme must employ a probabilistic (i.e., randomized) *encryption* algorithm. Otherwise, given the encryption key as (additional) input, it is easy to distinguish the encryption of the all-zeros message from the encryption of the all-ones message. The same holds for private-key encryption schemes when considering the security of encrypting several messages (rather than a single message as done before).[1] This explains the linkage between the foregoing robust security definitions and the *randomization paradigm* (discussed later).

B.1.2. Constructions

Private-key encryption schemes can be constructed based on the existence of one-way functions. In contrast, the known constructions of public-key encryption schemes seem to require stronger assumptions (such as the existence of trapdoor permutations).

B.1.2.1. Private-Key Schemes

It is common practice to use "pseudorandom generators" as a basis for private-key stream ciphers. We stress that this is a very dangerous practice when the "pseudorandom generator" is easy to predict (such as the linear congruential generator or some modifications of it that output a constant fraction of the bits of each resulting number [38, 84]). However, this common practice can become sound provided one uses pseudorandom generators as defined in Section 3.3. Thus, we obtain a *private-key stream cipher* that allows us to encrypt a stream of plaintext bits. Note that such a

---

[1]Here, for example, using a deterministic encryption algorithm allows the adversary to distinguish two encryptions of the same message from the encryptions of a pair of different messages.

stream cipher does not conform with our formulation of an encryption scheme, since for encrypting several messages we are required to maintain a counter. In other words, we obtain an encryption scheme with a variable state that is modified after the encryption of each message. To obtain a stateless encryption scheme, as in our earlier definitions, we can use a pseudorandom function.

Private-Key Encryption Scheme Based on Pseudorandom Functions. The key-generation algorithm consists of selecting a seed, denoted s, for such a function, denoted f_s. To encrypt a message $x \in \{0, 1\}^n$ (using key s), the encryption algorithm uniformly selects a string $r \in \{0, 1\}^n$ and produces the ciphertext $(r, x \oplus f_s(r))$. To decrypt the ciphertext (r, y) (using key s), the decryption algorithm just computes $y \oplus f_s(r)$. The proof of security of this encryption scheme consists of two steps (suggested as a general methodology in Section 3.6):

1. Prove that an idealized version of the scheme, in which one uses a uniformly selected function $f : \{0, 1\}^n \to \{0, 1\}^n$, rather than the pseudorandom function f_s, is secure.

2. Conclude that the real scheme (as presented earlier) is secure (since otherwise one could distinguish a pseudorandom function from a truly random one).

Note that we could have gotten rid of the randomization if we had allowed the encryption algorithm to be history-dependent (e.g., use a counter in the role of r). Furthermore, if the encryption scheme is used for FIFO communication between the parties and both can maintain the counter value, then there is no need for the message sender to transmit the counter value.

B.1.2.2. Public-Key Schemes

Here we use a collection of trapdoor one-way permutations, $\{p_\alpha\}_\alpha$, and a hard-core predicate, b, for it.

The Randomization Paradigm [123]. To demonstrate this paradigm, we first construct a simple public-key encryption scheme.

Key generation: The key-generation algorithm consists of selecting at random a permutation p_α together with a trapdoor for it; the permutation (or rather its description) serves as the public key, whereas the trapdoor serves as the private key.

Encrypting: To encrypt a single bit σ (using public key p_α), the encryption algorithm uniformly selects an element r in the domain of p_α and produces the ciphertext $(p_\alpha(r), \sigma \oplus b(r))$.

Decrypting: To decrypt the ciphertext (y, τ) using the private key, the decryption algorithm simply computes $\tau \oplus b(p_\alpha^{-1}(y))$, where the inverse is computed using the trapdoor (i.e., private key).

This scheme is quite wasteful of bandwidth. However, the paradigm underlying its construction is valuable in practice. For example, it is certainly better to randomly pad messages (say, using padding equal in length to the message) before encrypting them using RSA than to employ RSA on the plain message. Such a heuristic can be placed on firm ground if the following *conjecture* is supported: Assume that the first $n/2$ least significant bits of the argument constitute a hard-core function of RSA with n-bit-long moduli. Then, encrypting $n/2$-bit messages by padding the message with $n/2$ random bits and applying RSA (with an n-bit modulus) on the result will constitute a secure public-key encryption system, hereafter referred to as *Randomized RSA*.

An alternative public-key encryption scheme is presented in [35]. That encryption scheme augments Construction 3.4.4 (of a pseudorandom generator based on one-way permutations) as follows:

Key generation: As before, the key-generation algorithm consists of selecting at random a permutation p_α together with a trapdoor.

Encrypting: To encrypt the n-bit string x (using public key p_α), the encryption algorithm uniformly selects an element s in the domain of p_α and produces the ciphertext $(p_\alpha^n(s), x \oplus G_\alpha(s))$, where

$$G_\alpha(s) = b(s) \cdot b(p_\alpha(s)) \cdots b\left(p_\alpha^{n-1}(s)\right)$$

(We use the notation $p_\alpha^{i+1}(x) = p_\alpha(p_\alpha^i(x))$ and $p_\alpha^{-(i+1)}(x) = p_\alpha^{-1}(p_\alpha^{-i}(x))$.)

Decrypting: To decrypt the ciphertext (y, z) using the private key, the decryption algorithm first recovers $s = p_\alpha^{-n}(y)$ and then outputs $z \oplus G_\alpha(s)$.

Assuming that factoring Blum integers (i.e., products of two primes each congruent to 3 (mod 4)) is hard, one can use the modular squaring function in the role of the trapdoor permutation and the least significant bit (denoted lsb) in the role of its hard-core predicate [35, 5, 208, 82]. This yields a secure public-key encryption scheme (depicted in Figure B.1) with efficiency comparable to that of RSA. Recall that RSA itself is not secure (as it employs a deterministic encryption algorithm), whereas Randomized

---

Private key: Two $n/2$-bit-long primes, p and q, each congruent to 3 (mod 4).

Public key: Their product $N \overset{\text{def}}{=} pq$.

Encryption of message $x \in \{0, 1\}^n$:

    1. Uniformly select $s_0 \in \{1, \ldots, N\}$.

    2. For $i = 1, \ldots, n+1$, compute $s_i \leftarrow s_{i-1}^2 \bmod N$ and $\sigma_i = \text{lsb}(s_i)$.

The ciphertext is (s_{n+1}, y), where $y = x \oplus \sigma_1 \sigma_2 \cdots \sigma_n$.

Decryption of the ciphertext (r, y):

    Precomputed: $d_p = ((p+1)/4)^n \bmod p - 1$, $d_q = ((q+1)/4)^n \bmod q - 1$,

    $c_p = q \cdot (q^{-1} \bmod p)$, and $c_q = p \cdot (p^{-1} \bmod q)$.

    1. Let $s' \leftarrow r^{d_p} \bmod p$ and $s'' \leftarrow r^{d_q} \bmod q$.

    2. Let $s_1 \leftarrow c_p \cdot s' + c_q \cdot s'' \bmod N$.

    3. For $i = 1, \ldots, n$, compute $\sigma_i = \text{lsb}(s_i)$ and $s_{i+1} \leftarrow s_i^2 \bmod N$.

The plaintext is $y \oplus \sigma_1 \sigma_2 \cdots \sigma_n$.

Figure B.1: The Blum-Goldwasser public-key encryption scheme [35].

RSA (defined earlier) is not known to be secure under standard assumptions such as the intractability of factoring (or of inverting the RSA function).[2]

B.1.3. Beyond Eavesdropping Security

The foregoing definitions refer only to a "passive" attack in which the adversary merely eavesdrops on the communication line (over which ciphertexts are being sent). Stronger types of attacks, culminating in the so-called chosen ciphertext attack, may be possible in various applications. Furthermore, these definitions refer to an adversary that tries to extract explicit information about the plaintext. A less explicit attempt, captured by the so-called notion of *malleability*, is to generate an encryption of a related plaintext (possibly without learning anything about the original plaintext). Thus, we have a "matrix" of adversaries, with one dimension (parameter) being the *type of attack* and the second being its *purpose*.

Types of Attacks. The following mini-taxonomy of attacks certainly is not exhaustive:

1. *Passive attacks*, as captured in the foregoing definitions. Among public-key schemes, we distinguish two sub-cases:

   (a) A *key-oblivious* passive attack, as captured in the foregoing definitions. By "key-obliviousness" we refer to the fact that the choice of plaintext does not depend on the public key.

   (b) A *key-dependent* passive attack, in which the choice of plaintext may depend on the public key.

   (In Definition B.1.1 the choice of plaintext means the random variable X_n, whereas in Definition B.1.2 it means the pair of strings (x_n, y_n). In both of these definitions, the choice of the plaintext is non-adaptive.)

2. *Chosen plaintext attacks*. Here the attacker can obtain the encryption of any plaintext of its choice (under the key being attacked). Such an attack does not add power in case of public-key schemes.

3. *Chosen ciphertext attacks*. Here the attacker can obtain the decryption of any ciphertext of its choice (under the key being attacked). That is, the attacker is given oracle access to the decryption function corresponding to the decryption key in use. We distinguish two types of such attacks:

   (a) In an *a-priori-chosen* ciphertext attack, the attacker is given this oracle access prior to being presented the ciphertext that it will attack (i.e., the ciphertext for which it has to learn partial information or form a related ciphertext). That is, the attack consists of two stages: In the first stage the attacker is given the oracle access, and in the second stage the oracle is removed and the attacker is given a "test ciphertext" (i.e., a target to be learned or modified in violation of non-malleability).

---

[2]Recall that Randomized RSA is secure assuming that the $n/2$ least significant bits constitute a hard-core function for n-bit RSA moduli. We only know that the $O(\log n)$ least significant bits constitute a hard-core function for n-bit moduli [5].

(b) In an *a-posteriori-chosen* ciphertext attack the attacker is given the target ciphertext first, but its access to the oracle is restricted in that it is not allowed to make a query equal to the target ciphertext.

In both cases, the adversary can make queries that do not correspond to a legitimate ciphertext, and the answers will be accordingly (i.e., a special "failure" symbol).

Purpose of Attacks. Again, the following is not claimed to be exhaustive:

1. Standard *security*: the infeasibility of *obtaining information regarding the plaintext*. As defined earlier, such information must be a function (or a randomized process) applied to the bare plaintext and cannot depend on the encryption (or decryption) key.

2. In contrast, the notion of *non-malleability* [64] refers to generating a string depending on both the plaintext and the current encryption key. Specifically, one requires that it be infeasible for an adversary, given a ciphertext, to produce a valid ciphertext for a related plaintext. For example, given a ciphertext of a plaintext of the form $1x$, it should be infeasible to produce a ciphertext to the plaintext $0x$.

With the exception of passive attacks on private-key schemes, non-malleability always implies security against attempts to obtain information on the plaintext. Security and non-malleability are equivalent under a-posteriori-chosen ciphertext attack (cf. [64, 16]). For a detailed discussion of the relationships among the various notions of secure private-key and public-key encryptions, the reader is referred to [142] and [16], respectively.

Some Known Constructions. As in the basic case, the (strongly secure) private-key encryption schemes can be constructed based on the existence of one-way functions, whereas the (strongly secure) public-key encryption schemes are based on the existence of trapdoor permutations.

Private-key schemes: The private-key encryption scheme based on pseudorandom functions (described earlier) is secure also against a-priori-chosen ciphertext attacks.[3]

It is easy to turn any passively secure private-key encryption scheme into a scheme secure under (a posteriori) chosen ciphertext attacks by using a message-authentication scheme[4] on top of the basic encryption.

Public-key schemes: Public-key encryption schemes secure against a-priori-chosen ciphertext attacks can be constructed assuming the existence of trapdoor permutations and utilizing non-interactive zero-knowledge proofs see [176]. (Recall that the latter proof systems can be constructed under the former assumption.)

---

[3]Note that this scheme is not secure under an a-posteriori-chosen ciphertext attack: On input a ciphertext $(r, x \oplus f_s(r))$, we obtain $f_s(r)$ by making the query (r, y'), where $y' \neq x \oplus f_s(r)$. (This query is answered with x' such that $y' = x' \oplus f_s(r)$.)

[4]See definition in Section B.2.

Public-key encryption schemes secure against a-posteriori-chosen ciphertext attacks can also be constructed under the same assumption [64], but this construction is even more complex.

In fact, both constructions of *public-key* encryption schemes secure against chosen ciphertext attacks are to be considered as plausibility results (which also offer some useful construction paradigms). Presenting "reasonably efficient" public-key encryption schemes that are secure against (a posteriori) chosen ciphertext attacks, under widely believed assumptions, is an important open problem.[5]

B.1.4. Some Suggestions

B.1.4.1. Suggestions for Further Reading

Fragments of a preliminary draft for the intended chapter on encryption schemes can be obtained online [99].

In addition, there are the original papers: There is a good motivating discussion in [123], but we prefer the definitional treatment of [92, 94], which can be substantially simplified if one adopts non-uniform complexity measures (as done above).[6] Further details on the construction of public-key encryption schemes (sketched above) can be found in [123, 92, 35, 5]. For discussion of non-malleable cryptography, which actually transcends the domain of encryption, see [64].

B.1.4.2. Suggestions for Teaching

We suggest a focus on the basic notion of security (treated in Sections B.1.1 and B.1.2): Present both definitions, prove their equivalence, and discuss the need to use *randomness* during the encryption process in order to meet these definitions. Next, present all constructions described in Section B.1.2. We believe that the draft available online [99] provides sufficient details for all of these.

B.2. Signatures: Brief Summary

Again, there are private-key and public-key versions, both consisting of three efficient algorithms: *key generation, signing,* and *verification.* (Private-key signature schemes are commonly referred to as *message-authentication schemes* or *codes* (MAC).) The difference between the two types is again reflected in the definitions of security. This difference yields different functionalities (even more than in the case of encryption): Public-key signature schemes (hereafter referred to as signature schemes) can be used to produce signatures that are *universally verifiable* (given access to the public key of the signer). Private-key signature schemes (hereafter referred to as message-authentication schemes) typically are used to authenticate messages sent

---

[5]The "reasonably efficient" scheme of [57] is based on a strong assumption regarding the Diffie-Hellman key exchange. Specifically, it is assumed that for a prime P and primitive element g, given $(P, g, (g^x \bmod P), (g^y \bmod P), (g^z \bmod P))$, it is infeasible to decide whether or not $z \equiv xy \pmod{P-1}$.

[6]We comment that [92] follows [94] in providing a uniform-complexity treatment of the security of encryption schemes.

among a (small) set of *mutually trusting* parties (since the ability to verify signatures may be linked to the ability to produce them). In other words, message-authentication schemes are used to authenticate information sent between (typically two) parties, and the purpose is to *convince the receiver* that the information has indeed been sent by the legitimate sender. In particular, message-authentication schemes cannot *convince a third party* that the sender has indeed sent the information (rather than the receiver having generated it by itself). In contrast, public-key signatures can be used to convince third parties: A signature to a document typically is sent to a second party, so that in the future that party can (by merely presenting the signed document) convince third parties that the document was indeed generated/sent/approved by the signer.

B.2.1. Definitions

We consider very powerful attacks on the signature scheme as well as a very liberal notion of breaking it. Specifically, the attacker is allowed to obtain signatures to any message of its choice. One may argue that in many applications such a general attack is not possible (since messages to be signed must have a specific format). Yet our view is that it is impossible to define a general (i.e., application-independent) notion of admissible messages, and thus it seems that a general/robust definition of an attack must be formulated as suggested here. (Note that, at worst, our approach is overly cautious.) Likewise, the adversary is said to be successful if it can produce a valid signature to ANY message for which it has not asked for a signature during its attack. Again, this defines the ability to form signatures to possibly "non-sensical" messages as a breaking of the scheme. Yet, again, we see no way to have a general (i.e., application-independent) notion of "meaningful" messages (so that only forging signatures to them would be consider a breaking of the scheme).

Definition B.2.1 (Unforgeable Signatures [125]):

- *A* **chosen message attack** *is a process that on input a verification key can obtain signatures* (relative to the corresponding signing key) *to messages of its choice.*

- *Such an attack is said to* **succeed** (in existential forgery) *if it outputs a valid signature to a message for which it has* not *requested a signature during the attack.*

- *A signature scheme is* **secure** (or unforgeable) *if every* feasible *chosen message attack succeeds with at most negligible probability.*

We stress that *plain* RSA (like plain versions of Rabin's scheme [187] and DSS [169]) is not secure under the foregoing definition. However, it may be secure if the message is "randomized" before RSA (or another scheme) is applied [22]. Thus the randomization paradigm seems pivotal here too.

The definition of security for message-authentication schemes is similar, except that the attacker does not get the verification key as input.

B.2.2. Constructions

Both message-authentication and signature schemes can be constructed based on the existence of one-way functions.

B.2.2.1. Message Authentication

Message-authentication schemes can be constructed using pseudorandom functions [103]: To authenticate the message x with respect to key s, one generates the tag $f_s(x)$, where f_s is the pseudorandom function associated with s. Verification is done in the same (analogous) way. However, as noted in [15], *extensive* use of pseudorandom functions would seem to be overkill for achieving message authentication, and more efficient schemes can be obtained based on other cryptographic primitives. We mention two approaches:

1. *fingerprinting* the message using a scheme that is *secure against forgery provided that the adversary does not have access to the scheme's outcome* (e.g., using Universal Hashing [49]), and *"hiding"* the result using a *non-malleable* scheme (e.g., a private-key encryption or a pseudorandom function). (Non-malleability is not required in certain cases [209].)

2. *hashing* the message *using a collision-free scheme* [58, 59] and *authenticating* the result using a MAC that operates on (short) fixed-length strings [15].

B.2.2.2. Signature Schemes

Three central paradigms in the construction of signature schemes are the "refreshing" of the "effective" signing key, the use of an "authentication tree," and the "hashing paradigm."

The Refreshing Paradigm [125]. To demonstrate this paradigm, suppose we have a signature scheme that is robust against a "random message attack" (i.e., an attack in which the adversary obtains signatures only to randomly chosen messages). Further suppose that we have a *one-time* signature scheme (i.e., a signature scheme that is secure against an attack in which the adversary obtains a signature to a *single* message of its choice). Then we can obtain a secure signature scheme as follows: When a new message needs to be signed, we generate a new random signing key for the one-time signature scheme, use it to sign the message, and sign the corresponding (one-time) verification key using the fixed signing key of the main signature scheme[7] (which is robust against a "random message attack") [71]. We note that one-time signature schemes (as utilized here) are easy to construct (e.g., [161]).

The Authentication-Tree Paradigm [160, 125]. To demonstrate this paradigm, we show how to construct a general signature scheme using only a one-time signature scheme (alas, one where a $2n$-bit string can be signed with respect to an n-bit-long

---

[7]Alternatively, one can generate the one-time key pair and the signature to its verification key ahead of time, leading to an "off-line/on-line" signature scheme [71].

verification key). The idea is to use the initial signing key (i.e., the one corresponding to the public verification key) in order to sign/authenticate two new/random verification keys. The two corresponding signing keys are used to sign/authenticate four new/random verification keys (two per each signing key), and so on. Stopping after ℓ such steps, this process forms a binary tree with 2^ℓ leaves, where each leaf corresponds to an instance of the one-time signature scheme. The signing keys at the leaves can be used to sign the actual messages, and the corresponding verification keys can be authenticated using the path from the root. That is, to sign a new message, we proceed as follows:

1. Allocate a new leaf in the tree. This requires either keeping a counter of the number of messages signed thus far or selecting a leaf at random (assuming that the number of leaves is much larger than the square of the number of messages to be signed).

2. Generate or retrieve from storage the pairs of signing/verification keys corresponding to each vertex on the path from the root to the selected leaf, along with the key pairs of the siblings of the vertices on the path. That is, let $v_0, v_1, \ldots, v_\ell$ denote the vertices along the path from the root v_0 to the selected leaf v_ℓ, and let u_i be the sibling of v_i (for $i = 1, \ldots, \ell$). Then we generate/retrieve the key pairs of each v_i and each u_i, for $i = 1, \ldots, \ell$.

   It is important to use the same key pair when encountering the same vertex in the process of signing two different messages.

3. Sign the message using the signing key associated with the selected leaf v_ℓ. Sign each pair of verification keys associated with the children of each internal vertex, along the foregoing path, using the signing key associated with the parent vertex. That is, for $i = 1, \ldots, \ell$, sign the verification keys of v_i and u_i (placed in some canonical order) using the signing key associated with vertex v_{i-1}.

   The signature is obtained by concatenating all these signatures (along with the corresponding verification keys). Recall that the key pair associated with the root is the actual key pair of the signature scheme; that is, the verification component is placed in the public file, and the signature of the verification keys of the root's children (relative to the root's signing key) is part of all signatures.

Pseudorandom functions can be used to eliminate the need to store the values of vertices used in previous signatures [89].

Employing this paradigm, and assuming that the RSA function is infeasible to invert, one obtains a secure signature scheme [125, 89] (with a counter of the number of messages signed) in which the ith message is signed/verified in time $2 \log_2 i$ slower than plain RSA. Using a tree of large fan-in (and assuming again that RSA is infeasible to invert), one can obtain a secure signature scheme [67, 56] that for reasonable parameters is only five times slower than plain RSA.[8] We stress that plain RSA is not a secure signature scheme, whereas the security of its randomized version (mentioned earlier) is not known to be reducible to the assumption that RSA is hard to invert.

---

[8] This figure refers to signing up to 1,000,000,000 messages. The scheme in [67] requires a universal set of system parameters consisting of 1000–2000 integers of the size of the moduli. In the scheme of [56], that requirement is removed.

The Hashing Paradigm. A common practice is to sign real documents via a two-stage process: First the document is hashed into a (relatively) short bit string, and then the basic signature scheme is applied to the resulting string. We note that this heuristic becomes sound provided the hashing function is *collision-free* (as defined in [58]). Collision-free hashing functions can be constructed, assuming the existence of claw-free collections (as in Definition 2.4.6) [58]. One can indeed postulate that certain off-the-shelf products (e.g., MD5 or SHA) are collision-free, but such assumptions need to be tested (and indeed may turn out false). We stress that using a hashing scheme in the foregoing two-stage process without carefully evaluating whether or not it is collision-free is a very dangerous practice.

One useful variant on the foregoing paradigm is the use of *universal one-way hashing functions* (as defined in [175]), rather than the collision-free hashing used earlier. In such a case, a new hashing function is selected for each application of the scheme, and the basic signature scheme is applied both to the (succinct) description of the hashing function and to the resulting (hashed) string. (In contrast, when using a collision-free hashing function, the same function, the description of which is part of the signer's public key, is used in all applications of the signature scheme.) The advantage of using universal one-way hashing functions is that their security requirement seems weaker than that for the collision-free condition (e.g., the former can be constructed using any one-way function [192], whereas this is NOT known for the latter).

Theorem B.2.2 (Plausibility Result [175, 192]): *Signature schemes exist if and only if one-way functions exist.*

Unlike the paradigms (and some of the constructions) described earlier, the known construction of signature schemes from *arbitrary* one-way functions has no practical significance. It is indeed an important open problem to provide an alternative construction that can be practical and still utilize an *arbitrary* one-way function.

B.2.3. Some Suggestions

B.2.3.1. Suggestions for Further Reading

Fragments of a preliminary draft for the intended chapter on signature schemes can be obtained on line [100].

In addition, there are the original papers: For a definitional treatment of *signature schemes*, the reader is referred to [125] and [183]. Easy-to-understand constructions appear in [20, 71, 67]. The proof of Theorem B.2.2 can be extracted from [175, 192]: The first paper presents the basic approach and implements it using any one-way permutation, whereas the second paper shows how to implement this approach using any one-way function. Variants on the basic model are discussed in [183] and in [50, 137]. For discussion of *message-authentication schemes* (MACs) the reader is referred to [15].

B.2.3.2. Suggestions for Teaching

We suggest a focus on signature schemes, presenting the main definition and some construction. One may use [125] for the definitional treatment, but should *not* use it for the construction, the underlying ideas of which are more transparent in papers such as [20] and [175]. Actually, we suggest presenting a variant on the signature scheme of [175], using collision-free hashing (cf. [58]) instead of universal one-way hashing (cf. [175]). This allows one to present, within a few lectures, many important paradigms and techniques (e.g., the refreshing paradigm, authentication trees, the hashing paradigm, and one-time signature schemes). We believe that the draft available online [100] provides sufficient details for such a presentation.

A basic treatment of message authentication (i.e., motivation, definition, and construction based on pseudorandom functions) can be presented within one lecture, and [100] can be used for this purpose too. (This, however, will not cover alternative approaches employed toward the construction of more efficient message-authentication schemes.)

B.3. Cryptographic Protocols: Brief Summary

A general framework for casting cryptographic (protocol) problems consists of specifying a random process that maps n inputs to n outputs. The inputs to the process are to be thought of as local inputs of n parties, and the n outputs are their corresponding local outputs. The random process describes the desired functionality. That is, if the n parties were to trust each other (or trust some outside party), then each could send its local input to the trusted party, who would compute the outcome of the process and send each party the corresponding output. The question addressed in this section is the extent to which this trusted party can be "emulated" by the mutually distrustful parties themselves.

B.3.1. Definitions

For simplicity, we consider the special case where the specified process is deterministic and the n outputs are identical. That is, we consider an arbitrary n-ary function and n parties that wish to obtain the value of the function on their n corresponding inputs. Each party wishes to obtain the correct value of the function and prevent any other party from gaining anything else (i.e., anything beyond the value of the function and what is implied by it).

We first observe that (one thing that is unavoidable is that) each party can change its local input before entering the protocol. However, this is also unavoidable when the parties utilize a trusted party. In general, the basic paradigm underlying the definitions of *secure multi-party computations*[9] amounts to saying that situations that may occur in the real protocol can be simulated in an ideal model (where the parties can employ a trusted party). Thus, the "effective malfunctioning" of parties in secure protocols is restricted to what is postulated in the corresponding ideal model. The specific definitions

---

[9] Our current understanding of the definitional issues is most indebted to the high-level discussions in the unfinished manuscript of [165]. A similar definitional approach is presented in [11, 12]. The approach of [122] is more general: It avoids the definition of security (w.r.t a given functionality) and defines instead a related notion of protocol robustness. One minimalistic instantiation of the definitional approach of [165, 11, 12] is presented in [45] and is shown to satisfy the main conceptual concerns.

differ in the specific restrictions and/or requirements placed on the parties in the real computation. This typically is reflected in the definition of the corresponding ideal model; see the examples that follow.

B.3.1.1. An Example: Computations with Honest Majority

Here we consider an ideal model in which any minority group (of the parties) can collude as follows. First, this minority shares its original inputs and decides together on replacement inputs[10] to be sent to the trusted party. (The other parties send their respective original inputs to the trusted party.) When the trusted party returns the output, each majority player outputs it locally, whereas the colluding minority can compute an output based on all they know (i.e., the output and all the local inputs of these parties). A *secure multi-party computation with honest majority* is required to simulate this ideal model. That is, the effect of any feasible adversary that controls a minority of the players in the actual protocol can essentially be simulated by a (different) feasible adversary that controls the corresponding players in the ideal model. This means that in a secure protocol the effect of each minority group is "essentially restricted" to replacing its own local inputs (independently of the local inputs of the majority players) before the protocol starts and replacing its own local outputs (depending only on its local inputs and outputs) after the protocol terminates. (We stress that in the real execution the minority players do obtain additional pieces of information; yet in a secure protocol they gain essentially nothing from these additional pieces of information.)

Secure protocols according to this definition can even tolerate a situation where a minority of the parties choose to abort the execution. An aborted party (in the real protocol) is simulated by a party (in the ideal model) that aborts the execution either before supplying its input to the trusted party (in which case a default input is used) or after supplying its input. In either case, the majority players (in the real protocol) are able to compute the output even though a minority aborted the execution. This cannot be expected to happen when there is no honest majority (e.g., in a two-party computation) [53].

B.3.1.2. Another Example: Two-Party Computations Allowing Abort

In light of the foregoing, we consider an ideal model where each of the two parties can "shut down" the trusted (third) party at any point in time. In particular, this can happen after the trusted party has supplied the outcome of the computation to one party but before it has supplied it to the second. A *secure two-party computation allowing abort* is required to simulate this ideal model. That is, each party's "effective malfunctioning" in such a secure protocol is restricted to supplying an initial input of its choice and aborting the computation at any point in time. We stress that, as before, the choice of the initial input of each party cannot depend on the input of the other party.

---

[10]Such replacement can be avoided if the local inputs of parties are verifiable by the other parties. In such a case, a party (in the ideal model) has the choice of either joining the execution of the protocol with its correct local input or not joining the execution at all (but it cannot join with a replaced local input). Secure protocols simulating this ideal model can be constructed as well.

Generalizing the preceding, we can consider *secure multi-party computation allowing abort*. Here, in the ideal model, each of the parties can "shut down" the trusted party at any point in time; in particular, this can happen after the trusted party has supplied the outcome of the computation to some but not all of the parties.

B.3.2. Constructions

Theorem B.3.1 (General Plausibility Results, Loosely Stated): *Suppose that trapdoor permutations exist. Then*

- *any multi-party functionality can be securely computed in a model allowing abort* (cf. [211] for the two-party case and [113] for the case of more than two parties).

- *any multi-party functionality can be securely computed provided that a strict majority of the parties are honest* [112, 113].

The proof of each item proceeds in two steps [98]:

1. Presenting secure protocols for a "semi-honest" model in which the bad parties follow the protocol, except that they also keep a record of all intermediate results.[11]

   One key idea is to consider the propagation of values along the wires of a circuit (which computes the desired function), going from the input wires to the output wires. The execution of these protocols starts by each party sharing its inputs with all other parties, using a secret sharing scheme, so that any strict subset of the shares yields no information about the secret (e.g., each party is given a uniformly chosen share, and the dealer's share is set to the XOR of all other shares). A typical step consists of the secure computation of shares of the output wire of a gate from the shares of the input wires of this gate. That is, the m parties employ a secure protocol for computing the randomized m-party functionality $((a_1, b_1), \ldots, (a_m, b_m)) \mapsto (c_1, \ldots, c_m)$, where the c_i's are uniformly distributed subject to $\oplus_{i=1}^{m} c_i = \text{gate}(\oplus_{i=1}^{m} a_i, \oplus_{i=1}^{m} b_i)$. Repeating this step for each gate of the circuit (in a suitable order), the parties securely propagate shares along the wires of the circuit, going from the input wires of the circuit to its output wires. At the end of this propagation process, each party announces its shares in the output wires of the circuit, and the actual output is formed. Thus, securely computing an arbitrary functionality (which may be quite complex) is reduced to securely computing a few specific simple functionalities (i.e., given shares for the inputs of a Boolean gate, securely compute random shares for the output of this gate). Indeed, secure protocols for computing these simple functionalities are also provided.

2. Transforming protocols secure in the "semi-honest" model into full-fledged secure protocols. Here zero-knowledge proofs and protocols for fair coin-tossing are used in order to "force" parties to behave properly (i.e., as in the "semi-honest" model).

   Fair coin-tossing protocols are constructed using non-oblivious commitment schemes (see Section 4.9.2), which in turn rely on zero-knowledge proofs of knowledge (see Section 4.7).

---

[11] In other words, we need to simulate the local views of the dishonest players when given only the local inputs and outputs of the honest players. Indeed, this model corresponds to the honest-verifier model of zero-knowledge (see Section 4.3.1.7).

We stress the general nature of these constructions and view them as plausibility results asserting that a host of cryptographic problems are solvable, assuming the existence of trapdoor permutations. As discussed in the case of zero-knowledge proofs, the value of these general results is in allowing one to easily infer that the problem he/she faces is solvable in principle (as typically it is easy to cast problems within this framework). However, we do not recommend using (in practice) the solutions derived by these general results; one should rather focus on the specifics of the problem at hand and solve it using techniques and/or insights available from these general results.[12]

Analogous plausibility results have been obtained in a variety of models. In particular, we mention secure computations in the private-channels model [27, 51] and in the presence of mobile adversaries [182].

B.3.3. Some Suggestions

B.3.3.1. Suggestions for Further Reading

A draft of a manuscript that is intended to cover this surveyed material is available online from [98]. The draft provides an exposition of the basic definitions and results, as well as detailed proofs for the latter. More refined discussions of definitional issues can be found in [11, 12, 44, 45, 122, 165]; our advice is to start with [45].

B.3.3.2. Suggestions for Teaching

This area is very complex, and so we suggest that one merely present *sketches* of some definitions and constructions. Specifically, we suggest picking one of the two settings (i.e., computation with honest majority or two-party computation) and sketching the definition and the construction. Our own choice would be the two-party case; alas, the definition (allowing abort) is more complicated (but this is more than compensated for by simpler notation and a simpler construction that relies on relatively fewer ideas). We suggest emphasizing the definitional approach (i.e., "emulating a trusted party" as simulation of any adversary operating in the real model by an ideal-model adversary) and presenting the main ideas underlying the construction (while possibly skipping a few). We believe that the draft available online from [98] provides sufficient details for all of these.

---

[12]For example, although Threshold Cryptography (cf., [62, 87]) is merely a special case of multi-party computation, it is indeed beneficial to focus on its specifics.

Bibliography

[1] L.M. Adleman and M. Huang. *Primality Testing and Abelian Varieties Over Finite Fields*. Springer-Verlag Lecture Notes in Computer Science (Vol. 1512), 1992. (Preliminary version in *19th ACM Symposium on the Theory of Computing*, 1987.)

[2] W. Aiello and J. Håstad. Perfect Zero-Knowledge Languages Can Be Recognized in Two Rounds. In *28th IEEE Symposium on Foundations of Computer Science*, pages 439–448, 1987.

[3] M. Ajtai. Generating Hard Instances of Lattice Problems. In *28th ACM Symposium on the Theory of Computing*, pages 99–108, 1996.

[4] M. Ajtai, J. Komlos, and E. Szemerédi. Deterministic Simulation in LogSpace. In *19th ACM Symposium on the Theory of Computing*, pages 132–140, 1987.

[5] W. Alexi, B. Chor, O. Goldreich, and C.P. Schnorr. RSA/Rabin Functions: Certain Parts Are as Hard as the Whole. *SIAM Journal on Computing*, Vol. 17, April, pages 194–209, 1988.

[6] N. Alon and J.H. Spencer. *The Probabilistic Method*. Wiley, 1992.

[7] T.M. Apostol. *Introduction to Analytic Number Theory*. Springer, 1976.

[8] L. Babai. Trading Group Theory for Randomness. In *17th ACM Symposium on the Theory of Computing*, pages 421–420, 1985.

[9] E. Bach. *Analytic Methods in the Analysis and Design of Number-Theoretic Algorithms*. ACM Distinguished Dissertation (1984). MIT Press, Cambridge, MA, 1985.

[10] E. Bach and J. Shallit. *Algorithmic Number Theory. Vol. I: Efficient Algorithms*. MIT Press, Cambridge, MA, 1996.

[11] D. Beaver. Foundations of Secure Interactive Computing. In *Crypto91*, Springer-Verlag Lecture Notes in Computer Science (Vol. 576), pages 377–391, 1992.

[12] D. Beaver. Secure Multi-Party Protocols and Zero-Knowledge Proof Systems Tolerating a Faulty Minority. *Journal of Cryptology*, Vol. 4, pages 75–122, 1991.

[13] M. Bellare. A Note on Negligible Functions. Tech. Rep. CS97-529, Department of Computer Science and Engineering, UCSD, March 1997.

[14] M. Bellare, R. Canetti, and H. Krawczyk. Pseudorandom Functions Revisited: The Cascade Construction and Its Concrete Security. In *37th IEEE Symposium on Foundations of Computer Science*, pages 514–523, 1996.

[15] M. Bellare, R. Canetti, and H. Krawczyk. Keying Hash Functions for Message Authentication. In *Crypto96*, Springer-Verlag Lecture Notes in Computer Science (Vol. 1109), pages 1–15, 1996.

[16] M. Bellare, A. Desai, D. Pointcheval, and P. Rogaway. Relations Among Notions of Security for Public-Key Encryption Schemes. In *Crypto98*, Springer-Verlag Lecture Notes in Computer Science (Vol. 1462), pages 26–45, 1998.

[17] M. Bellare and O. Goldreich. On Defining Proofs of Knowledge. In *Crypto92*, Springer-Verlag Lecture Notes in Computer Science (Vol. 740), pages 390–420, 1992.

[18] M. Bellare, S. Halevi, A. Sahai, and S. Vadhan. Trapdoor Functions and Public-Key Cryptosystems. In *Crypto98*, Springer-Verlag Lecture Notes in Computer Science (Vol. 1462), pages 283–298, 1998.

[19] M. Bellare, R. Impagliazzo, and M. Naor. Does Parallel Repetition Lower the Error in Computationally Sound Protocols? In *38th IEEE Symposium on Foundations of Computer Science*, pages 374–383, 1997.

[20] M. Bellare and S. Micali. How to Sign Given Any Trapdoor Function. *Journal of the ACM*, Vol. 39, pages 214–233, 1992.

[21] M. Bellare and P. Rogaway. Random Oracles Are Practical: A Paradigm for Designing Efficient Protocols. In *1st Conference on Computer and Communications Security*, ACM, pages 62–73, 1993.

[22] M. Bellare and P. Rogaway. The Exact Security of Digital Signatures: How to Sign with RSA and Rabin. In *EuroCrypt96*, Springer-Verlag Lecture Notes in Computer Science (Vol. 1070), pp. 399–416, 1996.

[23] M. Bellare and M. Yung. Certifying Permutations: Noninteractive Zero-Knowledge Based on Any Trapdoor Permutation. *Journal of Cryptology*, Vol. 9, pages 149–166, 1996.

[24] S. Ben-David, B. Chor, O. Goldreich, and M. Luby. On the Theory of Average Case Complexity. *Journal of Computer and System Science*, Vol. 44, No. 2, April, pages 193–219, 1992.

[25] M. Ben-Or, O. Goldreich, S. Goldwasser, J. Håstad, J. Kilian, S. Micali, and P. Rogaway. Everything Provable Is Probable in Zero-Knowledge. In *Crypto88*, Springer-Verlag Lecture Notes in Computer Science (Vol. 403), pages 37–56, 1990.

[26] M. Ben-Or, S. Goldwasser, J. Kilian, and A. Wigderson. Multi-Prover Interactive Proofs: How to Remove Intractability. In *20th ACM Symposium on the Theory of Computing*, pages 113–131, 1988.

[27] M. Ben-Or, S. Goldwasser, and A. Wigderson. Completeness Theorems for Non-Cryptographic Fault-Tolerant Distributed Computation. In *20th ACM Symposium on the Theory of Computing*, pages 1–10, 1988.

[28] E.R. Berlekamp. Factoring Polynomials over Large Finite Fields. *Mathematics of Computation*, Vol. 24, pages 713–735, 1970.

[29] E.R. Berlekamp, R.J. McEliece, and H.C.A. van Tilborg. On the Inherent Intractability of Certain Coding Problems. *IEEE Transactions on Information Theory*, 1978.

[30] M. Blum. How to Exchange Secret Keys. *ACM Trans. Comput. Sys.*, Vol. 1, pages 175–193, 1983.

[31] M. Blum. Coin Flipping by Phone. In *24th IEEE Computer Conference (CompCon)*, February, pages 133–137, 1982. (See also *SIGACT News*, Vol. 15, No. 1, 1983.)

[32] L. Blum, M. Blum, and M. Shub. A Simple Secure Unpredictable Pseudo-Random Number Generator. *SIAM Journal on Computing*, Vol. 15, pages 364–383, 1986.

[33] M. Blum, A. De Santis, S. Micali, and G. Persiano. Non-interactive Zero-Knowledge Proof Systems. *SIAM Journal on Computing*, Vol. 20, No. 6, pages 1084–1118, 1991. (Considered the journal version of [34].)

[34] M. Blum, P. Feldman, and S. Micali. Non-Interactive Zero-Knowledge and Its Applications. In *20th ACM Symposium on the Theory of Computing*, pages 103–112, 1988. (See [33].)

[35] M. Blum and S. Goldwasser. An Efficient Probabilistic Public-Key Encryption Scheme

which Hides All Partial Information. In *Crypto84*, Springer-Verlag Lecture Notes in Computer Science (Vol. 196), pages 289–302, 1985.

[36] M. Blum and S. Micali. How to Generate Cryptographically Strong Sequences of Pseudo-Random Bits. *SIAM Journal on Computing*, Vol. 13, pages 850–864, 1984. (Preliminary version in *23rd IEEE Symposium on Foundations of Computer Science*, 1982.)

[37] R. Boppana, J. Håstad, and S. Zachos. Does Co-NP Have Short Interactive Proofs? *Information Processing Letters*, Vol. 25, May, pages 127–132, 1987.

[38] J.B. Boyar. Inferring Sequences Produced by Pseudo-Random Number Generators. *Journal of the ACM*, Vol. 36, pages 129–141, 1989.

[39] G. Brassard. A Note on the Complexity of Cryptography. *IEEE Transactions on Information Theory*, Vol. 25, pages 232–233, 1979.

[40] G. Brassard, D. Chaum, and C. Crépeau. Minimum Disclosure Proofs of Knowledge. *Journal of Computer and System Science*, Vol. 37, No. 2, pages 156–189, 1988. (Preliminary version by Brassard and Crépeau in *27th IEEE Symposium on Foundations of Computer Science*, 1986.)

[41] G. Brassard and C. Crépeau. Zero-Knowledge Simulation of Boolean Circuits. In *Crypto86*, Springer-Verlag Lecture Notes in Computer Science (Vol. 263), pages 223–233, 1987.

[42] G. Brassard, C. Crépeau, and M. Yung. Constant-Round Perfect Zero-Knowledge Computationally Convincing Protocols. *Theoretical Computer Science*, Vol. 84, pages 23–52, 1991.

[43] E.F. Brickell and A.M. Odlyzko. Cryptanalysis: A Survey of Recent Results. In *Proceedings of the IEEE*, Vol. 76, pages 578–593, 1988.

[44] R. Canetti. *Studies in Secure Multi-Party Computation and Applications*. Ph.D. thesis, Department of Computer Science and Applied Mathematics, Weizmann Institute of Science, Rehovot, Israel, June 1995. (Available from `http://theory.lcs.mit.edu/~tcryptol/BOOKS/ran-phd.html`.)

[45] R. Canetti. Security and Composition of Multi-party Cryptographic Protocols. *Journal of Cryptology*, Vol. 13, No. 1, pages 143–202, 2000.

[46] R. Canetti, O. Goldreich, and S. Halevi. The Random Oracle Methodology, Revisited. In *30th ACM Symposium on the Theory of Computing*, pages 209–218, 1998.

[47] R. Canetti, O. Goldreich, S. Goldwasser, and S. Micali. Resettable Zero-Knowledge. In *32nd ACM Symposium on the Theory of Computing*, pages 235–244, 2000.

[48] E.R. Canfield, P. Erdos, and C. Pomerance. On a Problem of Oppenheim Concerning "factorisatio numerorum." *Journal of Number Theory*, Vol. 17, pages 1–28, 1983.

[49] L. Carter and M. Wegman. Universal Hash Functions. *Journal of Computer and System Science*, Vol. 18, pages 143–154, 1979.

[50] D. Chaum. Blind Signatures for Untraceable Payments. In *Crypto82*, pages 199–203, Plenum Press, New York, 1983.

[51] D. Chaum, C. Crépeau, and I. Damgård. Multi-party Unconditionally Secure Protocols. In *20th ACM Symposium on the Theory of Computing*, pages 11–19, 1988.

[52] B. Chor, S. Goldwasser, S. Micali, and B. Awerbuch. Verifiable Secret Sharing and Achieving Simultaneity in the Presence of Faults. In *26th IEEE Symposium on Foundations of Computer Science*, pages 383–395, 1985.

[53] R. Cleve. Limits on the Security of Coin Flips When Half the Processors Are Faulty. In *18th ACM Symposium on the Theory of Computing*, pages 364–369, 1986.

[54] J.D. Cohen and M.J. Fischer. A Robust and Verifiable Cryptographically Secure Election Scheme. In *26th IEEE Symposium on Foundations of Computer Science*, pages 372–382, 1985.

[55] A. Cohen and A. Wigderson. Dispensers, Deterministic Amplification, and Weak Random

Sources. In *30th IEEE Symposium on Foundations of Computer Science*, pages 14–19, 1989.

[56] R. Cramer and I. Damgård. New Generation of Secure and Practical RSA-based Signatures. In *Crypto96*, Springer-Verlag Lecture Notes in Computer Science (Vol. 1109), pages 173–185, 1996.

[57] R. Cramer and V. Shoup. A Practical Public-Key Cryptosystem Provably Secure Against Adaptive Chosen Ciphertext Attacks. In *Crypto98*, Springer-Verlag Lecture Notes in Computer Science (Vol. 1462), pages 13–25, 1998.

[58] I. Damgård. Collision Free Hash Functions and Public Key Signature Schemes. In *EuroCrypt87*, Springer-Verlag Lecture Notes in Computer Science (Vol. 304), pages 203–216, 1988.

[59] I. Damgård. A Design Principle for Hash Functions. In *Crypto89*, Springer-Verlag Lecture Notes in Computer Science (Vol. 435), pages 416–427, 1990.

[60] I. Damgård. Concurrent Zero-Knowledge Is Easy in Practice. Theory of Cryptography Library, 99-14, June 1999. `http://philby.ucsd.edu/cryptolib`.

[61] I. Damgård, O. Goldreich, T. Okamoto, and A. Wigderson. Honest Verifier vs Dishonest Verifier in Public Coin Zero-Knowledge Proofs. In *Crypto95*, Springer-Verlag Lecture Notes in Computer Science (Vol. 963), pages 325–338, 1995.

[62] Y. Desmedt and Y. Frankel. Threshold Cryptosystems. In *Crypto89*, Springer-Verlag Lecture Notes in Computer Science (Vol. 435), pages 307–315, 1990.

[63] W. Diffie and M.E. Hellman. New Directions in Cryptography. *IEEE Transactions on Information Theory*, IT-22 (Nov.), pages 644–654, 1976.

[64] D. Dolev, C. Dwork, and M. Naor. Non-malleable Cryptography. In *23rd ACM Symposium on the Theory of Computing*, pages 542–552, 1991. (Full version available from authors.)

[65] D. Dolev and A.C. Yao. On the Security of Public-Key Protocols. *IEEE Transactions on Information Theory*, Vol. 30, No. 2, pages 198–208, 1983.

[66] C. Dwork, U. Feige, J. Kilian, M. Naor, and S. Safra. Low Communication Perfect Zero Knowledge Two Provers Proof Systems. In *Crypto92*, Springer-Verlag Lecture Notes in Computer Science (Vol. 740), pages 215–227, 1992.

[67] C. Dwork and M. Naor. An Efficient Existentially Unforgeable Signature Scheme and its Application. *Journal of Cryptology*, Vol. 11, No. 3, pages 187–208, 1998.

[68] C. Dwork, M. Naor, and A. Sahai. Concurrent Zero-Knowledge. In *30th STOC*, pages 409–418, 1998.

[69] S. Even and O. Goldreich. On the Security of Multi-party Ping-Pong Protocols. In *24th IEEE Symposium on Foundations of Computer Science*, pages 34–39, 1983.

[70] S. Even, O. Goldreich, and A. Lempel. A Randomized Protocol for Signing Contracts. *CACM*, Vol. 28, No. 6, pages 637–647, 1985.

[71] S. Even, O. Goldreich, and S. Micali. On-line/Off-line Digital Signatures. *Journal of Cryptology*, Vol. 9, pages 35–67, 1996.

[72] S. Even, A.L. Selman, and Y. Yacobi. The Complexity of Promise Problems with Applications to Public-Key Cryptography. *Information and Control*, Vol. 61, pages 159–173, 1984.

[73] S. Even and Y. Yacobi. Cryptography and NP-Completeness. In *Proceedings of 7th ICALP*, Springer-Verlag Lecture Notes in Computer Science (Vol. 85), pages 195–207, 1980. (See [72].)

[74] U. Feige. Error Reduction by Parallel Repetition – The State of the Art. Technical Report CS95-32, Computer Science Department, Weizmann Institute of Science, Rehovot, Israel, 1995.

[75] U. Feige, A. Fiat, and A. Shamir. Zero-Knowledge Proofs of Identity. *Journal of Cryptology*, Vol. 1, pages 77–94, 1988.

[76] U. Feige, D. Lapidot, and A. Shamir. Multiple Non-Interactive Zero-Knowledge Proofs under General Assumptions. *SIAM Journal on Computing*, Vol. 29, No. 1, pages 1–28, 1999.

[77] U. Feige and A. Shamir. Zero-Knowledge Proofs of Knowledge in Two Rounds. In *Crypto89*, Springer-Verlag Lecture Notes in Computer Science (Vol. 435), pages 526–544, 1990.

[78] U. Feige and A. Shamir. Witness Indistinguishability and Witness Hiding Protocols. In *22nd ACM Symposium on the Theory of Computing*, pages 416–426, 1990.

[79] W. Feller. *An Introduction to Probability Theory and Its Applications*. Wiley, New York, 1968.

[80] A. Fiat and A. Shamir. How to Prove Yourself: Practical Solution to Identification and Signature Problems. In *Crypto86*, Springer-Verlag Lecture Notes in Computer Science (Vol. 263), pages 186–189, 1987.

[81] M. Fischer, S. Micali, C. Rackoff, and D.K. Wittenberg. An Oblivious Transfer Protocol Equivalent to Factoring. Unpublished manuscript, 1986. (Preliminary versions were presented in *EuroCrypt84* and in the *NSF Workshop on Mathematical Theory of Security*, Endicott House (1985).)

[82] R. Fischlin and C.P. Schnorr. Stronger Security Proofs for RSA and Rabin Bits. In *EuroCrypt97*, Springer-Verlag Lecture Notes in Computer Science (Vol. 1233), pages 267–279, 1997.

[83] L. Fortnow. The Complexity of Perfect Zero-Knowledge. In *19th ACM Symposium on the Theory of Computing*, pages 204–209, 1987.

[84] A.M. Frieze, J. Håstad, R. Kannan, J.C. Lagarias, and A. Shamir. Reconstructing Truncated Integer Variables Satisfying Linear Congruences. *SIAM Journal on Computing*, Vol. 17, pages 262–280, 1988.

[85] O. Gaber and Z. Galil. Explicit Constructions of Linear Size Superconcentrators. *Journal of Computer and System Science*, Vol. 22, pages 407–420, 1981.

[86] M.R. Garey and D.S. Johnson. *Computers and Intractability: A Guide to the Theory of NP-Completeness*. Freeman, San Francisco, 1979.

[87] P.S. Gemmell. An Introduction to Threshold Cryptography. In *CryptoBytes* (RSA Laboratories), Vol. 2, No. 3, 1997.

[88] R. Gennaro and L. Trevisan. Lower Bounds on the Efficiency of Generic Cryptographic Constructions. *ECCC*, TR00-022, May 2000.

[89] O. Goldreich. Two Remarks Concerning the GMR Signature Scheme. In *Crypto86*, Springer-Verlag Lecture Notes in Computer Science (Vol. 263), pages 104–110, 1987.

[90] O. Goldreich. Towards a Theory of Software Protection and Simulation by Oblivious RAMs. In *19th ACM Symposium on the Theory of Computing*, pages 182–194, 1987.

[91] O. Goldreich. *Foundation of Cryptography – Class Notes*. Preprint, spring 1989. (Superseded by the current book in conjunction with [92].)

[92] O. Goldreich. *Lecture Notes on Encryption, Signatures and Cryptographic Protocol*. (Extracts from [91]. Available from http://theory.lcs.mit.edu/~oded/ln89.html. Superseded by the combination of [99], [100], and [98].)

[93] O. Goldreich. A Note on Computational Indistinguishability. *Information Processing Letters*, Vol. 34, May, pages 277–281, 1990.

[94] O. Goldreich. A Uniform Complexity Treatment of Encryption and Zero-Knowledge. *Journal of Cryptology*, Vol. 6, No. 1, pages 21–53, 1993.

[95] O. Goldreich. *Foundation of Cryptography – Fragments of a Book*. February 1995. (Available from http://theory.lcs.mit.edu/~oded/frag.html. Superseded by the current book in conjunction with [99].)

[96] O. Goldreich. Notes on Levin's Theory of Average-Case Complexity. *ECCC*, TR97-058, December 1997.

[97] O. Goldreich. *Modern Cryptography, Probabilistic Proofs and Pseudorandomness*. Algorithms and Combinatorics Series (Vol. 17), Springer-Verlag, 1999.

[98] O. Goldreich. *Secure Multi-Party Computation*. (In preparation, 1998. Working draft available from http://theory.lcs.mit.edu/~oded/gmw.html.)

[99] O. Goldreich. *Encryption Schemes – Fragments of a Chapter*. (December 1999. Available from http://www.wisdom.weizmann.ac.il/~oded/foc-book.html.)

[100] O. Goldreich. *Signature Schemes – Fragments of a Chapter*. (May 2000. Available from http://www.wisdom.weizmann.ac.il/~oded/foc-book.html.)

[101] O. Goldreich, S. Goldwasser, and S. Halevi. Collision-Free Hashing from Lattice Problems. *ECCC*, TR95-042, 1996.

[102] O. Goldreich, S. Goldwasser, and S. Micali. How to Construct Random Functions. *Journal of the ACM*, Vol. 33, No. 4, pages 792–807, 1986.

[103] O. Goldreich, S. Goldwasser, and S. Micali. On the Cryptographic Applications of Random Functions. In *Crypto84*, Springer-Verlag Lecture Notes in Computer Science (Vol. 263), pages 276–288, 1985.

[104] O. Goldreich, R. Impagliazzo, L.A. Levin, R. Venkatesan, and D. Zuckerman. Security Preserving Amplification of Hardness. In *31st IEEE Symposium on Foundations of Computer Science*, pages 318–326, 1990.

[105] O. Goldreich and A. Kahan. How to Construct Constant-Round Zero-Knowledge Proof Systems for NP. *Journal of Cryptology*, Vol. 9, No. 2, pages 167–189, 1996. (Preliminary versions date to 1988.)

[106] O. Goldreich and H. Krawczyk. On the Composition of Zero-Knowledge Proof Systems. *SIAM Journal on Computing*, Vol. 25, No. 1, February, pages 169–192, 1996.

[107] O. Goldreich and H. Krawczyk. On Sparse Pseudorandom Ensembles. *Random Structures and Algorithms*, Vol. 3, No. 2, pages 163–174, 1992.

[108] O. Goldreich, H. Krawcyzk, and M. Luby. On the Existence of Pseudorandom Generators. *SIAM Journal on Computing*, Vol. 22, No. 6, pages 1163–1175, 1993.

[109] O. Goldreich and E. Kushilevitz. A Perfect Zero-Knowledge Proof for a Decision Problem Equivalent to Discrete Logarithm. *Journal of Cryptology*, Vol. 6, No. 2, pages 97–116, 1993.

[110] O. Goldreich and L.A. Levin. Hard-Core Predicates for Any One-Way Function. In *21st ACM Symposium on the Theory of Computing*, pages 25–32, 1989.

[111] O. Goldreich and B. Meyer. Computational Indistinguishability – Algorithms vs. Circuits. *Theoretical Computer Science*, Vol. 191, pages 215–218, 1998.

[112] O. Goldreich, S. Micali, and A. Wigderson. Proofs that Yield Nothing but Their Validity or All Languages in NP Have Zero-Knowledge Proof Systems. *Journal of the ACM*, Vol. 38, No. 1, pages 691–729, 1991. (Preliminary version in *27th IEEE Symposium on Foundations of Computer Science*, 1986.)

[113] O. Goldreich, S. Micali, and A. Wigderson. How to Play Any Mental Game – A Completeness Theorem for Protocols with Honest Majority. In *19th ACM Symposium on the Theory of Computing*, pages 218–229, 1987.

[114] O. Goldreich, N. Nisan, and A. Wigderson. On Yao's XOR-Lemma. *ECCC*, TR95-050, 1995.

[115] O. Goldreich and Y. Oren. Definitions and Properties of Zero-Knowledge Proof Systems. *Journal of Cryptology*, Vol. 7, No. 1, pages 1–32, 1994.

[116] O. Goldreich and E. Petrank. Quantifying Knowledge Complexity. *Computational Complexity*, Vol. 8, pages 50–98, 1999.

[117] O. Goldreich, R. Rubinfeld, and M. Sudan. Learning Polynomials with Queries: The Highly Noisy Case. To appear in *SIAM Journal on Discrete Mathematics*.

[118] O. Goldreich, A. Sahai, and S. Vadhan. Honest-Verifier Statistical Zero-Knowledge Equals General Statistical Zero-Knowledge. In *30th ACM Symposium on the Theory of Computing*, pages 399–408, 1998.

[119] O. Goldreich and M. Sudan. Computational Indistinguishability: A Sample Hierarchy. *Journal of Computer and System Science*, Vol. 59, pages 253–269, 1999.

[120] O. Goldreich and S. Vadhan. Comparing Entropies in Statistical Zero-Knowledge with Applications to the Structure of SZK. In *14th IEEE Conference on Computational Complexity*, pages 54–73, 1999.

[121] S. Goldwasser and J. Kilian. Primality Testing Using Elliptic Curves. *Journal of the ACM*, Vol. 46, pages 450–472, 1999. (Preliminary version in *18th ACM Symposium on the Theory of Computing*, 1986.)

[122] S. Goldwasser and L.A. Levin. Fair Computation of General Functions in Presence of Immoral Majority. In *Crypto90*, Springer-Verlag Lecture Notes in Computer Science (Vol. 537), pages 77–93, 1991.

[123] S. Goldwasser and S. Micali. Probabilistic Encryption. *Journal of Computer and System Science*, Vol. 28, No. 2, pages 270–299, 1984. (Preliminary version in *14th ACM Symposium on the Theory of Computing*, 1982.)

[124] S. Goldwasser, S. Micali, and C. Rackoff. The Knowledge Complexity of Interactive Proof Systems. *SIAM Journal on Computing*, Vol. 18, pages 186–208, 1989. (Preliminary version in *17th ACM Symposium on the Theory of Computing*, 1985.)

[125] S. Goldwasser, S. Micali, and R.L. Rivest. A Digital Signature Scheme Secure Against Adaptive Chosen-Message Attacks. *SIAM Journal on Computing*, April, pages 281–308, 1988.

[126] S. Goldwasser, S. Micali, and P. Tong. Why and How to Establish a Private Code in a Public Network. In *23rd IEEE Symposium on Foundations of Computer Science*, pages 134–144, 1982.

[127] S. Goldwasser, S. Micali, and A.C. Yao. Strong Signature Schemes. In *15th ACM Symposium on the Theory of Computing*, pages 431–439, 1983.

[128] S. Goldwasser and M. Sipser. Private Coins versus Public Coins in Interactive Proof Systems. *Advances in Computing Research: A Research Annual*, Vol. 5 (*Randomness and Computation*, S. Micali, ed.), pages 73–90, 1989.

[129] J. Håstad, R. Impagliazzo, L.A. Levin, and M. Luby. Construction of a Pseudorandom Generator from Any One-Way Function. *SIAM Journal on Computing*, Vol. 28, No. 4, pages 1364–1396, 1999. (Preliminary versions by Impagliazzo et al. in *21st ACM Symposium on the Theory of Computing* (1989) and Håstad in *22nd ACM Symposium on the Theory of Computing* (1990).)

[130] J. Håstad, A. Schrift, and A. Shamir. The Discrete Logarithm Modulo a Composite Hides $O(n)$ Bits. *Journal of Computer and System Science*, Vol. 47, pages 376–404, 1993.

[131] R. Impagliazzo and M. Luby. One-Way Functions are Essential for Complexity Based Cryptography. In *30th IEEE Symposium on Foundations of Computer Science*, pages 230–235, 1989.

[132] R. Impagliazzo and M. Naor. Efficient Cryptographic Schemes Provable as Secure as Subset Sum. *Journal of Cryptology*, Vol. 9, pages 199–216, 1996.

[133] R. Impagliazzo and S. Rudich. Limits on the Provable Consequences of One-Way Permutations. In *21st ACM Symposium on the Theory of Computing*, pages 44–61, 1989.

[134] R. Impagliazzo and A. Wigderson. P = BPP if E Requires Exponential Circuits:

Derandomizing the XOR Lemma. In *29th ACM Symposium on the Theory of Computing*, pages 220–229, 1997.

[135] R. Impagliazzo and D. Zuckerman. How to Recycle Random Bits. In *30th IEEE Symposium on Foundations of Computer Science*, pages 248–253, 1989.

[136] R. Impagliazzo and M. Yung. Direct Zero-Knowledge Computations. In *Crypto87*, Springer-Verlag Lecture Notes in Computer Science (Vol. 293), pages 40–51, 1987.

[137] A. Juels, M. Luby, and R. Ostrovsky. Security of Blind Digital Signatures. In *Crypto97*, Springer-Verlag Lecture Notes in Computer Science (Vol. 1294), pages 150–164, 1997.

[138] J. Justesen. A Class of Constructive Asymptotically Good Algebraic Codes. *IEEE Transactions on Information Theory*, Vol. 18, pages 652–656, 1972.

[139] N. Kahale. Eigenvalues and Expansion of Regular Graphs. *Journal of the ACM*, Vol. 42, No. 5, pages 1091–1106, 1995.

[140] J. Kahn, M. Saks, and C. Smyth. A Dual Version of Reimer's Inequality and a Proof of Rudich's Conjecture. In *15th IEEE Conference on Computational Complexity*, 2000.

[141] B.S. Kaliski. Elliptic Curves and Cryptography: A Pseudorandom Bit Generator and Other Tools. Ph.D. thesis, LCS, MIT, Cambridge, MA, 1988.

[142] J. Katz and M. Yung. Complete Characterization of Security Notions for Probabilistic Private-Key Encryption. In *32nd ACM Symposium on the Theory of Computing*, pages 245–254, 2000.

[143] J. Kilian. A Note on Efficient Zero-Knowledge Proofs and Arguments. In *24th ACM Symposium on the Theory of Computing*, pages 723–732, 1992.

[144] J. Kilian and E. Petrank. An Efficient Non-Interactive Zero-Knowledge Proof System for NP with General Assumptions. *Journal of Cryptology*, Vol. 11, pages 1–27, 1998.

[145] J.C. Lagarias and A.M. Odlyzko. Solving Low-Density Subset Sum Problems. *Journal of the ACM*, Vol. 32, pages 229–246, 1985.

[146] D. Lapidot and A. Shamir. Fully Parallelized Multi-prover Protocols for NEXP-Time. *Journal of Computer and System Science*, Vol. 54, No. 2, April, pages 215–220, 1997.

[147] A. Lempel. Cryptography in Transition. *Computing Surveys*, Vol. 11, No. 4, pages 285–303, December 1979.

[148] A.K. Lenstra, H.W. Lenstra, and L. Lovász. Factoring Polynomials with Rational Coefficients. *Mathematische Annalen*, Vol. 261, pages 515–534, 1982.

[149] L.A. Levin. Average Case Complete Problems. *SIAM Journal on Computing*, Vol. 15, pages 285–286, 1986.

[150] L.A. Levin. One-Way Function and Pseudorandom Generators. *Combinatorica*, Vol. 7, pages 357–363, 1987.

[151] L.A. Levin. Randomness and Non-determinism. *Journal of Symbolic Logic*, Vol. 58, No. 3, pages 1102–1103, 1993.

[152] M. Li and P. Vitanyi. *An Introduction to Kolmogorov Complexity and Its Applications*. Springer-Verlag, 1993.

[153] J.H. van Lint. *Introduction to Coding Theory*. Graduate Texts in Mathematics (Vol. 88), Springer-Verlag, 1982.

[154] A. Lubotzky, R. Phillips, and P. Sarnak. Ramanujan Graphs. *Combinatorica*, Vol. 8, pages 261–277, 1988.

[155] M. Luby. *Pseudorandomness and Cryptographic Applications*. Princeton University Press, 1996.

[156] M. Luby and C. Rackoff. How to Construct Pseudorandom Permutations from Pseudo-Random Functions. *SIAM Journal on Computing*, Vol. 17, pages 373–386, 1988.

[157] C. Lund, L. Fortnow, H. Karloff, and N. Nisan. Algebraic Methods for Interactive Proof Systems. *Journal of the ACM*, Vol. 39, No. 4, pages 859–868, 1992.

[158] A.J. Menezes, P.C. van Oorschot, and S.A. Vanstone. *Handbook of Applied Cryptography*. CRC Press, Boca Raton, FL, 1996.

[159] R.C. Merkle. Secure Communication over Insecure Channels. *CACM*, Vol. 21, No. 4, pages 294–299, 1978.

[160] R.C. Merkle. Protocols for Public Key Cryptosystems. In *Proceedings of the 1980 IEEE Symposium on Security and Privacy*, pages 122–134, 1980.

[161] R.C. Merkle. A Digital Signature Based on a Conventional Encryption Function. In *Crypto87*, Springer-Verlag Lecture Notes in Computer Science (Vol. 293), pages 369–378, 1987.

[162] R.C. Merkle. A Certified Digital Signature Scheme. In *Crypto89*, Springer-Verlag Lecture Notes in Computer Science (Vol. 435), pages 218–238, 1990.

[163] R.C. Merkle and M.E. Hellman. Hiding Information and Signatures in Trapdoor Knapsacks. *IEEE Transactions on Information Theory*, Vol. 24, pages 525–530, 1978.

[164] S. Micali, C. Rackoff, and B. Sloan. The Notion of Security for Probabilistic Cryptosystems. *SIAM Journal on Computing*, Vol. 17, pages 412–426, 1988.

[165] S. Micali and P. Rogaway. Secure Computation. In *Crypto91*, Springer-Verlag Lecture Notes in Computer Science (Vol. 576), pages 392–404, 1992.

[166] G.L. Miller. Riemann's Hypothesis and Tests for Primality. *Journal of Computer and System Science*, Vol. 13, pages 300–317, 1976.

[167] R. Motwani and P. Raghavan. *Randomized Algorithms*. Cambridge University Press, 1995.

[168] National Bureau of Standards. *Federal Information Processing Standards*, Publ. 46 (DES 1977).

[169] National Institute for Standards and Technology. Digital Signature Standard (DSS). *Federal Register*, Vol. 56, No. 169, August 1991.

[170] M. Naor. Bit Commitment Using Pseudorandom Generators. *Journal of Cryptology*, Vol. 4, pages 151–158, 1991.

[171] M. Naor, R. Ostrovsky, R. Venkatesan, and M. Yung. Zero-Knowledge Arguments for NP Can Be Based on General Assumptions. *Journal of Cryptology*, Vol. 11, pages 87–108, 1998.

[172] M. Naor and O. Reingold. Synthesizers and Their Application to the Parallel Construction of Pseudo-Random Functions. In *36th IEEE Symposium on Foundations of Computer Science*, pages 170–181, 1995.

[173] M. Naor and O. Reingold. On the Construction of Pseudo-Random Permutations: Luby-Rackoff Revisited. *Journal of Cryptology*, Vol. 12, No. 1, pages 29–66, 1999.

[174] M. Naor and O. Reingold. From Unpredictability to Indistinguishability: A Simple Construction of Pseudorandom Functions from MACs. In *Crypto98*, Springer-Verlag Lecture Notes in Computer Science (Vol. 1464), pages 267–282, 1998.

[175] M. Naor and M. Yung. Universal One-Way Hash Functions and Their Cryptographic Application. In *21st ACM Symposium on the Theory of Computing*, pages 33–43, 1989.

[176] M. Naor and M. Yung. Public-Key Cryptosystems Provably Secure Against Chosen Ciphertext Attacks. In *22nd ACM Symposium on the Theory of Computing*, pages 427–437, 1990.

[177] N. Nisan and D. Zuckerman. Randomness Is Linear in Space. *Journal of Computer and System Science*, Vol. 52, No. 1, pages 43–52, 1996.

[178] A.M. Odlyzko. The Future of Integer Factorization. *CryptoBytes* (RSA Laboratories), Vol. 1, No. 2, pages 5–12, 1995. (Available from http://www.research. att.com/~amo.)

[179] A.M. Odlyzko. Discrete Logarithms and Smooth Polynomials. In *Finite Fields: Theory, Applications and Algorithms*, G.L. Mullen and P. Shiue, eds., Contemporary Mathematics,

Vol. 168, American Mathematical Society, pages 269–278, 1994. (Available from http://www.research.att.com/~amo.)

[180] T. Okamoto. On Relationships between Statistical Zero-Knowledge Proofs. In *28th ACM Symposium on the Theory of Computing*, pages 649–658, 1996.

[181] R. Ostrovsky and A. Wigderson. One-Way Functions Are Essential for Non-Trivial Zero-Knowledge. In *2nd Israel Symposium on Theory of Computing and Systems*, IEEE Comp. Soc. Press, pages 3–17, 1993.

[182] R. Ostrovsky and M. Yung. How to Withstand Mobile Virus Attacks. In *10th ACM Symposium on Principles of Distributed Computing*, pages 51–59, 1991.

[183] B. Pfitzmann. *Digital Signature Schemes (General Framework and Fail-Stop Signatures)*. Springer-Verlag Lecture Notes in Computer Science (Vol. 1100), 1996.

[184] V. Pratt. Every Prime Has a Succinct Certificate. *SIAM Journal on Computing*, Vol. 4, pages 214–220, 1975.

[185] M.O. Rabin. Probabilistic Algorithm for Testing Primality. *Journal of Number Theory*, Vol. 12, pages 128–138, 1980.

[186] M.O. Rabin. Digitalized Signatures. In *Foundations of Secure Computation*, R.A. DeMillo et al., eds. Academic Press, 1977.

[187] M.O. Rabin. Digitalized Signatures and Public Key Functions as Intractable as Factoring. TR-212, LCS, MIT, Cambridge, MA, 1979.

[188] M.O. Rabin. How to Exchange Secrets by Oblivious Transfer. Tech. Memo. TR-81, Aiken Computation Laboratory, Harvard University, 1981.

[189] R. Richardson and J. Kilian. On the Concurrent Composition of Zero-Knowledge Proofs. In *EuroCrypt99*, Springer-Verlag Lecture Notes in Computer Science (Vol. 1592), pages 415–413, 1999.

[190] R. Raz. A Parallel Repetition Theorem. *SIAM Journal on Computing*, Vol. 27, No. 3, pages 763–803, 1998.

[191] R. Rivest, A. Shamir, and L. Adleman. A Method for Obtaining Digital Signatures and Public Key Cryptosystems. *CACM*, Vol. 21, pages 120–126, 1978.

[192] J. Rompel. One-Way Functions Are Necessary and Sufficient for Secure Signatures. In *22nd ACM Symposium on the Theory of Computing*, pages 387–394, 1990.

[193] A. Sahai. Non-Malleable Non-Interactive Zero Knowledge and Achieving Chosen-Ciphertext Security. In *40th IEEE Symposium on Foundations of Computer Science*, pages 543–553, 1999.

[194] A. Sahai and S. Vadhan. A Complete Promise Problem for Statistical Zero-Knowledge. In *38th IEEE Symposium on Foundations of Computer Science*, pages 448–457, 1997.

[195] C.P. Schnorr and H.H. Horner. Attacking the Chor-Rivest Cryptosystem by Improved Lattice Reduction. In *EuroCrypt95*, Springer-Verlag Lecture Notes in Computer Science (Vol. 921), pages 1–12, 1995.

[196] A. Shamir. How to Share a Secret. *CACM*, Vol. 22, pages 612–613, 1979.

[197] A. Shamir. A Polynomial-Time Algorithm for Breaking the Merkle-Hellman Cryptosystem. In *23rd IEEE Symposium on Foundations of Computer Science*, pages 145–152, 1982.

[198] A. Shamir. IP = PSPACE. *Journal of the ACM*, Vol. 39, No. 4, pages 869–877, 1992.

[199] A. Shamir, R.L. Rivest, and L. Adleman. Mental Poker. Report TM-125, LCS, MIT, Cambridge, MA, 1979.

[200] C.E. Shannon. Communication Theory of Secrecy Systems. *Bell Systems Technical Journal*, Vol. 28, pages 656–715, 1949.

[201] M. Sipser. A Complexity Theoretic Approach to Randomness. In *15th ACM Symposium on the Theory of Computing*, pages 330–335, 1983.

[202] M. Sipser. *Introduction to the Theory of Computation*. PWS Publishing, Boston, MA, 1997.

[203] R. Solovay and V. Strassen. A Fast Monte-Carlo Test for Primality. *SIAM Journal on Computing*, Vol. 6, pages 84–85, 1977. (Addendum in *SIAM Journal on Computing*, Vol. 7, page 118, 1978.)

[204] M. Sudan. Decoding of Reed-Solomon Codes beyond the Error-Correction Bound. *Journal of Complexity*, Vol. 13, No. 1, pages 180–193, 1997.

[205] M. Tompa and H. Woll. Random Self-Reducibility and Zero-Knowledge Interactive Proofs of Possession of Information. In *28th IEEE Symposium on Foundations of Computer Science*, pages 472–482, 1987.

[206] S. Vadhan. A Study of Statistical Zero-Knowledge Proofs. Ph.D. thesis, Department of Mathematics, MIT, Cambridge, MA, 1999.

[207] A. Vardi. Algorithmic Complexity in Coding Theory and the Minimum Distance Problem. In *29th ACM Symposium on the Theory of Computing*, pages 92–108, 1997.

[208] U.V. Vazirani and V.V. Vazirani. Efficient and Secure Pseudo-Random Number Generation. In *25th IEEE Symposium on Foundations of Computer Science*, pages 458–463, 1984.

[209] M. Wegman and L. Carter. New Hash Functions and Their Use in Authentication and Set Equality. *Journal of Computer and System Science*, Vol. 22, pages 265–279, 1981.

[210] A.C. Yao. Theory and Application of Trapdoor Functions. In *23rd IEEE Symposium on Foundations of Computer Science*, pages 80–91, 1982.

[211] A.C. Yao. How to Generate and Exchange Secrets. In *27th IEEE Symposium on Foundations of Computer Science*, pages 162–167, 1986.

Index

Author Index

Adleman, L., 26, 89, 334
Ajtai, M., I., 91
Bach, E., 90
Bellare, M., 321
Ben-Or, M., 321
Blum, M., 89, 169, 321, 337
Brassard, G., 321
Carter, L., 170
Chaitin, G.J., 102
Chaum, D., 321
Crépeau, C., 321
Diffie, W., 26, 89
Even, S., 187
Feige, U., 321
Feldman, P., 321
Fiat, A., 321
Fischer, M., 26
Goldreich, O., 89, 170, 320–322
Goldwasser, S., 22, 26, 169, 170, 320, 321, 337
Håstad, J., 170
Hellman, M.E., 26, 89, 90
Impagliazzo, R., 170
Kilian, J., 321
Kolmogorov, A., 102
Krawczyk, H., 170
Lapidot, D., 321
Levin, L.A., 89, 91, 170
Lipton, R., 26
Luby, M., 170
Merkle, R.C., 26, 90
Micali, S., 22, 26, 89, 169, 170, 320, 321, 337
Naor, M., 320
Odlyzko, A., 90

Pratt, V., 90
Rabin, M., 26, 89
Rackoff, C., 26, 89, 170, 320, 321
Rivest, R.L., 22, 26, 89, 334
Shamir, A., 26, 89, 90, 321, 334
Shannon, C.E., 26
Sipser, M., 170
Solomonov, R.J., 102
Turing, A., 188
Vadhan, S., 322
Virgil, 195, 207
von Kant, P., 195, 207
Wegman, M., 170
Wigderson, A., 320, 321
Wittgenstein, L., 21
Yao, A.C., 89, 169

Subject Index

Arguments. *See* Interactive proofs
Averaging argument. *See* Techniques

Blum integers, 57, 60, 62, 283, 337

Chebyshev inequality, 10, 29, 70, 72, 137
Chernoff bound, 11, 28, 29, 106, 147
Chinese Remainder Theorem, 60, 335
Classic cryptography, 2, 26
Claw-free pairs. *See* One-way functions
Collision-free hashing. *See* Hashing
Commitment schemes, 223–240, 242–243, 252, 274, 276, 287, 320
    based on one-way function, 226–227
    based on one-way permutation, 225–226